C000001114

A HISTORY OF GONVILLE AND CAIUS COLLEGE

COLLEGIO DILECTISSIMO
HVNC LIBRVM D. D. AVCTOR
OLIM ALVMNVS DEINCEPS SOCIVS,
GRATO SEMPER ANIMO MEMOR PATRIS OPTIMI
ZACHARIAE NUGENT BROOKE
IPSIVS ETIAM SOCII,
NECNON IOANNIS VENN,
ANNALIVM CAIANORVM SCRIPTORIS DOCTISSIMI

The Gate of Honour, 1575

A HISTORY OF
GONVILLE AND CAIUS COLLEGE

Christopher Brooke

Foreword by the Master,
Professor Sir William Wade

Photographs by Wim Swaan

THE BOYDELL PRESS

© Christopher Brooke 1985

All Rights Reserved. Except as permitted under current legislation
no part of this work may be photocopied, stored in a retrieval system,
published, performed in public, adapted, broadcast,
transmitted, recorded or reproduced in any form or by any means,
without the prior permission of the copyright owner

First published 1985
The Boydell Press, Woodbridge

Reprinted with corrections 1996

ISBN 0 85115 423 9

The Boydell Press is an imprint of Boydell & Brewer Ltd
PO Box 9, Woodbridge, Suffolk IP12 3DF, UK
and of Boydell & Brewer Inc.
PO Box 41026, Rochester, NY 14604–4126, USA

British Library Cataloguing in Publication Data
Brooke, Christopher
A history of Gonville and Caius College.
1. Gonville and Caius College – History
I. Title
378.426′59   LF135

Library of Congress Catalog Card Number: 85–11639

This publication is printed on acid-free paper

Printed in Great Britain by
St Edmundsbury Press Ltd, Bury St Edmunds, Suffolk

Contents

List of Illustrations   vii
Foreword by Professor Sir William Wade, Master of Gonville and Caius
    College   ix
Preface   xi
Note to the 1996 reprint   xvi

1 FOUNDATIONS   1
1348 – Edmund Gonville – God and Mammon on the 14th
Century – William Bateman – Gonville's foundations –
Bateman's foundations – John Colton

2 GONVILLE HALL, 1353 – 1500   21
Building Gonville Court – Fellows and scholars – The
library and its books – The Masters

3 PRELUDE TO DR CAIUS   41
Cambridge 1450 – 1550: the formation of the academic quarter
– The Masters of Gonville Hall, 1483 – 1557 – The mid-16th
century and Bishop Shaxton

4 CAIUS   55
Scholar, humanist and physician – Gonville and Caius
College: preparations – The foundation – Caius Court and
the gates – Rewriting the statutes – John Caius and
Matthew Parker: 'much ado with the quarrels of Gonville
Hall' – The catastrophe

5 THOMAS LEGGE AND THE ELIZABETHAN COLLEGE   79
The tombs of Legge and Perse – The matriculation register:
Caius and the wider world – Thomas Legge – The Catholic
recusants – William Harvey – Charity and Mrs Frankland –
Junior and Senior Fellows – Stephen Perse

6 BEFORE THE CIVIL WAR   104
William Branthwaite – John Cosin – John Gostlin – The
community in the early 17th century – The Gawdys –
Thomas Batchcroft – Jeremy Taylor – Epilogue: Charles
Scarburgh

7 THE ENGLISH REVOLUTION   127
William Dell and revolution – William Bagge and continuity
by Z. N. Brooke – Epilogue: transition to 1660

8 THE RESTORATION AND DR BRADY 143
Robert Brady, physician and antiquary – Brady and the
intellectual life of Caius – Bartholomew Wortley – The
clergy of Caius: Samuel Clarke – The East Anglian connection – Titus Oates

9 THE EIGHTEENTH CENTURY 159
Clerical fellows, and College livings – Cambridge and
politics: Tory and Whig – Sir Thomas Gooch – Sir James
Burrough, architect and Master – John Smith – Smith as
professor – Caius and the Antiquaries – The letters of
Framlingham Willis – The society in the late 18th century

10 CAIUS IN THE AGE OF REFORM 188
Winds of change – The young Caians: William Wilkins,
Robert Woodhouse, Hamnett Holditch and George Green –
Henry Bickersteth – Bickersteth and the Perse scandal –
Robert Willis – George Paget – The flow of recruits –
Martin Davy as Master – Benedict Chapman – Edwin Guest
– The works of Salvin and Waterhouse

11 INTERLUDE: THE COLLEGE IN THE 1850s 218

12 THE AGE OF E. S. ROBERTS 223
The Statutes of 1860 and the abolition of celibacy – Norman
Ferrers as Master – Cambridge in the late 19th century –
Religion in Caius – The educational programme of the 1860s
and 1870s – E. S. Roberts – Education and learning, c. 1900
– Sir William Ridgeway – The natural sciences, the medical
tradition and Sherrington – The humanities and music:
Charles Wood – Professorial fellows – The entry of women
to Cambridge – The Barnwell estate and the age of timber –
Clubs, societies and the Mission – Benefactors

13 1912 – 1984 I THE MASTERS 259
Prologue: the historian's dilemma – Sir Hugh Anderson – J.
F. Cameron – Sir James Chadwick – Harvey Court – Sir
Nevill Mott – Darwin College – Joseph Needham as Master
(1966 – 76) – Sir William Wade – The admission of women

14 1912 – 1984 II EDUCATION, RELIGION AND LEARNING 280
Education – Religion – Learning and research

Epilogue and Addenda 302
Appendix 1   The Masters 309
Appendix 2   The Presidents, by Mark Buck 311
Appendix 3   Notes on the changing pattern of schools, courses and
careers in the late 19th and 20th centuries 314

Bibliography and List of Abbreviations 323

Index 340

List of Illustrations

All the photographs are by Wim Swaan, unless otherwise noted

Front Endpaper Gonville and Caius College about 1690, by David Loggan (from *Cantabrigia Illustrata*: photo Cambridge University Library, by courtesy of the Syndics)

Frontispiece The Gate of Honour, 1575

Plates (between pages 140 and 141)
1 The Gate of Virtue, 1567 – 9
2 Portrait of Dr Caius
3 a. Dr Caius' caduceus
  b. *Fortuna*, from the Gate of Virtue
4 Gonville Court
5 Caius Court
6 The tomb of John Caius
7 The College organ
8 The Chapel, looking east
9 a. The tomb of Dr Perse, c. 1615
  b. The tomb of Dr Legge, c. 1619
  c. Bust of Lord Langdale in the Public Record Office (photo. by courtesy of the Public Record Office)
10 Matthew Parker's flagon, 1571, and two 15th century coconut cups
11 Tankard or flagon given by Richard Branthwaite and William Webb in 1609; and Matthew Parker's chalice, given in 1570
12 The nef or bonbonnière, early 19th century, attributed to Pugin (Venn, VI, 524): from an imitation of a 15th century French secular vessel, but adorned with religious symbolism.
13 Portraits: a. Dr William Butts, by Holbein, in the Isabella Stewart Gardner Museum, Boston (photo. by courtesy of the Isabella Stewart Gardner Museum)
  b. John Gostlin, Master 1619 – 26
  c. John Smith, Master 1764 – 95, by Joshua Reynolds
  d. Martin Davy, Master 1803 – 39, by William Beechey
14 Portrait of Sir Charles Sherrington, by Augustus John, in the University of Liverpool collection (photo. by courtesy of the University of Liverpool)
15 A room in Caius Court, panelled in the 1690s
16 The drawing room in the Master's lodge, 1795
17 The hall roof, by Salvin, 1853 – 4

18 The Great Gate, by Waterhouse, 1868—70

19 Harvey Court, by Sir Leslie Martin and Colin St John Wilson, 1960—2, from the garden

20 Caius from above; the old courts

21 St Michael's Court from above, with St Michael's Church

22 The panelled combination room, 1431—1905

23 'Dessert' in the panelled combination room, by Paul Gopal-Chowdhury, 1984

24 The Gate of Honour and Caius Court, from the steps of the Squire Law Library

Plan, (p. 20) The windows of hall, library and chapel in the 14th and 15th centuries, by Hugh Richmond

Final Endpaper Plan of the College, by Hugh Richmond

Foreword

by Professor Sir William Wade,
Master of Gonville and Caius College

A College which has so long a history as Caius needs a versatile as well as a scholarly historian. If in addition he has a talent for bringing the past back to life, and writes with vivacity and charm, his college is more than twice blessed. Christopher Brooke shows all these qualities in this volume. Himself the son of a medieval historian who was a fellow and librarian of Caius, he has the history of the College in his blood and almost a hereditary right — or perhaps duty — to be its historian.

It is no disparagement of the author's distinction as a medievalist and antiquary to say that he is especially successful in his account of the later centuries and of the great changes in the life of the College and of the University which occurred in those times. As he himself says, a college historian is at his most vulnerable as he approaches his own day. John Venn, the pioneer of the College's history, brought both his shorter narrative account and his massive prosopographical volumes to a close in 1900. He had been a fellow, and subsequently president, since 1857, so that he lived through the revolutionary times which saw the end of the rule of celibacy for fellows and the monopoly of the established church. Now, at a century's distance, Professor Brooke is better placed to see these great events in perspective. But he has not been daunted from carrying his story right up to his own time, culminating with what is arguably the greatest event of all, the admission of women to the College.

All who have lived within the walls of Caius will have had the feeling of continuity with the past and will have wondered about the conditions of life of their predecessors over more than six centuries. In this book we now have a splendid panorama of college society, in which room is found not only for staple commodities such as the deeds and misdeeds of Masters, the achievements of fellows and the growth of the buildings, but also for the Boat Club, the bedmakers and the son of the College cook who became a fellow in 1674 and ended as Regius Professor of Physic. The hijacking of the Jesus gun, long famed in Caian song and story, now takes its place in our official history. Readers will admire the art with which Professor Brooke spices the solid meat of his narrative with anecdote and humour and occasionally with light-hearted gossip. He has done full justice to the many-sided corporate life of the College.

There is much that is sobering for a Master to read. All too many of my predecessors lived embattled in the Lodge, more or less continually at war with the fellows. Even the less belligerent of them sometimes acquired bad names, one being known as 'the devil of Caius' and another provoking the comment that 'the Master of Caius was as tiresome as ever' (pp. 152, 210). Well within living memory, moreover, were the stirring events of 'the Peasants' Revolt'. But, viewed in proper proportion, the College's story is one of academic peace and industry, ornamented by the work of many distinguished scholars and scientists. My predecessor Joseph Needham, who has won renown in both capacities, handed over to me a thriving and harmonious community, for which I have great reason to be thankful. In Dr Caius' statutes was one, *de nimia familiaritate*, which forbade friendly associations between doctors, masters, bachelors and scholars. But I am glad to find that this, like so many of our early statutes, has been more honoured in the breach than the observance.

Dr Caius' statutes provided also that the annals of the College should be kept up to date by the Master. Fortunately he can now leave this duty to expert historians such as Professor Brooke, whose wide knowledge and literary skill have produced a far finer work than a mere magisterial college chronicle. It will provide good reading not only to the 'greater Caius', the 7000 or so members of the College (not old members — for once a member, always a member) dispersed across the world, but also to all interested in university and college history.

Preface

A few years ago someone said to me: 'In former times Colleges had divine and saintly names — Jesus, Christ's, Trinity, Magdalene, St John's — now they are called after their human founders, Wolfson and Robinson' — at which I smiled and responded drily 'Have you not heard of Gonville and Caius?' What's in a name? A German scholar visiting Cambridge in the early 18th century sent his servant to prepare for his coming to Caius to look at manuscripts, after taking careful note that it should be called 'Kies' College.[1] The servant asked the way to Cheese College, to the amusement of his master and the people of Cambridge, but in truth many difficult explanations over the centuries would have been avoided if Cheese College it had been, instead of commemorating an obscure country parson of the 14th century whose name was Gonville and a celebrated *savant* of the 16th who insisted that his name was Caius. A notable stretch of history lies behind such a curious name, and it is part of the business of this book to explain it.

But a deeper question follows. What is a college? It is a visible collection of stones and bricks and concrete — and they have their own fascinating history, which is an essential part of our theme. But few of us think of the stones as the College: it is above all a gathering of folk. How can one write a coherent, yet truthful, story of many thousand men and a few hundred women too — the vast majority of whom lived here briefly, many of whom thought little of it till they had gone? It is an intensely interesting and challenging task for a historian and a Caian; but it is baffling too. I have spent much time writing the history of cathedral chapters, where the problem is even more acute. Thomas Gooch, Master of Caius from 1716 to 1754, was a 'resident' canon of Chichester from 1719 to 1738 and can be proved to have joined in local politics, and met his second wife, in Chichester.[2] He was there almost every year; but he has little place in the history of Chichester. John Smith, Master later in the 18th century, was Chancellor of Lincoln Cathedral and so tenant of the Chancery in Lincoln Close. It cannot be shown that he ever visited it, though it is probable that he kept some residence most years. We can claim more in all our alumni, but in some, not much more.

The first Master, John Colton, was an ambitious young canon lawyer; he rapidly became an absentee and probably an advocate in the papal court at

1 Mayor 1911, pp. 133–4.
2 I am much indebted to Joyce Horn for evidence on Gooch in Chichester: see p. 168n.

Avignon. It is a miracle that so precarious an institution survived, but it did, and it was partly his doing – more for the contacts and the influence he was able to exert from afar than for anything we can believe he did on the spot. William Harvey was here from 1593 to 1599 or 1600; he left Caius for ever when he was twenty-one; his later links with the College were few. Doubtless it had an influence on him, and equally surely the inspiration of his name and work has greatly affected the College; its lasting memory of him is recorded in Harvey Road and Harvey Court; he has helped to make the College the home of distinguished doctors and physiologists ever since. But it is equally evident that his discoveries and books are not part of the College history as were, say, Dr Caius' or Dr Brady's, which were partly or largely written within its walls. Still less can it claim a great share in Titus Oates, who was only two years resident, or in the immensely popular historical novelist G. A. Henty, who only kept three terms.

Yet there has been extraordinary continuity too. If Colton flitted, Richard Pulham, Master for forty years or more, stayed on to see the tiny foundation struggle to life. Pulham lived into the 1390s and by the end of the decade Thomas Wood was already a fellow; many years, later, as Master, he was to build the old hall and library whose shell still stands. He was succeeded as Master in or about 1456 by Thomas Boleyn, great-great-uncle to Queen Anne, and when he died John Barley was a fellow, and he was to die as Master in 1504 – 5; already in 1488 William Buckenham appears as fellow, and he in his turn was Master from 1513/14 to 1536. Buckenham was the Master who presided over the early years of John Caius, who was a fellow from 1529 and himself died founder and ex-Master in 1573. By then Stephen Perse, who had come in 1565, was already a fellow, and he died a fellow in 1615. In 1615 the young Thomas Batchcroft had been twenty-five years in residence, and he was to survive – though excluded for many years in the days of the English Revolution – till 1660, when he briefly returned as Master. Before his removal the young John Ellys had come into residence, and in residence he remained until his death, as Master, in 1716. By this date James Burrough had arrived in Cambridge, and from 1720 he was a tutor; in 1732 came the young John Smith – and Burrough and Smith as tutors and Masters spanned most of the rest of the century down to 1795. One of the last fellowship elections over which Smith presided was that of Benedict Chapman, fellow from 1792 to 1820, Master from 1839 till his death in 1852. Only a year later John Venn matriculated, and when Venn died as president in 1923 Joseph Needham was a research student: from 1924 he was a fellow and he was to be fellow for over seventy years, Master for ten of them, 1966 – 76.

This inspiring vision of longevity and continuing service to the College presents, however, one particular problem to the historian. To keep a coherent narrative on the move – and above all to see each shift and turn in the fortunes of the College in the wider perspective of the University and of the world of education and culture and religion, and even of politics, without which it makes no sense – would be much easier if no major character was on the stage for more than ten or twenty years. But the story of the College would have been fundamentally different had this been so; and the bewildering tricks of chronology, which every historian is tempted to hide or suppress, form one of the most intriguing and important challenges to the historian of a College. Thus William Harvey belongs to the 1590s, sure enough – but also to the 1640s, when he encountered the young Charles Scarburgh, and to the 1880s and 1960s when Harvey Road and Harvey Court were built. By the same token the young Charles Sherrington who played a very vigorous game of rugger and laid the foundations of immortal fame in the lab in the 1880s, and returned as a very senior honorary fellow to live in College in the 1940s; and the Sherrington Society doubtless, and his fame in Caius, owe as much to the second phase, and to all that lay between, as to the first.

The Governing Body of the 1850s and '60s swept away much of the College's ancient traditions: they abolished named fellowships and scholarships (for a time) and they invited Waterhouse to obliterate the older buildings of Tree Court. But they showed some sense of history in the statues of founders and benefactors with which they adorned the Waterhouse building, and they admitted the young John Venn and made him a fellow.

To write a brief and comprehensive history of the College without many years of detailed preparation would be impossible now were it not for the incomparable foundation laid by Venn – in his *Biographical History*, I – III (1897 – 1901), his shorter *Caius College* (also of 1901) and other works. He had a great mastery of the College archives and very little escaped his notice. He loved amassing biographical detail, and he and his friends set to work with immense toil and care over a wide range of sources; he lived long and passed his mantle to two other men who carried it through two generations more: his son, J. A. Venn, president of Queens', who arranged for the completion of their *Alumni Cantabrigienses* (modelled on the *Alumni Oxonienses* of Joseph Forster), and Dr A. B. Emden, whose *Biographical Registers* have reordered and transformed our knowledge of Oxford and Cambridge down to the early 16th century – for Oxford, to 1540. John Venn was a pioneer: he was not by profession a historian, but a mathematician and philosopher, and Venn's diagram has made his name known to a wide circle who know nothing of Caius. His mathematical skills came out in the tables and statistics with which, quite in the modern fashion, he adorned his *Admissions* and the masterly introduction to the first volume of the *Biographical History*. But he was in a real sense an amateur; he knew far less than modern scholars of the background of his story. Like most professionals, he made mistakes. There is something left for a successor to do. Yet every page of this book which is worth anything contains a tribute to his hobby and his learning. I have never scrupled to use his material or repeat his stories; this history would be gravely impoverished if I had. In the famous phrase of the grammarian of Chartres, I am a dwarf on the shoulder of a giant, and so long as I stay firmly planted there, may see a little further than he did.

In my efforts to do so I have been greatly helped by many generous friends and colleagues. First of all, the Master and the College Council have given my efforts a kind welcome and smoothed my task in many ways, the Master above all by reading the book in draft and contributing the Foreword; and he and the Senior Bursar have been a constant support in its planning and production. It had originally been hoped that Philip Grierson would write the book, and when he passed the task on to me he generously provided much material and many notes besides — and his friendly interest and criticism have been invaluable, for he too has read it. It has also been read in whole or in part by Paul Binski, Patrick Brooke, Jonathan Clark, Eamon Duffy, Elsie Duncan-Jones, Richard Duncan-Jones, Anthony Edwards, Catherine Hall (see below), Roger Highfield, Roger Lovatt, Neil McKendrick, Noel Malcolm, Joseph Needham, Michael Oakeshott, Dorothy Owen, John Sturdy, and by my wife, Rosalind Brooke — and all have contributed generously to its improvement. Jonathan Clark and John Sturdy have provided indeed a sheaf of notes, and my wife the criticism, advice and encouragement that only she can give. Sections of the book have been vetted, to my great advantage, by Lord Bauer, Charles Brink, Jane and Stephen Hawking, Peter Tranchell, and Sir Vincent Wigglesworth; and I am also very grateful to Charles Brink for the dedication. In the College library, I have had generous help from the librarian, Jeremy Prynne, and his assistants. I have had kind approval from Edward Timms, editor of the *Caian*, and those he has interviewed in its pages, for many quotations from the *Caian*; for quotation and citation of copyright matter from Michael and Nicholas Brooke (see p. 131), David Cressy, Damian Leader, Victor Morgan and John Twigg. I have had valued help and advice also from Melanie Barber, Mark Birkinshaw, Thomas Cocke, Elizabeth Danbury, Sir Sam Edwards, Vic Gatrell, Elizabeth Hallam, Sandy Heslop, David Howlett, Derek Ingram, Konrad Martin, Brian Outhwaite, Quentin Skinner, Sandra Raban, Miri Rubin, Peter Stein, Malcolm Underwood and Betty Wood.

For the plans of the College I am deeply indebted to Hugh Richmond. The Loggan engraving (front end-paper) is reproduced by kind permission of the Syndics of the Cambridge University Library. Plate 9c was kindly furnished by Elizabeth Hallam with the permission of the Public Record Office; plate 13a by the Director of the Isabella Stewart Gardner Museum, Boston, Massachusetts; plate 14 by the kind help of the Registrar and University of Liverpool. For help in typing I am grateful to Patricia McCullagh, Edna Pilmer, Jean Durrant and Lorraine Ostler.

Mark Buck, former fellow, nobly provided the substance of the list of presidents (Appendix II), hitherto curiously difficult to disentangle from

Venn. Stanley Price generously wrote the account of his impressions of Caius thirty years ago specially for this book. Richard Barber and his colleagues in Boydell and Brewer have greatly eased the process of publication.

My chief helper in this work has been Mrs Catherine Hall, College archivist, who has acquired over many years a unique knowledge of its early records and of many of the problems of interpreting them, which she has generously shared with me. She has opened many paths of enquiry and solved innumerable problems: to her I and all users of this book owe special thanks.

It is adorned with splendid photographs by my friend Wim Swaan, architect and photographer, who generously set time aside specially to add the distinction of his craft to this book; for this all who open it will be grateful, and I most of all.

There are passages in this book which an incautious reader might suppose disrespectful to those old oligarchs the Governing Body of senior fellows and their lineal successors the College Council. This Council has twice, in 1949 and 1977, elected me a fellow and joined me to the society whose membership has been one of the supreme delights and privileges of my life; and I must disown with a hasty *mea culpa* any hint of ungraciousness, and repeat my heartfelt thanks.

I have had for many years in my possession the manuscript of a paper written by my father, the late Professor Z. N. Brooke, fellow of Caius from 1908 till his death in 1946, on the College under the Commonwealth; and it is a special pleasure for me to include it (in modified form) in chapter 7. My father died in October 1946, when I was entering my second year as an undergraduate. I was old enough to have learned something from him of his devotion to the College and to have chosen for myself to apply to Caius for a scholarship. I had served a brief apprenticeship to him already in the techniques of historical research. But I was young enough to be a heavy burden on my mother's straitened income; and in this crisis – with some aid from generous friends and a leaving exhibition from my school – I was supported by the generosity of the College. This book is a modest thank offering for this and other benefits past counting.

Christmas Day 1984   Christopher Brooke

Since this was written I have had generous aid in proof-reading from Paul Binski and Margaret Freel; and valuable new evidence on Thomas Gooch from Joyce Horn (see pp. xi, 168n.) and on Lord Langdale from John Cantwell (cf. p. 200n.). For all this help I am deeply grateful.

July 1985   C.B.

Note The spelling of quotations from 16th and 17th century texts has usually been modernised except for a few texts published here for the first time.

Note

In this reprint an Epilogue describes the major events in the history of the College in the late twentieth century; Addenda correct some of my errors and describe advances in knowledge between 1985 and 1996. Minor corrections have been made to the text. To all who gave this book a kind welcome, and to all who have helped me to correct it, I offer warm thanks.

1996   C.B.

1

Foundations

1348

On 28 January 1348 letters patent were issued from the royal chancery of King Edward III granting licence to Edmund Gonville, king's clerk, rector of Terrington St Clement in Norfolk, to found 'a college of twenty scholars in the University of Cambridge'.[1] The petition had been backed by the distinguished warrior, Walter Manny or Mauny, and authorised by writ of privy seal on payment of a handsome fee. The Chancellor who presided over the issue of this charter was John of Ufford, and the Keeper of the Privy Seal Simon Islip; they were to succeed one another with great rapidity as archbishops of Canterbury in the following year.

The modest beginning of a small college was an item on the agenda of royal government at a remarkable moment in the reign of Edward III.

1348 saw the foundation of the Order of the Garter and the outbreak of the Black Death, fit symbols of the splendour and panache, and horror and suffering, of mid-14th century England. Edward's chivalry was immortalised in the pages of the chronicler Jean Froissart, who came to know the court through the patronage of another native of Hainault, Queen Philippa, the shrewd, tactful, enchanting wife of Edward. It was also through her patronage that her fellow countryman and domestic carver, Walter Manny, entered the king's service; and their common origin helps to explain how Manny came to be one of Froissart's principal heroes among the English soldiers in the Hundred Years' War.[2] He was clearly a gifted warrior. In 1347 Manny had the effrontery to claim safe-conduct from the siege of Aiguillon, where he had been trapped, to the siege of Calais. This was granted by the duke of Normandy — but in Orleans Manny was arrested and sent to Paris, and only after fierce expostulations between the duke and the French king, his father, was Manny released, in time to join Edward III

---

1 Venn, III, 325; and for what follows, Venn, III, 1–4; Grierson in *VCH Cambs*, III, 356. The title king's clerk shows that Gonville had attracted royal attention and done the king service; it does not imply regular employment at court. For Ufford and Islip, esp. Emden, *Oxford*, II, 1391–2; II, 1006–8; Emden, pp. 431–3; *DNB*; *Fasti 1300–1541*, IV, 3–4: Ufford died in May 1349 before consecration; Bradwardine was archbishop from May–June to his death in August; Islip from late 1349 to 1366. On Manny, see *DNB*: Knowles and Grimes 1954; Jean le Bel and Froissart, *passim*. For the 1340s Jean le Bel was Froissart's source; for the later passages of Manny's career, Froissart was independent — though never the most reliable of chroniclers (see Gransden 1982, pp. 87, 89–91).
2 For what follows, Jean le Bel, esp. II, 117–20, 166–7.

for the final stages of the siege of Calais. After the fall of Calais, when Edward's savagery towards the leading citizens had been prevented (first by the appeal of Manny, if we may believe Jean le Bel and Froissart, and then by the characteristic intervention of Queen Philippa), Manny was among the young soldiers high in royal favour who accompanied the court on its return to England. One of his first acts was to help Edmund Gonville win the royal approval for his new foundation.

The origin of Manny's friendship with Gonville is unknown, but it looks as if the rector of Terrington had made a deep impression on the soldier. In 1348 Gonville embarked on the foundation of his College in Cambridge, and the seal he devised for it leaves no doubt that it was from the first his intention that it be dedicated to the Annunciation of the Blessed Virgin Mary. In 1349, in the wake of the Black Death, Manny dedicated, also to the Annunciation, an open space in the City of London as a cemetery for victims of the plague; and his intention was to found a college of chantry priests to sing mass for his own soul and those of the folk buried round about. Years later, at the suggestion of Bishop Michael Northburgh, he turned his thoughts towards the Chartreuse, and eventually, in 1371, he founded the London Charterhouse.[3]

Edmund Gonville

Manny, Ufford, Islip, Queen Philippa: here are major figures of the royal court to make a splendid frame for the portrait of the founder. What is lacking is the picture in the centre. We have to search deeply to discern any of the lineaments of Edmund Gonville. He himself inspired or founded two other religious houses before he embarked on the academic college in Cambridge which has preserved his name and secured it from oblivion.[4] He came of a well-to-do English family of French extraction, which held property in Norfolk, and it is reasonable to suppose that he owed his prosperity in some measure to his gentry relations. His father William Gonville was lord of the manor of Larling: he acquired it by a settlement which involved his elder son Nicholas marrying the heiress to the manor. Edmund himself had the most securely East Anglian of all names — that of the saint of Bury — and was successively rector of Thelnetham in Suffolk (1320–6), and of Rushford and Terrington St Clement in Norfolk (1326–42, 1343–51).

---

3 Knowles and Grimes 1954, chap. 1, esp. p. 5. For Gonville's seal, see Stephenson and Brooke 1933.

4 On Gonville and his family, see esp. Bennet 1887, pp. 8–18, 63–71; Venn, III, 1–4; cf. C. Brooke in *Dict. d'Histoire et de Géographie ecclésiastiques*, s.v. Gonville. For Gonville's rectories, see Norfolk and Norwich Record Office, NNRO Reg I/1, f.87v; I/2, f.10; I/3, f.66; II/4, f.134v; see NNRO Tanner II, REG/31, p. 715, and Bennet 1887, pp. 90–2, esp. for the date of his surrender of Rushford to the College there. The NNRO references have been kindly verified for me by Dr Miri Rubin.

These were substantial livings; but even in the 14th century country parsons could not endow religious houses out of their tithes or their glebe; nor yet could the younger sons of gentry families out of their family estates. There must be a hidden source of wealth. A country parson could hardly be a merchant or a banker; but he was extremely well placed for managing estates and tithes. In the 14th century the holders of estates great and modest drew their revenues, often from afar, very largely from rents; and the management of estates for absentee landlords, and the collecting of rents, must have been among the most lucrative, as it is certainly among the most obscure, of professions.

God and Mammon in the 14th Century

Of the Church's wealth a great part consisted in tithes and offerings to parish churches. Originally conceived as God's portion, for the maintenance of all those who could not maintain themselves, the young and the poor and the old, tithes had long before the 14th century become concentrated into the hands of the clergy. Their prime purpose was reckoned to be to provide the clergy with stipends; but not only the resident clergy, for two apparently contradictory views of their function were widely held, sometimes within the capacious minds of the same 14th century ecclesiastics: that they were for the clergy who actually performed the pastoral duties of the parish; or that only a share, a third, was needed for the vicar who (in principle at least) cured the souls — and that the rest, the greater tithes, the two-thirds share, should go to other worthy clergy, sometimes to monasteries, sometimes to absentee clergy whose chief vocation lay elsewhere, sometimes, as we shall see, to colleges. In the minds of the Church's leaders the service of God and Mammon, as we should understand them, were much confused — and not in the 14th century alone, for the mingling of spiritual and temporal of which we catch a glimpse here was a characteristic of every age at least from the 12th to the 19th century. But in the 14th century the confusion (if such it is) had a vigour, and in retrospect an irony, which gives a special interest to its working; and for the outcome anyone who has enjoyed the patronage of Edmund Gonville — or William Bateman, or William of Wykeham — must be duly grateful.[5]

Let us consider three examples of this confusion. If I am right that Gonville was engaged in managing land and tithe, then he was a country parson engaged in very secular activities. But tithe had to be managed or the Church's finances would have collapsed: who more suitable than an educated clerk? By the same token a mingling of different vocations — of rector and man of affairs — was quite acceptable, and it was assumed he

5 Cf. Pantin 1955; Brooke 1957, pp. 81–90. For tithe see especially Constable 1964, and for their original use, p. 43.

would find time for both. After Gonville's death William Bateman diverted the tithes of three East Anglian churches to support Gonville's College. This was not the purpose for which tithes had been instituted. But so great a portion of the Church's wealth lay in tithes, and so ill-distributed were they, that it seemed to many — then and for centuries to come — only reasonable that some of them should be diverted to support religious and academic institutions. William of Wykeham, before he was a bishop, was canon of eleven cathedrals and other churches. They all had far more canons than were needed; this was a recognised method of supporting a man engaged in the service of pope or king or bishop; and it might provide the church itself with a notable ally in high places. But was not eleven excessive? — So many thought at the time; and it was hard then, and is impossible now, to draw a line between the useful and sensible redeployment of the Church's resources, and mere abuse. If Gonville dabbled in Mammon on a modest scale and Wykeham on the largest, they certainly employed their resources in an admirable way.

Bateman and Wykeham were great pluralists and rich bishops; Gonville was neither. In the account of the founding of the house of Dominican Friars at Thetford in Norfolk in 1335 the eminent 18th century Caian and Norfolk antiquary Francis Blomefield asserted that it owed its origin to the patronage of Henry earl of Lancaster, acting on the advice of Edmund Gonville, who was steward of his Norfolk estates, as he had been to his predecessor the Earl Warenne. Contemporary evidence shows that Gonville, Warenne and Lancaster were involved, but gives us no indication so precise as this statement, and Blomefield had the qualities of his kind — an immense capacity for exploring hidden records, a failure in critical sense, and a blithe incapacity adequately to reveal his sources.[6] Yet some such story as this must underlie Gonville's achievement: as steward, that is land agent, for a great estate, and doubtless for lesser men too, he could honestly and readily have acquired a great fortune; the little evidence we have about him shows that he was involved in land transactions and administration as a Commissioner of Marshland, and had the command of ready money; there is no other known explanation of his wealth. His service of Henry of Lancaster, furthermore, may explain his friendship with Manny — Earl Henry and his greater son, the first duke, were close associates of Manny's

6 See below, pp. 7, 177; Blomefield 1739, I, 192, 427. No trace has so far been found of Gonville in the Duchy of Lancaster records, but very little is known of the East Anglian administration in the period; and if Gonville was rather an adviser and an agent than a formally appointed steward, as seems very likely, he might be hard to trace even if the records for his period were more copious (he is not noted among the estate officers in Sir Robert Somerville's *History of the Duchy of Lancaster*, I (London, 1953; see esp. p. 362). There are fairly numerous references to Gonville in the Patent and Close Rolls showing him involved in land transactions and especially in advowsons and in modest tasks of royal administration (*CCIR 1333—7*, p. 56; *1343—6*, p. 552; *CPR 1334—8*, pp. 141—2, 439; *1340—3*, p. 188; *1343—5*, p. 337; *1345—8*, p. 176 — appointment as Commissioner *de walliis et fossatis; 1348—50*, p. 77; etc.).

in the French wars; and Duke Henry himself was to play the role in the foundation of Corpus Christi College in 1352 which Manny had played for Gonville Hall in 1348. All these are hints rather than solid facts; but a closer look at William Bateman, Gonville's bishop, and Duke Henry, very likely his patron, can make much clearer the social, political and religious world in which Gonville moved.

William Bateman

When Gonville died in 1351 leaving his work unfinished, it was completed by William Bateman.[7] He was a Norwich man and a canon lawyer trained in Cambridge. He had risen to be archdeacon of Norwich (1328 – 40) and dean of Lincoln (1340 – 4), and a pluralist, though on no very scandalous scale. But he can have been only an occasional visitor to Lincoln, for the main centre of his career lay in the papal court at Avignon, where he was a judge evidently high in the pope's favour. Leading churchmen of this age commonly amassed a variety of jobs and attended to each of them at least occasionally. We have no reason to suppose that he was permanently resident at Avignon even in the early 1340s. Certainly he was in touch with the royal court too, and served the king as well as the pope. In diplomatic circles he became a key figure. It was commonly alleged, with some truth, that the so-called Babylonish captivity of the papacy at Avignon in the 14th century was unpopular with the English, since the popes, and most of the cardinals, were French; and Avignon in Provence, though from 1348 an enclave of papal territory, lay close to the realm of the French king. At the outbreak of the Hundred Years' War this had some modest effect in sharpening anti-papal feeling in England. The popes had come to claim the right to make numerous appointments in the English church by papal provision, and so far as bishoprics were concerned, they were well on the way to making their claim good. Edward III was the most cynical of kings in his relations with the Church: with one hand he fanned the campaign against 'provisors', with the other he ensured that the pope provided his royal nominees, not always without difficulty, but always showing himself ready to work a system so palpably to his personal advantage. Pope Clement VI played into his hands by a rapid series of provisions in 1342 – 3; and Gonville himself was occupied in royal measures against appeals to the papal curia in 1348. When Edward accepted the papal provision of William Bateman to the see of Norwich in 1344 his letter to the pope laid emphasis on the dangerous murmurs he had to quieten in the process; and Bateman himself was converted from a papal judge who occasionally served the king into the central figure of Edward's diplomatic manoeuvres at the height of

7   On Bateman, see Thompson 1935; Emden, p. 44; Crawley 1976, pp. 1 – 15; *Warren's Book*,
    pp. 3 – 7; Ullmann 1967, p. 466, n. 39.

the first decade of the Hundred Years' War.[8]

When Francis Blomefield in his great *History of Norfolk* described the charities of Bateman's distant successor as bishop of Norwich (1738—48), Sir Thomas Gooch, he piously observed that he prayed 'that it would please God long to preserve him amongst us' — 'I am apt to think that the bishop did not heartily say amen to this' was the tart comment of their friend William Cole, 'as he had an eye to a future translation to Ely.'[9] Gooch passed with some despatch from Bristol to Norwich to Ely, gaining handsomely in stipend as he went — and also acquiring sees nearer to the College of which he was still the Master. He was doing what innumerable bishops had done between the 14th century and the 18th, accepting translation to a richer see. To Bateman's credit it may be said that he, a Norwich man, never left his see — though whether that was from choice, or due to early death, or because he lived a generation before such translations became an inevitable ambition, we cannot now tell. In 1350 he followed Gonville's example and founded a college, Trinity Hall; and in the years which followed, conscientiously taking up a task imposed by Gonville's will, he became the second founder of Gonville Hall.

Henry of Lancaster the younger is one of the most attractive figures of the secular world of the mid-14th century. He answered to the better aspect of Edward III: he was chivalrous, a good soldier — he rejoiced in tournaments and war without revelling in their more sordid side; he knew the weaknesses of his own kind, and he had a powerful and active sense of human sinfulness. All this may have been not uncommon among the better English warriors of the day; what was unique in Duke Henry's case was that he was an author and left a book in which he describes and reveals these attributes. The *Livre de Seyntz Medicines* is an allegory in French, written in 1354, the year after he had helped to found Corpus: Christ is the doctor, diseases are sin; specifics, lotions, and other medical stock in trade formed the aid and treatment Christ can give.[10] The whole is infused with a pleasant, ingenious, imaginative spirit, and is evidently the work of a person genuinely devout. As a soldier he doubtless worked with Manny, as a diplomat with Bateman, as a landlord (we may presume) with Gonville; he was a Knight of the Garter even before Manny, and founded a college of chantry priests on his own account in Leicester, which greatly enlarged a hospital founded by his father, the earl.

8 Crawley 1976, p. 6; Thompson 1935, pp. 104—9. For Gonville and royal measures against appeals see *CPR 1348—50*, p. 77; and for the background to the Statute of Provisors, see esp. J. R. L. Highfield in *History*, New Series XXXIX (1954), 331—2.
9 Blomefield 1739, II, 430, quoted Venn, III, 115.
10 Pantin 1955, pp. 231—3. It was ed. by J. Arnould in the Anglo-Norman Text Soc., 1940.

Gonville's Foundations

It had evidently been by an arrangement with the same Earl Henry, the father of Duke Henry, that Edmund Gonville organised the founding of the house of Dominican Friars at Thetford. The only contemporary document known is a puzzle. It is a royal confirmation of 1335 of the foundation of the house on lands recently granted by the Earl Warenne to Edmund Gonville and since surrendered.[11] But the Earl Warenne had handed over Thetford and his estates nearby to Thomas, Earl of Lancaster in 1318, as part of the price of peace in a great feud; and in the subsequent political confusion of Edward II's last years they had passed through various vicissitudes, returning to his son Earl Henry in the late 1320s. The only sense one can make of the letters patent of 1335 is that they represent a scheme, formed perhaps before 1318, which was allowed to mature, evidently by agreement between Gonville — who appears here at least as agent, and perhaps himself truly the founder — and the earl of Lancaster. All Gonville's foundations show a pastoral concern. We might think from what we know of his career that he was a country rector who neglected his flock for his business as a land agent. A part of his benefactions may be attributed to his conscience; like Duke Henry he was evidently a man acutely conscious of sin and the difficulty of curbing and atoning for it; as a priest we may suspect that Gonville had this doctrine deep in his system. But the scale of his benefactions and the period of time over which he fostered them tell a different story, for in each there is a clear pastoral aim. The Dominican friars had been founded to provide a corps of trained, professional preachers to supplement or replace the inadequate resources of the parish clergy; and by the secular priests, especially in the universities, they were often seen as unpopular rivals. But it would doubtless be truer to say that there was occasional friction and anger between friars and seculars, rising in the university cities to a mingling of hate and love wholly characteristic of the urban and student populations of the Middle Ages — but that there was also a widespread appreciation of their value and their aid. A practical and professional man like Gonville — not himself, so far as we know, an academic or trained in a university — might well appreciate the Dominican Friars above all. Their houses lay in a wide circle round Thetford, in Cambridge, Sudbury, Ipswich, Yarmouth, Norwich and Lynn; but at the centre, in south Norfolk and northern Suffolk, was a substantial gap; this the house of Thetford could fill.[12]

His second foundation was a college of chantry priests at his living at Rushford, not far from Thetford, also in southern Norfolk.[13] In the late Middle Ages there was no form of religious endowment more popular than the chantry. Literally and fundamentally, this involved no more than funds

11 *CPR 1334–8*, p. 158.
12 Hinnebusch 1951, pp. 59, 83n., etc.; *VCH Norfolk*, II, 433–4.
13 Bennet 1887.

to support the singing of masses for the souls of the founder, his family, friends and patrons. But in practice the chantry often took a more substantial or material form, endowing specific priests in perpetuity, to celebrate at altars in parish churches or cathedrals; sometimes providing an independent church and house in which they could worship and work and live. At Rushford Gonville built a substantial house (of which part remains) and established a small community of five priests who were to serve the church of St John the Evangelist of which he had been rector; pastoral care and direction lay in the hands of the Master, who was one of them and elected by his brethren. Thus far he formed a group ministry to serve a large parish. But a special importance doubtless attached to the opening clause among his statutes, which enjoined every one of the five priests, unless excused for reasonable cause, to celebrate mass daily for the founder's soul and those of his ancestors and heirs and all the faithful departed. Five daily masses would be regarded in the 14th century as a reasonable investment for a man of strong but not eccentric conscience and ample resources. A college in this sense was a community of priests and a chantry; and Gonville's college combined a sort of modest religious life — though without the formal rule of monk and friar — with pastoral work and the central duty of daily and ceaseless prayer for Edmund Gonville and his kin.

His third foundation was also a college, and called a college largely because it had close affinities with the type of community we have seen grow up at Rushford. It was a religious community; it had at its centre a chantry; prayer for the benefactors of the college was to lie at the heart of its being and its raison d'être. But it was not a community of priests. Some academic colleges were; more were not; almost all had a substantial priestly element within them till the 19th century. Gonville Hall was a community of students and scholars, and this set it apart from Rushford; but we must not set it too far apart, for a medieval college in Cambridge was an academic chantry; it was a *collegium*, a community, formally established and endowed for both an academic and a religious purpose.[14]

In the late 12th and early 13th centuries England acquired two universities, the first in Oxford, long a centre of learning, but only in the late 12th century a university in the full sense. Its character derived from the greatest centre of learning in northern Europe, the University of Paris. In Cambridge learning seems to have been a more recent and superficial presence when some local difficulties in Oxford led the first group of serious scholars to set up school in Cambridge under the friendly eye of the bishop of Ely and the learned clerks who served him. In 13th and 14th century Paris colleges of various kinds, religious gilds or small communities or roofs to provide a context for scholarships and bursaries, grew up in some numbers. Various attempts were made in the course of the 13th century to form such at

14 For what follows, see Cobban 1975, esp. chap. 6; Highfield 1984; Hackett 1970, chaps. 3–4; Gabriel 1955 and 1962.

Oxford, but the first to acquire a full collegiate status (as we understand the term) was Merton, in 1264.[15] Walter of Merton was a great royal servant and statesman, and also a man of affairs with a genius for buying land at a discount. He bought it from Jewish moneylenders who might foreclose on land but could not hold or manage it; or — where it suited him — from spendthrift Christians, including some of the leading citizens of Cambridge. From these he acquired the splendid house, now a part of St John's, known as 'the School of Pythagoras', and a handsome property lying about it, in case his scholars should ever need to migrate to Cambridge. His scholars remained in Oxford; but his ideas crossed from the Isis to the Cam, and in 1284, after one false start, Hugh of Balsham, monk and bishop of Ely, established Peterhouse. In both cases a group of scholars was attached to a parish church, which was presently rebuilt primarily as a college chapel; from Merton indeed the parish has since departed; and Merton at the outset was much better endowed. The communities were formed of advanced arts students and graduates working for higher degrees (see p. 12). When they had completed their studies, they were expected to go out and serve the church in pastoral work; or in the household of bishop, king and pope, in the various ways that Edmund Gonville and William Bateman had served it. For the most part they were small communities of young scholars; even the Master or President was commonly as young as his colleagues; not always, for in due course, in two ways, an element of older men began to appear within the Colleges and the Universities. There were a few dyed-in-the-wool academics who only left the university in their grey hairs; of these the most famous in Oxford was John Wyclif.[16] Much more common were those who retained an office in a college while conducting their main careers elsewhere. A college office was a source of income, like any other church benefice; and following the example of the bishops, churchmen of all kinds from the 14th to the 19th century often combined office in Oxford and Cambridge with offices in other spheres, not necessarily or always or in intention compelling them to be absentee; and not wholly to the disadvantage of their communities, who often benefited or hoped to benefit greatly from the power and authority of their absent members; but they were not in full time residence as the founder had nearly always intended. A substantial proportion of the Masters of Gonville Hall, and of Gonville and Caius College down to the 19th century, were absentees or partly resident; and it will be a very delicate matter to discern the balance of profit and loss the College sustained thereby.

In intention, the early fellows of Gonville Hall were students working for degrees. In a university perhaps 500 strong all told, with schools informally arranged in the region round Great St Mary's, and the first beginning

15 Highfield 1964 and 1984.
16 For whose career see Emden, *Oxford*, III, 2103–6; K. B. McFarlane, *John Wycliffe and the beginnings of English Nonconformity*, London, 1952; J. A. Robson, *Wyclif and the Oxford Schools*, Cambridge, 1961.

made with the original quadrangle of the Old Schools, Gonville Hall was an inconspicuous newcomer, quietly following Peterhouse, the King's Hall and Michaelhouse (now Trinity), Clare and Pembroke into the world, and at first, in Free School Lane, quite remote from the centre of the University. Put another way, it was a tiny religious foundation in a town in which Barnwell Priory and St Radegund's (now Jesus College) flourished in the suburbs, substantial houses for the four main Orders of Friars within the town and other lesser religious houses besides; one among many modest religious and academic foundations under the shadow of the houses of friars, and the King's Hall, which were substantial. The fellows of Gonville Hall were a small group of East Anglians of modest means.

Thus, in principle, the early fellows were students. With the fellows of other colleges they formed a tiny proportion of the University community; they were men of modest means. It was for such that Edmund Gonville formed his plans. He was an East Anglian. It was therefore natural to look to Cambridge as the place for an academic college. Doubtless he knew that Peterhouse had been followed by Clare and Pembroke, founded by great ladies though in close association with Cambridge clergy.[17] It is also likely that he knew something of the other foundations in Oxford; and there is a striking resemblance between Gonville Hall as it came to be established and Exeter College, or Stapeldon Hall, founded by Walter de Stapeldon, Bishop of Exeter, in the 1310s.[18] Stapeldon, though an eminent royal servant, cared for his diocese, and left a great monument in the rebuilding of his cathedral. His college at Oxford was intended to improve the quality of the clergy of his see: from the diocese they were to come, and the college was originally endowed out of the tithes of a Cornish living. By the same token the students in Gonville Hall were mostly to come from the diocese of Norwich, and very many of them did, down to the 19th century.[19] The college was originally endowed by William Bateman with the tithes of three (later four) livings in Norfolk and Suffolk; we may reckon that it was assumed, not so correctly, that they would return to serve the diocese which had fed and educated them.

It is impossible to show how much was already in Gonville's mind when he founded the college, how much it owed to the initiative of Bateman. For Gonville we have little information save the very earliest charters and a draft set of statutes.[20] The statutes are full of puzzles, starting with the initials of the Chancellor of the University who was supposed to be confirming them. In the copy of 1472 used by Dr Caius his initials appear as 'A. de G.' and so they were printed by Venn. Dr Caius interpreted this as representing 'Anthony of Grantchester'; Dr Venn improved the name to 'Adam of

17 *VCH Cambs*, III, 340 – 1, 346 – 7; for the prehistory of Clare, see Chibnall 1963.
18 Buck 1983, chap. 5.
19 See below, p. 16.
20 Venn, III, 341 – 5; for what follows, ibid. p. 345; John Caius, *Historiae Cantabrigiensis . . . Liber ij* (ed. 1912, Caius, *Works*), p. 105; *VCH Cambs*, III, 332.

Grantchester'; but neither is known to history, either as native of Grantchester of this epoch or as a chancellor of the university. In the 14th century
fair copy in the College Archives, however, he is A. de B. — as we might
say X. of Y.: the letters are evidently ciphers, for chancellors came and
went, and Gonville knew not who would ratify his provisions. The draft
itself represents Gonville's intentions in the last years of his life, between the
foundation in 1348—9 and his death in 1351.

Probably they reflect an early stage in the development of Gonville's
ideas, though they show a very precise appreciation already of the kind of
studies he hoped his fellows would pursue. He states his motives for the
foundation as being to enhance and adorn the number of students in the
university, to support poor scholars, above all to do honour to God and the
Church and promote the health of his own soul — and thus, he hoped, 'the
precious pearl of learning acquired by their long hours of study shall not be
hidden under a bushel, but spread abroad in the university and for the profit of the realm'.[21] It has often been observed that the dedication of the College is not laid down: it is to be called 'Aula de G.', Gonville Hall, and so it
was in common parlance from his day to the advent of John Caius. But
from Bateman's statutes on, its official title has been the hall or college of
the Annunciation of the Blessed Virgin Mary. Nor can there be any doubt
that the idea of the dedication was Gonville's, for on the seal he used as
founder of the College the Annunciation is charmingly portrayed.[22] It looks
as if his draft statutes were made early, though not before the appointment
of John Colton as first Master. Indeed, the most surprising omission is any
detail of the religious duties of the fellows, such as are laid out at the start of
the statutes of Rushford College.[23] It is hard to believe that Gonville gave no
instructions to his protégés that they were to pray 'for the health of his soul';
in this and other ways they seem to be a draft of c. 1348—9, never properly
revised.

Early college statutes commonly prescribe the studies to be pursued and
the parts of the land from which the fellows shall come. Most early colleges
provided primarily for graduates, that is for students of higher degrees,
usually in theology or law or both. Some from the first allowed an element
of what we should call undergraduates — students of the arts courses who
had not yet achieved an MA — especially the King's Hall in Cambridge,
founded to meet the practical needs of young men in the chapel royal; and
New College in Oxford, founded (to cut a long story short) to provide for
the higher education of boys already grounded in the sister college at Winchester.[24] The general explanation of these varieties seems to be twofold.
First, every academic founder had his own predilections: William Bateman

21 Venn, III, 341.
22 Stephenson and Brooke 1933.
23 Bennet 1887, pp. 38—9.
24 Cobban 1969, chap. 1; Buxton and Williams 1979, chap. 1.

was an eminent lawyer, and laid a legal mark on Trinity Hall, and would evidently have liked to do the same for Gonville Hall. Henry VI wanted to combat heresy, and so planned a King's College which was to be a haven of conservative theology. Dr Caius was a man of the broadest intellectual interests – except perhaps in theology – yet he set a medical stamp upon his College which has never faded. The second element was an appreciation based on more objective advice, as to where the shoe pinched, what class of worthy scholar most deserved support. University courses were long, and a great number never concluded their studies – sometimes because they ran out of money or lost heart, sometimes because they prospered in another university or another world. But it must always have been difficult to finance a full course. In principle the arts course, comprising the ancient seven liberal arts – grammar, rhetoric and dialectic (or logic); arithmetic, geometry, astronomy and music – which were still studied and had not been infused in earlier studies, took seven years; and the higher studies of theology or law several years beyond that.[25] There were short cuts in practice; and many of the seven arts were ignored. Grammar was supposed to have been mastered, though the foundation of God's House in the 15th century specifically to train grammar masters showed how little this could be assumed.[26] Rhetoric as such was not deeply studied; geometry, arithmetic, astronomy and music somewhat eclectically; all took time. The study which entered most deeply into the curriculum of successful *artists*, arts students, was dialectic – as we should say, the study of logic and philosophy. It was in this area, Gonville was told, that the need was most acute. He assumes that his fellows will all start 'in arte dialectica' and study it for up to four years; then they may go on to theology or, he adds, as it seems, a little reluctantly, some other higher course; he allows any one or two fellows at a time to be studying another discipline – 'except that anyone who wishes to study canon law is free to do so . . . for up to two years'.[27] This odd phrase seems clearly an afterthought, not surprising in statutes designed for a college to which an exceedingly able young canonist had just been appointed first Master.

In the event Gonville established a Master and a small group of fellows, and purchased a site for the College in Free School Lane, where the Master of Corpus now has his garden. But he proceeded no further with his endowment or establishment. It may be that the Black Death interrupted his schemes; he may himself have been aging and sick. In any event he survived the Black Death, but died in November 1351, leaving William Bateman, his bishop, to complete the task.

25 Fletcher 1984, p. 397; Hackett 1970, pp. 124 – 5.
26 *VCH Cambs*, III, 429 – 30.
27 Venn, III, 344. Cf. Highfield 1984, p. 245, for the studies in early Oxford colleges: at Merton, as at Gonville Hall, most of the early scholars were to be advanced arts students.

Bateman's Foundations

Bateman meanwhile had embarked on his own foundation.[28] His cathedral was dedicated to the Holy Trinity, and so his college was the hall of the Holy Trinity of Norwich. He was a canonist, and it was designed for graduates studying in the two laws, canon and 'civil', that is Roman, the closely allied discipline which, however little relation it bore to English Common Law, was the foundation both of medieval jurisprudence and of many areas of canon law. 'As he was father to Trinity [Hall]', said Fuller, 'so he was foster-father to Gonville Hall'. Early in 1350 he had completed the formalities of the foundation of Trinity Hall; in December 1351 he issued a confirmation of Gonville's foundation, calling the college the Hall of the Annunciation of the Blessed Mary; in June 1353 he agreed to an exchange with the guilds of the Corpus Christi and the Blessed Mary, and their alderman Duke Henry, so that the college received the nucleus of its present site, and the old plot in Free School Lane became part of the new college of Corpus Christi.[29] In September 1353 he presided over an agreement or 'treaty of amity' between his own two colleges, for friendship and common action and good fellowship — and for the Hall of the Annunciation to be led by its elder sister, as he regarded it, Trinity Hall. By what means the elder sister came to be reminded of Gonville's foundation and its priority, we do not know; but whenever the Praelector of Caius takes his flock into the Senate House ahead of the Praelector of Trinity Hall, he obeys the University Statutes, and is in breach of the 'Treaty of Amity'.

It is a nice question which college might claim to have priority in historical fact. Doubtless Gonville took formal steps first; but the real issue is: did he found a college at all? Or does it owe its very existence to Bateman? To this there is no clear answer. Common sense suggests that Bateman could have commanded sufficient from the resources of a relatively rich man like Gonville to have accomplished most of what was needed; and the modest scale of the foundation Bateman confirmed strongly suggests that he did not add greatly to it from his own resources. Gonville had allowed for a college of up to twenty fellows; Bateman established a college of five or six. There is not much significance in these figures, however, since Bateman did exactly the same at Trinity Hall — allowed in his statutes for up to 20, in his endowments for a much smaller number. If both had lived as long as William of Wykeham after the foundation of their

---

28 See n. 7; see esp. Thompson 1935, p. 124, for lack of evidence that Bateman visited his foundations; but one of his Trinity Hall documents is dated in Cambridge.

29 Fuller 1662, p. 276; Crawley 1976, p. 9; Venn, III, 327, 329; for the 'treaty of amity', ibid. pp. 329–30. Catherine Hall has pointed out to me that it was a remarkable achievement to see through so advantageous an exchange so rapidly; and although it cannot be proved that Bateman often visited Cambridge after he became bishop, his hand and power may be seen behind every move in this complex property transaction. By this date Henry, duke of Lancaster, one of Gonville's patrons, had become 'alderman' of the guilds founding Corpus, *VCH Cambs*, III, 371.

colleges, the story might have been different – from their own and their friends' resources much might have been added. What is clear is that if Gonville had not begun, Bateman would not have thought of founding a second college; and that if Bateman had not set the college on a better site and properly (if modestly) endowed, it would not exist.

Doubtless the founders of Gonville Hall and Corpus discussed their common aims and problems together; and it proved convenient for Corpus to release land where Gonville Court now stands. The history of the island site between Trinity Street – then the High Street – and Trinity Hall Lane is very complex. In 1311 an active speculator in town property called John of Cambridge acquired a substantial part of the site, including a stone house which may already have been a hundred or even two hundred years old.[30] It was this house and its neighbour, standing on what is now the northern side of Gonville Court, which formed a convenient nucleus for their tiny college when the agents of William Bateman negotiated the exchange in 1353. If we look at Loggan's print of *c.* 1690 (front endpaper), we see on the further side of Gonville Court the walls and some of the windows – already much altered – of these two houses, linked by a gateway into Trinity Lane, which was the entrance to the College till the time of Dr Caius.[31]

From this nucleus by slow stages the College was to grow round Gonville Court in the 14th and 15th centuries. East and west through the middle of the island site ran a tiny street, Henney Lane, which is now lost and swallowed long since in the College buildings. But its line may still be discerned by the strange orientation of the chapel, which was not parallel to the old houses on Trinity Lane; nor is Gonville Court to this day a perfect square. When the old houses were rebuilt in the 18th century, their site and their line were respected. But the chapel, projected already in 1353 and built in the course of the next forty years, was never completely rebuilt;[32] the original walls still stand behind the present ashlar surface – and so the original line is preserved, following a strange angle which commemorates the departed Henney Lane.

The exchange with Corpus was completed on 1 June 1353, and on 7 September the Master and fellows of Gonville Hall or their representatives waited on William Bateman in his manor house at Hoxne in Suffolk to receive their statutes, duly sealed. The document they received survives and is full of surprises. It told them in essence that the fellows were to be arts men nearing their term – thus far, following Gonville; but they were to go on to civil or canon law or medicine. They were given elaborate injunctions how to conduct their devotions and to pray for their benefactors; and for

30 Willis and Clark, I, 159 – 60; IV, plan 8. The details in Willis and Clark have been considerably modified by Catherine Hall's researches, which I hope will shortly be published.
31 See below, pp. 21, 65.
32 For this and the next paragraph, see Richmond, Hall and Taylor 1981, pp. 95 – 100. It is probable from the evidence of his books that John of Terrington (not to be identified with Colton), one of the first generation of fellows, was a theologian.

the rest, they were to follow the statutes of Trinity Hall. Evidently the fellows asked two pertinent questions. Gonville had wished them to study theology, and one of them was already a theologian — very good, the bishop agreed, and in his own hand, or that of a scribe under his personal direction, the word 'theologie' has been added to the text. Then, they asked, how are we to live? — And the same hand has added detailed injunctions for yearly payments till the endowments of the College shall be complete.[33] That is all. In January 1355 Bateman died, and the document which the notary drew up in that year, which he claimed to be a true copy of the bishop's statutes, also dated 7 September 1353, is very different from the draft we have been inspecting: not different in intent or basic purpose; but omitting the temporary provision of funds and spelling out the clauses of the statutes of Trinity Hall, though not naming the other College. The bishop had died without completing his foundation, and we may take it that his officials tidied the statutes up in this way after his death; and very likely we should see behind the enterprise the benevolent hand of Walter of Elveden, vicar general of the diocese, keeper of spiritualities — that is caretaker — after Bateman's death, and himself a benefactor, at least in books and instruments, to Gonville Hall.

Bateman's endowment followed a pattern familiar from Stapeldon Hall, and adumbrated less perfectly elsewhere. He arranged for the appropriation of the three rectories of Mutford, Foulden and Wilton, all in his diocese; when the process was complete, two thirds of the tithe became the College's main steady income; one third in each case fed a vicar. Until John Caius' refoundation, these tithes, and those of Mattishall, added in the late 14th century, formed the nucleus of the college income. A handsome sheaf of tithes went to Cambridge as cash to pay for the support of a small group of poor scholars; and it came to be assumed, as in the case of Stapeldon Hall, that the tithes were given by the diocese in return for service to it.[34] The fellows of Gonville Hall should come from the diocese of Norwich, and in an ideal world, should return there to give back in service to the souls of East Anglia what they had been given from their pockets.

Such schemes are always easier to propound and to justify than to put into effective execution. The links between Gonville Hall and Norwich and East Anglia remained close and intimate for centuries, though never quite as close as this principle might suggest. East Anglia was one of the most prosperous parts of England in the mid and late Middle Ages; even a superficial acquaintance with its medieval churches must convince us of what other evidence abundantly confirms. It was also relatively remote from Oxford. It

---

33 Archives I, 15. It was Catherine Hall who kindly drew my attention to this document and she and Elizabeth Danbury who saw its significance: I hope they will publish a fuller study of it. On Walter of Elveden, see Emden, pp. 210—11. The version of 1355 is Archives I, 28.

34 Venn, III, 7; for the link with the see of Norwich, see p. 16. It was never *prescribed* that the fellows should go back to the see of Norwich, but the logic of the endowment surely implied the hope that many would.

was bound to be a recruiting ground for Cambridge students; and there was, from early days, an element among the founders and benefactors and rulers of medieval colleges which liked to see close links with particular places here and there about the country. Some founders took exactly the opposite line and forbade local ties of this character; others, like William of Wykeham, took a broader view, not too exclusive of either. There is an intriguing variety in college statutes on the point. But admission tutors, then as now, had a practical task to perform, and it did not always allow them — or they were not always inclined — to conform precisely to the tidy rules laid down in college statutes. Notoriously, medieval statutes give a plan or plot of how a founder or superior wishes a college to be run — they may give little idea of how it actually worked. But there is a special piquancy about the local tie in the case of Gonville Hall: it was a matter of pride, and matter of dispute, for centuries; but how it was originally defined we cannot be sure.

If we had asked Dr Caius, he would have said that it was enshrined in the statutes of William Bateman; and so it was in the official copies used, at least by 1472, and possibly earlier. In the statutes as they were copied in 1472, but not in the earliest version of 1353 and 1355, there is a clause proscribing personal affection, conspiracy or partiality as grounds for electing Master or fellows. It goes on to say that in all elections the good of the College shall be the first concern, and one of the fellows or some other well known figure of the diocese shall be preferred in electing the Master; and in the election of fellows the 'scholars of our diocese shall be preferred to all others, and those without benefice to those who have such, and poorer to richer'.[35] There can be little doubt that this clause was missing from the original statutes of William Bateman; if we were handling a document of the early middle ages or the 12th century, we would have little hesitation in pronouncing it a later interpolation added when the origin of Master or fellows was a matter of serious dispute. In the 14th and 15th centuries forgery and interpolation were rather less common; but by no means unknown. It is noticeable indeed that this clause first appears in surviving manuscripts immediately after a contested election to the Mastership. All the Masters down to Thomas Boleyn were, or were claimed to be, Norfolk or Suffolk men, and Boleyn, though the brother of a Lord Mayor, was alleged to come from the see of Norwich, and had certainly been a fellow of Trinity Hall. But when he died in 1471−2, it seems that one Hamond Bothe, who had no known connection with the College or the see, and was a member of a rapacious north country family which battened on many of the plums of Cambridge and the English Church at large, tried to infiltrate

35 Venn, III, 352. It is curious that Venn elsewhere shows himself unaware of the significance of the absence of this clause from the earliest copies — although it had been observed in the controversies following Guest's election as Master in 1852 that the clause was not in the original MS (Winstanley 1940, p. 265, quoting 'olim socius' writing in the *Cambridge Chronicle* of 11 Dec. 1852).

himself.[36] The successful candidate was John Sheriffe, whose origin is unknown; and it may well be no coincidence that the clause first appears in the records immediately after this unseemly dispute.

The genuine statutes of Bateman came swiftly to the detailed provision for daily prayers and masses so strangely absent from Gonville's draft.[37] Every fellow shall hear or sing mass daily, repeat the Ave Maria fifty times, and pray for the benefactors of the College; every Saturday the dedication of the College was to be celebrated with a Mass of the Annunciation and 150 Aves. The statutes are not long; but they are redolent of serious purpose, pastoral concern and of an authentic tone of moderate austerity; these are coupled with a very worldly-wise concern for efficient administration; and they prescribe a way of life of genuine devotion mingled with the very curious spiritual arithmetic so characteristic of the late Middle Ages. The fellows of Gonville Hall were to recite 50 Aves a day; 150 years later, so St John Fisher assures us, even in her arthritic old age, the Lady Margaret Beaufort, foundress of Christ's and St John's, knelt for each of 63 Aves daily.[38]

Both Gonville and Bateman assumed a free election of the Master by the fellows — with provision only for reference to the Chancellor if serious difficulties arose.[39] The election was in any case to be formally notified to the Chancellor in a manner which was not meant to imply that he had any other jurisdiction. Similarly all the fellows joined with the Master in the election of a new fellow, so long as it was completed within a month; after that term the Master could act alone, according to Bateman's statutes, a clause more than one Master was to use to his advantage. Each election was to be reported to the bishop and chapter and synod of the diocese of Norwich — and every Master and fellow had to swear to do nothing injurious to the church of Norwich or engage in litigation against it — and it may well be in practice that the close link with the diocese in its foundation and endowment, and in the mind and intent of the founders and early Masters, involved a rapport which made the notorious clause confining elections to men of the see a fair statement of tradition. But it was not, either in the founders' statutes, or in practice, an invariable rule.

In another statute we can observe the opposite trend: a clause which stated an ideal rarely attempted, the statute of residence. Bateman clearly expected Master and fellows to be resident most of the year, even in vacations; and the majority of the early fellows were doubtless poor or relatively poor scholars — at first without benefice, and, even as they came to pile up emoluments, normally expecting to reside a fair amount of their time — or depart. We have no college accounts before the 1420s, but when they come

36 Hall and Brooke 1983, p. 47.
37 Venn, III, 346–7; see above. The revised Statutes in general follow those of Trinity Hall closely: see Crawley 1976, pp. 10–11 and n.
38 See Fisher 1840, p. 114.
39 Venn, III, 342, 348.

they reveal a small community mainly resident.[40] It was otherwise with the Masters from the start. One marked feature of the 14th century church was the tendency to regard all offices of the church, and especially of cathedrals and chantries and colleges, as places of emolument and profit. Thus Bateman was by no means unusual in drawing the revenues of the deanery of Lincoln with (as we may suppose) only minimal residence. We shall find in due course that the Masters of the 15th and 16th centuries were often men of varied profession and scattered offices, some of them sinecures. But none of this quite explains why the first Master of all was an absentee.[41]

John Colton

John Colton of Terrington was evidently a young man who caught the eye both of Gonville and of Bateman. We need not doubt that he owed the first step in his career to the patronage of his rector, Edmund Gonville; and it is certain that he early won the attention of William Bateman, who made him one of his chaplains, that is, a member of his personal administrative staff. John Colton was evidently a young man of remarkable ability, on his way to higher places. He was made Master by Gonville, and just as Gonville had devised a special seal for his role as founder, so Colton had a seal for his role as scholar, with St Catherine, patron of scholars, upon it.[42] But he was not able to use it very often, for the early deeds of the College make it abundantly clear that between 1349, when he was established as Master, and about 1360, when he resigned his office, he was rarely resident. On a number of occasions documents were approved in the presence of a group of fellows, with no mention of the Master. A medieval clerk or student depended on patronage — and patronage will be the principal burden of our next chapter. John Colton may have been Gonville's man, and the trusted deputy of both the first founders for forming the college; but he was also, and one suspects increasingly, close to Bateman the bishop. If a man was absent from his cure in the 14th century, one commonly soon learns that he is at the schools — that is, at University — or about the business of a bishop or a king, or the pope; doubtless Colton had spent much time in attendance on the bishop in and about the diocese. But there are indications that he followed his master in preferring a more southerly clime, and that he was carving a new career for himself in the papal court at Avignon. In fairness one may say that he was also following the example of the first Master of Trinity Hall, Robert Stratton, and no doubt both were acting on the orders of their bishop, who perhaps thought they could best serve their very young foundations by active service in the papal curia. But it was an odd way of starting a new college.[43]

40 Archives, *Compotus Book*, containing accounts, 1423–1523, with many gaps.
41 For Colton, see Watt 1981; Hall and Brooke 1983, p. 45 and refs., esp. to Walsh 1981, p. 453.
42 It is attached to Archives, IX, 6. I am much indebted to Dr A. Heslop for his advice on this seal.
43 For Stratton at Avignon, see Ullmann 1967, p. 466, n. 39.

It is likely that he was at Avignon in January 1355, when Bateman himself died there; and we know that he was at Avignon in the late 1350s, when we find John Colton established as chamberlain to the celebrated Richard FitzRalph, archbishop of Armagh, who was there from 1357 till his death in 1360.[44] On FitzRalph's death Colton looked for pastures new — but not in Cambridge; for it was in or about 1360 that he resigned the Mastership and in 1361 he took the vital step, with the aid of a papal provision, of establishing himself in Ireland, in the service of church and king. First treasurer, then dean of St Patrick's Dublin, he rose by 1372 to a leading place in the royal service: he was Treasurer of Ireland for a time in 1372−5, Chancellor 1380−2, and Justiciar, the highest office of all, in 1382. But for all his political skill and diplomatic expertise, he evidently wished to be a master in Church, not state; and though he continued to play a leading part in Irish politics, helping Richard II in the one area of politics in which that king had some lasting success, his main energies were spent as archbishop of Armagh from 1383 to his retirement and death in 1404, in the same year as William of Wykeham. Recent study has shown him to have been a very notable and effective archbishop; and one hopes that he spared a thought in later life for the College he had helped to found and the patrons who had made him. But he is a classic example of the destiny of medieval tithes: the tithes of the churches of Foulden and Wilton and Mutford might go to support good men of the diocese in Cambridge — but where those men, and especially the ablest of them, would go, was beyond the ken of the peasants of East Anglia who paid them.

Gonville had expected his fellows to be arts men completing their courses, or theologians; but he appointed as first Master a Doctor of Canon Law. Bateman slightly modified Gonville's intent. He allowed that the fellows might be in the later stages of the arts course, but reduced this element to a year of study; he clearly expected them mainly to be graduates, MAs, working in 'law, civil and/or canon, theology or medicine, at their choice' — but never more than one or two in medicine, and the Master always in the faculty of his choice.[45] One fancies that this rigmarole was meant to allow for as much of Gonville's intention as a strong-minded and successful lawyer, founding a College presided over by another able lawyer, could really accept. Trinity Hall was destined to be a nest of lawyers, and we may well believe that if Bateman had lived longer and Colton stayed longer in residence, their influence would have been more strongly felt in this direction. As it was, so far as the scanty evidence goes, the study of theology was to predominate in the later Middle Ages; but if we pay due attention to the most substantial surviving piece of evidence, the College library, we shall see that neither Roman nor canon law was neglected.

44 See Hall and Brooke 1983, pp. 45−6 and refs. in p. 49 n. 12.
45 Venn, III, 346.

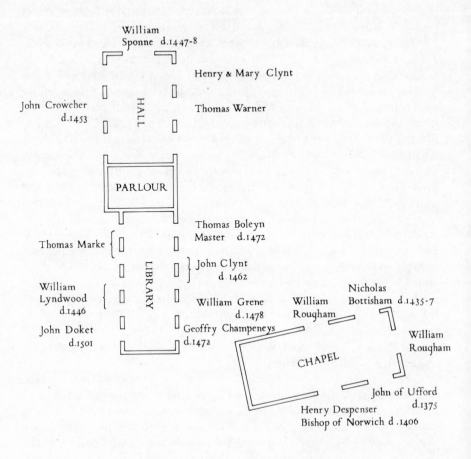

A plan of the old hall, library and chapel to show the windows: 14th—15th centuries. See pp. 21—8.

2

Gonville Hall, 1353 – 1500

Building Gonville Court

For its first hundred and fifty years or so Gonville Hall was a modest institution, with a community of fellows of no more than five or six, a tiny element in a growing university. Yet it was by no means negligible. A visitor to the library in 1500 could contemplate two windows commemorating the most celebrated English ecclesiastical lawyer of the late Middle Ages. 'Pray for the good estate of William Lyndwood, bishop of St Davids, formerly commoner of this College'.[1] A college in which Lyndwood had been prepared to spend his time as a fee-paying student was no mean place; and the library and windows mark its growth in size, academic pretension and outward show. Between 1353 and 1500 it gradually crept round what is now Gonville Court: a quadrangle of buildings was completed, the community increased a little in size, very slowly its endowment improved.

The four or five fellows – already including Richard Pulham and William Rougham – who formed the resident community in the 1350s, while John Colton, the Master, disported himself in Avignon or elsewhere, had to be content with the two stone houses on Trinity Lane, joined by the gateway which formed the entry to the college till the advent of the Gate of Humility in the 1560s. Loggan's print of c. 1690 (front endpaper) shows two Gothic windows of apparently 14th century character on the first floor of John of Cambridge's house, which suggests that where the senior parlour now is there may have been a modest hall and library. But this is conjecture: most of the houses must have furnished living rooms for the fellows and the college servants.

By 1400 the pattern of student rooms in Oxford and Cambridge had been clearly established, and it was to last with little alteration till the 17th century. When Robert Willis, the great architectural historian of the 19th century, was an undergraduate and a fellow of Caius, the Legge and Perse buildings of the early 17th century still stood in Tree Court, soon to be overwhelmed by the new buildings of Alfred Waterhouse. In their attics the young Willis was able to explore student rooms unaltered since they were

---

1 'Orate pro bono statu rdi. domini dni. W(illel)mi Lindwood Menevensis episcopi, hujus collegii quondam commensalis', copied in Matthew Wren's 'De Sociis Aulae Pembrochianae Analecta' in Pembroke Coll. archives, pp. 13 – 14; from Wren, in Baker's MS BL Harleian 7029, f. 157. I owe kind help with Wren's MS to Catherine Hall and Jayne Ringrose. On Lyndwood, see p. 26 and nn.

built; and from these he was able to reconstruct a pattern for which much evidence has since been found, especially by W. A. Pantin and others in 14th and 15th century Oxford, probably already from the first formation of student chambers in the 13th century.[2] This allowed for two or three fellows or other students to live together in a single room. In the corners cubicles were formed to make separate, tiny studies, often lit by single-lancet windows, such as one may still see in numerous college sets first built between the 14th and the 17th centuries. The centre of the room was common ground, and there beds were laid at night for the group to sleep. Before the late 17th century it was rare for fellows to have rooms to themselves: college seniors and Masters might have their own chambers, and rich visitors and pensioners.[3] It could be that William Lyndwood, who was already a man of some means, had such better quarters. It is even more likely that the first known commoner or pensioner, John of Ufford, son of the earl of Suffolk, had one; and reasonably certain the Humphrey de la Pole, Doctor of both Laws and a pensioner in the 1490s, enjoyed ample space — but by then the buildings had been much enlarged.[4]

At the time when Bateman set the college by Trinity Lane, the foundress of Pembroke, and Bateman himself in Trinity Hall, seem to have been projecting enclosed quadrangles containing hall and kitchen and library and chambers and chapels.[5] The earliest to survive tolerably in its original form is the Old Court of Corpus Christi, which lacks only a chapel since it was attached to St Benet's, but otherwise shows clearly the model of a small college of the late Middle Ages: a miniature of what William of Wykeham was able to build at New College or of the King's of Henry VI's dreams, but a remarkably substantial and handsome provision for a tiny community of between three and twenty young fellows. This ample provision reminds us that the founders were conscious that they were building for eternity, and building religious foundations comparable in their more modest way to the houses of monks and canons and friars.

In early days, one suspects, Gonville Hall was a poor relation to Trinity Hall and Pembroke and Corpus. But the first fellows seem to have conceived a group of buildings which might one day form a court, for they laid out the chapel more or less parallel to the houses in which they lived. In 1353 they had obtained a licence from the bishop to build a chapel a few months before leaving Free School Lane, and this was renewed by the bishop in 1389 and by the Pope in 1393. It has been cogently argued that the

2 Willis and Clark, III, chap. III, esp. pp. 298, 304–11; cf. below, p. 118; Pantin 1959, pp. 244–7 and fig. 88; Highfield 1984, pp. 255–6; Buxton and Williams 1979, pp. 183–5. It seems likely that in the late 16th and early 17th centuries in some cases the beds had been moved into corners where the studies had originally been placed.
3 See below, pp. 53, 99 (Nicholas Shaxton, Stephen Perse).
4 Emden, pp. 180–1, 603; Venn, I, 1, 14.
5 Willis and Clark, I, 121–38 (Pembroke), 209–22 (Trinity Hall); cf. Crawley 1976, pp. 28–35. For what follows, Willis and Clark, I, 241–62; RCHM Cambridge, I, 48, 49, 53–7.

chapel was not finally completed until the early 1390s and that a series of valuable books were pawned by fellows in the previous years in the university chests partly to help with the cash flow in its building.[6] If so, this is remarkable evidence of the financial straits of the college in its early years.

The visitor to Merton College Chapel today may see a series of beautiful windows probably of the 1290s each adorned with a kneeling figure under a canopy and recording the benefactor who paid for them.[7] By the same token, the college chapel of Gonville Hall was completed by a set of five windows recording the 'principal donors to the building fund'.[8] We know the shape of the chapel, which was about half the length it now is, since it has been extended both east and west; and from Loggan's engraving we can form an impression of its outward aspect – plaster lined to look like stone laid over a structure basically of clunch and brick – and of the tracery of the windows. But of the glass we know only the inscriptions. Two, the east and the north-west windows, commemorated William Rougham, whom we may suppose to be the prime mover in the scheme, even if the name in the south-western window, Henry Despenser, bishop of Norwich, was the 'ultimate source of the greatest part of the funds', as has been conjectured.[9] Despenser was bishop from 1370 to 1406, and sprang from a family of warrior nobles. He himself is chiefly remembered as the leader of a preposterous crusade in the 1380s.[10] Amid scenes of great enthusiasm he set off to confound the rival pope of the Great Schism in Flanders, failing to observe (so it seems) that the count of Flanders supported the same pope as he. The crusade brought disaster and disgrace and suspension for a time to the bishop, which may help to explain the delay in completing the chapel. William Rougham had been a fellow in the 1350s, and has from the time of John Caius been supposed to have been the second Master of the College; but it is clear that he was a leading and active fellow when Colton and Pulham were Masters. By 1366 he was a Bachelor of Medicine, and as a physician he seems to have prospered.[11] We know that he was also a priest and held livings in the diocese of Norwich; tradition has it that he was the bishop's personal physician. Whether or not Despenser's aid reflects his gratitude to Rougham for his body's health, we may hope that the prayers of countless fellows in the chapel have helped the bishop's soul – for he seems to have needed it. The two other windows record John of Ufford, the earl's son and the college's first pensioner, who died in 1375; and Nicholas Bottisham, who studied canon and civil law and was probably either fellow

6 Catherine Hall, personal information based on *cautiones* in early MSS and the interpretation of the windows; Richmond, Hall and Taylor 1981, pp. 95 – 6, 99 – 100. The licences for the chapel are in Venn, III, 328, 331.
7 Catto 1984, pl. V (1296 – 1311); but H. W. Garrod, *Ancient Painted Glass in Merton College Chapel* (London, 1931), pp. 12 – 20, cited evidence suggesting a date *c.* 1289 – 96.
8 Hall in Richmond, Hall and Taylor 1981, p. 97.
9 Ibid.
10 Hector and Harvey 1982, pp. 34 – 7, 46 – 55, 522 – 7 and nn.
11 Emden, p. 491; Venn, I, 1 – 2; Hall and Brooke 1983, pp. 45 – 6.

or pensioner — but he is a shadowy figure whose dates are far from clear.[12] Thus we have in the chapel the mixture we are later to meet in hall and library, of fellows and friends and patrons, who between them financed the extension of the buildings in their slow progress round Gonville Court.

Meanwhile in the 1380s William Fiswick or Fisshewicke, university bedel, had bequeathed his house in Trinity Lane, almost opposite the college gate, to Gonville Hall; and after his death it became known as Fishwick or Physwick Hostel.[13] It is common to talk of hostels or halls as rival homes for students to colleges; but it was also common for them to be or to become attached to colleges; and Physwick Hostel was a part of Gonville Hall throughout its life — presently drawing with it its neighbour St Margaret's Hostel, which had originally been attached to Michaelhouse. Where the 16th century Queen's Gate of Trinity now stands lay once the entrance of a small street called Foule Lane, which headed away towards the centre of what is now the Great Court of Trinity, where it met the entrance of the King's Hall. On its left as it departed from Trinity Lane lay Michaelhouse, much of whose structure can still be seen in the walls of Trinity at this corner. On its right lay the two hostels of Physwick and St Margaret; and in 1467 Gonville Hall acquired St Margaret's Hostel and about 1481 rebuilt the two as a single, substantial complex with hall and gate-tower. Meanwhile Physwick Hostel added greatly to the space in which the students of the college lived.

The second Master, Richard Pulham — of whom more anon — and William Rougham presided over what must have been a poor, struggling community for the first forty years of its existence. The next step forward was primarily the work of another long-lived fellow, Thomas Wood, or atte Wode, fellow from 1399 or earlier, Master from 1426 to the mid 1450s.[14] In 1431 he embarked on the most ambitious building project so far, comprising hall and library and Master's chambers or lodge. By 1441 the work was finished, and the west side of Gonville Court had been enclosed. A little can still be seen within the Monro Reading Room and the Panelled Combination Room of the timbers of the hall and library; and the structure and shape of the building survives, heavily disguised within and without. Beyond this wing lay stables and gardens, and so both rooms had windows to west as well as east; as in the chapel they commemorated benefactors, though in this case more specifically the donors of the windows (so it seems) rather than the patrons of the rooms themselves.[15] John Caius in his *Annals*

12 Emden, p. 603; *Fasti 1300–1541*, III, 66; IV, 33; Venn, I, 1 (Ufford); Emden, p. 80, cf. p. 69; Venn, I, 7 (Bottisham).
13 Emden, p. 231; Willis and Clark, I, p. xxvii; II, 415–19; Stokes 1924, pp. 95–6 (for St Margaret's Hostel, p. 85).
14 Emden, p. 23; Venn, I, 4; Hall and Brooke 1983, p. 46; for what follows, Richmond, Hall and Taylor 1981, pp. 97–8.
15 *Annals*, p. 28; for Lyndwood, see above, n. 1. He was bishop 1442–6, which seems to date his window quite precisely, since the inscription was 'pro bono statu' not 'pro anima'.

tantalisingly says that Wood was aided by 'John Warrocke, John Preston, and other good men'. But Warrocke and Preston seem to be alternative names for a single fellow of Pembroke Hall of the 1390s, a native of the Norwich diocese who studied theology at the turn of the century and lived till c. 1436.[16] We may well believe that he helped Wood — he may even have been a member of the College; but he and his contribution to the stone and timber work are shadowy; we know more of the glass. The hall windows all seem to have been inserted about the time the room was built, for they recorded the generation which built it. In the north window overlooking Trinity Lane one encountered William Sponne, a considerable local figure and pluralist, who had won patronage from the bishops of Norwich and been a king's clerk, as well as Justice of the Peace for Cambridge.[17] On the window he was called archdeacon of Norfolk, so it seems, an office he held from 1419 till his death in 1447 or 1448. Meanwhile at various times between 1434 and 1447 he appears in our records as a pensioner, evidently staying for long periods in College while he pursued his studies in canon law. The window next to the archdeacon's looking over the court was the gift of Mary Clynt and her brother Henry, doubtless close relations of Dr John Clynt, fellow, who gave a window in the library. John Clynt was a theologian, as was the Master himself and most of the fellows whose discipline we can descry; and these included John Crowcher, another donor of a hall window, who had been a fellow in 1407—8, had established himself in the chapter at Chichester when John Rickinghall, Wood's predecessor as Master, was bishop there, and was dean from c. 1426 to 1447, as his window bore witness.[18] Crowcher, like Sponne, was a pluralist and a career ecclesiastic of means; but he maintained his interest in books: we have his hand in one of our manuscripts which may have come to us from him, and the University Library still preserves his copy of Boethius' *Consolation of Philosophy* with Chaucer's translation.[19] Of the other donor in the hall, Thomas Warner, we know in contrast little but his name, and entries in the accounts which show him as a fellow from c. 1425 to 1433.[20]

South of the hall lay the Master's parlour now the white combination room with the fellow's parlour below, and beyond the Master's parlour, the library.[21] Here we might encounter in glass as remarkable a cross section of the interests of two generations of the College as they could have found among the books themselves. Of the generation of the builders we meet the theologian John Clynt, looking out upon the court; opposite to him in two

16 *Annals*, p. 7; Emden, pp. 460, 620, who, however, gives two entries for him, and it is possible that two men have been conflated. Cf. *Fasti 1300—1541*, V, 29 for his death. Caius in *Annals*, p. 39, talks of 'William Warrock', but this may be an error.
17 Emden, p. 546; cf. Venn, I, 8; *Fasti*, IV, 29.
18 Emden, pp. 141—2; Venn, I, 6—7 (Clynt); Emden, p. 170; Venn, I, 4—5; *Fasti 1300—1541*, VII, 5.
19 Emden, p. 170; CUL MS Ii.3.21.
20 Emden, p. 620; Venn, I, 6—7; Archives, *Compotus Book*, pp. 17—25, s.a. 1426—32.
21 Willis and Clark, I, 198—200; Venn, III, 197.

windows toward the garden, William Lyndwood, bishop of St Davids, the most eminent figure of the century in the history of Gonville Hall.[22] Born about 1375 in Linwood near Market Rasen in Lincolnshire, son of a wool merchant, he was never, one may assume, a poor scholar, though he is alleged to have been at one time a fellow of Pembroke. He gained his earliest preferment in 1396, and his career as a student was presumably well under way at that time; but the studies in canon and civil law which formed the basis of his fame came in the years c. 1400—7. It may well have been then that he lived in Gonville Hall, though there is no record of his presence save his windows and their inscription. Like many successful career ecclesiastics of the late Middle Ages, his progress proceeded simultaneously down several profitable channels. We cannot trace the details of the early patronage he enjoyed; but by 1402 he was already a royal clerk, and from 1417 on he was frequently abroad on diplomatic missions — most important of which was the delegation to the Congress of Arras in 1435 which marked the beginning of the end of the Hundred Years' War. Through much of this time, from 1432 to 1443, he was Keeper of the Privy Seal and a highly placed royal councillor. Meanwhile in 1414 he was chancellor to Henry Chichele, archbishop of Canterbury and founder of two Oxford colleges, and by 1417 Official of his Court. This was the most fruitful of his offices, since it gave him the authority and experience which issued in his famous *Provinciale*, an analysis of the local legislation of the English provinces of the western Church, which remained one of the most important textbooks of canon law till the Reformation. It is a book which reflects a sharp, clear, intelligent, practical mind — purposeful in making short work of insoluble difficulties; he was not a man to get lost in loving contemplation of the complexities of canon law like some of his more academic colleagues — yet a real lawyer who knew the schools as well as the courts.[23] He was a princely collector of benefices, canon at one time or another (and sometimes the same time) of Salisbury, Exeter, Wells and Hereford; archdeacon of Stow in his native see of Lincoln; rector of many country livings. He ended his days in a poor bishopric (as these things were understood in the 15th century), doubtless expecting a richer to come his way. It must have been difficult for him to keep count of the many churches with which he had been connected; and this makes the more impressive his continued interest into later life in the small Cambridge college where he had once stayed and studied; this also doubtless reflects Wood's skills as a fundraiser. Appropriately, there are six early manuscripts of his *Provinciale* in the College Library, of which four may have been there by 1500; none, alas, can be associated with the author himself, nor can we identify any of his own books in the collection. But it is likely that there are a number still there which he handled.

22 Emden, pp. 379—81, 679; Venn, I, 8; *DNB*; and see n. 23.
23 Cheney 1973, pp. 158—84.

The other library windows seem to belong to the next generation. At the north-east corner, looking into the court, one met Dr Thomas Boleyn, Master.[24] Boleyn had been a canonist and a fellow of Trinity Hall in the 1420s. He was a Norfolk man by origin, but had a brother who became Lord Mayor of London, and was great-great-uncle of the future queen; and he did not lack for patronage. He was precentor of Wells throughout his mastership. In 1434 he went to the Council of Basel in company with Edmund Beaufort. From 1456 to 1472 he was Master and evidently gave, or joined in, a new initiative to fill the library windows. Some of the donors were not (it seems) members of the College. John Doket, nephew of Thomas Bourgchier, cardinal and archbishop (1454 – 86), was one of the notable figures of 15th century Cambridge.[25] An early product of Eton and King's, he studied in Cambridge, Padua and Bologna, and deployed an extraordinarily wide if eclectic range of learning. He ended with degrees in both canon law and theology, but is best remembered for his commentary on Plato's *Phaedo*, a modest excursion in the direction of Italian Humanism. In the window he figured as archdeacon of Chichester, his earliest major preferment (*c.* 1460 – 78), and he may well have given the window on his return from Bologna about 1470; he was, however, still a young man, and lived till 1501. Another window was given by Thomas Marke, archdeacon of Norfolk and Cornwall, offices he held simultaneously in token of the two sees, of Exeter and Norwich, where he made his career, in the 1460s and probably the 1470s.[26] In 1477 he exchanged the archdeaconries of Norfolk and Norwich with John Morton, the future cardinal, and soon after disappeared from view.

Very different were the careers of William Grene and Geoffrey Champeneys, who gave the other two windows. They had both been fellows in the 1430s and 1440s; both studied theology and became doctors; both went out to become incumbents of country livings, one at a time. Both ended as rectors of town livings, Champeneys in Norwich, Grene in London; neither was a pluralist.[27] They represent a different side of the 15th century church from Lyndwood or Doket or Marke, and one equally characteristic – the increasing element of university men in quite ordinary parishes; the avoidance of pluralism by some in an age used to the remarkable accumulation of apparently incompatible offices – which culminated in the successive wardens of the King's Hall in the 1480s, Henry Bost, who was head of three colleges at once, all in different places, and Christopher Urswick, the humanist, who worked his way through five archdeaconries.[28] Yet William Grene, though in later life only rector of the single church, not rich, of St Andrew Holborn in London, was not

24 Hall and Brooke, pp. 46 – 7; Emden, pp. 70 – 1; Venn, I, 9; III, 18.
25 Emden, pp. 190 – 1.
26 Emden, p. 391; *Fasti 1300 – 1541*, IV, 29; IX, 17.
27 Emden, pp. 130 – 1; Venn, I, 7 (Champeneys); Emden, p. 270; Venn, I, 7 – 8 (Grene).
28 Emden, pp. 74 – 5, 605 – 6; Cobban 1969, pp. 288 – 9.

impoverished. He managed to leave twelve valuable books to the library at Gonville Hall and at least one to Pembroke, after paying for his window.[29] He must have had other resources than his church's tithes — a fact which underlines how little we may know, even with a conscientious parson like Grene, of these men's way of life and means of livelihood.

Beyond the library was a stair which linked it to the Master's chambers and on this stair was a window portraying the two sons of the duke of Suffolk in doctors robes, if Caius has got it right.[30] This leads us into a curious puzzle. A most interesting altar book, a Sarum Manual printed in Paris in the late 1490s and bound in Cambridge about the same time, was presented to the College by Humphrey de la Pole, one of the ill-fated family of the second duke, who married the sister of Edward IV. The children were thus close to the throne, a fatal situation in the days of the Yorkists and Tudors, and of the men only those who took orders died natural deaths. One such was Humphrey. But in another treasure in the College library, a very handsome 12th century copy of Gratian's *Decretum*, one of the earliest and finest in England, is an inscription of 1499 attributing the gift to Geoffrey de la Pole, likewise doctor. Some have thought this evidently an error for Humphrey;[31] others have agreed with John Caius that there were two brothers, both doctors of law, both pensioners of Gonville Hall. There is no certain solution, and Geoffrey is a shadowy figure.

Beyond the staircase came the lodge; and from the upper chamber the Master had access to an oratory, also probably part of the building works of the 1430s, which linked the lodge and chapel and extended beyond the present gallery, so that the original piscina is still in view, strangely isolated high upon the chapel wall.[32] In recent years repairs to the plaster have revealed other elements in this oratory and the doorway which led to the turret which can be seen in Loggan's view, containing a staircase by which the Master might descend from his oratory to the ante-chapel below.

Thus far the works of 1431−41. Later in the century, building work was resumed. Henry Costessy, Master 1477−83, was also Master of Rushford College and a parson in Norfolk and Norwich; and he inspired two substantial gifts from Norwich citizens, with which (it seems) stables and garden walls and other works were completed, and Physwick Hostel largely rebuilt.[33] It became an imposing little college in its own right. Caius indeed maintained that it could house more than thirty or forty students; the figure may be exaggerated, but he himself had been President of the Hostel;[34] and

29 See n. 27.
30 *Annals*, p. 29; Schneider 1928, p. 35, no. 86; James 1907−8, I, 4−6, MS 6/6; Venn, I, 14−15; Emden, pp. 180−1; *CP* XII, i, Appendix I, pp. 22, 24; cf. XII, i, 448−50, Appendix, pp. 21−5.
31 Thus Emden, pp. 180−1.
32 Richmond, Hall and Taylor 1981, pp. 98−9 and fig. 1.
33 Hall and Brooke, p. 47; Willis and Clark, I, 168; II, 416−17; *Annals*, pp. 8−9.
34 *Annals*, p. 9; cf. Caius, *Hist. Cantab. Academiae*, I, 38 in Caius, *Works*.

it was a grievous loss when Henry VIII confiscated it to form part of Trinity, granting Gonville Hall a compensation of £3 per annum which the Treasury paid till it was finally commuted in 1983.[35]

A part of the same fund from Norwich went to private hangings for the College hall, the Master's bedchamber and inner chamber 'together with linen cloths and ornaments for the common table'.[36] Soon after, Elizabeth Clere, a Norfolk heiress and widow of a Norfolk landowner, gave substantial sums from which first a fellowship was endowed, then the chambers on the east side of Gonville court were built; if Caius' summary in the *Annals* was correct, she paid for this shortly before her death in 1492, but the final completion of the chambers linking the east side to the chapel was provided by Nicholas Buckenham, brother of the Master, William Buckenham, about twenty years later.[37]

Fellows and Scholars

Our early alumni were listed, and their careers studied, in loving detail in Venn's *Biographical History*; and his details have been greatly increased and improved, and brought up to date, in A. B. Emden's *Biographical Register of the University of Cambridge to 1500*.[38] From these data modern scholars have worked out statistics of the fellows and scholars of the colleges and the university and the subjects they studied.[39] For Gonville Hall such statistics are of limited value. It was a small community and we know little of the studies of many of its members; the names of a large proportion of the early generations may have been lost. It is only when the college accounts are extant, as in the second quarter of the 15th century, that we have any comprehensive picture of the community; and even then it is defective, telling us little or nothing of Physwick Hostel. It is only the survival of a record of its windows that shows us that William Lyndwood was a member of the college; the extent of our ignorance is large. To understand the studies of medieval fellows we have to penetrate the jargon of their world, which is almost as alarming and unnecessary as the jargon of modern economics. It is an extraordinary mixture of the familiar and the totally unfamiliar. The ruling bodies of Oxford and Cambridge took decisions by passing graces of the regent house, then as now; and by graces they conferred degrees of BA and MA and doctorates of theology and law and medicine, much as now. But amid this striking continuity there are equally

35 Venn, III, 201; *Annals*, pp. 35—6; but the payment passed through various vicissitudes (e.g. during the Commonwealth) before final extinction.
36 *Annals*, p. 8; Emden, p. 161; Venn, I, 12; III, 20. I am grateful to Catherine and Philip Hall and David Howlett for help with this passage.
37 *Annals*, p. 8; Willis and Clark, I, 168; Venn, III, 214—15.
38 Emden, on which much of the present chapter is based.
39 Cf. Cobban 1980, 1982; Aston, Duncan and Evans 1980.

striking differences. 'The questionist was a determining bachelor' wrote a modern scholar in a book intended for the general reader, and for most of us he only revealed that we are in an impenetrable jungle.[40] A young student had to be admitted to a course and finish it before he passed to a degree or went on higher; so much is plain: that is all that is involved in many graces, and all that is meant by determining is ending. But after a bachelor has determined he had to incept, and to us 'inception' appears to be a beginning, whereas in the medieval university it signified the end, or the beginning of the end, for permission to incept allowed a student to embark on the final exercises which gave him his degree. Thus inception, like 'commencement' which replaced it in early modern times, marks the end of a stage in academic life, as the natal day of a saint marked his entry into heaven, or to speak more plainly, his death. With inception we meet a precious piece of jargon going right to the roots of our university history; for the incepting master or doctor had not only to give an inaugural lecture and disputation and other exercises, but to feast his colleagues; and the feast was the heart of the matter.[41]

If we look again at the statutes of Gonville and Bateman we should expect to find the early fellows of Gonville Hall BAs at least — or rather, since the BA was a stage not a degree in the sense we understand the term, veterans of the arts course with years of grammar and dialectic under their belts; not far short of the day when they could incept in arts or turn to theology or law.

In the period 1350—1400 we know the names of about eighteen fellows, including the Masters, which we may conjecture represent the majority of those on the foundation; we can name three pensioners or commoners, or occasional visitors, but there may have been quite a number more — though the shortage of space makes it unlikely there were anything like the number of the late 15th century.[42] Of the studies of six of the eighteen fellows we know nothing. Gonville and Bateman had both prescribed in their statutes that the fellows were to be advanced students in arts, completing the arts course and going on to higher studies; and four at least of the fellows of these early generations did just that, completing and incepting in arts, and going on to theology, law and medicine; one only may have spent all his years in arts, and that is far from certain.[43] Two went on from arts to theology, and four more (so far as our knowledge goes), read theology throughout.[44] John Colton, first Master, was a canonist; Richard Pulham, the second Master, had started in arts and proceeded to civil law;

40 E. F. Jacob, *The Fifteenth Century 1399—1485* (Oxford, 1961), p. 672n. For a more precise definition of 'questionist' see Fletcher 1984, p. 381.
41 See e.g. Mullinger 1873, pp. 357—8.
42 These figures are based on Emden and Venn.
43 John Osborne and Robert Tunstall went on to theology, Pulham to civil law, Rougham to medicine (Emden, pp. 436, 598, 462, 491).
44 Richard Dereham, Roger Rande, William Somersham and Alan Tilney (Emden, pp. 184—5, 471—2, 541, 601).

Nicholas Bottisham, celebrated in the chapel, was student of both laws; Henry Thompson, fellow in the 1370s and 1380s, and rector of Stoke by Nayland thereafter, was a canonist.[45] One only, William Rougham, the central figure of the chapel-building, was a doctor of medicine.[46] Medicine indeed figures very little among the early fellows — only one other MD occurs before 1500 to prepare us for the world of John Caius.

In broad outline, the original pattern was preserved, so far as the evidence allows us to perceive it. Between 1400 and 1450 there are seven or eight fellows whose studies are hidden from us, and two more of whom we can only at best know a part. The striking feature of this period — the age, we may suppose of Lyndwood and Sponne (see pp. 25—6) — is that we cannot name a single fellow who studied law or medicine. The majority of the known completed arts courses and went on to theology, as Gonville would have wished; one may never have passed beyond his MA; four at least seem to have been theologians throughout their tenure. But this includes John Rickinghall, who came to Gonville Hall as Master, having already risen to be Chancellor of the University and a doctor of some standing.[47] The absence of lawyers is perhaps surprising, but partly compensated by the fact that all three pensioners of this age whose higher studies are known — as compared with five whose disciplines are not — were lawyers.[48] In the late 15th century the numbers rise. Our information improves; the turnover of fellows seems somewhat to have accelerated; the number of fellows slightly increased, and the size of the community increased still more.

Venn reckoned that down to 1478 the permanent establishment consisted of the Master and four fellows; but he conceded that the accounts showed some fluctuation — from two to five in fact — and concluded, doubtless correctly, that the number of fellows fluctuated with the state of the funds.[49] There was a modest extra endowment with the advowson of Mattishall in the late 14th century — and a substantial addition when Mattishall church was appropriated in 1393—5; henceforth the chief single source of income was the tithes of four parishes.[50]

From 1478 to 1500 came a series of modest additions to the endowment, each intended to support a fellow with special duties to pray for the benefactor's soul: Stephen Smith, Elizabeth Clere and Thomas Willowes — Norfolk parson, wealthy widow of a country gentleman and Cambridge glover respectively — all provided for students in divinity, and preferably priests who could sing masses for their souls.[51] The executors of the Lady

45 See above; for Thompson, Emden, p. 581.
46 Emden, p. 491. I have not attempted to give detailed notes for the statistics which follow.
47 Hall and Brooke 1983, p. 46; Emden, p. 480.
48 The lawyers were Lyndwood, Sponne and Thomas Walsingham (above, pp. 25—6; Emden, pp. 613—14).
49 Venn, III, 213—14 and 213 n. 1. Five is the correct maximum, not nine (as Venn), so Catherine Hall tells me.
50 See p. 15; for Mattishall, ER, p. 60.
51 Venn, III, 214—15.

Anne Scroop handed over a property in the manor of Mortimers mainly in the west and east fields of Cambridge to support 'one well disposed priest or . . . one good young man disposed to learn, born in the diocese of Norwich' to be nominated by the executors while they lived and elected by the College, 'which young man shall within the space of one year be priest, and be called Dame Anne's priest'.[52] Anne Scroop was the last surviving descendant of Edmund Gonville's brother, and she showed an interest in both Rushford and Gonville Hall. She was married three times, but had no children: her considerable wealth passed mainly to a nephew, but she managed to distribute gifts in her lifetime and after her death to a number of institutions and to almost everyone of note in Norfolk. In 1490 she had made elaborate provision for enlarging Rushford to provide additional fellows and a school there, as well as a chantry for her first and second husbands and herself. Her provision for Gonville Hall was more modest and more laconically expressed. But it meant much to a small college, for it included pasture land in Newnham and arable in Newnham and Barnwell; and in due course this became some of the college's most valuable land.[53] Mortimer Road commemorates her manor and Scroope Terrace her name — and a stretch of Cambridge was developed in the 19th century scoring the map with College names, Gonville, Harvey, 'Lyndewode' among them. The pasture closes in Newnham run from West Road to the south end of the Backs, and supply the lung for a college whose island site in central Cambridge has always been circumscribed; on Dame Anne's pastures now lie a line of gardens and buildings from Harvey Court to the Fellows' garden.

Thus the late 15th century saw a slight increase in the Fellowship and a substantial increase in the accommodation for the college; and we have more details of the fellows' studies than for former generations. The preponderance of arts and theology remained. We know the names of 28 fellows, which must be a high proportion of the total; but of these six studied we know not what, and three began in arts and passed to a higher discipline unknown. For the rest, the pattern is much as we should expect in a conservative institution following earlier models and (as far as they were intelligible) the founders' statutes. At least ten started their fellowships in arts; three more may have been arts men throughout. Ten studied theology, of whom five have been numbered already among the arts; one of the 'artists' went on to medicine, and one to civil law.[54] Four more studied law, and so we may say that the theologians were roughly twice as numerous as the lawyers.[55] Exactly the same proportion holds among the pensioners —

---

52 Venn, III, 215—16; for what follows see esp. Bennet 1887, pp. 19—23, 107—12.
53 See pp. 252—3; Venn, III, 215—16.
54 The last two were Edmund Albon and Thomas Cabold, both of whom prospered greatly, Albon to be physician to Edward IV, Cabold a papal penitentiary (Emden, pp. 5, 116, 673).
55 The lawyers in this reckoning include Thomas Boleyn, the Master, and William Barley, who were both advanced in years when they came to the College; also John Carter and Thomas Croppe: Emden, pp. 39, 70—1, 124, 169.

four are known to have been theologians; two lawyers, including a Florentine bearing the famous name of Bardi, who had made his career in England; and Humphrey de la Pole; if Geoffrey existed he may be reckoned to add a third.[56] In any case there were nine pensioners whose studies are unknown — and far more, in all probability, if we include Physwick Hostel, of whom we know nothing. Thus in 1500 theology still predominated; it was a markedly clerical community; priestly functions played a large part in it and the priests must have needed all the altars that the two college chapels and an aisle in St Michael's could provide.[57] But the strength of the arts shows that some preparation for the spread of new types of humanistic learning had been made, even if Gonville Hall counted no notable precursor of the new learning in this age. We shall be wise to recall indeed that the new learning came slowly and was not so radical a break with older scholastic traditions as its enthusiastic propagandists would have had posterity believe.

The library and its books

The most considerable body of evidence for the studies of Gonville Hall lies in its library — a rich and tantalising source not yet fully sifted. Unlike Merton or Peterhouse or Queens' there is no medieval catalogue to help us assess the original scope of the collection; but, like Balliol, we have the books.[58] As with all Cambridge college libraries, the collection of manuscripts was catalogued by M. R. James, the great pioneer at the turn of the 19th and 20th centuries in manuscript studies — and ghost stories. His catalogue provides a fine foundation, though much still remains to be investigated. But if we exclude from the eight hundred or so catalogued by James all of later date, or known to have been given after 1500, we are left with a nucleus of about three hundred and fifty which could be members of the medieval library.[59] Of these we can assert from references to Gonville Hall or to donors or to fellows or other signs, such as shelf marks, that at

56 See above, p. 28; for Bardi, Emden, p. 36. There was also at least one arts student, called Medfield, in Physwick Hostel (Emden, p. 398) — who reminds us of our ignorance of that substantial hostel 'artistarum'.

57 See pp. 23–4, 28; Brooke in *History, Society and the Churches*, ed. D. Beales and G. Best (Cambridge, 1985), pp. 66n., 75.

58 James 1907–8 (with Supplement, 1914), which shows all the flair, and glaring faults, of James's catalogues — in particular his ignorance of legal books; but if it is regarded as notes towards a scholarly catalogue, it was a marvellous achievement. For Merton, see Powicke 1931; for Balliol, Mynors 1963; for Peterhouse and Queens', James 1899 and 1905; Searle 1864; and esp. Lovatt 1983–4. I have had much help in this section from successive Librarians, Philip Grierson and Jeremy Prynne, as well as from Catherine Hall, College Archivist.

59 My exact count is 355; but such precision is illusory, for these are many obscure problems, many shades of probability in identification or attribution — and what is now one book may have been two or three in the 15th century: see p. 35.

least 131 were in all probability in Gonville Hall before 1500; and there is no indication among the notes and shelf marks that the collection contains any substantial element from another college or library. There is indeed a marked absence of any sign that other colleges (most of which simply lost their medieval libraries in the conquest of print in the 16th century) contributed to the collection.[60] Furthermore, we have lists of some medieval bequests; and even allowing for some difficulties of interpretation and identification, they mostly encourage us to think that the college still preserves the bulk of what it received. Walter Crome, fellow in the 1420s, left seven volumes to Gonville Hall on his death in 1453, of which at least six can still be identified in its collection; with a generosity less prudently displayed he left ninety-three to the University Library, of which only eleven are still there.[61] In 1473 died John Beverley, fellow from c. 1425 – c. 1441, then canon of Lincoln; and he left sixteen volumes, all of which seem to be still there. These are startling proportions, for they suggest unusual vigilance in preserving not only the chained books in the main library, but the rest of the collection, which would normally have been lent for long periods to fellows. Thus from the rich records of the medieval library of Merton it appears that the college kept a firm grip on the chained books and the fellows took the rest.[62] A 15th century fellow of Gonville Hall might have said to his colleague in Merton that his college had a better record for preserving its library — and the fellow of Merton might have retorted that the books in his library were more assiduously read. However this may be, it seems likely that the main body of the medieval collection survives in the library still; and that Matthew Parker knew what he was doing when he made his colleagues in Gonville and Caius the watchdogs of his own great collection of manuscripts, the choicest pillage of some of the greatest of medieval libraries.[63]

No medieval library passed down the centuries unaltered. It would be absurd to suppose nothing was lost or that every one of the three hundred and fifty was in the library before 1500 — and indeed when Thomas James catalogued them in 1600 he found only 324, of which a small number are probably now missing.[64] There are vagaries in all such calculations. Thomas

60 A medieval catalogue was promised in the colophon of the register of 1472, Sheriffe's Evidences (MS 706/692); see James 1907–8, II, 683. But the promise is not fulfilled in the book as it stands. In its absence, there is an inevitable weakness in the argument here conducted. Yet if the collections were notably different from the library of c. 1500 it would be very strange, in so markedly academic a collection, if there was no substantial intrusion from other college libraries, or if such intrusion had left no trace; and it would be equally strange that we can point to so few losses from the bequests whose contents are known.

61 For Crome and Beverley (below), see Emden, pp. 168, 60; for their surviving books, see also James 1907–8, II, p. xix.

62 Powicke 1931, esp. p. 16.

63 MS 710/743 is the catalogue of the Corpus Library intended for audit by the Master of Caius and his colleagues; see James 1909–12, I, pp. xii–xiv.

64 James 1907–8, I, pp. ix–x. M. R. James's figure of 324 is probably an underestimate and he was unsure of the identification of many volumes; but he reckoned 'only one or two

James was far from infallible and he may have overlooked some books; and rebinding has a way of altering the number of surviving manuscripts — one volume may become two, and three be bound as one. Future research will add to the 131. We shall never know the whole story in detail; but we shall probably not greatly err if we reckon that about three hundred of the present collection or somewhat more were in the library in 1500. If so, it is the most substantial medieval academic library surviving intact in Cambridge.

A table below will show how the books are distributed among subjects. Such numeration is full of hazards — for quite heterogeneous themes may be collected under a single cover, and each of the categories is really much wider than it seems. Some liturgical books will be reckoned theology; some philosophical treatises by famous theologians appear under arts — and so forth. But when all allowances have been made, it is satisfactory to record that the proportions in the different subjects make reasonable sense, both among those marked as Gonville Hall's and those without specific evidence of their early history, and in the balance of subjects and the balance of studies in the college. Theology predominates, counting over twice as many as arts; canon and civil law come a distant third, with medicine still further behind. But the overall impression is of coherence; no-one who has worked extensively in these books could doubt that they comprise a working scholastic collection: the stock-in-trade of a run of the mill medieval

Medieval manuscripts

Subject area	Number with indications of Gonville Hall provenance	Number with no medieval indication of Gonville Hall
Arts	20	50
Canon Law	16	36
Civil (Roman) Law	11	28
Medicine	16	15
Theology (including liturgical books in brackets)	64 (1)	90 (4)
Etc.	4	5
Total	131	224
Combined total	355	

volumes' definitely missing since 1600. I have not attempted to check James's work on his namesake; when this has been undertaken this paragraph may need modification. The story will be clarified by future research, such as the work Mrs Hall is doing on the fellows' borrowing register of c. 1400.

academic library, a genuine reflection of a medieval college.

To all this it may be objected that a college library until quite recent times was the product of casual and occasional giving, not of carefully pondered purchase. No-one doubts that most books came by gift; nor that a great single bequest, like that of Dr Branthwaite in the early 17th century, could alter the whole balance of a collection (see p. 106). But gift and purchase do not automatically lead to quite divergent results. Most of the substantial gifts of books in 15th century Cambridge were distributed to more than one library — as was apparently common in 14th century Oxford; and the distributions presumably took some notice of the library's needs.[65] Gifts could be solicited or the result of negotiation; and buying can be at times remarkably unsystematic. There is a test in miniature in the medical books, for the bulk of them came from a single bequest, from Roger Marshall, who had been fellow of Peterhouse from *c.* 1437 to 1460, and who then established himself as a court physician to Edward IV and built up a practice in London.[66] He divided his fine library of medical and arts books between Peterhouse, Gonville Hall and King's and possibly others; sixteen or seventeen survive in the Caius Library, three (out of fifteen) in Peterhouse, and one in King's. Those he left to Gonville Hall did not form a perfectly balanced or complete collection, but they were a very tolerable foundation in a library evidently weak in medicine before his gift. It would be naive to expect an exact correspondence between the interests of the fellows and pensioners of 15th century Gonville Hall and the books which filled the library in 1500; but it is evident that there was a rough correspondence, and the balance and content of the collection is our best evidence of what happened in Gonville Hall in the late Middle Ages.

The catalogue of 1569 shows that the main reference books were still chained to desks disposed in bays between the five windows on either side and at the end of the library.[67] Doubtless the furniture in use in 1569 was still that of the 1430s. (The cases which now survive, and were moved to the new library in the 1850s, are of the 17th and 18th centuries.) The library of the 15th century seems likely to have been in the form common at that time, with lecterns in each bay, and two shelves for the chained books below the lecterns on either side.[68] The fellows of the 1430s made provision which would have done justice to a larger institution — and Peterhouse indeed began their library in the same year, and it was a key period in the development of monastic and college libraries. But it is likely that the shelves were

65 Cf., for Balliol and Oxford, Mynors 1963, pp. xi—xlix, esp. xi—xii; for Peterhouse, Lovatt 1983—4, pp. 64—8.
66 Emden, pp. 392—3; James 1907—8, II, p. xix.
67 Leedham-Green 1981.
68 Clark 1901; Streeter 1931. The 15th century library survives in Queens', but the furniture has been altered in the 17th century; the lecterns at Trinity Hall, though later (16th century), preserve the original form of a medieval library. For early Oxford libraries, see Highfield 1984, p. 257. For a wider view of medieval libraries, Wormald and Wright 1958. For Peterhouse, Lovatt 1983—4, p. 72.

designed to hold approximately two hundred and fifty volumes laid on their sides, so that we need not assume echoing spaces in the earliest days. But it was a lordly provision for five fellows and a few pensioners.

Of special interest to the modern scholar must be the law books, for it is hard to parallel such a collection in this country. Law books fared particularly ill in the 16th century holocaust, for Roman canon law departed with the pope, and Roman civil law never played the same role in this island that it did on the continent after the reception of Roman law in the late Middle Ages.[69] Indeed, there was evidently a spirit of conservation in Gonville Hall even before the advent of Dr Caius, since the handsome set of the *Corpus Iuris* printed in Venice in the 1490s, which has probably adorned the library shelves since the early 16th century at latest, by no means led to the loss of the relevant manuscripts. These included a manuscript of the *Digest*, books 25–38, which is the only English manuscript to play a part in Theodor Mommsen's great edition of 1866–70.[70] The Master and fellows of Caius, getting wind that Mommsen was at work, actually posted the manuscript to him — and by good fortune it escaped the fire in his house which disposed of some others of his materials. In his introduction Mommsen duly thanked them; but proceeded to abuse the book itself, which is a fine 13th century copy from a good tradition, but full of scribal errors. It once belonged to Master William of Louth, bishop of Ely at the end of the 13th century; and by the early 15th century, as a shelf-mark shows, it had come to Gonville Hall.

There are few rarities among these manuscripts; they rather reflect the working of practical academic needs. There once existed larger collections of legal manuscripts, we need not doubt; in the King's Hall, for example, canonist studies played a much larger role, in a much bigger college, than in Gonville Hall.[71] But the wind has blown them away. The books at Merton and Balliol are philosophical and theological; so are the bulk of those which survive from the Cambridge libraries, such as Peterhouse and Pembroke.[72] The interest of the books from Gonville Hall is that they are a very rare survival of such a working collection of legal texts — and that among them must be a number of books which helped to form the young William Lyndwood.

69 But see p. 85.
70 Mommsen, *Digesta*, I, pp. XXXXVIIII–L (*sic*); the MS is 15/131 (James 1907–8, I, 12–13), the editions of the 1490s, Schneider 1928, nos. 35–40. There is no indication when they came to the College, but they are in the catalogue of 1569 (Leedham-Green 1981, p. 38) and not indicated in any mid-16th century bequest, and it seems likely they were acquired soon after publication.
71 Cobban 1980, 1982, esp. pp. 69–71.
72 Powicke 1931; Mynors 1963; James 1899 (and his catalogue of Pembroke, 1905).

The Masters

If at the end of this rapid survey of the first 150 years of the College's life we stand back to take stock, it seems evident enough that in the 14th century, after the rapid disappearance of two founders and the departure of the brilliant young Master, John Colton, it was a struggling institution dependent on the devotion and prudence of a small group of young fellows, and such help and patronage as they could obtain. Better times, or anyway easier times, were to come in the 15th century; but the regime of Richard Pulham must have seemed precarious indeed. However, in his later years he witnessed the completion of the chapel under the direction of his colleague, or former colleague, William Rougham — not for the last time a successful physician brought a prosperous touch to the college; and doubtless both enjoyed mulcting their ruffianly bishop to preserve the heritage of his predecessor. In other ways too the Norfolk and Suffolk connections stood them in good stead. Early in Pulham's time, so it seems, a local family in Mutford helped to rebuild the church and put it in shape for its long support of the college's finances; and in the 1370s another East Anglian family added Mattishall, also after considerable additions to the church, to Bateman's endowment.[73]

It is often said that the fellows of medieval colleges were young men on the move, enjoying their fellowships for a short spell, then departing to richer pastures. Of many this was true, and John Colton is doubtless an example. But longevity was equally characteristic of the early Masters of Gonville Hall. When Pulham drew to the end of his days in the 1390s, Master William Somersham of Lynn was already a fellow of at least twenty years' standing; and by 1401 he had succeeded as Master and held office to his death in 1416.[74] Then came a remarkable change. Whether because Gonville Hall had achieved a measure of stability and was worth the attention of a notable figure in the University — or perhaps for the opposite reason, that it was in the doldrums and needed a shot in the arm — the next Master, John Rickinghall, was already Chancellor of the University, and seems to have combined the offices of Chancellor and Master, anyway for some years, a plurality always unusual. He was indeed a Norfolk man, and already established as a Doctor of Theology and a person of note. In 1426 he was consecrated bishop of Chichester, and a fortnight later resigned the Mastership; for a short spell, till his death in 1429, he combined the roles of bishop and confessor to the regent, the Duke of Bedford. Thus for the first time the Master's lodge or chamber came near to being a corridor of power.

---

73 For Mutford, *ER*, p. 66: tombs of the Hengrave family show their continuing interest in the church and may help to explain the fabric of the chancel, which seems to have been rebuilt *after* its appropriation to the College (I am indebted to the advice of A. Baggs and D. A. H. Richmond on Mutford church). For this the College cannot have paid. For Mattishall, *ER*, p. 59.

74 Hall and Brooke 1983, p. 46. For Rickinghall ibid. and Emden, p. 480.

Rickinghall had already been, while Master, chancellor of York, and archdeacon of Northumberland, as well as holding other preferment nearer to hand. But he was a man of Cambridge too and our accounts, which first survive from his Mastership, show him to have been often in residence.

With Thomas Wood we return to the earlier pattern: a fellow of many years standing who was evidently still young on his election, for he remained Master from 1426 to 1454 or later — may still have been Master when he died in 1456.[75] He was a modest pluralist, and he asked in his will to be buried at Elsworth not far from Cambridge. Of his regime, and the building of hall and library and lodge, we have spoken at length. The first two Masters had been canonists; the next three were theologians, concluding with Wood. Thomas Boleyn was a canonist, and like Rickinghall a mighty pluralist — canon of St Stephen's Westminster and Hereford and Abergwili at various times, and precentor of Wells, as well as enjoying rectories, some of them nearer home. While Master he received a papal dispensation — such as the rich could command and the not so rich sometimes beg for at this date — to hold three 'incompatible' benefices, that is, to which cure of souls was supposed to be attached.[76] Small wonder that the Master's lodge at Gonville Hall seemed a desirable home to ambitious men of the late 15th century.

A 16th century fellow has left us a garbled account of a disputed election on Boleyn's death in 1472.[77] The most likely explanation is that a young man called Hamond Booth or Bothe tried to usurp the Mastership. It was an act characteristic of the remarkable family to which he evidently belonged. Hamond became a canon of Exeter in the same year; and the bishop of Exeter was John Bothe, nephew of the half-brothers William and Laurence, both in their turn archbishops of York; rapacious members of a family which took much of the pickings of the English church of their day, and never lacked nephews to carry on their work. In Cambridge Laurence has a better fame than elsewhere, for he was a devoted Pembroke man, who added to the buildings of Pembroke Hall; and evidently his college found it worthwhile to keep so adroit a politician as its Master through the turmoil of the Wars of the Roses, for they continued the practice of electing political Masters after his death.[78] Laurence was Master of Pembroke 1450—80, while he was bishop of Durham (1457—76) and archbishop of York (1476—80) — and also for a time chancellor of the University. In spite of this strong connection, Hamond failed, and another pluralist without known links with the college, Edmund Argentein or Sheriffe, succeeded. Sheriffe was probably at least a local man, if not from the diocese of Norwich; and he marked his accession by drawing up the register and cartulary

---

75 Hall and Brooke 1983, p. 46; Emden, p. 23.
76 Emden, pp. 70—1; Hall and Brooke 1983, p. 47.
77 For this story see Hall and Brooke 1983, p. 47.
78 Emden, pp. 78—9; VCH Cambs, III, 348, 355.

known as Sheriffe's evidences, which contains the copy of Bateman's statutes in which the local limitation on the recruitment of Master and fellows first appears.[79] Whether it was directed for or against him we cannot say; nor whether he spent more of his reign in the government of the college or of his archdeaconry of Stow and canonry in Lincoln Cathedral.

In any event, his reign was short, and from 1477 the East Anglians resumed.[80]

First came Henry Costessy, a former fellow of King's Hall and already Master of the college of Rushford, who seems to have combined residence in Cambridge with residence in Norfolk, not only at Rushford, but at Norwich, where he and his successor made contacts profitable to Gonville Hall and its buildings. He died in 1483; and for the next twenty years John Barley or Barly was Master, another Norfolk man devoted to Norwich, but also a man of Gonville Hall, where he had been fellow since 1466. He died in 1504, requesting that he be buried in the churchyard of his Norwich rectory, St Michael Coslany.[81]

Thus ten Masters filled the space between Edmund Gonville and the chancellorship of John Fisher, the era of the Lady Margaret. In the same time, twenty-five men had held the office of warden of the King's Hall.[82] We have seen that there was considerable variety in the Masters of Gonville Hall. Some were men of note and substance, one on his way to a bishopric; but several were men who made of the College — often in combination with a country living or a home in Norwich or elsewhere — a way of life. The wardens of the King's Hall were rising men, academics who had won patronage from the king already and were likely to enjoy more. It is interesting that one of the longest lived was an ex-fellow of Gonville Hall, Richard Dereham, warden (in two spells) from 1399 to his death in 1416—17. Most of them represented a pattern common in University life in the late Middle Ages — men to whom the University was a stage in a career in the wider circles of royal or papal or episcopal service; men who might become bishops themselves. The striking feature of Gonville Hall is the prevalence of long-lived Masters who kept their offices, and though this may not always have been for the College's health, they provided it at least with a continuity otherwise difficult to establish in a young and modest institution.

---

79 Emden, p. 523; Hall and Brooke 1983, p. 47; the MS is 706/692.
80 For Costessy and Barley see Emden, pp. 38—9; Hall and Brooke 1983, p. 47; Venn, I, 11—12; III, 20—2.
81 His will is Public Record Office PCC 25 Holgrave (f. 200); cf. Hall and Brooke 1983, p. 47.
82 Cobban 1969, pp. 280—90; for Richard Dereham ibid. pp. 283—4; Emden, pp. 184—5.

3

Prelude to Dr Caius

Cambridge 1450—1550: the formation of the academic quarter

The period from 1450 to 1550 saw the transformation of both Oxford and Cambridge into the familiar pattern of collegiate universities. Before 1450 the colleges had formed an interesting, prestigious element in the universities, but harboured a minority — in Oxford a tiny minority — of the students. From 1450 on the transformation began. It is very difficult to pinpoint what precisely was new in that period; but some of the major causes of change and the forms it took are clear enough. For many decades they affected Gonville Hall relatively little; until under Dr Caius it emerged as a new college, part of the world of richer, larger colleges, dominating the academic, social and religious life of the universities.

In 1450 most students lived in hostels. Some of these already belonged to colleges, others were gradually absorbed. In Oxford there were 69 halls in 1444; already by 1469 they had fallen to 50, by 1501 to 31, by 1514 to 12 and by 1552 to 8.[1] It is more difficult to give figures for Cambridge, since evidence is less and research less advanced. But it has been established that there were about seventeen *c.* 1450, all of which had been absorbed by colleges or disappeared in the course of the late 15th or 16th centuries.[2] Probably there were originally more. One of the main differences between Oxford and Cambridge, however, was that Oxford was much larger, and that its hostels were normally rather smaller, than those of Cambridge, The most recent estimate, made by Dr T. H. Aston, suggests that Oxford as a whole numbered in the region of fifteen hundred students in the late 14th century, and perhaps slightly more in the mid 15th; while Cambridge had somewhere between four hundred and seven hundred in the mid to late 14th century, but by 1450 had risen to a figure much nearer Oxford's, say thirteen hundred.[3] These are admittedly rough estimates, and others have calculated differently. All are agreed that the growth of colleges and of collegiate teaching in the second half of the 15th and early 16th centuries brought Cambridge nearer to an equality with Oxford, an equality which was by the late 16th century fully established.

1   Pantin 1964, pp. 34—5.
2   Aston, Duncan and Evans 1980, pp. 14—15, estimates about 17, basing the figure primarily on the list by Rous in Toulmin Smith 1908, p. 157. Larger numbers are given in Willis and Clark, I, pp. xxv—xxviii and Stokes 1924, but these include doubtful cases and duplicates and need further critical scrutiny.
3   Aston, Duncan and Evans 1980, pp. 12—17. For Oxford in this period see esp. McConica 1975.

By 1550 almost every student in either university was a member of a college, and non-collegiate students virtually disappeared in the 1580s; although they reappeared for a time in the 19th and 20th centuries, the virtual identity of the university with the colleges is the essence of the system which separates these universities from all others in western Europe.[4] It is thus a crucial stage in the history of the universities, and still only partially understood. We can see that it reflected changes in every aspect of college and university life, academic, social, economic, religious and political; but some of these elements have been only very partially explored, and a general view is essential if we are to understand both the prelude to Caius and the work of Dr Caius himself.

Visitors to Cambridge are always struck by the modest extent of the central university buildings. The Old Schools are overshadowed by colleges on every side; and the first university building, the church of St Mary the Great, looks very modest when compared with King's Chapel over the road. In recent times the university has built or acquired very extensive faculty buildings and laboratories, above all the University Library. But until the library was built in the early 1930s library and university administration shared a single complex in what is now the Old Schools. Essentially this was possible because, between the 15th and 16th centuries and the 19th, the bulk of teaching took place within the colleges; lecturers gave courses and tutors arranged their pupils' programmes within the colleges, and they only had to emerge to take examinations and receive degrees. The origins of this system go back to 14th century Oxford and the tutors — at first little more than overseers and prefects — who were established by William of Wykeham in New College.[5] In the 15th century there is copious evidence from the King's Hall in Cambridge that a large number of fellows could act as tutors, which meant that they received their pupils' fees and organised their teaching and domestic life; this is the beginning of the undergraduate arrangements of later times, and evidently spread more rapidly in the larger colleges with younger students.[6] How soon it impinged on the smaller, graduate colleges, is very hard to tell. But it is evident that the appointment not only of tutors but of lecturers, at first in the basic arts, later in a wider range of subjects, became widespread in the second half of the 15th century.[7] Parallel with this went the break-down of the old university system of teaching in the arts. The 'necessary regents' — the young MAs whose necessary duty was to lecture in the arts — became less and less necessary and were relieved of their duties. It used to be said that it was the decay of

---

4 Russell 1977, pp. 734−5, throws considerable doubt, anyway for Oxford, on the confident view often expressed that non-collegiate students had virtually disappeared by 1550. There still had to be legislation against them in the early 1580s. But they were no longer numerous or respectable.
5 See esp. Cobban 1976, pp. 196−9.
6 Cobban 1969, esp. chap. 2.
7 Leader 1981, esp. chap. III; Cobban 1976.

university teaching in arts, and its failure to grasp the new needs of the humanist era, that made it essential for the colleges to take over such teaching. But recent research has shown that the seeds of the new system appeared first; and we may reasonably suppose that the two went hand in hand – the university provision was allowed to die because it was ceasing to be needed. The colleges were taking over.[8] But the details of the system are hard to discern, and in a number of colleges, like Gonville Hall, we have no clear evidence of tutors and lecturers until the 16th century was well under way.[9] The obscurity of the change is unfortunate, for it is undoubtedly one of the central features in the larger changes of the period. The appointment of college lecturers, for example, gave greater freedom of manoeuvre, and enabled colleges with forward-looking fellows to embark on humanist studies in the late 15th century. Nor was the movement all in one direction. The centrifugal tendency naturally made some feel strongly that a measure of central academic control was all the more necessary, and above all that there should be provision for salaried, permanent university professors in the central subjects of the curriculum. Under the inspiration of her confessor, John Fisher, the Lady Margaret provided for a preacher and a Professor of Divinity – the University preacher is a particularly significant feature of the age, for the love of sermons was assuredly no new discovery of the reformers. Not long after came Henry VIII's endowment of the first Regius Chairs, in Divinity, Greek, Hebrew, Civil Law and Physic[10] – Latin was too basic, Canon Law too risky, ever to achieve a Regius Professor. They were fine appointments in principle, and some of them had great influence in the 16th century; but so strongly had the tide run to the colleges in academic instruction that many of them had little to do in the early centuries of their existence, and by the 18th century a proposal that professors should be required to lecture was regarded as distinctly radical.

The appointment of lecturers and tutors was at first often on a very *ad hoc* basis, and it is difficult to document because clearly a good deal of the time it was fairly informal. But from the first this development must have favoured the larger and better endowed colleges. At least they set a pattern which the small foundations followed as they could. One of the most marked features of the history of Cambridge from the 15th to the 20th centuries has been the tendency for colleges to strive for equality of status and academic prestige. There is a paradox here, for they are also notoriously individual, and guard with jealousy their customs and peculiarities. But until the 1950s, with modest exceptions, the process of assimilation between smaller and larger, poorer and richer, went steadily on; only recently has it become fashionable to carve out a new line, of which the young graduate colleges are particularly clear examples. The race has not always been to the

8 Leader 1981; Cobban 1976.
9 Venn, III, 244 – 7.
10 Roach 1959, pp. 166 – 8, 177.

wealthy: the highest reputation of all in late 19th century Oxford (in the eyes of a wider world) lay with Balliol, then one of the poorest. But in the late 15th and 16th centuries there can be little doubt that the pattern of the future, and the greatest authority, lay with the largest colleges, the giants, really quite a new feature of the academic scene. Gonville Hall was a small college; Gonville and Caius has never been a giant; but the efforts of John Caius were aimed to bring it nearer into line or into competition with King's and St John's and Trinity.

The first of the very large colleges were the King's Hall in Cambridge, now absorbed in Trinity, and New College at Oxford: William of Wykeham more than doubled the number of fellows in Oxford colleges; and the King's Hall remained far and away the largest fellowship in Cambridge until Henry VI laid the foundations of King's College.[11] If he had completed it, then King's would have been a more splendid version of New College, and much the same can be said of the more effective foundation of Magdalen at Oxford by Henry VI's schoolmaster friend turned bishop of Winchester, William Waynflete. But in scale of foundation and grandeur and ostentation all these were overshadowed by Thomas Wolsey's Cardinal College, which survived as Christ Church, the most ostentatious royal monument in Oxford after its revival by Henry VIII — a theme he repeated in Cambridge when he united two colleges and much else besides in the formation of Trinity.[12] Nor had anything so substantial as Cardinal College been seen since the heyday of monastic foundations 300 years earlier. It is a constant source of astonishment to students of the 12th century that monasteries large and small were built for communities of varying size — but never as large as a modern school or large college — on a scale and with a solidity which the resources of the 20th century can rarely rival. They were sometimes intended for communities of monks vowed to poverty and an ascetic life, yet provided with buildings which the advanced economies of the modern world would consider expensive and grandiose. By the same token the colleges of the late 15th and 16th centuries, with their solid quadrangles, splendid halls and chapels and impressive gate towers, seem amazingly generous provision for relatively small communities of poor clerks.[13] The more one studies these buildings, indeed, the more one's amazement grows. For it is precisely in this period that the academic quarter was formed which has made Cambridge a famous and beautiful city. As one contemplates the ranks of colleges from Queens' to St John's one cannot doubt that many of their makers were conscious of the formation of this quarter; that it did not grow by accident. Yet it cannot be attributed to any man's policy — not to Henry VI who moved God's House away to its site

11 Buxton and Williams 1979, chap. 1, esp. pp. 3—4, 7 and nn.; Cobban 1969, esp. chaps. 1, 2.
12 VCH Oxford III, 228—35; Trevor-Roper 1973, chap. i; VCH Cambs, III, 462—3.
13 They are lavishly described in Willis and Clark and RCHM Cambridge.

outside the Barnwell Gate where its successor, Christ's College, still stands; nor to Bishop Alcock who seized and beautified St Radegund's, likewise outside the King's Ditch, on the east side of the town, and made it into Jesus College; nor John Fisher, on whose advice the Lady Margaret first turned her attention and resources to enlarging God's House into Christ's.[14] Yet it was precisely the same Henry VI and John Fisher who took the most crucial steps towards the creation of the academic quarter, Henry by cutting a great slice out of the west side of the town for his King's College, Fisher by urging and aiding the Lady Margaret to convert St John's Hospital into the College which marks the culmination of the quarter at its northern end. If we were to ask William Bateman or his advisers why they chose the sites for Trinity Hall and Gonville Hall, a variety of economic and practical considerations might come first in their answer. That part of Cambridge was always less built over, and sites were presumably cheaper than those closest to the High Street — especially after the Black Death; we may be sure that this affected Henry VI's choice of site for King's. Again, the site for Gonville Hall was evidently affected by the holdings of the Corpus Christi Guild with whom Bateman made exchange. But it can hardly be chance that he set both his colleges so close to the centre of the University. The first part of the Old Schools was begun very shortly before Bateman's foundations;[15] and already the area was graced, not only with Great St Mary's itself, but with Clare, Michaelhouse, and not far off, the King's Hall. From Bateman's time on, this region was always the nodal point of college development. By a combination of planning and chance, and owing to the curious shape of medieval Cambridge and the way it related to the river, the great academic quarter was formed in the period between 1350 and 1550.

In the 15th and 16th centuries we see the academic quarter not only filled in and beautified, but also punctuated with colleges of an unprecedented size and grandeur. Cardinal College was preserved as Christ Church by Henry VIII's desire for a monument in Oxford. No other college has a cathedral attached; it is a unique, astonishing combination, and reflects an enhanced view of the grandeur of a college. It was not wholly new — New College was splendid, King's in conception even more so; but a modest poor relation like Gonville Hall looks small indeed beside these growing giants. The next step on this path was the completion of King's Chapel, which was mainly a chantry, and an amazing monument to Henry VI's love of college chapels and Henry VIII's megalomaniac sins; and the next the foundation of Trinity, Cambridge, into which Henry VIII and his aides swept two earlier colleges.[16] Beside the splendour of the foundations, these colleges tended to

14 *VCH Cambs*, III, 421, 429—30. Henry VI's original site for King's is now the west court of the Old Schools; he soon after planned on a much more lavish scale, taking in virtually the whole site of modern King's between the High St and the river.

15 Willis and Clark, III, 10—11; *RCHM Cambridge*, I, 12—15.

16 Above n. 12; for King's Chapel, esp. Willis and Clark, I, 465—84; *RCHM Cambridge*, I, 99—131 (A. R. Dufty); *VCH Cambs*, III, 388—91 (J. Saltmarsh).

develop a new status for their heads, which is reflected in larger provision of lodges. Doubtless this was also partly because, after the Reformation, Masters might marry and have children. But the display is even more striking than the size of the new lodges. The long gallery at Queens' and the even longer gallery at St John's (now the Fellows' Combination Room) are among the most splendid of the Elizabethan age anywhere in the land, and among the most magnificent of any period in Cambridge.[17] Both were built for the parade of their heads; the Master of a Cambridge college was someone to reckon with, and the larger colleges at least wished it to be visible to their visitors and their fellows. Gonville and Caius has never acquired a lodge of this magnificence — it was scarcely large enough for children till the 18th century — but these events nearby help us to understand both how Dr Caius was inspired to enlarge a small foundation and bring it closer to its richer brethren, and how a man whose life was at London and in the circles of the court could be invited, and could agree, to be Master of a Cambridge college. In the 16th century indeed, there were no heads of quite the panache of Laurence Booth;[18] but it became common for Masters to be great men of the realm and the church, often combining their Masterships with deaneries elsewhere or similar offices. Thus Thomas Nevile as Master of Trinity (1593—1615) converted a tumble of buildings into Great Court and started the court which bears his name, and as dean of Canterbury (1597—1615) built the Deanery by a similar conversion of older foundations.[19]

Never before or since have the University and the colleges been so close to the centre of politics. If John Caius owed his wealth and authority to his standing as a physician to the great and the rich, his entanglement in religious disputes was nearly his undoing. It was above all the Reformation which made Cambridge so important politically. Yet the relationship started before that. It was indeed one of the martyrs of the Reformation, St John Fisher, who laid the foundation of these developments. As a devout Cambridge man he was president of Queens'; as the Lady Margaret's principal confessor he guided her hand in her endowment of her Professorship, her Preachership, and her Colleges, Christ's and St John's; as bishop of Rochester likewise he was involved in politics and government; as chancellor of the University for thirty-one years (1504—35) he greatly enhanced the political importance of the office.[20] In early days the chancellors had been elected annually and often only served for short spells. Thomas Rotherham, archbishop of York, had started the tradition of long-serving absentees;[21] but Fisher was the first whose influence in the

17 Willis and Clark, II, 21—36 (probably dating Queens' long gallery too early), 248—63; *RCHM Cambridge*, I, 168, 174 (re-dating the Queens' gallery), 194—5.
18 See p. 64. For Booth, *VCH Cambs*, III, 348; Emden, pp. 78—9.
19 Willis and Clark, II, 474—95, 517—18, etc.; *RCHM Cambridge*, II, 212—13.
20 Porter 1958, chap. 1.
21 Emden, p. 289.

University was constantly felt. When Henry VIII broke with Rome and had Fisher beheaded, the significance of Cambridge — both as a source of support and a potential source of danger — was reflected in the appointment of Thomas Cromwell, the all-powerful minister, as chancellor; and in the reign of Elizabeth the queen's leading minister, Lord Burghley, was chancellor (1559—98) and tirelessly concerned in the minutiae of Cambridge affairs — whether it be the religious complexion of professors and students, or the tendency of the fellows of Queens' to waste their assets and spoil the Backs by cutting down trees.[22] Political chancellors succeeded him through several generations, but the role of the office gradually changed; at first and particularly because no minister could attend to its business as Burghley had done, and because as the Reformation receded no government ever felt quite so sensitive again to its thoughts and its teaching.

The most remarkable of the figures linking Cambridge and the political world were Thomas Cranmer of Jesus, who rose with only a slight intermission from a Cambridge fellowship to the see of Canterbury; and Matthew Parker, who rose to the same throne, after a spell of exile, from the Mastership of Corpus. Parker was an important figure both in the history of Cambridge and of Gonville and Caius. He and his friend William May, president of Queens', — with John Redman, who helped Henry VIII to find his vocation as founder of Trinity — had been the leaders in the late 1530s and 1540s, who saved Cambridge colleges from the threat of dissolution by their adroit manoeuvring of college accounts to convince the king that they were insolvent bodies not worth dissolving, and by exploiting their political influence in the later stages of the Henrician Reformation.[23] Under Mary they both were in eclipse, but when Elizabeth came to the throne, Parker passed rapidly to Lambeth; and May would have become archbishop of York had death not intervened. Parker was naturally Burghley's right hand man in the management of Cambridge, and his personal friendship with John Caius and confidence in him helped to save Caius from disgrace and his college from destruction in the late 1560s and early 1570s. They had a common interest in colleges and in antiquities: both were men of wide and curious learning and extreme credulity. But in religious matters, as contemporary report had it, they seemed far apart in the 1570s.

The Masters of Gonville Hall, 1483—1557

We may now turn back and trace the fortunes of Gonville Hall in the last years of its existence. The links between the college and Norfolk and

---

22 Roach 1959, pp. 180—9; see below, pp. 91—3; for the Queens' trees, Searle 1867—71, II, 371—4.

23 Roach 1959, p. 177; Documents 1852, I, 105—294. On May, see Searle 1867—71, I, 211—44, 285—94; on Parker, below, chap. 4.

Norwich remained at first as close as ever, and were symbolised by the three successive Masters, John Barley, Edmund Stubb and William Buckenham (1483–1536) who were also rectors of St Michael Coslany in Norwich and who evidently divided their time between Norwich and Cambridge. Barley began the rebuilding and refurbishment of the rectory at Norwich — he 'edified out of the ground the . . . parsonage and the wall, sealed and glazed all the chambers therein'; Stubb extended the house in Norwich and 'built the stable there'; Buckenham 'bought a little piece of ground' to enlarge the yard 'where standeth the coop for capons and the privy, and made the wall'.[24] All this has a somewhat remote and rustic air; but William Buckenham was also a figure in the University. He is indeed a remarkable link between two worlds. He was a fellow from 1488 and lived to sign in 1535 as Master the acknowledgement of the royal supremacy over the Church; he died in the same year as Thomas Cromwell, in 1540. In 1508 he was executor to the most considerable Cambridge scholar of the generation before the coming of Erasmus, John Argentein, provost of King's, physician and Doctor of Divinity, who had probably studied his medicine in Padua, as Caius was later to do.[25] In 1508 Buckenham also became vice-chancellor and must have had close contact with the chancellor, John Fisher — perhaps too with Fisher's friend Erasmus, who came to Cambridge in 1506 and again in 1511.[26] Erasmus reckoned that the Cambridge of Fisher was a new place, in which it was possible to study Greek seriously and to lay humanist foundations for a sound study of theology. The humanists always exaggerated the difference between themselves and their predecessors, and Erasmus' judgement seems largely to be a compliment to Fisher, whom he justly admired. There is no doubt that humanism in the sense of serious and extensive classical study on the Italian model, and any deep knowledge of Greek and Hebrew, came very slowly to Cambridge — and that it had arrived in time to inspire the young John Caius in the 1520s and 1530s.[27] We shall not be far wrong to conclude that it interested him a good deal more than the current theological controversies which were stirring Cambridge and Gonville Hall in particular. Yet he cannot have been unaffected, for his elder colleagues included Nicholas Shaxton, and Matthew Parker, his contemporary, was in the long run to become one of his closest friends.

The first stirrings of Protestant doctrine in Cambridge are associated with the circle of Thomas Bilney of Trinity Hall and Hugh Latimer of Clare; and with them for a time at least Nicholas Shaxton of Gonville Hall. By the 1530s Cranmer and Parker were its rising stars. In 1533 Cranmer was consecrated to Canterbury, and in the next two years Shaxton became bishop of Salisbury and Latimer bishop of Worcester. Henry VIII's conscience, or

24 Hall and Brooke, pp. 47–8, citing Archives X, 1aa.
25 For Buckenham, Hall and Brooke, p. 48; Emden, pp. 103–4; for Argentein, Emden, pp. 15–16, 669.
26 Porter 1958, chap. 2; Thomson and Porter 1963.
27 See below, pp. 56–8.

some other parts of his psyche, had troubled him, and Queen Anne had replaced Queen Catherine. Anne had long been patron of a group of Protestant divines and sympathisers.[28] In the college where her great-great-uncle Thomas Boleyn had been Master, her influence was for a short time strong. A leading go-between was the royal physician William Butts, formerly of Gonville Hall; and Shaxton had been her almoner before he became a bishop. One of the senior fellows, John Skipp, was her chaplain, and later her almoner, and her companion in her last days; and the most outspoken of the Gonville Hall Protestants, Edward Crome, a friend of Bilney and Latimer, was presented by her to the living of St Mary Aldermary in London in 1534.[29] A majority of the fellows, indeed, seem to have had Protestant leanings or sympathies. But there is a substantial part of the community whose beliefs are unknown to us. The pensioners included a contingent of monks and canons, and Venn seems to have assumed that these would have been Catholic and conservative.[30] The ground for his opinion is not clear. It is true that two came from a house where there was reputed to be trouble when Thomas Cromwell's visitors inspected the monasteries in preparation for their dissolution; but all of them belonged to monasteries which submitted without a murmur both to the royal supremacy and to their final surrender. All whose later history is known received pensions at the dissolution; two became canons of Norwich of the new foundation, one archdeacon and canon of Winchester. The most remarkable, William Repps, became bishop of Norwich in 1536, soon after the elevation of Latimer.[31] But he had departed from Gonville Hall long before; and of the monks and canons it is in general reasonable to suppose that they accepted change without actively seeking it — and that above all they had no defence, in political ideas or theology, against the will and supremacy of the monarch.

In 1535 the Royal Supremacy — which effectively ended the jurisdiction of the Pope in England — was subscribed to in the College by the old Master, William Buckenham, a DD for nearly 30 years; by Roger Overy, whose later sympathies at least seem to have been mildly Protestant; by John Styrmin, later to succeed John Skipp both as archdeacon of Hereford and as Master, and evidently of his mind, and inclined to the new doctrines; Laurence Maptid, who in later years was to accept the Mastership of Corpus under Mary when Parker was ejected — and so was of Catholic sympathy in the 1550s; Andrew Deane, who was also received in Corpus in

---

28 On Queen Anne and Gonville Hall see now Dowling 1984; on Butts esp. pp. 35, 38, and below, pp. 56—7, pl. 13a; on Shaxton, pp. 53—4.

29 On Shaxton and Skipp, Dowling 1984, p. 38; Hall and Brooke, p. 48; Venn, I, 19—21; III, 25—7; on Crome, Dowling 1984, pp. 38—9; Venn, I, 28. William Betts, also a chaplain of Anne, had been a pensioner at Gonville Hall: see Dowling 1984, pp. 37, 40; Venn, I, 27.

30 Venn 1912, p. 3, contrasting them with Shaxton and Skipp; for a full account of them, which allows for some influence from the reformers on them, see Venn 1913, chap. VI.

31 On Repps see Venn, I, 18; he was bishop of Norwich 1536—50 (*Fasti 1300—1541*, IV, 25).

Parker's absence under Mary; John Caius himself: and William Barker, of whose opinions we know nothing, save that he was a good friend of John Caius, and in the early 1570s was making gifts to the College chapel.[32]

If we add to this list the small number of pensioners known to have Protestant links[33] — and an absent fellow, John Skipp himself, soon to become Master, who was evidently signing the Supremacy elsewhere — there appears to be a solid group of sympathisers both with the royal will and with Protestant doctrine in the College and a smaller group of more conservative temperament. But some of the evidence is sketchy — a man might hold very different opinions in 1535 and 1555; and the Reformation brought out every nuance of doctrine and attitude.

There was already at this time a group of eminent physicians linked to Gonville Hall. Caius tells us that William Butts, whom we have met as a patron of Anne Boleyn's Protestant chaplains, and who went with him to Padua and returned to treat Henry VIII and die in 1545, was for a time a member of the College; so also Henry Walker, who became Regius Professor of Physic c. 1555, and Thomas Wendy, a notable benefactor to the College, who studied in Ferrara and was royal physician to Henry VIII and all his children, including Queen Elizabeth, dying in 1560.[34] All these men studied in Italy in milieux principally Catholic; Butts had harboured Protestant sympathies none the less; but Walker was, or became, so convinced a Catholic that he played an active part in Cardinal Pole's visitation of the University in 1557. Wendy and Caius, however, faithful London physicians and men of international learning, seem to have stood a little apart from doctrinal disputation and to have cared more for what united the academic commonwealth of letters than for its divisions. John Caius himself spent a part of his early years translating some of Erasmus' theological works, an activity neither very conservative nor revolutionary.[35] His main interest before he went to Padua seems to have lain in humanist studies, in Latin and Greek and Hebrew; even in Padua he taught Greek while studying medicine; nor did his affection for things humanist desert him when he became an eminent physician.[36] Thus in the 1530s Caius was a fellow in a group with close links with Queen Anne, ready to sign the royal supremacy, among whom several had advanced Protestant leanings, and some were to emerge as conservatives and catholics. He himself, though he studied theology, may never have been deeply involved in these controversies; but he was sufficiently sympathetic to make friends with Parker,

32 Venn, I, 30.
33 On Sygar Nicholson, the printer, see Venn, I, 25; Black, 1984, pp. 12−13, 21: he has been supposed a pensioner of the College, but may simply have been a tenant.
34 *Annals*, p. 29; Caius, *De methodo medendi* (edn. of Basel, 1544), Praef. On Wendy, Venn, I, 24; III, 217; *Ann. Coll. Medicorum* in Caius, *Works*, pp. 18−51. On Butts see n. 28; Venn, I, 17; on Walker, Venn, I, 27−8.
35 Caius, *De libris suis*, in *Works*, p. 70.
36 See below, p. 57.

sufficiently aloof to travel happily in Catholic and Protestant universities on the continent.

In May 1536 Queen Anne was executed; but her chaplain and almoner did not suffer in her fall, and was elected Master in or shortly after June.[37] He was evidently no fervent Lutheran, for in 1539, when Shaxton and Latimer resigned their sees after refusing to accept the king's conservative Six Articles, Skipp rose to be bishop of Hereford; in 1540 he resigned the Mastership. No modern study has been made of him, but he appears from what we currently know to have grown more catholic as the years passed. He died in London in 1552, surrounded by a group of Norfolk friends, recalling his origin, not his bishopric; the witnesses to his will included Dr Wendy who was doubtless attending to his sickness. John Styrmin, Skipp's successor as Master, and colleague at Hereford, where he was archdeacon, had also died in 1552 – in death as in life a close colleague of Skipp.[38]

In 1552 Thomas Bacon succeeded, the last Master of Gonville Hall, the first of Gonville and Caius College. His memory has suffered grievously from the assaults of John Caius; he may have been a little easy in his ways and (if Caius' most serious accusation was true) inclined to hand over to his brother, a London merchant, money he owed the College.[39] He occasionally came late to audit – perhaps because he had to share his attention between the College and a scatter of livings in Kent and East Anglia. But the accounts were kept and the library and much else of the College's past survived to be garnered and fostered by Caius himself. There can be little doubt that Caius enlarged his own achievements by belittling his predecessor; yet if the College were to compare what it owed to Bacon and to Caius, doubtless it could reasonably forget Thomas Bacon. Like Caius himself, he seems to have been quite at home with the regime of King Philip and Queen Mary; and on 14 January 1557 he entertained in the lodge the vice-chancellor and a group of leading heads, including Laurence Maptid, ex-fellow and Master of Corpus, and witnessed the sealing of the instrument condemning the great reforming theologian Martin Bucer and his friend the Hebrew scholar Fagius, both happily some years dead.[40] Their bodies were solemnly burnt in the Market Place, one of many violent acts of the period.

In 1530 Richard Nykke, bishop of Norwich, had written to Archbishop Warham that 'I hear of no clerk that hath commen out lately of' Gonville Hall 'but savoureth of the frying pan, though he speak never so holily'; and

37 On Skipp, see Hall and Brooke, p. 48 and refs.; Venn, III, 25 – 7; *Fasti 1300 – 1541*, II, 3; III, 9; IV, 34.
38 Hall and Brooke, p. 48 and refs.; Venn, III, 27 – 8. Skipp had voted against the Act of Uniformity of 1549, i.e. against the Prayer Book of 1549, evidently because he took a more conservative view of eucharistic doctrine than Cranmer and most of his colleagues (Cuming 1982, pp. 54 – 6).
39 *Annals*, p. 42; cf. Hall and Brooke, p. 48, q.v. for Bacon's accounts; on Bacon see Venn, II, 28 – 42.
40 Venn, III, 29.

in 1531, when Bilney had been burnt and Shaxton had for the moment recanted, he is alleged to have exclaimed — 'I fear I have burnt Abel and let Cain go'.[41] But the College passed quietly on — some of its members suffered imprisonment for a while at one or another crisis between the 1520s and the 1550s; but none, so far as we know, slipped into the fire.

The mid-16th Century and Bishop Shaxton

In 1506 John Fisher had preached his famous sermon before Henry VII in which he spoke of the 1490s as a time when there was 'weariness of learning and study, so that not a few did take counsel in their own minds how that they might effect their departure so as it were not to their own hurt' — observing that royal bounty offered a modest improvement in more recent years.[42] When Caius returned to Cambridge in the late 1550s after nearly twenty years of study in Padua and prosperous medical practice in London, he was saddened by the signs of change which he saw in the students about him, and looked back to a golden age in the 1530s. In Venn's admirable paraphrase, 'he contrasts them, sadly to their disadvantage, with the short-haired, long-gowned lads of his remembrance, who found their only joy, not in games, but in admiring and critical attendance on each other's disputations in the schools; who never missed a public lecture, or visited a public house; who spent their scanty pocket money not on clothes which would wear out, but on books which might endure for ever. They seldom stirred from the College walls except on their way to the Schools; and were ever on the lookout reverently to salute their elders . . .'[43] Both have been taken to portray a time of decay, even if it was to be checked by their own endeavours. But Fisher simply described the outward-looking view which has always been essential for most university students — towards the career or the benefice which would lead them on to life and livelihood; and Caius' lament has an eternal quality which can be paralleled in every age from Noah's to the present, and can only be taken seriously by those who think that continual decadence is the human lot. In Cambridge one might almost think that the opposite was true. A university which was once a modest satellite of Oxford now commanded the centre of the stage. The decades which linked the heyday of John Fisher, the rise of Matthew Parker and John Redman, and the return of John Caius, may be seen as the first golden age in the history of Cambridge — for all the anxieties and set-backs, for all the rancour and the flames of the Reformation and Counter-Reformation. But there is a paradox in such a view, for it also witnessed the silencing of

41 Strype 1812, II, 696 (with text corrected by Henry Ellis; the original is BL Cotton Cleop.E.v, f.389; spelling here modernised); Foxe, IV, 650. Cf. Dowling 1984, pp. 35, 38, citing Venn 1901, pp. 34, 39; Morgan 1975, p. 207.
42 Mullinger 1873, p. 427, from Lewis 1855, II, 269; also quoted Roach 1959, p. 165.
43 Venn, III, 43; Venn 1912, pp. 3–4.

many leading academics, the first major incursion of politics into Cambridge, and a sharp decline, apparently, in numbers.

In Gonville Hall we have two striking testimonies to this decline. When Henry VIII and John Redman united the King's Hall and Michaelhouse to make Trinity, they swept up Physwick Hostel, cutting off in one blow perhaps a half, very likely more than a half of the rooms of Gonville Hall. Yet in spite of this the aging Bishop Shaxton, who had twice been involved in Protestant advance and twice recanted, now in his conservative old age under Queen Mary a respectable suffragan to the bishop of Ely, was able to find an ample suite of two chambers, one above the other, and two small rooms beside, in Gonville Court, in which to settle his splendid collection of books and end his days.[44] While he lived, he gave some fine books to the library and money to warm the Hall and Parlour on saints' days in winter. In College he died, in August 1556. In his will he asked to be buried in the College chapel and divided his goods between the College and a friend called Thomas Alabaster in Hadleigh in Suffolk where Shaxton had been rector, 'to the behoof and profit of his lad by him named Thomas Dratsab'. The patent reversal of 'bastard' in the boy's name has led to the assumpton that he was Shaxton's own son, and this is possible. In his Protestant days the bishop had taken a wife. At his second recantation in 1546 he had been made to preach at the burning of Anne Askew, a 'heretic' whom he had formerly supported, and then to return to his home at Hadleigh in Suffolk to repeat his recantation and repudiate his wife. From then on he was a chastened and, apparently, a convinced Catholic. He tried to reconcile Mrs Shaxton to her lot by composing for her some verses of doggerel urging her to celibacy.

> '. . .Voyde evil thoughtes, studie in scripture
> Kepe thine eye, ill company eschue . . .
> The ryme is base, the medicine is good . . .'

and so on for some 60 halting lines. All this we know because a former friend and persevering Protestant, Robert Crowley, a master printer who later rose to be an archdeacon, published a rebuttal of Shaxton's recantation, and set at the head of these verses, 'The copye hereof was had at hys wyves handes', adding a vigorous commentary of his own. Even St Paul

---

44 The evidence for this is his will and inventory (CUL, Vice-Chancellor's Court, Probate Wills, 1501 – 58, f. 100; and Inventory, 1556), which describe upper and lower chamber, little chamber and study in a manner very similar to the suite Stephen Perse occupied at his death in 1615 (below, p. 99). On Shaxton, see also Venn, I, 19; *DBN*; *Fasti 1300 – 1541*, III, 3; Porter 1958, pp. 42 – 3, 61; BL Lansd. MS 979, ff. 148v – 151v. On his books see Leedham-Green 1981, who shows that none of the books in his Inventory can be identified in the library catalogue of 1569 and many must certainly be lost. My own view is that the library received the books listed in *Annals*, p. 14, in his lifetime, with the other gift there, which is not in his will, and somehow failed to absorb the books in his inventory even though they must have been in college at his death.

'durste prescribe no remedie
Agaynste fleschlye incontinence: (1 Cor: vii)
But onely chaste matrimonie,
Whyche kylleth all concupiscence.'[45]

But Shaxton's return to Catholic discipline was final, and we hear no more of his wife; and after his death, no more of the lad Thomas. When the bishop died, he left all his books or so many as were 'wanting in' Gonville Hall Library to the College, 'for the use of such as are lawfully admitted to study in the' library. But apart from those he had given in his lifetime they cannot now be found. He also gave a house in Cambridge whose rent was 'to solace the company at home yearly in Christmas[tide]' — and that bequest from the first fellow known to have been married was happily remembered in the 1940s so that the fellows and their wives are summoned yearly, soon after Twelfth Night, to Bishop Shaxton's Solace.

---

45 R. Crowley, *The Confutation of xiii. articles, whereunto Nicolas Shaxton . . . subscribed . . .*, London, 1548, ff. Aii — A(v) (original spelling).

4

Caius[1]

John Caius laid an indelible mark upon his College. That is as he would have wished; for he loved it with a dedicated, possessive affection, and he was a man in whom generosity and egoism, selfless devotion and fanatical self-will were strongly mingled. He was also a man of very various learning, of imagination deep and rich; a character, one of the ripe eccentrics of British history; a man who could not fail to leave his mark. He loved symbolism, and his years in Italy had made him a humanist to the core – hence the Gates of Humility, Virtue and Honour, in spirit and design emanations of the Renaissance – even if the Gate of Honour reflects a characteristically personal, eclectic taste in the fusing of Gothic ornament with the high Renaissance. He was a great medical practitioner, whose practice in the city of London and among the nobility must have provided the wealth which enabled him to double the endowment of the College and enrich it with beautiful buildings. He laid his mark also on the College of Physicians of which he was many times president; over the centuries since his death, his name and college have had a medical flavour in the public image.[2] He was an intensely vivid personality; a man who did nothing by halves; a man of some magnetism who made friends in many places; but also sharp, quick-tempered, crabbed, cantankerous, authoritarian, dictatorial – a man who stirred opposition and faction about him, expelled his more contumacious colleagues from their fellowships (if we may believe the charges made against him) and put the less offensive in the stocks.[3] He could reduce even his friend the masterful diplomat Archbishop Matthew Parker to exasperation.[4] His fate was to have his name and profession and oddity – if nothing else that was genuinely his – immortalised in the *Merry Wives of Windsor*.[5] But he enjoyed too a better destiny. He lies in his college chapel in a peace he never knew in its walls when he was alive; his monument is one of the most inspired memorials ever a man raised to himself; and the

1 The chapter is based on Venn, III, 30 – 63, revised in Venn 1912, pp. 1 – 78, (which is usually cited below), and on Caius, *Works*. I have greatly benefited from Grierson 1978 and Raven 1947, pp. 138 – 53; see also *DSB*, III, 12 – 13 (C. D. O'Malley); *DNB*; Clark 1964, pp. 107 – 24; McNair 1969; Nutton 1979; O'Malley 1955. Since this was completed I have seen a deeply interesting forthcoming study of Caius' work on Galen etc. by Dr V. Nutton.
2 See esp. pp. 93 – 5, 187, 288.   3 See pp. 70 – 77, and 74 n.3.
4 See p. 74.
5 But see McNair 1969, for a fairly sceptical view of the influence of Caius on Shakespeare. Yet some connection seems almost certain; and on Dr Caius' 'counting-house' (McNair 1969, p. 338) see Catherine Hall's paper in *The Caian* 1987.

College remembers his kindly gifts and honours his name, making some amends for the fierce ingratitude of his contemporaries.

Scholar, Humanist and Physician

His name reminds us of the humanist: it turns into classical form the name of his family, Keys or Kees or what-you-will — John Venn counted ten different spellings in the accounts of Caius' time as student and fellow.[6] He was born in Norwich of Yorkshire stock, in October 1510, six years after the birth in the same city of Matthew Parker. He came to Gonville Hall in September 1529, eighteen years old.[7] He was a scholar from 1530 to 1533, leading the University in the exercises for his BA early in that year; on 6 December 1533 he was elected a fellow, and spent his first two years (in accordance with the original intention of the college statutes) completing his MA. He seems to have been seriously interested in theology at this time; but he never embarked on a theological degree and his course was diverted, we may think, by two influences. In the 1530s the College had close links with the household of Anne Boleyn and the first stirrings of Henrician Protestantism, if the phrase may be allowed.[8] John Caius may well have found the breath of new ideas confusing, as many did — for although Cambridge was to be so vivid a centre of Reformation ideas and influences, the number of students of theology fell for a time dramatically in the mid-16th century. In any case, Caius was duly impressed by the distinction of some of the College's theologians, for he puts at the head of his list of its worthies at this time in the *Annals* William Repps, later bishop of Norwich, and its two most notable reforming bishops, Nicholas Shaxton of Salisbury and John Skipp, Master and bishop of Hereford.[9] But we may well reckon that the next two names on his list counted for more in his life: William Butts, who as royal physician and patron of reformers is now regarded as the major link between the College and Queen Anne; and Thomas Wendy, another eminent court physician, nearer in age to Caius himself, and a figure in the College's history for many years to come.[10] We may reckon that these men first turned his thoughts to medicine.

But the surest influence on him in these years lies in his growing affection for the classical past, his classical learning, and his evident desire to mingle in the cosmopolitan humanist life of the continent.[11] Love of humanism and

6 Venn 1912, p. 2.
7 For this and what follows, Venn 1912, pp. 1—5.
8 See above, pp. 48—51.
9 *Annals*, p. 29.
10 See above, pp. 49—50 and pl. 13a.
11 This is abundantly clear from a wide range of evidence, especially his *De libris propriis* and *De pronunciatione Graecae et Latinae linguae* (in Caius, *Works*), but his learning and his library were both eclectic — see Grierson 1978, p. 523.

the lure to study medicine doubtless combined to inspire his wish to visit Italy; and it seems that he went with William Butts to Padua — certainly it was a meeting with Butts at Dover in 1539 which was the immediate prelude to his journey.[12] In Padua he studied medicine under J. B. Montanus; and the most famous of his teachers was Vesalius the anatomist.[13] For eight months Caius and Vesalius lodged in a house called the Casa degli Valli. His humanist studies continued; and for a time he was 'Professor of Greek Dialectic', an office which doubtless helped to support him through the years of study, although he also retained his fellowship in Gonville Hall. His chair involved lectures on Aristotle based on his Greek text. In 1541 he proceeded to the degree of Doctor of Medicine at Padua, but continued his studies there for two more years. In 1543 he moved to Florence, and then to Pisa; and over the next two years toured northern and central Italy, down to Siena and Rome.[14] Although he had been fascinated with the anatomical dissections of Vesalius and was to make dissection a central part of his own teaching of medicine in England, the central principle of his medical theories, which he had learned at the feet of Montanus and pursued with a logic and a rigour beyond his master's, was that the essential foundation of all true medical science lay in the ancient works of Hippocrates and Galen. If, as the moderns rashly asserted, Galen was found to err, it was due to the corruption of his texts not the failure of his genius.[15] With this in mind he toured Italian libraries searching for manuscripts of Galen and other ancient authorities which he could copy, purchase or borrow. At every stage of the formation of his mind his imagination was fired by the new learning; but his scientific progress was hampered by his humanist fundamentalism and the love of ancient texts. The young fellows of Caius of the 1560s were to accuse him of atheism; and if this meant more than occasional outbursts of ill-temper, in which he uttered warm and blasphemous words — it surely only meant that in his heart he loved Galen above St Paul. More immediately, it led him to view the original scientific work of men like Vesalius with a distinct reserve; and to compose his first substantial treatise, 'On the art of healing', which is essentially a commentary on Galen and Hippocrates developing the methods of Montanus.[16] The first step in the art of healing was a proper understanding of Hippocrates and Galen: briefly at the outset he outlines the necessary stages of learning in a manner which may remind a medievalist of the way in which late antique writers like Cassiodorus made the study of all the liberal arts a necessary foundation to theology, and the study of ancient authors as authorities the basis of all branches of learning. Caius displays a humanism solidly based on medieval academic methods. But this did not hinder him from finding

12 *De Medendi Methodo*, edn. of Basel 1544, Praef.
13 Venn 1912, pp. 5–6; O'Malley 1955.
14 Venn 1912, pp. 6–7. [See n. 1.]
15 Grierson 1978, p. 522; Nutton 1979, esp. for Montanus, pp. 381–2; O'Malley 1955.
16 *De Medendi Methodo*, Basel, 1544; the edn. of 1556 is in Caius, *Works*.

new matter for intellectual excitement. His book was published in Basel in 1544, on the first stage of his journey back to England; and it was presumably at that time that he met and made friends with Conrad Gesner of Zürich, the great Swiss naturalist, whose friendship inspired Caius to another of his most characteristic interests, in the natural world, especially in animals — he was to provide Gesner with material for his *Historia Animalium* and to compose a neat little treatise of his own 'Of English dogs'.[17] He has left fine descriptions, for example, of a dolphin and a sturgeon he saw in London; and of the 'Hippelaphus' from Norway, evidently an elk — though Caius was deeply convinced it could not be an elk, since he knew, or thought he knew, from Caesar, that elks have no joints in their legs.

Gesner's sudden death in 1565 inspired some pages of lament and reflection on human mortality and fate in Caius' autobiographical account of his own writings, *De libris propriis*, printed in 1570. He talks of Gesner as his dearest friend, his death as an event from which it took him a great while to recover. 'That happy man rests in peace — good, just, set apart from the storms and sorrows of this life — this wretched life which we mortal men still drag on in our unhappiness, however rich in earthly goods we are . . .' and he quotes 'Posidippus' for the reflection that it is better for a man never to have been born, or, if he must be, to perish quickly.[18] The news had fallen on him at the height of his quarrels with the fellows of Caius, which may have sharpened the edge of his sorrow. The passage shows a gleam of light when it talks of the after-life — 'post funera vivere', a phrase recalled in his epitaph; but in its essence it is a humanist's lament with nothing specifically Christian in it.

His contributions to natural history show an extraordinary combination of shrewd observation and learning with much credulity and philological pedantry. Philip Grierson, in his fascinating study of Caius' library, has shown how deep and yet how eclectic was the learning reflected in the collection of books he bequeathed at his death. Hippocrates, Dioscorides, Celsus — and above all, the great master Galen — were richly represented; and there was much other medical and scientific matter, but within certain marked limits, for physical science and metaphysics have little place, and even medical and surgical tracts fall sharply off after the mid 1540s. 'One

17 For all this see esp. Raven 1947, pp. 138—53; also Venn 1912, p. 7; *De canibus* and *De rariorum animalium . . . Historia* in Caius, *Works*; and esp. *De libris propriis* (ibid.), pp. 94—8, for his lament on Gesner's death. For what follows see Raven 1947, pp. 142, 145.

18 *De libris propriis* (in Caius, *Works*), pp. 94—8, at p. 95 (edn. of 1570, f. 22). Charles Brink tells me the saying is attributed to Posidippus, among others, in the Palatine Codex of the *Greek Anthology* (*Hellenistic Epigrams*, ed. A. S. F. Gow and D. L. Page, Cambridge, 1965, I, 173, II, 501—2), and suggests it may have been known to Caius through Stobaeus' collection of famous sayings, *Flor*. iv. 34, 57. This suggestion is the more appropriate since the current Latin version of Stobaeus was by Gesner himself (Zürich, 1543, p. 465); unfortunately the copy in the College library came there later, from William Branthwaite, but this was surely Caius' source.

has the feeling that, in a period when medicine was rapidly changing and new works were constantly seeing the light, Caius was largely living in the past'.[19]

In humanist studies and medical science, and even in natural history, Caius advanced little beyond the experience of the early and mid 1540s. Late in 1544 or in 1545 he returned to England, resigned his fellowship at Gonville Hall and settled in London.[20] In 1547 he became a fellow of the Royal College of Physicians; about the same time he began his series of lectures on the theory and practice of anatomy, with demonstrations of dissection, at the Barber-Surgeons' Hall; in 1551 he set up house in the close of St Bartholomew's Hospital in the city of London.[21] Of his lectures a contemporary said that they revealed 'unto this fraternity — the Barber-Surgeons — the hidden jewels and precious treasures of Cl. Galenus, showing himself to be the second Linacre'.[22] In another way he showed himself a worthy successor to Linacre, as a central figure in the progress of the College of Physicians, whose *Annals* he wrote and whose president he was to be over the years 1555 − 61 and again in 1562 − 4 and 1571 − 2; for whose authority and dignity and traditions he showed the same love he gave his Cambridge College.[23] But what is most obscure about these years is his activity as a practising physician, and the way he made his fortune. His *A Boke or Counseill against the disease commonly called the sweate or sweatyng sicknesse* (1552) owes something to his observations in Shrewsbury and other places — but more to Galen and the pattern of medieval tracts. He is alleged to have been physician to successive sovereigns and to have served the court; and there is no doubt that he had ready access to William Cecil (later Lord Burghley), Queen Elizabeth I's Secretary of State and Lord Treasurer, both as the leading minister and as Chancellor of the University of Cambridge.[24] With Archbishop Parker he was on terms of friendship which must have taken him not infrequently to Lambeth. Late in 1557, in a letter excusing himself for missing the Master of Gonville Hall, Thomas Bacon, on a visit to London, he explains that when he had reached home on Michaelmas Day, 'straight I was sent for to Heningham Castle [Castle Hedingham] to my Lady of Oxford' — a rare glimpse of Caius in attendance on an

---

19 Grierson 1978, p. 522.

20 Venn 1912, pp. 4, 9.

21 Venn 1912, pp. 7−10. For the site of Caius' house see N. Moore, *The History of St Bartholomew's Hospital* (London, 1918), II, 416. He is not known to have had any formal relationship with the hospital.

22 Quoted Venn 1912, p. 9.

23 Clark 1964, pp. 107−24; Venn 1912, p. 8; *Annalium Collegii medicorum Londini Liber,* in Caius, *Works,* pp. 21−70. On Linacre see Maddison, Pelling and Webster 1977; Nutton 1979.

24 See below, p. 60. It has often been asserted that Caius was physician to Edward VI, Mary and Elizabeth, but I have found no evidence earlier than Fuller 1662, p. 275. There is no such evidence for Caius as readily identifies Thomas Wendy as royal physician (*CPR 1547−8,* p. 102; etc.). For the book on *The Sweat* (1552), see Nutton 1979, p. 381.

aristocratic patient.[25] But the house in the city, which was his London home from 1551 till his death, clearly points to a practice among the city fathers, where rewards were great and comparatively sure — rather than at court or among the nobility, who were inclined to reward their professional advisers erratically, and whose demands might have prevented him for long periods from concentrating on his London and his Cambridge colleges, as did the Countess of Oxford.[26] Whatever the source, he undoubtedly amassed a substantial fortune in the years between 1547, when he received recognition at the College of Physicians, and 1557, when he began to refound and re-endow his College in Cambridge. To that year belong two of his most characteristic acts — the provision of a new monument in St Paul's for Thomas Linacre, founder of the College of Physicians, and his first approach to Gonville Hall to offer reendowment.[27]

He had meanwhile prepared for the events of 1557 by making the acquaintance of William Cecil, soon to be Chancellor of the University and Elizabeth I's chief minister. How Caius and Cecil first came together we do not know. The doctor may have cured the young Cecil; they may have met at city dinners. But there is another possibility. Among the worthies of Gonville Hall celebrated in Caius' *Annals* was Thomas Gresham, the eminent merchant, who built the Royal Exchange in the City, Caius himself tells us, in the very years that Caius was rebuilding his College in Cambridge; and who later founded Gresham College and had Gresham's Law thrust upon him. Gresham was intimate with Cecil; it was the kind of friendship between the great City magnate and the Westminster mandarin which we may witness a little later between Sir Wulstan Dixie and Sir Walter Mildmay — out of which much endowment came to Emmanuel College. It is only a conjecture; but there was undoubtedly a bond between the physician, the merchant, the politician — and the divine; for Matthew Parker too was a member of this group. It may have played an important role in the events of 1557−9, but in later years the College passed out of Gresham's view. By combining political influence and diplomacy with a grasp of finance and a lack of scruple almost equally breath-taking, Gresham managed the Antwerp exchange for successive English governments. He built up an epic fortune in the process; and in later life he gave much to many good causes — to the building of the Exchange, for example, and of Gresham College; but nothing to Gonville and Caius.

---

25 Venn 1912, p. 15. He visited Shrewsbury (ibid. p. 8), Kenilworth, Warwick and Cumbria (Raven 1947, pp. 140, 142), presumably to attend patients.
26 See preceding note; for his City house, Venn 1912, p. 10.
27 For Linacre's tomb, Venn 1912, p. 11; Maddison, Pelling and Webster 1977, pp. xxv−vi, xlviii. For Thomas Gresham see *Annals*, p. 29; Venn, I, 28; *DNB*; and esp. Burgon 1839 and Salter 1925.

Gonville and Caius College — preparations

The College was much reduced from the state Caius had known in the 1530s. Physwick Hostel had been lopped off to form part of Trinity, taking with it possibly half or more than half its chambers; the College had also (it seems) shared in the sharp fall in numbers characteristic of the anxieties of the mid-century.[28] Caius at first approached them obliquely — he had encountered a likely benefactor and wished to know if they were willing to accept such a gift and their benefactor as a third founder, and allow Caius to act as mediator. The Master and fellows 'after good deliberation' readily agreed 'and are very glad that it hath pleased God so soon after the stormy and evil times to have given us such a great benefactor or founder'.[29] The benefactor had prepared the ground well. The Master's reply was sent from Cambridge on 3 June 1557: by the 13th, Trinity Sunday, after taking legal advice, Caius met John Boxall, the Secretary of State, and other eminent men, including 'Master Cecil', who conveyed the Queen's approval of his petition to be allowed to refound and reendow Gonville Hall.[30] In his *Annals* Caius makes great play with the legal advice he received, that Bateman's foundation had never been properly valid, since it received only a licence, not a charter of incorporation;[31] but indeed his lawyers' advice was better law than history, for no such process was expected in the 14th century. In any case, all this was speedily set to rights, and on 4 September — after a procedure by modern standards incredibly rapid — the royal charter was engrossed and sealed, in letters patent under the name of Philip and Mary, king and queen of England, Spain, France, the two Sicilies, Jerusalem and Ireland, defenders of the faith, archdukes of Austria, dukes of Burgundy, Milan and Brabant, counts of Habsburg, Flanders and Tyrol.[32] The marriage of Philip II of Spain and Queen Mary gave England for a brief space a cosmopolitan standing it had never enjoyed before, even if the flavour of the titles was enhanced by some empty realms and the structure was based on the frail health of a queen whose reign was soon to be, for many, a hated memory. But the protocol of the letters patent provided a fitting context for a foundation in which the local loyalties of Cambridge were to be enriched by the learning of Padua and Zürich and the College adorned with the trappings of the high Renaissance. At a more practical level, the presence of Cecil at the meeting on Trinity Sunday may help to explain his later reluctance as Chancellor to countenance the charges against Caius as Master of the College. Meanwhile, the royal charter converted 'the house or hall hitherto called the College or Hall of the Annunciation of the Blessed Virgin Mary, commonly (*vulgariter*) named Goneville Halle or

28 See above, p. 53.
29 Venn 1912, p. 11.
30 Venn 1912, pp. 12–13.
31 *Annals*, pp. 42–3; for the explanation, see Maitland 1898, pp. 19–20.
32 Ibid. pp. 43–56.

Gonvell Halle or Gonwell Halle' into 'the College of Gonville and Caius, founded in honour of the Annunciation of the Blessed Virgin Mary' and this new foundation and title the king and queen 'name, make, erect, create, establish, and declare' by their charter.

The charter specifically refers to certain new features of the foundation — that Caius was to add two or more new fellowships (in the event he added three) and twelve or more (later twenty) scholarships; that he might appoint and remove his own fellows and scholars at will, and make new statutes for the College so long as they were compatible with Bateman's.[33] The first step had been speedily concluded; but there was much to be done. In the months which followed he seems particularly to have relied on the help of two close colleagues in the College of Physicians, Dr Wendy and Dr Huys. Thomas Wendy had been a fellow of Gonville Hall, and clearly his own studies in Italy in the 1520s had been a part of the inspiration of Caius' early life. He was a leading royal physician and was to act for the second time as a commissioner sent to visit the University in 1559; he was also squire of Haslingfield and lord of much of the Barnwell estate in Cambridge; on his death in 1560 he left the College a valuable collection of books, mostly relics of his Italian journeys.[34] They are works of general humanist culture, with only a few medical items among them, and the most notable are the earliest printed edition of Thucycides and of the complete works of Plato (1502, 1513); Wendy was a man of like outlook to Caius, and may well have helped to form his mind and inspire his foundation. In other respects this has the marks of the founder's own characteristics upon it. By the end of September plans for the new college seal were well in hand — the charming Gothic annunciations of Gonville's seal and of the later seal of Gonville Hall have yielded to a renaissance or mannerist composition under a triumphal arch.[35] The new founder was busy and cheerful — his letters to the College mingle details of his medical practice and of his preparations for the College's benefit; these were surely the happiest months of his life. By March 1558 he had even moved into action the land conveyancers and the three manors of Croxley, near Rickmansworth in Hertfordshire, and Burnham Wyndhams and Runcton Holme in Norfolk, could be handed over to the College: all of them had been monastic property and came to him (for a price of £1033.12.6) from the Crown.[36]

---

33 Ibid. pp. 54—6. For Caius' fellows and scholars, see Venn, III, 217, 227. For Wendy see above, p. 50; and for Wendy and Huys, Venn 1912, p. 15.
34 Venn, I, 24; Grierson 1978, p. 510; P.V. Danckwerts in *Proc. of the Cambridge Antiquarian Soc.*, LXX (1980), 212; Leedham-Green 1981, p. 30.
35 For Gonville's seal see p. 2; the later medieval seal and Caius' seal face p. 39 in Venn, III. The iconography of the Annunciation on Caius' seal is unusual: there is a figure (perhaps meant to be God the Father) in the sky, and the angel enters right, not left as was common in medieval and early Renaissance Annunciations. Both features occur in the Annunciation by Lorenzo Lotto in the Pinacoteca Civica Recanati (probably of 1527). Caius may well have seen this or a similar picture on his travels.
36 Venn 1912, pp. 16—17, 21.

The Foundation

Later the same month he came at last to Cambridge, and suffered his first disappointment. The College and the University were places of his dreams, and we may reckon that the Cambridge he had left was far different from his memories of it; in any event he has described to us the bitter disillusionment of Cambridge as it was[37] — and he evidently found the College and its Master part and parcel of this decadent modern world. But for the moment all was ritual and festivity. He had come bearing the first of his gifts, symbols of tradition and authority — such as he had already given to the College of Physicians the year before.[38] On Lady Day, the Patronal Festival, he was led by four servants carrying these gifts from his chamber between the library and the hall to Chapel, for solemn Mass for the College's dedication; and then he laid his gifts in the hand of the celebrant who placed them on the altar.[39] There was a book containing Annals and the Statutes, in such form as they then were; the silver caduceus, still the Master's symbol of office, a narrow rod of exquisite delicacy surmounted by four serpents supporting a coat of arms; there was a cushion to kneel on — still used after much repair to support the caduceus; and a great salver. After mass followed a feast, at which the founder entertained the Vice-Chancellor and leading members of the University and Colleges, and the fellowship of Gonville and Caius. After the feast Caius arose and expounded what he had done, laid the royal charter before the assembly and announced that it named the former Master, Thomas Bacon, Master of the new College. Then he handed over the gifts — 'We give you the cushion of reverence . . . We give you the rod of prudent governance' explaining with each the significance of its symbolic form and function; 'We give you the book of knowledge, that you and your fellows and all who follow you, may understand that this College stands and abides on knowledge and prudent counsel — and so will stand and abide in the time to come.' Next he handed over the salver, and on it the royal charter and the other documents recording and establishing his own foundation; and he pronounced Thomas Bacon Master. And finally he 'prayed for all happiness for his College', and dessert and spiced wine and merry-making brought his great day to a close. As they parted, the Vice-Chancellor, Robert Brassie, Provost of King's, offered the University's thanks and invited the founder to accept the degree he had received at Padua, of Doctor of Medicine, from his own University; this duly was conferred on the following day; and on Friday 1 April a public celebration of the new foundation was made in full Senate.[40]

37 Venn 1912, p. 17; *Historiae Cantebrigiensis Acad. Lib. i* (in Caius, *Works*), p. 3.
38 *Annales Coll. Medic.*, p. 42.
39 *Annals*, pp. 57−8. The coat of arms on the caduceus consists solely of six flowers gentle, and seems most probably to represent an earlier version of Caius' arms, before the full scheme confirmed in 1560−1 was developed (pl. 3a).
40 *Annals*, pp. 58−60. Caius' narrative makes clear that he received the degree *ad eundem gradum* on the day after the feast, 26 March, and that this was followed by a public meeting of the Senate on Friday, 1 April.

Nine months later, on 1 January 1559, Thomas Bacon died; and on the 24th Caius himself was elected Master.[41] He tells us in his *Annals* that he was reluctant to accept office, 'both because he was not a theologian, nor a priest, and because he would be compelled owing to his manner of life to be almost always absent' but the Vice-Chancellor and the Heads of Houses, as well as the senior fellows, urged him to accept; and as he reckoned the College in a parlous state he could not refuse. Rescue the College he undoubtedly did, however much he may have exaggerated its condition and his predecessors' failings. Nor was it exceptional to have an absentee Master. Pembroke had tolerated Laurence Booth for thirty years (1450−80), while he was bishop and archbishop and a busy royal official; and the College not only remembered him as a benefactor but continued to have eminent absentee Masters for two generations. We have seen that many of the Masters of Gonville Hall had ecclesiastical offices elsewhere, and Bacon had died in his rectory in Kent.[42] This was quite accepted, and a man of Caius' connections evidently brought benefits to the College. But he and the College would have been spared the quarrels of his later years if he had refused.

He immediately put in hand some repairs to the building and the cleaning and paving of Gonville Court; but it seems likely that he spent most of the next few years in London, where he was still President of the College of Physicians in 1558−61 and again in 1562−4.[43] It was during these years (in 1560) that he presided over the famous session in the College of Physicians in which John Geynes was accused by Thomas Wendy of impugning the authority of Galen, and made to subscribe a solemn statement that Galen had not erred in the points he had asserted against him.[44] He also characteristically made use of his residence in the City to call on the College of Arms to provide him the Grant of Arms which was to set beside the simple medieval chevron attributed to Gonville the strange symbolic fantasy of Caius.[45] As on the caduceus, a sengrene or houseleek or sempervivum sits upon the heads of two serpents; their tails are knit together and rest on a marble stone with a book between them and flower gentle or amaranth set about in the field around them: 'betokening by the book, learning; by the two serpents resting upon the square marble stone, wisdom with grace founded and stayed upon virtue's stable stone; by sengrene and flower gentle, immortality that never shall fade . . . — that is to say, by wisdom and learning grafted in grace and virtue men come to immortality'.

41 For this and what follows, *Annals*, pp. 77−8.
42 See pp. 38−40, 48, 51.
43 *Annales Coll. Medic.*, pp. 46−58.
44 Ibid. pp. 53−4, cf. 56−8; Clark 1964, p. 109.
45 Venn 1912, pp. 21−2. Of the flowers in Caius' arms the houseleek is readily identifiable, but the name 'amaranth' was and is applied to several different species for which the Greek word meaning everlasting was somehow appropriate.

Caius Court and the Gates

As the years passed he began to form his plans for an extension of the buildings of the College. In 1563-5 he completed the purchase of gardens and houses which extended the college to include the whole of its main island site – all of Gonville and Caius and Tree Courts – except the south-east corner, where the Great Gate now stands, which was not acquired until 1782.[46] Cambridge builders of this period looked upon the dissolved monastic houses of the region as quarries of good building stone – much of the structure of the Cambridge houses had gone already, and ambitious eyes had been cast as far afield as Bury. On 1 May 1564 Caius concluded an agreement with Henry Cromwell of Hinchinbrooke near Huntingdon, Oliver's grandfather, for a substantial heap of stones from Ramsey Abbey.[47] In May – June he resigned the Presidency of the College of Physicians (which he was to resume only once more, in 1571 – 2), and cleared up his affairs there, partly to be free for his building works in Cambridge, and also to be present when Queen Elizabeth I visited the University in August.[48]

He made the College more spacious, set about with gardens; he extended it to the south, and built a court deliberately open to the south and to the sun; he gave it a new and more attractive entry, replacing the dark gateway in Trinity Lane with an avenue stretching across Tree Court; and he made immortal his love of symbols and his aesthetic flair by adorning his avenue and his court with the Gates of Humility and Virtue and Honour. The men of his College would enter in humility, live in virtue and pass out to take their degrees and to a life of honour. There is nothing specifically Christian in his scheme – nor anything anti-Christian, needless to say; it derives from the ancient Roman moralists filtered through an Augustinian vision of humility as the gateway to the other virtues.[49] The portrayal of the goddess Fortuna on the Gate of Virtue enforces its secular aspect; the rewards she holds in her hands include a palm, symbol of glory, as well as a bag of money, fortune in its most worldly sense. The Gate of Humility rapidly decayed and in the 19th century was removed first to Senate House Passage, then to the Master's Garden; its present form attempts to preserve, not its original appearance which we only know distantly from Loggan's engraving of c. 1690, but the first restoration of about 1815.[50] It was basically a plain arch with Corinthian capitals. Virtue has two faces. As one approaches it across Tree Court it is a delightful sample of panelled stonework, a

46 Venn 1912, pp. 28 – 9; Willis and Clark, I, 160 – 4; below, pp. 208 – 9.
47 Venn 1912, p. 28; Richmond, Hall and Taylor, 1981, pp. 100 – 3. Cf. D. Purcell, *Cambridge Stone* (London, 1967), pp. 33 – 4 for this stone (and ibid. p. 66 for the King's Cliffe stone in the Gate of Honour).
48 *Annales Coll. Medic.*, p. 58. For the queen's visit, see Mullinger 1884, pp. 187 – 92; Venn 1912, p. 41 – Caius himself disputed in the medical act but so quietly that the queen had difficulty in hearing him. The queen's maids-of-honour were lodged in Caius.
49 I owe this information to Professor Quentin Skinner, who has kindly advised me on this question. Pl. 3b shows one of the two images of Fortuna.
50 Willis and Clark, I, 177 and n. (note by John Lamb).

peaceful renaissance composition in marked contrast to the formidable castellated gatehouse of Queens' or the ornate yet still militant gates of Trinity and St John's. Within, the Gate of Virtue is plainer, matching the extreme simplicity of the two wings of the court, only adorned with an inscription to Wisdom, the general dedication of the College, as on the foundation stone of 1565[51] — though the sky-line was broken by a posse of turrets, originally four, on the Chapel, the Lodge, and the two Gates (see endpapers). The life of virtue — though it might compass all the heroic qualities of renaissance *virtù*, all the manly and military overtones of classical *virtus*, was based on a plain and simple life; and every line of Caius' own buildings in Caius Court tells us as much — save for the Gate of Honour whose rich ornament stands in a contrast all the more marked for the simplicity of the rest of the design. It was finished after Caius' death, but there is no doubt that the Gate of Honour represents in almost every detail his conception, even if the relative shares of the founder and the architect can never be precisely determined. It is a miniature triumphal arch, on a scale suited to the modesty of the court and that of the little street which originally ran from it to the Schools. The arch itself is Gothic in shape, four-centred and adorned with some Gothic ornament; yet above it there rise capitals and architrave and cornice purely classical, reminiscent of Roman tomb architecture. There is little doubt that the designer was strongly influenced by Sebastiano Serlio's work *Regole generali di architettura . . .*, published 1537−47' in Venice, as Dr F. C. Powell has pointed out.[52] On the summit of the gate originally there was a weathercock formed of a serpent and dove; above the turret staircase on the chapel there rose a figure of Mercury; and above the elaborate, fantastical column with 60 sundials which Theodore Haveus of Cleves erected in the court in 1576 was a weathercock in the shape of Pegasus; and two years later a fountain was set beside it surmounted by Aquarius. The weathercocks and the mythical figures have departed; the Gate of Honour and the Court have been more than once extensively restored;[53] the medieval chapel has been faced in stone; but in its essence Caius Court is still a faithful monument to the founder's plans.

The *Annals* tell us that Theodore Haveus 'artifex egregius et insignis architecturae professor', dedicated his column as a sign of his goodwill towards the College.[54] We know also that he was the chief craftsman of

---

51 The inner face of the Gate of Virtue is often called 'the Gate of Wisdom' since it bears the legend 'Io. Caius posuit Sapientiae 1567', but this clearly follows the foundation stone, which read 'Io. Caius posuit Sapientiae anno 1565 mense Maio' — and is the general dedication of his foundation (*Annals*, p. 113; cf. Willis and Clark, I, 177).

52 Venn, VII, 534 n. 11; cf. p. 535 and n. 12, and the reproduction of Serlio's engravings, pp. 536−7; and Pevsner 1970, p. 78. Dr Powell's account of the Gate and its restoration (pp. 534−40) has much valuable information. Our knowledge of Caius' iconography would be enriched still further if we could know more of the lost 'frontispieces' once on the walls of the passage from Humility to Virtue (Venn, III, 49).

53 *Annals*, p. 190; Venn, VII, 534−40 (F. C. Powell).

54 *Annals*, p. 190; for Theodore Haveus see p. 187, the account for the tomb of Dr Caius of which he was evidently the chief craftsman. Cf. *RCHM Cambridge*, I, 73−81; Pevsner 1970, p. 79; pls. 6, 15.

Caius' tomb. It has long been supposed that he was Caius' chief architect in all his works, and especially in the Gate of Honour. It cannot be proved; but the phrase about the column in Caius court is hardly intelligible unless Theodore's own involvement in the works of John Caius had been large.

The sequence of humility and virtue in the student's life may seem to betoken the vision of a man better endowed with imagination than ordinary human understanding, a suggestion only too fearfully confirmed by the record of his mastership. The peaceful aspect of the Gate of Virtue somehow provokes an echo of Lady Bracknell's remark: 'The general was essentially a man of peace, except in his domestic life'. And it is a curious reflection that the only one of Caius' statutes which has been wholly and consistently obeyed is that which prohibits the erection of any building closing the south side of his court 'lest the air, being prevented from free movement, should be corrupted, and so do harm to us, and still more to those of Gonville's College' (i.e. perhaps court), 'and bring on us sickness and death'.[55]

Rewriting the statutes

College statutes, however, were commonly before the 19th century reforms subjected to the most various treatment — some obeyed with fundamentalist fervour; others reinterpreted in a mode reminiscent of the 'old Chancery draftsman' in Iolanthe, who inserted a 'not' to improve the sense of the law; others plainly disregarded. Caius' statutes appear to us fussy and verbose, but they only differ in degree from the many others of their kind. The picture they conjure of College life sometimes resembles Dotheboys Hall more than a modern College; and we are amazed to read that any who presume to enter the College by any route save the gates will be expelled from the society for ever.[56] Many of them are of more practical sense than this, and the clause which observes that the Master should be a model and pattern of goodness and learning — but that it is more important that he understand practical affairs than be academically distinguished — reminds us of the debates of more modern academic societies.[57] In general, however, they seem much overwritten. We know little in detail of the process of composition; but we can discern three stages.[58] First, some draft provisions must

55 Statutes, c. 30, Venn, III, 364. For the Statutes of Bateman and Caius, see Venn, III, 345–53, 353–89. The versions in the text are my own translations from the Latin original. Pevsner 1970, p. 77, mentioned French analogies for the three-sided court, including Anet, and Paul Binski has pointed out to me that Anet also had a gate pavilion and a frontispiece showing figures similar to those on the Gate of Virtue (A. Blunt, *Philibert de l'Orme*, London, 1958, pls. 4, 8).
56 c. 52, p. 371.
57 c. 4, p. 354.
58 Venn, 1912, pp. 47–50 (= Venn, III, 58–61). An early stage is represented by draft English notes for statutes printed in Venn 1912, pp. 49–50; but the first major effort at drafting is now CUL MS Mm. 4.20 dated 1557 (for 1558 — and see n. 75), of which an attempt at an edition, at once heroic and hopeless, was made in *Documents 1852*, II, 321–65.

have been included with Bateman's Statutes in the Book of Knowledge he handed to Bacon — and which is now unhappily lost. Next, we have a draft which shows much activity in writing and rewriting, but little resemblance to the final form; and finally, we have the version promulgated in 1573 and printed by the Commissioners of 1852 and by Venn.[59] Since this was not published until 1852, when it was about to go out of use — and only a garbled version of the draft was available in print with it — we do not have far to seek for the explanation, or excuse, for a general ignorance of some of their provisions. For the present, let us content ourselves with two of the most characteristic.

'c.45 On prayers . . . We will that all the fellows and scholars of our own foundation . . . [i.e. supported by Caius' endowments], shall at the accustomed time of prayer in chapel, every day at 5.00 a.m., be on their knees in their stalls or seats, the fellows in the higher, the scholars in the lower, facing the east and on their knees, . . . and in a clear voice pray in this manner' — And there follows a form of confession for the scholars, and another for the fellows: 'Lord Jesus Christ, fount and sea of mercy, have mercy on the soul of John Caius our founder, pardon his sins and grant him life eternal' — to which the scholars said 'Amen'. It would be interesting to know how long this practice survived in a world increasingly suspicious of the Popish tendency of prayers for the dead, even if they were not formally forbidden.[60]

'c.14. On celibacy. We ordain also that all members of your College, Master, fellows, scholars and pensioners, be celibate, and living in celibacy perpetual and honest for as long as they remain in the College . . .'.[61] This was a stringent version of a law universal to the colleges of Oxford and Cambridge between 1561 and the mid-19th century. Although marriage was permitted to Anglican clergy after the Reformation, Queen Elizabeth notoriously disapproved of it, and issued an edict in 1561 designed to prevent it in many colleges and cathedral closes.[62] Among the cathedral clergy it had no effect; many of them were older men, and over their habits presided Mrs Parker, a partner in one of the happiest of recorded marriages; but in Oxford and Cambridge, reinforced by the Cambridge University statutes of 1570 and the statutes of many colleges in both universities, it remained the fundamental law, and also — unlike many such laws — the custom and the practice. But not universally; for already in the 16th century the Heads of Houses were great men of the world and could not be constrained by rules appropriate for younger men, most of them embarking on the earlier stages of a clerical career. Thus the custom arose in some colleges that the Heads alone were allowed to marry, and the great extension of

59 Venn, III, 353—89.
60 c. 45, pp. 368—9 (for the 3rd prayer, see p. 294).
61 c. 14, p. 357.
62 Parker 1853, p. 151; cf. University Statute of 1570 in *Documents 1852*, I, 493.

some Lodges in the late 16th century already bears witness to the growth in their families as well as in their status.[63] John Caius was a layman, not innocent of all anti-clerical bias; but he was also a confirmed bachelor, and evidently felt very deeply that wives and womenfolk were distracting intrusions in his society. Partly for this reason the Master's chambers remained relatively modest and the married Master was slow to come — the first to be married was the Puritan intruder Dr Dell in the 1640s; the first (so far as we know) to bring a wife to visit the Lodge was Dr Brady after the Restoration.[64] The tradition of celibacy had a curious and ironical effect on the future history of the colleges. It undoubtedly postponed, in a way which might have been disastrous for the survival of Oxford and Cambridge, both the possibility of fellows normally making university teaching a lifelong career and any serious prospect of these places opening their doors to the education of women. But the rule of celibacy also saved the colleges from consisting wholly of aging, married absentees — as was the fate of many a cathedral close — and provided them with close-knit resident communities. When the abolition of celibacy was being discussed in the 19th century, it was held by some that it would make the societies more diffuse, less close to their pupils.[65] This has not proved wholly untrue, and there has on any showing been loss as well as gain in the changes of the last century. But few would doubt that the colleges have been immeasurably enriched by the presence of fellows' wives, and of women fellows and students; nor can anyone reasonably deny that Dr Caius would have been appalled to encounter them.

The most famous sentence in his statutes was that in which, with medical precision, but following other founders' precedents, he listed ailments which might disqualify from membership. No-one shall be elected Master, fellow or scholar who — 'is deformed, dumb, blind, lame, maimed, mutilated, a Welshman, or suffering from any grave or contagious illness, or an invalid, that is sick in a serious measure'.[66] The Welshman, *Wallicum* in the Latin original, is an absurd intruder in this list, and heroic efforts have been made to save the founder's credit by finding a sickness of that name. Had he but said 'Gallicum', French, then we might detect a reference to the *morbus Gallicus*, venereal disease, which is referred to in his Annals of the College of Physicians under a date only months before these Statutes were finally promulgated.[67] But Wallicum, Welsh, is a different word. So it has been supposed that the irascible Master had encountered a Welsh antagonist and added him to his list of human aberrations; and a likely candidate has been found in the lively and voluble Welsh physician, Dr Hugh Glyn, fellow of the College, who mysteriously departed to an obscure

63 See p. 46.
64 See pp. 131, 146.
65 See Engel 1983, pp. 106–14, for Oxford.
66 c. 12, p. 357.
67 *Annales Coll. Medic.*, p. 70.

practice in Chester a few months after Caius was installed as Master.[68] That Caius was quick to anger is undoubted; but it is not equally clear that he was so eccentric on a solemn matter as to list Welshry as a disease in the definitive edition of his statutes. Probably it is a scribal error for *Gallicum*. The intrusion remains an intriguing puzzle; and the statute, by a merciful dispensation, a dead letter.

Of greater moment for the future of the College were such clauses as defined the functions of the officers, and especially the office of President (c.31), which seems to have been formalized in Caius' time. He was the Master's nominee and deputy – not elected by the fellows until the statutes of 1904 came to effect. As in other colleges with Masters often absent, a prestigious official was needed to guide the College's affairs.

John Caius and Matthew Parker – 'much ado with the quarrels of Gonville Hall'

Thus the years 1564 – 5 saw Dr Caius more often in Cambridge, more continuously in his Master's Chamber in his College, and it is probably no coincidence that they also saw the first quarrels between Master and fellows come to a head. He could make friends readily enough with those who shared his interests – be it medicine with Dr Butts or Dr Wendy, natural history with Conrad Gesner, or antiquarian pursuits with Matthew Parker. But it is abundantly clear that he was at his worst in handling a lively group of young fellows in his College. The Master had more authority in the 16th century than any wise Head of House would try to assert in the 20th; but then as now he established it by mingling the firm guiding hand with personal relations widely spread through the community. We must allow that the documents tell us of enemies, victims and rebels among the fellows – much less of his friends, who may have been numerous. But the effect is only too plain: Dr Caius behaved like an old-world headmaster handling an unruly group of schoolchildren.

The storm finally broke in the Christmas season of 1565, a few days after the death of Gesner, when the aging Master was doubtless at his most morose.[69] On 7 January 1566, two anxious fellows, Stephen Warner and Robert Spenser, wrote to the Chancellor, William Cecil, who was also Lord Treasurer of England, a tearstained plea that the Master's threat of expulsion should be prevented; and they proceeded to ask for certain reforms – that no man be put in the stocks or flogged 'for keeping his right until the

68 For a careful discussion, see Cule 1969. Welshmen were in fact numerous in Cambridge at this time, specially in St John's. Dr David Howlett, Editor of the *Dictionary of Medieval Latin from British Sources*, tells me no alternative meaning for Wallicus is known, except 'youth', 'valet' or 'yeoman' (by some attraction to 'valettus'); but even at his gloomiest Dr Caius would not have excluded youths from his College.
69 See above, p. 58.

matter be decided' and that 'our Master may be ruled by some good man's counsel hereafter and not to drive the fellows to such chargeable suits and troubles wherein he delighteth to undo poor men, he never being quiet since he came to the College, as may appear in the number of his expulsions which have been above twenty, with an infinite number of injuries to the old founders and benefactors and their fellows which is well known to the whole University.'[70] Even granted that the expulsions related to the fellows of his own foundation, over which he had special powers, the accusations suggest a violent and disorderly manner of government. In these years the University was anxiously watched over from afar by two powerful men, exceedingly benevolent to it in intent, yet not at all inclined to countenance charges against so eminent a man as Caius: the archbishop of Canterbury at Lambeth and the Lord Treasurer across the river at Westminster. On 29 December, a few days before the appeal from the two fellows, the archbishop had written to Cecil a letter which remains a masterpiece even among the jewels of that master of diplomatic English.

'I have had very much ado with the quarrels of Gonville Hall from time to time. The truth is, both parties are not excusable from folly. At the first controversy betwixt the Master and one Clarke and Dethick, my lord of London and I so compounded the matter, that we perceived it very needful to the quiet of that society to remove both Dethick and Clarke from their fellowships. Dethick, after a year, made suit to me to have a room again in the College. Upon his importunity I was importune upon the Master to accept him, with the condition of my promise that if by him any trouble should arise, I would take him from him again. Which promise made me to receive him into my house, after this last expulsion by the Master and more part of the company. From that they do appeal to your honour. I cannot see how rightly they can do it, or how your Vice-chancellor can deal in order with their College matters. The parties sued to me; I promised them to deal with the Master to obtain of him more commodity than I take them worthy to have; only restitution to their fellowships I would not move. Wherein I see good cause; for if they be there, there will ever trouble arise. These fellows have divers drifts they shoot at, which I think good to be disappointed. I see the faction hath laboured very much in this matter. Although I see over much rashness in the Master for expelling fellows so suddenly etc. (?), he hath been well told of it, as well of my lord of London as by myself; and surely the contemptuous behaviour of these fellows hath much provoked him. The truth is, I do rather bear with the oversight of the Master (being no greater than yet I see) in respect of his good done and like to be done in the College by him, than with the brag of a fond sort of troublous factious bodies. Founders and benefactors be very rare

70 Venn 1912, pp. 23–5; PRO SP 12/39/11, pp. 262–4.

at these days; therefore I do bear the less with such as would (but in a mere triumph) deface him, and respect more that conquest than any quiet in the house; and the rather, for I think that if this matter be ended, there will arise no more trouble in such kind there, for the Master hath firmly assured me to do nothing in such innovations, but partly with my knowledge and approbation first, and other of his friends. But undoubtedly in my opinion, *computans omnibus circumstantiis*, I think it nothing meet to have them restored again, what other commodities so ever they may have of favourable departing. If your honour will hear their challenges, ye shall hear such cumbrous trifles and brabbles, that ye shall be weary. And I would not wish particular Colleges (in these times) should learn to have, by forced appellations, a recourse to your authority as Chancellor, for the precedents' sake hereafter. And again, I would not have your time so drawn from better doings in the weighty causes of the realm. Scholars' controversies be now many and troublous; and their delight is to come before men of authority to shew their wits &c.; and I cannot tell how such busy sorts draw to them some of the graver personages to be doers, *an ex sinceritate et ex bona conscientia nescio*. My old experience there hath taught me to spy daylight at a small hole. Thus ye hear my fancy, which I pray your honour to take in good worth. To write much more my dull deaf head will not suffer me. I pray you if any offence be taken for my not oft attending, and to come over the reumatike Tempsis [Thames], answer for me.

Thus God be with your honour, this 29 December, 1565.

Yours assuredly,

MATTH. CANT.'[71]

What lay beneath these violent arguments? It has often been supposed that Dr Caius was a crypto-Catholic, and that a body of young fellows sympathetic to the rising Puritan fashions of the Cambridge of the 1560s found his devotion to the old religion, his theological conservatism, genuinely repugnant. In his study of Caius' library, Philip Grierson has argued very cogently that the Master was not a man of strong theological views.[72] It is true that he was by this date aging, conservative in outlook, backward-looking, a great admirer of an imaginary past. It is also true that he hoarded the medieval books of the College, including altar books — two at least of which we still preserve[73] — at a time when Parker himself was ordering the

71 Parker 1853, pp. 248 – 50, corrected by PRO SP 12/38/124 – 5 (here, as throughout, I have modernised the spelling).

72 Grierson 1978, pp. 523 – 4.

73 The Sarum Manual, Schneider 1928, no. 86, which was evidently brought back into use in the 1550s — see p. 28; and the 14th century MS Breviary, 394/614, which has a charming verse inscription threatening hanging to any thief, because —
   Where so ever y be come over all
   I belonge to the Chapell of Gunvyle Hall
(James 1907 – 8, II, 459 – 60; *Caian* I (1891 – 2), 127).

mass books of All Souls to be sent to him for inspection;[74] worse still, he hoarded vestments and other treasures, and it is quite evident that he saw no incongruity in preserving prayers for dead benefactors, and much of the world of a medieval chantry, in a notionally Protestant chapel.[75] Undoubtedly grounds could be found for charging him with popery. Yet if he were truly a Catholic at heart, he must surely have undergone some manner of conversion; for he seems to have signed the royal supremacy in 1535 without demur, and he mingled comfortably then in a college in close touch with Queen Anne, and in particular with William Butts, physician and reformer. Yet it is improbable that Caius thought deeply on theological matters. Theology is conspicuous by its absence from his library. He had studied the Old Testament in Hebrew and Greek as a young man, but parted with his copies of the Old Testament in these languages in course of time, and passed into old age, so far as the evidence goes, with nothing of Augustine or Gregory the Great or Bernard or Aquinas or Nicholas of Lyra to hand.[76] His real interests lay elsewhere, to such an extent that in his lament on Gesner,[77] conceived in these dark Christmas days in 1565 and printed in 1570, only three years before his death, he writes as a humanist, scarcely as a Christian at all — and on his tomb it is *virtus*, the quality of the man, which lives on — Caius is past: 'I was Caius, *fui Caius*'. It may be guessed that after the flurry of the 1530s, the experience of travelling in Catholic and Protestant Europe and enjoying deep academic friendships with men attached to a variety of communions, he cared little for current controversy. There must have been many such in 16th century Europe, though they tended to leave sparse evidence behind them. He had Catholic friends: Dr Clements, another eminent humanist President of the College of Physicians, fled to the Continent to die in Catholic Malines.[78] It may be that Caius had a certain liberality towards men of catholic sympathy — we soon find them flourishing in his College when he was gone, under his chosen successor; there may have been an honourable corner of tolerance in this most intolerant of men. But we cannot reasonably doubt that he was also an entirely conforming Christian who subscribed with his whole heart to the supremacy of his sovereign — whether it be Henry or Edward or Philip and Mary or Elizabeth. Even under the cool and relatively permissive guidance of Parker and Cecil, eight heads of houses were replaced in 1559—60, though only two by direct dismissal;[79] and even allowing for Parker's

74 Parker 1853, pp. 296—8.
75 cc. 18, 45, pp. 359, 368. Naturally these clauses of 1573 are much less explicit on the commemoration of the dead than the draft of 1558: see *Documents 1852*, II, 331—3.
76 Grierson 1978, p. 523.
77 *De libris propriis* in Caius, *Works*, pp. 94—8, in which he spells out that 'post funera vivere' means that though life is short, glory — i.e. basically fame — can last for ever — 'cum cursus vitae brevis sit, cursus gloriae possit esse sempiternus', p. 98.
78 On him see *DNB*; Clark 1964, I, 69—73; and see the list of 'papists' in the College of Physicians, ibid. pp. 129—30, which includes by implication Caius and Clements.
79 Porter 1958, pp. 104—6.

tolerance towards friends and colleagues — especially for one who shared his view that Cambridge was much older than Oxford, and cured the sick about him — he could hardly have protected the old Master so long if he knew him to harbour popish doctrines.

But the strongest evidence of all comes from the next letter the archbishop sent across the rheumatic Thames, on 4 January. 'No sooner than yesterday, I was informed of certain articles charged upon Dr Caius, not only sounding and savouring atheism, but plainly expressing the same, with further show of a perverse stomach to the professors of the gospel, of the which if I were credibly persuaded, I would take him *tanquam ethnicum et publicanum*, and would not vouchsafe him within my house. There is a difference betwixt the frailty of a man's mutability, and a professing of plain impiety' — and he proceeded to defend his own former part in the proceedings, and to surmise that Dethick himself hoped one day to be Master of the College.[80] This letter was hastily written and suggests that Parker had received some message which exasperated him with the Master — as well as giving him a nagging fear that the charge of atheism might stick. On the day it was written Cecil made his decision (possibly before this letter had reached him), confirming the archbishop's former proposals — the expulsion of the insurgent fellows and a charge on the Master to proceed in more orderly fashion in his handling of essential domestic business.[81] Though many of the fellows were very young, Dethick and Clarke were in their 30s, and if Dethick's later career is obscure — he is supposed later to have fled the country as a recusant — Clarke became a respectable Vicar General in the see of Canterbury under Archbishop Grindal in the following decade.[82]

Thus far the quarrels of 1565—6; then silence falls. But we have no reason to suppose that the Master's temper became milder, or that resentment at his rule died away, with the departure of the leaders of opposition. Certainly he grew closer to Parker, who shared his passionate interest in antiquarian pursuits. In 1566 or 1567 Parker showed Caius the modest *Assertio* of his namesake, Thomas Caius of Oxford, claiming that Oxford was the older University; in April 1567 Caius submitted a draft of his own reply 'On the Antiquity of the University of Cambridge', with a letter of fussy and somewhat obsequious friendliness. 'Your man Mr Josselin [in fact the most distinguished of Parker's antiquarian secretaries] I fear will shew it to everybody, and give out copies *ante maturitatem*, and do little good in it himself. I beseech your grace remember what I wrote to you in that matter heretofore. I am sorry that the book is no better written for your grace . . . Because all things should be readier to your grace I have put to every *pagina* his number. If anything your grace will note, the number is ready to tell the

80 Parker 1853, pp. 251—3. Some of the charges against Caius, including use of the stocks, are confirmed in a letter from Andrew Perne to Parker of 11 Jan. 1565/6 ed. P. Collinson, *Godly People* (London, 1983), p. 332 (a reference I owe to John Sturdy).
81 *CSPD 1547—80*, p. 267; checked by PRO SP 12/39/9—10.
82 Venn, I, 38—9, 43.

place.'[83] Parker doubtless gave it his blessing, and next year the book was published with the extremely disingenuous pseudonym 'Londinensis' – by a Londoner; the archbishop himself, as Caius' literary executor, reissued it with its author's name in 1574. This and the accompanying *History of the University of Cambridge* are the largest and most calamitous of its author's works; a farrago of invention and credulity. No modern reader progresses further than King Cantaber and the age of the giants;[84] and they owe their immortality to the famous saying attributed to F. W. Maitland that the first Oxford and Cambridge contest was a lying match. Indeed the *De Antiquitate* does its author little justice, and we sympathise with the comment attributed to James I when offered a copy – 'What shall I do with this book? Give me rather Caius *De canibus*';[85] though even for his dogs Caius could not claim to be an interpreter equal to Van Dyck, who made all the dogs of James' son's court and nobility noble creatures, sometimes much more so than their masters.

We must contemplate the sad and heroic vision of the aging Dr Caius, ceaselessly generous in the care and resources he poured into the building and endowment of his College, ceaselessly at variance with many of his younger colleagues. One particular bone of contention was that he swore his fellows to obedience to his statutes, but still continued to add to and revise them, they knew not how. As his life drew to a close, he at last determined to put them in final shape, and this sharpened the edge of the fellows' anxieties.

The catastrophe

Meanwhile in 1570 the pope had excommunicated Queen Elizabeth I and absolved her faithful subjects from their allegiance; thus popish recusancy could henceforth be viewed as potential rebellion.[86] It is clear to us now that in the eyes of the large majority of those of Catholic faith or sympathy Elizabeth was queen, and they had no wish and no intent to depose her. But it was not so clear at the time; and from 1570 on popery was the subject of genuine fear, as well as an ever-tempting bogey for the cynic and the disaffected. We may well reckon that both motives were at work among the fellows: that some were genuinely apprehensive that the old Master might involve them in recusancy, and that others welcomed the new wind which blew in the 1570s to bring their intrigues into harbour. The insurgents of 1570 knew that Caius was highly respected in Lambeth and Westminster, and looked for a new ally in Edwin Sandys, the eminent Protestant divine

83 Parker 1853, pp. 298 – 300.
84 *Historiae Cantebrigiensis Academiae lib. i* in Caius, *Works*, p. 12.
85 Fuller 1662, p. 276; cf. Venn 1911, p. 51n.
86 Morey 1978, chaps. 3 – 5, esp. pp. 55 – 7.

who had once been Master of St Catharine's, then a Marian exile — while Caius was refounding his College — and was now passing through the see of London en route for the primacy of York, where he was to end his days (1577 – 88).[87] He was given a hint of popery in the College, which he continued to suspect and denounce under Caius' successor.

It was probably for his eye — though it ended at Lambeth — that the anonymous 'Articles concerning the preposterous government of Dr Caius, and his wicked abuses in Gonville and Caius College' was drawn up.[88] 'Imprimis he maintaineth within his college copes, vestments, albs, tunicles, censors, crosses, tapers, also all kinds of mass books . . . with all massing abominations and termeth them the college treasure.' This and other charges shrewdly deployed the complaint of Catholic abuses at the outset and invited visitation. But it is clear that the fellows who drew up the document were equally concerned with his tyrannical attitude to statutes and government. 'Item he lying upon his bed did threaten a preacher and in a rage he rising up would have beaten him away for saying that we deserved not God's favour by our works. The said Dr Caius adding moreover that he desired God's favour according to his deserts'.[89] It was written by an enemy, yet in substance it may well be true; we can picture the elderly, sick Master, growing exasperated with the sophistical arguments of the 'preacher'. His words could doubtless be interpreted as Pelagian — but it is the heresy par excellence of the intelligent layman in every age of the Church's history; not for nothing had Dr Caius kept Augustine out of his library. Calvin and St Thomas would have been equally shocked. 'Item his college inhabitants are neither instructed nor encouraged in religion as is usual in all other colleges nor yet examined of false belief, and himself did never contrary the antichristian doctrine or confirm and allow the true religion either by his statutes or otherwise'.[90] As a statement of overt popery is it pitifully inadequate, but it was well designed to arouse suspicions among the heresy-hunters.

Bishop Sandys wrote 'very earnestly' to the Vice-Chancellor, Dr Byng, who gathered Dr Whitgift, Master of Trinity and future archbishop of Canterbury, and Dr Goade, Provost of King's, extracted an inventory of the 'treasure' from the fellowship, and from noon to 3.00 p.m. one December day they carried out all they could find, burning what could be burnt, smashing what could not be burnt.[91] The next day the Vice-Chancellor wrote to the Chancellor an account of his proceedings, 'which was accomplished yesterday with the willing hearts, as appeared, of the

87 See DNB.
88 Venn 1912, pp. 26 – 7; for the date see Grierson 1978, p. 524 n. 10. I have corrected the text from Lambeth MS 720/2 with the kind help of Miss Melanie Barber: e.g. Venn printed 'swinches' for 'tunicles'.
89 Venn 1912, p. 27.
90 Ibid.
91 Annals, p. 185; Venn 1912, pp. 37 – 8 (dated 1570 for 1572 in p. 37 n. 1); CTPC, I, 124 – 5.

whole company of that house' — a rather different account is enshrined the
the College *Annals*.[92] This was evidently a shattering experience for the
poor Master, even if he did succeed in saving some books from the flames,
as the College library still bears witness.[93]

In a final effort he completed the revision of the Statutes and promulgated
them on 1 January 1573. The spring found him lying sick in his London
house 'at Little St Bartholomew's'; and on 2 June he wrote to Lambeth to
excuse his long failure to visit the archbishop.[94] A bout of illness 'ceased not
until the 28 of May last, leaving me in great weakness which I can not yet
recover, nor shall not, I fear me, yet this fortnight and more. I am so faint I
can not go twice about my house, but I must sit down; but when I may wait
upon your grace, it shall be the first thing I shall do'. On 14 June he signed
his will, completing his many generous gifts to the College, anxiously setting his friend the archbishop to supervise and give aid in the execution of
the will and the disposal of his writings; giving a few small bequests — especially to eminent lawyers whose support he may have hoped in seeing his
wishes fulfilled, and two noble ladies whom we may suppose to have been
his patients — but most to the College; appointing 'My trusty and
wellbeloved friend Thomas Legge, of Jesus College in Cambridge to be
Master of my said College of Gonville and Caius after my decease, which I
may lawfully do' under a concession he had extracted from the fellows the
previous September.[95] After all his troubles with the College, the immense
generosity of his will makes even so formal a document intensely moving.

On 23 June he arrived in Cambridge for his final visit 'wearied much with
my horselitter, but after a day or two with a little rest somewhat more
quieted', as he wrote in his last letter to the archbishop.[96] He described the
progress of his illness, and commended 'all my things to your grace, as in
my will' and 'for shortness take my leave, committing your grace to the
tuition of Almighty God. . . I have done here at Cambridge all things
according to my mind and discharged myself of all things to thintent I
would give [yield] myself from the world, and depend on God's mercy
only. . .' To this the archbishop replied on 4 July: 'I am glad to hear how
obediently you submit yourself to almighty God's good will toward you. . .
That *fiat voluntas tua* is alway a good prayer to agree unto which argueth
our undoubted election. And though it be God's pleasure you go a little
before us, yet we trust shortly to follow you. . . In the mean season I shall
offer you to God in my prayer. Thus God bless you and send you the comfort of his Holy Spirit, as I wish to myself when my turn shall be'.[97]

Meanwhile, on 27 June he handed over the Mastership to Legge; and the

---

92 Cf. *CTPC*, I, 125 (and Venn 1912, p. 37) with *Annals*, p. 185.
93 See above, n. 73.
94 Venn 1912, p. 39.
95 Venn, III, 389−92; but see below, p. 87.
96 Venn 1912, p. 39.
97 Venn 1912, pp. 39−40.

first days of July were spent ordering his tomb.[98] In his will he had said 'I commend my soul to God Almighty and my body to be buried in the Chapel within my College of Gonville and Caius in Cambridge under the tabernacle wherein the image of Our Lady sometime did stand, in a tomb there to be made of alabaster.'[99] The tabernacle has long since departed, and the tomb, raised from the floor in 1637, now stands above the 18th century panels and benches. But otherwise it is perfectly preserved: a skull rests on a book above the elaborate, pedimented canopy; while below, a sarcophagus lies under a richly adorned architrave supported by Corinthian capitals. On the architrave is inscribed in Roman capitals the same epitaph he had inscribed on the tomb of Thomas Linacre – 'Vivit post funera virtus' – '*Virtue* lives on after death' – or after the rites of death; and among the symbols of immortality, 'Fui Caius', 'I was Caius'; on its base: 'he died on 29 July 1573, aged 63'.[100] Thus at the end Theodore Haveus and his colleagues portrayed in a deeply imaginative symbolic and decorative scheme of great and vivid beauty the virtue, the immortal quality, of 'that great and generous man, John Caius'. And within the arches of the tomb, most delicately portrayed, they set his sengrene and flower gentle, 'immortality that never shall fade'.

98 Venn 1912, p. 40.
99 Venn, III, 389; see p. 168 and facing for the tomb; Venn 1912, p. 11, for Linacre's tomb.
100 I.e. in his 63rd year. Plate 6. Cf. Venn 1912, pp. 40 – 1; for Theodore Haveus, above, n. 54.

5

Thomas Legge and the Elizabethan College

The Tombs of Legge and Perse

High on the chapel walls on either side kneel two figures in doctor's robes, Stephen Perse and Thomas Legge, close colleagues for well over thirty years. Perse was a fellow from 1571 until his death in 1615, Legge was Master from 1573 till he died in 1607.[1] Perse was a physician, but also a financier and a man of the widest charity in College and town; Legge was a lawyer and a minor dramatist — author of 'a Tragedy of the life of King Richard the third, presented with great applause [in Latin] . . . in St John's College hall' and 'The Destruction of Jerusalem' which 'some plagiary filched . . . from him' — but also a very notable tutor, a man to whom the young flocked, genial and friendly. In their time the College expanded greatly and took its full share in the rapid growth of Elizabethan Cambridge. Dr Caius had laid the foundations and wisely chose a much younger and easier man to succeed him. Legge provided the humane leadership which gathered the human flock; the prudence and munificence of Perse helped to keep the College solvent and pay for its enlargement. But there is more than this to be discovered in the tombs. They are almost identical: both figures kneel under arches, and in both the arch is surmounted by architraves supported on Corinthian capitals closely imitating those of the founder's tomb; and the architraves have lofty obelisks above them echoing those on the Gate of Honour. Legge was the first to die and it has usually been assumed that his tomb was erected first. But Perse's tomb has on it a lengthy epitaph including 'This epitaph by me Perse was devizd'; whereas Legge's has in place of the epitaph a heart, and beneath the heart:

Junxit amor vivos sic jungat terra sepultos
Gostlini reliquum cor tibi Leggus habes.
'Love joined them living, and so may the same earth link them in their tombs; Gostlin's heart you still have with you, O Legge'.[2]

1   On Perse see Venn, I, 57−8; III, 169, 218, 231; Mitchell 1976, chap. 1; Gray 1921, chap. 1 (to be read with caution, see below, p. 98). On Legge, Venn, I, 73; III, 64−9. There is an unpublished paper on him by Lord McNair in the College library. Professor Peter Stein is preparing a paper based on his legal common-place book (CUL MS Ely Consistory Court F/5/49) and has kindly advised me on his legal career. The quotation below is from Fuller 1662, p. 276.
2   Venn, III, 169. See pls. 9a, b.

When Legge died John Gostlin was chosen to succeed him, but the election was overruled, and Gostlin went into exile to Devon, where he practised as a doctor. In 1614 – 15 he returned to Caius and in 1619 he was elected Master. A few days before his election it was determined at a meeting that a monument to Legge should be made.[3] In 1619 there was also begun a set of buildings in the north-east corner of what is now Tree Court named after Legge and funded by his legacy; and surviving drawings and photographs of it make it seem identical to the Perse building adjacent to it – as identical as the tombs.[4] It seems clear that John Gostlin was deeply devoted to the memory of Thomas Legge and thought it wholly appropriate that Legge and Perse should be viewed as twins in the memory of future generations. This strongly argues that Perse had worked in closest harmony with the Master, and all the evidence suggests that Legge was an amiable, magnetic personality. There seems little doubt that Legge's tomb was commissioned in 1619; but whether the inscription was put there in anticipation of Gostlin's burial, or added after he had himself died in 1626, seems now impossible to tell.

The matriculation register – Caius and the wider world

It is against this picture of good fellowship that must be set the other picture which the records portray, of a fast-growing, tumultuous, noisy community. The College matriculation register has long been recognised as a major source of English social history.[5] As John Caius decreed, it contained details of each new student admitted to the College – his place of origin, his parents' names and occupation, his age, his tutor – even, in early days, the room in which he lived.[6] The parents' occupation is particularly unusual and valuable to the historian, and these details play a leading role in many modern discussions of social and educational history of the 16th and 17th centuries. In various ways John Venn himself was a pioneer in all these

3 The decision is recorded in a part of the *Gesta* preserved by Moore in the *Annals* (p. 278), where it is said that the monument was to be 'in illa structura' which seems to mean in the Legge building, and Moore notes that it was not built – having previously referred the making of the tomb in Chapel to 1607 (*Annals*, p. 214). But something is wrong: if the tomb is of 1607 why does it have Gostlin's inscription at the foot, and how was it financed? – and why was another monument needed? It seems much more likely that it was made under Gostlin's eye *c.* 1619, made to resemble the Perse tomb as he made the Legge building resemble the Perse building – and that the plan to put it 'in illa structura' was modified. The *Annals* of these years were not written till the late 1640s. On Gostlin, see below, pp. 114 – 17.
4 The memorial stones are now in the bicycle shed in Tree Court (cf. Venn, III, 69).
5 Venn 1887 – it is the basis of Venn, I; see also Curtis 1959, pp. 60 – 1; Simon 1963; Cressy 1970; Morgan 1975, pp. 184, 203 – 10.
6 Thus when Perse arrived as a pensioner in 1565 (Venn, I, 57) he was 'assigned to the third lower chamber' (in Gonville Court, probably in the north-east corner) – I hope to publish a reconstruction of the chambers and their inmates in the 1560s and 1570s in a forthcoming *Caian* [see *The Caian* 1987, pp. 56 – 67].

adventures. He first saw the real interest of the document, transcribed and interpreted and distilled it into print; and being an eminent mathematician he enjoyed reducing its elements to statistics. Being a pioneer, he made mistakes — though not many. But one was fundamental. As he himself explained, he translated *generosus* and *ingenuus* alike as 'gentleman', and a number of statistical tables have showed the exceptional proportion of the sons of the gentry in the Caius of Elizabeth and the early Stuarts.[7] In 1970 Dr David Cressy pointed out that *ingenuus* meant a 'yeoman' — a word covering a very wide range in the farming community, approximately from the 'forty-shilling freeholder' (i.e. who owned or tilled land worth 40s. *per annum*) to the prosperous farmers too modest or too mean to purchase a coat of arms and a genealogy from the heralds and set up as gentlemen. There are indeed many qualifications to be set to these statistics. The harassed registrary and tutors who compiled them had little thought for the modern demographer and his machines: they used categories of evident imprecision. But they help greatly to focus our view of the community in the college at the time, and as no other College can provide comparable details so early, they have a much wider interest too. Here is Dr Cressy's revised table.[8]

	Gentlemen	Clergy/ Professions	Merchant/ Trades	Yeomen/ Husbandmen	Mediocris fortunae/ unclassified
		(The figures are all %)			
1580−9	34	6	7	11	42
1590−9	33	10	8	10	38
1600−9	38	19	6	17	20
1610−19	30	24	10	16	19
1620−9	28	20	23	22	7
1630−9	39	20	16	19	6

and let us compare these with the figures Mrs Simon has extracted from the admission registers of St John's for the years 1630−5.

35	21	14	18	12[9]

The most obvious shift in these figures over the decades is, as Dr Cressy noted, in the last column. If we suppose that many of the unclassified were 'unregistered tradesmen' as both he and Mrs Simon thought likely,[10] then it

7 Venn 1887, p. xxiii, corrected by Cressy 1970.
8 Cressy 1970, p. 114. There is a very interesting account of the Caius figures in their wider context, and discussion of their significance in Cressy 1972, chap. 7, esp. pp. 254−61, and table 31 p. 257, which shows e.g. that though the percentage of gentry slightly dipped in the 1620s the actual numbers stayed steady. Cf. below, p. 156.
9 Simon 1963, p. 63.
10 Simon 1963, p. 60; Cressy 1970, p. 115.

is only the second column which shows any significant shift from the 1580s to the 1630s — and since the majority of the parents here were married clergy, this column may partly reflect the end of the rule of celibacy for country clergy which enabled the clerical Cambridge graduates, slowly at first but with increasing momentum, to breed their own successors as they could not before. Here there is a real novelty; but for the rest, one is bound to say that the size of the last column and its indeterminate nature may invalidate any conclusions drawn as to the proportions of small tradesmen and modest farmers among the parents. We should dearly like to know if the comparable figures from St John's and other colleges would show a like pattern in the reign of Elizabeth, but the evidence is lacking; and it may be that the very low proportion of sons of clergy in the 1580s in Caius also reflects the fact that the College had a lay master and a reputation for popery. To this we shall return.

But first of all, how do these figures relate to the wider history of the College and University? They have been used as a central part of the evidence for the thesis that the University grew very rapidly in the reign of Elizabeth, and that the gentry and secular folk in general were the chief patrons or beneficiaries — that there was a cultural revolution in which the universities, long centres of theology and clericalism, were sought after by many who had no intention to be ordained, and often no wish for a degree; and that Oxford and Cambridge were valued for their wider educational values, as higher boarding schools or places of liberal learning. In general terms there is much to be said for this way of looking at the history of Oxbridge in the late 16th century.[11] Men like Sir William Cecil, Lord Burghley, clearly valued Cambridge as a home of sound learning quite apart from the orthodox Anglican theology it was supposed to foster. It became an integrated part of the social life of aristocracy, gentry and middling folk who cared for education. At the same time, the old higher faculties lost ground. Canon Law was officially abolished at the Reformation, though Dr Legge's membership of Doctors' Commons — and the absorption in that extraordinary City club of most of the energies of Trinity Hall — will presently reveal to us that it crept back in again by the back door.[12] It was to be many centuries before medicine became a major school of study, in spite of the notable physicians from John Caius to William Harvey which this college produced over these decades. Theology remained a primary interest, but the shifting sands of argument as to what academic theology should be, made the search for higher degrees a much more uncertain and unstable business than in the days when scholar after scholar glossed the *Sentences*. Meanwhile, the elements of humanist learning came to figure more largely in the college libraries and basic liberal studies — selectively, but clearly — flourished.

11 Curtis 1959, modified by Kearney 1970, Morgan 1975 and Russell 1977. For the wider context of university history see Porter 1958; Roach 1959, pp. 180ff.; Mullinger 1884.
12 See below, p. 85.

Yet to this picture of a university secularised, liberalised, de-clericalised, two major objections can be made. First of all, Hugh Kearney, in his forthright study of *Scholars and Gentlemen*, sets out to show that at no date before the 19th century did Cambridge cease to be primarily a grandiose seminary for clergy in the bud; that the proportion of Cambridge men who completed their arts course and took degrees, and then went on into the church, remained high; that it remained a predominantly clerical institution.[13] In broad terms this is undoubtedly true; and it is possible that the social historians had been deceived in any case by an excessive reliance on the Caius matriculation register; for Caius was the only major college to have lay masters at its head throughout the reign of Elizabeth I.

Yet the real difficulty is that we have no comparable document before the time of John Caius with which to compare it. No other college in either university has a comprehensive admissions register so early as this; and the universities have only very defective registers of degrees. It has never been the case that every student entering the university departed with a degree; even today there are a few who do not; at most earlier periods they were very numerous. In the 1560s the large majority of students entering Caius did not in the end proceed to degrees. They were not for that reason failures — most of them presumably came for a spell of study and of Cambridge and went their way to complete their studies in the Inns of Court, or to a profession elsewhere, or to till their father's fields. So may an innumerable number of their predecessors who have left no trace in our records.

We can be sure that the college expanded very rapidly in the reign of Elizabeth. The matriculation book starts at the very beginning of the reign and the figures are reliable: the annual intake in the 1560s averaged 18 − 19, in the 1570s 32 − 3.[14] That figure was artificially inflated by the advent of Dr Legge with a flock of disciples, and there was a falling off thereafter to 24 in the 1580s, 26 in the 1590s, rising again to the peak of 34 − 5 in the 1620s and 1630s. But these figures are affected by two crucial local circumstances. All the indications are that Legge in his prime was a popular tutor of exceptional reputation; no-one would have used such phrases about Caius. The College was likely to prosper and multiply whatever the national averages and trends. Furthermore, after the theft of Physwick Hostel by the king in the 1540s, the accommodation available to the college was very limited indeed. It was doubled by the building of Caius Court, and greatly increased again by the building of the Legge and Perse buildings in the 1610s. These two major building campaigns closely preceded the great expansions of the 1570s and the 1620s. We can, of course, point to other building campaigns which fit the same pattern: to Trinity Great Court and Nevile's Court under the inspiration of that frenetic builder Dean Nevile at the turn of the 16th and 17th centuries; or to the second court of St John's whose

13 Kearney 1970. For the next paragraph see also Russell 1977.
14 Venn, III, 392.

drain-pipes bear the elegant legend 1599.[15] These are important examples, since these were the largest colleges at the time — and were only challenged in numbers and distinction in the 17th century by Emmanuel, founded in 1584. But if we turn back and compare the general provision of student accommodation in the reign of Elizabeth and before — we compare the known with the unknown. We have a fair idea of what existed in the late 16th century when colleges had won the monopoly of student admissions. But while hostels of quite uncertain size still flourished before the mid-16th century, we have little idea of the accommodation, or the total numbers, of students. It would be excessively sceptical to deny altogether the increase in numbers of Elizabeth's reign; it would be credulous to extrapolate the figures from the Caius matriculation book to the whole student body. We can look back to the 15th century and see that William Cecil's predecessors already counted many educated laymen; that lay folk in court and country house were often literate, and some of them already enjoyed university experience or coveted it for their sons.[16] The interest of the nobility and the gentry in Cambridge was in evidence before 1559. Behind the foundation of the giant colleges in Henry VIII's reign must lie a growing interest in the universities in court and aristocratic circles. Queen Katherine Parr may have taken a hand, but it was surely this wider concern which mainly explains why Henry VIII withdrew from the project of dissolving the colleges and expanded them instead. By the same token, Dr Caius' scheme for the refounding of his own college was fostered — not in Cambridge, which gave him a rude shock when he returned there in 1558 — but in a house in the City of London and in a practice among the nobility and perhaps at court. To this extent Professor Curtis was justified in seeing a new relation between society and universities in *Oxford and Cambridge in Transition, 1558—1642* (1959); but he surely dated its start too late, and underestimated the clerical continuum.

Thomas Legge

Thomas Legge was born in Norwich and spent his days in Cambridge; this may account for his friendship with John Caius. His family claimed an Italian origin, which may excuse the heavy Italian pun on his name and profession — 'Legge' and 'legge', the law — which adorns his tomb: 'Col legame della legge' — 'with the chain of the law'.[17] He was trained in civil law, a civilian — that is, he was an expert in Roman law. He was also, like Caius,

15 It was completed in 1602—3. Willis and Clark, II, 248—63; *RCHM Cambridge*, II, 187. For Nevile see Willis and Clark, II, 474 ff., etc. — he also built the Deanery at Canterbury.
16 For an example, see pp. 28, 33; and for what follows, above, pp. 43—4.
17 Whatever other meaning the words have eludes me, but I note that the inscription 'hides' the Latin words 'collega, medella', colleague and remedy or healing, which might naturally appeal to Gostlin.

a layman; but his expertise in Roman law gave him an entrée into some of the hidden chambers of the law of the Church, for if Roman Canon law was abolished, the courts were not; and the proper training for professional office in them was in civil law, partly because there had always been close links between Roman and Canon law in court procedure.[18] Civil law was also much valued in Tudor court circles as a training for the royal service and for diplomats; but Legge's talents did not lead him to be a courtier. He took his LLD in 1575, and from 1579 until his death he was Commissary of the Vice-Chancellor's court — itself an ecclesiastical court in tradition and practice if not in name; and in this office he presided over all cases which concerned students not yet masters. He was also Commissary to the bishop of Ely. In 1580 he was admitted to practise in the Court of Arches, the Provincial Court of Canterbury in London, and in 1590 he and Richard Swale his President were admitted as Advocates of Doctors' Commons, a strange legal institution in the City of London. By a curious irony the vacancy caused by Henry VIII's condemnation of the old canon law was filled by Civil or Roman law, and in Doctors' Commons Legge and his fellows were civilians practising ecclesiastical law. Legge's surviving notes show him to have been a man who studied Roman law in order to practise it — a *conoscente* of the practical, Italian manner, not a man of high theory like the French.[19] In its years of decline the young Charles Dickens was for a time a clerk there — and Steerforth introduced David Copperfield to it. Here proctors and advocates — the solicitors and barristers of Doctors' Commons — prepared cases in ecclesiastical law and for the court of admiralty — strange bedfellows in 'the lazy old nook near St Paul's churchyard. . . . It's a little out-of-the-way place, where they administer what is called ecclesiastical law, and play all kinds of tricks with obsolete old monsters of Acts of Parliament, which three-fourths of the world know nothing about, and the other fourth supposes to have been dug up, in a fossil state, in the days of the Edwards. It's a place that has an ancient monopoly in suits about people's wills and people's marriages, and disputes among ships and boats.' Doctors' Commons was like a miniature Inn of Court — a tiny collection of chambers and offices and a sort of lawyer's club, but with a court attached. In later times it became exclusively a haunt of laymen — strange fate for the centre of the church's legal practice — and this explains, or is explained by, the predominantly lay character of the fellowship of Trinity Hall, which became for two centuries the Cambridge club of the leading members of Doctors' Commons.[20] But this was still mainly

18 Squibb 1977, esp. chap. 1. For what follows, see Venn, III, 64. Legge is sometimes said to have been Regius Professor of Civil Law, but I have found no evidence of this: and Professor Peter Stein tells me he cannot be fitted into the known sequence of professors. For his commonplace book (n. 1) see D. Owen in *Journal of Soc. of Archivists*, II, 468.

19 Though he can on occasion show knowledge of this fashion. On Legge's approach to Roman law I am indebted to the kind help of Peter Stein. On Doctors' Commons, see Squibb 1977, pp. 163–4 (Legge 16 May, Swale 3 Oct.), replacing Coote 1804, p. 60. For what follows, *David Copperfield*, chap 23.

20 Crawley 1976, chap. IV.

in the future in Legge's time, when laymen and clergy freely enjoyed the commons together. His membership was an illustration of the respect in which his legal talents were held, and probably led him to be more often absent from Cambridge:[21] he was also a Master in Chancery and a JP in Cambridge in the 1590s.

Early in life Legge had been a student at Corpus, a scholar and fellow of Trinity, and a fellow of Jesus (1568−73).[22] Even before he became Master, the numbers in college had been rising — thirteen were admitted in 1568−9, 14 in 1569−70 (including two new tutors), 17 in 1570−1 (one a tutor), 22 in 1571−2; space was more ample and, one may judge, the reputation of the College growing in spite of its quarrels.[23] In 1572−4, which included Legge's first two years, the entries were 33 and 34, and they remained at this level for the rest of the decade. Many of the early recruits came from other colleges, from Corpus and Trinity and elsewhere, but above all, with Legge himself, from Jesus. Legge's arrival also signalled a wider variety of geographical origins for the new admissions, even though he himself was a Norfolk man as much as any of the founders. The complexion of the College had early been, and always remained, until the 19th century, predominantly East Anglian; in the 18th century Norfolk and Suffolk were to achieve a virtual monopoly. But in earlier centuries there had always been some variety, and this was notably so in the time of John Caius. Thus in the lean year 1565−6, when only 6 students were admitted, three were from Yorkshire — Simon Davys of Howden whose brother was already in the college, George Vavisore, who migrated from Clare, and his brother Ralph who came straight from school in South Cave.[24] The three East Anglians came from Stoke by Clare and Norwich — and from Great Massingham in Norfolk and from school in Norwich came Stephen Perse, son of John Perse of modest fortune, aged 17; he was to die in College 50 years later after a career of unique stability. The generation which came in 1573−4 included many from Norfolk and Suffolk, a sprinkling too from Essex and Hertfordshire and Cambridgeshire.[25] From Yorkshire came John Green, formerly of Corpus and Jesus, who ended his days a Yorkshire rector; John Price from Merionethshire, a migrant from Clare; Richard Kirkby from Lancashire, who had been at school at St Bees and Giggleswick. Of the 34 admitted this year eleven at least, and probably more, became country parsons; one a schoolmaster at Norwich who presently sent one of his own pupils to Caius; three at least followed the Master's bent into the law; one may have become a physician. But the general trend towards

---

21 The *Liber Rationalis* 1581−93 and *Exiit Book* (from 1592) show him to have been little absent in the 1580s, but often away for periods of weeks at a time from *c.* 1590. The pattern of Perse's absences was the reverse — he was little absent from 1590 till his death in 1615.
22 Venn, III, 64.
23 Venn, I, 63−71, and 71−80 for what follows.
24 Venn, I, 57−8.
25 Venn, I, 75−80.

the established church seems clear, and it is in this light that we come to examine the most remarkable names in the list, John Fingley, the Recusant martyr, Edward Osburne, his close associate, and their enemy John Paman, the convinced Protestant.

The year 1570 witnessed three dramatic events which dominated many men's thoughts in Cambridge for a generation to come. The Pope excommunicated Queen Elizabeth and pronounced her faithful subjects freed from their loyalty to her; and contrariwise statutes of the University were revised in a manner calculated to tighten ecclesiastical discipline and the control of heads of colleges; and the great Puritan preacher, Thomas Cartwright, Lady Margaret Professor of Divinity and fellow of Trinity, was condemned and driven into exile — both on the initiative of John Whitgift, Master of Trinity, Vice-Chancellor and future archbishop of Canterbury.[26] Whitgift was a man of great intellectual and administrative gifts, with a view of the Anglican *via media* by no means narrow; but he regarded the vestments of John Caius and the strong puritanism of Thomas Cartwright with an equal and impartial abhorrence. If in the year 1574 Thomas Legge presided over the election of Paman to be fellow and tutor, and allowed the admission of John Fingley — who was quickly suspected of recusancy and yet promoted by the Master to the office of College butler, not infrequently a scholar's perk — we must assume that Legge was either obtuse to theological distinctions, or, much more probably, a man of genuine tolerance.[27] No doubt he laid up much trouble for himself; but these admissions are only part of the copious evidence that he liked to have a lively, active, contentious community about him; and however much those who have lived through stormy times may prefer the peace which follows, it must be allowed that argument and controversy are a sign of life in a young community, and their absence not necessarily a sign of health.

It is most improbable that Legge was himself a crypto-Recusant. After due enquiry, the Chancellor and the royal court had allowed his succession to Caius[28] — and he was no obscure hidden academic at that time. He was later to see the inside of the Fleet Prison for a while owing to the College's failure to answer a royal letter with sufficient rapidity.[29] But there is no indication that the Chancellor, or Archbishops Parker or Whitgift, held him in personal disesteem, and it is hardly likely that he would have survived well over thirty years as Master — and latterly very active in the ecclesiastical courts — had his theology been suspect. It is more probable that like Caius he was a man of conventional religious practice, sufficiently devoted to the

---

26 Morey 1978, chaps. 3–5; Porter 1958, chap. VIII, esp. pp. 174–8.
27 Venn, I, 76, 79; on the recusants in Caius, see esp. Venn 1913, chap. VII.
28 *CSPD 1547–80*, p. 474; PRO SP 12/75/30: draft order for an election to the Mastership dated 21 Jan. 1574; doubtless this was followed by acceptance or confirmation of Legge's status. But the document speaks as if the College had no Master and was a prey to faction, which suggests that some false rumour had reached Burghley.
29 Venn, III, 66–7.

established church and to the royal supremacy. Whether he understood the extent to which powerful influences among his students might lead Popery and Puritanism to flourish under his complacent sceptre is another matter: that we cannot tell. It is certain that he was easy-going and refused to cast too shrewd an eye on those under his care or demanding his favour.[30] When Legge died, he left over £570 in debts due to him which could readily be recovered, for like many of his contemporaries, including Perse himself, he lent most of his spare cash to those in need. It is sufficient commentary on their business acumen to observe that with Perse good debts outmatched bad by roughly three to one, with Legge the debts doubtful were over £200, the debts desperate well over £800.[31] He was a man of easy charity.

The Catholic recusants

In due course Archbishop Sandys turned once again a malevolent eye on the college. Recusancy was spreading in his diocese, and he suspected the college of fostering it among its Yorkshire students. This was not wholly untrue. One of the Vavisores 'being a sober, wise young gentleman, said unto Mr Church that he thought that his Tutor was a Papist'[32] – and the tutor was the President of the College, Mr Swale, who was widely accused of helping the College recusants. Of the Master himself the archbishop crossly wrote: 'All the Popish gentlemen in this country (county) send their sons to him. He setteth sundry of them over to one Swale of the same house, by whom the youth of this country is corrupted'.[33] Richard Swale was one of Legge's Jesus men, a Yorkshireman, a lawyer – like the Master he later became an LLD, and an advocate in Doctors' Commons, and also a Master in Chancery; in later life he was an MP and in 1603 a commissioner 'for suppressing unlicensed books'.[34] He was accused that 'in his first commonplace, in chapel, Abraham and David for lying were commended to be examples as a point of wisdom in the serpent to be followed' which perhaps savours of humour rather than Popery.[35] Like Legge, he is much more likely to have been guilty of tolerance than recusancy; he seems to have had little difficulty in convincing Burghley of his integrity; and a 20th century historian cannot avoid honouring both of them for fostering a group of notable, and some of them heroic, Catholics in their midst. Both Swale and

---

30 See esp. Venn, III, 66 – 7, citing the Vice-Chancellor's opinion in 1582.
31 CUL, Vice-Chancellor's Court, Inventory of Legge dated 10 Dec. 1607; of Perse dated 4 Oct. 1615.
32 Venn 1913, p. 86; Venn, I, 97. The depositions of 1582 are from BL Lansdowne 33, ff. 91 – 128; substantial extracts from these, and other papers relating to Caius disputes of this time, are in CTPC, I, 314 – 41, 344 – 69.
33 Venn, III, 65 from Strype, *Annals of the Reformation*, II, ii (edn. of Oxford, 1824), p. 342; cf. Morgan 1975, p. 208.
34 Venn, I, 85; DNB; Squibb 1977, p. 164; cf. Venn 1913, pp. 86 – 7.
35 Quoted Venn, I, 85.

his young pupil and room-mate, Thomas Vavisore, were later knighted.[36]

The most celebrated of the recusants was Richard Holtby, the Yorkshire Jesuit, who was Provincial of the Jesuits in England from 1606 till his death in his late 80s in 1640, 'a little man with a reddish beard' who survived many dangerous encounters and died in the odour of sanctity. But he only spent one year in Caius (1573 – 4), in the room now known as I2 Caius Court, between two years' study at Christ's and the completion of his arts course in Oxford.[37] In 1573 another Yorkshireman arrived, John Fingley, who came to be regarded as the ring-leader of the papists, especially after his promotion to be butler. 'There was very much speech of a mass reported to be said by Fingley in the Master's great chamber, and that he was by some suspected to be a priest'.[38] This story we may readily disbelieve, since he was not then a priest: he went to Rheims in 1580, was ordained priest there in 1581, and returned to England with his Caius contemporary, Edward Osburne, a Norfolk man. Osburne had a chequered course: under family urging he abandoned his faith for a time, then returned, and is alleged to have ended his days a Franciscan friar. Fingley kept to his course, was caught and imprisoned in York in 'a deep and darksome dungeon', was tried, condemned, hanged and quartered in August 1586. In his fascinating paper on the Caius recusants, Venn listed about 15 more names of those who had passed through Caius to the ranks of the Jesuits or the secular Catholic priesthood in the reign of Thomas Legge.[39] Their places of birth were as diverse as those of the College, but most came of gentry or yeoman stock. They include no other major figures among the recusants of the age, but Christopher Walpole, one of a number from East Anglia, was a younger brother of Henry Walpole, member of a famous Norfolk clan and himself one of the most celebrated of the martyrs.

Some of these men came from Catholic recusant homes or environments sympathetic to the development of recusant ideals; but we cannot doubt that there was a fervour of Catholic idealism abroad in the College in the 1570s and 1580s, probably going much wider and deeper than the Master had at all anticipated.[40] Yet Protestant fervour seems to have flourished even more; for when the storm broke early in 1582 seven fellows – a majority of the fellowship, since only five beside the Master refused to join

36 Venn, I, 84 – 5.
37 Venn, 1913, p. 90; Venn, I, 75; he was assigned 'the first lower cubicle (chamber), to the south, on the West side of the Caius Court'.
38 For this and what follows, Venn, I, 76; for Osburne ibid. 77.
39 Venn 1913, chap. VII, esp. 89 – 99.
40 Venn, III, 65 – 8; Venn 1913, pp. 84 – 9. What is evident from the original depositions, preserved among Cecil's papers in BL Lansdowne MS 33, but not from the extracts and summaries in Venn and CTPC, is that when the leading Protestants of Cambridge were summoned to the enquiry, they refused to testify for the most part to any of the detailed charges of popery against the Master and Swale. Thus on f. 98 Laurence Chaderton knew nothing against Swale and only voiced suspicion against Legge by hearsay: 'he thynketh he hathe been suspected'.

the protest — propounded a comprehensive list of 88 charges against the Master and other colleagues.[41] Most of the seven insurgents became beneficed clergy and there is no precise or satisfactory evidence of their theological views; but some of the charges against Richard Swale suggest a Puritan tendency in his enemies. One solemn young student thought Swale a Papist, 'because that when he requested him to buy a Calvin's Catechism, or Beza's Confessions, he was offended with him. . .' — and another complained that he failed to take adequate steps against card-playing on Sunday.[42] The virulence of the attack on Popery suggests a Puritan sympathy; but you did not have to be a Puritan to denounce the recusants. The insurgents won some support indeed from leading Cambridge Puritans such as William Whitaker, Master of St Johns, and Laurence Chaderton of Christ's, later first Master of Emmanuel; but in the further enquiries their testimony amounted to little more than the general reputation of the College as a harbour of Papists.[43] The heat of the dispute naturally raised so much smoke as to obscure the real opinions of many of the combatants; faction breeds absurdity, and we must not lay too much stress on the details of the charges. Richard Garrard, one of the leaders, complained 'that the College is much annoyed with hackney horses' and of 'excessive lewd singing and organs' and of those who 'spend a great part of their time idly in music to the great trouble of others' — which wrung from Venn the comment 'and all this complaint before the piano had been invented'.[44] Evidently the Master's fondness for music and drama offended his Puritan colleagues.

It is interesting to observe quite a clear-cut division of age between the insurgents and the other fellows. Only the Master was over 40 — he was about 46 at the time; next in age came Swale and Perse, in their mid-30s, and Robert Church, about 32.[45] The ringleaders of the insurgents, Paman and Gerrard, were both about 30, Gould in his early 30s, the rest in their late 20s. Richard Gerrard himself was the son of an old friend of Dr Caius and Legge made things difficult for him by complaining to his father. The three youngest fellows, all in their early 20s and recently elected, stood by the Master; and one of them, Remigius Booth, appears as a hammer of the insurgents.[46] The heart and core of the complaint was that Popery was rife and the Master condoned it. Some of the detail in the charges gives us vivid glimpses of life in College. Richard Gerrard deposed that 'Barnham was reported to be the bringer up of Huddleston deceased — [a young member of the well-known recusant family who had died as a student in the College] — which Huddleston had been instructed in papistry, and that the report

41 Venn, loc. cit.; *CTPC*, I, 316–26.
42 Venn 1913, pp. 86–7.
43 See n. 40.
44 Venn 1913, pp. 88–9.
45 Legge died in July 1607 aged 72, according to his tomb; for the rest, see Venn, I, 57–9, 85, and for the younger fellows, Venn, I, 78–110.
46 Venn, I, 110. For earlier charges of immorality against Booth, see *CTPC*, I, 227–62.

was that Barnham did read popish prayers unto Huddleston in the time of his sickness; and that the said Barnham had written certain verses in commendation of the papists of our College. And further this deponent affirmeth that he did see wax candles carried to the said Huddleston's chamber by a serving man which he believeth were burning about the dead body until ten of the clock. . .'[47]

The most serious of the charges related to popery; the most numerous to the administration of the College and its estates. The truth of these is difficult to penetrate; many are natural emanations of heated minds when faction and argument were in riot. The Master evidently kept the affairs of the College much in his hands, sharing from time to time with bursars of his own choosing, and especially with Stephen Perse; and it is noticeable that Perse defended him against many charges. Probably the most deeply felt, and frustrating, of his measures was the exercise of the negative vote — by which he vetoed proposals approved by a majority in the fellowship. This was to be a bone of contention time and again in the future; and in a community in which it was common for the Master to be the one elder statesman among a group of young and ardent fellows, we can understand that he might quite often feel the need to use it, and that they would see it as the ultimate sign of maladministration or tyranny. That the Master strongly objected to their proceedings would hardly need proof, but it does indeed emerge from several of the complaints against him. One young man called Thomas Mudde, an accomplished musician, was forbidden his degree for popish leanings, and the Master remonstrated with his colleagues to no effect; so he arranged his transfer to Peterhouse which on this occasion was more complaisant — and the College lost its first known composer.[48] Yet the Master on the whole seems to have kept his temper. Not so Richard Swale who spoke out in College and before the Chancellor, to whom the insurgents' complaints presently came. They had failed to get redress from the Master or the Vice-Chancellor or the Visitors, so they turned at last to Burghley. All of these potentates were doubtless used to such complaints by now, and by no means inclined to lend too ready an ear to ardent young Protestants even if denouncing popery. The matter was compounded by a dispute on the nomination of a proctor — a nomination Swale claimed as his of right and his enemies denied — which brought the jurisdiction of Vice-Chancellor and Chancellor directly into play. Burghley set the Vice-Chancellor to a full investigation, and listened personally to Swale's plea for mercy.[49] The Master was made to return some money he had charged the College for his expenses in visiting the Fleet prison, but otherwise the

---

47 Venn 1913, p. 88; BL Lansd. MS 33, f. 106. The list of charges against the Master are in *CTPC*, I, 316–26.
48 On Thomas Mudde see Venn, I, 90; *DNB*; S. Jeans in *The New Grove Dictionary of Music and Musicians*, XII (1980), 758. He evidently fell under the puritan disapproval of music and drama.
49 *CTPC*, I, 344–69, esp. 366–9.

charges against him seem to have gone away on the air, and Gerrard himself and some of his colleagues found themselves out in the cold, begging the Chancellor for help.[50] By the end of 1587 all the insurgents had departed the College, most of them onto country livings. The Master could sleep more peacefully; and it may be that the excitements of 1582 taught him caution, though it seems clear they did not cure him of his tolerance. For tolerance a man must have cared deeply, who — however inadvertently — reared a nest of papists and at the same time allowed a majority of the fellows to be fervent Protestants.

Swale himself stayed in the fellowship until 1589; of the others, Church and Burton remained fellows until well after 1600 and Stephen Perse until his death in 1615.[51] They provided, with the Master, a continuity and common purpose through the changing kaleidoscope of fellows, scholars and pensioners coming and going. We need not take the charges against them too seriously, though a special interest must attach to that against Perse.[52] He was in orders, they claim, yet moved to a medical fellowship and back; they evidently thought him a half-hearted minister of the word, and there is no reason to suppose (as has sometimes been asserted) that he had Puritan sympathies. The only clear evidence of his position is that he made Valentine Carey, dean of St Pauls, later bishop of Exeter, one of his executors; and Carey was a high churchman, almost a Laudian before Laud — who as Master of Christ's was engaged in putting down the Puritans there.[53]

In 1587—8 Legge was Vice-Chancellor, and presided over the opening ceremonies at the Puritan College of Emmanuel.[54] Now he seemed at peace with the world, whatever its complexion. But the excitements of his reign were not over. In 1587 he also presided at the election to the fellowship of the distinguished mathematician Edward Wright; and in due course the College gave him leave to sail to the Azores with the earl of Cumberland, the only known occasion when sabbatical leave has been granted for the pursuit of piracy. But Wright's role was as navigator and surveyor; and his later work with Hakluyt involved major advances in map-making. Meanwhile the Puritans were on the move again, led by William Whitaker, the Master of St John's; and moderate or high churchmen felt themselves beleaguered. In 1592 William Barrett of Trinity was appointed Chaplain, and in April 1595 preached a University sermon in which he 'laboured to prove that justifying faith may finally decay and be lost, and consequently did maintain and teach the popish doctrine of doubtfulness of our salvation, against the comfortable certainty of true faith taught and preached in this

50 Venn, III, 67.
51 Venn, I, 57—9, 85, 103.
52 Venn, I, 57.
53 See below, pp. 101, 110.
54 F. Stubbings in *Emmanuel Statutes*, p. 94. For Edward Wright, see *DSB*, XIV, 513—15 (P. J. Wallis); *DNB*; Venn, I, 88—9.

our Church ever since the first planting of the Gospel amongst us: with most bitter railing upon those worthy men Calvin, Peter Martyr, Beza, Zanchius, and others, to the great offence of the godly'.[55]

Thus spoke Barrett's Calvinist critics; and although it has been shown that his intent was defensive, he roused more widespread opposition than solely among the godly, for he was evidently arrogant and aggressive. Like others who have preached intemperately with the hope of stirring a hornet's nest, he was deeply hurt by the behaviour of the hornets. They first made him recant, then, deciding his recantation was inadequate, raised a petition against him, which was signed not only by known Puritan sympathisers but by four fellows of Caius, including Perse, who evidently found him an intolerable bedfellow.[56] Whitgift, now archbishop of Canterbury, tried to smother the dispute; Burghley, the Chancellor, with a like aim but opposite result, tried to ignore it and leave it in Cambridge. There, as Whitgift indignantly pointed out to him, it festered — and indeed, the archbishop himself discovered that some of Barrett's doctrines, though offensive to Calvin, were matters on which the Church of England had not pronounced. And on one point — assurance of salvation — H. C. Porter has shown that Barrett was following doctrine pronounced many years before by Whitgift himself; 'although the Christian be persuaded that nothing can separate him from the love of God, the persuasion is of faith and hope, not of infallible fact.'[57]

Whitgift, himself a moderate Calvinist, reckoned that the Cambridge Puritans were using the Barrett case as an opportunity to impose extreme Calvinist doctrines on their colleagues; and he was determined to see that they failed. But in the end his sympathies lay rather with them than with Barrett, and when he eventually met the young man, he realised that he was not a sound prop of the establishment. In due course (after a fuss in College) his chaplaincy expired, he went abroad and became a Catholic.[58] Through all this the Master kept a low profile: he had nurtured another lively young man, but Perse and other colleagues evidently warned him against rising to his defence.

William Harvey

In the same year that William Barrett came to Caius from Trinity came also a 15-year old yeoman's son from Folkestone and King's Canterbury, called

55 Porter 1958, pp. 344—63, esp. 344—5, quoting Trinity Coll. MS B. 14.9, p. 23. Cf. Venn, I, 145. His fellowship lapsed at Michaelmas 1595. For a sympathetic view of Barrett, and the beleaguered moderates, and a modification of Porter's account of Whitgift's position, see Lake 1982, chap. 9.
56 Porter 1958, p. 346.
57 Porter 1958, p. 353; cf. pp. 347—63; but see the careful study in Lake 1982, pp. 218—26, stressing Whitgift's agreement with the Heads and modifying some of Porter's conclusions.
58 See n. 55. For evidence that Barrett's chaplaincy gave much dissatisfaction in College, see *Annals*, p. 340, laying down the duties of his successors.

William Harvey.[59] In 1593 he acquired a scholarship on Matthew Parker's foundation, which had a Kentish and a medical bias, which may well help to explain his choice of college. In any case he remained a scholar till 1599–1600, and evidently in this period found a vocation to study medicine like that which had inspired John Caius two generations earlier. So he migrated to Padua, and there proceeded MD. Thus William Harvey's residence in Caius was over when he was 22, and his later links with the College were relatively slight. Like Caius, he built up his practice and his name in London, and became for the Royal College of Physicians in the early 17th century what Caius had been in the mid-16th. But he was incomparably the more original scientist; and his demonstration of the way blood circulates reoriented human knowledge of the body and its functioning and founded the science of physiology. At first it was treated with opprobrium; but the tide turned, and Thomas Hobbes said of him, 'he is the only man, perhaps, that ever lived to see his own doctrine established in his lifetime'.[60] Unlike Caius again, he was a man of lively wit: 'he was wont to say', so Aubrey tells us, 'that man was but a great mischievous baboon'.[61] Later in life he became a court physician too, and was in attendance on Charles I at the Battle of Edgehill in 1642. For a time he revived his academic career on the fringe of the royal court in Oxford during the Civil War, and was made Warden of Merton in 1645. In this period the Caian Charles Scarburgh 'in whose conversation he much delighted' became his assistant.[62] Harvey survived the Civil War to die in honoured old age in 1657. Legends have grown up round him and his links with the College. John Aubrey alleged that he gave it the house in which he was born — which was apparently not so; and Venn, who sadly scotched this error, himself observed 'We have a portrait of him attributed to Rembrandt'.[63] No-one now attributes it to Rembrandt, and few believe it is a portrait of Harvey;[64] but it is a fine picture and it came to the College because a later hand had put his name upon it; and it is a splendid symbol of the fact that Harvey as legend has performed much

59 On Harvey see Keynes 1966; Whitteridge 1959, 1964 (editions of his works with full commentary); Venn, I, 149. Harvey was born on 1 April 1578 and admitted to Caius 31 May 1593 (Keynes 1966, p. 6; Venn, I, 149).
60 Aubrey, I, 301; revised text in Keynes 1966, p. 435.
61 Aubrey, I, 299; revised text in Keynes 1966, p. 433.
62 Aubrey, I, 299; in Keynes 1966, p. 433.
63 Venn, I, 149, citing Norman Moore (DNB) for the doctrine that Harvey left property to Caius, which Venn denied — rightly, for the College is not mentioned in his will; and it has been suggested that there has been confusion with Henry Hervey (died 1585), after whom a scholarship was named (cf. Venn, III, 231). But Aubrey, I, 295 (Keynes 1966, p. 431) says that William Harvey gave the house where he was born with 'some lands there' (i.e. in Folkestone) to Caius. See Keynes 1966, p. 4 and n. 4. If he intended so the gift seems never to have matured; there is no evidence of communication with Harvey in Bagge's correspondence (p. 131). It seems likely, as Philip Grierson has suggested, that the royalist ex-Warden of Merton was disaffected with the regime of Dr Dell.
64 See Keynes, 1949, p. 41, no. 5. But good judges have thought Sir Geoffrey too dismissive of the claims of the portrait in Caius. It was given to the College by the earl of Leicester in 1798.

service of his College which Harvey the man omitted. To him we owe it that the reputation of the College as a nursery of physicians — first fostered by Caius, continued by Perse into and beyond Harvey's boyhood — has outlived the later generations when it was sometimes difficult to discern a living tradition of medical teaching in the College.

Stephen Perse was by turns divine and doctor and financier. We have seen how little we know about him in the first guise; and we know not much more in the second. It may reasonably be supposed that he built up and sustained a profitable practice in and around Cambridge, since by some such means he laid the foundations of a fortune comparable to that of Caius himself, of aldermanic proportions indeed.[65] He was undoubtedly the foremost medical fellow in the 1590s, when Harvey was a student; but he was only one of a galaxy. Thomas Grimstone was fellow 1582 — 95 and proceeded MD in 1601; John Gostlin, the Master's close friend and disciple, was fellow from 1592 and Master 1619 — 26; Robert Welles was fellow from 1592 till his death in 1632; and Matthew Stokes may somewhat doubtfully be added to this list, for although for most of his even longer tenure of the fellowship, from 1592 to 1635, he seems to have been primarily a divine, in his later years he also practised medicine.[66] It is evident that Harvey was bred in a congenial atmosphere, and probable that the atmosphere owed much to Perse. Yet Perse lives mainly as a founder and benefactor.

Charity and Mrs Frankland

Perse's charity, however, we must postpone awhile, and explore other benefactors of his time and the consequences of their bounty. Two are of outstanding interest. First, in 1563, early in the reign of Caius, Joan Trapps, widow of Robert Trapps, a rich London goldsmith, left money to buy land for the endowment of four scholarships to be named after her husband and herself. The origin of her interest in the College was evidently personal friendship with the founder: 'on our persuasions' says Caius in the *Annals* — and we may conjecture that she was a grateful patient.[67] At first the legacy seemed likely to bring nothing but trouble, for the executor, Sir Roger Manwood, was more interested in founding Sandwich School than in benefiting the College, and eventually, nearly twenty years after her death, he made a settlement which tied half the scholars at least to the school. But of much greater benefit to the College was the link thus provided with the Trapps' daughter Jocosa or Joyce.[68] She married in turn two substantial London citizens, and by the first had one son, William Saxey; she had no

65 See below, pp. 99—102.
66 Venn, I, 115—16, 122, 124 (and for Gostlin, also below pp. 114—17).
67 *Annals*, p. 89; Venn, III, 227—8.
68 For what follows, Venn, III, 229—30; Venn 1901, pp. 90—1. It is an oft repeated tale, but no history of Caius would be complete without it. On Nowell, see *DNB* and references.

children by the second, William Frankland, and his own sons by a former wife died before her, so that she was at the end of her life a widow of very substantial means. Her last years were darkened by tragedy. In 1581 she was visited by that notable beggar, Alexander Nowell, dean of St Paul's and former fellow of Brasenose, who wrote to Archbishop Whitgift five years later, after her death: 'One Mrs Frankland, late of Hertfordshire, widow, having one only son, who youthfully venturing to ride upon an unbroken young horse, was thrown down and slain. Whereupon the mother fell into sorrows uncomfortable; whereof I, being of her acquaintance, having intelligence, did with all speed ride unto her house near to Hoddesdon to comfort her the best I could. And I found her crying, or rather howling continually, "Oh my son! my son!" And when I could by no comfortable words stay her from that cry and tearing of her hair; God, I think, put me in mind at the last to say: "Comfort yourself, good Mistress Frankland, and I will tell you how you shall have twenty good sons to comfort you in these your sorrows which you take for this one son." To the which words only she gave ear, and looking up asked, "How can that be?" And I said unto her, "You are a widow, rich and now childless, and there be in both universities so many poor toward youths that lack exhibition, for whom if you would found certain fellowships and scholarships, to be bestowed upon studious young men, who should be called Mrs Frankland's scholars, they would be in love towards you as dear children, and will most heartily pray to God for you during your life; and they and their successors after them, being still Mrs Frankland's scholars, will honour your memory for ever and ever. This being said, I will, quoth she, think thereupon earnestly. And though she lived a good time after, yet she gave in her Testament to the College of Brasen Nose in Oxford a very great sum, and to Gonville and Caius College she gave £1540 in money, and in annual rents besides for ever £33.6s.8d.' – not to mention other legacies to Emmanuel and Lincoln Colleges, and Newport Grammar School which she founded; and she left the portraits of her parents and herself to Caius to be hung in the chapel.[69]

Junior and senior fellows

The legacy of Joyce Frankland and the arrival of her fellows in the early 1590s had a consequence quite unforeseen, we may be sure, by the pious lady or the dean. Their arrival was a little delayed – her wealth, like Perse's was largely in other folks' debts, and these had to be collected.[70] When the process was complete in 1592, six new fellows arrived. The old fellows found themselves flooded, as it were, by new stock. They were in

69 Venn, III, 229 – 30.
70 *Annals*, pp. 193 – 4. For what follows, and especially the entry fines, corn rents, etc. see below, pp. 102 – 3.

process of devising the admirable system — admirable, that is, to the beneficiaries — by which, for centuries to come, the rising value of the College estates was realised, not by rising rents but by such devices as larger entry fines, which were distributed to the fellows. The twelve in possession had other rights and privileges; with the Master, they ran the College. They were determined to keep Mrs Frankland's fellows in their place. And so they devised the distinction between 'senior' and 'junior' fellows, which persisted till the reforms of the 19th century — and in a measure is with us still; for the College is still governed by a committee of the Master and twelve fellows; the seniors have become the College Council.[71]

There may be other reasons for the survival of this sacred number: in the late 19th century it seems to have been supposed that 12 was a sound number for a committee, for the 'seniority' of St John's and Trinity were increased to 12 and 13 respectively from 7 and 8 — and the 12 of Caius and the 13 of King's were clearly among the influences upon this change.[72] But in the 1590s the influence evidently flowed from King's, Trinity and St John's — perhaps especially from Trinity, Legge's original home. There the concept of senior fellows was already established, and statutory; it had been first devised for King's in the 15th century.[73] In the statutes of Caius there is no justification for any such distinction. It is true that Mrs Frankland's fellows are not mentioned at all, since they did not then exist. But Caius envisaged a fellowship of 13, for he included Wendy's fellow.[74] Wendy's will, however, was not implemented until after 1600, so his fellow never became a 'senior'. Thus the sacred number of twelve seniors — who, with the Master, ruled the College and divided the spoils between them for three hundred years — was achieved by an act of silent revolution — for the event itself is entirely unrecorded in the *Annals* and mentioned in no surviving document; but the language of the records quietly changes, and from 1592 all fellows are designated 'senior' or 'junior'.[75] It was a characteristic event in the history of such institutions: a remarkable example of the way in which custom and tradition mingled with the statutes to form the structure of the College as it worked in practice. Few members of the College Council in this century, I fancy, have realised that they were heirs to this act of usurpation in the 1590s. However it was engineered, it was exceedingly effective, and from then on the juniors only received their basic stipends and their commons; all else, in cash and government, lay with the seniors and with the Master.

71 See below, p. 271; for the twelve, Venn, III, 217, cf. 353; and for the duties of fellows, and complexities introduced by the rules as to what they might study, Venn, III, 204–12. But so far as I can see, Venn did not fully appreciate the nature of the change which took place in the 1590s.
72 Cf. *VCH Cambs*, III, 383, 402, 438, 444, 464.
73 *VCH Cambs*, III, 383.
74 Venn, III, 353, cf. 217 for Wendy's fellow.
75 Thus Venn, I, 145, etc.

Perhaps it is wrong to talk of usurpation; for the increase in the fellowship created a problem which required some adjustment; and it is evident that Perse himself, when he founded new junior fellowships and supplemented Mrs Frankland's by his will, had come readily to accept the distinction.[76] Indeed, he may have been — with Legge — its architect.

Stephen Perse

There is no doubt that Perse had a shrewd eye on ways of making money, and that when he came to make his will in 1615 he fully understood the financial inequality of the Frankland fellows and the status his own would enjoy. Our most solid information about Perse relates indeed to his wealth and financial acumen. On his death he left somewhat over £11,000, a small part of it in the furniture and plate in his College rooms, nearly £600 in house property and leases, £360 in ready money, and no less than £10,000 in debts 'esteemed to be good debts' — apart from £3,311 9s. 6d in 'desperate debts'.[77] The roll of his debtors is an extraordinary document listing a great many of the gentry, middling and lesser folk of Cambridge and the neighbouring shires.[78] There is abundant evidence that his was a normal method of investment among men too occupied to be merchants or invest in trade and not inclined to be land agents on any substantial scale — as well as among wealthy widows like Mrs Frankland. Joyce Frankland and Stephen Perse were exceptional only in the scale of their transactions and the scope of their bounty. Perse left nearly half his fortune to support his many charities; most of the rest was divided between his sister and his stepmother and their families, and his distant relative Martin Perse, who became the effective executor of his will.[79] The stepmother has caused confusion among historians, for she is called his 'mother-in-law' in his will; and some have on her account endowed him with a wife.[80] But in spite of all the evasion of law and statute in which the colleges of Oxford and Cambridge indulged between the 16th and the 19th centuries, certain vagaries were rigorously excluded. A fellow could not be a Catholic or a Dissenter; and he could not marry. It is inconceivable that Perse could have been a resident fellow for over forty years and be married; and 'mother-in-law' was normal usage for a stepmother. This is strange enough; but it seems that Perse's

76 See below, p. 100.
77 CUL, University Archives, Records of the Vice-Chancellor's Probate Court, 1615, Perse's Inventory.
78 Caius Archives, LXIV, 4. For what follows see *Annals*, pp. 193–4 (Joyce Frankland) and Inventories of Legge and Branthwaite, CUL (as in n. 77) 1607, 1619.
79 For the complete text of Perse's will, see CUL, Vice-Chancellor's Court, Wills 1602–58, III, ff. 87ᵛ–94ᵛ; there is a modern transcript in CUR 69, no. 152; extracts in *Annals*, pp. 245–56 and elsewhere.
80 See esp. Gray 1921, pp. 8–9; Mitchell 1976, p. 5, is more cautious. For 'mother-in-law' see *Oxford English Dictionary*, s.v.; for a possible exception to the rule of celibacy, see p. 203.

father remarried late in life a woman so much younger than himself that she outlived her stepson, and was very likely younger than he.

Like David and Jonathan, Thomas Legge and Stephen Perse were not divided in their death — they still preside each over one side of the chapel; and we have seen that the close identity of their effigies and tombs reflects the deliberate symbolism of John Gostlin in his devotion to the memory of Legge, and probably to both.[81] In the College's history they complement one another. Legge was the warm-hearted Master who gathered disciples of many persuasions about him and after a chaotic period of religious strife left peace and goodwill behind; and Perse was the bursar, the master of the money-bags, the founder of many charities, of the Perse School, the Perse Fellowships and Scholarships and of the Perse Feast.[82]

Stephen Perse came in October 1565, and was set under Matthew Trott his tutor in the third lower chamber in Gonville Court. He was then 17; from 1571 he was a fellow; and as fellow he died, still resident in College, in 1615. He proceeded to the MD in 1581 and evidently had a good practice as a physician; and we may also believe the tradition that he lived frugally, saving his wealth for his many charitable interests. What is certain is that he was a money-lender.[83] The word to a modern ear carries a pejorative sense; but Perse's profession was entirely respectable — he was a kind of banker before there were accessible banks in our sense of the word; and his will proves that he regarded his own kind of money-lending as a charitable good work. We do not need to suppose that all his debtors took the same view — one of them hauled him into Chancery for extortion, but failed in his suit — nor do we know what interest he charged. When he died his will was proved in the Vice-Chancellor's court, and the inventory shows that he had a chamber in college, with a study and bedchamber with books and furniture and plate; he had lands and leases; but clearly his main financial interest lay in money-lending.[84] His own choice of investment is reflected in the opening of his will in which he directs that the sum of £5,000 (out of an effective total of about £11,000) was to be the handed over to the Corporations of Norwich (£2,000), Cambridge, Bury St Edmunds and King's Lynn (£1,000 each) to be lent 'to several young tradesmen' of these towns 'by several sums of £30 or £40 at the most upon good security' at a rate of interest not exceeding 5% per annum. Thus £5,000 would produce £250 which he proceeded to parcel out. In the event the towns refused to accept the legacy on these terms, and his executors, under the active leadership of his distant cousin Martin Perse, invested it in land. The plan and its failure set Perse's whole outlook on finance in perspective — he believed that investment and charity should go hand in hand, and that they could; by helping young

---

81 See pp. 79−80.
82 For what follows see Venn, I, 57−8; III, 218, 231; Gray 1921, chap. i; Mitchell 1976, chap. i.
83 See nn. 77−8; Mitchell 1976, p. 3 (q.v. also for the Chancery suit).
84 For the inventory see n. 77, for the will n. 79.

tradesmen you invested in their prosperity and could use the proceeds for wider educational and charitable purposes. His own lending was certainly not confined to young tradesmen and a private fortune could hardly have been built up by lending at 5% but he had evidently enlarged his wealth by relatively modest, well-placed loans.

His will shows how deeply he was committed to educating the boys and young men of Cambridge. The first task he lays upon his executors, after the abortive investments in the five towns, was to take in hand the whole of his property on the site of the Austin Friars in Free School Lane in Cambridge, and 'erect and build a convenient house to be used for a Grammar Free School with one lodging for the Master and another for the Usher' or second master, who were to be graduates of the University of Cambridge. There were to be taught 100 scholars of Cambridge, Barnwell, Chesterton and Trumpington, and to be taught free. In the same complex were to be built six almshouses for 'six several poor almsfolks', 'aged', by which he meant over 40, and from the parishes of St Edward and St Michael in the heart of the city and the neighbourhood of his college – or failing that of St Benet. Next he willed and ordained six fellowships and six scholarships in Gonville and Caius College, the most expensive and munificent of his charitable arrangements. Thus he provided for the young, the middle aged and the decrepit of his community, and he then detailed how the £250 annual income from the investment of £5,000 was to be distributed, with minute and fascinating detail; £40 to the master of the school, £20 to the usher, £24 to the six almspeople, £60 to the six fellows, £24 to the six scholars, and a host of items for the repair of college buildings, the increase of Mrs Frankland's fellowships, to the cook, the butler, the 'caiter' (caterer) and the porter, to repairs of the New River (Hobson's Conduit), to building a new causeway – Maids' Causeway and parts of the Newmarket Road – and repairing them; for the poor of Great Massingham and Harpley in Norfolk from which he sprang; to the Master of Caius £3 and to the four senior fellows 30s. for ever for managing his charities; to the College £2 for a dinner each year when the accounts were audited – 13s. 4d. for a preacher to preach a sermon before it;[85] 20s. in exceedings to the scholars that day; £1 to the Vice-Chancellor for attending the dinner and 3s. 4d. each to the three Esquire Bedells; and £2 to the 'Register' or Registrar or Bursar of his fund, whose business it was to present the account to these dignitaries and the Master and senior fellows for their edification and approval. Over and above all this £500 was provided for an addition to the College buildings.

The name Stephen Perse is remembered and honoured in two great schools, that for boys which was founded under his will, and the school for girls founded out of his endowment in the late 19th century. In the College his tomb and his feast stand as perpetual reminders of his generosity, and to

85 The sermon, long disused, has been revived since 1973, though it has proved too difficult to hold it just before the dinner.

the feast the Vice-Chancellor and the Esquire Bedells still come. His almsfolk still enjoy his hospitality, though on another site. Along the road to Newmarket the traveller may still pass dryshod, if not quite as Perse expected; and one hopes the poor of Great Massingham and Harpley are fed. In a broad and general sense his wishes are now fulfilled; but as they crossed the causeway of the centuries they encountered as many obstacles as Bunyan's Pilgrim; and they provide many a contrast, in Jane Austen's words, 'as time is for ever producing between the plans and decisions of mortals, for their own instruction, and their neighbours' entertainment' — and, be it said, scandal. At first things went tolerably well. The three executors were Valentine Carey, Master of Christ's and dean of St Paul's, Robert Spicer, Stephen's solicitor, and Martin Perse, his distant relation. The first two rapidly stood aside and left the whole management to Martin.[86] The chief beneficiaries were Stephen's stepmother and his half-sister, Mrs Katherine Becke, widow of William Becke, and the charitable endowment. Martin prudently married Katherine and set to work in a forthright manner to execute the rest of the will. When the offer to the towns failed the £5,000 were invested in land. The tomb was set up in Caius chapel and the Perse building built — the Persian, as it came affectionately to be called in the 17th and 18th centuries; and, above all, in March 1618, the school was opened. It set off to a flying start, with an excellent first master in Thomas Lovering, and a first decade of pupils which included Jeremy Taylor, one of the earliest and most notable ornaments of Perse's foundation, and one of the two great Anglican divines — Taylor himself and John Cosin — whose portraits still hang in the College hall. But after Martin Perse's death the appointment of Lovering's successor in the school fell to the Master and senior fellows, and they appointed one of themselves, Richard Watson, who neglected it. He was a high churchman who rapidly departed at the onset of the Civil War, to the school's lasting benefit. Thereafter it had its ups and downs, till it came onto a steadily declining slope in the 18th century.[87] The Trustees failed in their duties but collected their salaries. Inflation and changing land values, meanwhile, enormously increased the nominal value of the Trust until by the late 18th century the income was often well over five times the £250 envisaged by Perse himself. But it was not until 1837 that an eminent judge, who had been himself a senior fellow, gave a judgement which ushered a new dawn for the school and the Trust.[88]

The judgement of 1837 went against the Trustees. Perse's real intention, to found a flourishing school, had been flouted; the income from the Trust had been misapplied. But the judge very reasonably observed that the seed of the mischief lay in the will itself. The founder's intentions were clear, but

---

86 For what follows, see Mitchell 1976, pp. 11−18; cf. Gray 1921, chap. ii.
87 Mitchell 1976, chap. iii; see below, pp. 201−3.
88 See below, p. 203. In the second half of the 18th century the income of the Perse Trust was fluctuating between approximately £1000 and £1800 a year, and frequently over £1250.

the disposal of his charity was tied to a rigid formula, which made no allowance for inflation. It is the more surprising since Perse was college bursar and financier through a long period of inflation himself; and this was the reason why he had to augment the Frankland fellowships to bring them into line with current standards.[89] There is indeed an artificial tidiness about his will which might make one wonder if he was losing touch with reality. £5,000 was to be invested at exactly 5% to bring in £250 a year in perpetuity; and every penny of the £250 was accounted for. Yet the state of his finances and the general grasp of affairs revealed by his actions and his will do not at all suggest a man of failing powers. We cannot penetrate his mind; but it is a striking example of the strength of other elements in deciding a man's outlook on money, investment, and economics. He inherited an immense tradition of medieval suspicion: every account must be audited, not to strike a balance of profit and loss, but to see that the bursars and registraries and clerks had done their job precisely and honestly. Further, the tendency to simplify the facts of finance is fundamental even among many men of business. Readers of Jane Austen are familiar with the habit of mind which puts a precise label on every man's income and capital, and on every woman's dowry. In the 1780s or so 'Miss Maria Ward of Huntingdon, with only seven thousand pounds, had the good luck to captivate Sir Thomas Bertram, of Mansfield Park' in Northamptonshire, though 'her uncle, the lawyer, himself, allowed her to be at least three thousand pounds short of any equitable claim to it'.

Yet there is more to it than that. The view of a college as a kind of charitable company, with measurable assets, and gross, assessable income, is very modern. Between the 16th and 19th centuries, as in the cathedral chapters, every office, every fellowship and scholarship was a kind of benefice, separately funded, separately endowed. The bursars kept accounts of the colleges' estates and income, for estate management was an essential part of their task. But the accounts which mattered most were the *Libri rationales* or *Computi*, which showed the account of every member of the foundation as an individual. Most college lands were let out on lease; and in the mid 16th century these had sometimes been for very long periods.[90] Dr Caius ruled in his statutes that no lease should be granted for more than twenty years, to ensure that the College kept its grip on its lands and tenants, and could from time to time raise the rent. None the less he and his like really assumed that rent in the long run was a constant item, so that the income of an office or element in the College economy could be foreknown and foreordained. It became the practice never to raise the basic rent even though leases were commonly renewed in the later 17th and 18th

89 On the inflation of this era, see Outhwaite 1982.
90 For what follows, see *ER*, pp. i—x, for a full account of how the system worked and some of its results; Caius' statute is no. 86 (Venn, III, 380—1). I am especially indebted to Catherine Hall for guidance in this obscure region.

century every seven years or so. The increased value of the land, or the product of inflation, was realised in other ways. Under an Act of Parliament of 1576 colleges were bound to draw one-third of their rents in kind: these 'corn-rents' ensured that a proportion of their income was hedged against inflation. Furthermore, if the rents were not raised, the fines for grants or renewals of leases were — and entry fines became the normal and fundamental way of keeping pace with changing values. They had, however, the curious effect that college incomes which the founders and benefactors had tried to render stable became extremely variable, according to the number and value of leases renewed. Furthermore, the fixed rents still provided the income of many offices and fellowships; and the surplus from corn-rents and entry fines was distributed among the Master and twelve seniors, who each received their 'dividend'. In these ways the Elizabethan inflation was observed and harnessed by the bursars and senior fellows of the late 16th century; and this was a major reason why the senior fellows in 1592 were so keen to keep the newcomers from sharing the pickings. Yet this story makes all the more strange the apparent indifference of the old bursar, Stephen Perse, to the risks of inflation. These arrangements gave the seniors an acute interest in the management of the College's estates. But it also led to the paradox that after some generations of inflation a college with large resources could not afford to pay its junior fellows a living wage. In the 18th century the endowments for most of the junior fellows were not sufficient to feed them.

That, however, is to anticipate. For the moment, Perse's will may reveal to us the strangeness of college finance in earlier centuries; but it also reflects the marvellous generosity of a rich man whose life was centred in the work of the college and the welfare of the young and old of the city of Cambridge.

6

Before the Civil War

William Branthwaite

Stephen Perse held us long in the Bursary and with Mammon, without which the College could not exist or prosper. It is time to return to the library, which was enhanced on a scale unprecedented by the bequest of William Branthwaite, Master from 1607 to his death in 1619.[1] Branthwaite was one of the good gifts of Emmanuel to Caius. In 1584 Sir Walter Mildmay had founded Emmanuel College to be the nursery of trained preachers of the word, like the Dominican Convent on whose site it nestled. Mildmay was an ancient colleague of Lord Burghley in the royal administration, a survivor of the reigns of Edward VI and Mary; but a man of pronounced religious views and of evident Puritan sympathies — so long as these sympathies could be contained within the royal supremacy and the fold of a national Church to which his whole life had been dedicated. Among the earliest of the fellows of Emmanuel was William Branthwaite, a Norfolk man who had studied first at Clare. He was evidently well regarded as a theologian, for he proceeded BD and DD in the 1590s, and in 1604 was chosen to be one of the editors of the Authorised Version of the Bible.[2] The story of the Authorised Version is remarkably ill-documented; but we know that Branthwaite was one of the 4th 'classis', or group of editors, to whom was entrusted the Apocrypha. Branthwaite apart, it consisted of two Emmanuel men and four others from St John's, King's and Trinity, and included the Regius Professor of Greek. Their work was evidently done in Cambridge, and was completed by 1608−9.[3] Branthwaite was not one of those involved in the final revision of 1610−11. The Apocrypha represented the parts of the Old Testament discovered, when the serious study of Hebrew revived in the 16th century, to have no Hebrew original, but to exist only in Greek — one book, indeed (II Esdras), only in Latin; and so it was a deep knowledge of Greek and Latin and English which the panel required. The state of the text and the prejudices of Protestant reformers

1 On Branthwaite, see Stubbings, 1983, no. 4; Venn, III, 70−3; DNB. There is a detailed account of his election and its background, with interesting new material, in Morgan 1984, pp. 622−8. Morgan 1984 is full of valuable information and insights on the themes of chaps. 5 and 6.
2 For what follows, see Westcott 1905, pp. 347−8; Pollard 1911, p. 50 — cf. pp. 51−2; Scrivener 1884; Allen 1969−70.
3 Scrivener 1884, pp. 47−8; Allen 1969−70, pp. 4, 6−7, 139−40, based on the notes of John Bois, a member of the same panel and also of the revision panel.

made this a difficult and relatively unrewarding task; and the Apocrypha are commonly reckoned the least satisfactory part of the AV. But this is comparative, for the whole remains a marvel of literature and learning, and some of the credit must go to Branthwaite. One would like to know where his contribution lay, but neither the documents nor his library have yielded any clue so far, though the major texts were probably at his disposal among his own books and Dr Caius'.[4] It is indeed his library which is the only major source for his life and learning.

Branthwaite had lived for many years in Emmanuel under the benign rule of the moderate Puritan, devout, learned, first Master, Laurence Chaderton, chosen by Mildmay as the embodiment of everything he admired. Chaderton could preach for two hours without intermission and still, we are told, his congregation cried 'For God's sake, Sir, go on!'.[5] Chaderton combined total loyalty to the queen and government and Mildmay, with a strongly based Calvinism and a deep learning both in ancient texts and contemporary continental scholarly Protestanism. He gave lectures on the influential French Huguenot professor Ramus, Pierre de la Ramée. Ramus had revised the textbooks on logic and rhetoric, and searched the classics for material which was congenial to the Protestant conscience, and so laid emphasis on those areas of ground where humanism and Calvinism could comfortably meet.[6] As so often happens, his textbooks were heady wine to his younger contemporaries, and seem to us prodigiously dull. They were sometimes associated with radical opinions, but they were essentially textbooks popular in universities where the earnest young teachers wished above all to see both Cicero and Calvin flourish in some sort of harmony together.

But we must not exaggerate the Puritanism of Chaderton or his disciples. They were not dissenters; they were not primarily party men; they were above all the inspiring teachers of a generation of faithful Anglican pastors, and it was this which gave Emmanuel its early prestige. A succession of pastors, scholars and teachers — after a while far removed in theological interests from Chaderton himself — rapidly gave Emmanuel a substantial leadership among Cambridge colleges, even surpassing the pre-eminence of Trinity and St John's, unchallenged under Elizabeth I. In 1595 the mantle of Puritan leadership among the divines of Cambridge passed from William Whitaker, Master of St John's, who died that year, to Chaderton, and some of Whitaker's books were acquired by William Branthwaite.[7] Yet the

4 Crucial texts included the Complutensian Polyglot completed in 1517 and Aldus' Greek Bible of 1518; the former was in his own library, the latter in the College library by the gift of Dr Caius (Venn, VII, 521, no. 133). For Branthwaite's library, see Caius MSS 648/353, 734/782, 735/783, three contemporary copies of Branthwaite's library catalogue made at the time of his death for the annual audit. There is another copy in Emmanuel.
5 Stubbings 1983, no. 3. On Chaderton see also Lake 1982, chaps; 1, 3; Porter 1958, esp. pp. 239−41, 398−403.
6 Kearney 1970, chap. iii, esp. p. 63.
7 As may be gleaned from inscriptions in some of Branthwaite's books.

impression of Branthwaite's books is not of advanced Puritanism, but of a broad and catholic taste in the university disciplines of the day, in humanist studies as well as in theology, and in the mingling of traditional university texts — medieval glossed bibles, Bernard, Bonaventure and Aquinas, Gratian's *Decretum* and Peter the Lombard's *Sentences* — with an exceptionally wide range of contemporary continental Protestant literature. His thousand books do not match the five thousand of the other great library of the early fathers of Emmanuel, that of William Sancroft, who in the 1660s, 70s and 80s was to be chaplain to the Caian John Cosin, Master of Emmanuel and archbishop of Canterbury. Sancroft was the richer man and books were more plentiful in the 1660s. For its day Branthwaite's is a noble collection, and if one inspects it now, gathered in one large bay in the Caius library, as the eye roams up from the folios below to the tiny octavos among the ceiling joists, one seems to follow a course in the history of learning, from the medieval Bible and its glossators to the continental Protestant divines of the late 16th century. Branthwaite was a learned man; and as befitted a translator of the AV, one finds some Greek and a little Hebrew. But the overwhelming drift of his culture was Latin; and it is intriguing to find that the large majority of his biblical texts are copies of, or based on, the Vulgate. It is sometimes said that a man's library consists of the books he did not read; it can never be a precise mirror of his mind or his knowledge; but there is solid traditional matter here beneath and beside the Protestant divines; just as a handsome copy of Foxe's *Book of Martyrs* sits side by side with the stately Catholic volumes of the *Annales* of Cardinal Baronius; we have little other evidence of Branthwaite's mind, and must accept it that these were the books he liked to have by him.

On 12 July 1607 Thomas Legge died.[8] Stephen Perse, now senior of the senior fellows, and a group of his colleagues, strongly wished to follow the advice of the dying Master, and elect John Gostlin, another senior medical fellow, as their head. He was in his early forties, vigorous, a very capable physician and evidently a man of ability and charm. The senior fellows in residence gathered and six or seven of them — the seventh vote was somehow in doubt — voted for Gostlin, and immediate efforts were made to secure the approval of the chancellor, the Earl of Salisbury, the powerful royal minister, and Burghley's son, and the royal court. Gostlin's account of his expenses in this adventure show that these approaches were long and costly.[9] First of all, the Chancellor objected that the election had been too precipitate: during vacation many fellows were absent and not enough time had been allowed to summon them. So the fellows staged another election with larger numbers. But this, said the Chancellor, was too late: a valid

8 Venn, III, 68; *Annals*, p. 214; for what follows Venn, III, 70–1; *Annals*, pp. 214–16. On Gostlin, Venn, I, 116; III, 74–85, and below.
9 Venn, III, 74–5 — the year is not recorded, but the details of Gostlin's movements confirm that it relates to events of 1607.

election had to take place within a month. 'That second election . . . I esteem no otherwise of it than a mere confused and disorderly attempt of a headless body, utterly void by statute . . .'[10] All this was evidently pretext; it was the man not the election which was truly objectionable; the Chancellor had no intention of letting the fellows of Caius choose their Master. The Gunpowder Plot was but two years old; Caius in Legge's day had been a notorious harbour of papists; Dr Gostlin, being a layman, was naturally charged with popery. His friend George Montaigne of Queens', in supporting Gostlin's successful election in 1619, defended him indignantly against the charge; and this defence, and the friendship with Montaigne — an eminent Laudian before Laud — strongly suggest that he was a high churchman in his personal sympathies. But the royal court was doubtless already determined to see a respectable Protestant divine, whose theology was known and above suspicion, in charge of so dangerous a College; Laurence Chaderton was a close friend of Archbishop Bancroft, who may well have influenced the decision. Branthwaite, evidently a moderate Puritan in high favour, was an admirable choice. The Chancellor complacently interpreted the statutes in his own sense, and ignored the stipulation that if the fellows failed to elect within a month and it fell to him, he should choose a fellow of the College 'if any be found suitable'.[11] In 1587 Dr Bridges, dean of Salisbury and a Cambridge man — his enemies alleged he had been 'a very patch and a duns, when he was at Cambridge'[12] — in a general defence of the Anglican establishment, had attempted to sketch the qualifications needed for a Head of House. Here is Mullinger's summary: 'The Puritan denounced the Heads as drones; to which Bridges replies that all the Heads are by no means drones, and that even a drone may do far less harm in a hive than "an angrie waspe". To the Puritan demand that no-one should be appointed a Head who was not also a sound and competent divine, he makes the somewhat inadequate rejoinder that in some societies the special studies pursued render it desirable that the master should be rather a civilian or a physician'.[13] It is not as clear to us in the 1980s as to Mullinger in the 1880s that this was at all inadequate, and the statement seems prophetic of the situation twenty years later in which the civilian Legge looked to be followed by the physician Gostlin. But it is evident that opinion in general was with the Puritans on this point; that the Heads had been rendered immensely powerful by the University Statutes of 1570; that they were held responsible by those in the royal court and a little removed from the facts of life in Cambridge colleges for the opinions of their charges; and so they were increasingly expected to be safe Protestant theologians. Such was William Branthwaite.

10 Venn, III, 71; and see n. 1.
11 Venn, III, 348−9. For Chaderton's friendship with Bancroft, see Mullinger 1884, pp. 476−7.
12 Mullinger 1884, p. 282n.
13 Mullinger 1884, pp. 382−3.

So far as we can tell, the early years of Branthwaite's rule were relatively peaceful. The Master was normally resident[14] and we may presume that most of his work for the Authorised Version was conducted in the Master's Lodge and in his own and the College library. In later years he was more often absent, and his relations with the fellows were certainly far from peaceful. It may be that advancing age and the distance which this set him apart from the fellows — especially after the death of the elderly Dr Perse — sharpened some of the difficulties for Branthwaite as it had for Caius, and was to do for some of his successors. It may be that Gostlin's return to residence reminded the fellows of former battles. What we know of Gostlin does not at all suggest a factious man. None the less the chronology is striking. Gostlin went into Devon on his failure at court and set up a lucrative medical practice in Exeter.[15] The surest signs of residence or absence are the accounts for fuel in the *Bursar's Books*, which start in 1609. Almost no fuel allowance was paid to Gostlin in the years 1609–14; and in the spring and early summer of 1614 he was in London representing Barnstaple in Parliament. Later in 1614 preparations were made for a royal visit by King James I in March 1615, and the Medical Faculty summoned Gostlin back to play a leading part in the medical exercise laid on for the king's edification.[16] On 8 December he was back and his allowance for fuel suggests he stayed in residence till after the king had come and gone. It was a famous winter — the same account notes payment of six labourers shovelling snow[17] and doubtless he needed it. In the summer of 1615 he was away, presumably in Exeter; then at Michaelmas old Stephen Perse died, and throughout the winter Gostlin was in residence. On Perse's death his fellowship was filled by the translation of a junior fellow, Robert Wells, and the fellows wished to fill Wells' place, significantly, with a Devonian, John Allen, already a Frankland fellow. The Master studied his statutes and found it firmly stated by Dr Caius that the Master had a negative vote, and by Bishop Bateman that if no election to a fellowship took place within a month, the election fell by default into the Master's hands.[18] Dr Branthwaite was the first, but far from the last, of the Masters after Caius who tried the recipe of the negative vote to ensure an election they had set their mind to. In due course he declared Thomas Cooke of Norfolk, another Frankland fellow, to have been elected; and the *Annals* of the College sourly note that the whole of the year 1616 was filled with litigation on the election.[19]

14 See p. 104: these facts can be inferred from the *Redit Book*, and from the fuel account in the *Bursar's Books*; but they are not always easy to check in detail in the absence for most of his reign of the *Computus*.
15 *Annals*, pp. 325–6; Venn, III, 74–7 (Venn, p. 75, exaggerates the length of Gostlin's stay in Devon).
16 *Annals*, p. 326; Venn, III, 73–4. The entries in the *Bursar's Books* for fuel are confirmed by the *Redit Book* and by occasional entries in *Annals*. For the repairs to the Gate of Honour etc. for James I's visit, see *Annals*, p. 233.
17 See Venn, III, 73.
18 Venn, III, 349, 354.
19 *Annals*, p. 257; for all this, Venn, III, 71–2.

Even in the spring and summer Dr Gostlin drew a part of his fuel allowance, and one fears that his patients in Devon may have suffered from his zeal in the cause of their fellow countryman in Caius. Thereafter he was increasingly resident and Branthwaite more often away. The *Annals* record that the fellows took counsel's opinion,[20] and one of the learned civilians they approached confounded the Master out of Bartolus, Baldus and Jason — and others — good papists all, though also the normal authorities of the eminent civilians.

In 1617 these disputes came to a head in a meeting of fellows in which a two-thirds majority admonished the Master under the statute 'On an incapable Master' and suggested he resign.[21] Instead the case was put before the Chancellor, the earl of Suffolk, who summoned the parties to Audley End, and brought them to concord.[22] On most of the various points in dispute, and especially on the election of Mr Allen, the Master gave way. In the last two years of his life, however, somewhat better accord seems to have been achieved, and he and Gostlin and the other fellows joined in making contracts for the construction first of the Perse, then of the Legge buildings;[23] Gostlin's return seems to have ensured proper attention to Legge's memory both in the building and in the chapel. In 1618 Branthwaite — in spite of the odium he had incurred only shortly before — was elected Vice-Chancellor; but in the course of the winter he fell ill. The symptoms described in the *Annals* suggest consumption, and he died on 14 February 1619.[24]

Even while Branthwaite lay ill not far from Newmarket, royal letters were sent to the fellows from that same town intimating the royal pleasure that a divine congenial to the king, and in any case one 'sound and untainted in religion', should succeed.[25] Evidently the Mastership was a theme for intrigue in the royal court, for a confusing instruction was drawn up demanding the appointment of Sir Thomas Wilson, keeper of State Papers. But this time the fellows had won support sufficient to counter such manoeuvres. Two days after Branthwaite's death, on 16 February, the fellows elected Dr Gostlin, and on the following day confirmed their election. The matter was thrown temporarily into confusion by Gostlin's friend and ally, George Montaigne, now bishop of Lincoln, who wrote from

20 *Annals*, pp. 257−62.

21 *Annals*, p. 262; for the statute, see Venn, III, 349.

22 *Annals*, pp. 262−70.

23 *Annals*, pp. 270−83.

24 *Annals*, p. 293. Venn, III, 72, says 'he died about the end of January', but the *Annals* are quite specific. A letter in *CSPD 1619−23*, p. 9, shows that his death was reported in late January (cf. Venn, III, 75); but presumably the report was premature and this may be why the letter was not sent. The course of events seems to confirm that the election followed his death by a very short interval.

25 For what follows see Venn, III, 75; PRO SP 14/105/101, endorsed 'copie of His Majesty's letter to Cayus Coll. 30 Jan. 1618[−19] not sent', demanding Wilson's appointment and, if correctly dated, anticipating Branthwaite's death.

Buckden (then in Huntingdonshire) advising that the election be postponed until the royal assent to a free election had been received. But it seems that the testimonials which he also sent — and doubtless Gostlin's reputation — carried the day in the court; for on 23 February the Chancellor wrote confirming the election, and soon after he was elected Vice-Chancellor to fill the other office Branthwaite had vacated by his death.[26]

Doubtless in the troubles of Branthwaite and Gostlin there was a religious and theological element, as in almost every crisis in Cambridge in this epoch. But in Caius in this period it has left only a faint trace. When Perse's friend Valentine Carey became Master of Christ's in 1609 he attempted to weaken the Puritan element there — 'Woe is me for Christ's College' said a fellow of Emmanuel, though Carey was no extremist[27] — and this may partly account for the rapid growth of Emmanuel in the years which followed. The Master of Emmanuel, Laurence Chaderton, was a man who won almost universal respect. But feeling between Puritans and non-Puritans — whether one calls them Arminians in the 1610s and 1620s or Laudians in the 1620s and 1630s — ran high, and seems often to have followed a kind of party line rather than any strict distinction of doctrine; though even the word 'party' may overstate the case. The little that we know of religion in Caius at this period suggests that high churchmen had strong influence; but there is no doubt William Branthwaite was of Puritan leaning, and that Thomas Batchcroft, Master from 1626, was a low churchman at times.[28]

John Cosin

The most notable product of the College in the 1610s was John Cosin, who came from Norwich, aged 14, in 1610.[29] His tutor was John Browne, whom

26 The documents in *Annals*, pp. 287−8 and Venn, III, 75−6, are confusing, for they seem to show the bishop of Lincoln, George Montaigne — who was at Buckden in Huntingdonshire (now Cambs.) at the time — advising Gostlin on the day after the election that it be postponed. There is some confusion here, perhaps due to the speed of events. That the Chancellor confirmed the election on 23 Feb. after hearing evidence from the bishop and others seems not in doubt. I have checked the dates in MSS 602/278 and 714/570 in which the original letters are gathered.

27 Quoted in Porter 1958, p. 420.

28 See the evidence cited in Venn, III, 87n., and below, p. 122.

29 Aged 15 according to our matriculation register (see Venn, I, 207), but the ages are sometimes a little flattering to the boys. Thus Jeremy Taylor was 13, claiming 15 (Venn, I, 278). Cressy 1979, ignoring this point, argues for a normal age of entry of 16−17. Cosin was born on 30 November 1595 according to his own notes, quoted in Osmond 1913, p. 1. What follows is mainly based on Osmond; much has been written on Cosin and his world since, but for solid information (thought occasionally to be treated with reserve) it has not been replaced. See however the admirable introduction to Stanwood 1967, esp. pp. xiii, xliv n. 1; on his letters, Stanwood and Doyle 1969; and on his early life R. C. D. Jasper in *The Bishoprick*, 1954, pp. 5−9. For Browne see Venn, I, 151. For the events of 1624, see Cosin 1869, pp. 11−20 and below, pp. 115−16. (On Cosin I have had particular help from John Sturdy.)

we may reckon a high churchman from the influence he seems to have had on Cosin, but was himself a humanist and a civilian — doubtless a disciple of Legge; Cosin was a junior fellow from 1620 to 1624, and intrigued unsuccessfully for a senior fellowship in that year. But by then he had begun to tread the path outside the College which ended in the see of Durham. He attracted the early attention both of Lancelot Andrewes, the celebrated Anglican divine, then bishop of Ely, and of John Overall who had passed from the Regius Chair of Divinity to the see of Lichfield, after a stormy controversy on the nature of election and grace and on the Eucharist.[30] On his tutor's advice he chose the service of Overall, and indulged his lifelong passion for books as Overall's librarian. Soon he passed into the service of the bishop of Durham and became a canon of Durham and a pluralist — yet always deeply involved in all his various tasks. In 1635 he returned to Cambridge as Master of Peterhouse, and until the outbreak of Civil War he was extremely active as a builder and leading high churchman in Cambridge, and as Archbishop Laud's principal informant on the affairs of the university.

John Cosin was the very type of the Anglican triumphalist; and in our own ecumenical world it is not an attractive type, even (or especially) to those of us who are Anglicans. Yet there was a heroic quality both about his survival during the Civil War and Commonwealth, and about his role as bishop of Durham after the Restoration. As a disciple of Laud and a hammer of Puritans he was a marked man, and had to flee to France in the early 1640s. There he was appointed chaplain to the Anglican members, especially the maids of honour, of the household of the Catholic queen of England, Henrietta Maria.[31] As the years passed he became increasingly absorbed in controversy with Roman Catholics, and it is hardly surprising that Henrietta Maria, now a widow, began to wonder why she paid a salary to a ferocious Anglican controversialist in her midst. In short she stopped payment, but did not drive him out of Paris, and Cosin went on his way unabashed, living on charity, supporting himself a little like old Dorrit when he was Father of the Marshalsea, by tips. When he was well over 60 he returned to England to the see of Durham, and set his mark upon the Restoration church with boundless energy, astonishing in a man who had never been robust since he had undermined his constitution (so it was thought) by excessive fasting as an undergraduate and junior fellow in Caius.[32] To the end he remembered his family and friends, and every institution to which he had been attached; and he spent with a lavish hand in restoring his castles and preparing benefactions, including three scholarships and a feast in Caius.[33] In spite of all, he

30 Porter 1958, pp. 397—413, *passim*, for his view on election and redemption; p. 402 for his view on the Eucharist.
31 See Osmond 1913, chap. v.
32 Osmond 1913, p. 329 (the source is not stated).
33 Venn, III, 232; for all this, Osmond 1913, esp. pp. 309—13. Cosin's letters to Brady about the scholarships are in Caius MS 570/714, ff. 161—76; see also Archives xlvii; Stanwood and Doyle 1969, p. 78, n. 3.

died a rich man. The income of a bishop of Durham was princely; but even so, Cosin's methods of ensuring an adequate flow of funds were harsh. Yet it is wrong to see him merely as an Anglican exploiting the astonishing reaction of the 1660s. In a part of his mind he was a Reformation divine, and in his anti-Roman tracts one hears the monotonous thunders of the reformers. In part of his mind he was a devout Anglican, who loved Cranmer's liturgy and King James's Bible, and was an influential figure in the preparation of the Prayer Book of 1662, whose Ordinal enshrines his version of the 'Veni Creator' — 'come Holy Ghost, our souls inspire', in his words among the most familiar of English hymns.[34] He sincerely believed that 'the Constitution of the Church of England is eminently sweet and merciful'[35] — a sentiment which would have astonished some of the recusants and dissenters who fell under his lash; but he was one of the divines who stood for a measure of comprehension for those of Presbyterian tenets in 1660 – 1, and he shocked his colleagues by a tenderness towards non-episcopal orders which was evidently the fruit of his friendly dealings with the Huguenots in his exile. In other ways he showed the effect of exile: his controversies had strengthened his sympathy with Protestant doctrine on the Eucharist.[36] But he remained in essence a high churchman and a lover of fine timber and stately ritual; and he was every inch a medieval bishop. He was medieval in the sense that he believed it to be his duty to preserve every item of his privileges and every penny of his rent, cost what it might in human suffering and hate. To these ends he refused to allow any compromise in the antique privilege of the bishop to be sole representative of his county palatine in Parliament, as if the events of the 1640s had never occurred.[37] The ancient metaphor of the Church 'Militant' had a natural appeal. To his son who turned Catholic he was unspeakably harsh. Yet he could be warm and kind and brilliant company. Perhaps the most characteristic of all his activities as bishop was his lavish expenditure on the great staircase and the font cover and the stalls at Durham. For throughout his life he had loved good carving and had filled almost every church in which he had held office with panelling and screens and craftsmanship in wood.[38] His earliest benefaction to Caius was a grant of £10 for an altar table in Chapel when

---

34 Cosin produced the 'Durham Book' (see Cuming 1961) on a basis provided by Matthew Wren, and this was then extended by Sancroft, his chaplain at this time; but the presiding figure in the final revision was Sheldon, bishop of London and later Archbishop of Canterbury — especially in the revision of the Communion service (Cuming 1982, p.116 – 27, cf. Osmond 1913, chap vii).

35 Osmond 1913, pp. 270 – 1.

36 On Cosin's view of Huguenots and on his eucharistic doctrine, see Cuming 1983, chap. 7, esp. pp. 137 – 9; cf. Osmond 1913, pp. 332 – 6. He was one of a long line of Anglican divines who thought remarriage after divorce permissible where adultery was the cause, and his intervention in the case of Lord Roos in 1670 had much influence in inaugurating the process of divorce by Act of Parliament which was to flourish in the 18th and early 19th centuries (Winnett 1958, chap. 7; on the background, see chaps. 4 – 6).

37 Osmond 1913, pp. 287 – 9. On his relations with his son, ibid., pp. 316 – 7.

38 See Osmond 1913, plates facing pp. 20, 209, 283.

the fellows were planning the new ceiling of the 1630s.[39]

It would be pleasant to imagine that his love of the Authorised Version and of books came from his contact with William Branthwaite. But in truth it really seems more likely that from his early days in Caius he was inspired by a love of high church practices uncongenial to an ancient fellow of Emmanuel. In the old age of Laurence Chaderton, and the first spring of Emmanuel and Sidney, it was a marvellous time to be a young Puritan in Cambridge; but equally, while Lancelot Andrewes was bishop of Ely (1609 – 19) or George Herbert public orator (1619 – 27), it was a time of life and hope for high churchmen, even before the accession to power of William Laud. Above all, Cosin loved orderly and elaborate ritual and dignified vestments. At Durham when he was a canon he took the initiative in spreading the use of copes and his greatest love was for white candles and white surplices. For the candles he was alleged to have brawled with the dean at Durham about the number to be lit on the altars in the 1620s or 30s; and the surplice be believed a fitting vesture for angels: 'White linen, which resembles purity and beauty, wherein angels have appeared (Revelation 15:6), fit for those whom the Scripture calls angels: and this habit was ancient.'[40] This characteristic passage unites two of his special devotions – to the surplice and to angels. The chapel of Peterhouse had been built by Matthew Wren, his predecessor as Master, and was already adorned with some angels, it seems; but he may have added to them and certainly loved them dearly; and when we contemplate the innumerable cherubs of the ceiling of Caius chapel, designed in 1637 when Cosin was at Peterhouse, and clearly in imitation of Peterhouse, we may think it no coincidence.[41] They are at least the charming survival of the high churchmen of Caius of the generation before the Civil War, counterparts in wood of the surpliced human angels below.

John Cosin's career shows us what a Caian might be and do in the 17th century. Yet it seems clear that the tradition of the College was far from exclusively high church, nor its studies predominantly theological. When Cosin himself or a colleague reported to Laud in 1636 on the state of the colleges and their chapels, Caius was not commended.[42] Communion was received by the fellows and scholars seated in their pews, not kneeling at an

---

39 See *Annals*, p. 399; Venn, III, 161; Willis and Clark, I, 193.
40 Osmond 1913, p. 173; for vestments, cf. p. 19; Cosin 1869, p. 70 and n.; for candles ibid., p. 162, and esp. 174 n.
41 For Peterhouse chapel see Kersting and Watkin 1984, pls. 35 – 8 and architectural notes to them. Dowsing removed 100 small cherubs and at least two large ones. Willis and Clark, I, 46 – 7; and, on the angels, Osmond 1913, pp. 81, 109. Osmond (p. 81) asserts that the angel roof was Cosin's – this cannot be correct, and he gives no evidence. But we can readily believe that Cosin enhanced the angelic presence. For Caius chapel ceiling, see Venn, III, 161 – 4; Willis and Clark, I, 194. The Angels of Caius were restored after 1660.
42 These reports are preserved in Harleian MS 7033 (Baker 6), ff. 161 – 5 (formerly 152 – 5); they are printed in Cooper, *Annals*, III, 280 – 3 (Caius, p. 282); for Caius see also Venn, III, 87 – 8; cf. Osmond 1913, p. 85. Baker thought they were either by Cosin or by Sterne of Jesus.

altar rail as Laud would have wished, and the use of the surplice was not as mandatory as for the angels. The reforms of 1637 doubtless put this right and some remnants of a Laudian altar rail survive; to the chapel furnishings we shall return.[43] But it seems that for many years the fellows had been content with an easy give-and-take not at all congenial to high churchmen or to Laud. Nor, apart from Branthwaite and Cosin, and Jeremy Taylor a little later, were Caians of this generation conspicuous as theologians. The College evidently appealed for the breadth of its education, which included humanists and lawyers and mathematicians and doctors of medicine. When he visited the royal court in the 1640s, Dr Cosin may well have met the elder Caian Dr Harvey. In the College itself he encountered lesser men, yet serious students too of many disciplines. We have seen that his own tutor, John Browne, was a humanist and a civilian; Browne's closest friend, Thomas Orrell, taught Latin and Greek, and when he died in 1603 Browne wrote an epitaph for his tomb in chapel (now lost) which anticipated the devotion of the grander monument of Gostlin and Legge.Of the same year as Cosin was Aquila Cruso, a Fleming, also a noted Greek scholar.[44]

John Gostlin

Gostlin himself is a reminder that the teaching of medicine had flourished in the 1590s, when Harvey was a scholar, and continued to flourish throughout the 17th century. Gostlin had a high reputation in his own day both as a practising physician and as a teacher of medicine. Many years after his death, in the late 1640s, his younger friend and disciple, William Moore — best known to us as a book-collector and University librarian — was instructed to write the College *Annals*, which then stopped short in 1603;[45] and of Gostlin he had much good to say. As Regius Professor 'he entered upon this high office endowed with the most happy memory, with a sound and well-regulated judgement, and with a great fluency of speech; in which qualities he so much excelled that the Chair of Medicine was never more worthily filled, nor was that profession ever more highly regarded among the men of Cambridge.'[46] This is not very precise, and Moore was not a medical man; but Gostlin evidently adorned the Chair, and had a hand in rearing the most eminent Caius physician of the age after Harvey, Francis Glisson. Glisson had arrived from Dorset in 1617, and was a fellow from 1624 to 1634. He was to be Regius Professor himself from 1636, and only relinquished the chair finally on his death in 1677, when it passed to another Caian, Robert Brady, the Master, who held it till his death in 1700

43 See p. 122. The remnants of the altar rails are now in the organ gallery. For the changes
    between 1636 and 1641, and the reputation of the College in this period, see pp. 122–3.
44 *Annals*, p. 233; Venn, I, 142–3, 151, 209.
45 *Annals*, p. 210.
46 *Annals*, p. 326, as translated in Venn, III, 77.

— to be succeeded in his turn by Christopher Green, who held it till 1741.[47] Thus the Chair became almost a monopoly of Caians and the mantle of John Caius was passed on into the 18th century. When civil war threatened, however, Glisson withdrew from Cambridge, and played a role as peacemaker in the siege of Colchester in 1648. A little later he settled in London, and after the Restoration he became a founder fellow of the Royal Society and an elder statesman of the College of Physicians. His treatise on rickets, often regarded as the first scientific monograph on such an illness, was published in 1650, and followed by other influential treatises — and by philosophical writings still showing marked scholastic influence.[48] Though his links with Caius became tenuous as a result of the Civil War, he stayed long enough to preside over a group of younger medical fellows, including his brother Henry. Of these the most considerable was Charles Scarburgh, who was admitted as a sizar in 1633 and showed a precocious interest in mathematics, and early developed remarkable medical skills.[49] In the 1640s he became a fellow, but moved to Oxford where he was drafted into the army until William Harvey made him his assistant — 'Prithee leave off thy gunning, and stay here; I will bring thee into practice' — and where he graduated MD. He later joined Francis Glisson among the first fellows of the Royal Society, and became a royal physician, attending Charles II and James II in the 1680s in the company of Robert Brady. Thus the College continued to foster young medical students, who went on to prosper elsewhere.

Medical skill was only one of the accomplishments of John Gostlin. We met him first as a fervent friend and admirer of Thomas Legge; and the impression of the various accounts we have of him is of a man of charm mixed with firmness, and diplomatic skill. 'He secured to us the tranquillity we had so long and earnestly been wishing for, and to himself the reputation his deserts so richly merited.'[50] Thus Moore; yet he goes on to say — as those who have contemplated his striking portrait (pl. 13b) can understand — 'that his features somewhat resembled those of a lion'; but those who inferred from this that he had a ferocious temperament greatly erred, for although he could be severe when he had to inflict punishment, and was a man of 'invincible resolution' yet he was also noted for the 'gentleness and flexibility of his manners'.

This probably explains the happy end to an extraordinary flurry of activity revealed in the correspondence of John Cosin.[51] His old friend Oliver

47 On Glisson, see *DSB*, V, 425−7 (O. Temkin); Venn, I, 236−7; *DNB*.
48 *De rachitide*, London, 1650. His other most celebrated treatise is *Anatomia hepatis* (London, 1654).
49 On Henry Glisson, Venn, I, 272; on Sir Charles Scarburgh, Keynes 1966, pp. 304−7; Venn, I, 308; *DNB*; Aubrey, I, 299 (quoted below); and below, p. 126.
50 This and the following passages are from *Annals*, pp. 325−7, as translated in Venn, III, 77−8.
51 Cosin 1869, pp. 11−20, nos. VIII−XII, contain five letters from Naylor to Cosin written between March and June 1624. When most if not all of them were written Naylor was in Tawstock and Cosin with the bishop of Durham in London. Cf. Morgan 1975, p. 187. For

Naylor, learned, friendly, much liked, so the *Annals* tell us, was settled at Tawstock in Devon in 1623 by the generosity of the earl of Bath and his son, who lived there; indeed Naylor's letters show that he had been commuting to Tawstock for some years before this.[52] Venn noted that between 1560 and 1680 at least 65 Caians sprang from Devon, and attributed this connection in origin to the same earl, who came to Caius as fellow-commoner in 1575, and whose tutor, Thomas Hinson, was appointed agent to the earl for his Devon estates, and moved to Tawstock.[53] Naylor evidently continued the link, but after surrendering his fellowship in 1623 tried to keep in touch with College from a distance. Early in 1624 Cosin had wind that Thomas Wake — presumably because he had been presented to the living of Bincombe — must get a dispensation or resign his fellowship. He was a senior, and a vacancy in the senior fellowship naturally caused a stir among the juniors, of whom Cosin was one. The Master, however, was known to favour Edmund Michell. A tremendous intrigue got under way, recorded in surviving letters from Naylor to Cosin. Cosin must see that Wake did not let on that he was resigning till all was prepared; and then spring letters from 'your Lord' — the bishop of Durham — or get up a petition to the Chancellor to stay the proceedings. In later letters some of the background to this is revealed — the passionate dissatisfaction and anxiety of junior fellows, especially of Frankland fellows and Perse fellows, as they waited for their chance to become seniors. There is talk of what the statutes said, of the need to study Dr Perse's will; to call in this or that great man, even the king himself. There was a hint of the way in which Branthwaite had been thwarted. A tremendous storm seems to be brewing. But it rapidly blew away. It was not Wake but Christopher Husband who resigned: a very worthy physician and a good college man, who retired onto his family estate and soon after married. He announced his resignation many months in advance and the Master and fellows pre-elected Michell — contrary to the statutes, said the intriguers helplessly. The Master was in command; Wake was one of his closest friends; and Wake and Naylor remained intimate in spite of all these démarches. These personal links remind us that much of the excitement was doubtless quite superficial. It seems clear that a firm hand applied at the right time by a strong but genial Master could still a storm. The senior fellows evidently thought Cosin too ambitious, too much involved with great prelates; and at Michaelmas his fellowship lapsed. Gostlin's qualities help to explain his re-election as Vice-Chancellor in 1625, a time of anxiety and ferment. But in October 1626 he fell fatally ill, and we

---

Naylor, the earl of Bath, Hinson, Wake, Michell, Husband and Cosin, see Venn, I, 158, 81 (bis), 169, 210—11, 140, 207 (and above); for the earl see also *CP*, II, 17—18. The old earl (the 4th) died in July 1623, to be succeeded by his son, also a Caian, who evidently made Tawstock his main residence, and died in 1637 (ibid., pp. 18—19; Venn, I, 183).

52 Cosin 1869, pp. 1—6, nos. I—IV. For the earls, see n. 51.

53 Venn, I, p. xiii (cf. p. 81) — by a slip Venn says William for Thomas Hinson: William was the son of Thomas and matriculated in 1594 (ibid., p. 152.).

have a moving account of his deathbed from Thomas Wake himself. Gostlin summoned Wake and made confession and received absolution 'according to the form set down in our Book of Common Prayer'; and then the Master asked for Communion, 'which the next day was administered to him by myself, seven of the senior fellows being communicants with him: and albeit very feeble, yet with help being brought down unto his lower chamber, . . . he began thus: "It pleased God yesterday to send his angel unto me, for so I term his priest upon earth, unto whom I made a general confession of my sins . . .",' and he proceeded to repeat it before the larger gathering, with learned asides from Cicero and Augustine. The Master 'having spoken this, I administered the sacrament. Then, having received the Communion, calling on us again he spoke thus: "When I am dead and gone, observe strictly the prescript form of the Liturgy. For let them say what they will, that invert and alter it by pieces, it is the true obedience and service to God, to observe what the Church hath commanded. Let me entreat you to love one another, to bear with one another's infirmities, and not to retain malice in your hearts." '[54]

The community in the early 17th century

The Master and senior fellows represented the inner cabinet, the governing body of the College, the upper echelon of a hierarchy longer and more subtly graded than in a modern college.[55] In the 19th century a much sharper division came to be drawn between fellows and students, and between students and servants, in accordance with the ethos of the Victorian age; and by a curious irony the egalitarian 20th century has in some respects enhanced, not narrowed, these divisions. But in early days the distinctions were much less sharply drawn. It was not that society in or out of College was egalitarian — there were sharp distinctions in the outer world, and they were not forgotten. Yet down to the late 17th or 18th century the distinctions in the College did not at all precisely conform to the outer world, and the conditions of life within ironed out or rearranged many external distinctions. Many a student of modest means came first as a sizar, that is to say, as a student-servant; for most of the work of college servants, and especially waiting in hall and personal service to the older fellows and to the Master, was performed by young students, of about 15—18 years old, in return for their board and keep. Thus the poor and relatively poor student could live almost for nothing; but indeed many a sizar was really a probationary scholar, and his sizarship much like fagging in a boarding school; and many sizars proceeded to other grades very

54 Venn, III, 78—9.
55 For the grades of fellows and scholars, see especially Venn, III, 204—20, 271—5; Venn 1913, chap. ix; Winstanley 1935, chap. iv, esp. pp. 197—203.

rapidly. Many came to be promoted to the scholars' table, then to be junior fellows; and some went on to be senior fellows and even to be Masters. In the 16th and 17th centuries there was no stigma attached to such a position; it did not necessarily represent any difference of social origin outside the college. Such distinctions were preserved among the students by payment of fees: the moderately well to do came as pensioners, that is, they paid for themselves; the rich came as fellow commoners, with special rooms and special privileges, and seats at the high table. Yet here again there were no watertight compartments. A sizar might have a pensioner for elder brother; a pensioner might become a scholar. And most of the community lived, gathered in chambers about their tutors, usually young fellows little older than themselves, without any outward sign of their different status. Unless numbers were very pressing, it was evidently possible by this date for the fellows and tutors to live in some style in their first-floor chambers, with their charges arranged in the chambers below and the cocklofts above; but full segregation of fellows and undergraduates only came with declining numbers in the mid and late 17th century. It was at the turn of the century that the elegant panelling which adorns the finest of the sets in Caius and Gonville Courts was made; it was then that all the resident fellows began to expect a chamber or two for their private use.[56] At the opening of the century only the very old and the very grand, like Stephen Perse, were thus provided.[57]

It is in the first half of the the 17th century that we first learn many details of student life. Cosin or his friend who reported to Archbishop Laud on the condition of Cambridge in 1636 noted with disfavour the long hair and ruffs worn by fashionable students — a practice Cosin himself was later to forbid his own scholars — and explained at length to the archbishop, whom no detail escaped, the habit of dress of the students of Cambridge.[58]

'The clerical habit appointed for students here is generally neglected unless it be in King's College only, wherein they retain the ancient manner both for colour and fashion, with the use of square caps from the first entrance. At Trinity, and otherwhiles at Caius, they keep their order for their wide sleeve gowns, and for their caps too when they list to put any on, but for the rest of their garments they are as light and fond as others. And others, all that are undergraduates, wear the new fashioned gowns of any colour whatsoever, blue or green or red or mixed, without any uniformity but in hanging sleeves. And their other garments are light and gay, some with boots and spurs, others with stockings of diverse colours . . . and round rustic caps they wear (if they wear any caps at all) . . ., though the

---

56 See pl. 15 and p. 156; Perse's inventory (above, pp. 98−9) already shows a senior fellow in 1615 with at least two chambers. Already in 1652 a College order prescribed a separate chamber for every fellow, scholar and student (Willis and Clark, III, 303 n., if that is what 'de proprio' means).

57 See p. 99; and for the grades of fellows in this era, pp. 96−8.

58 Venn 1913, p. 117 (for the source, see n. 42); for Cosin, see Venn, III, 232.

fashion here of old time was altogether "Pileus quadratus" [the square cap], as appears by retaining that custom and order still in King's College, in Trinity, and at Caius, whose governors heretofore were more observant of old order than it seems others were . . .'

The Gawdys

Among the material which John Venn put together in his *Early Collegiate Life* was a collection of letters of the Gawdy family of West Harling in Norfolk.[59] In the early 17th century Squire Framlingham Gawdy sent six of his sons to Caius, and one other, poor relation besides. It is characteristic of a wealthy landlord of this period that he should send his sons to university, of a Norfolk squire that he should send them to Caius — and of the young men of the age that only one of them stayed long enough to take a degree. We must not think of modern statistics of 'failure rates'. The degree was a professional qualification, primarily for the clergy. For a lawyer or a soldier, or a country gentleman, Cambridge was only a part, and a small part, of their training. 'Most of the men of this class' wrote Venn, '— with the exception of the . . . clergy — treated the College life as an episode in their general training for social life.'[60] They were none the less important to the College and the university, for it was their presence — and of many more who went without thought of a clerical career — that encouraged the Cambridge tutors to see their vocation as providing something wider than a clerical seminary could provide, and it was their zeal which helped to make this a golden age in the ancient universities. Between 1610 and 1640 came well over thirty new students a year on average, and these figures were not equalled or surpassed till the mid 19th century.[61] Under the Commonwealth the numbers fell to 21 or 22 a year, and one might attribute the fall to the impoverishment of the squirearchy or doubts about clerical education. But in fact the proportion who were sons of gentry rose to nearly 50% in the 1650s, and the decline persisted after the Restoration — down to seventeen or so in the 1680s, twelve in the 1690s, eleven in the decade 1700 – 10; and then, after some fluctuations, to seven in the 1760s, after which it slowly revived. The 18th century undergraduates were predominantly clergy in the making — but so were very many of their predecessors in the 16th and 17th centuries. The full reasons for the blossoming in early Stuart times are hard to penetrate; but at least we can see that it was a time of intellectual excitement, of rich promise in the Church, and of unparalleled interest in the middle and upper strata of society in the kind of education a university

59 Venn 1913, chap. xi.
60 Venn 1913, p. 192.
61 The figures are based on Venn's table, Venn, III, 392. For what follows see esp. Cressy 1972, p. 228, Table 25, who gives the figure of 49% for gentry in the 1650s, falling to 22% by the 1730s.

could provide.[62] Beyond that it is difficult to penetrate, and the Gawdy letters are exceptionally valuable evidence since they show us this world from the inside.

It is a common heresy among university dons to think that they have been the only creative forces in the history of universities; and it is salutary to be reminded from time to time that colleges have always been made by the students as much as by the teachers. This must have been especially true when the centre of college life was a little knot of students gathered in a chamber. It is in the ardent conversation of a chamber, rather than in fellows' parlour or the Master's lodge, that one should seek the explanation for the heroism of the Caius recusants of Dr Legge's time, and for the fervour for Anglican worship represented by John Cosin and his like. Having said that, let us confess that the Gawdy letters, like most surviving student letters from any age, talk more of money, travel and sport. The sons talk of travel or books – sometimes a bible or Josephus, or Camden's *Britannia* – or a 'spare hawk' – a sparrowhawk, one presumes, for a modest hawking in the fens – and arrangements for sending the horses to Barton Mills, the first stage out of Cambridge, half-way home, for their journeys.[63] The poor relation talks much of tutors' bills, for the tutors looked after all their charges' financial affairs, and struggles to show that he is a student. 'If I should strive violently to extract somewhat out of my obtuse brain, which might challenge the title of wit, in my own conceit, yet I know when it should make his appearance before your judicious censure, it would be but dew against the sun' – and so to the 25s. for which he had asked in his last letter and other such matters.'[64] But occasionally the sons tell us something of more special interest. In November 1631, just after the opening of the London season, to which the squire had evidently gone, William Gawdy wrote to his father:

'Dear father we did expect you here at Cambridge at your going to London. I was chosen by the proctors to be senior brother [he evidently means as one of the senior students who helped the proctors to organise the candidates for disputations] in the Commencement house this year, which is a place of great credit, but withal very chargeable, for I should have given the proctors each of them a satin doublet and should have invited all the doctors and chief men in the town to supper: my Tutor took some time to consider of it, hoping that you would have come this way, but you coming not I was constrained to refuse it . . .'[65] William was the eldest son, and a fellow-commoner and so reckoned well-to-do, and fair game for such charges. But he was a serious student too who took his BA, and went on to

62 There is a large and fascinating modern literature on this, represented by Curtis 1959; Simon 1963; Kearney 1970; Cressy 1970, 1972; and several papers in Stone 1975, I, esp. Morgan 1975.
63 Venn 1913, chap. ix, esp. pp. 204, 209, 214, 219.
64 Venn 1913, p. 195.
65 Venn 1913, p. 201; for William Gawdy, Venn, I, 289, and for other members of the family, pp. 252, 295, 300.

the Inner Temple, and after the shadows of the Civil War had passed, rose to be a baronet in the 1660s. The Gawdy connection comprised a fellow-commoner, pensioners, scholars and a sizar, and spread through a range of social strata; their links and connections help us to understand how the fame and attraction of the College went about East Anglia — as the career of the Glissons suggests its wider influence in counties far from Norfolk or Suffolk or Cambridgeshire.

Thomas Batchcroft

In October 1626 John Gostlin died, and there was another flurry before the court and the Chancellor were prepared to confirm the election of his successor.[66] It was a sensitive year. John Cosin's friend and mentor, Richard Montague of King's, had published his *Appello Caesarem*, a statement of Anglican doctrine on many points including predestination, on which he claimed that the Church had no fixed doctrine, and by this and other means greatly incensed the House of Commons, in which the Puritans were strong.[67] When they had done attacking Montague they impeached the Duke of Buckingham — and Charles I promptly asked the University of Cambridge to make him Chancellor, which was accomplished by a very narrow majority, or, as some suspected, by none at all. A gale blew briefly through Cambridge; passions rose high. These storms were always more complex than appears on the surface, but broadly, it was the royalists and the high churchmen who voted for Buckingham, the Puritans and the Commons men who voted for his rival, the earl of Berkshire; it is interesting to note that in Caius ten fellows were for Buckingham, two for his opponent.[68] We can understand why a college election in October was a delicate matter, but in view of these figures it must be judged very ungrateful of Charles I and Buckingham to doubt the wisdom of the fellows of Caius. When Batchcroft was elected royal letters came objecting that the court, that is, the duke, had not been consulted — some more eminent figure had been thought of, and it was alleged that Sir Robert Lane of St John's had been intriguing for the place.[69] An enquiry was demanded, and although the Heads were divided, in the end plentiful good testimony was sent to the Chancellor, the College paid out £55 in expenses, fees, tips — and, one assumes — bribes; and Batchcroft was confirmed. The events of the 1630s

---

66 Venn, I, 85−6.
67 For this and what follows, see Mullinger 1911, pp. 25−64, esp. 25 ff.; cf. Porter 1958, pp. 415−17; Morgan 1984, chap. 1.
68 Mullinger 1911, pp. 53−60, esp. p. 58. Cosin was one of the royal agents in this affair; but we do not know whether this influenced the fellows of Caius, or in what direction.
69 For this and what follows, Venn, III, 85−6; *CTPC*, I, 349−51; CUL Add. MS. 22, ff.7ᵛ−8ᵛ — a reference I owe to David Hoyle. The analysis in Morgan 1984, pp. 33−51, has confirmed that some of the high churchmen had doubts about Batchcroft.

and 40s suggest that Batchcroft, though perhaps (as David Hoyle's researches suggest) more inclined to the Puritan party, was not really a party man — he was a reed prepared to bend before the wind; perhaps something of a vicar of Bray. He was by all accounts a theologian of no distinction, and so safe, and a conscientious and thoughtful Master whom most were glad to serve, and who managed the affairs of the College in an efficient manner. The oft-quoted report to Laud in 1636 shows that surplices were voluntary,[70] and not as consistently worn as by John Cosin, or the angels — and a certain informality in chapel services was noticed in the practice of receiving the sacrament in the fellows' stalls. This degree of old-fashioned informality did not suit the Laudians, but Batchcroft and his colleagues made up for it in the next year by filling the sky with cherubs and by a general improvement in the furnishings of the chapel. The chapel was extended, the tomb of Dr Caius lifted off the floor to make more space for stalls and worshippers. All this was accomplished by Woodroofe the joiner and carver and John Westley, builder and perhaps architect as well, who went on to major works at Clare in 1638.

Thus in 1637 Batchcroft bent before the winds blowing from Peterhouse, as the cherubs — abolished in the 1640s but brought back after the Restoration and still with us — bear witness. But in 1640−1 the Long Parliament was taking a close interest in the universities from a different angle from Laud's, and the Puritans in Cambridge reported to Westminster in a fascinating document which David Hoyle has rediscovered and dated to the early months of 1641.[71] Among 'The novel practices in particular colleges', here is the entry for Caius.

'The chappell of this Colledge of late yeares by the overbearing sway of the major part of fellowes (the Master being rather passive then otherwise) hath had much cost bestowed upon it in wainscotting and gilding to the expence of some hundreds of pounds. The east end is ascended by steps, and an high erected frame of wood placed to the proportion of an altar, but the table never placed here, because this part of the chappell was newly taken in from an out peece of ground and was not consecrated, soe that the table stood beneath the steps, turned formerly altarwise by Mr Ling late fellow of that howse, but of late it hath been turned againe table wise. In the east end there were formerly two hallow places for images, which now at the reedifying of that part of the chappell are againe fitted for any the like

70 See n. 42. For the building works of 1637, see Colvin 1978, p. 879; Willis and Clark, I, 193−5; Venn, III, 161−4.
71 I am greatly indebted to David Hoyle, who kindly furnished me with the reference to BL Harleian 7019, ff. 52−93, and generously lent me his notes and transcripts and a copy of his forthcoming paper on these reports (though for any errors in the details given here I must take responsibility). The account of Caius chapel is on f. 79, and of Normanton's sermons on ff. 55−6. Other references to Caius occur on ff. 59, 63 (a sermon by Mr Pickerill), 66, 68. For Normanton, London and Tinckler, see Venn, I, 248, 255−6, 325. Pickerill was a fellow till 1645, when he was ejected, but he survived as rector of Burgate in Suffolk from 1649 till his death in 1681 (Venn, I, 265).

purposes. Adoration towards the east is practised by the greatest part of the fellowes and schollers and this soe farre promoted, that for these late yeares none have bene admitted into fellowship that used not that gesture. Standing towarde the east at the doxologie and hymnes is generally practised together with bowing at Venite exultemus. Singing of psalmes in the accustomed way of the church is omitted contrary to the former practise of the Colledge. Mr Pickeril fellow of this College was soe earnest for the aforesaid innovations that he whipped a student of the house for not observing them. Many of the fellows of this howse are very ill affected to the religion established in the Church of England, and great favourers of Popish doctrines and ceremonies, some of them having crucifixes in theire chambers, and being suspected to use beades and crossings. One of the fellowes, to witt, Mr Normington, hathe of late renounced the Protestant religion. Another of them Mr London is supposed very popish, and is now or late was at Rome or in the parts of Italy. And a yong scholar one Tinckler of the same Colledge is reported to have forsaken our religion and to have left the kingdome.'

Allowing that this is a report by Puritans, there was yet much in the practice of the College to alarm the conforming Batchcroft. He felt the wind blowing from another quarter and showed solidarity with the low church party; the altar was turned 'table wise'. Normanton and London did in fact become Catholics — London after taking his MD at Padua in the steps of Caius and Harvey, and of Tinckler no more is known. The most offensive of the fellows in the eyes of the Puritans was John Normanton or Normington, whose sermons savoured of 'popery', as we can readily understand if the extracts from them are at all reliable. After giving a lively account of the benefits of auricular confession, he went on. 'I have read somewhere I am sure that the devil appeared to Christ in the habit of a monk with his hood and cowl, but I think a man may as well say he appeared in the fashion of a Puritan, for he lyeth most abominably in the next words: "All these things [will I give thee] . . ." '.

These words were uttered in Great St Mary's, and he was presently hailed before the Vice-Chancellor and the Heads. 'Dr Cosin said that he was undiscreete and was willing that he should be censured for some indiscretion, but for any popery or propension there to he discovered none'; and when it was objected that Normanton called Aquinas 'St Thomas' Cosin said that if he were in the pulpit of Great St Mary's he could call him 'St Thomas Aquinas'. But the Puritans had the last word, for already before 1639 Normanton had gone abroad and failed to return; for this he was deprived of his fellowship — it seems indeed that he had become a Roman Catholic.

Jeremy Taylor

A few months before Batchcroft became Master, when already the most experienced tutor in College, he had taken under his wing a young Cambridge boy called Jeremy Taylor.[72] He was apparently only thirteen, though claiming to fifteen years in the matriculation book. His father was a barber in the city and churchwarden of Holy Trinity Church; he was a pupil at the Perse school in its first blossoming; and after a spell as personal sizar to Batchcroft as tutor and Master, he became Perse scholar and Perse fellow on the nomination of Martin Perse, doubtless on Batchcroft's advice. But after two years as fellow, in 1635—6, he found loftier patronage. We do not know who introduced him to Laud — but it is hard not to see the finger of John Cosin, recently promoted Master of Peterhouse, in the sudden elevation of a fellow-Caian; and the effect was that Laud imposed the young Jeremy on All Souls and made him a fellow there. Laud indeed was greatly impressed by the young man, observing in a famous exchange that his only fault was his youth — which Jeremy undertook, if he lived, to mend. In 1638 he married and relinquished his fellowship, but in compensation became chaplain to the king as well as to the archbishop and received other preferment — and doubtless would have risen yet higher had not his doughty patron's ruinous career been cut short by the events of the 1640s, culminating in his execution in 1645. In the civil war and Commonwealth Taylor attempted, not unsuccessfully, to lead a quiet life in Wales, then in London, and eventually reaped his reward — if such it was — with the bishopric of Down and Connor and the post of Vice-Chancellor of Trinity College, Dublin. A man of piety, rich and deep, a pastor, and a writer, he was not at his best as a bishop; and the divine who was reputed to have lost the chance of an English bishopric for showing too much tolerance in his *Liberty of Prophesying* found himself cornered (as he seems to have thought) into persecuting the Presbyterians of Down. His formal links with Caius ceased in 1635—6; but we need not doubt that the piety and mellifluous style which gave him his lasting fame were learned in Cambridge, partly at least under the kindly guidance of Dr Batchcroft. One cannot help wondering if the fall of Laud was not a blessing to Taylor, however fearfully disguised; for it ushered in that lengthy period of pastoral work in

72 For Taylor in Caius, see Venn, I, 278—9. There is a useful summary of his career and achievement in Hughes 1960: for his birth, p. 3; for his jest to Laud, p. 4; his Irish career, pp. 11—14; his works of devotion, chaps. iii—iv. For a deeper treatment, Stranks 1952; see especially p. 294, where Taylor's originality is summarised, and he is claimed as the first man to write a whole treatise on religious liberty, the first to write a life of Christ in English, the first to provide a complete manual of casuistry. On his moral theology see McAdoo 1949; Dewar 1968, esp. pp. 117—18 for his anticipation of Newman's famous saying about the appalling weight of venial sins; on his work in Ireland, Bolton 1958; and on his liturgical work, Porter 1979; Grisbrooke 1958, chap. ii (I am much indebted in this note to John Sturdy). The hymn 'Heaven' seems to have been first published in *The Golden Grove . . . also Festival Hymns*, London, 1655, pp. 157—8 (here and in the edition of 1664 at least the reading in 1.9 is 'on').

relative obscurity which gave him the opportunity to develop his pastoral understanding and elaborate moral theology, and to write his famous Treatises on *The Rule and Exercises of Holy Living* and *Holy Dying* (1650−1) which were to be a part of the prescribed reading for innumerable devout Anglicans, down to George Eliot's Dorothea Brooke in *Middlemarch* (1871−2) and beyond.[73] Taylor cannot stand high as a poet in the century of Donne and Milton, or the circle of George Herbert; but the best of his hymns have a delectably fresh, even mystical quality, familiar to Caians in the setting of his Heaven by Charles Wood now embedded in the service for the Commemoration of Benefactors.

> O beauteous God, uncircumscribed treasure
>   Of an eternal pleasure,
>   Thy throne is seated far
>   Above the highest star,
> Where thou prepar'st a glorious place
> Within the brightness of thy face
>   For every spirit
>   To inherit,
> That builds his hopes [up]on thy merit,
> And loves thee with a holy charity.
> What ravish'd heart, seraphic tongue or eyes,
>   Clear as the morning's rise,
>   Can speak, or think, or see,
>   That bright eternity?
> Where the great King's transparent throne
> Is of an entire jasper stone:
>   There the eye
>   O' th' chrysolite,
>   And a sky
> Of diamonds, rubies, chrysoprase,
> And, above all, thy holy face
> Makes an eternal clarity.
> When thou thy jewels up dost bind: that day
>   Remember us, we pray,
>   That where the beryl lies
>   And the crystal, 'bove the skies,
> There thou may'st appoint us place
> Within the brightness of thy face;
>   And our soul
>   In the scroll
> Of life and blissfulness enrol,
> That we may praise thee to eternity.

73 For evidence that Dorothea's religious interests derived from Frances Strong, Mrs Mark Pattison, see Green 1957, p. 212 n.

Epilogue — Charles Scarburgh

Down to the outbreak of Civil War, Batchcroft's Mastership was almost as peaceful as Gostlin's — not quite, for in 1635—6 a barrack-room lawyer called Thomas Cooke brought on the College a committee of enquiry, but this found in the Master's favour.[74] He seems to have been an earnest, peace-loving, conscientious man. He lives most memorably in the oft-quoted passage in Aubrey's *Brief Lives*.

'In Sir Charles Scarburgh's time (he was of Caius College) . . . the head of that house would visit the boys' chambers, and see what they were studying; and Charles Scarburgh's genius led him to the mathematics, and he was wont to be reading of Clavius upon Euclid. The old Dr. had found in the title ". . . *e Societate Jesu*", and was much scandalised at it. Said he, "By all means leave off this author, and read Protestant mathematical books".'[75] One may doubt if Clavius much inclined the young Scarburgh to Rome; but it is curious to recall the epilogue to this story: when the Old Pretender was born to the Catholic James II on 10 June 1688, in the queen's chamber, among the royal physicians, though a little late for the event itself, were Sir Charles Scarburgh and Dr Robert Brady, Batchcroft's chosen successor as Master of Caius.[76]

74 Venn, III, 86—7. Cf. Morgan 1975, pp. 222—3, for the interest of the enquiry in its bearing on the College's East Anglian links.
75 Aubrey, I, 94—5; *CC*, p. 64; Venn, III, 92; etc.
76 Full details of the event and witnesses were published in a sort of 'white paper' *At the Council-Chamber in Whitehall, Monday the 22. of October 1688* (London, 1688), later reprinted as *The Several Declarations . . . made in Council on Monday, the 22nd of October, 1688 . . .* and quickly answered in *A Full Answer to the Depositions; and to all other the Pretences and Arguments whatsoever Concerning the Birth of the Prince of Wales* (London, 1689). The arguments about the genuineness of the event rumbled on until the 1750s, and were lent a certain colour by the late arrival of the two Caius physicians — which may have been partly due to a mistake by Scarburgh as to the date of conception. I owe the substance of this note to the generous help of Jonathan Clark.

7

The English Revolution

William Dell and revolution

Thomas Batchcroft held on as Master through the Civil War till after the execution of the king. He was finally ejected in 1649; but even then he was to make a brief return as Master in 1660 before handing over to Brady.[1] Yet it would be false to see the Commonwealth as a mere interlude. In all manner of ways it opened new windows and blew away the dust; and even if the most conspicuous consequence of the Restoration was a mighty reaction in favour of the Anglican establishment — a reaction which was in the long run to turn the Cambridge of Harvey and Scarburgh and Brady, and of Newton and Bentley, into a modest Anglican seminary, and the College into an East Anglian finishing school — some of the new ideas and perspectives of the English Revolution struck root, and some cast long shadows before them.[2]

Godmanchester and Kimbolton were formerly in Huntingdonshire, now in the county of Cambridge. The eminent judge Henry Montague, when elevated to an earldom in 1626, had his seat in Kimbolton and took his title (so it is said) from Godmanchester, but in his piety left God's name out of his title. And so it was as earl of Manchester that his son, in alliance with the MP for Cambridge, Oliver Cromwell, set to work to purge the University in the fateful year 1644.[3] In December 1643 William Dowsing had ejected 68 cherubs from the chapel; by the summer of 1644 the earl had also ejected several fellows of Caius, and he sent a questionnaire to the Master demanding further information — 'of the names of all such in your College as have practised bowing at the naming of the name of Jesus, adoration towards the East, or any ceremony in divine service not warranted by law'. The Master was in no hurry to reply; but a month later he felt able to send, not only a list of fellows present and fellows absent and fellows ejected — 8 and 10 and 8, though 4 of the 8 seem to have survived a little longer — but a reply which stated that these practices 'have been so by degrees left, as there are none in our whole Society that do use or practise any of them, as far as we know'; in due course the Puritan service book, the 'Directory' was

1 Venn, III, 90−2. On Cambridge in this age see Mullinger 1911, and especially the fine reappraisal in Twigg 1983.
2 See esp. Hill 1965; Hunter 1981, with useful bibliography.
3 Mullinger 1911, pp. 272−80 (for Dowsing in Caius, p. 269); Venn, III, 88−9; Walker 1970, pp. 100−4; Twigg 1983.

introduced. More fellows were yet to go.[4]

As in so many areas of English life, the English Revolution presents us in the small compass of one College with a heap of paradoxes. The times were violent and revolutionary; the Master and most of the senior fellows were ejected; among old and young a sword of division was thrust which bred much hard feeling and personal tragedy. Into the Master's seat came a fire-eating Puritan, more at home in the camp than in a college chapel; more ready to denounce the University as the throne of Satan than to engage in the humdrum of college business.[5] Yet there were compensations here, for it was a time alive with new ideas. In academic circles it has now come to be seen that some of the most original thoughts attributed to Puritans and revolutionaries were anticipated in the generations which preceded 1640, so that in mathematics and some of the sciences no sudden wind of change blew in this epoch.[6] But the winds blew none the less; and some of them blew about William Dell, who for all his fire and folly remains one of the most interesting and alive of the Masters of the College.[7] And if one ignores the intruded Master and the ejected fellows, and looks first and foremost at the new recruits — at sizars, scholars, pensioners and junior fellows, at the source of recruitment and the pattern of their careers — it is as if nothing had changed. In February 1644, two months before the first ejections, arrived Robert Brady from Denver, aged 16 — and though he was never a fellow he was rarely far from the College till he died, after very nearly 40 years as Master, in 1700.[8] In June 1644, three days after the fateful letter from Lord Manchester, William Adamson was admitted as sizar; and he is the symbol of a continuity even more startling; for in the course of 25 years of continuous residence, during nearly 18 of which he was a fellow (1651–69) he not only survived every vicissitude, but compiled the *Registrum Magnum* — with the help and perhaps under the inspiration of William Bagge — the great register of College estates and College deeds, which was still used as such till the 1970s.[9]

By 1645 eleven colleges had seen their Heads removed, and in the next few years Caius and Magdalene followed; only a tiny minority escaped the

4 Venn. III, 88–9. For the Directory, see Twigg 1983, p. 123. There are problems about the list of ejections, for of the 8 noted as ejected, 4 went in 1644, but two apparently survived till 1645 and two more till 1646; but the list itself must be genuinely of 1644 and includes as 'absent' one fellow who was ejected later in 1644 and another who died in 1645 (Venn, I, 255–6, 265, 286, 289, 294, 304, 310–11). Presumably four of the eight 'ejected' were under threat or rumour of expulsion.

   Twigg 1983, p. 154, cites evidence that Batchcroft's ejection was due to dissensions among the fellows; for the ejections in general, see ibid., pp. 82, 274.
5 Walker 1970, esp. chap. vii.
6 Contrast Hill 1965 and Feingold 1984.
7 As we have been taught anew by Walker 1970, to which I am much indebted; and see esp. Joseph Needham's Preface, quoted below.
8 Venn, I, 351: on Brady see below, chap. 8, and esp. Pocock 1950–2.
9 Venn. I, 352–3. For Bagge see below, esp. p. 135. Both Bagge's and Adamson's names are on the title-page, but the chief original hand is evidently Adamson's.

purge. In their place were set men good, bad and indifferent; but mostly good; and if one contemplates Ralph Cudworth at Clare and Benjamin Whichcote at King's, one must say that the appointments of this period included the most distinguished men, in intellect and character, who held such office in the 17th century.[10] Whichcote and Cudworth were the leaders of the group known still as the Cambridge Platonists, who grew up in the 1620s and 30s in Emmanuel, at that time the most fertile intellectual soil in Cambridge; and who joined to the Puritanism they learned at Emmanuel a strong dose of tolerance, a wide and deep learning (in Cudworth's case) of terrifying dimensions, and a breadth of intellectual vision which might have given Cambridge a golden age in the 1640s and 50s if they had not all been entangled in the net of politics. However friendly the eyes of Manchester and Cromwell — Sidney men both, but fully aware of the merits of Emmanuel — they had little idea of academic freedom. And some of the new men of the 40s and 50s were of a different stamp.

William Dell had the misfortune in his own lifetime of attracting the attention of the eminent Presbyterian divine Richard Baxter, who characterised him thus: 'Mr Dell, the chaplain of the Army, who, I think, neither understood himself, nor was understood by others any farther than to be one, who took reason, sound doctrine, order and concord to be the intolerable maladies of Church and State, because they were the greatest strangers to his mind.'[11] Nor was he much more kindly treated by John Venn, who observed that as Master, 'his career seems an almost entire blank'.[12] But in recent years he has received more sympathetic treatment in the careful and thoughtful book of Mr Eric Walker.[13] Dell was a product of Emmanuel, different in outlook from William Branthwaite, equally different from the Cambridge Platonists. These men built new academic edifices on old foundations: humanist learning and traditional Protestant theology were their sources of inspiration. Dell was a brilliant revivalist preacher, who had been early rewarded in 1641 when the Long Parliament turned a noted Laudian out of the living of Yelden in Bedfordshire, and the earl and countess of Bolingbroke presented Dell in his stead.[14] Yelden was his parish, and in a sense his home, until he was ejected after the Restoration — and even then he continued to make it his base. But he was destined meanwhile for higher things, and in 1644 he attracted Cromwell's notice as one of the most effective preachers in the armies of Parliament, and a man marked with Independent theological views not far removed from his own. Late in 1644 Cromwell was still hoping for accommodation with the Presbyterians and he left Dell for a time out to grass at Yelden. But in 1645 Dell returned

10 Walker 1970, p. 101; for Whichcote and Cudworth, see Stubbings 1983, nos. 12, 14.
11 Baxter 1696, I, i, 64, quoted Walker 1970, p. 105 n.
12 Venn, III, 95.
13 Walker 1970. On Dell as Master see also the interesting discussion in Twigg 1983, pp. 153−7.
14 Walker 1970, p. 23.

awhile to be one of the leading ministers of the New Model Army, and clearly a preacher of fervour and eloquence, high in Cromwell's confidence.[15] There is indeed a force and eloquence in his printed utterances which still has some power to move; but the sermons of the dead are notoriously damp tinder; Dell had the misfortune to be a contemporary of John Milton, and to compare the two is bound to seem an act of cruelty to Dell. He was a preacher, and none of his works effectively counters Baxter's stricture on his reasoning faculty. Yet there is a fire and sparkle in his best utterances which helps us to understand the power he had when he preached to the Army in 1645. He was a man of ideas, as is brilliantly summarized in Joseph Needham's Preface to Walker's life.

'To have said, in the middle of the 17th century, that the young men should study geography and mathematics, not philosophy and scholastic theology; to have maintained that they should spend half their time in practical work, in learning an honest trade or profession as well as their booklearning; and finally, to have urged and preached that there should be a university in every great city of the Commonwealth, . . . — would make anyone a pioneer covered with glory. Now that we know him better . . . he has come down to a more human size. He could be as tedious a Puritan preacher as any, and it is certain that not everyone can sympathise with his intense dislike of philosophical theology. Yet . . . he was a friend of John Bunyan, and we would give a lot now to know all that the tinker said when Dell yielded up his pulpit to him on Christmas Day so long ago. Whatever may have been his faults and imperfections, William Dell remains in a way a lovable figure, a man who responded to the call of a revolutionary age . . .'[16] His *Right Reformation of Learning, Schools, and Universities . . .*, published in 1654, though attached to a large and querulous pamphlet complaining of the universities as they were, has reasonably been viewed as a work of vision and originality; and when he advocated placing 'universities or colleges . . . in London, York, Bristol, Exeter, Norwich, and the like', he may be accorded a measure of prophetic insight.[17] It is not so clear that he brought these gifts to bear on the College under his charge. In his first two years as Master he seems to have spent more time in London and Yelden than in Caius; and when tricky problems of College business came to light, messengers had on more than one occasion to be despatched to Dr Batchcroft, living in peaceful retirement in Suffolk, to seek his advice.[18] He was a preacher and pastor and parliament man first and foremost. Yet he was not wholly absentee, and he deserves full credit for helping to ensure that university life went on in spite of all the alarms and excursions, and for providing an umbrella in the face of the outside world behind which the College

15 Walker 1970, pp. 28—9, 45—56.
16 Needham in Walker 1970, pp. v—vi.
17 Walker 1970, p. 151; John Twigg tells me that he cites evidence in a forthcoming article that there was also a strong conservative vein in Dell's writings.
18 Venn, III, 91.

continued and in its own way prospered. In or about 1648 he married a wife; and this may have been part of his excuse for not residing at once when he was appointed Master in 1649.[19] For he never departed so far from the tradition of his predecessors (as far as we know) as to bring his wife to live in the Master's Lodge; that revolutionary step seems first to have been taken by the high Tory Robert Brady.

William Bagge and continuity

By the late Zachary Nugent Brooke

[Shortly before the Second World War, Mr Donald Paige, Assistant Librarian, made a remarkable discovery among the bindings and pastedowns in the College library; he found a considerable archive of 17th century letters. With the encouragement of the Librarian, Dr (later Professor) Z. N. Brooke, he extracted the letters, restored and transcribed them, and it was hoped that he would later edit them. But early in the war he was called to military service and was never able to return to the task. What follows (pp. 131–40) is condensed from a paper written by my father at the time about the find and its bearing on the history of the College.][20]

The whole collection amounts to about seventy letters, some of them mere scraps; sometimes only the addresses survived. The letters had been cut to make them fit into the required space; the larger the book the more complete the letter; in one or two cases it was possible to piece together a letter from portions extracted from different books. Sometimes the date was missing, or even the signature of the writer; not infrequently these could be supplied from internal evidence, and missing words could often, with reasonable certainty, be inferred. Perhaps the most remarkable fact about this collection of letters, extracted from over 70 different volumes, is that they were all written within a period of four or five years, and that practically every item in it is certainly connected with one person. William Bagge, who was admitted scholar at the age of 14 or 15 in 1637, became a junior fellow in 1646, a senior fellow in 1651, held in turn most of the minor offices, was a Doctor of Medicine and a University Proctor, and was President of the College from October 1655 to his death in July or August 1657.[21] The majority are letters written to him — including some 13 by parents of

19 Walker 1970, pp. 95, 106; Venn, III, 95.
20 The archive is now MS 816. The numbers are those assigned by Donald Paige, to whose notes we are much indebted. It was originally given as a paper to the Caius Historical Society, and included extracts from the letters; with the kind approval of my brothers, Dr Michael Brooke and Professor Nicholas Brooke (Venn, VI, 212, 237; VII, 86, 90) I have revised and edited it to fit the present context. Donald Paige, who died in 1968, was never able to resume work on the letters; it is hoped that they will be edited before long.
21 For Bagge's career, see Venn, I, 324, and below. The figures which follow can only be approximate.

undergraduates, 12 by fellows, 6 by BAs or undergraduates, 2 by old pupils of the College, 2 by members of other colleges, 4 by tenants of college estates, 2 by his father, and one by a lady patient. There are also 8 undergraduate exercises, 7 Latin essays and one set of Greek verses, some of which are signed by three undergraduates, all of whom had the same tutor, Adamson. They may, however, have been written for Bagge, or submitted to Bagge by their tutor as evidence of their proficiency.

The obvious inference is that the books from which they came all belonged to Bagge; the books are practically all medical books, as we should expect his library to have been. He was a Doctor of Medicine, was consulted on matters medical, and was keenly interested in acquiring new medical books, as letters to him from two fellows show. We know that his books came to the College.[22]

After the ejections of 1644, a number of the remaining fellows were under suspicion, and had had heavy fines imposed upon them, and an inventory made of their goods for sequestration. The most notable of these, William Moore, eventually resigned his fellowship in 1647, though he continued to live in Cambridge, and from 1653–9 was University librarian ('the model librarian', one of his more modern successors has called him); he was one of the greatest benefactors to the College library, for on his death in 1659 he left to the College his magnificent collection of manuscripts.[23] The confusion and insecurity of the time may be judged by the fact that only one of the first intruded fellows retained his fellowship for as long as ten years. In October 1645 a commission was appointed by Parliament to view the statutes of the colleges and to suggest alterations, and also a committee to take into consideration the filling up of vacant fellowships and scholarships. After this committee had reported the College was allowed, in February 1646, to exercise again its statutable authority in filling vacancies. One of its earliest actions under this authority was to elect William Bagge and Edmund Barker to junior fellowships.[24] This gracious concession did not, however, prevent Manchester and his committee from continuing to intrude fellows when they thought fit.

The execution of Charles I in 1649 introduced a new period of stress. The Chancellor of the University, the earl of Holland, soon followed Charles to the block, and on 15 March Manchester succeeded him as Chancellor. A month later Dr Batchcroft was ejected from the Mastership of the College, and to replace him Manchester intruded William Dell.[25] In 1649–50, all graduates were ordered to subscribe to the Engagement. 'I do declare and promise that I will be true and faithful to the Commonwealth of England, as the same is now established, without a king or a House of Lords.' This

22 Venn, I, 324.
23 Venn, I, 192–3; *Annals*, pp. vii–ix; James 1907–8, I, p. viii, II, pp. xix–xx; below, pp. 135, 141.
24 Mullinger 1911, pp. 329, 334–5; Venn, I, 324–5.
25 Mullinger 1911, pp. 358–60; Venn, III, 90, 94; Walker 1970, chap. 7.

produced a new batch of ejections, including two fellows of Caius, Blanckes and Sheringham, the latter a distinguished orientalist.[26] Intrusions continued as before, but the College was not now disposed to submit without a struggle. At the College meeting on 6 March 1651 it was 'Ordered that the Master and Mr Harrington [himself an intruded fellow] go to London to reverse if possible the Orders [for the election] of Sir Stockton and Sir Hickhorngill appointed fellows by the committee for regulating the University.'[27] It is interesting to note that the Master joins the fellows in protesting against the committee's interference, even though Stockton was a Puritan after his own heart and Hickhorngill, like himself, had been a chaplain in the Parliamentary Army. Their protest was unavailing, however, and on 12 June 1651 a minute of the College meeting records 'An Order from the Committee for regulating the University read, for augmenting the stipends of Sir Stockton and Sir Hickhorngill to £25 per annum' — no inconsiderable increase, since £5.6.8 was the normal stipend of a fellow.[28] Augmentations were not uncommon; Dr Dell had received one of £60 a year by order of the committee. The College often acted on its own: thus at the meeting on 6 March 1651 it was agreed 'That £10 per annum be allowed to Mr Barker and Mr Bagge *durante beneplacito*'.[29]

While Parliament and the Cambridge commission were thus busy weeding out the unfaithful, they were at the same time equally interested in the general conduct of the University and its teaching. In 1645 Parliament had appointed a committee to consider how godly preaching was to be established in the University church and parish churches of the town, and in its report the Heads of Colleges were ordered personally to supply the 'morning course' at Great St Mary's on the Lord's Day, and to provide good preaching in the afternoon and on fast days and days of thanksgiving. In 1649 the commission decreed that only Latin and Greek were to be used in colloquial discourse among the students in the colleges.[30] This ought to have been no hardship in Caius, for the same rule was laid down in Dr Caius' statutes, but it doubtless had not been obeyed, and it certainly was not customary in the University. When Archbishop Laud imposed a test of colloquial Latin for the MA degree at Oxford, a number of Oxford BAs migrated to Cambridge to obtain the MA without having to undergo the test. About this time, the Council of State decided that all communications with foreign powers were to be carried on in Latin — John Milton was known as 'Latin secretary' — and this may have added point to the

26 Blanckes went at the end of March 1649, Sheringham in 1651, but both doubtless as part of the same campaign; Charles Scarburgh departed in 1649 (at Michaelmas), presumably also by ejection. Venn, I, 204, 243, 308; cf. Mullinger 1911, pp. 366—7.
27 *Gesta* 6 March 1651. There are two copies of the *Gesta* for 1650—5, one more informal, the other a more formal copy, containing only Orders. This is in both copies.
28 Informal *Gesta* 12 June 1651.
29 *Gesta* 6 March 1651.
30 Mullinger 1911, pp. 329—30, 335—6, 367—9 (also for what follows).

injunction. A few years later Cudworth, as Master of Clare, writing to Thurloe, Cromwell's Secretary of State, recommended to him certain members of the University 'proper to be employed in political and civil affairs', and especially commended some of them as good Latinists; for instance 'Dr Bagge, fellow of Caius College and Doctor of Physick, a singularly good and ready Latinist'.[31] Bagge seems to have seen to the maintenance of the rule; at any rate, the three letters in the collection written to him by undergraduates were all written in Latin.

Criticism of university education was common at this time, and was particularly directed against the low standard of Latinity and the conservative adherence to Aristotelian metaphysics. The Master of Caius abused the current teaching because of the stress it laid on 'the wickedness of the heathen' or pagan classical learning.[32] One of Cromwell's earliest acts as Protector was to appoint a University Commission in 1654 with powers of visitation and reform. The Commission sat for three years, and in 1657, in justification of a further extension for six months, it was asserted that 'it had been a great means to regulate the University, and to purge it of loose and profane persons'.[33] Considering all the purges of the University that had taken place before, there would seem to have been little for this Commission to have done, and the evidence of its work, other than the irritation caused by its presence, is slight. As the Commonwealth came to an end, the University was passing into a more peaceful mood. The last injunction to it was an Act of Parliament in January 1658 against the non-residence of Heads of Houses.[34] This might seem to have been particularly applicable to the Master of Caius, but during the three months previous to the passing of the Act he had a remarkable record of attendance at College meetings, which was continued for some months longer.

The difficult circumstances do not seem to have disturbed unduly the normal working of College life. If distinguished scholars like Sheringham were ejected, many of those intruded were obviously men of learning. These letters — and their evidence is supported by that of the College *Gesta* — show the ordinary interests of peace time: the management of the College estates engrossed much of the time of the Governing Body; there is the constant correspondence of a tutor with the parents of his pupils, making arrangements about their studies or their degrees, the settlement of their accounts, and the like. There is little evidence of internal friction. The intruded fellows were as devoted to the interests of the College as anyone; one at least was a benefactor.[35] We might expect to find considerable ill-will between those who continued as fellows and those who had been ejected or

31 Mullinger 1911, p. 611 and n.
32 Walker 1970, p. 149; see above, p. 130.
33 Mullinger 1911, p. 501, n. 1; for the Commission, ibid. pp. 484−8, 500−9.
34 Mullinger 1911, pp. 503−4; and see below, p. 137, for what follows.
35 Owen Stockton (Venn, I, 381): see above, n. 27; he left his books and £500 to the College, for a scholarship.

voluntarily absented themselves from College. But there is no trace of this. In 1655 Bagge was instructed to 'continue and endeavour to perfect the College Annals etc.' and the outcome seems to have been the *Registrum Magnum* itself, executed by William Adamson. He was also to visit Dr Batchcroft, the ejected Master, and to seek the assistance of Mr Moore for that purpose; he duly made the journey to Wangford in Suffolk to visit Dr Batchcroft, and the payment of his expenses is recorded in the bursar's book.[36] As to Moore, the entry in the *Gesta* of 28 July 1659 is memorable: 'This day the manuscripts bequeathed to the College by our ancient and worthy friend Mr Moore were received into the College Library.'[37] Moreover after the Restoration, when the ejected fellows were reinstated, only one intruded fellow was ejected. This was Wheeler, who had been made President by Dr Dell shortly before the Master's own retirement. The record of his departure in the *Gesta*[38] shows that he was thoroughly unpopular, but his is a solitary case. There was indeed one disturbing element in the College during our period — the Master — and had his residence been more regular the friction might well have been greater. There are some letters in this collection which seem to bear this out, and at the same time emphasise the general good feeling among the fellows.[39]

It is not unlikely that many of the fellows, whether elected or introduced, were more interested in College life and the pursuit of learning than in politics, secular or religious, and were willing to conform in order to be left undisturbed. Indeed it was said at the time that so many oaths had been imposed upon the University that little regard was paid to the taking of an oath.[40] And if strict Puritans objected to the taking of oaths, their secular engagements were no less binding. It may be that there were a number of vicars of Bray among the fellows — and they were certainly not allowed to neglect their religious duties — though probably most of them were rather actuated by the desire to be left in peace. And on the whole it would seem that College society, so often turbulent in peaceful times, was fairly peaceful in these days of turbulence. It there was some friction between the Master and the fellows, that was not unusual.

I think it not fanciful to suggest that Bagge can be given as much credit as anybody for the preservation of amicable relations in College, at any rate during the years covered by this correspondence. The fact that it was to him that the most senior fellow, Rant, wrote to act on his behalf during his absence, the cordial tone of the letters from him and other fellows, testify to

---

36 *Gesta* 16 May 1655 (both copies). There is in fact no continuation of the *Annals* of this period after Moore had ceased to write them; and it is very probable that the *Registrum Magnum* was the fruit of this decision, as Catherine Hall has pointed out to me: it bears the joint names of Bagge and Adamson upon its title-page (see p. 128).

37 See above, p. 132; for his death and funeral sermon, see Mullinger 1911, pp. 513–14.

38 28 May 1661; cf. Venn, I, 376.

39 Letter 22 from Edmund Barker shows clear ill-feeling towards the Master.

40 Cf. Mullinger 1911, pp. 332–4, 539 ff.

the amiability of Bagge's character.[41] The grateful terms in which parents wrote to him for his kindness to their sons may be only the formal language of politeness but probably were a genuine tribute to his kindliness. It is, perhaps, not justifiable to take at its face value the flattering language in which the junior members of the College themselves wrote of his greatness and his goodness to them. Doubtless in duty bound the three undergraduates wrote in Latin, and in a turgid rhetorical Latin; but to one of them (no. 40), addressed by an 'indignissimus . . . alumnus' to his 'venerande Praeses' — 'most unworthy pupil' to his 'revered President' — a special interest attaches, for its author, Stephen Camborne, as a country parson with a modest living, was able to leave £3000 to 'Keys College'.[42] Those who reached the grade of BA were not afraid to write in English; and the cream of the collection, from Henry Harcock to his tutor in January 1655, was a letter which Jane Austen's Mr Collins might have been proud to write.

'Worthy Tutor,

Rather than shew myselfe ungratefull, an illiterate pen (undeckt with flosculent Rhetoricke) have here presumed to commend these impolish'd characters to the candid eye of your acceptance; which though rusticity of style may prompt you to reject with one hand, yett in this am I emboldned, that so ingenuous a nature, so affable a disposition will not be wanting to imbrace with the other.

. . . For my owne part, far be it from me to be so unnaturall, as to disrespect those brests, that have afforded such pleasant milke, or to imitate that hard hearted offspring which are wont to calcitrate their dame in recompence of her kindnes; I shall rather make it my τὸ ἔργον to become thankfull for what I have receyved, endeavouring to be responsible for what I may receyve. Sir, I know not how that little pittance of mony held out, which I left in your hands. . . What you have disbursed I shall repay at my returne, with thankes, which shall be with as much expedition as conveniency will permitt. Mr Rant had you commended upon his leaving the Coll., who commanded mee to make mention of his name to you, to the intent, his desire with my hearty cravings might be so prevalent as to persuade with you to goe for the obtayning a Junior Fellowship for me. Tis further the humble request of your observant pupil, that in his absence you would be pleased to open a dore of preferment for his intended presence. I know your interest, as to that particular, far exceeds any one mans in the Coll., which if you please to improve in your pupil's behalfe, you shall for ever oblige

your humbly devoted

---

41 The cordial tone of the letters from absent fellows testifies to this; and the most senior, John Rant (see below), gave him commissions which the *Bursar's Books* confirm that he performed.
42 See below, p. 160.

> pupil and servant
> Hen: Harcocks.

My Father presents his best respects to you.'[43]

Even this did not suffice to win him the junior fellowship he asked for. Though we discount the language of undergraduates and BAs about Bagge, we get from the correspondence the impression of a conscientious and kindly man, serving the College well, a good friend and a good tutor, and one who had won the confidence of his colleagues.

At the same time he had the confidence of the Master as well. For Dr Dell, who had left the office of President vacant for some years, appointed Bagge to that office in October 1655 and renewed the appointment a year later. During the two years that Bagge was President, the Master attended only ten of the forty-six College meetings that were held. Bagge died in the Long Vacation of 1657, and the Master was present at every subsequent meeting from 8 October to 1 May in the following year — a record for him of fourteen consecutive meetings. This seems to show that he had been quite content to leave things in Bagge's hands, but for several months after Bagge's death was careful to be present. Bagge, therefore, was *persona grata* with both groups in the College. The office of President was again left vacant until 4 April 1660, when the Master, little more than a month before his resignation, appointed the unpopular Wheeler as President.[44]

During the years covered by this correspondence, certainly during the period from January 1655 to July 1657, Bagge was the real ruler of the College. He had been one of the senior fellows since 1651, and the entire government of the College was in the hands of the Master and the twelve senior fellows. Dr Caius laid it down that the senior of the twelve had no authority by virtue of his seniority: what was to happen when Master and President were both absent is not clear.[45] What did happen in this period is that one fellow known as the *Locum Tenens* presided over College meetings. From 1651 to 1654, this title rarely appears; but from 1655 it was regularly used, and it may have been assumed that the senior in standing should hold that position. From 2 January 1655 Bagge, then the senior fellow, was regularly *Locum Tenens* until he became President the following October. From the same date he was also Registrary ('Register' or Secretary), so that during the last two and a half years of his life he wrote and signed the minutes in the *Gesta*, which were much more neatly and carefully kept than before. During this period he also presided over most College meetings, and was the chief person in the College in the long absences of the Master. This is the more remarkable in that he was only 35 at the time of his death. If there were older fellows, they had been intruded,

---

43 On him see Venn, I, 380.

44 For the details in this paragraph, see *Gesta* 1655−6.

45 See Caius' Statutes cc. 31−2 (Venn, III, 364−5). It was however possible under c. 32 for Master or President to delegate power to a senior fellow — and cf. below for Gooch's practice.

and he was senior to them in standing. It shows how rapidly the personnel changed in this period and how important it was that there should be someone like Bagge of high character and ability to act as a stable element and preserve both continuity and peace. His personal interests were in medicine. His book on the stone probably served as a thesis for his doctorate, which he took in 1655; and a letter from Joan Lightfoot, almost certainly the wife of the Master of St Catharine's, shows that he was regarded as an authority on that and similar disorders.[46] He was constantly concerned with keeping his medical library up to date, and John Rant more than once wrote to him about new medical books: no. 9 is a pleasant mixture of College business and personal concerns with discussion of books on the market, and concludes with salutes to his friends in Caius, 'and please to receive to yourselfe the salutes and cordial affection of' the author. Another fellow, Thomas Allen, himself later an MD and FRS and fellow of the College of Physicians, sent him (no. 34) an opinion on certain books Bagge was seeking. 'As for Greg. Horstii *Observat: Medicinalium* my friend hath them, but something differing both in the time and place of their impression, as is specified to you in this inclosed note, neither doe they agree in the price, with thoes you mentioned in your former letter. I did meet with some imperfect Horst: in some other places, but none so intire. For Amatus Lusitanus it is not to be had . . .'

He would also seem to have been an efficient man of business, for he was often engaged in visiting the College estates,[47] and handling all kinds of College business. No. 33 is a classic debtor's excuse to his son's tutor — he had arrived in Caius too late to see Mr Bagge. 'By the loss of my way in yesterday's mist I finde myself inconvened with the greater loss of not meeting with you which maynly ingaged mee in this journey and retarded the advance of my sonns supply . . . I have left with my sonn 8li sterling to be delivered to you upon youre retourne. I hope by the spring I may undertake a more seasonable voyage, I have stayed a month for weather, I wish I had stayed twoe more.' In no. 6 (1653) a Caian, Jermyn Wright, rejoices that his son, whose tutor had had to resign, had chosen Bagge, and is happy to 'applaud his circumspect, provided and discreet election of such a Maecenas of learning and favourer of modesty, civility and piety as your selfe.' In no. 9A John Rant, fellow since 1632, wrote to him from Norfolk:

'I thank you for your satisfying letters in answere to my last, and in particular for the chamber for my younge nephew. When he comes he shall take his choice whether he will have that under me where Sir Bolt lives [John Boult, fellow], or that in the new building [presumably Perse or Legge] which you commend; wherefore let that chamber be still kept void,

---

46 Her letter, full of the touching anxiety of a sick woman, is no. 39. Bagge's thesis on the stone was completed *c*. 1655, the year that he took his MD.
47 There are four letters in the collection from College tenants concerning various matters of estate business.

and lett not Sir Bolt as yet remoove. I beleeve the yonge gentlemen will be with you in the first or second weeke in June at the furthest, about which time I also intend (God willing) to meete them at Cambridge. [He is evidently writing of Humphrey Rant and William Branthwaite, who were actually admitted on 22 June 1653.][48] But in the meane time I desire that you would receive for me all such moneyes as are due to me from the Colledge of the Bursar and the Steward and the Register for the admission of fellow commoners . . . You are to receive of the Bursar for this last halfe yeares corne money and the small dividends, and for what is due to me in *Libro rationali* [p. 102]. . . When you have received all these moneyes let me know (without faile in your next weekes letters) the totall summe, and keepe it by you till you have order from me how to dispose of it, which will be verie soone. I pray faile not in this . . . I am glad that all thinges are quiett in the Colledge. How long it will so continewe I know not. You are likely to see verie suddenly great changes in this whole Nation: and I hope all for the better. Deare Mr Bagge, I wish you all happiness, and that we may meete each other with ivy and comfort. The vote of

Your most affectionate friend

Jo: Rant.'

John Rant's position was precarious; he had been granted leave of absence, and in no. 10 he writes again, full of business, about books and tenants of the College in and around Foulden in the neighbourhood in which he was evidently living; but also about further leave and the possibility that he would have to resign; and in 1655 he resigned his fellowship. When he finally made up his mind it was evidently a surprise to Bagge, for his last letter, no. 35, tries to explain and excuse. 'For if any action of mine was hammer'd upon the anvill of deliberation, this was. If I could find in myselfe propensions to returne, yours and many others of the fellowes loving invitations (which I gratefully commemorate) would be to me very strong attractions.'[49]

In 1653 Bagge's standing already was shown by the College choosing him to be University proctor. Bagge had a favourite pupil, a fellow-commoner called William Hovell, of whom Venn records that he was 'B.A. 1653−4; 1st, out of 15, in the list'.[50] It was unusual for a fellow-commoner to proceed to the BA degree, still more to be 'in the list', that is, the Tripos list. The list was not an order of merit as in more modern times but merely an order which gave seniority, and little heed was paid to it, for instance, in the awarding of fellowships. It was a prerogative of the proctors to have a say in drawing up the list, and Bagge was proctor when Hovell was placed first;

48 Venn, I, 388; for John Rant, I, 276.
49 Rant speaks only of withdrawal, but the weightiness of his decision makes it seem clear that it refers to his resignation, or was a prelude to resignation; and he goes on to talk of commencement business, not wholly intelligible, but evidently relating to Bagge's acts for the MD in 1655.
50 Venn, I, 376.

three other pupils of Bagge's appeared high on the list that year.[51] Hovell was the son of Sir Richard Hovell of Hillington, and he entered the College in October 1649; at the same time his cousin Henry Chicheley, son of Thomas Chicheley of Wimpole, Cambridgeshire, was also admitted as fellow-commoner.[52] Both these young men are described as educated at Wimpole for four years under Mr Bagge — whom Donald Paige conjectured to be our William Bagge, which seems very probable. If so, he spent the first three or four years of his time as junior fellow as tutor to these two boys at Wimpole, and came into full residence with them in October 1649, when they were both admitted to Caius as his pupils.[53] It is the more remarkable that a young man (he was then barely 27) could have achieved so predominant a position in the College in so short a time, and have won, apparently, such general esteem.

His death in 1657 must have been very sudden. He and the Master were both present at the College meeting of 8 July 1657, and his will was proved on 15 September of the same year. In the interval he went on a visit to Hillington — presumably to the home of his former pupil — and there he died.[54]

Epilogue: transition to 1660

Of continuity the matriculation book remains the chief witness. It shows us some remarkable cases of stability, among them that of John Ellys, who arrived in 1648, aged 14, was successively sizar, scholar, fellow, tutor and Master — and died as Master in 1716 after a unique record of service to the College.[55] It shows that though the numbers somewhat declined, the entries to the College went steadily on — still mainly from Norfolk and Suffolk, but with an ample sprinkling from Cambridgeshire and from many other parts of the country. It would be extremely interesting to determine the religious complexion of the College, but this is impossible. Many doubtless cared little for the religious movements of the 1640s and 50s, and among these we may reckon Thomas Shadwell, who has a substantial niche in restoration drama — and is remembered in the Shadwell Society and the drama of Caius in the 1980s. His *Virtuoso* portrays the intellectual world of his time, though, not, we may think, of his College. He was a pupil of William Naylor under the presidency of Bagge, and we may hope that his tutor never had to write a report like that with which his enemy John Dryden immortalised his name.

51 Tanner 1917, p. 407; cf. pp. 41, 350−1.
52 Venn, I, 376.
53 Wimpole is not so far from Cambridge as to preclude frequent visits, but there is practically no record of Bagge in the College in these years.
54 *Gesta* 8 July 1657; for his will and death, see Venn, I, 324.
55 Venn, I, 370 and below, pp. 159−60.

1   The Gate of Virtue, 1567 – 9; see pp. 65 – 7

QVI STVDIO EXCOLVIT MVSAS FLORE[
COTVLIT & PATRIÆ C[ ]MODA MAGN
QVI STRAVIT FACILES ADIT[ ]D APOLL
ET FECIT GRAIOS VERBA LATINA
QVI CÃTABRIGIÆ GONVILLI ICÆPT
AVXIT & EPARVO NOBILE FECIT
ET QVI MAUSOLEV LIÆCRO DONAVIT
QVÆ NVC DE PAVLI NOIE NOME[
QVI LVCE DEDIT & SOLATIA MAGNA C[
VT SCIRET PARTES ANOTOMÆ
ARTE MACHAOIA GALEVS FINE S[
ET PATRIÆ ATQ[ ]ÆVI GLORIA [
TALIS ERAT CAI QVALE SVB IMAGI
PENE HIC VIVÈTE PICTA TAB[ ]LA

2 Portrait of Dr Caius, by an unknown artist: probably a contemporary portrait,
   presented by John Caius himself

…e head of Dr Caius' caduceus, a slender silver staff,
…minating in a group of four serpents supporting a
…at of arms. This is not Caius' usual arms, but may
…resent an earlier form, and be a field of
…naranths', signifying immortality: see p. 64

…ere are two figures of *Fortuna*, one on either side of
…arch of the Gate of Virtue, facing the entry of the
…llege: that on the right, shown here, offers worldly
…osperity, a bag of gold and a cornucopia; that on
…e left worldly honour, a palm and a laurel wreath

4 Gonville Court. The façade of the Chapel is of 1718 – 26, of the rest of the court, including the lantern, 1753 – 4; the oriel window is of the 19th century: behind the façade to its left, the library of 1431 – 41, remodelled as the panelled combination room in 1905; see pp. 24 – 7, 172 – 3, 253 – 4

5 Caius Court. Chapel, 1718–26, and Gate of Virtue, 1567–9: see pp. 65–7, 172

6 The tomb of John Caius, by Theodore Haveus of Cleves, 1575: see p. 78

7 The College Organ, by Johannes Klais of Bonn, 1981, under the ceiling of 1637: see
  p. 289

8 The Chapel. The basic structure is of *c*. 1390, the ceiling of 1637, the stalls of *c*. 1718 – 26, the apse of 1870. On the left, the tombs of Perse and Caius, on the right of Legge. See pp. 22 – 4, 113, 172, 216 and Plates 6, 9a – b

(above right) Tomb of Stephen Perse,
1615: see p. 79
(below right) Tomb of Thomas Legge,
1619: see pp. 79–80
(below left) Bust of Lord Langdale
died 1851) in the Public Record Office:
e pp. 196–203

10 Matthew Parker's flagon, and two coconut cups. Parker gave identical silver gilt flagons to Caius and Trinity Hall in 1571, and a similar one to Christ's. The coconut cups are both 15th century with silver gilt mounts and covers, that on the right of *c*. 1470. It is not certain that either cover was intended for its cup, nor how they came to the College (C. A. Crighton, *Cambridge Plate*, Fitzwilliam Museum, 1975, pp. 17, 54; Venn, III, 302–3).

11 Tankard or flagon given by Richard Branthwaite and William Webb in 1609, and
Matthew Parker's chalice, given in 1570. Parker gave a similar cup to Corpus.
Branthwaite and Webb were nephews of the Master; Webb died young and is
buried in Chapel. Tankard and chalice are both of silver gilt (Venn, III, 303;
Crighton, p. 55).

12 The nef or bonbonnière, early 19th century, attributed to Pugin and given by Sir
   Clifford Allbutt (died 1925)

13 Opposite: Portraits: a (above left) Dr William Butts, by Holbein: see pp. 49 – 50, 56 –
                      b (above right) John Gostlin, painter unknown: see p. 115
                      c (below left) John Smith, by Joshua Reynolds: see pp. 177, 183
                      d (below right) Martin Davy, by William Beechey: see pp. 209 –

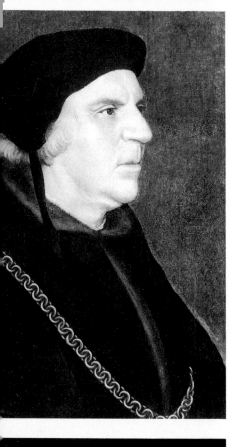

CATERA SACCVS

14 Portrait of Sir Charles Sherrington, by Augustus John, in the University of
Liverpool Collection: see pp. 239 – 40

15 A room in Caius Court, panelled in the 1690s. The portrait in the recess is of Theodore Haveus, Caius' mason: see pp. 66 – 7

16 The drawing room in the Master's lodge, by the elder William Wilkins, 1795

17 The hall roof, by Salvin, 1853 – 4, with coats of arms of founders and benefactors added in 1909

18 The Great Gate by Waterhouse, 1868 – 70, with statues of founders: Caius and Bateman above, Gonville below

19 Harvey Court, by Sir Leslie Martin and Colin St John Wilson, 1960 – 2, from the garden: see pp. 275 – 6

20 Caius from the tower of Great St Mary's: the old courts, with the Senate House to the left and Trinity beyond

21 St Michael's Court and St Michael's Church from the tower of Great St Mary's

22 The Panelled Combination Room: the library of 1431–41, represented by the moulded beams in the ceiling, remodelled in the 18th century and again in 1905: see pp. 253–4. The portrait to the right of the fireplace is of Sir Vincent Wigglesworth by Paul Gopal-Chowdhury

23 'Dessert' in the Panelled Combination Room, by Paul Gopal-Chowdhury, 1984. In
their order at table, from the left: Noel Malcolm, John Casey, Peter Bayley, Mark
Birkinshaw (behind), Stephen Hawking, Neil McKendrick (standing), The
President, Sir Vincent Wigglesworth, Nicola Nichols, Robin Holloway (standing),
Peter Tranchell, Richard le Page (behind), Joseph Needham. Also standing, Mr
Quintana, the butler, and Mr Healey, the deputy butler.

24 The Gate of Honour and Caius Court, from the steps of the Squire Law Library

'The rest to some faint meaning make pretence,
But Shadwell never deviates into sense.'

The Caian, however, had his revenge, and briefly succeeded Dryden at the Glorious Revolution of 1688−9 as Poet Laureate and Historiographer Royal.[56]

For the rest, one of the alumni was marked down in later life 'a moderate presbyterian', others were deprived of their livings in 1660 or soon after; others again profited from the Restoration. But the majority, even of those known to have had Puritan sympathies, survived the various changes; and though they may have undergone agonies of conscience or changes of faith, the formal record of their lives rarely has anything to say of their inward views. Doubtless it exaggerates the continuity; but it remains very striking.

Let us dwell for a moment on the admissions in 1644. Robert Brady was admitted on 20 February under the Master's surety; he was one of Batchcroft's last tutorial pupils, and sizar, or servant, to him. From the autumn of 1644 till 1650 he was a scholar, and his chief study was evidently in medicine.[57] So far, one does not have to search very deep to understand the career of an able young East Anglian in Caius who became a physician. He was evidently too much of a royalist already to be entirely respectable in the 1650s, and so missed a fellowship, and had to wait till 1660 to complete his MD. By 1660 he had already performed services to the royal cause and was furthermore well known to Dr Batchcroft, his former Master and tutor — and so he was reckoned a suitable choice for Batchcroft's successor; and his medical career continued, within and without Cambridge. He was Regius Professor of Physic from 1677 to his death in 1700, and royal physician in the 1680s. None of this prepares us for Brady's lasting fame. For he was one of the eminent historians of his century, and one of the most distinguished Caius and Cambridge have fostered. Yet the first origin and beginnings of his interest in historical records and the medieval past are quite obscure. Possibly he was allowed to potter in the University library by the Caius antiquary William Moore. Today he is remembered as the hammer of parliament — and to this we shall return; perhaps it may owe something to the harsh experience of his youth. The only thing certain is that of all the scholars of the early 17th century, Sir Henry Spelman, antiquary and Norfolk squire, influenced him the most.[58] The matriculation book records that in November 1644, nine months after Brady, Charles Spelman entered the College; and in March 1645 his elder brother Roger.[59] They were sons of Sir John Spelman of Heydon in Norfolk, a noted antiquary, and grandsons of

---

56 On Shadwell, see Venn, I, 393−4; *DNB*; Dryden, *Mac Flecknoe*. For what follows, Venn, I, 300, and many entries in Venn, I.

57 Venn, I, 351; Pocock 1950−2; below, chap. 8.

58 See Pocock 1950−2, pp. 191−2, 194−5, showing the clear influence of Spelman on Brady's interpretation of the history of Parliament.

59 Venn, I, 355−6; on the Spelmans, cf. *Annals*, p. 416.

Sir Henry Spelman. In one of his works Brady noted Charles Spelman's service in preserving one of his grandfather's major works.[60] If the young Spelmans influenced the formation of his interest, it would be a striking example of the way in which students can often influence one another, in all manner of ways, academic bent not excluded, more than their tutors, teachers and professors.

60 Brady 1684, pp. 229–30.

8

The Restoration and Dr Brady

Robert Brady, physician and antiquary

Robert Brady, Master from 1660 to 1700, was a royal physician, a Regius Professor and a man of many parts. Above all, he was a medieval historian, and he used his exceptional knowledge of English history in the service of Charles II and James II and in defence of royal authority and of a doctrine of the royal succession which allowed little place for any elective or democratic principle.

Among the eminent scholars who have adorned the College and the Master's Lodge, Brady was, until the 1950s, one of the most neglected.[1] A man who was celebrated for his defence of Stuart absolutism hardly appealed to the liberal mind in the 19th century; and neither his extreme royalism nor his attendance in the train of James II when he went to purge the fellowship of Magdalen College, Oxford, are any more congenial today.[2] But as a scholar he has come into his own. However we may delight in the fantasy that the Anglo-Saxon Witan was a democratic body which freely elected the Anglo-Saxon king, as it was described by Edward Augustus Freeman in 1867, it has now come to be recognised that the account of the royal succession which Robert Brady was propounding in the 1680s — and tried to explain to James II even as he prepared to flee the country in 1688 — was very much better history.[3] He was not a major editor of texts, and so unlike the amazing student prodigy Henry Wharton, also a Caian, who worked and died while Brady was Master and whose *Anglia Sacra* is still in the hands of numerous medievalists, Brady's books are not now well known. But in their day and world — in the scientific revolution of the 17th century, the age of Newton and Leibniz — they put the study of medieval English history on a scientific basis; and although Brady was not so remarkable an archivist, or so exciting a character, as the heroic and eccentric Puritan William Prynne, who presided over the public records immediately before Brady worked there, he was a much better historian. He was a physician and antiquary combined, a very fitting

1 See now Douglas 1951, chap. vi; Pocock 1950—2 (on which much of what follows is based); Pocock 1957, pp. 194—228.
2 Pocock 1950—2, p. 202.
3 E. A. Freeman, *History of the Norman Conquest of England*, I (Oxford, 1867), pp. 111—23; cf. C. Brooke, *Saxon and Norman Kings* (Fontana edn., 1967), pp. 22—4. For Brady as historian see esp. Brady 1684, 1685, 1700 and above n. 1. For Wharton, see pp. 147—50.

combination for a successor of Dr Caius — yet whereas Caius really did important work for the advance of medicine but was a quack of an anti- quary, Brady was no more than an efficient and observant working physi- cian; as a historian he was a man of stature. Though he employed assistants, he worked hard among the records himself; after his death the seat at which he had sat long hours in the Tally Court at the Exchequer of Receipt was remembered by his younger colleagues; and doubtless he had studied Domesday Book there, for he was the first modern scholar seriously to unfold its riches.[4] As with almost every major historian of his century, history and politics were inextricably entwined in his outlook and interests; but as with Cotton and Spelman, on whose shoulders he climbed — or Dugdale and Sancroft and Wharton, whom he knew personally — the scholarly achievement was a real and sincere and lasting part of the man.

In Sir Robert Cotton's youth in the reign of Elizabeth it was largely taken for granted that the famous broadside of the 1320s, the *Modus tenendi parliamentum*, 'How to hold a Parliament' — which propounded the doc- trines of the 1640s in the idiom of the 1320s — was a historical document; and as it purported to describe parliament as it had been in the days of Edward the Confessor, it was supposed that the House of Commons as Cotton knew it — and Pym and Hampden in the 1630s and 1640s — was older than the Conquest.[5] Cotton was above all a book-collector, and his library is still one of the greatest treasures of the British Library. It con- tained at least eight copies of the *Modus*, and a great proportion of all the Anglo-Saxon charters which survive — many of them adorned with innumerable 'signatures' of the Witan, whom Cotton presumably took to be early MPs.[6] He was a passionate antiquary who became also a passionate parliamentarian, and in due course the king separated him from his library, which he believed to contain explosive material. But Cotton was a true scholar, and may himself have come to know that the doctrine of the *Modus*, however congenial, was not historical. This was certainly known to Spelman, on whose shoulders Cotton's mantle fell; and it was from Spelman that Robert Brady first learned that Parliament as we know it was a product of the 13th and 14th centuries, and was not derived by any direct or simple evolution from the Witan — that the Norman Conquest inter- vened, bringing feudal institutions of a character very different from parliamentary. It was Brady who first made scientific, historical sense, of the nature and history of Anglo-Norman feudalism. In doing so, with a

4 PRO SP 64/139. I owe this information to Elizabeth Hallam: see her forthcoming *Domes- day Book through Nine Centuries* (London, 1986).
5 N. Pronay and J. Taylor, *Parliamentary Texts of the later Middle Ages*, Oxford, 1980, p. 68: 'temporibus regis Edwardi filii Ethelredi regis.'
6 Ibid. pp. 118 (lost copy), 202−4 for texts of *Modus*; P. H. Sawyer, *Anglo-Saxon Charters* (London, Royal Hist. Soc., 1968), pp. 50−4. Dr Colin Tite has a full study of Cotton's library in hand and has given me most helpful advice — but is not to be held responsible for my conjectures.

lively pen and vigorous argument, he manhandled opponents even more for-
midable than the defenders of parliamentary antiquities. For among the
Common Lawyers of his day, who already regarded the English Common
Law with that mystical devotion so puzzling to the layman of any age
acquainted with its workings, it was generally believed that the English
Common Law was eternal and owed nothing to any medieval king. When
Brady coolly answered that medieval law was largely king-made, that *Magna
Carta* itself was a royal charter, the lawyers and the Whigs saw in this propaganda for a repellent political royalism — but they failed to see that it was
also very good history, based on a deep knowledge of the public records,
only surpassed in the 17th century, one may conjecture, by Prynne. We can
admire the scholar without necessarily condoning the politician.

Brady was a Norfolk man, like so many of his line; he was born at
Denver in 1627 and inherited a modest estate there which in the end he left
to the College.[7] He had his first schooling at Downham Market, then
entered Caius under Batchcroft in 1644. He specialised in medicine, but the
troubles of the Commonwealth prevented him from completing his degree;
for his brother Edmund was caught as a royalist 'traitor' and hanged in
1650, and Brady had to fly; after various adventures in the Low Countries
and the Scilly Isles and France, he was able to return to Cambridge in 1652
and resume his studies.[8] But for some reason not clear — though doubtless
related to his royalist sympathies — he was refused leave to proceed MD
and was even imprisoned at Yarmouth for a time. In the late 1650s he was
practising as a physician and perhaps as a royalist spy, for he claimed in
1660 to have been active 'in many services tending to his Majesty's restoration'.[9] In May 1660 Charles returned to the throne; in September a
royal patent ordered Brady's admission to the MD and in December the
aged Batchcroft combined with the king to designate him Master of Caius,
to which office he was duly elected. He was then thirty-three and held the
Mastership for close on forty years, till his death in 1700. In 1671 he
succeeded Glisson as Regius of Physic, and he evidently remained in touch
with the Court, where he served especially in the 1680s as a royal physician.

Venn succeeded in giving the impression that he was largely an absentee
Master, though he acknowledged his 'keen interest in our domestic records'
which is fitting in a great student of the public records.[10] But the *Exiit Books*
are complete for this period and give very precise details of the time he spent
in College; and it is clear that throughout his forty years as Master he was
never absent for any great length of time.[11] The pattern is indeed strange

7 Venn, I, 351; III, 105—8; *ER*, pp. 36—8; Pocock 1950—2, p. 187.
8 Ibid.
9 Ibid.
10 Venn, III, 107; and for his work with the Public Records, Pocock 1950—2, pp. 197—8: he
was Keeper *de facto*, though Sir Algernon May, 'a person deservedly obscure' continued
apparently to draw the salary; but Brady had a handsome salary too from 1686 to 1688.
11 This is based on the *Exiit Books* 1619—1677, 1678—1747.

and intriguing. In 1661 he visited College at least twelve times, once for only a few hours, usually for a few days, never for more than a week — and this remained very roughly the pattern throughout his early years. As he grew older he grew steadily less fidgety — or less of a commuter, as we might say. By 1672 his visits to Caius were normally of at least a fortnight in length, and as the years passed steadily increased. What we do not know is where he spent the rest of his time — in Norfolk, perhaps at Denver, where his early medical practice seems to have been, and where he retained the country seat to which in the end he returned to die — or perhaps in London, where he must have gone very frequently in the 1670s and 1680s not only to the royal court but to the public records, even though he came increasingly to rely on a research assistant.[12] Doubtless he went elsewhere: to Newmarket, a favourite royal home from home; or to Windsor, where he is recorded in 1684. Venn quoted documents which showed that in 1684, as Charles II's life was drawing to a close, Brady attended on him regularly in Windsor and Winchester and Newmarket, and deduced from the allowances he was given that Brady was absent from Cambridge throughout this period.[13] Not so, however, for in the 144 days for which he was given allowances for attendance at Windsor between April and August 1684, the *Exiit Book* shows that he was in Caius for about forty-one.[14] The calls of the ailing king were moreover exceptional — he was never absent so long as in that year.

The most interesting of these entries is that which shows an unusually long stay in College early in 1680, from 9 February to 12 March; for during this period his wife Jane or Jean — daughter of Luke Constable of Swaffham — died and was buried on 6 March in St Michael's Church.[15] It is reasonable to suppose that Mrs Brady died in the Caius Master's Lodge and was the first Master's wife ever to reside there. We know little else of her, save that she had no children to survive her.

Brady and the intellectual life of Caius

What is much less clear is the extent of Brady's contact with the students in College. Some influence he must have had, and one notes the arrival of the brothers Robert and Thomas Barber from Denver in 1668 and 1671 — Robert came specifically on the Master's surety and evidently shared some

---

12 Pocock 1950—2, pp. 196—7; see above, n. 4.
13 Venn, III, 106—7 (checked by MS 602/278).
14 *Exiit Book*, 1678—1747: the number of days depends, of course, on whether the counting was inclusive or exclusive.
15 Pocock 1950—2, p. 188, n. 11 ('1679' for 1679/80); Venn 1891, p. 127; Venn, III, 106. Her epitaph is recorded in BL Harleian MS 6121, f. 23ᵛ, dating her death 4 March 1679 for 1680. For her father, see *The Visitation of Norfolk A.D. 1664*, ed. A. W. Hughes Clarke and A. Campling (Harleian Soc. 85, 1933), p. 31.

of his antiquarian interests, for though he died young he lived long enough to acquire and give the College Dugdale's *Baronage,* when it was published in 1675—6.[16] One might also, a little more remotely, sense the Master's influence behind an entry in the same year 1668 that brought Robert Barber: Francis Hartstongue, whose father was a Norfolk squire who had recently moved to Ireland, and who gave the library a fine set of the *Annales* of Cardinal Baronius.[17] His brothers Standish and John came later, in 1676, bringing the breath of a wider academic air, for they had been at Trinity College, Dublin, and the University of Glasgow before following their brother to Caius; and John was to return to Ireland as archdeacon and bishop.[18] But Brady was also Regius Professor of Physic, and one may suppose had some influence on the medical studies in the College. One observes such names as John Dade, brother, son and grandson of Caians, who came in 1666, was a fellow from 1674 to 1694, held several college offices, took his MD in 1683 — and after his marriage practised at Ipswich.[19] We look even more attentively at Christopher Green, son of the college cook, born in Cambridge in 1651—2, 'at school under Mr Griffith', that is, at the Perse, who entered the College on a December day in 1667, was a fellow from 1674 to 1688 and then married, but went on to succeed Brady as Regius Professor of Physic, a post he held till he died in extreme old age in 1741.[20] The college offices these men held — Green, though a physician, was in turn ethical lecturer, Greek lecturer, bursar, steward and dean — strongly suggest a link of confidence with the Master, even though we cannot tell how much attention he paid to their training as doctors in his flittings to and fro. The best known name among the physicians was not of a fellow, but Thomas Dover, who devised the celebrated specific 'Dover's powder' and was, as Venn coolly observed, 'more distinguished as a buccaneer'. He set up in medical practice, it seems, in Bristol, from which he set sail in 1708 on a three year privateering expedition, which seems to have added substantially to his wealth; in later years he was able to practise in London, where he died in 1742.[21]

But the link between Master and students is most obscure where we should expect it to be clearest. For in his time two very eminent young historians grew up in College, Henry Wharton and Jeremy Collier. Neither became a fellow, which perhaps suggests that they did not win Brady's favour; and in the surviving portions of Wharton's autobiography Brady is

---

16 Venn, I, 435, 446. Barber's gift is recorded on a slip inserted in the book itself; but it seems that in fact and in accordance with John Knight's will our copy was exchanged for one with painted coats of arms belonging to Knight, and the slip transferred (I owe this to evidence collected by Heather Owen; on Knight see Venn, I, 246; James 1907—8, I, pp. viii—ix; II, 585—618).
17 Venn, I, 435—6.
18 Venn, I, 456.
19 Venn, I, 426.
20 Venn, I, 433; cf. Mitchell 1976, p. 23.
21 Venn, I, 481—2; *DNB.*

never mentioned.[22] It is an astonishing omission, for it is hard to believe that one of the most remarkable medieval scholars of the century could be brought up in the college presided over by another without any influence having passed between them.

Nor can we doubt that Henry Wharton's bent was already clear when he was a scholar in the College.[23] He died aged thirty having published numerous books and tracts, and in two stout volumes of *Anglia Sacra* edited enough important texts to make several reputations.[24] He was a remarkable character, devout, dedicated, neurotic, impatient — a prodigious worker, as his books dramatically show; and in his personality (like others of his day) he anticipates the characteristic young and ardent divine of the Oxford Movement, pious, devoted and over-anxious. He came of a family already closely linked to the College: his father had been a Caian in the 1650s, and he himself enjoyed the scholarship founded by his great-uncle Matthew Stokes, former fellow.[25] When he arrived at Caius aged fifteen early in 1680 he reckoned to work twelve hours a day, making secure foundations in classics, theology and mathematics — he is said to have been Isaac Newton's 'last private pupil'.[26] His scholarship ran till 1687, and he narrowly missed a fellowship, it seems; but by then he was already occupied elsewhere, as amanuensis to William Cave in his *Historia Literaria* — an uneasy collaboration, since Wharton felt the master exploited him — but probably a useful apprenticeship.[27] In the late 1680s he became a fervent disciple of William Sancroft, archbishop of Canterbury, and was one of his favoured chaplains when the revolution of 1688 broke on them. Sancroft was an Emmanuel man who had been chaplain to John Cosin, and in the early 1660s Master of Emmanuel; and he united the tradition of piety in which he had grown up at Emmanuel — in a manner considerably modified as the years had passed — with Cosin's love of Anglican ritual and the tradition of Anglican worship; he was a solitary, austere man of great dedication; and a scholar who loved to toil for many hours at his desk and left immense quantities of notes, and a splendid library, which he bequeathed to his college.[28] Sancroft was determined to maintain Anglican supremacy and Stuart legitimacy, and his plans foundered on James II, who as a Catholic wished to see a toleration alien to the triumphalist Anglican archbishop,

---

22 What survives of Wharton's autobiography is printed in D'Oyly 1821, II, 105–54; cf. Douglas 1951, p. 141 and n. 2; also chap. vii and pp. 200–2 for Collier; and Overton 1902, pp. 121–9.

23 Though not quite so precocious as Douglas makes him by dating an early work '1680' (p. 142) — this is corrected to 1689 in p. 143 n. 1. It was published in 1690 (after approval in 1689).

24 Wharton 1691. He was born on 9 Nov. 1664, and died 5 March 1695 (D'Oyly 1821, II, 105; Douglas 1951, pp. 139, 154; Venn, I, 464).

25 Ibid.; Venn, III, 232.

26 Douglas 1951, p. 140; for his career at Caius, D'Oyly 1821, II, 107–9; Venn, I, 464.

27 D'Oyly 1821, II, 110 ff.; Douglas 1951, p. 140. Early in 1687 he expected a fellowship which did not materialise: D'Oyly 1821, II, 116.

28 Stubbings 1983, no. 16; D'Oyly 1821; cf. Douglas 1951, p. 143.

and then lost his throne and fled, carrying, in Sancroft's view, the true succession with him.[29]

By 1688 Wharton was established at Lambeth and in his element. He could join the rejoicing when his master led the successful resistance to James which issued in the trial of seven bishops and their acquittal. But then disaster followed. Early in 1689 two royal chaplains came to Lambeth to ensure the archbishop's recognition for William and Mary. Wharton was to say prayers that day and consulted the archbishop, who refused to give any new instruction to him. We can see that Sancroft laid a mild test on his chaplain: James was king, no change was authorised. But Wharton, young, unstable, without any clear directive, would not or could not see his meaning. He prayed in the chapel of Lambeth palace for the new sovereigns.[30] This was a bitter blow for Sancroft, who refused to recognise them and was preparing to go into dignified retirement, the natural leader of those who had refused the oaths to William and Mary, the non-jurors. Sancroft sent for Wharton in white heat and upbraided him — and although the dignified and kindly old man quickly forgave his young protégé, and extended advice and help to him down to his death in 1693, the rebuke went far to break Wharton's spirit. He had failed in the moment of crisis; and his failings continued to the point of swearing the oath to William and Mary.[31] It did him little good: the livings to which Sancroft had presented him lapsed with the fall of the patron. Wharton went on to complete *Anglia Sacra* and dedicate it to Sancroft — and to write several more books and die, worn out by anxiety and toil, in 1695. In *Anglia Sacra* a rich collection of ecclesiastical chronicles and similar works are strung together in a series of diocesan histories. The work is marred by the intense haste of its author; and yet a prodigious work of scholarship too — with a scope and a scale, and knowledge of sources, which sets him among the greatest scholars of his day. He had not the flair of Jean Mabillon or the shrewd sense of Robert Brady; but it is an astonishing achievement of learning and devotion. 'Great numbers of learned men have published civil histories of the English, and are still at work on them today. Very few of our ecclesiastical histories have come forth.' This is the nearest to an acknowledgement to Brady that he gets, and it shows that the *Anglia Sacra* was designed to do for the Church what Brady had done for the feudal monarchy — 'I resolved to bring out of darkness into light a number of our ecclesiastical histories . . .'[32] When we consider that the project must have been conceived in the 1680s when

29 For Sancroft's aims see esp. G. V. Bennett in *Studies in Church History*, XV (1978), 267−87.
30 D'Oyly 1821, II, 135−7; cf. Douglas 1951, pp. 152−3 (which needs correction in detail). It is possible that Wharton really differed in principle from Sancroft, but this is not clear from what survives of his autobiography.
31 D'Oyly 1821, II, 136−7. For Wharton's moving account of his final visit to the dying archbishop, ibid., pp. 151−2.
32 Wharton 1691, I, p. ix; cf. the letter quoted in Douglas 1951, pp. 145−6.

Wharton was a scholar of Caius, and soon after the publication of Brady's major works — and that Wharton was already (by his own standards) a mature scholar before he left Cambridge, can we really believe that he was not in some sense influenced and inspired by Robert Brady? I do not believe so myself; I am sure there was a link; but it is difficult to trace with precision.

The other ecclesiastical historian bred in Caius in this time, Jeremiah or Jeremy Collier, became an unequivocally fervent non-juror.[33] He was an older man than Wharton, but much slower to mature. He was sizar and scholar from 1666 to 1676, then chaplain to the countess of Dorset and rector of a Suffolk parish. After the revolution he had to abandon hope of a regular benefice, and ministered to a non-juring congregation in London. In 1713 he was even elevated to the non-juring episcopate, and died a bishop in 1726. Meanwhile he had made his name as the hammer of Congreve and Vanbrugh and the theatre of his day, whose immorality he fervently denounced. He was one of the authors of the non-juror's service book, which in its turn influenced the Scottish Episcopalian liturgy and, more remotely, the Prayer Book of 1928. He was technically an outlaw but in practice left in peace. His most lasting book, the *Ecclesiastical History*, is a kind of complement to Brady; for it tells the story of medieval England from the Church's point of view, and denies the right of kings to control it. Though far from being a Catholic, he was a strong defender of Becket against Henry II; and it was the most notable study of its kind for over a century — yet he was not perhaps quite of the stature of Wharton or Brady.[34] Nor was he the only non-juring bishop bred in Caius. Richard Welton, scholar 1688–95, was a colleague of Collier in London, who, after preaching in 1710 on the advantage of navigation and commerce to the nation, was consecrated *c.* 1722 and shipped to Philadelphia, but died in Portugal on his return journey in 1726.

Bartholomew Wortley

The pattern the careers of Wharton and Collier suggest is of great interest for the history of the College. They show that the historical, antiquarian tastes of the Master spread down into the student body in this age, sufficiently to produce two of the most notable medieval scholars of the late 17th and early 18th centuries. They show a tide of Tory ecclesiastical idealism which went far beyond the Master's personal convictions. For

33 Cf. Douglas 1951, pp. 200–2; Venn, I, 428; *DNB*: article in *Oxford Dict. of Christian Church* (2nd edn. ed. F. L. Cross and E. A. Livingstone, Oxford, 1974), p. 314 and refs.
34 Douglas 1951, pp. 201–2. On Collier's consecration, see N. Sykes, *William Wake*, II (Cambridge, 1957), pp. 178–9. On his liturgical work, see Cuming 1982, pp. 141–6; Grisbrooke 1958. On Welton, see Venn, I, 484, and esp. his *The Substance of Christian Faith and Practice* (London, 1724 — to which Jonathan Clark kindly drew my attention).

Cambridge produced a multitude of non-jurors, including a score of fellows of St John's; and that Caius did not follow this example – and yet had the reputation later on of being the home of Tory and non-juring sympathies – we may in good measure ascribe to the Master's steady nerve and firm insistence in 1689. In 1691 the Master made a return about the oaths to the new regime: all the fellows, he was able to declare, had sworn the oaths, except the unfortunate Malachi Thurston, who 'is a distracted man', and Bartholomew Wortley, who was absent – and no-one knew where he was. It was, however, asserted that he too had sworn them, but the details were not known.[35] By this date Wortley had been in College for just on twenty years, and a fellow since 1679; he was by now a senior fellow and remained so till 1706, holding many college offices, including at this time that of Hebrew lecturer. He is included in at least one list of Cambridge non-jurors,[36] and Brady's statement about him sounds like an ingenious face-saving device. It is highly likely that he was in sympathy, and perhaps, in fact, a non-juror. If so, the College successfully protected him; for after he had been a fellow for over a quarter of a century, he was presented to the College living of Bratton Fleming in Devon which he held for forty-four more. He died in 1749, in his mid-90s, and left £7,000 and lands in Norfolk and Devon to the College, the steady accumulation of a long bachelor life. Well might it be said that he 'retained a strong attachment to the place of his education' – and perhaps of gratitude too, for sheltering him from the consequences of a deep-seated Jacobitism.[37] His will provided for two new fellowships, and was full of minute stipulations: 'one of my fellows shall always be of the name of Wortley, exclusive of the name of Wortley Montague or Montague Wortley, the other a North Devonshire man . . .' preferably from Bratton Fleming itself or the neighbourhood; his fellows should inspect the estates on which their foundations rested, and then might travel abroad for four of the years of the fellowship.[38] In the event, £400 was put towards the refacing of Gonville Court, and a substantial sum was laid out in buying property in Cambridge itself. The chief vestiges of this today are the playing fields on Barton Road and the south-east corner of Tree Court, where the Great Gate and the tower now stand. Here a charming statue of the late 1860s of Mr Wortley in the costume of his day presides over the staff bicycle shed; here and in Barton Road he has acquired a certain sporting aspect which would perhaps have surprised the old, retired, solitary rector of Bratton Fleming. The reason for the statue is that when Waterhouse was commissioned to replace the old buildings by the great French château which now dominates Tree Court, it was arranged that

---

35 Venn, I, 339, 445, from MS 602/678, p. 9, dated 17 Oct. 1691. For Wortley, see Venn, I, 444 – 5; III, 218 – 19.
36 Overton 1902, p. 496.
37 For the history of his bequest, see Venn, III, 218 – 19; ER, pp. 29 – 30. The will is in the Archives, Leases, Wills etc., pp. 253 – 66.
38 Leases, Wills etc., p. 254. For what follows, ER, pp. 29 – 30.

statues of the benefactors who had provided the buildings swept away should adorn the new. Thus Perse is to be seen where his building lay about the north-east corner; and where Wortley stands once stood a group of charming houses of the late 17th and 18th centuries, the chief of them called Barraclough's, which were bought in 1782 with his bequest, and provided lodging for students in the last half-century of their life. For particularity, Wortley's will seems modelled on Stephen Perse's, which the ex-bursar and senior fellow presumably knew well; and like Perse's and many others, his bequests were crowned with the endowment for a feast to lend warmth to a February evening.[39]

Bartholomew Wortley's tutor was John Ellys, and however much or little contact Brady may have had with the students of his day, we may reasonably suppose that the main work of tuition, of contact with schools and schoolmasters, with members old and new, lay with the tutors.[40] Whiston, in his *Historical Memoirs of the Life of Dr Samuel Clarke*, refers to Ellys as 'that eminent and careful tutor', a happy reminder that in his heyday he was probably just that — and that he and a group of younger men sustained the College in its academic side and inner life over the long years of Brady's mastership and beyond.[41] Ellys was only a little younger than Brady. He arrived, aged fourteen, from the customary Caian sources — he was a man of a Norfolk family, brought up in Suffolk; he was one of the last fellows elected under William Dell in 1659. In 1661 he became a senior fellow and held his fellowship till he was promoted Master in 1703; he died Master in 1716. He was by turns ethical lecturer, registrar, bursar, steward and dean; an admirable servant of the College until his last years, when he proved an exceedingly (if not altogether exceptionally) cantankerous Master and earned the soubriquet of the 'Devil of Caius'.[42] Meanwhile he was a symbol of continuity even more remarkable that Mr Wortley.

The clergy of Caius — Samuel Clarke

We have surveyed a few of the physicians and historians who grew up in the College in this era and observed something of the range of intellectual interests which could be fostered there. Nothing, however, is more difficult than to write an intellectual history of an academic society, however much it be the heart and core of its existence and its raison d'être. The great scholar like Brady had his contacts everywhere about the land, and hardly looked for close intellectual companionship among the fellows. Even though Newton spent many of his early years in Trinity great part of his life

39 It was to be held on 23 February when Wortley's obit was celebrated (it was not the day of his death, 8 May 1749): Venn, I, 445.
40 For Ellys see Venn, I, 370; III, 110−4.
41 Whiston 1730, p. 5.
42 Peter Le Neve, cited Venn, III, 111.

lay elsewhere, and a Trinity history of Newtonian physics would be a strangely mutilated affair. If Richard Bentley, Newton's younger colleague and friend, had found intellectual companions to his taste in Trinity, he would have talked with the fellows instead of belabouring them with insults and lawsuits; and the history of 18th century Cambridge would have been far different. In a measure we can still wander in the world of 18th century Caius among the books which survive in the library from that epoch — but even with them the question remains, how much were they read — is it not the least read which best survive? — And to what extent were the generality of students able to gain access to the library at all?[43] To that we have no answer, no clear answer indeed till 1928. But Wharton in the 1680s and Francis Blomefield a generation later very evidently found their way into the College library; and we may conjecture that this was always possible for a few especially privileged or persistent; that most hard reading men needed relatively few books by modern standards, most of which they would buy; and that the less assiduous needed none at all. Yet the problem remains. Trinity fitted up a magnificent library with ample space for the hard reading men to escape from the noisy fellow-commoners in the courts to peace and quiet in a large collection of books. Books there were in plenty in Caius, but no reading room worth the name — nor was one thought necessary when the library was rebuilt in 1853—4, nor in the modern sense till the 1920s. The young men of Caius did not have to escape from the gentlemen of Trinity. But this is not sufficient answer.

Yet the library urges us to think — and Venn's biographies demonstrate — that even Caius, with its medical and antiquarian tradition so firmly maintained, was first and foremost a seminary for Anglican clergy. The library shows a very wide range of intellectual interest, from Dugdale's and Brady's works and Blaeu's atlas to the treatises of Harvey and Glisson and their colleagues. But here is much solid theological fare too — sermons and biblical texts and editions; only what one misses is the wide, almost ecumenical flavour of Branthwaite's reading: popish literature and the best of the dissenters are noticeable by their absence. But for what it is worth, the general pattern confirms the evidence of the historical record, that the College mainly bred parish clergy.

Among the clergy two names stand out preeminent: Samuel Clarke, who came in 1690, and Thomas Gooch, in 1691.[44] Gooch rose to be Master and three times a bishop — he belongs to a later page, for he was essentially a

---

43 On college libraries in the 17th and 18th centuries, see Wordsworth 1877, chap. 1 — and for curricula and reading lists ibid., *passim*; cf. Ferguson 1976, pp. 4—5. Wordsworth's prejudice against the lesser colleges sometimes misleads him, e.g. into confusing Uffenbach's account of the upper room in Caius, where the MSS were kept, with the library; but his pride in Trinity was natural and just. See Wordsworth 1877, p. 3; Mayor, 1911, pp. 133—5; Gaskell and Robson 1971; below, p. 215. For fellow-commoners, see p. 185.

44 On Gooch, see chap. 9. On Samuel Clarke see esp. Ferguson 1976; also Venn, I, 488, 504; *DNB*; and the contemporary life, Whiston 1730.

political prelate and a college politician. Clarke was a major figure in the intellectual history of the late 17th and early 18th centuries. He was the son of a Norwich alderman and MP; he and his younger brother John (who came to Caius in 1699) both had a strong mathematical-physical bent and were ardent disciples of Newton. He was a junior fellow from 1696 to 1700, then married a Norfolk wife, and by her had seven children, none of whom, it seems, followed him to Caius. From 1709 he was rector of St James, Piccadilly, and a familiar figure in London clerical and intellectual society.

His first book (1697) was an improved Latin translation of Rohault's *Physica*; for Latin was more intelligible than the French of the original to an English academic audience.[45] This text-book of Cartesian philosophy was basic reading in Cambridge, and it was Ellys, his tutor, who set him to work on it. Already, however, he was under the spell of Newton, whose physical theories had much modified the Cartesian basis of Cambridge teaching in this field; and in 1706 Clarke published a Latin translation of Newton's *Optics* — which had been written in English — to make it available to the academic communities of Europe. Newton was delighted, and gave Clarke £500 — £100 apiece for the five children that had come so far.[46] His work with Newton brought him into close touch with William Whiston, who later wrote Clarke's *Life*, and the three between them formed a heretical trio: Newton the original mind, penetrating through his cosmological speculations and biblical study to doubts of the traditional theology of the Trinity; Clarke the lecturer and preacher, ready to publish and engage in controversy, but wishing to avoid a scandal so violent as to lead to schism; and Whiston, always urging on Clarke the logical consequence of his doctrines, pressing him on the dangerous road to denial of the 39 Articles. Newton was cautious, and for the most part kept his silence in these heretical regions. Clarke went forward from his Boyle Lectures, published in 1704−5, on the bases of Natural Religion; through the act for his DD in 1709, celebrated in the annals of the University Schools — when the Regius Professor of Divinity, after hours of fluent argument in Latin, urbanely closed the disputation by saying 'you have sufficiently proved *me*'; to *The Scripture Doctrine of the Trinity* in 1712.[47] In this he argued for the primacy of God the Father in a manner which went at least as far as the Arians of the 4th century, and in tendency beyond — in his later years he was helping to lay the foundations of 18th century Unitarian thought. This work produced a storm of controversy; and Clarke himself rejected the Athanasian creed,

45 Ferguson 1976, pp. 6−7; Mayor 1911, pp. 280−1.
46 Ferguson 1976, p. 35; for what follows see ibid. esp. chaps. 3, 5.
47 Mayor 1911, pp. 333−4; Ferguson 1976, pp. 40−1. On Newton and his influence on Clarke, see Hunter 1981, pp. 186−7, 216 and works there cited (nos. 309−11); and esp. E. Duffy's forthcoming paper in the *British Journal for the History of Science*. On the affair of the Trinity Sunday Communion see Ferguson 1976, pp. 57−8; on Wigston's Hospital, pp. 152−3, 208; on the meeting with Walpole, p. 209. I am very grateful for the help of Eamon Duffy and Jonathan Clark in this passage.

even on one occasion refusing to celebrate Communion in St James's on Trinity Sunday to avoid the Trinitarian formula of the Proper Preface. In later years he refused to subscribe the 39 Articles, and the only preferment he would accept was the Mastership of Wigston Hospital at Leicester, for which no subscription was needed. But he held St James's till his death. He had powerful friends among the bishops and at court; and the princess of Wales — later Queen Caroline — engaged him in her efforts to reconcile Newton and Leibniz, which led Clarke into a correspondence with the German philosopher on natural theology which was closed by Leibniz's death in 1716. When Caroline was queen she set to work to make Clarke a bishop, and Kensington Palace witnessed in 1727 the curious spectacle of Samuel Clarke and Sir Robert Walpole deep in theological discussion till far into the night. Clarke knew well that though he had friends in the episcopate, the leading bishops would never consecrate him, and so he died in 1729 rector of St James's — by some reviled as the heretic of the age, by others revered as preacher and pastor, and honoured by a few as the mouthpiece of rational theology. He was not in the front rank of theologians, but an eminent exponent of a theology and biblical exegesis deeply imbued with the rationalism of the enlightenment.

The East Anglian connection

Brady, Ellys, Wortley, the Clarkes — all were East Anglians, from places and people who had bred most of the scholars and fellows of Gonville Hall and of Caius College for 350 years. Throughout the period between Caius and Brady there is a substantial element from other regions.[48] We have met the Yorkists and the Devonians of c. 1600. In the 1660s there is an element of Londoners, and a scatter from every region, including Cheshire and Lancashire.[49] There is a notable element of Cambridge men. In 1661 John Green, son of a Cambridge tailor, came from the Perse, and with him William Peters, son of the College butler; both became fellows, Peters for nearly twenty years.[50] The College servants prospered indeed: the son of the former butler of King's appears in the list in 1674. We have already encountered Christopher Green, another Perse boy and the future Regius Professor of Physic.[51]

Yet East Anglia prevails, and increasingly. The scatter of names from other regions grows less as the decades pass. It never disappears, but by 1700 we are prepared for the characteristic situation of the 18th century, when the recruitment was more local, and the College more provincial,

48 Cf. Venn, I, pp. xiii—xiv and *passim*.
49 See esp. Venn, I, 418, 425—6.
50 Venn, I, 415.
51 Venn, I, 433, 450, and above, p. 147.

than at any time since the 14th.[52] At the same time the numbers entering the College dwindled. It is hard to interpret these declining figures. When Venn prepared the statistical tables on which all study of university statistics has since been based, he observed that the rise and fall of Caius admissions — unlike most of the larger- or medium-sized colleges — has usually followed quite closely the general pattern in the university.[53] This precludes us from regarding local causes of declining numbers as decisive; yet such must have existed, and there are some significant differences between Caius and university trends. The College had held its numbers well in the 1630s when university decline was already under way; but the sharp decline of the 1640s struck everywhere: Caius fell from 34 or 35 a year to 27 and down to 21 or 22 in the 1650s and 1660s. In the university at large, however, there was a sharp increase in the 1660s not reflected in the College, then a decline till 1700. The College figures fell to an average of 12 a year in the 1690s, 11 in the 1700s; but they rose somewhat in the 1710s, to fall away again to 9 a year in the 1730s and less still later in the century. Compared with the heyday of Elizabethan and Jacobean Caius these were pitiful figures indeed. Equally striking are the figures of the chosen professions of Caians. In the five years 1680−5, out of 103 admissions, some 36 became clergymen, and all but a handful country parsons; 9 succeeded to family estates; 19 went to Inns of Court, en route for a legal profession or to return home to live as gentry; 5 became physicians; of 28 the fate is unknown; and 4 died while they were students. A hundred years later, in 1780−5, only 45 entered; 3 died as students; one was a fellow-commoner and a baronet; two, including the celebrated Dr Wollaston, became physicians — while 39 became clergy. The College had become a seminary.

In the declining numbers there were some compensations for the resident community. Space was more plentiful at a time when standards of living and of elegance were rising; and the splendid panelling of the best sets in Caius Court, and the more modest panelling of their neighbours, belongs to this time. In 1696 a College Order decreed that 'If any fellow desired to have his chamber wainscotted, and it was done at the College charge, the common chest should receive yearly' a wainscot rent of £5 per cent per annum — and one substantial charge for such work appears in the accounts for 1697 (see pl. 15).[54]

Some of the reasons for the decline are clear. After the Civil War and Commonwealth a university dedicated to educating members of the Anglican Church alone could not command the support of the Catholics or Dissenters — they looked for their education elsewhere. Furthermore, even

52 The proportion c. 1700 was roughly 2 from Norfolk and Suffolk to 1 from elsewhere: Venn, I, 504−6, etc.
53 Venn, III, 392 and chart. The statistics of professions are based on Venn, I, II, but the figures are deceptively precise for the late 17th century, since there are a number of insecure identifications.
54 Venn, III, 109; Bursar's Book s.a. 1697 etc.

if the Cambridge of Newton and Brady must be regarded as one of the major intellectual centres of the age of the scientific revolution, the real centres of intellectual life moved inexorably away.[55] Newton was as much at home in the Royal Society in London as in his garden outside the Great Gate of Trinity. The university had shown much more adaptability to new ideas and new subjects in the late 16th and early 17th centuries than it was to do in the late 17th and 18th — even though mathematics won through at this time as a major field, and began its climb to the eminence it held by the late 18th century, when university eminence was measured by the mathematical wranglers alone.[56] Cambridge — not just Caius — was becoming a provincial backwater.

Titus Oates

We have looked at some of the heroes of our story, and to bring the matter into a proper proportion and balance, we must conclude with a word on its villains. We may doubt if John Clarke, famous in the annals of the university library as the only fellow of Caius (so far) to be expelled from his fellowship for stealing books from the library (1696), was really in this class — even if the library had to pay for a cart to move its property back home.[57] But of Titus Oates there can be no doubt. This remarkable man came in 1667 — and it is slightly misleading, as a worthy Caian of the same generation, Adam Elyott, said of him, to say 'that he and the plague both visited the University in the same year', for the other plague struck in June 1666; but it lasted into 1667 and a few months after it had departed it was replaced by Titus Oates.[58] Adam Elyott was later to have adventures much more interesting than Oates' — on his way back from a tutoring trip to Italy he was captured by Barbary pirates, sold as a slave and only escaped after some adventures out of the Arabian Nights.[59] These were described in a pamphlet he wrote to rescue himself from another scrape — from a charge by Oates that he was a Jesuit in disguise. Elyott portrays his fellow-Caian as having been 'very remarkable for a canting fanatical way conveyed to him by his Anabaptistical education; and in our Academical exercises when others declaimed Oates always preached.'[60] His tutor, John Ellys, alleged,

55 See Hunter 1981 and its admirable bibliography.
56 See Feingold 1984; cf. below, p. 189. Mathematical Tripos lists were published from 1748, wranglers placed in order from 1753 (Tanner 1917, pp. 352, 443).
57 An older man than Samuel's brother — Venn, I, 468; see the forthcoming *Cambridge University Library: a History*, by John Oates and David McKitterick. Charles Burney was detected removing books from CUL in 1777; but he was a pensioner, not a fellow; and though he rapidly departed from Caius he later made good, returned briefly in 1807—8, was given a Lambeth DD and 'his large library was bought for the British Museum' (Venn, II, 99). There is a monument to him in Westminster Abbey.
58 Venn, I, 43; Venn 1913, p. 176. On Oates see esp. Kenyon 1972, chaps. 3, 8.
59 Venn 1913, pp. 174—90.
60 Quoted Venn 1913, p. 176.

perhaps with the wisdom of hindsight, that he 'was a liar from the beginning: he stole or cheated his tailor of a gown, which he denied with horrid imprecations'.[61] He came to Caius in 1667, and moved to St John's in 1669, going down without a degree.[62] By 1677 he was a spy in the Jesuit College in Valladolid, from which he was expelled even more expeditiously than from Cambridge – and returned to spread his notorious invention, the Popish Plot. It is horrifying to recall how many of his lies were believed, how handsome a living he made of them; and even after his exposure and condemnation to the pillory and brutal punishment, he staged a come-back and found a following. The only thing genuine about Oates was his love of preaching, and he was still preaching in Wapping about 1700; but in 1705 the plague finally departed with his death.[63] Among Caians he enjoys a fame only approached by William Harvey.

61 Quoted Venn, I, 431.
62 *Admissions to the College of St John the Evangelist in the University of Cambridge*, II (Cambridge, 1893), p. 20: admitted sub-sizar 2 Feb. 1668/9, formerly admitted to Caius 29 June 1667.
63 *DNB*.

9

The Eighteenth Century[1]

Clerical fellows and College livings

After Brady's death in 1700 the College was presided over by three elderly men who had all been resident for forty years or so. John Gostlin, great-nephew of the Master, sprung from a family of Norfolk merchants, had had to flee to Peterhouse in the 1650s to escape from William Dell. He returned to be fellow of Caius in 1661, and President from 1679 till his death in 1705; a devout Caian, as appears from the brief history of the College in his time which he wrote, from his tomb in the chapel and from some substantial gifts to the College: a man 'of the greatest skill in good literature and in the happy art of healing' — an MD like his great-uncle and Brady.[2] The second was James Halman or Holman, who came in 1655 and was a fellow from 1662; after long service in many College offices and as University Registrary, he was elected Master in 1700, and died in 1702, to be succeeded by the old tutor John Ellys.[3] Ellys had a moment of glory in 1705 when he was Vice-Chancellor, and Queen Anne came to Cambridge and knighted him. But he lived too long; and well before his death in 1716 he was locked in hopeless conflict with the fellowship.[4] From early in 1709 he took to exercising his negative vote on every issue from the appointment to a College living to an annual audit or a fellowship election. In 1714 the Visitors overruled him on this issue and thereafter some decisions could be made in his absence. But he became steadily more difficult and more querulous. An attempt to unseat him altogether in 1715 failed: the reason is not clear, but the Master's policy was to stay firmly in the lodge, and external authority was always slow to move. His own complaints are noted in one surviving list, and it is evident that he thought the younger fellows disrespectful, and too inclined to follow their own courses. Venn was evidently right to see in the quarrels the gap between age and youth. No doubt Ellys had been accustomed to a community in which the aging Brady had been supported by the equally senior triumvirate of Gostlin, Halman and Ellys; and when his comrades departed Ellys tried to carry on alone. A new generation had arisen

---

1 In this chapter, as well as the writings of Venn, I have made much use of Winstanley 1922 and 1935 — and for the early 18th century, as all students must, of Monk's *Life of Bentley* (Monk 1830).
2 Venn, I, 369; for his tomb, III, 168.
3 Venn, I, 391; III, 110.
4 Venn, I, 110–14; cf. I, 370.

which wished — and needed — to have a say; and the old man failed in sympathy and temper. His one ally was his nephew, John Ellys, a fellow since 1690.[5] In his will the old Master left him executor and residuary legatee, for 'the affectionate and faithful care, labour and vigilance' he had shown, and the vexation he had suffered and was likely still to suffer. The fellowship enquired of the younger Ellys if the College was concerned in his uncle's will — and he informed them that the College was 'not at all concerned'. It was a sad end to a career of lifelong service.

As the College grew smaller its function as a nursery of country clergy became more pronounced. The young scholar of promise or talent, or supported by the right kind of patronage, was promoted fellow; and when he wished to marry he hoped for a College living to provide for his wife and family and career. For 150 years the College livings were, in the eyes of many of the fellows, the most valuable property the College possessed. It is no accident that the centre of Gostlin's benefaction should be an advowson, or the start of many a quarrel within the fellowship a presentation.[6] When Hethersett in Norfolk came to the College from Gostlin's will, Caius already had the advowsons of the four churches which were its original endowment; also of St Michael Coslany in Norwich, which was acquired in 1441 and formed a vacation home for a succession of Masters in the late 15th and early 16th centuries; of Bincombe (Dorset), acquired with the manor by Dr Caius; of Bratton Fleming (Devon), which had come in 1667 in good time to provide for Mr Wortley; and a few others. Between 1705 and 1736 nine more were added, including Hethersett from Gostlin and Denver, also in Norfolk, from the estate of Brady — after a transaction of infinite complexity made by Brady's executor; and no fewer than six from a handsome bequest from Stephen Camborne, a Caian who died rector of Lawshall in 1704.[7] Camborne's relations pointed out that he had left £3,000 for the purchase of an advowson — and everyone knew it would purchase several — and that he had spelt the college Keys which no Caian in his right mind would do; and they took the will into Chancery. After careful local enquiry the Lord Chancellor decided with commendable despatch, after only two years' delay, that it was a perfectly reasonable way to spell the College — 'Caius College is commonly called Keys College' — and that advowson or advowsons was neither here nor there to a chancery draftsman; so the College won the suit and no fewer than six were bought wholly or partly with the money, including the valuable living attached to the magnificent

---

5 Venn, I, 472; for what follows, III, 113–14. But the nephew was never a senior. In 1710, to judge from the indications in Venn, one senior, John Lightwine, was well over 50, 2–3 40 or more (one died in 1710); 4 in their 30s; 5 in their 20s; Ellys was by then in his late 70s.

6 Venn, III, 111. For the College livings, see ibid. 280–1, 311–22; VI, 558–63; VII, 545–7 and ER *passim*; some of the information has been brought up to date in an unpublished paper by Catherine Hall and C. B. For Denver see *ER*, p. 38.

7 See p. 136; and for what follows, Venn, I, 395, based on *Registrum Magnum*, pp. 683–4. There is a copy of the will in Archives, *Leases, Wills etc.*, p. 61.

church of Lavenham in Suffolk.

Camborne lived much like Wortley, though a poorer man in a poorer benefice; 'yet by living with great frugality to a good old age, he raised a considerable estate', and nourished the ambition to be remembered as a benefactor. Wortley himself expected a part of his benefaction to be used for buying livings, and so it was, but not till much later, in the 1810s. By then the main tale of college livings was made up, though a few additions came later, right down to the acquisition of St Mary's Stockport — far removed from the College's normal pastures — by the gift of a Caian incumbent in 1910. Meanwhile they remained possessions greatly treasured by the fellows until the mid and late 19th century. When the rule of celibacy for fellows was abolished in 1860 and teaching became a profession for life — and above all, with the secularisation of learning and even of Cambridge — they gradually lost their role for the fellowship. H. B. Swete continued to enjoy the college living of Ashdon in Essex (since lost to the College by exchange for Chatteris) while he was Professor of Pastoral Theology at King's London; but when he returned to Cambridge to the Regius Chair of Divinity in 1890, he resigned it.[8] Meanwhile a junior fellow called Woodhouse had been presented to Bratton Fleming in 1875, and held it till 1913.[9] Arthur Duncan-Jones' departure to Blofield in 1912 was the last such move so far. By then the fellowship's grip on the college livings had relaxed. The large majority of clergy presented to them remained Caians till the Second World War; but the concern of the fellowship had subsided. None the less, the Patronage Committee is still an active body and the role of colleges in patronage was defended with great vigour and success in the National Synod of the Church of England by Professor Geoffrey Lampe in the 1970s when he was a professorial fellow. Few Caians now present themselves as candidates, but the College is still sole patron of five livings, shares patronage of nine — mainly in Norfolk and Suffolk — and has a vestige of patronage in two.[10]

In the 18th century, in spite of the preponderance of clergy in the fellowship, and the great interest they took in the college livings, the society still had a significant lay element, and three of the Masters of the century, James Halman, Sir John Ellys and Sir James Burrough, were laymen. In compensation, the Master who filled the space between them, Sir Thomas Gooch, Bart., was first an archdeacon, then thrice a bishop.

---

8 Venn, II, 316; III, 321.

9 Venn, II, 327—8; VI, 560.

10 See n. 6. One likes to think that Theodore Venables, 'sometime Scholar of Caius Coll: Camb:', in Dorothy Sayers' *Nine Tailors*, was a characteristic Caius incumbent of the 1920s and 30s.

Cambridge and politics — Tory and Whig

In contrast to those of the 17th century, the elections of Halman and Ellys were noteworthy for the absence of outside intervention. No one who has read Winstanley's books and followed the amazing adventures of the duke of Newcastle as Chancellor (1748—68) will imagine that Cambridge became a backwater, free of politics and the court. Newcastle in his way was to be as active as Fisher or Cecil in the 16th century, but it was not their way.[11] He proceeded by patronage and intrigue. The universities had asserted a measure of independence in the early 18th century and the attempt to force appointments on them tended to languish or be resisted; furthermore, the Chancellor of Cambridge before Newcastle, the duke of Somerset, who reigned from 1689 to 1748, had lived in retirement since 1716 and had neither the power nor the will to do much harm.[12] Newcastle never reckoned to have the direct fiat some earlier chancellors had wielded, but so long as he held high office in the government — that is, till 1762 — he had the power of patronage, especially compelling to the clergy; and even after his fall from power in Westminster he managed by a virtuoso combination of the techniques of political management, intrigue, bad temper, fuss and sheer activity, to keep a remarkable grip on some sections of Cambridge society. When he fell from power in Westminster Dr Zachary Brooke of St John's made the fatal error of abandoning his flag — and so lost the chance to become Master of St John's. The secret of Newcastle's success lay wholly in politics. He was the arch-Whig, grand master of patronage, corruption and Whiggery — though he never took bribes himself, and had some awareness of political principles. Caius was throughout this period predominantly a Tory College, and his influence there was slight; he rarely if ever tried to intervene in its affairs. But without visible effort he won a convert in Thomas Gooch, the Master; and Gooch was for years one of his principal helpers in Cambridge, and in return enjoyed promotion to three bishoprics. He paid for it by falling ever more out of sympathy with the fellows of Caius.

If we ask the question, what did Whig and Tory mean in this context? — we shall find no easy answer. Sir Lewis Namier preached the doctrine a generation ago that they were meaningless labels and that the keys to 18th century politics must be sought elsewhere, thus rendering the Cambridge politics of the century unintelligible.[13] Now a group of scholars has arisen

11 See esp. Winstanley 1922.
12 On Somerset as Chancellor, see *DNB*; for his death, and Newcastle's election, Winstanley 1922, pp. 36—47.
13 I am very much indebted to Jonathan Clark for help in this passage. The classic study is L. B. Namier, *The Structure of Politics at the Accession of George III* (2 vols., London, 1929). The chief contributions to revision of his views on the Tories before 1750 have come from Linda Colley (Colley 1977, 1982), Eveline Cruickshanks (Cruickshanks 1979) and Jonathan Clark (Clark 1978, 1982, 1983) — and his forthcoming *English Society 1688—1832* will stress the continuing importance of Jacobite and royalist ideology.

who have revived the Tory party, but not yet made it much easier for modern spectators to understand. An exciting historical argument is in full swing, and it is far from clear what will emerge. It is now agreed that the Tories survived as a coherent political group down to about 1750. There is no agreement yet how large a place opposition to the Hanoverian dynasty, Jacobitism of varying complexions, played in preserving the Tory image. But it is already apparent that the Tories, like most political parties in recorded history, were a complex mixture of personal alliance, tradition and ideology; and that even the Whigs had principles as well as devising an impressive machinery of political corruption. Yet if one cares anything for political morality one cannot but sympathise with the moral implied in the *Beggar's Opera* of 1728 — commenting on the world of Robert Walpole — 'that the lower sort of people have their vices in a degree as well as the rich: and that *they* are punish'd for them'.

The first Whig, according to Dr Johnson, was the devil; the first Whig in Cambridge — in stature though not in time — was Dr Bentley, Master of Trinity from 1700 to 1742. He was an immortal classical scholar whose fame alone would have prevented Cambridge seeming quite the provincial backwater most of his colleagues were conspiring to make it. He was over forty years Master of Trinity and behaved in a manner so outrageous to his colleagues as to earn A. E. Housman's famous jest that when he was at his most cavalier as a critic he treated the manuscripts of Manilius as if they were fellows of Trinity.[14] At the very end of his life the lawsuits fell away from him and the attempts to remove him from the Trinity Lodge ceased; and then (one suspects) the old man lost heart and died. Except in his own hearth and home, he loved strife above all else, and he found an opponent almost worthy of his steel in Dr Gooch of Caius. Bentley's chosen weapons were the law's delay, which he traded on with such success that on one occasion one of his judges, a bishop of Ely, died on the eve of giving judgement against him; on another, his affairs fell into the hands of Sir E. Northey who, 'though a lawyer of great fame, did not possess the gift of despatch'; and on yet another the whole House of Lords found the affairs of Trinity so entertaining they voted to dedicate a Saturday to an entirely fruitless debate upon them.[15]

Sir Thomas Gooch

Thomas Gooch came of a well-to-do Norfolk family, and his younger brother rose to be Lieutenant-Governor of Virginia and was awarded a baronetcy, which Thomas inherited.[16] Thomas was born in 1675 and came

14 A. E. Housman, *Manilii Astronomicon*, I (2nd edn., Cambridge, 1937), p. xviii; for what follows, Monk 1830.
15 Monk 1830, pp. 285, 324, 596.
16 On Gooch, see Venn, I, 489; III, 115–25.

to Caius as a pupil of Ellys in 1691, rising in due course to be junior and senior fellow, and to hold a succession of College offices, culminating in the bursarship in 1710. About this time he became chaplain to Compton, the bishop of London, and to Queen Anne, and laid the foundations in Compton's service of his later career. He was a notable pluralist, but for many years his chief benefice was the archdeaconry of Essex, in Compton's diocese, which he held from 1714 to 1737.[17] Already by 1710 he was well known in Cambridge as a staunch Tory, and there was a famous story of how the Proctor had tried to break up a dinner party in the Rose in that year, at which the two MPs for the University, and Sir John Cotton, MP for the City, were present — and among them Mr Gooch of Caius.[18] He was clearly a man of parts. He preached before the Commons in 1712, and before the Lord Mayor in 1713, in honour of his dead master the bishop of London. He had a growing circle of friends, led by his brother-in-law, Thomas Sherlock, Master of St Catharine's from 1714 to 1719 and dean of Chichester — to whom Gooch doubtless owed the 'residentiary' canonry he enjoyed at Chichester from 1719 — and later, like Gooch, bishop of three different sees.[19] The reputations of Cambridge men of his era have suffered from the profuse and caustic pen of the Jacobite William Cole — as have those of the late 18th century from the friendlier, but equally candid, pen of Henry Gunning. But though Cole has many harsh things to say about Gooch, he saw his charm too. 'As I have hinted that he was a man of as great art, craft, design, and cunning, as any in the age he lived in, so I must also bear my testimony that he was as much of a gentleman in his outward appearance, carriage, and behaviour as ever it was my good fortune to converse with. He was a man also of the most agreeable, lively, and pleasant conversation, full of merry tales and lively conceits, yet one who well knew the respect that was due to his character; . . . always free and easy of access to all those who had any sort of pretension to it. His company and conversation were coveted by everyone . . .' — and he characteristically goes on to instance his enjoyment of the company of hearty drinkers — 'not that I would insinuate that he was ever given to that vice'. He was always neatly and cleanly dressed and 'wore his own fine grey locks without a powder in them, so his scarf, gown and cassock were never soiled'.[20] Such was the man the fellows of Caius chose for their Master in 1716, when he was forty-one

17 Horn 1969, p. 9.
18 Monk 1830, pp. 224–5.
19 Venn, III, 122; Horn 1971, pp. 8, 53, 78; for Sherlock see *DNB*; Carpenter 1936 (esp. pp. 47, 314–16 for his relations with Gooch). He was successively bishop of Bangor, Salisbury and London. Owing to the patronage of Queen Caroline, Sherlock was able to become a bishop and a courtier without ceasing to be a Tory, and one of the Tory clergy who drew close to Newcastle. By the time he became bishop of London in 1748 the old distinction of Whig and Tory was fading away. He and Gooch remained firm friends, and he stoutly supported Gooch's promotion, though he underwent no such 'conversion' as Gooch's. (I owe help here to Jonathan Clark.)
20 Cole, quoted in Venn, III, 118–19.

— doubtless for his friendly disposition and good fellowship, as well as his reputation as an influential Tory.

The Vice-Chancellor of the University was by custom nominated by the Heads of Houses for election by the Senate; and to save undignified confusion, they normally chose the senior Head who was a doctor and had not held the office before. Thus it rotated annually and was usually held by one of the most junior of the Heads.[21] But in the age of Bentley and Gooch affairs were differently conducted, for every election was a political event; and the conflicts which swirled round the Master of Trinity, as a leading Whig, naturally concentrated the minds of the Tories. On 4 November 1717 came the election of the Vice-Chancellor, and the Tory Master of Caius triumphed over the Whig Master of Corpus (Dr Bradford) by 95 votes to 51.[22] One may reckon Sherlock, his brother-in-law, the brains of the university government, but the Vice-Chancellor was its active and effective hand. The Vice-Chancellor was Visitor of Corpus, and he proceeded against his defeated rival, who had recently had his son elected fellow by a tiny caucus. But Bradford was a Whig, and in an instant promoted bishop of Carlisle — and he obtained a royal Order in Council preventing Gooch interfering in Corpus, and had him deprived of his royal chaplaincy, which was given to another of the victims of his jurisdiction.[23]

None of this impeded Gooch's steps against the Master of Trinity. At the Rose in 1710 had also dined Conyers Middleton, a man of much greater academic stature than Gooch, and one of the most implacable enemies of Bentley. He complained to the Vice-Chancellor of a fee which Bentley as Regius Professor of Divinity had extracted from him, and Bentley was threatened with arrest. In fairness to Gooch, he consulted the other Heads and really tried to settle the matter out of court — but to his letter Bentley made answer by paying his celebrated visit to the Caius Lodge and saying to the Master's face that 'he would not be judged by him and his friends over a bottle'.[24] He was convinced that the Tory Gooch would do him no justice and played for time till another Vice-Chancellor should sit in his place — a foolish manoeuvre, one would have thought, since the Tories predictably kept Gooch in office for three years running to undo this device.[25] Bentley was summoned time and again to the Vice-Chancellor's court, and failed to appear or to answer, and when the Esquire Bedell was sent to Trinity Lodge, the Master of Trinity repeated his reference to Gooch and the bottle. There followed a solemn meeting of the Court at which the Esquire Bedell's evidence, exasperated 'by the joint action of resentment and of gout', led to a peremptory sentence: Gooch declared Bentley deprived of all his degrees.[26]

21 Winstanley 1935, pp. 8—16, esp. 13.
22 Monk 1830, p. 368.
23 Monk 1830, pp. 371—2.
24 Monk 1830, p. 373; ibid., pp. 372—83 describe this part of the saga.
25 Monk 1830, pp. 373—8, 420 ff.
26 Monk 1830, pp. 374—7, esp. 376.

The sentence was later confirmed by the Senate, but ultimately, after long and bitter argument and endless delay, declared null by the Court of King's Bench in a classic application of the principles of natural justice — and its only known effect on Bentley was to give him an excuse, since he could not wear his hood, of absenting himself from College Chapel for some years; for so long indeed that it was said that when he returned he found his pew locked and could not gain entrance.[27] Meanwhile Gooch had acted with decision, but not wisely; yet it was difficult to act wisely in the face of the most redoubtable and unscrupulous of university politicians. By a curious irony, Gooch and Bentley had much in common: they were both arch-deacons, longing for bishoprics. Bentley, being also king's librarian, had wished to be on good terms with Harley when he was Tory minister — and was ever after viewed with suspicion by the Whigs; Gooch was simply a Tory. Years later, in 1724, Bentley was offered the bishopric of Bristol:[28] he refused, since it was too poorly endowed for his rapacious tastes; but it may well be that this event had some influence on Gooch, for not long after he himself became a Whig, and after an almost intolerable delay was himself consecrated bishop of Bristol in 1737, at the age of sixty-two: such was the price he had paid for his long years as a Tory. Meanwhile, at the height of the dispute with Bentley, the story was told that one of the Master of Trinity's heated supporters fired a shot into the Lodge at Caius, and years afterwards the hole in the panelling where it entered was shown to their visitors by those who had been courageous enough to enter so dangerous an office.[29] To a medievalist this vision of the archdeacon of Ely embattled against the archdeacon of Essex inevitably brings to mind the picture of John of Salisbury, in the 12th century, congratulating an old friend just promoted archdeacon on having his ancient doubts resolved as to whether archdeacons could be saved.[30] It was a nice question.

But the epic conflict across Trinity Lane has a happier epilogue. Both men were fond of children: Bentley made his son a member of the College at ten, a fellow at fifteen; Gooch was more modest, only admitting his sons at sixteen, and only making one of them a fellow, when he was twenty. Bentley's grandson recalls how 'Once, and only once, I recollect [my grand-father] giving me a gentle rebuke for making a most outrageous noise in the room over his library and disturbing him in his studies; I had no appre-hension of anger from him, and confidently answered that I could not help it, as I had been at battledore and shuttlecock with Master Gooch, the bishop of Ely's son. "And I have been at this sport with his father", he replied; "but thine has been the more amusing game; so there's no harm

27 Monk 1830, pp. 494−6, 555−6 and 556 n.
28 Monk 1830, p. 499.
29 Monk 1830, pp. 396−7; Venn, III, 117. Monk alleges that the bullet was actually found during repairs a few years before he was writing (i.e. early in the 19th century).
30 *Letters of John of Salisbury*, II, ed. W. J. Millor and C. N. L. Brooke (Oxford Medieval Texts, 1979), pp. 24−5, no. 140.

done".'[31]

Thus Bentley must take some share in the responsibility for the corruption of Gooch — if such it was; for in a sense it was a true conversion, from the world of Harley and Swift in which he was brought up, to that of Walpole and Newcastle; and from one profession to another, for Gooch had nothing more to contribute to academic life. In this progress he followed his brother-in-law, Bishop Sherlock, who eventually became Newcastle's leading episcopal supporter. It was probably in 1727 that Mr Dixie Windsor, MP, another of the diners of 1710, came to visit Gooch when he came canvassing in Cambridge, 'whom he found shaving himself' says Cole; and he complained that the University was much altered and that if the court party sent up a broomstick they would vote for it, he believed; to which Gooch 'said very gravely "and so must I too" '.[32] 'Gooch' was pronounced 'Gotch' by Bentley — a dialect word for jug — 'that empty Gotch'; but after this incident it seems he acquired the nickname Broomstick. In 1730 he drew the first fruits of Whiggery, a canonry in Canterbury Cathedral, and he offered to resign the Mastership.[33] But at this date his relations with the fellows were still good, and they dissuaded him. The leading characters of the College were, however, Tory, and the Master's conversion was bound to cast a shadow over the Combination Room, still more when he became a bishop. In 1737 Gooch became bishop of Bristol, 'where he stayed so short a time' so Cole alleged, 'as never to have visited his diocese'.[34] In 1737 the duke of Newcastle began his career of management and control in the University. A genuine affection for Cambridge entered into his motives; and if managing the House of Commons was his profession, managing the University of Cambridge was his hobby. But it had a serious side, for his patronage greatly affected the prosperity of the University; while giving it a savour of political life which saved it from becoming hopelessly provincial, he gave it more than a savour of the political corruption of the day. Of this Gooch must in the end be taken to be a notable example. In 1737 Newcastle was elected High Steward; in 1737−8 Gooch became in rapid succession bishop of Bristol and Norwich.[35] In 1739 the Caius antiquary Francis Blomefield published the first volume of his

31 Monk 1830, p. 650; cf. ibid., pp. 423, 528; Venn, II, 43, 58. In fact Gooch must have been bishop of Norwich at the time.

32 Quoted by Venn, III, 118. The date seems confirmed by Monk 1830, p. 564, which shows Gooch acting in the Whig interest in the University in 1730. For 'Gotch' see Monk 1830, p. 374; for 'broomstick' Venn, III, 118 n. On Sherlock see above, n. 19.

33 Venn, III, 119; Horn 1974, p. 33; he held it *in commendam* with the bishopric of Bristol 1737−8 and resigned it on translation to Norwich. It was normal then to hold other preferment with bishoprics as poor as Bristol, which Bentley reckoned would not pay the expenses of attendance in the Lords, let alone a visit to Bristol (see n. 28).

34 Venn, III, 115.

35 For Newcastle's election, Winstanley 1922, p. 37; for Gooch's promotions, Venn, III, 115; cf. II, 20. For the support he received from his brother-in-law, Bishop Sherlock, who had earlier tried to secure for him the bishopric of St Asaph, see Carpenter 1936, pp. 47, 314−16.

History of Norfolk, and in reference to a charity which Gooch had revived in his new see said it 'must make others, with the author, pray that it would please God long to preserve him amongst us'. 'I am apt to think', said Cole, 'that the bishop did not heartily say Amen to this, as he had an eye to a future translation to Ely'.[36]

In 1747 Newcastle apprehended that the duke of Somerset, Chancellor of the University, could not live much longer, and was rallying his forces, among whom 'our old friend' Dr Gooch was preeminent; and Gooch was rewarded with the see of Ely early in 1748.[37] The duke's rival was the Prince of Wales and presently the king made it clear that he would be much displeased if the prince was elected. In July 1748 there was an alarm — Somerset was thought to be dying in full long vacation; there came a response which gave Newcastle much encouragement: 'many of the Tories, particularly those of Caius College, have declared their obedience to his Majesty's pleasure' he was told.[38] Somerset cheated these hopes by living on; but when he died at the beginning of December there was in effect no opposition, though a few abstained from voting in the great Whig manager, including 'all the fellows of pure Emmanuel . . . several of Caius . . . and some few of St John's'.[39]

But though Gooch's conversion had helped both Gooch himself and the duke of Newcastle to secure the offices of their dreams, the fellows of Caius remained predominantly Tory and increasingly disaffected with their Master. In the early days of his Mastership he was mainly resident in the College and it seems to have been a relatively harmonious community. Even then there are signs of negligence — but this may be primarily because Gooch trusted over much to two bursars who failed to balance their accounts; and the Master was Vice-Chancellor, and deep in his battles with Bentley.[40] Chichester claimed occasional residence, Essex hardly any.[41] As he warned the fellows, when he accepted the canonry at Canterbury, more was involved, and he was absent half the year in the early 1730s, sometimes more. After he became bishop he scarcely resided at all for a while — even if he did not visit Bristol it was not for assiduous residence in Caius — and presumably London was his main home from then on, and the House of Lords and the court his forum. It was during this era, in March 1739, that a

36 Blomefield 1739, II, 430 — and for Gooch ibid., pp. 429–30; Venn, III, 115.
37 Winstanley 1922, pp. 37–54, esp. p. 44 for Gooch as 'our old friend'; Venn, III, 115–6 for his promotion.
38 Winstanley 1922, p. 46.
39 Winstanley 1922, p. 48.
40 See Venn, III, 122–3.
41 Joyce Horn has very kindly checked evidence of Gooch's presence for me in the Chichester muniments in the West Sussex Record Office and drawn my attention to L. P. Curtis's delightful *Chichester Towers* (New Haven, 1966), pp. 13–27. The Caius *Absence Books* show that he was continuously in residence when Vice-Chancellor and not scandalously absent till he became bishop of Norwich. For Canterbury see Venn, III, 119; *Absence Book* 1730–1821; *Exiit Book* 1678–1747 (absent 12 March–14 Sept. and 27 Sept.–14 Oct. 1731).

junior fellow called Tinkler Ducket was expelled from the College and University for professing atheistical opinions — though recently ordained — 'a little wave on the flood of deism', which carried him out to sea; he is last heard of living in Constantinople.[42] The affair of the Newcastle election and his translation to Ely brought Gooch more to Cambridge; but even so he was more often out of Cambridge than in until the closing years of his life; then the *Absence Books* note a remarkable change, and in the half year between Michaelmas 1751 and Easter 1752 he was absent only four days — and only three days the next winter. 'For above three years before his death', said Cole, 'he has been in a very declining condition, residing for the most part at Cambridge, and often going out in his coach for the air to Gogmagog Hills; but removing up to town for his health in 1753, he gradually and visibly decayed apace'.[43] In his last year he was absent for nearly 45 weeks and died in Ely House in Holborn in February 1754.

Thus the Lodge had been his chief home for the greater part of his time as Master, and there presumably was born his son John, the future fellow, in 1729;[44] there, one after the other, his three wives lived and reared their families. The children were few and far between, which perhaps helps to explain why comparatively little extension of the Lodge took place, though it was substantially refurbished in his day. But once he became bishop he became a rare visitor to Cambridge, and his relations with the fellowship deteriorated rapidly.[45] He had not fought Bentley for nothing: he well understood the law's delays, the difficulty of putting down a man with political influence, the simple benefits of doing nothing. But he never exercised sway again in the College, and when he died, Newcastle — who could move heaven and earth in a more hopeful case — did not interfere in the election of his successor.

In September 1737 the Master exercised his negative vote in a fellowship election, and the fellows feared he would make use of this, and of Bateman's statute which gave the Master authority to act if Master and fellows could not agree; and they took Counsel's opinion.[46] The blessings of the English law to men like Bentley and Gooch were happily illustrated, and they received two opposite opinions. Meanwhile the Master had appointed John Berney as President, a senior fellow whose term was about to expire; there was a dispute about the length of his tenure and the confusion gave the

---

42 Venn 1901, pp. 175—6; Venn, II, 28; Venn, *Alumni*, I, s.v. For Gooch's movements, *Absence Book* 1730—1821. Cf. *Exiit Book ut supra*.

43 Venn, III, 121—2.

44 John was born in Cambridge; Thomas, his elder brother, in London *c*. 1721 (Venn 1891, p. 40; Venn, II, 43, 58). Thomas was son of Mary Sherlock, Gooch's first wife, John of Hannah Miller, his second; he had no children by his third, Mary Compton. Venn, III, 116 records Cole's peevish comments on the second and third.

45 Venn, III, 116, 120, seems to exaggerate his residence in Cambridge while bishop, and to miss the relation between his absence as bishop and his failure to perform his role as Master.

46 Venn, III, 120.

Master the excuse to appoint no President at all[47] — or, at least, that is how one interprets the chain of events; but it may really have been as much that the Master was a busy absentee, deep in the charities of Norwich and the intrigues of Westminster, and simply let things slide. He nominated the most senior, respected and popular of the fellows, James Burrough, as 'locum-tenens', expressly excluding him from electing fellows or other major business, and as he found this expedient worked very happily for him, he left things as they were.[48] Presently the living of Mattishall was vacant and they could not present. The fellows took Counsel's opinion again, and on this occasion the voices were not divided — power they might truly have, but it would be very unwise to proceed against a bishop and a peer. So the benefice lapsed to the bishop, that is, to Gooch himself; and whether from tact or (more probably) from negligence, he let it lie; presently it passed on to the archbishop, who appointed Henry Goodall — and whether one should lay greater stress, as does Venn, on the fact that he was (then or later) Gooch's chaplain — or that he was a fellow of Caius — there is no evidence to determine. But though there is copious evidence of dissatisfaction by the fellows and negligence by the Master, it would be imprudent to assume there was permanent rift and strife.[49] Their Master was a bishop and at court, the centre of patronage and hope, even if most of them loyally remained Tories. Fellowships and livings apart, they did well under James Burrough's genial guidance; and when Gooch died they made him Master.

Sir James Burrough, architect and Master

However many excuses might be found for this convivial Whig, Gooch was neither an admirable man nor an exemplary Master, and it is a pleasure to turn to Burrough.[50] In early days indeed they seem to have worked closely together. One of Gooch's initiatives as Vice-Chancellor had been the active promotion of a new University building between the Old Schools and Great St Mary's. Where we see now the Senate House and lawns was a tumble of houses and streets.

As often as not in Cambridge an ancient lawn is the monument to a building scheme long forgotten — the lawns of King's of Henry VI's mighty schemes, lost in the Wars of the Roses, the lawns before the Old Schools of

47 Venn, II, 20 notes this; but the account under III, 120 is truncated.
48 For what follows, Venn, III, 121; for Henry Goodall, II, 19. Venn, III, 121 n., sadly observes that the popular version — 'that the Master let the living lapse to the bishop, who at once appointed the Master's son' — is a better story, but not true. But John Gooch was amply provided for.
49 Gooch's letter of 1742 (Venn, III, 121), however, suggests a good deal of bickering.
50 On Burrough, see Venn, I, 517−18; III, 126−9; Colvin 1978, pp. 168−70; DNB; Cocke 1984; Kersting and Watkin 1984, pls. 49−58 and architectural notes on them.

the battle of Senate House yard. Like all military engagements its beginning is obscure and its course confused. But the whole episode started peacefully enough, with the establishment under Gooch's benevolent eye in 1719 of a Syndicate to arrange for new buildings in this area – to which James Burrough was added in March 1721.[51] In March 1722 James Gibbs came from London and was entrusted with 'Mr Burrough's plan of the intended publick buildings' which he was to improve as he thought fit – and to be 'retained to supervise and conduct' the building.[52] Burrough has much other architectural work to his credit – in 1752 he collaborated with James Essex on a scheme for a new east front of the Old Schools and about the same time he was evidently at the centre of the plans for rebuilding and refacing Gonville Court. He has in recent years won recognition as a major amateur architect of the 18th century; and we need no longer doubt that the pure classical geometry and exquisite detail of the Senate House were indeed the fruit of a design for which both Burrough and Gibbs deserve credit.[53] Burrough was still comparatively young: he was twenty-nine in March 1721; Gibbs was eight or nine years older; and we may assume that the building of the Senate House went forward with the active encouragement of the Master of Caius. An observer today, standing in Caius Court and looking south, sees an enchanting anthology of styles – the late 14th century in a corner of the Regent House, the 15th and 16th in King's Chapel, the 16th in Caius Court and the Gate of Honour, the early 18th, severely classical, in the Senate House, Palladian on the east front of the Old Schools, and 19th century neo-Classical in the Cockerell addition to the old University Library, now [1996] the Caius Library. Even as it is, the Gate of Honour, designed as a triumphal entry to a modest street running to the Old Schools, is overpowered. But if the original scheme of the 1720s had been completed, the Senate House would have been linked to a complex of buildings including the Old Schools and another building parallel to it across Senate House yard.[54] As the Senate House proceeded west and began to appear looming over Caius Court, the fellows of Caius took alarm. It is indeed surprising the Burrough and Gooch had not foreseen this. Burrough supervised the digging of trenches in 1725 – 6 to make the foundations of the new link between the Senate House and the Old Schools, and this finally

51 For all this see Willis and Clark, III, 43 – 71; *RCHM Cambridge*, I, 9 – 14; cf. Pevsner 1970, pp. 199 – 203.
52 Willis and Clark, III, 44.
53 Colvin 1978, pp. 168 – 70, gives a full and balanced account of Burrough's known work; and see ibid. 297 – 300 and Cocke 1984 for his influence on James Essex. Colvin still reckons Gibbs mainly responsible for the design of the Senate House, but the instructions to Gibbs, to 'take with him to London Mr Burrough's plan of the intended public buildings and make what improvements he shall think necessary upon it' (Willis and Clark, I, 44) certainly suggest that Gibbs had accepted a preliminary scheme of Burrough's as the basis for his work – though it is not incompatible with other interpretations of the relations between them.
54 For what follows see Willis and Clark, III, 44 – 54, esp. 49 – 52 for Gooch's intervention.

revealed to his colleagues what was afoot. On 31 May 1727 the Master, from the safe distance of his canonry in Chichester, addressed a fervent remonstrance to the Vice-Chancellor against blocking up the street running south from the Gate of Honour. It was 'a scheme that will so effectually shut out all view of that noble fabric King's Chapel, that I wonder how the University or that College can bear it; and a scheme so injurious to Caius College, that I am fully resolved not to bear it. What ground you have already to build on I myself contracted for: but I am sure I never contracted for the street in front of the Schools, nor could anybody convey it to me.'[55] Whatever the truth of this, it provided a colourable basis for the College's defence; and on 6 July a College Order was passed empowering the Master to procure an injunction from the Court of Chancery to protect the king's highway; and to Chancery went Burrough's scheme and all chance of completing it. It must have been exceedingly galling to him; but Burrough was evidently a man of amiable and resilient character, and he recovered from the blow to become the leading tutor and central figure in the fellowship in the 1730s and 1740s, and to keep such peace as existed between the Master and fellows.

As Gooch sank into dotage the College itself prepared for major building enterprises; and we need not doubt that Burrough was their inspiration and mainstay. Already between 1718 and 1726 a start had been made with the recasing of Gonville Court. John Lightwine, the President, had been slowly disentangling the complex benefaction of Dr Brady, of which he was executor, over many years, to the eventual benefit of the College and of many of the fellows. In 1716 he sold to the benefaction the advowson of Denver, which he had himself acquired, for £500, and generously set this money to the task of extending and refurbishing the chapel; from other sources this was raised to £2746. To this work may be attributed the ashlar facing and the buttresses of the exterior, and most of the stalls and panelling within — all of it executed to the designs of John James, architect of St George's Hanover Square. Thus Francis Blomefield, who was a scholar when the work was completed, describes the chapel in its first fresh glory.[56]

'The roof is covered with lead on the outside, and is inwardly arched and coloured with blue, beautified all over with cherubs' heads in rays of light; the altar piece is wainscot, having four large pillars on each side, and in the midst a large picture of the Salutation in a gilt frame [a copy by the painter Ritz of an Annunciation by Carlo Maratta]. On the top stands [sic] seven mock candlesticks and tapers, and on each side of the picture are fruits, corn, flowers, etc. finely carved in wood. The altar is railed in, and paved with black and white marble; the cloth for the Table is of velvet, on which

55 Willis and Clark, III, 50−1. The College Order is cited by Venn, III, 123−4.
56 Brady's will is in CUL, Vice-Chancellor's Probate Court, dated 24 Aug. 1694; see Venn, I, 441−2; III, 107, 124−5, 164; ER, pp. 36−8. For what follows, see Blomefield 1750, p. 101; Willis and Clark, I, 195 and n. 1; RCHM Cambridge, I, 74.

stands two large silver gilt candlesticks with wax tapers, a large silver dish, two Books of Common Prayer, and two velvet cushions, all fringed with gold. The cloth and cushion of the Litany desk are of velvet, laid with gold lace and fringed with gold, as are the Master's and President's cushions . . .' In the years 1751—4 the recasing of Gonville Court was completed, and the north side, where the original medieval houses in which the College was founded had stood, was completely rebuilt.[57] We need not doubt that Burrough was the master mind of this operation. He had worked with Essex on Trinity Hall in the previous decade, and more recently at Sidney;[58] and by this time the College was effectively run by two Tutors, of whom Burrough himself was the senior, and Smith, later to succeed him as Master, the other. When Gooch died in 1754, and the buildings were nearing completion, Burrough was translated to the Master's Lodge.

Meanwhile he had suffered another setback in his career as university architect. In the early 1750s the schemes for the Old Schools, and especially to provide better accommodation for its main component in that era, the University Library, were floated once more; the Chancellor became extremely active. In conjunction with James Essex, who was already much involved in the preservation of Ely Cathedral and was later to adorn Cambridge with the west front of Emmanuel, Burrough devised a scheme for building a new east front to the Old Schools — but not impinging on the king's highway — in harmony with the Senate House.[59] The duke, however, had his own candidate, Stephen Wright — and anyway, Burrough was a Tory — so his design was overruled and in a famous vote in the senate the duke's was passed. Burrough and nine other fellows of Caius, and a tiny handful of others, voted against the scheme; the overwhelming majority supported the copious fountain of patronage; they voted in Cole's phrase 'for the lucrative side'.[60] The story has a happier sequel, for in 1759 the duke summoned a deputation from the University to make a Loyal Address to the king on the occasion of the capture of Quebec. These addresses were anxious occasions for Newcastle, since he was always concerned lest the University officials muff their lines or show him inadequate respect; they were occasionally used by rebellious Cambridge Heads as opportunities for modest displays of independence; and in any case the duke thought they were the most important activities in which the University engaged. Imagine his horror when he discovered, on 5 November, that the University had the day before elected a Tory Vice-Chancellor in James Burrough. But Burrough was a tactful man who saw no reason to make trouble. As Winstanley observed, 'he earned his reward'.[61] On 12 November a small

---

57 Willis and Clark, I, 188—9; *RCHM Cambridge*, I, 74, 76—7; Venn, III, 125—6.
58 *RCHM Cambridge*, II, 246; Pevsner 1970, p. 158 n. (on the hall at Sidney, 1749—52, and later (1762) the new arch in Sidney Street, now in Jesus Lane — ex inf. R. C. Smail).
59 For all this Willis and Clark, III, 61—9; Winstanley 1922, pp. 223—7, cf. Cocke 1984.
60 Quoted in Venn, III, 127; for details of the vote, Willis and Clark, III, 63—4.
61 Winstanley 1922, pp. 155—7, at 156.

deputation led by Newcastle and Burrough attended on the aging king at St James's, 'and His Majesty was pleased to confer the honour of knighthood upon James Burrough, Esq., Vice-Chancellor'. Burrough indeed had been Esquire Bedell from 1727 till 1754 and knew much of such occasions; and was probably more dedicated to the University and the College than to politics. But the front of the Old Schools remains, however delightful in itself, a strange monument to the vanity of the duke — and a Whig Old Schools to this day frowns at a Tory Senate House.

Like Gooch, Burrough was a convivial man; and unlike his predecessor, he was universally liked. Even Cole said of him 'He had no enemies' — which drew from Winstanley the comment that 'any prominent person in an university, of whom this can be said, must be either singularly fortunate or remarkably amiable'.[62] He was also a man of genuine talent who made a fine collection of prints and medals. He shared with John Smith, his successor, a keen interest in the arts and a tendency to monopolise the tutorial work of the College. After Burrough became Master, Smith was for a time sole tutor.[63] It is true that they were not overstretched — entrants averaged no more than seven or eight a year; the total numbers were smaller than at any time since the advent of Dr Caius; the College and the University were at the nadir of their reputation as places of learning and education. In 1728 King George II had paid a visit to Cambridge, and Dr Bentley, as Regius Professor of Divinity, presented fifty-eight DDs, a remarkable inflation since the visit of George I eleven years before, when Bentley had been content with the creation of thirty-two.[64] This event would hardly have inspired George II with a lofty notion of Cambridge academic standards, and in 1734—7 he founded at Göttingen a university which rapidly became far the most distinguished in his dominions, even Edinburgh not excluded. At a time when the enrolments were steadily falling in both Britain and Germany, Göttingen almost alone saw no decline, and the scholarly and educational standards it maintained inspired the whole of Europe two generations later with the notion, quite foreign to most 18th century intellectuals, that universities were the natural centres of intellectual life and academic advance.[65]

John Smith

Meanwhile Dr Smith became a DD and a Professor. On 7 August 1764 Burrough died, and on the 17th John Smith was elected to succeed him; he was to hold office till his death in 1795 at the age of eighty-four or so; and

62 Winstanley 1922, p. 224 n. For Burrough as Master, Venn, III, 126—9.
63 Venn, II, 69—82.
64 Monk 1830, pp. 361—3, 542—3. Jonathan Clark tells me that the purpose was to increase the number of Whig voters for the University constituency.
65 Cf. Turner 1975.

if we reckon all the years that Burrough and Smith were tutors and Masters, from 1720 to 1795, we have a remarkable record of continuous service; not perhaps academically distinguished, but within the limits the 18th century set itself, honourable and good.[66] Handsome black marble slabs in the ante-chapel preserve their memories. Smith became Master at a moment of high drama in university politics: the epic struggle between Lord Hardwicke and Lord Sandwich for the High Stewardship was in full swing, and Newcastle as Chancellor was in a state of extreme excitement. His immediate anxiety was to place one of his supporters as the next Vice-Chancellor. It was at first assumed that he need not worry about Smith, although he was a Tory – in so far as the word had any meaning after 1750. Smith, like Burrough, was not a doctor, and would have to wait his turn for the Vice-Chancellorship. Smith, however, immediately applied to the Vice-Chancellor for a DD by royal mandate, and this appealed to the duke's loyal supporters, since Smith had hinted that he was not expecting to upset the usual order of election to the Vice-Chancellor's office. As there always had [till the 1990s] to be two nominees for the office, it was thought an excellent idea to have Smith as a man of straw and second nominee after the Master of Corpus, who was Newcastle's man for the job. In the affair of the High Stewardship Tories like Smith were inclined to line up with the earl of Sandwich, who though a Secretary of State was more congenial to them than Newcastle the former Whig leader. The defeat of Sandwich was the supreme opportunity for Newcastle to show that his loss of office in Westminster did not abolish his influence in Cambridge. Smith was a Sandwich man, and his colleagues in Caius refused to be tied by his statement that he would not upset the order of batting. Newcastle got into the wildest anxiety. On 1 November he wrote, 'If we lose our Vice-Chancellor all is lost'.[67] But a happy end was not far off. On the 3rd the Heads duly nominated the Masters of Corpus and Caius and on the 4th the Master of Corpus was duly elected, without dissension; and by May Newcastle's candidate had been declared High Steward.

Smith as professor

Smith had only to wait till 1766 to become Vice-Chancellor, and he had the reward of presiding over the completion of the Senate House to the designs of Essex with the help of a bequest from Burrough, and laying the foundation stone at the south-west of the western pediment in 1767.[68] In 1769 he turned his attention to a Professorship. The Master of Peterhouse, Dr Law,

66 Venn, I, 518; II, 14, 35; III, 129 – 32; for the Vice-Chancellorship, Winstanley 1922, pp. 131 – 6; for Smith's age see tombstone in the ante-chapel.
67 Winstanley 1922, p. 135.
68 Willis and Clark, III, 70. For what follows, Winstanley 1935, pp. 138 – 42.

was also Knightbridge Professor of Divinity; and when he became bishop of Carlisle — since the Chair was a sinecure of modest worth and he had twelve children — he rather thought of keeping it; but the archbishop of Canterbury advised against, and he resigned. The founder of the Chair had stipulated that the holder must be over fifty. So the Vice-Chancellor declared the obvious candidates ineligible and Dr Smith was one of those who offered themselves.[69] It was then discovered that the Court of Chancery had been in the business and the stipulation had faded away; and so Smith missed this Chair, and had to content himself with the Lowndean Professorship of Astronomy.[70] Cambridge tutors have by custom held professors in contempt, and it may be wondered why Smith, a most experienced and respectable tutor, but a man quite without academic pretensions, so far as we know, coveted such an office. The 18th century attitude to professorships is bewildering. On the one hand, a century which vividly recalled the career of Newton as Lucasian Professor and witnessed many years of Bentley as Regius Professor of Divinity knew that the office could be held by academics and intellectuals of immortal fame. But the stipends they commanded and the work they were able to do meant that most conscientious professors were inspired school masters: an extreme case was the celebrated Bishop Watson of Llandaff who was a professor of chemistry for a time and gave some of the best lectures anyone could remember. But when he was elected he had known nothing of the art.[71] True, he took the Regius Chair of Divinity more lightly, but by no means so easily as Dr Zachary Brooke, who had the Lady Margaret Professorship, which was 'a valuable sinecure'. Reform was in the wind: when Brooke died in 1788 the electors received a petition that they would make his successor undertake to give lectures.[72] But his successor soon found one could promise to lecture, but to collect an audience could prove more difficult. So a few 18th century professors were notable figures in the world; a few more gave a little elementary teaching; most did little or nothing. Smith cannot have been in the first category, and was probably in the third. But he had paved the way for his election, according to 18th century standards, in the most exemplary manner, by arranging with the College for his transit telescope to be set up on the chapel roof with 'such alterations in the south parapet, over the antechapel, as may be thought necessary' and by seeking influence at court.[73] The only thing certain is that he held the Chair for twenty-four years and no trace has been found of any teaching that he gave. Yet the College bred at least one astronomer of high distinction in his later years.

---

69 Winstanley 1935, p. 141.
70 Winstanley 1935, p. 173.
71 Winstanley 1935, pp. 144−5; for the context, ibid., chap. iii *passim*.
72 Winstanley 1935, pp. 98−9, 359 n. 10 (for 'a valuable sinecure').
73 Venn, III, 129; Winstanley 1935, p. 173 (citing Cole for the court influence). For what follows see p. 186.

Caius and the antiquaries

Smith had the merit of sharing in Burrough's taste for the arts and anti-
quities, and the supreme merit, in the eyes of his successors, of being
acquainted with Sir Joshua Reynolds, who painted his portrait (plate 13c).
At the end of his life he called in Sir John Soane, no less, to refurbish the
Hall. Both Burrough and Smith were fellows of the Society of Antiquaries.
Burrough had helped John Battely to write the history of his native town of
Bury St Edmunds, contributing a plan of the abbey, a drawing of the
abbot's lodging, and a list of the abbots.[74] But over and beyond and surpass-
ing all this he was tutor to Francis Blomefield. When Blomefield arrived in
Caius from Fersfield in Norfolk and Thetford School in 1724 as a pupil of
Burrough's, he had already, so it is said, begun to collect notes for his life
work, the *Essay towards a topographical history of the County of
Norfolk*.[75] His little book on Cambridge, the *Collectanea Cantabrigiensia*,
though not published till 1750, is also alleged to have been put together
while he was a student. In any case he came to Cambridge passionately
committed to antiquities and evidently had encouragement from Burrough
and the run of the College library. He did not stay for a fellowship but went
straight into the living of Fersfield while still a scholar, married young and
died, aged forty-six, of the smallpox, in 1752; but by then he had already
had three daughters and completed most of three volumes of his great work,
which was finished by Charles Parkin and others. Although Blomefield
found Caius a congenial place for his studies, his real links lay elsewhere,
with the great antiquaries Peter Le Neve, whose collections formed the basis
of his work, and who was one of the founding fathers of the Society of Antiquaries, of which Blomefield became in due course a fellow; and Thomas
Tanner, one of the notable survivors of a former generation of antiquaries,
who gave generous help to many younger men.[76] Blomefield shared with
others of the antiquaries of the century a tendency to leave out his
references, which spoils some of his work for a modern scholar. Yet he was
a good, careful, patient compiler; and this makes especially frustrating the
details he gives of Edmund Gonville's career which can be traced to no
earlier source.[77]

A much younger Norfolk antiquary, Sir John Fenn, was to find a like
encouragement under the tutorship of Smith.[78] Fenn was born in 1739 and

74 On Soane's work in 1792, see below, pp. 194, 254. Burrough's work is in Battely 1745, esp.
   p. 161, a list of abbots from 1279 'e collectaniis Jacobi Burrough' and Pls. II and III, plans of
   the church and the abbot's 'palace' by Burrough dated 1718, 1720.
75 First 2 vols., Blomefield 1739; for what follows see Blomefield 1750. Cf. Venn, II, 20.
76 Douglas 1951, pp. 158−9.
77 See above, p. 4.
78 Venn, II, 73; and for what follows, Serpell 1983. On Fenn's edition of the Paston letters,
   their most recent editor, Professor Norman Davis, has kindly told me that he reckons that
   'Fenn's editorial work still seems good, even very good, for its time'. Like many 18th and
   19th century scholars, he used an amanuensis; but he evidently took considerable pains

came to Caius in 1756; he rose to be a fellow for a short time in 1764, but soon resigned to marry Eleanor, daughter of Sheppard Frere, the sister of his close friend and fellow-Caian John Frere. Thus Fenn entered the East Anglian squirearchy and lived the life of a modest country gentleman. But meanwhile, even before he came to Caius, he seems to have fallen in with the fanatical Norfolk antiquary, Thomas Martin, who was, like Blomefield, a disciple of Peter Le Neve and an FSA, and in whose vast, eccentric collections Fenn was to discover the celebrated Paston letters, the outstanding source of East Anglian social and political history in the late Middle Ages. He was the first editor of the Paston letters, and for this he was knighted. Martin was a cousin of Sir James Burrough, and when Fenn came to Caius he came by request of one of his own cousins, Bartholomew Edwards, who was a Caian, and with an introduction to Burrough. Fenn's reminiscences, recently studied by the late Michael Serpell, are a prime source for the College in the mid-18th century. Soon after his arrival, he describes how 'I was walking one day after dinner backwards and forwards in Caius Court by myself' when he was joined by John Norris, a year his senior, who invited him to tea, and they became fast friends; next year they added John Frere to their company.[79] Fenn 'applied himself chiefly to Natural Philosophy and the Mathematics, the then prevailing studies'; his comrades combined classics with mathematics; and in the event Norris was third wrangler in 1760, Fenn fifth in 1761, and Frere second in 1762.[80] 'My acquaintance was chiefly amongst young men, whose pursuits were similar to my own. I never found time hang heavy on my hands. I loved cheerful company, and both in College and at home mixed in the amusements of the place and neighbourhood. Drinking I always had an aversion to . . . As I never kept late hours, I was constantly an early riser; by which means I always found time for both study and amusement . . .' 'Having no particular fondness for Country Diversions', like Blomefield, he was able to spend many hours in College studying history, especially the 'history and antiquities of his own country' — presumably in the College library.[81] He gives a fascinating list of his close acquaintances in Cambridge, who were by no means confined to Caius — they spanned Clare, St Catharine's, Peterhouse, King's and Trinity as well; and their common interests have been thus summed up by Serpell: 'three became prosperous landowners in Norfolk and Suffolk; five became fellows of the Society [of Antiquaries]; three were well-connected clergymen; one, the senior wrangler of Fenn's

---

himself and learned from his experience. The next editor, Gairdner, thought Fenn's work so accurate he need not check all his texts. 'This was rash, for Fenn was far from perfect; but he had done a very creditable job all the same.' For the history of Fenn's edition and of the letters, see Davis 1971, pp. xxiv – xxx.

79 Serpell 1983, p. 99.
80 Serpell 1983, p. 99.
81 Ibid.

year, rose to be a Commissioner of the Great Seal; and one, having achieved a joint secretaryship to the Prime Minister, Rockingham, resigned under the strain of office and committed suicide through a Treasury window.'[82] Norris died young, and Frere and Fenn lived on to be friends and brothers-in-law and colleagues in many other ways. In the long run Fenn became a leading Norfolk antiquary and handed on the tradition of Le Neve and Blomefield in Norfolk and the Antiquaries in London. Meanwhile the East Anglian traditions of the College, narrow as they made it in the eyes of many later commentators, had ensured that the library was a place suited to the tastes of Blomefield and Fenn, two of the most eminent of 18th century antiquaries.

The letters of Framlingham Willis

Among the most notable benefactors of the Society of Antiquaries was Thomas Kerrich of Magdalene, University librarian at the turn of the 18th and 19th centuries. From his archives have survived a clutch of letters written to him when he was shivering on the brink of Cambridge by a young freshman at Caius called Framlingham Willis, who went into residence on 25 June 1767.[83] This was the time of year when the modern undergraduate is going home; but to many students in former centuries term and vacation were much alike. By 1767, however, very few resided in the long vacation, and many kept only a part of each term. Kerrich was a year or two older than Willis, but reluctant to take up his place in Magdalene — he had the anxieties familiar to every generation of freshmen, and was furthermore recovering from smallpox. Five days after his admission, Willis writes to him:

'Dear Sir,
    Since I had the happiness to see you last I have been admitted of this college, where I am now resident. From the observations I have been able to make, I must be of opinion that a College life, for one of a serious turn, and contemplative disposition, is the most delightful situation imaginable. My residence here, however, was at first, a little uncomfortable, where I could hardly see a single person whom I had met with before, or anyone who might instruct me in the ways and customs of the place. But this awkwardness is worn off now, and I am almost as perfectly settled in College as one who has led the greater part of his life in it. Since my being here I have taken a view of all the Colleges, which has been I think the pleasantest time I ever spent in my life. You would

82 Serpell 1983, pp. 99–100. The last was Edward Chamberlayne (1741–82), ibid., p. 116, n. 56.
83 Venn, II, 85; and for what follows, Venn 1913, chap. xii.

hardly believe it is in the power of art to furnish out such a multitude of noble buildings as you here meet with. Here is every convenience allotted to the students that can possibly be expected from the benefactions of kings and queens. I do not believe, as good a painter as you are, that you can fancy finer walks than those about Trinity College, or a more magnificent edifice than the College itself. I am, however, so singular as to prefer Clare Hall to any of the rest. It is neat beyond description; and though it might not at first sight strike your fancy so much as Trinity, yet the more you consider, the more you admire it; whereas the surprize occasioned by a magnificent appearance wears off, after once or twice seeing, and the beauty of it is lost insensibly. I have to-day seen the public Library where the Learning of all ages is represented, and to which something is added every day. The number of books in it is supposed to be upwards of seventy thousand.'[84]

On 18 July he wrote further:

'Dear Sir.

Your not coming up to College as soon as you expected, I assure you, is a cutting disappointment to me. I had laid my account with having a friend resident here, during the whole vacation, with whom I might in agreeable converse pass away the minutes, which every one must allow for a recreation from study. Such a disappointment is the more severely felt at this time, as the University is always very thin during the long vacation; and there will not, in a week's time, be one Undergraduate left in Caius besides myself. The objection you make to coming up immediately, I must beg leave to say, is very frivolous. Your being already admitted will prevent the examination you so much dread: and let me tell you the examination at a person's first being admitted, though it were much more strict than it generally is, is very easily passed through, and hardly deserves to be styled any thing else than a mere matter of form. My Tutor, when I first went to him, only desired me to construe an ode in Horace, a few lines in the beginning of a Satire in Juvenal, not more than three sentences in one of Cicero's Orations, and as many verses out of the Greek Testament. A Homer indeed was produced; but as it had a Latin version quite uncovered, which, if there had been occasion, I might with one single glance of my eye have had recourse to, it hardly deserves to be mentioned. The examination by the Master and Dean was still more easy than the Tutor's.'[85]

Then comes a notable concession, to tempt Kerrich further:

'Your opinion that Magdalen(e) is the worst College in the University

84 Venn 1913, pp. 241 – 2.
85 Venn 1913, pp. 243 – 4.

seems founded upon prejudice, rather than on reasonable ground. The College is but badly situated, and, I think, not overstocked with Undergraduates, but it has one ornament, by which it outshines not only all the Colleges here, but perhaps all the Universities in the world — the best mathematician and most able astronomer of them all. The Library there I have not seen. I apprehend it will be an easy matter for you to avail yourself of any advantage, which might be open to you from it, if you had liberty to go and come as you please; for as long as I have been in Cambridge I have not once got admission into our Library.[86]

In August he wrote twice again, first to describe a busy day —

'As I can do anything I please at this time especially, I spend a part of my time in a manner very different from what the rest of my acquaintance here do, in a manner which perhaps you may call whimsical. I generally rise at five, and then read for an hour; at six I take a pretty long walk, but so as to be back to chapel at seven. After chapel is done, three times a week I go to the cold bath, and after that I come home to breakfast, which I take care to have over before nine. Then I set down to read for three hours and a half, and at half an hour after twelve my hair-dresser comes to me, and I begin to dress for commons [dinner]. You will be obliged to comply with the custom of putting on a clean shirt every day and of having your hair dressed. After commons, if ever, 'tis allowable to lounge away an hour at a friend's room and drink a glass of wine, but this is what I seldom do. At five I sometimes go to a Coffee-house, where you meet with all the new pamphlets, magazines, newspapers, &c., and drink a dish of tea, coffee or chocolate. At six I return to chapel, and after that I take a walk on the walks if it be fine weather, if not, in some college cloisters. At eight, your bed-maker comes to ask what you please to have for supper, and gives you a bill of fare, which they call here a size bill. They have always very good things, but they are exorbitantly dear, as you may guess by 3d for a common tart. Persuade your father to let you have a good allowance; if you keep whole terms, an hundred pounds a year will not be sufficient. You will be glad to hear that the custom of drinking is entirely exploded in polite company; but I would advise you never to seem afraid of drinking, for the bucks here will imagine by that, that they can make you drunk very easily; and to make a freshman drunk is excellent fun to them. Your Tutor or your Master will probably ask you to sup with them; if they do not I shall be glad to see you with me the night of your admission and then you will be in no danger to be led into any excess.'[87]

---

86 Venn 1913, pp. 244—5. The mathematician was Edward Waring, Lucasian Professor.
87 Venn 1913, pp. 246—8. Venn identifies the cold bath as 'a bathing place in the Fellows' Garden, like those still existing at Christ's and Emmanuel'.

In his second letter he admits that not every day was for work:

'. . . I have been somewhat more gay and idle than I should have been this last fortnight, in making parties to go on the water, and in riding out to Newmarket and the country round about Cambridge in little one-horse chaises . . .'[88]

The society in the late 18th century

Willis's letters are a remarkable survival, giving a rare glimpse of the view of Cambridge of a student in the 18th century — active, conscientious, yet well aware of the bloods and bucks he needed to avoid if he was not to fall into idleness and debt. Willis was duly rewarded with a fellowship, which he held from 1772 to 1776.[89] Although the majority of Caians were East Anglians preparing for orders, or gentry's sons at finishing school, the society was not monochrome. There were hard-reading men and moderate readers and the totally idle. It was precisely in the mid-18th century, when academic work is supposed to have been least regarded, that Francis Schuldham, a fellow from 1720 to 1776 — and most of that time absent on medical practice in Walsingham and perhaps elsewhere in Norfolk — formed the idea of the Schuldham prize or plate which has been the most coveted of College awards since his death, and is given 'after due examination' for prowess in the tripos. There were to be plenty to deserve it in the years ahead.

Nor were all Caians of this era Norfolk and Suffolk men. In 1741−3 came Lewis and Joseph Williams from Jamaica, pensioner and fellow-commoner from a wealthy colonial home, under the benevolent eye of Mr Burrough. A few months before Willis came Thomas Lynch from Charlestown, Carolina, the harbinger of a group of four boys from Carolina who came in the years 1767−70, illustrating the interest of some well-to-do colonists in British education on the eve of the War of Independence.

Beside the hard-reading men like Francis Schuldham and Framlingham Willis Caius also doubtless had its share of black sheep; and the most famous of these among the pupils of John Smith was Edward Thurlow, who had to leave the College in haste in 1751 owing to 'his insolence to the

88 Venn 1913, p. 249.
89 Venn, II, 85. For what follows, see Venn, I, 530; and for the Americans, II, 51, 54, 85−9. There was an epilogue in 1792 in Henry Cassin from Nevis, West Indies, subsequently poisoned by a servant on a voyage to England, with his family (Venn, II, 125) — nonetheless a descendant, James Bourne, was happily able to enter the College in 1981 (*Caian* 1982, p. 25). Sons of rich settlers in Cambridge and elsewhere in England are being studied by K. G. Southernwood of Jesus College; and I am indebted to Dr Betty Wood and to my wife for kindly drawing my attention to them.

dean'.[90] Thurlow subsequently rose, by a nicely calculated mingling of legal skills and political corruption, to be Lord Chancellor for most of the period from 1778 to 1792; he was a royal toady, the king's spy over successive cabinets; ardent in defence of British rule over the American colonies and of the slave trade. He 'was very far from being an admirable or even a respectable character' observes Winstanley — but he does so in the act of chronicling a case in which Thurlow behaved with notable fairness and tact in restoring peace between the Master and fellows of Trinity in 1787.[91] Robert Goodrich, the offended dean of 1751, was soon after given compensation in the rectory of Bincombe which he held till his death in 1797. Meanwhile in 1780 the Lord Chancellor, who enjoyed large patronage, among his earlier disposals of it, presented Goodrich to another Dorset living, that of Pentridge, to hold in plurality with Bincombe — 'in a manner as flattering to Mr Goodrich, as it was honourable to his lordship', as Hutchins, the historian of Dorset, recorded.[92] Institutions, like families, tend to be proud of their black sheep, and in 1894 the College bought his portrait by Thomas Phillips. It may lack the colour and panache of the better known portrait by Lawrence; but it is a fine picture, and the head — of an old man in deep meditation, perhaps on his sins — is magnificent. Half a century after it was painted a greater artist than Phillips portrayed in *Bleak House* the evil and corruption spread by 'that most pestilent of hoary sinners', the Court of Chancery. Doubtless Dickens' indictment was overdrawn; but for the truth in it Thurlow must take his share of the blame.

Of John Smith, the Master, we have not only the portrait by Reynolds but pen sketches by Cole, who had known him since they entered Eton together on the same day.[93] Like all Cole's sketches, the character varies with his mood. He never wavers in paying tribute to his honesty; nor to his generosity — 'he has a brother's widow and her children; a Mrs Smith who lives with him and keeps his house'. But Smith starts shy and reserved and grows more irascible as the sketches go on; evidently in his later life there were occasional gusts of temper, and occasional quarrels with the fellows apparently about College livings — but nothing to compare with the arguments with Ellys or Gooch, still less any sign of a weakness for change or reform such as one occasionally meets in his friend Dr Powell, the Master of St John's.[94] 'This downright honest man is the son of an attorney in Norfolk who had but one leg . . . Dr Smith has no other preferment [late in life he was chancellor of Lincoln]; but, as he is a bachelor, with a private

90 Venn, II, 62; cf. p. 40.
91 Winstanley 1935, pp. 253−4.
92 Hutchins, III, 443 n., cited Venn, II, 40.
93 For these, see Venn, III, 129−31.
94 For the quarrel see Venn, III, 130 (1777). This seems to be connected with the presentations of Bartholomew Edwards to Hethersett and Edward White to Hockwold and Wilton in 1782 (Venn, II, 64, 75). Archives LV, 2 contains Counsel's opinion dated 1782 that the Master can nominate to Hethersett; but the *Gesta*, 3 July 1782, record his nomination of his nephew Joseph Smith (see p. 210) and the fellows' refusal.

fortune, he lives very hospitably and much esteemed by his acquaintance. There is an excellent picture of him in the Lodge by Reynolds, very like him. Smith is . . . an eternal smoker of tobacco; pretends to a taste in painting, and may possibly understand it, though he looks as if he did not, and such an inarticulate way of expressing himself that very few people understand what he says.'

Smith presided over a modest and intimate community. In theory there were nearly thirty fellows — twelve seniors and fourteen juniors, to which the Wortley fellows added two more. But since in practice the senior fellows absorbed the fines for leases and most of the other sums which reflected the change in the value of money, the stipends of junior fellows, many of them fixed at rates thought appropriate in the early 17th century, could not support men in residence. Some took on auxiliary tasks, taught at the Perse, acted curate in local churches, acquired livings compatible with occasional residence, or became, like Cosin and Naylor in the 1610s and 20s, chaplain or tutor to a bishop or a great man's household. Increasingly the junior fellowships came to be regarded as prizes or pocket money, and the junior fellows ceased to reside. The turning point came soon after 1700 and was no doubt equally due to the poverty of the fellowships and the general habit of the 18th century to regard non-residence with a lenient eye.[95] It spread even to the undergraduates. In practice it was accepted that three years' residence and a term qualified for the BA and that no further residence was needed for the MA; and that residence might be taken to mean up to or rather over half of each term.[96] This varied considerably, but the exercises and disputations and tutorials were not exacting — though they could be for those who wished to have them so — and the result was that for much of the year the College was very lightly peopled. On a normal day in term we may presume that 10−15 fellows and 20−30 students might take dinner. On feast days the numbers may have been much higher, but these figures help to explain why the tiny College hall survived so long. As Willis shows, dinner was a formal dress affair, taken by the whole community in the early afternoon. The hour lagged behind that normal to the quality. Readers of Jane Austen will be familiar with a dinner hour of 4 or 5, of Trollope with one which had gone forward to 7 or 7.30; even when Venn was an undergraduate in the 1850s dinner in Caius was still only at 4 or 5.[97] We have little information about the practice of hall and combination room in the 18th century, but it may be that the community at Caius was not so different from Christ's as Gunning describes it in the 1780s, where after a major feast the whole community gathered at two tables in the combination room to drink the numerous toasts. Christ's was 'a college more remarkable for its cordial

95 The progress of non-residents can be clearly traced in the *Absence Books*.
96 See in general, Gunning, I, 12−17, 29−32, and *passim*; for Caius scholars, the *Absence Books*.
97 Venn 1913, p. 270; cf. A. Palmer, *Movable Feasts* (Oxford, 1952).

hospitality than for the refinement of its manners';[98] and the evidence of the Caius Betting Books suggests that by the late 18th century at least the Combination Room was normally a fellows' preserve. There was no JCR at this time, however, and the separation of senior and junior community was in many ways less marked than later.

Apart from the Master and a tiny nucleus of older fellows, most of the fellows were near in age to the undergraduates; a junior fellow was far less privileged than a senior, the distinction between a fellow and a scholar, originally a fine one, had not grown large; fellow commoners dined with fellows, and pensioners were often better off than the scholars. In the 16th century the parlour — predecessor of the Combination Room — had been a dark room on the ground floor, where the undercroft now is; and here on cold days fellows and scholars could huddle over a fire until some kindly benefactors paid for a fire in hall.[99] Over the parlour was the Master's room for entertaining guests, and in the course of the 17th century this became the Combination Room and fellows' parlour; and so it is today, though much extended in the 19th century and refurbished in the 20th. It is clear that in original conception it was not a separate apartment for the fellows, and only slowly became such. That there was a sense of community and privacy among the fellows in the Combination Room by the late 18th century, however, is revealed in the manner in which they celebrated 1789, the year of Revolution, by instituting the first fellows' Betting Book. In one of the earliest bets 'Mr Davy bets Mr Brinkley 1 bottle of Port that there are 50 undergraduates on the boards' — and loses; but Charles Davy, a notable teacher and educationalist, was perhaps too involved in his efforts to revive the Perse School of which he was Master, to command the details of College life — even though he was also dean; and he was right to think that numbers were growing.[100]

The small community of less than fifty was shortly to be swollen by a young man called Henry Tilney, preparing to become a country parson.[101] He bears the name of the hero of *Northanger Abbey* and was almost exactly of the same age; and although it is not very probable that Jane Austen had heard of him, he may represent the archetypal Caian of this age, who — as we have seen — was on his way to a country parsonage.[102] But the name of Brinkley reminds us that some of the parsons were destined to a wider

---

98 Gunning, I, 50.

99 Willis and Clark, I, 198−9; Venn, III, 197.

100 On the *Betting Books* see Buck 1982, esp. p. 46. On Davy, see Venn, II, 97; and on Davy's father, Venn, II, 46; Mitchell 1976, p. 26; for Davy as Master of the Perse, 1789−91, Mitchell 1976, p. 29.

101 Venn, II, 118. Frank Stubbings in *Emmanuel College Magazine, Quatercentenary Issue, 1984*, pp. 77−81 (repr. from ibid. XLVII, 1964−5), reveals a talkative fellow of Emmanuel, Samuel Blackall, visiting Jane Austen in 1798, so that it is far from impossible that she had heard the name of his Caius contemporary.

102 See the figures quoted on p. 156;

view.[103] John Brinkley was a fellow from 1788 to 1792; but in the early 1790s he was already Professor of Astronomy in Dublin, and from 1792 first Astronomer Royal of Ireland; and from then on he steadily mounted as scientist and divine, ending bishop of Cloyne (1826—35) and Copley Medallist of the Royal Society. This he achieved in 1824 for his distinguished work on the mathematics of stellar parallaxes; he devised a way of measuring the distance of stars by this means, which — though it proved erroneous — inspired a major breakthrough in astronomy: many a great scholar has taught more by his errors than by being right. About this time the College fostered a brilliant entomologist in William Kirby, who stayed in Caius from 1776 till 1782—3, and then lived out a long life as curate and vicar of Barham in Suffolk, happily observing the plant and insect life of his own and his neighbours' parishes.[104] Just as Brinkley was departing came Thomas Manning, a remarkable mathematician who taught and published without ever troubling to complete his degree; and began while in Cambridge 'to brood upon the mysterious empire of China'; having learned Chinese in Paris, 'he was the first Englishman to penetrate to Lhasa, where he used to play chess with the Dalai Lama; afterwards he was Chinese secretary and interpreter in Lord Amherst's Embassy of 1817 to Peking'.[105]

Thus the homogenous appearance of the College as a seminary of country clergy hides a remarkable, and growing variety of talent, which was to blossom in the days of Wilkins, Bickersteth and Woodhouse.[106] Yet it remains the fact that the large majority of Caians of this era were in search of livings. If we ask, in what measure and by what means did any academic tradition survive, save the mathematics in which they were examined and the theology they somehow absorbed, we can only give a very partial answer. In fairness to Dr Smith, the Master, we may say it was when he was Professor of Astronomy that Caius produced, in Brinkley, its most notable astronomer before the 20th century; and if we look among the two physicians who almost alone checked the monopoly of the clergy in the early 1780s, we find William Wollaston. Even in Caius, a young physician must have felt himself a fish out of water in that age. But only thirty years before, in 1754, one Christopher Tancred had died, leaving a trust to provide support for students in medicine in Caius, in divinity in Christ's, and in law at Lincoln's Inn — 'of such low abilities as not to be capable of obtaining the education directed without the assistance of such a charity'. Though singularly inappropriate to a scientist of the first rank, a Tancred studentship no doubt helped to make Caius attractive to the young Wollaston.[107] He also found it possible, as a medical student of exceptional promise, to step straight into a senior fellowship, which he held from 1787 till his death

103 Venn, II, 107—8; DSB, II, 468—9 (Susan M. P. McKenna); DNB; Gunning, I, 87 ff.
104 Venn, I, 98—9; DNB.
105 Quoted from a note by Joseph Needham in a College prospectus of c. 1970.
106 See chap. 10.
107 Venn, III, 233; for Wollaston, see Venn, II, 106; DSB, XIV, 486—94 (D. C. Goodman).

in 1828. Meanwhile he had embarked on scientific studies in Cambridge, some botany and astronomy, and above all chemistry. From 1797 he was settled in London, mainly engaged in careful, persistent enquiry into the nature of certain metals. Long before Brinkley he was to win the Copley Medal (1804) for his remarkable studies of palladium and platinum: he was one of the foremost chemists of his day, and a leading figure in the Royal Society of which he was President in 1820. But he was a rare visitor in Caius, and an outstanding example of the way in which the special endowments of the College for medicine enabled some vestige of the tradition of John Caius and William Harvey to survive, even when medical teaching had ceased to exist in Cambridge and medical skill was hardly known in Caius. Martin Davy, who as tutor, president and Master, was to preside over a modest revival of the College's medical fame, was a younger contemporary of Wollaston's.

Meanwhile, by modern standards, the Master, fellows and scholars of Gonville and Caius College in the 1780s and 90s were a very small, intimate, provincial body. Presently the young Mr Pitt became member for the University; then Prime Minister; and with the outbreak of war with France in the 1790s, so the radical Gunning informs us, everyone became Tory once again: 'Scarcely a Whig was to be found.'[108] On 17 June 1794 a present of wine was made to celebrate Earl Howe's victory over the French at sea.[109] It was amid the sound of distant battle that old Dr Smith died, aged eighty-one, on 17 June 1795.[110]

108 Gunning, I, 189.
109 Buck 1982, p. 43.
110 Venn, III, 171. For his age, see tombstone in ante-chapel.

10

Caius in the Age of Reform

Winds of change

When John Smith died in 1795, he was succeeded by the President, Richard
Belward (or Fisher, as he had been in earlier years), a man in his mid-forties
but already long a senior. Of all the Masters of recent centuries he is the
most shadowy, and only two events of note are recorded of him. In the year
of his election a major extension was made to the Master's Lodge by
William Wilkins, senior, to whose designs the drawing room and dining
room were made — and who thus brought the name of Wilkins into its first
close relation with the College; and on his death he left the College ten
shares in the Grand Junction Canal, a modest bequest which none the less
reveals that he knew he lived in times of economic advance.[1]

But the most famous incidents of his time were the two silver robberies of
1799 and 1800. They were planned by a gardener and clock-maker of great
ingenuity called Kidman, who worked in collaboration with a chimney-
sweep named Grimshaw. Together they relieved several colleges of a great
quantity of silver plate; and then Grimshaw tried his hand in the house of
Alderman Butcher. But Butcher was a suspicious and determined man, and
had Grimshaw's house demolished; and thus his plate was found, and
Grimshaw was hanged. Meanwhile he was known to have been friendly
with Kidman, and constables went speedily to search Kidman's house,
where a silver pint-pot and 27 teaspoons, with the Caius marks still on
them, were found. Kidman was saved from the gallows by an able barrister
and his wife's ready tongue, and transported 'for life'; but by good conduct
and good gardening in the colony to which he was sent he was able to return
in 1810, and the kindly Henry Gunning, the Esquire Bedell, who 'knew a
source of good stories when he saw one, . . . took him on as a temporary
gardener', as Philip Grierson has observed, 'to his profit and ours' — for
Gunning wrote down Kidman's account of the proceedings, and doubtless
to Kidman we owe the story that the elder Wilkins provided a 'burglar-
proof safe' after the first robbery in Caius, which was broken into only a
few weeks later in the second robbery. We may believe that the loss was
considerable, including, according to Gunning, 'a most superb and massive
silver waiter' — doubtless Dr Caius' salver; but there is no corroboration in

1 Venn, III, 132−3; cf. II, 82−3; Willis and Clark, I, 202; on Wilkins the elder of Norwich
   see Colvin 1978, pp. 892−3. Fisher's change of name was presumably due to a legacy.

the College records of the special safe, and it may probably be attributed to Kidman's yarns. The College has always attributed its relative dearth of old silver to the thefts, and they were considerable (about 2000 oz.); but the main reaction of seniors to the thefts, 'apart from recording the Master's gift of £100 towards replacing' the loss, 'was indeed to order that 100 oz. of what had survived should be melted down and turned into something "more convenient" for daily use'.[2]

Richard Belward, the Master, died, still comparatively young, in 1803, and Martin Davy held sway in his stead; and when Davy died in 1839 the land had felt the first shocks of parliamentary reform, and even Caius had been touched by some marks of the world to come.

In the present state of knowledge the early 19th century is the most difficult of all for a college historian to map; for we know too little of the University about it, and the little that we know — or seem to know — is often wrong. D. A. Winstanley's splendid books on 18th century Cambridge may be thin in intellectual history, but in every other region they provide a wealth of balanced information wittily presented. He followed these by two books on Victorian Cambridge which are far from balanced, rich though they are in useful and entertaining matter.[3] For they are a history of Trinity College in the 19th century, with due respect to the significance of St John's, and occasional droll stories about other houses — the tragic tale of how the endowment of Downing College was decimated in Chancery; of the Master of St Catharine's who elected himself; and so forth. But though much has been written since, including some fine recent studies sketching the intellectual world of 19th century Cambridge,[4] the heresy still persists that the history of Cambridge down to the middle of the 19th century may be equated with the history of Trinity and John's. No one doubts that they were the largest colleges, and that they produced many leaders in almost every sphere of university activity; but most colleges contributed something of substance, and the University was always conscious of all its members. Even the great Dr Whewell of Trinity had the humiliation of being second wrangler only; the first was a Caian.[5] The office of Vice-Chancellor continued to rotate among all the Heads of Colleges, and a long-lived Master like Davy was liable to have two terms of office irrespective of the House to which he belonged. More significant, perhaps, is the view at a

2 Philip Grierson, in an unpublished note on the robberies, to which I am much indebted. The chief sources are Gunning, II, 45, 125–31, 268–73, and *Gesta*, 29 Oct. 1800, 14 Jan. 1801. For what follows, see Venn, III, 133–7; cf. II, 114.
3 Winstanley 1940, 1947.
4 Garland 1980; Rothblatt 1968/81. Garland, p. 18, gives an account of the modest role of smaller colleges compared with Trinity and St John's closely modelled on Winstanley 1940, p. 385, but lacking some of his qualifications — such as that Caius had six senior wranglers between 1800 and 1860. For Trinity itself there are very valuable studies in Robson 1967; Robson and Cannon 1964.
5 Clark 1900, p. 22. Clark, pp. 1–76, is still one of the best accounts of Whewell; cf. esp. Robson and Cannon 1964.

lower level, for much of the initiative and inspiration of change in 19th century Cambridge came from students and would-be students. The catalysts
of intellectual change are most visible to us in the private essay and debating
societies, of which the Apostles is the most famous; and although it is true
that the founder was a Johnian and the second generation was dominated
by F. D. Maurice and his friends in Trinity, it was always an inter-collegiate
group and two of the original members of 1820 were Caians.[6]

In another sphere the University Boat Club may be considered the key to
eminence in university affairs — and for the College, we have the authority
of E. S. Roberts for the view that 'of the various clubs and societies which
largely contribute to the vigour and wholesomeness of College life on its
lighter side the Boat Club is, and from the date of its foundation always has
been, the most important'[7] — a sentiment not echoed, perhaps, in all its
parts, by every Head Porter who has supervised the measures taken on the
morning after a bump supper. Sure enough, Trinity and St John's founded
their first clubs in 1825; but the University and four other colleges — and
the Third Trinity — came in 1827, and the four included Caius.[8] In 1836 the
second University Boat Race was held, and the Cambridge crew included
three Caians; in the May Races the College's first boat had a brief moment
of glory at the head of the river, while the second boat, after some heroic
adventures — it made an over-bump at the very beginning of the week —
ended last on the river. It has even been claimed that Caius gave to Cambridge its familiar light blue. This is an obscure region of scholarship. The
most circumstantial account is that it was achieved by an oarsman in the
race of 1836 hastily laying hands on a piece of Eton blue silk. But Caians,
following the historian of the Caius Boat Club, H. Claughton Scott, may
reckon it a remarkable coincidence that light blue was first adopted by a
boat containing three Caians; for light blue silk had already been consecrated for the College boat some years before.[9]

Wherever the winds of change blew from in early 19th century Cambridge, they were not inspired by its official mentors. The young Charles
Darwin, drifting from course to course in the 1820s, tried first Edinburgh
for medicine, then Cambridge to prepare for a clerical career. He got little
from Edinburgh, and wasted his time in Cambridge — though he derived a
vital impetus from J. S. Henslow, Professor of Botany, and Cambridge in
return was to receive everything from him and his descendants. Doubtless it
was in the nature of his genius not to find its fruition in formal instruction;
but it also reflects the extremely narrow curriculum of the day. This consisted of a little classics and an immense deal of mathematics. Those who

6 Allen 1968, pp. 219—20. The 13th member, 'Guest', tentatively identified by Allen as
   Benjamin Guest of Queens', could have been Edwin Guest of Caius, later Master, who
   matriculated in 1819 (see p. 214).
7 In Venn, III, 306.
8 For this, and what follows, see Scott 1927, pp. xiv—xv, 16—18.
9 Scott 1927, p. 18.

have erected the history of Trinity into the history of Cambridge have made of Dr Whewell, Master of Trinity from 1841 to 1866, a reformer.[10] All admit that he hated change; but he had a creative energy which compelled him to be at the forefront of every movement, so long as it was not a desperately radical movement. The recent restoration of Whewell's Court in Trinity, which he inspired, has revealed the romantic, antiquarian, medieval Whewell. This shows his creative spirit at its most characteristic. In matters of curriculum he believed fervently that the Mathematical Tripos which had adorned the land with so many eminent Trinity wranglers deserved its preeminence;[11] and only with reluctance did he join the Gadarene plunge into moral and natural science. However greatly we may admire the Mathematical Tripos, few today would regard it as fitted for the multitude of students. To the historian, it seems to have achieved its unique eminence by the accidents of 17th and 18th century history; but Whewell erected a dusty tradition into a mighty principle of education. According to his lights Whewell was not wholly illiberal: he believed that the Mathematical Tripos should be broadened to include occasional pieces of Greek, for example; nor did he wish to suppress the Classical Tripos, which had won through to recognition in the 1820s. But in education and curriculum he was a powerful conservative force. In his own personal tastes and aptitudes he was quite different. He could master a new science and publish a book on it almost in an instant. It need hardly be said that some of his contributions were superficial and all were deeply flawed. But his enthusiasm and his errors stimulated many minds more accurate than his; his work for the history and philosophy of science has lasting value; and his love of Gothic architecture fostered and was fostered by the genius of his friend Robert Willis. His enthusiasm for German professors, however, seems more likely to have impeded than advanced the cause of the professors of Cambridge. He believed in his heart that one course alone was best for all the truly first rate men as fervently as did the great headmasters of the early 20th century. The difference was that for them it was the classics; for Whewell it was mathematics. Both are splendid disciplines — but to claim monopoly for either seems now to most of us absurd.

It is indeed a wonder that reform in any real sense ever came to Cambridge. The Whewells of this world were enthroned on high. If we may peer into the future we see a university in which a German was to be Chancellor, and since genuine reform existed in Germany — and scholarship in many fields of a high order — that might seem a hopeful thing; and in the discussions between Whewell and Prince Albert the prince consort had the better of the Master of Trinity.[12] But the prince had an excessive deference for

10 See esp. Winstanley 1940; Roach 1959, pp. 241−5; and above, n. 5.
11 The most balanced account still seems to be Clark's (n. 5) , and for his academic work, see Robson and Cannon 1964.
12 Winstanley 1940, chaps. 10−12, esp. pp. 198−201.

Cambridge tradition, and this led him to place a check on the politicians who thought that radical measures were needed; so that the first Royal Commission of the 1840s and 50s proceeded in a manner so timid that when the Master of Caius, Dr Chapman, refused to show them the Statutes of John Caius, they failed to press the matter, and sought them elsewhere.[13] Yet in a halting way reform came, even to Cambridge, even to Caius.

How this happened is still obscure. But we may gain some insight into the nature of the society, and the winds which blew upon it, by studying a group of distinguished young Caians of Dr Davy's time before we proceed to the Master himself.

The young Caians: William Wilkins

In 1795 William Wilkins of Norwich executed the new extension of the Master's Lodge, and in the following year his son, the future architect of Downing and Corpus and King's — not to mention the New Court of Trinity — entered the College as a pensioner, and was soon after a scholar.[14] In 1798 the father proceeded to build a charming Italian villa on College land beyond the Backs, now Newnham Cottage, and here one may suppose father and son had their home while William was a student.[15] In him were united the antiquarian tradition of the College and the architectural vocation of his father. On graduation he was immediately elected FSA. His exquisite drawings of the Gate of Honour now in the Antiquaries' collection were probably executed in 1799, though not published till ten years later;[16] and he was to show his appreciation of the Gate by imitating its dome in the Gate of King's. In 1801 he had the fortune to receive a University scholarship endowed in the early 18th century by William Worts, best known to the people of Cambridge as the patron of Worts Causeway. He had prudently laid down that in recognition for his bounty — which gave his scholar £100 for three years to travel — a report should be sent in Latin to the Vice-Chancellor every month giving full details of the countries he visited. Wilkins' letters describing Sicily and Greece and other parts of the classical world are a fascinating source for the history of antiquarian learning and taste in this age, and the transmission of classical antiquities to Britain, and they have been admirably used — and compared with the findings of other travellers, especially Lord Aberdeen, who were

13 See below, p. 213.
14 Venn, II, 130–1; Liscombe 1980; Colvin 1978, pp. 893–6.
15 ER, p. 27; RCHM Cambridge, II, 375–6; cf. map of enclosure of 1804–5 in College Archives.
16 See Liscombe 1980, p. 233, for the drawing of 1799, supposed lost — but this is very likely the drawing, one of three published by the Society of Antiquaries in 1809, in Vetusta Monumenta IV, pls. 21–3. John Hopkins, librarian of the Society of Antiquaries, has kindly checked for me that the Society's records show that the drawings were received in 1808 and engraved in 1809.

exploring the Mediterranean in these years.[17] It was a crucial experience, for, as H. M. Colvin has written 'Wilkins was an architect for whom scholarship was in some danger of inhibiting invention . . . His was an architecture based essentially on archaeological investigation.' That the Mediterranean was safe, or moderately safe, for British travellers, was due to the victory of the son of a Caian, Horatio Nelson, at the Nile in 1798, and Wilkins travelled indeed for a time in a survivor of the French fleet; and though it is not recorded that he and Nelson met, his monument to Nelson at Yarmouth is one of the finest of its kind.[18] In these travels Wilkins added a rich classical heritage to the Gothic of his native land, and both flowered in a triumphal progress of successful designs between 1805 and the 1830s. Meanwhile, he became a fellow of Caius in 1803, Master of the Perse in 1804; senior fellow and junior dean in 1805. The senior fellows of Caius found it embarrassing to have the juniors starving in their midst, and were inclined to appoint them to office in the Perse school, augmenting their stipend without adding materially to their work, for pupils were rare birds in the school at this time. But in 1805 he submitted successful designs for both Downing College and Haileybury, and any ambitions he had to shine as a schoolmaster are buried under the lawns and porticoes of Downing. He remained a fellow till his marriage in 1811, but by then he was a busy architect. His work is a remarkable expression of its age and an impressive document of Cambridge on the eve of reform; but many will regret that he came to dominate Cambridge building to so great a degree, and few Caians will be sorry that his mighty scheme for enlarging the High Street of Cambridge, to make it a worthy cousin to Nash's Regent Street in London, did not mature.[19] It would have involved — not indeed the plan to obliterate the front of Caius with a new Fitzwilliam Museum propounded by the preposterous Mr Bankes in 1824 — but stepping back the front of Caius to create a nobler Trinity Street.[20] Nor need we regret too much that Wilkins' designs for Tree Court of the 1820s, which would have created something very like his King's where the Waterhouse building now stands, were considered too expensive.[21] In his later years indeed Wilkins' achievement lay further afield, in University College London and the National Gallery, and though abundantly creative to the end he suffered many disappointments. But in the New Court at Corpus he was not disappointed, and in Corpus Chapel, at his death in 1839, he asked to be buried.

17 Liscombe 1980, pp. 18−45. The quotation which follows is from Colvin 1978, pp. 893−6.
18 Liscombe 1980, pp. 114−17 and pl. 45. For Edmund Nelson, Nelson's father, see Venn, II, 50; but see below, p. 224n.
19 Liscombe 1980, esp. pp. 33, 46−54 (Downing and Haileybury), pp. 136−8 (High St.). The line of streets now known as Trumpington Street, King's Parade, Trinity and St John's Streets was, down to the 19th century, normally called the High Street.
20 Liscombe 1980, p. 135.
21 Liscombe 1980, p. 237 and pl. 54; but Venn, III, 136−7 is probably correct in dating this 1822.

Robert Woodhouse, Hamnett Holditch and George Green

However little John Smith and Richard Belward may have contributed to any branch of learning, it is a remarkable tribute to their taste that they brought Sir John Soane and Wilkins senior — who heartily disliked one another — into Caius;[22] and so paved the way for the career of William the younger. In Caius too the younger Wilkins made one of the most lasting of his friendships. In 1795, when he was still at school in Norwich, the senior wrangler was another Caian sprung from Norwich, Robert Woodhouse, who also carried off the first Smith's prize in the University and the Schuldham prize in the College. From 1798 to 1823 he was a fellow, and he appears among the subscribers to Wilkins' *Magna Graecia* in 1807.[23] His fellowship was cut short in 1823 by an event in the chapel of the British Embassy in Paris, when he married Harriet Wilkins, William's sister.[24] But his career as a mathematician continued. Rouse Ball called him 'an apostle of the new movement', and his numerous works on mathematics and astronomy, and especially on the calculus, earned him first the Lucasian Chair of Mathematics in 1820, and then the Plumian in 1822; his brilliant career ended prematurely in 1827, when he died in his early 50s.[25]

In a University primarily designed to produce mathematicians and divines, it is hardly surprising to find some of the best minds in Caius devoted to mathematics; and the College certainly had its share. Six senior wranglers between 1800 and 1860 was a reasonable number for a college of medium size — a good number indeed, when one recalls the grip Trinity and St John's tried to keep on this pinnacle.[26] As often happens, however, it was not the senior wranglers for the most part who stayed the course as eminent mathematicians. Robert Murphy, the brilliant Irish mathematician who became an FRS while still a junior fellow in 1834, and who made original contributions to the study of algebra and electricity, had had to be content with being third wrangler. Venn noted his exceptional brilliance, but sadly observed that his 'dissipated habits' proved his undoing; that he had to sequester his fellowship 'for the benefit of his creditors' and leave Cambridge, and died an early death in 1843.[27] But Hamnett Holditch, senior wrangler in 1822, was spoiled even as a mathematician by his early success, and Venn — himself the most distinguished mathematician in the College in the mid and later years of the century — coolly wrote of him that 'he would

22 See p. 254; cf. Liscombe 1980, pp. 147—9. The elder Wilkins came from Norwich, but lived in his later years in Newnham Cottage and is buried in St Giles' Church, where a single monument records himself, his wife, and their three daughters, including Harriet Woodhouse.
23 Venn, II, 119—20; *DNB*; cf. Liscombe 1980, p. 34 (Dr Davy also subscribed: ibid. p. 33).
24 Liscombe 1980, p. 34; Venn, II, 120.
25 Ball 1901, p. 450; cf. pp. 450—1 and Ball 1889, pp. 118—20; Venn, II, 120. The date of death on his tombstone reads X kal. Jan. 1828 ('X' omitted in Venn, III, 173), 23 Dec. 1827.
26 Winstanley 1940, p. 385.
27 Venn, II, 196—7; *DNB*.

probably have distinguished himself had he been compelled to work'. As it was, he was successively Hebrew lecturer, registrar, steward, Greek lecturer, salarist and bursar — but never taught anyone save a few who came to him for coaching; and after rising to the presidency in 1835 — an office he held till his death in 1867 — he abandoned every temptation to work. In the summer he fished in Scotland or Wales, and in the winter he lurked in his rooms in College. He imagined 'some ancient slight' and 'absented himself from Hall and Chapel'; and the story is told that a friendly undergraduate, mistaking the President of the College for a stranger, showed him round.[28] It is alleged that he was genuinely shy, but his career remains a paradigm of the oddest features of the ancien regime in a Cambridge college.

These men undoubtedly helped to foster an interest in mathematics in the College, and Woodhouse was one of a group of original mathematicians who brought Cambridge into the 19th century in this field. But in truth his importance perhaps lies more in the history of the University than of Caius, for what was crucial was the development of the subject as a fit and eminent academic discipline which could make Cambridge once again, as it had been in Newton's time, a leading centre of the science; and here Woodhouse must take his place as the man who inspired even greater names, such as Babbage, Peacock and DeMorgan, who provided an adequate content to justify Whewell's faith in the Mathematical Tripos. So far as the teaching of the subject was concerned, this lay primarily with the coaches and private tutors — and to them we shall return.

Woodhouse was a very able interpreter of current continental advances in mathematics, rather than a creative thinker. Soon after his death Caius received the most original mind among its 19th century mathematicians in George Green.[29] His father was a baker and miller in and near Nottingham, and until his death in 1829 the son helped him. But meanwhile he had been developing mathematical theories and had published an 'Essay on the application of Mathematical Analysis to the Theories of Electricity and Magnetism' in 1828. Green's is an astonishing story, full of puzzle and irony. The puzzle is to know where he learned his mathematics — apart from well-placed encouragement by a local schoolmaster — and how he came to know the continental literature which helped to inspire his own discoveries. The irony is that owing presumably to a difference of opinion with his father, he did not marry the lady of his choice, Jane Smith, and so was able in due course to accept a fellowship at Caius — even though he had by her six children, and was to have a seventh. In 1828 he sent a copy of

28 Venn, II, 170.
29 On Green (1793–1841) see esp. *George Green, Miller Snienton* (Nottingham, 1976), with studies by R. M. Bowley, L. J. Challis, F. W. Sheard, F. M. Wilkins-Jones and D. Phillips, and full account of other literature; also *DSB*, XV (Supplement), 199–201 and references (P. J. Wallis); Venn, II, 224; *DNB*. For Bromhead, see Venn, II, 151–2. For the colleagues and successors of Woodhouse, see Winstanley 1940, pp. 157–60; Garland, chap. 3.

his essay to a country gentleman called Sir Edward Bromhead. Bromhead was a Caian who claimed founder's kin by relationship to the Gonvilles, and had retained from his Cambridge days a strong interest in mathematics. He helped Green to publish later studies in Cambridge and Edinburgh, and encouraged him to enter Caius, where he flourished — though he had to be content to be fourth wrangler — and became a fellow. In Cambridge he was able to develop his theories further. His first paper, enshrining what was later seen as his most important discovery, laid the foundation of what are now called 'Green's functions', which made a notable advance in applied mathematics or theoretical physics — but have come into their own in the last thirty-five years or so since they became one of the pillars of modern nuclear physics; and Green has risen from being an obscure genius to be one of the founders of modern science. In later papers he developed principles of elasticity fundamental to the progress of engineering and studied the motions of waves on liquid surfaces by a method which marked a significant development in fluid mechanics. But his career in Caius was short: he died very soon after winning his fellowship, and his works lay in relative obscurity till they were published by the Caius tutor Ferrers in 1871, to reap their reward when 'Green's functions' became famous in more recent times.

Henry Bickersteth

If Woodhouse inspired reform in the study of mathematics, his younger colleague in the fellowship, Henry Bickersteth, seems to represent, in a wider sphere, the age of reform itself.[30] Born in 1783, the son of a surgeon in Kirkby Lonsdale, then in Westmorland, he died a peer and Master of the Rolls in 1851. His *Memoirs* by Thomas Duffus Hardy were published in 1852, in the same year that *Bleak House* began to appear: there are extraordinary echoes in Dickens' onslaught on the Court of Chancery of Bickersteth's own more measured schemes for its reform; and there is even a curious resemblance between his career and that of Richard Carstone. Like Richard, he tried or thought in turn of all the professions open to a man of breeding — medicine, law, church and war — and he seriously studied as a medical student and a lawyer. Unlike Richard Carstone, he was touched by almost every intellectual wind which blew — by turn romantic, Benthamite, and liberal reformer — and he was a man who found a purpose and vocation in life which led him to creative work among the Whig reformers. He was born in the north-west and early fell in love with the Lake District; when his time came to choose a title, he called himself Lord Langdale, though the Langdales only received a passing mention in the vivid narrative of a Lakeland tour he wrote in the year he entered Caius, in 1802. 'We proceeded through Langdale, between and over the Pikes,

30 Hardy 1852 — on which most of what follows is based; *DNB*; Venn, II, 139.

through a wild, but by no means uninteresting country' — and on to Coniston and Furness — 'Furness Abbey, whose vaulted roof once rung with the praise of Heaven, is now the abode of birds and reptiles . . .; and the high altar itself, formerly consecrated to the holiest of uses, is now become open to that vast expanse, and the same praise is now reiterated by the warblers of the forest'.[31] Though he was later to be a friend of Bentham and James Mill, and in the inner counsels of Grey and Melbourne, he always combined a powerful sense of the romantic past with the zeal of the reformer.

At the age of fifteen, after early schooling at Kirkby Lonsdale and possibly at Sedbergh, he set up as a medical student in the house of his uncle, Dr Batty (like Richard in the house of Dr Bayham Badger) in London late in 1798; and after just over two years' study there and at a school of anatomy, he went on in 1801 to the true centre of medical education in Britain at that time, in Edinburgh.[32] But after only a few months he was summoned home to help his father for a space; and within a few months again he had matriculated at Caius, at the age of twenty, evidently in the hope of continuing his studies notionally as a medical student while working for a Cambridge degree. Cambridge was no place for a serious medical student at this time, but he seems to have seen it as a stepping stone to a better place in London — and he perhaps had some inkling of his future. In any case he was from the first a reading man, and his early letters show the intensely serious nature of his studies, perhaps not surprising in a man of twenty determined to make good use of his time in Cambridge. His reading was wide — his early letters are full of Bacon and philosophy; but 'Lectures on Euclid began yesterday, and will be continued every morning, but Sunday and Thursday, till the end of term. Classical lectures begin on Tuesday evening, with the Medea of Euripides three evenings in the week, and Greek Testament two . . .' The date on the letter, 17 November, reminds us how short was the lecturing term.[33] None the less, he was soon 'working very hard at Mathematics. Cambridge you know [he is addressing his Edinburgh friend Alexander Henderson], is everywhere celebrated for knowledge of this kind' — and he intended 'to make use of it' — and by good fortune it suited his talents well.[34] And to his little sister: 'I have to get up every morning at seven o'clock, to go to chapel, and have also to go in the evening. I have likewise to attend lectures twice a day. Now these lectures are something like your lessons, only longer and on more difficult subjects. You will think two lessons a day very little, . . . but in fact I am fully engaged, and have scarcely time for anything.'[35] It seems indeed that he worked too hard and worried too much about his growing disaffection for medicine; for by March 1803 his health was breaking down, and his uncle despatched him

31 Hardy 1852, I, 92—4; cf. the whole passage, pp. 80—95.
32 Hardy 1852, I, 11—14, 28.
33 Hardy 1852, I, 135.
34 Hardy 1852, I, 140—1; on Henderson, see *DNB*.
35 Hardy 1852, I, 145.

to Italy — via Paris, where he saw Napoleon himself at the opera, in the brief interval of peace after the Treaty of Amiens — to become personal physician to the earl of Oxford, then enjoying an Italian tour.[36] In Florence he caught up with the earl and his party, and started one of the chief friendships of his life — and with his little daughter Lady Jane a friendship even closer which culminated over thirty years later in their marriage. Immediately, the omens for a peaceful stay in Italy were extremely unfavourable; war was soon in the air again and the party fled via Venice to Austria and Germany, and in September 1804 they were settled at Eywood in Herefordshire, the earl's favourite seat.[37] In March 1805 Bickersteth returned to Caius and was finally rescued from a medical career by an extraordinary chance.[38]

When Bickersteth first came to Caius his tutor was Martin Davy, then President; in 1803 Davy became Master and when Bickersteth returned he had just served a turn as Vice-Chancellor. Davy was a practising physician — though he intermitted his practice while Vice-Chancellor — and he and the Regius Professor joined together in a campaign to prevent anyone who had practised 'any trade or profession whatsoever' from being admitted to a medical degree. Davy proposed and passed at a meeting of Heads an interpretation of the relevant statute which simply added this extraordinary codicil. The fact so far is clear; the rest of the story depends wholly on the *Reminiscences* of Henry Gunning written long after the event. Gunning had a clear memory, in this case a little clouded, one may think, by growing dislike of Davy in later years. But he certainly tried to be fair.

'Davy and I had always been on very friendly terms; he had treated me with marked kindness and respect, and had not unfrequently canvassed with me subjects relating to the University. Upon this occasion . . . he drove to Ickleton [where Gunning had a farm] to converse with me on the subject; he supported the expediency of the interpretation, which, he remarked, appeared to him necessary to prevent the degradation of the medical profession, by introducing low and improper persons into the University.'[39] Gunning resisted him to his face, with little or no result, for Davy could evidently be an obstinate man, and on this issue Gunning showed no understanding of the physician's viewpoint. The victim's trade had been that of surgeon. We seem to be the witnesses of the ancient feud of physician and surgeon; and the successor to Dr Caius evidently felt bound to join the Regius of Physic: Mr Thackeray, the occasion of this flurry, was unlucky to find the Regius and the Vice-Chancellor thus locked in prejudice together, but many years later the interpretation was rescinded and he was able to proceed to a degree.

36 Hardy 1852, I, 160−96.
37 Hardy 1852, I, 196−7.
38 Ibid., and for what follows, pp. 216−17; Gunning, II, 191−6; Winstanley 1940, pp. 161−3.
39 Gunning, II, 191−6, esp. 192−3; cf. Winstanley 1940, pp. 161−3.

Meanwhile Henry Bickersteth returned to Caius after serving as a professional medical attendant on the earl, and 'found a probability of obstacles to his obtaining a medical degree'.[40] Indeed he was rather in Mr Thackeray's position, of whom Gunning had said that his father 'had sent him and his two brothers to Edinburgh, as well as to Paris, for the express purpose of improving themselves, and of acquiring that professional knowledge for which our University was confessedly an indifferent school' — and though Bickersteth had not fallen under suspicion of surgery, Davy's situation was evidently delicate, and gave the young scholar the opportunity he sought.[41] After toying with a military career he settled in earnest to work for his degree, following the advice of his new tutor, Dr Chapman — who recalled, not without the benefit of hindsight, that he had advised him to take an arts degree (that is, ultimately in mathematics), 'and to read hard for his degree' — and becoming, as Professor Sedgwick, the eminent geologist, recalled 'a desperately hard student'.[42] The flight from medicine worked a wonderful improvement in his health. He explained to Henderson that 'I have resolved to remain at Cambridge. At the end of that time, if my studies are prosperous, I may become a fellow of my college, and thus I should secure to myself an agreeable retirement whenever in future life I choose to quit the scenes in which I may be engaged. In the meantime my studies must be adapted to the character of the place: they will be chiefly mathematics, partly classics, and partly moral philosophy, and belles lettres.' He confesses that he has derived great comfort from the prospect, though the plan 'is plainly a mere temporizing one'.[43]

In January 1808 Bickersteth's labours were rewarded: he became senior wrangler and senior Smith's prizeman in a distinguished year; and in March he was elected fellow of Caius.[44] Neither then nor at any future date — at least till the 1830s — does it seem to have occurred to this deeply conscientious reformer of the abuses of the world that his fellowship carried any obligations to residence or toil. When faced with the prospect of a clerical career open to all fellows, he speedily fled to the bar; and Duffus Hardy's account of how he came finally to his vocation reads a little like another chapter in the meanderings of Richard Carstone — medicine, the army, the church had been put on one side; the bar remained. Perhaps in later life Lord Langdale so described his early progress; but it is hard to believe his life in Cambridge had not affected his choice more positively. Hardy himself noted that four of the senior wranglers of the decade, two from Trinity and two from Caius, became judges.[45] The law school was moribund and hardly contributed to this result. The academic exercises of the

40 Hardy 1852, I, 215—16.
41 Gunning, II, 193; Hardy 1852, I, 215—27.
42 Hardy 1852, I, 228, 231.
43 Hardy 1852, I, 234—5.
44 Hardy 1852, I, 236—8; Venn, II, 139.
45 Hardy 1852, I, 237. For law studies in this epoch, see Crawley 1976, pp. 87—9.

age, which involved public disputation, may well have contributed something. But the heart of the matter seems likely to lie among the young men themselves. In public instruction, in scholarly example, Caius and Cambridge had little to offer. But both were the happy hunting grounds of growing numbers of young men of unusual talent. We may suppose that the presence of Robert Woodhouse in the fellowship was a stimulus to the wranglers of Caius. We may reflect how short a distance separated Caius and Trinity. And we may reckon it no chance that the other eminent Caian of this age to become a judge, Sir Edward Hall Alderson, was a younger contemporary of Bickersteth and followed him as senior wrangler in 1809.[46] If we are ever tempted to think meanly of the Caius high table of the early 19th century, let us reflect what it might mean to compete with Woodhouse, Wilkins, Bickersteth and Alderson.

If we consult the Absence Book, however, we shall discover that in all the twenty-four years Bickersteth was a fellow, he was rarely in residence. His interest to us lies not in what he contributed directly and at first hand to the life of the College, but in what he reflects of the place of Caius in the lives of its most talented members, and for what he shows of its place in the age of reform. Slowly he came to prosper at the bar; but the fellowship, specially when he became a senior in 1814, meant much to him for support for many years. At last in the 1820s he achieved some independence; in the 1830s he felt prosperous enough — or perhaps enough of an abuse — to resign his fellowship, and after a space to marry the Lady Jane Harley whom he had known since her childhood;[47] the reticence of Victorian biographers has doubtless hidden from us a charming romantic tale, and one would like to know if Mr Knightley's success with Emma encouraged him to persevere. Meanwhile his progress had been slowed down by suspicion that he tended to radical views, and he was indeed a friend of Burdett and Bentham: he was to come into his own in the 1830s and 40s when the Whigs came to power and he was offered the woolsack — but refused to take the office till Chancery was reformed, and preferred to be Master of the Rolls.[48] In that office it fell to him to see into operation the Public Records Act of 1838; and his bust in the Public Record Office in Chancery Lane is the monument to a very notable public service for which all historians should hold his memory in benediction.[49] That many of his subordinates held him in warm regard is attested by Duffus Hardy — a man more familiar perhaps to medievalists than Langdale, and the most notable scholar among the early Deputy Keepers; and indeed it seems that only Sir Francis Palgrave, the first DK, himself, failed to appreciate Langdale.[50] To the end he was a 'desperately

46 Hardy 1852, II, 144−5.
47 On 17 August 1835: Hardy 1852, I, 444 — cf. p. 231 n.; Venn, II, 139.
48 See Hardy 1852, I, chaps. xxiii−v, xxxiii−iv; II, chap. xvi.
49 Pl. 9c. Hardy 1852, II, chaps. viii−xii.
50 See the moving account of his farewell in Hardy 1852, II, 189−93. On p. 190 Hardy notes that only one failed to sign the farewell address, and Palgrave's signature is notable by its absence on p. 192. [See now J. Cantwell's illuminating study in *Archives*, XVII (1985), 22−37.]

hard' worker, and he died well short of seventy, in 1851, full of honours. Thomas Duffus Hardy, with the breath-taking speed so familiar to those who use his works, stitched together a final memorial to him in time to be published the next year.

But his image in the eyes of posterity has been marred by his role in the Gorham case, in which he acted as the leading member and mouthpiece of the Judicial Committee of the Privy Council and uttered its findings in the matter of baptismal regeneration, a subject which many persons of many persuasions have doubted if judges should be invited to determine; nor was the case much improved by the presence as assessors of both archbishops and Bishop Blomfield of London — the third wrangler of 1808.[51] In such a case Lord Langdale felt it his conscientious duty to act within the law and interpret the law. He may well have thought the Judicial Committee a tolerable body for such a purpose; he certainly much disliked his task. But he really believed that in law what mattered was not the theological doctrine but the proper interpretation of the 39 Articles and their enforcement; and the notes he left leave one in little doubt that when the judgement was delivered he knew far more than Mr Gorham or the bishop of Exeter — or probably than either archbishop — on the history of the Articles of the Anglican Church and the true obligations of bishops and incumbents. There is little evidence of the wider vision of what was involved, but a very powerful attempt to see that justice was done according to established law in the particular instance. And thus it had been in the curious case of the last will and testament of Stephen Perse.

Bickersteth and the Perse scandal

In 1823 Bickersteth became one of the four senior fellows of the College, and so a trustee of Perse's will, and a beneficiary of it. 'From the time when I first became a fellow of Caius College, I always understood that the four Senior Fellows had some peculiar benefit from the Perse Foundation', he wrote himself, 'and as I approached seniority, hints were frequently given to me of the advantages I should have when I became one of the four Seniors . . . I thought that the Perse Foundation was, amongst other things, a special benefaction to the Master and four Senior Fellows. I became one of the four Senior Fellows in 1823, and received an increase of stipend to the amount of sixty pounds a year, without thinking that there was, or could be, any doubt of my right. I rarely attended College meetings, and when I did so, ran down to Cambridge and concurred in what passed upon the information I then received, and in the reliance that what they proposed was for the general benefit. In 1825, at a meeting of the Master and Seniors,

51 Hardy 1852, I, 237; cf. II, chaps. xvii−xviii; Nias 1951, esp. pp. 97−104, who, however, ignores the evidence of Hardy's *Memoirs*.

it was proposed to increase their stipends. I asked if it was clear that we were entitled to do so. I was told that it was, and . . . giving entire confidence to the Master and the other Seniors, but particularly the Master, who said he knew the Foundation, etc., I concurred in the vote of increase. I pretend not to justify or excuse the proceeding . . .', and he went on to lay particular blame on himself.[52] But he did nothing till 1830. The seething discontent among the junior fellows — the Perse fellows, no doubt, who saw so little of the colour of Perse's money — was reported to Bickersteth by the Master in May 1830. Now Bickersteth determined to see Perse's will, to the evident annoyance of the Master, who presently left him in the hands of the bursar, Hamnett Holditch, — the senior wrangler of 1822, but also the future silent President, the idlest man, so far as the records go, among the fellows of Caius of the century. Eventually in October, after unlocking (so he alleged) four locks and finding the necessary books for the purpose, he sent Bickersteth a copy of the will; Bickersteth came in haste to Cambridge to protest at the way it had been interpreted; the Master and four seniors failed to calm him, and he appealed to a general meeting of all the senior fellows; and at meetings on 27—28 October 1830 'a new and just scale of payments' was adopted, and Bickersteth placed in the astonished bursar's hands £748. 15s., which he reckoned the amount he had wrongfully received. He subsequently checked the calculation, which included 4% per annum interest for each years' taking, sent a further payment of £25, and the full account — the autograph original is one of the treasures of the College archives — was duly printed by Hardy in his *Memoirs*.[53] 'The sequel to this beautiful trait of character', as Hardy loyally observed, was that the Perse scandal began to leak out.[54]

Perhaps so: but some of it had been notorious for many years, and efforts had been made by the townsfolk to improve the condition of the school long before Wilkins was Master of the Perse, two generations before 1830. Only a man so rarely at large in the streets of Cambridge as Henry Bickersteth could have passed so long in ignorance that something was amiss. None the less it was a noble act, and doubtless made his seat among the seniors a hot one, and this may have led to his resignation in 1832.

In the wake of the Reform Act of the same year the smell of sulphur was in the air. A few years later 'A bill in Chancery was . . . filed against the college praying the Court to compel the Master and fellows to do, by a decree in equity, the same as had been so nobly done by one Fellow . . .; and it is curious enough that the judge who heard and decided the case was no other than the identical Fellow who seven years before had acted thus. The judge

52 Hardy 1852, I, 297—8.
53 Hardy 1852, I, 296—7 and n. (where, in totals for year 25 . . ., read not 22 but 22½). By general meeting of fellows he means a meeting of the twelve senior fellows with the Master, the Governing Body. See *Gesta*, 27—28 Oct. 1830 (which makes no mention, however, of Perse Trust business).
54 Hardy 1852, I, 299; for what follows, see above, p. 100—1.

at first declined, out of delicacy, to hear the cause, and only consented to do so at the earnest solicitation of both parties.'[55] It was a tribute to his high repute — and, be it said, to the goodwill of the parties in a dangerous case. Lord Langdale, as he now was, found, as Mr Bickersteth, fellow, had done, that much money had been misappropriated; but he softened the blow by observing how difficult Perse's will had now become to implement; and — showing himself ever the careful judge as much as the reformer — he saw no ground in law for removing the Master and four seniors from the charge over the trust which they had thus betrayed.[56] In the measured words of his judgement the bad deeds and good intentions of the fellows of Caius were displayed before the world in 1837 as a fitting epilogue to the years which had seen the Reform Act and its many sequels. The scheme which followed his judgement first mooted the idea for a girls' school; but this was not realised until the more radical reforms of the 1860s and early 1870s, from which the original school emerged like the phoenix, with the Girls' School beside it founded out of the school's share of the Trust. The College retained a formal link with the Boys' School, and is still represented on its Board of Govenors; E. S. Roberts was to be one of the early Chairmen of Governors of the Girls' School. But the old Trustees were relieved of their charge of the school just at the time when the College was becoming more aware of its role in the world of education; and the College's share of the Trust was put into the hands of the Official Trustee of Charitable Funds, who invested it so cautiously that it is now of little worth. From the well-meaning intervention of public bodies with as little idea of inflation and investment as the earlier Trustees, the great endowment of Stephen Perse can hardly hope to recover.

Robert Willis

Robert Woodhouse and Hamnett Holditch came from the traditional sources of Caians, from Norwich and Lynn; and Henry Bickersteth came in search of a medical scholarship or at least of a college whose tutor was a physician. William Wilkins and Robert Willis came because their fathers had a link with Caius. Dr Willis had been a junior fellow in the 1790s and by some device had held his fellowship till death; and his son waited till his death in 1821 before setting off to Caius at the age of twenty-one.[57] He was

55 Hardy 1852, I, 299—300.
56 Ibid.; there is an extract from his judgement at II, 414—20. Cf. Gray 1921, pp. 114—16; Mitchell 1976, pp. 39—40 (which needs correction in detail from Hardy, loc. cit.). For what follows see Scott 1981, esp. pp. 1—2; Mitchell 1976.
57 For the father, Venn, II, 101. Mrs Hall and I have checked the records, and there seems no doubt that Dr Willis senior kept his fellowship till death — whether by bravado or by the complacency Dr Davy may have felt towards an eminent court physician. Since no wife is mentioned in J. W. Clark's *DNB* entries on the family it seems likely that Robert and his sister (J. W. Clark's mother) were illegitimate. For the son, Venn, II, 182; *DNB* (J. W.

ninth wrangler and won the Schuldham prize and a Frankland fellowship in 1826, which perhaps suggests that the competition in the College was not so severe as twenty years before. Yet Willis is the only fellow of Caius of the age of Davy whose works are well known to undergraduates still. He was ordained in 1827 but never, so far as I know, practised in a parish and eventually renounced his orders; he is not remembered in the Faculty of Divinity. He was a pioneer in the Cambridge School of Engineering, a remarkable teacher of mechanical contrivances; a man of wide repute for his knowledge of metals and their use in railway construction and mines. From 1837 till his death in 1875 he was Jacksonian Professor of Natural Philosophy, but in fact it was mechanical engineering that he taught. He is now greatly honoured in the Faculty of Engineering – and though he had a collection of mechanical models he had no laboratory or museum in which to keep them; the conditions of his work must have been somewhat rough and ready, but he had considerable private means to provide the models a comfortable home and he doubtless performed his exercises with exquisite precision.[58] It is in the Department of the History of Art that Willis is read today; and his name is revered wherever the study of medieval architecture lives and flourishes. He was a fellow from 1826 – a senior from 1829 – till his marriage, in 1832, to Mary Ann, daughter of Charles Humfrey, architect and mayor of Cambridge – now remembered for his speculative development south-east of Christ's Pieces, and as architect of the tower of St Clement's. Then Willis's fellowship lapsed and was never revived, and although he was sometimes later called 'Willis of Caius' his links with the College do not seem to have been very close. One hears more of him in Trinity, where he dined with Whewell, and where his nephew J. W. Clark, later Registrary and joint-author of his greatest work, was to be a fellow.[59] With Whewell he formed a friendship, and it may be that Whewell's extravagant book on the origins of Gothic of 1830 inspired his own similar study of 1835; and their cast of mind – mathematical, scientific, and yet romantic too – made it natural that Whewell should influence Willis. But Whewell's book is only remembered now for its influence on Willis; for the younger man was a much greater scholar. Willis's delight was to lead the Royal Archaeological Institute from cathedral to cathedral, expounding each with a learned paper based on patient measurement and a deep insight into the mechanics of medieval architecture. Nor was that all: he was a

---

Clark); and esp. Pevsner, *Willis*. Venn says that he was 22, but he was born in 1800, according to *DNB*. See Romilly, p. 115, for his admission as professor.

58 Venn 1913, p. 265. For Willis's inherited wealth, see Romilly, p. 91. For his father-in-law see Colvin 1978, pp. 438 – 9.

59 See e.g. Romilly, pp. 38 – 9 (the christening of Willis's daughter and of J. W. Clark), 109; preface to Willis and Clark, I, pp. xvii – xxvii – esp. p. xviii, for his friendship with Whewell, and p. xx for the encouragement by Guest. Pevsner, *Willis*, p. 27, describes an occasion in 1851 when Ruskin, Whewell and Willis visited Ely together. For 'Professor Willis of Caius' see Francis 1923, p. 118.

pioneer in the study of archival evidence for buildings. The golden year of 1845 saw the publication of his papers on Canterbury and Winchester Cathedrals;[60] in 1869 he expanded his study of Canterbury to all the monastic buildings and in the 1980s I have seen one of the most distinguished living art historians exploring Canterbury Cathedral, Willis in hand. The most remarkable of all his works is *The Architectural History of the University of Cambridge and of the Colleges of Cambridge and Eton*, which his nephew John Willis Clark published in 1886 from his notes and drafts. The scheme and the best of the book were Willis's; its completion a labour of love, all the more welcome to its users because Clark meticulously noted by a system of brackets where Willis ended and Clark and his helpers began; and for Caius he had the help of the Reverend John Lamb, fellow from 1849 to 1880, son of the Master of Corpus and brother-in-law of the Master of Caius, N. M. Ferrers.[61] Venn evidently regarded Lamb as a valued predecessor in the study of College history, as well as honouring him as a man 'well known in Cambridge for his genial social qualities, and in his own college as the most active and efficient of bursars'; and Lamb's notes are valuable. But the heart of the matter was Willis's own, and his account of the College, its topography and history, and state before the great changes of the mid 19th century, is one of the chief foundations of our history to this day; and the whole book has long been the envy of Oxford. Yet it seems sadly true that Willis never received the recognition which was his due within his College while he lived.

The antiquarian tradition in Caius was indeed continued for a time by J. J. Smith, a great-nephew of the former Master, who had been both captain of the Boat Club and fellow in 1828; he was later to be one of the founders of the Cambridge Antiquarian Society, and he produced a catalogue of the College manuscripts which was a notable work for its day. In 1835 he became a tutor, and to his antiquarian researches we may perhaps attribute the discovery that Dr Caius had suggested in his statutes that the gown worn by the members of the College might be violet in colour — though (unusually for Caius) he did not insist on it. Whoever was responsible, the fact is certain that in 1837 the seniors determined — and successfully petitioned the Chancellor to this end — that Caius undergraduates should wear the blue and velvet gown which has marked them out ever since. Legend has it that a deputation went to E. S. Roberts when he was Master to ask for a change, which he answered with the *mot*: 'Caius men change their gowns by *degrees*'.[62]

---

60 Willis 1845, 1 and 2.
61 Venn, II, 265; cf. 278. Lamb's work was to provide a nucleus for Gross's in *ER*; he may himself have been partly inspired by his father's work in the archives of Corpus, as Catherine Hall has pointed out to me.
62 Personal information from the late Z. N. Brooke. On the change of gown in 1837, see Venn 1901, p. 212; Venn, III, 137. The decision is recorded in the *Gesta* under 13 May 1837, and a draft petition to the Chancellor apparently in J. J. Smith's hand dated 20 May has very

George Paget

I have surveyed the careers of an architect, two mathematicians, a lawyer, and an engineer turned architectural historian; in such a selective view many disciplines and spheres of work are naturally left on one side. But in the history of Caius a place must be found for medicine, and the outstanding candidate from the young fellows of Davy's era is George Paget, the 'beloved physician'. Paget is the very type of the all-round Caian. His elder brother was a founder of the College Boat Club, rowing in the first recorded crew; George himself rowed in 1830—1.[63] He was eighth wrangler in 1831, and was suddenly promoted to senior fellow in 1832 owing to a happy vacancy in a fellowship which the arcane traditions of the seniority reserved for medical men from Norfolk. He was catechist in 1834, later bursar and steward, and though evidently conscientious in the latter offices he was also rapidly advancing as a physician and one of the leaders of Cambridge medicine; he was later to be Regius Professor of Physic from 1872 till 1892; and he was a man of great popularity and charm. He might well have been elected Master in 1839 or 1852 but for two involuntary failings. In 1839 he was too young, and when, like Jeremy Taylor in the service of Laud, he had cured this error, it was held against him in 1852 that he had been born in Norfolk. To this sad tale we shall return. But he had meanwhile committed another misdemeanour and married, and so he had to abandon his fellowship in 1851. Paget, though never able to forge the link between the reviving medical school and the College which some thought he might have done if he had been both Master and Regius Professor, kept his close links with Caius, and saw many Caians in his school and hospital; and when the image of a professorial fellow was traced in the wake of the Royal Commission in the early 1880s, and Guest, his successful rival as Master, was dead, Paget was duly re-elected a fellow in 1881, at the age of 72.

He is chiefly remembered as one of the architects of the medical school. But his hand was everywhere — presiding at the celebration of the centenary of the College in 1848, attending the young Venn when he fell sick of small pox in College in the 1850s, debating the future of the ordinary degree in the 1860s, a major figure in the medical, academic and social life of Cambridge.[64]

---

recently come to our notice by the courtesy of the librarian of Queens', in whose Archives it was discovered. This establishes that the basis for the colour was the word 'violaceo' in Caius' Statute 27 (Venn, III, 363), as was ingeniously conjectured in Hargreaves-Mawdsley 1963, p. 132. On Smith, see Venn, II, 189. His *Catalogue of the Manuscripts* (Smith 1849) was a valuable work for its day, and was extensively used by M. R. James (see James 1907—8, I, p. v).

63 A. C. Paget was Secretary in 1828 — for all this see Scott 1927, pp. 3, 173, 176—7. For George Paget, 'the beloved physician', see A. G. Day in *Caian* II (1892—3), 3—10, at p. 10; Venn, II, 202. Paget is duly commemorated in a memorial window in chapel, containing a picture of St Luke, among others — opposite the window to his rival Dr Guest (see pp. 213—14, 226).

64 *Caian* II, 5—6; *Caian* XXXI (1922—3), 109; Winstanley 1947, pp. 151—3.

1864 found him insisting in public debate that poll-men, students for the ordinary degree, should profit from the lectures of professors — before Paget himself was professor — and that clergymen should enjoy some smattering of natural science and philosophy — to be told for his pains by Ferrers, the future tutor and Master of Caius, that 'the value of poll hydrostatics was absolutely zero'.[65] He is a powerful link, in the whole range of College activities from the medical school to the boat club, between the world of Dr Davy and the 1890s, between Caius unreformed and the new world of E. S. Roberts, who was firmly in the saddle as tutor when Paget died in 1892.

The flow of recruits

The College which contained these men of remarkable and varied talent had grown from a modest entry of 11 or 12 a year between 1790 and 1810 to 15 a year in the 1810s, then to 23 a year in the 20s and to 29 a year in the 1830s.[66] It was not until the 40s that it recovered the figures of the 1570s or 1610s, nor till the 1850s that it finally surpassed the 1620s and 30s. But it was growing fast in Davy's later years. Perhaps a little may be attributed to the special qualities of the college, and a very little to the Master himself. But applicants and their parents have always looked more to the tutors than to the Heads, and more credit should perhaps be given the tutors, who included Dr Chapman, the future Master, and Mr Alderson — presumably Samuel Alderson, the brother of the judge, for Edward must already have been busy at the bar.[67] But in truth the increase was universal in Oxford and Cambridge, and the main causes lay outside the College. The later 18th century saw a growing population with an element of middle-class parents of unprecedented prosperity. Many still favoured the more varied, more practical academies of the 18th century; but first a trickle then, in the end, a flood, came to Oxford and Cambridge.

It is hard to put a finger on the moment of change, but after a while a new pattern becomes clearer. The entry of 1800 — 1 was still small — 5 from East Anglia, a Wykehamist from Wiltshire, a migrant from St John's, and a farmer's son from Banffshire.[68] But as the numbers grew a slow and steady shift away from Norfolk and Suffolk gradually becomes perceptible; one observes an increasing element of prosperous middle class parents, and especially professionals, and later in the century the inexorable advance of the Victorian public schools. Yet throughout the 19th century the vast majority continued to come from local grammar schools, and throughout

65 Winstanley 1947, p. 152; cf. pp. 151—3.
66 Venn, III, 392.
67 Venn, II, 144—5.
68 Venn, II, 136—8.

the history of the College — for all the family dynasties which have occasionally formed — the vast majority of Caians in every decade have been of the first generation of their family in the College. We may presume that for many the reason of choice has always been fairly haphazard; and in the early and mid 19th century this was reasonable enough. Increasingly the young who came to Cambridge could expect a serious education if that is what they came for. College lecturers lectured, if a trifle perfunctorily; professors professed, if rather intermittently. But the real hope of teaching lay with the private tutors, and it was they, more than any professors or reformers, who created the educational traditions of 19th century Cambridge — they and their charges, who paid for their services and looked with a critical eye at the pabulum they received.[69] Choice of a college could make a substantial difference — in the pursuit of scholarships or fellowships, in the pursuit of friends; and sometimes in the atmosphere and currents of the place. The moderate Whiggery of Davy may have been some encouragement to the liberal tendencies of Bickersteth and his like. Much more cogently, in the mid-19th century, when an eminent Evangelical, Charles Clayton, was sole tutor, it became a natural haunt for the son of Henry Venn, an evangelical of like distinction, even though he himself had once been a fellow of Queens'.[70] But for serious tuition, the young had to look outside the Colleges.

The flow of recruits in all but a handful of colleges put a great strain on the buildings available. This continued right through the century, and a steady increase took place in the numbers who lived in lodgings. But the colleges which could afford it also built new courts or extended old ones. The works of William Wilkins at Trinity, King's and Corpus, as well as the very existence of Downing, are a monument to this expansive phase. Caius had produced the architect himself, and was not a poor College; and it is strange perhaps that it had to wait till the 1850s and 60s for any substantial new building. In the 1820s a scheme for remodelling the Persian and the Legge buildings was prepared by Wilkins, but never executed.[71] Three grounds for this are known — though arguments of taste may well have entered too. Living space may not at first have been so acute a problem as in other colleges. Increasingly ample fellows' sets and the development of greater privacy even for undergraduates meant that buildings which could house large numbers in the early 17th century could not revert to their original capacity. But most of the fellows were non-resident and made little or no demands on the space; and the ample and handsome 17th and 18th century houses — especially Barraclough's — standing where the Great Gate and Tower now are had been bought from Mr Wortley's bequest in the

69 See below, pp. 219–20; cf. Winstanley 1940, pp. 410–13.
70 See chap. 11.
71 See n. 21.

1780s and were ready to be converted into student sets in the early 1850s.[72] By this and other means quarters were found. Meanwhile the College funds were so organised that no regular building fund existed, and it was the formation of this, and the gradual accumulation of a large reserve, which made possible the giant schemes of the mid-19th century. It is clear indeed that many fellows felt the need for building, for many contributed to the fund long before results were likely to be seen from their generosity.[73] Finally, Caius has always notoriously lacked space for building. It was only towards the end of the century that St Michael's Court was added or the idea of moving the fellows' garden to the ancient meadows beyond the Backs seriously considered.[74] Every extension of the College buildings removed the narrow amenities, for Master and President and fellows — and in a measure for the whole society — of lawns and gardens. Meanwhile the growing numbers, from sources more diverse, with a range of talent of which we have had some glimpses, prepared the way for a new world. It will be debated till the end of time whether the revival of College and University may be attributed more to the rising zeal of young private tutors, to the growing earnestness of undergraduates, and undergraduate societies, to the formation of the college and university boat clubs, to the lectures of Professor Woodhouse and Professor Willis, or the general zeal for reform of which Henry Bickersteth was so shining an example. But the significant fact is that the issue can be debated at all. The flickers of reform in 18th century Cambridge — the movement to allow fellows to marry, to provide serious teaching at the Perse, to encourage or compel professors to lecture[75] — had faded away. Yet as the long rule of Martin Davy went on, it became apparent that Cambridge was astir.

Martin Davy as Master

Martin Davy had the misfortune of earning the dislike of the two most active gossips of Cambridge of his time, Henry Gunning and Joseph Romilly. Romilly only knew him in his decline, when a natural tendency to be opinionated, and a great capacity for absurd conversation seem to have grown on him. He met Davy in the 1830s at the celebrated dining club known as 'the Family'. 'Dr Davy was more absurd than ever: he says the

---

72 *ER*, p. 29 (and see p. 152); Venn, III, 147.
73 Venn, III, 139, 280: Dr Chapman himself gave £1,000 in 1840, and later £1,000 more. Other donations are noted in Venn, II — e.g. pp. 115—6, 119, 125, 142, 164, 170, 174 (£1,000 from Dr Guest in 1853); III, 280.
74 See p. 253.
75 William Cole in *CC*, p. 151 (1766) — 'At Cambridge they seem to be going mad. Last week a grace was actually prepared in the Senate House in order to petition the Parliament for leave that the Fellows of colleges might marry'; Mitchell 1976, pp. 26—32; Winstanley 1935, chap. iii. Hans 1951 and Wordsworth 1877 show the solid content of the 18th century curriculum — but not reform in the sense intended here.

Alps were either formed in the air or thrown out from the moon'; or again 'the Master of Caius was as tiresome as ever . . .'.[76] Gunning acknowledged Davy's genial kindliness to him in earlier days; but the old Esquire Bedell evidently found the aging Master very trying when he came to he Vice-Chancellor for the second time. 1827: 'When Dr Davy was elected . . . to take the office of Vice-Chancellor a second time, he exclaimed vehemently against (what he called) the drudgeries of the office; but the fact was, he had been so long accustomed to self-indulgence, that whatever interfered with his settled habits never failed to put him out of temper'.[77]

Davy was a Norfolk man who showed an early interest in the classics and in medicine, and studied in Edinburgh in the circle of which the great Whig Henry Brougham was a member.[78] He came to Caius in 1786 at the age of twenty-three on the advice of the celebrated Dr Parr, sometimes called 'the Whig Dr Johnson', then a schoolmaster at Norwich, who had befriended him, and was fortunate, even before graduating as MB, to acquire a senior fellowship – Dr Caius' medical fellowship. After completing his medical studies in Edinburgh he returned to Caius and became steward and registrar; and in 1795, according to Gunning, was a candidate already for the Mastership at the age of thirty-two.[79] In compensation, Dr Belward made him President and in 1803, after some further medical study and years of successful practice as a physician and as tutor of Caius, he was elected Master. 'Davy was represented by Dr Parr as a very staunch Whig' says the discontented Gunning, who suffered, or thought he suffered, for his own political radicalism in the era.[80] Down to the 1760s, as we have seen, the political pivot of Cambridge life had been the duke of Newcastle; now it was William Pitt, whose secretary, Joseph Smith, was an ex-fellow and nephew of the former Master.[81] Pitt avoided corruption in any financial sense; but as MP for the University he was a frequent visitor, and loyalty to king and university – especially at the height of the French wars – tended to be measured by loyalty to Pitt. In the age of Walpole, the fellows of Caius had mostly been Tories; now in the age of Pitt, when everybody called himself a Whig, and the word 'Tory' was only used by radicals like Gunning, their dominant tendency came to be opposition or Foxite Whig. And Davy showed courage in supporting his convictions by vetoing on the 'Caput' the scheme for a statue to Pitt in the Senate House – he claimed it was due to the manner not the matter of the grace, but it was a bold defiance none the less; and many years later, by vetoing a petition against the Dissenters Bill – that is to say, by declaring his support for a move to

76 Romilly, pp. 70. 92; cf. Winstanley 1940, p. 399.
77 Gunning, II, 359 – 60; on Davy, see Gunning, II, 189 – 202, 359 – 66.
78 For what follows, Venn, II, 114; III, 133 – 7; DNB (Davy, Parr).
79 Gunning, II, 189.
80 Gunning, II, 189 – 90.
81 Venn, II, 95.

abolish religious tests – he showed again his genuine liberalism.[82] Gunning alleges that his Whiggery was skin deep and tells of how, when Davy was first Vice-Chancellor in 1803 – 4, and Pitt was returned unopposed, he amazed Gunning first by arriving in the Senate House so early as 8 a.m., and then by signing Pitt's indenture – and concludes that he did it to curry favour with Pitt.[83] This seems hardly fair: it is much more likely that Davy was only doing what he thought correct and proper in a Vice-Chancellor.

Davy was an active and successful doctor; but he was also a man of wide culture with many friends. He was elected to the Royal Society in 1801 and to the Antiquaries in 1812. In 1808 he wrote a letter which is a pleasant mixture of banter and learning to the great scholar Richard Porson: first excusing his delay in writing 'as I have been for two or three days much engaged in slaying partridges instead of patients', he goes on to ask for copies of Porphyrius, Apollodorus, and Philostratus and asks for news of Porson's Aristophanes.[84]

But in 1810 – 11 a great change came into his life. He fell in love with an heiress called Ann Stevenson, who turned his thoughts to divinity; he became a DD and married Miss Stevenson in 1811 – but sadly, she died in the Master's Lodge in October in the same year.[85] The rest of his life, according to Gunning, was largely spent reading in his study and his fine library. He had had the reputation of being unorthodox, and was clearly a man of perceptive and original mind; but he directed that his manuscripts should be burnt after his death, and they were boiled 'in the great kitchen copper of the College'.[86] He indulged in a little divinity and was even a prebendary of Chichester, as Gooch had been, in the 1830s; but Davy's canonry was not residentiary.[87] He suffered in his last years from deafness, which reduced the sociability for which he had been noted. He continued to indulge in country sports. The same letter to Porson in 1808 had included: 'I have a design of going into Norfolk early in October, and will then send you some game'.[88]

Davy was in easy circumstances after his wife's death, and he purchased an estate of 200 acres at Heacham in Norfolk and with it acquired the Queen Anne house there which became his country retreat. After his death he left the estate to his successors, subject to a life interest to his sister.[89] And so from 1869 when she died, till 1933, Heacham Lodge was

---

82 Venn, III, 134 – 5; Gunning, II, 190; Willis and Clark, III, 60; Romilly, p. 57; Winstanley 1940, p. 93 and n. The Caput was the curious body redefined under the Statutes of 1570, consisting of the Vice-Chancellor, a doctor from each of the three ancient faculties, and two MAs, which initiated all university legislation – and every member of which had a veto. In the 1850s it was replaced by the Council of State.
83 Gunning, II, 190 – 1.
84 Venn, III, 135 – 6.
85 Venn, III, 134; Gunning, II, 201, 360.
86 Venn, III, 135, quoting Pryme.
87 Venn, III, 135; Horn 1971, p. 36.
88 Venn, III, 136.
89 ER, pp. 112 – 113.

a country house for the Master of Caius, who had to support it as best he might from the revenues of the farm, and to reside there for at least sixty days each year. From these burdens J. F. Cameron withdrew in 1933 by an arrangement which handed the Trust over to the College;[90] in return he continued to stay in the lodge when he wished, and other fellows might use it for occasional visits. Under this benign dispensation my parents enjoyed its shelter while they were building a new house in Cambridge; and so it was my home for several months in 1934. In the Second World War it was let and never resumed; and in the early 1970s the College made a handsome profit by selling some of the fields near it for development. The world in which Heacham Lodge had flourished was no more, and the house itself has been sold — though the College still manages a farm there — but the consequence is that the Davy Trust, which scarcely supported the Lodge fifty years ago, now pays for a posse of young fellows.

Benedict Chapman

On 18 May 1839 Dr Davy died and on the 25th Romilly, as University Registrary, walked behind Dr Paget in the procession to his funeral — 'verses were pinned to the pall: the coffin lay in state in the hall: — we met in the Combination room — we marched round the inner court: — Stokes read the service tolerably well: — no music or singing: — not over till 12.'[91] The verses survive and show a more than formal respect for the old Master; and over his grave was laid a fine brass on which a mature student of the College called William Shoubridge and the engraver T. W. Archer portrayed Martin Davy beneath the Gate of Virtue. But when the fellows gathered in chapel to elect his successor, they chose a former fellow and tutor on the verge of seventy. Such an election might have meant that they had endured Davy too long and wished to ensure a brief tenure; that they could not agree and played for time; or that they had a candidate in mind too young, and looked for a brief space for him to gather a few grey hairs. Tradition, which we need not doubt, voted for the last and named Paget, then only twenty-nine, as the future Master. After the election Paget himself wrote to Romilly describing the event and although there were ten scrutinies they all took place in one morning, and Dr Chapman's supporters gradually increased. Paget describes the vacillations of the senior fellow, John

90 Venn, VI, 534.
91 Venn, II, 114; Horn 1971, p. 36; Romilly, p. 170. The 'inner court' sounds like Gonville Court, but later practice certainly was for the procession to go round Caius Court (see Venn, IV, 155 for Ferrers' funeral in 1903, 'according to ancient custom'). For the brass, which was the spearhead of the revival of this art, see Venn, II, 239; (and for Shoubridge ibid. and Colvin 1978, p. 733), and esp. D. Meara, *Victorian Memorial Brasses* (London, 1982), pp. 5–7 (a reference kindly supplied by John Sturdy). The signatures of both Shoubridge and Archer are inscribed on the brass.

Woodhouse, brother of Robert, an elderly local physician, a well-known eccentric (according to the entry in Venn's *Biographical History* which is signed by Paget) with 'a special taste for cock-fighting'. 'The poor old doctor . . . stood by the altar with a pencil in one hand, and what I believe was an old betting book in the other, looking more knowing than I ever knew him before or since.'[92] Paget suspected that the old doctor hoped to win the election himself, and switched his vote to prevent their agreeing. But in the end Chapman was elected, a man 'in all respects, political and academical, a strong conservative', and lived a blameless life between the Lodge and his rectory at Ashdon (then a College living), fourteen miles away, riding between the two, dignified and elegant.[93] When the Royal Commissioners sent their enquiries to him in 1850−1, he was outraged — he did not absolutely refuse to answer, as did some Heads, but replied 'under a strong and earnest protest', refusing to let them see a copy of the sacred statutes; and then, in October 1852, he passed to his rest.[94] The Commissioners published the statutes from Archbishop Parker's copy at Lambeth and a draft in the University Library;[95] and later in the decade, the Statutory Commissioners appointed in 1856 set to work and in 1858−9 substantial revisions to the statutes were agreed.

Edwin Guest

The distant echoes of these changes were already foreshadowed, it is clear, in Chapman's later years and while the Commission sat. There were a number of younger fellows more ready for change than the Master. Their anxieties boiled over in the election of 1852. Tradition and the statutes of Caius had hitherto constrained the Master to be a native of the diocese of Norwich, and the two most eminent ex-fellows in the eyes of the world, Paget and Alderson, both fitted this prescription; Paget indeed had clearly been the favoured candidate until he married and left the fellowship; and doubtless he was still supported in the 1840s by the two most remarkable men in the active fellowship, J. J. Smith and J. W. Crowfoot.[96] We have encountered Smith as a noted tutor and antiquary; Crowfoot was active in proposing educational reform, and taught theology both in Caius and King's. But in 1849 Smith, and in 1850 Crowfoot, took wives and left the fellowship. Meanwhile there were other reformers among the younger fellows to whom the Norfolk tie was anathema. On the third scrutiny

92 Venn, III, 137 (cf. II, 134).
93 Venn, III, 137−40, at p. 138.
94 Venn, III, 139; Winstanley 1940, pp. 235−6.
95 *Documents 1852*, II, 241−306, 320−65: see above, p. 68. For what follows, Venn, III, 150.
96 On Paget and the Mastership, see *Caian* II (1892−3), 6−8; Winstanley 1940, pp. 265−6; for Smith and Crowfoot, above, p. 205; Venn, II, 189, 234; Garland 1980, p. 18.

Edwin Guest, who had been a fellow since 1824, but came from Birmingham, and so was safely outside the statute, was elected.[97] Frantic efforts were made to unseat him, led by Smith and Crowfoot — but supported by Paget and others too — who cited the statute against Guest, but failed to observe, as Venn points out, that the same statute prescribed that the Master be celibate and so might equally have excluded his rivals. The efforts failed, since the Visitors refused to countenance an appeal unless supported by a majority of the fellowship; but it has cast a certain shadow over Guest; and Venn himself clearly found him too remote, too conservative in educational affairs — his 'rule in college', he says, 'was uneventful'.[98] Doubtless his mind was on the quarrels of Gooch and the reforms of later decades; for to those who contemplate the buildings of Salvin and Waterhouse, or the statutes of 1860, the phrase seems astounding.

Guest was an able practising lawyer and a cultivated scholar — fellow of the Royal Society and of the Antiquaries. He was also a country gentleman with a handsome estate in Oxfordshire. His *History of English Rhythms* (1838) was a remarkable pioneer work which stimulated later studies in a marked degree. His 'speculations on Ancient History, as contained in the *Origines Celticae*' were published after his death in 1883, and already when Venn wrote opinions differed on their value.[99] They differ no more: Guest's later work carried him into the world of scholarly dreams, and while Brady is honoured as a pioneer and Wharton and Willis are read, Guest now gathers dust upon the shelves. But if his scholarship was doubtful and his views on education blindly conservative, his influence on the building programme seems to have been decisive. The poet Longfellow, in a letter to the young Charles Sherrington in 1882, described a visit to Caius in 1868 and 'its amiable and excellent Master Dr Guest who had a mania for building'.[100] The building fund had slowly built up, and Barraclough's building had been brought into use in the early 1850s; but the Hall had become hopelessly inadequate to feed the growing College, which had long since flowed out into lodgings about the town. As for the library, it could scarcely hold the books it contained and had no space for readers.

Curiously enough, the last failing does not seem to have caused concern. We are in a very obscure area, but if we ask — where did an undergraduate read? — we have no clear answer until the Monro Reading Room was

---

97 Venn, II, 174; III, 140–53; see pp. 142–3 and Winstanley 1940, pp. 264–6, for what follows; the protest signed by a whole group of ex-fellows, including Paget, is in Caius MS 714.

98 Venn, III, 143. See ibid. p. 149 n. for the draft statutes proposed in 1853, soon after Guest's entry to office, but postponed owing to the onset of the general revision of College statutes.

99 Venn, III, 145; see esp. Stevenson 1902. It is fair to say that his book on *Rhythms* and his philological work — which partly no doubt reflected his travels in Germany in the heyday of the Brothers Grimm — had much more lasting value.

100 Sherrington 1957, p. 4; for Guest's influence, see Willis and Clark, I, 190. For the use of Barraclough's see Venn, III, 147.

thrown open in 1928.[101] College libraries were not designed for undergraduates, though they had frequently enjoyed access to them — but on an occasional basis for the favoured few, so far as the evidence goes. Things were better in Trinity, where some access was permitted from the early 18th century.[102] But if one contemplates the numbers in that college and the space for readers even of the majestic Wren Library, one can see that until the formation of extensive reading rooms well into the 20th century, demand was not too pressing. Doubtless many courses were studied in a restricted number of textbooks. The University Library had wonderful resources of books, and the more they grew the less chance there was for many readers, until the opening of the new library in 1934. But serious efforts were made from time to time, culminating in graces of the late 1860s and 70s which permitted undergraduates to read there, with tutors' recommendations, at special hours outside the normal routine of working seniors.[103] As for Caius, when the new library was built in 1853—4, it provided ample resting place for books and for the library furniture, but almost no reading space at all.

The works of Salvin and Waterhouse

The Hall was different; Guest and his colleagues had chosen Salvin, the grand master of baronial castles of his day, who had recently been at work in Trinity Hall, and was soon after to design Whewell's court for the Master of Trinity.[104] His Hall is a fine version of the hall of the Middle Temple, with Tudor brick exterior and a fine double hammer-beam roof within; and by lifting its floor to a considerable height he was able to fit together with it a new library, kitchens and a large extension to the Master's Lodge. By the mid-1850s the men of Caius could feed, and the fellows could borrow books; lecture rooms were provided in Dr Gooch's stable; but the living quarters were becoming exceedingly cramped. In December 1866 it was decided to consult Mr Waterhouse, and in 1868—70 the present buildings of Tree Court were built; and an immense addition made to College rooms.[105]

Willis attributed Salvin's work to 'the influence of the present Master, Dr Guest'; and we may suppose that Guest himself played a leading part in the decision to build on the grandest scale in Tree Court, and to choose Alfred Waterhouse to do it.[106] It was a bold decision, for Waterhouse was still

---

101 See below, p. 254.
102 Gaskell and Robson 1971, pp. 33, 36.
103 I owe this information to the kind help of John Oates and David McKitterick, whose forthcoming *Cambridge University Library: a History*, will give more precise details.
104 Venn, III, 190; Willis and Clark, I, 190, 197, 200; Pevsner 1970, pp. 80, 176. For the interpretation of the hall, I owe special thanks to Paul Binski; for later changes, see p. 254.
105 Venn, III, 147—8 and 147 n.; cf. *RCHM Cambridge*, I, 74.
106 See n. 100.

comparatively young; but he was a coming man. He had already built much in Manchester, he had embarked on the South Kensington Natural History Museum, and he had made a start in Cambridge with the Union in 1866 when he was chosen to work for Caius.[107] Contemporaries were immensely impressed, and he went on to build for Jesus, Pembroke and Girton. A later generation regarded it as the ugliest building in Cambridge, and some of its knobs and excrescences were given to my father to build a rockery in the 1930s. 'Remarkably self-possessed and insensitive', said Pevsner still in 1954.[108] But the tide of fashion turns, and there are many now who regard Waterhouse as one of the most under-valued of the great Victorian architects; we still possess his sketches and need not wonder that the College seniors found them alluring. He was evidently given the brief to build as massively as space permitted, and this he achieved under the inspiration of the châteaux of the Loire. It is abundantly clear that he had studied and drawn at Blois and Chambord and Chenonceau. If one contemplates the face which Chenonceau offers to the waterfront, the source of the main design, especially of the windows, seems manifest; yet Chambord evidently inspired the dormers and the spiral staircase (now S); and Blois has also influenced the staircase, the dormers and above all the gargoyles. The whole conception is closely modelled on the grand French manner of the age of François I, of the childhood of Dr Caius. Ruthless Waterhouse undoubtedly was, and the tower and Great Gate are somehow out of temper with the Senate House and Great St Mary's alike. But within one cannot but admire the boldness of his solution. He had to reconcile a lofty castle with the ancient buildings of Caius and Gonville Courts, of a charming modesty of proportion. This he accomplished by bringing his château to an end well before it impinged on the older buildings; and the transition from high to low – crude in detail, but noble in conception – is the portion of his design most generally admired. He tinkered and pottered with the back of Gonville Court and partly re-shaped the chapel – giving it an apse at one end and a new organ gallery at the other. The west end of the chapel was extended to allow space for a new organ by J. W. Walker and Sons. In the late 1860s sung services had been reintroduced after two centuries without music; and the new organ led on to the gradual development in the 1880s and 1890s of a musical tradition in the College, culminating in the arrival of Charles Wood in 1889 as organ scholar, and his promotion to music fellow in 1894. Meanwhile Waterhouse had greatly altered the chapel at either end.[109] When the new organ was installed in the 1980s the Organ

107 Pevsner 1970, p. 205; cf. pp. 37, 90, 127, 190.
108 Pevsner 1970, p. 37 (unaltered from the first edn. of 1954, p. 32). Here as later I quote Pevsner, not for a final judgement, but for a representative view held by an eminent critic of recent date from outside the College. In what follows I am much indebted to Paul Binski.
109 See below, pp. 242 – 4. The Walker Organ was financed by an appeal, and the original accounts, a Subscription Book, and a Building Fund Accounts Book for the works by

Committee and the German designers were careful to treat Waterhouse with a sympathy greater than he himself had shown to his predecessors. In the 1860s the sense of historic continuity was preserved by placing monograms and a statue on the parts of the building where Perse and Legge had been — and a statue of Mr Wortley on the site of Barraclough's, bought with his legacy. What could not be disguised was the affront to Humility, for though the word is still inscribed over the front entry to the College, the Gate of Humility was banished to a distant corner, eventually to find rest in the Master's garden.

But greater changes were to come. The lecture rooms, also by Waterhouse, were only a modest preamble to the great changes of the late 19th century which converted Caius from a grand and ancient hostel in which study and prayer could be conducted, or neglected, at the student's choice, to a place of active education in several disciplines. The Waterhouse building, furthermore, though ample and magnificent, was extremely austere within. It was the reign of E. S. Roberts as tutor and Master, which was to see fundamental changes in the educational work of the College and its role in scholarship, that also witnessed the arrival of baths in three courts between 1904 and 1909.[110] 'Soap and education', said Mark Twain, 'are not as sudden as a massacre, but they are more deadly in the long run'. The fatal infection still lay far in the future when John Venn entered the College in 1853.

Waterhouse, survive in the Archives, as Catherine Hall has pointed out to me. For the châteaux, see L. Hautecoeur, *Histoire de l'Architecture classique en France*, I (Paris, 1963), pp. 170, 191, 205, 427, 459.
110 Venn, IV, 167; VI, 509.

11

Interlude: The College in the 1850s

In 1853, the young John Venn arrived as a pensioner; from 1854 he was a scholar, and a fellow from 1857 till his death in 1923. In 1913 he published an account of 'College life and ways sixty years ago', the gem of his collection on *Early Collegiate Life*; and this and the memoir written on him by his friend H. T. Francis, who joined him in 1856, and shared Venn's vivid memories in later years, are our chief documents for the College in the mid-century.[1] Not only are they precious in themselves, but they reflect a changeless moment in many aspects of College life, and especially in its scheme of education. Venn recalled that 'the elder Mr Weller . . . rather prided himself on the educational advantages which he had conferred upon his . . . son; he had . . . let him run about the streets and pick up information for himself. The College authorities of my day adopted a somewhat similar plan.'[2] Venn's devastating condemnation of a system in which no personal direction or supervision was offered by the College, and College lectures — there were very few others — were performed in a perfunctory manner to audiences in which potential wranglers and poll-men sat shoulder to shoulder, was calculated to show the old regime at its most indefensible. Venn had been much involved in reform, and doubtless painted a bleak picture; but the essence of the matter was that the Master, for all his wide learning, thought classics and mathematics the only serious undergraduate courses, the President did little but sleep and fish, and even the tutor 'never lectured'.[3] Charles Clayton, the tutor, was a remarkable man: he knelt at the desk of Charles Simeon as vicar of Holy Trinity, and was a leading evangelical, eloquent in the pulpit, friendly and welcoming to his guests at tutor's breakfasts and missionary teas. Francis describes the breakfasts: 'His butler would go round and distribute haphazard invitations . . . to some twenty or more men. The central figure . . . of this entertainment was usually a missionary, recently returned home from India or, it might be, from China' — and Caius, it may be added, played a notable part

1 Venn 1913, pp. 253–82 and Francis 1923 are our main sources for this chapter; on Venn's and Francis's early careers, see Venn, II, 313, 329. Francis was for many years on the University Library staff and a leading Buddhist scholar; he was a man of wide literary tastes.
2 Venn 1913, p. 262; cf. ibid. pp. 256 ff. for what follows.
3 Venn 1913, pp. 262–3; on Clayton see ibid. pp. 268–9; Francis 1923, pp. 106, 108, 119–20. He is otherwise remembered for his fierce disapproval of clergymen who danced, and his unbending opposition to the abolition of religious tests in Cambridge (Winstanley 1940, p. 405; Winstanley 1947, p. 68).

in recruiting 19th century missionaries. 'This ill-assorted gathering of undergraduates would be separately introduced to this chief guest, with reference to his Evangelical progenitors or relations' — and Francis goes on to describe how, 'after some humming and hawing Clayton' introduced him as 'a friend of Mr John Venn' — for Venn came of a line of distinguished evangelicals and his was a name to conjure with.[4] Under Clayton the College acquired a distinctly evangelical cast, and in the early 1850s was divided very roughly between the evangelicals and the Boat Club rowdies — for both sets Venn had more sympathy than Francis; and the latter observes a great improvement in quality with the entry of 1855, which included such men as Clifford Allbutt.[5] Venn came as a convinced evangelical, and his picture of Clayton is the more telling for being in intent extremely sympathetic: 'He was a very kind-hearted and worthy man; and I am convinced that if any of us had gone to him in difficulty or in doubt, he would have given all the assistance in his power. But that was not the custom.'[6] And then, in the account of his parish and involvement 'in religious movements', there is a faint hint of Mrs Jellyby and Borrioboola-Gha. It seems to us astonishing that the whole of a large college should have been entrusted to one such tutor; but so it was from 1848 — 1851 rather, when he acquired the parish — till 1865, when he departed with his wife (he had married under the revised statutes in 1863) to a living in County Durham.[7] He did not direct studies, though doubtless he gave an occasional word of advice in the brief twice-termly meetings he had with all his pupils. 'We selected our coaches by mutual advice and comparison; we decided for ourselves what line of studies we would follow' — and in practice this meant ordinary or honours, classics or mathematics; the birth of the moral sciences and natural science tripos in the late 1840s had hardly impinged, and the provision for the specialist teaching of science — spreading over seven or eight acres of the Downing site by the time Venn wrote in the 1910s — 'was a small table, such as two people might take their tea at; a table not in constant use, but brought into the Arts School three times a week during the May term.'[8] He admits that there was a medical school and the Sedgwick Geological Museum, within the University Library, and occasional practical teaching elsewhere by Professor Willis and others; but the table was the perquisite of Professor Stokes, and with it he expounded physical optics. Venn's description sounds more like an optical illusion; but in essence he must be right — such is the measure of change which overtook Cambridge in the second half of the 19th century.

Meanwhile he chose his coach with anxious care. First, William Hopkins,

4 Francis 1923, p. 119; cf. Venn 1913, p. 263; and on the Venn family, Venn 1904; Yates 1978; Hennell 1979, chap. 5.
5 Francis 1923, p. 108.
6 Venn 1913, p. 263.
7 Ibid.; Venn, II, 218, 285–372.
8 Venn 1913, pp. 263–4.

the most eminent mathematical coach of his day — who had already reported to Gunning in 1849 that 'From January 1828 to January 1849 . . . I have had among my pupils 175 Wranglers. Of these, 108 have been in the *first ten*, 44 in the *first three*, and 17 have been *Senior Wranglers*.'[9] Gunning took pride in having Hopkins as his colleague as Esquire Bedell; but Venn found his classes too much like public lectures, and in 1855 he passed to Isaac Todhunter, who aimed too obviously, however, for Venn's taste, at exam results.[10] Such were the men who created the Cambridge tradition of teaching. It is surprising to us that Venn did not seek out younger men less well known — for there is abundant evidence of good informal teaching long before this; and it is significant that a man like Whewell, notorious for his brusque inattention with his pupils when tutor of Trinity, had been greatly valued by his first, private pupils.[11] So was Venn himself to be by his own pupils, who included A. J. Balfour and F. W. Maitland.[12]

In the social life of the College Venn mixed little at first; but gradually his circle in Caius and Cambridge grew. The most obvious difference between the 1850s and the 1980s is that there were no women. 'My cousin, Leslie Stephen, of Trinity Hall, who was three years my senior, used to say that about the only lady he had ever spoken to during his College course was, he believed, his bedmaker . . . The female element in University society was epigrammatically described as consisting of five or six wives of Masters of Colleges, who sat apart; of five or six wives of professors, upon whom the former did not call; and of one other lady, wife of a well-known classical coach.'[13] It is an epigram and has about as much truth as most; and the married fellow was not far away. Meanwhile even May week did not exist and visits from parents and sisters were rare events, anyway in Caius.

Life was austere, without water laid on or adequate provision for heating. As a Perse scholar, Venn lived in the Persian building, and had a bedroom in the unconverted attics of the early 17th century in which he observed, as Willis had done, the original arrangement for students' chambers.[14] He also observed, in the Crimean winter of 1854−5, ice on his jug for two months on end; and earlier in 1854 Dr Paget had found him in his bedroom sickening for small pox and had him moved for a time to his sitting room.[15] In 1853 he dined in the old Hall, with the freshmen, at 4.00; later a single sitting was possible in Salvin's Hall, and this was at 5 — but gradually, as Venn grew older, hall advanced too, until it settled at 7.00 or soon after by the end of the century.[16] The food was plain. 'I should say that breakfast did

9 Gunning, II, 359; cf. pp. 358−9.
10 On Hopkins and other tutors, see Winstanley 1940, p. 411−12.
11 Clark 1900, pp. 23−4.
12 Francis 1923, pp. 118−19.
13 Venn 1913, pp. 266−7. On Stephen, Annan 1951.
14 Willis and Clark, III, 298, 304−11; Venn, III, 83−4.
15 Venn 1913, pp. 272−4; Francis 1923, p. 109.
16 Venn 1913, pp. 269−70.

not often go much beyond eggs and bacon; that lunch (if the term may be used) was secured by cutting bread and cheese at the cupboard door; and that the place of supper was occupied by tea and bread and jam. And the dinner itself was of the simplest. Nothing was regularly provided for the table beyond joints, potatoes and cabbage. There were . . . waiters . . . but we did all the carving for ourselves, pushing the dish from one to another in turn. The wasteful hacking of the joints . . . may be conceived; as each operator followed out his own ideas as to the method of carving.'[17] For the fellows the monotony was broken by fairly frequent feasts — even after the catastrophe of 1780 when nineteen were abolished by a single minute in the *Gesta*[18] — and in a few of these the scholars at least partook. And dinner was a formal occasion for which all still dressed. Dress indeed was a curious mixture of formality and informality, and many wore their silk hats or the new-fangled bowlers, on their way to the river; and on Sunday 'no one ever walked except in cap and gown' — otherwise used for lectures, dinner, visiting a tutor and wandering at night — much as it still was down to the 1950s; save that the practice of waiting on the Master of Trinity, for seniors and juniors alike, in cap and gown, did not survive Dr Whewell.[19] For less formal dress, the Lady Margaret blazer gradually set the pace and in the course of the century boat club blazers spread through other colleges, and other clubs less ancient than the Boat Club.

Daily chapel services were held at 7.45 and 4.45.[20] 'We were a very church-going, sermon-attending folk. Hall, on Sundays, was at 4, Chapel at 6 . . . and a very large number of us were in the habit of attending the sermon at one or the other of the parish churches' — most of all at Clayton's Holy Trinity; many too at St Edwards, where Harvey Goodwin, ex-fellow and future bishop of Carlisle, and a noted high churchman, was then vicar (1848 – 58).[21]

Walking 'was, with the majority of us, the sole mode of exercise. There was of course the river, for those who had a taste that way, and there was some cricket for a few weeks in May. But that was all. Lawn tennis and croquet were unborn. Real tennis and hunting were . . . confined to the wealthy few. Hockey and football were left to boys.'[22] — Here however he exaggerates, perhaps because he rarely walked past Parker's Piece, where the young men from Eton, Rugby and Harrow in particular were giving football its first real blossoming in Cambridge. The Boat Club indeed retained its popularity, boosted by a Guild Challenge Oar presented by G. A.

17 Venn 1913, p. 270.
18 Venn, III, 131. Since the original minute (14 Jan. 1780) is largely concerned with increasing the cook's stipend, one suspects that the feasts were sacrificed to justify a general improvement.
19 Venn, 1913, p. 276 (also for what follows); cf. pp. 266 – 7 n.
20 Francis 1923, p. 106.
21 Venn 1913, pp. 268 – 9; for Harvey Goodwin, see Venn, II, 234 – 5.
22 Venn 1913, pp. 279 – 80.

Henty, who had resided for three terms in 1851 and, as an immensely popular historical novelist, probably had more influence on the historical views of young Britons in the rest of the 19th century than other Caius historians, even J. R. Seeley.[23]

'I have been asked before now what I have found to be the main formative educational influences here. I have replied, with strict truth, that I had learnt something from my lecturers, more from my coach, but most of all from conversation with friends; and the main opportunity for such conversation was the daily walk. What comes back to my mind most vividly in such a connection?' – and Venn concludes with a moving account of 'hours spent on Welsh mountains, and in Yorkshire dales, and over the breezy commons of Surrey, with the most stimulating of companions by my side,' J. R. Seeley. In later life Sir John Seeley was to be pictured as 'grave, dignified, and possibly somewhat lethargic. I wish I could adequately portray the slim, active form of one who was then one of the keenest and most subtle of dialecticians, brimming over with happy illustrations and humorous fancy, and with a memory stored with poetry and philosophy. Those were the early fermenting years, when *Ecce Homo* was taking shape in his mind.'[24] Seeley had been a student at Christ's, and the friendship flowered after he left Cambridge for a while. *Ecce Homo* was to help Seeley to the Regius Chair of Modern History at Cambridge; and in 1882, no doubt partly or largely by Venn's initiative, he was to become a fellow of Caius.[25] Meanwhile, we can understand how the young Venn, the narrow evangelical, yet a cousin of Leslie Stephen and a friend of Henry Sidgwick, deeply influenced by the speculative bent of C. H. Monro,[26] and intimate with the author of *Ecce Homo*, gradually passed through many of the phases of Victorian religious sentiment until he came near to lose his faith altogether. But we are anticipating.

After reminiscing of his many walks in the roads and lanes round Cambridge and elsewhere, Venn's last words to his 20th century audience were:

'I do not doubt that your interest in the problems of Ethics, Politics, and Philosophy is just as keen as ours, and that it exists with equal intensity during a scrimmage on the football field, or a lively rally at tennis, but it will be admitted that the free expression of that interest is comparatively hampered at the time.'[27]

23 Scott 1927, p. 70; Venn, II, 301.
24 Venn 1913, pp. 280 – 1.
25 See below, p. 246. Wormell 1980, p. 42, reasonably doubts that *Ecce Homo* was the reason for Gladstone appointing him, but there is no doubt he knew he was the author and greatly admired the book: ibid. p. 190.
26 Francis 1923, pp. 112 – 13.
27 Venn 1913, p. 282.

12

The Age of E. S. Roberts

Ernest Stewart Roberts arrived in Caius in 1865, and died in College in 1912.[1] For most of the time he was tutor or President or Master, and for all of it he was resident in Caius. He presided without fuss or fireworks over one of the most rapid transformations in the history of the College. The Caius of the 1850s which we have just been inspecting under the guidance of John Venn and H. T. Francis was little altered from its 18th century *persona*; by 1912 Cambridge and Caius were centres of education and learning of international repute in many fields, and the ideal of 'education, religion, learning and research' had been stamped upon them. It would be foolish to attribute so spectacular a change to a single man; but Roberts embodies it within the College — and in a much more limited sense was deeply influential in the University at large. This is all the more remarkable, since he was not a colourful man of brilliant conversation or dazzling mind. Yet he seems now without question the central figure in the history of the College in the age of Venn.

The statutes of 1860 and the abolition of celibacy

Much had happened even before the arrival of Roberts. The statutory changes of the 1850s canonised in the statutes of 1860 gathered together and swept away all the minute, personal, particular elements in the endowments of the College, with the exception of the intractable Trusts of Perse and Davy which retained their special character in spite of the ruthless reforms of the Statutory Commissioners.[2] The consequence is that Drosier and Tapp are recalled much more clearly today than any of the early benefactors, for their gifts were made after the holocaust of the 1850s. Venn commented drily on the lack of historical sense or interest which the Master and seniors of the 1850s had shown; and of Ferrers, tutor for the later years of Guest's Mastership and Master himself from 1880 till 1903, it was oberved that he was a reformer in clearing away this element of the College's past, but not in the education appropriate to the College.[3]

---

1 This chapter is primarily based on J. S. Reid's memoir, Reid 1912; on Mrs Roberts reminiscences, Roberts 1934; and on Venn, VI, 505—14.
2 See above, pp. 100—1, 211—12; for Drosier and Tapp, below, pp. 225, 257.
3 Venn, III, 211; IV, 152—3 (Roberts on Ferrers).

The other great change which came with the statutes of 1860 was the abolition of celibacy. So far as I can ascertain Caius was the first College to sweep away all bars to matrimony on every member of its foundation.[4] Other colleges went a certain distance in 1860 – 1; Oxford began slowly to follow in the late 60s and 70s; and by the end of 1882 when the statutes forbidding fellows to marry were finally wound up only small pockets of celibacy survived. These changes were made amid a babble of controversy. Some thought celibacy the bar to making a serious, lifelong career for a don; others thought it a ridiculous anachronism; others again just wanted to get married. But there was another view, which held that celibacy was the only check on lifelong, idle fellows absorbing the whole endowments of the Colleges; and some who feared not only that the old club-life of college would wither away but that colleges might cease to be resident communities at all.[5] None of these views, on the one side or the other, was wholly without foundation; and one wonders above all at the courage of the first generation of wives. Even as late as 1919 when my mother came to Cambridge as a bride, it was a strange world for a young woman without any academic qualifications of her own – and one conjectures that but for the abundant kindness of the College wives, led by Mrs Cameron, it would have been still a repelling, uncomfortable world.

One of the few other colleges to make a move against celibacy in 1860 – even though only a partial move – was Trinity Hall, where Venn's cousin Leslie Stephen was a leading proponent of the change, and has left a full account of the manoeuvres by which it was accomplished.[6] It is sad that Venn, who laboured so indefatigably to preserve the College's history, and

4 For Caius, Venn, III, 150: 'Every single member of the College being statutably at liberty to marry'. It is difficult to be precise about some other colleges, but Trinity Hall and Queens' gave restricted permission to marry and Sidney allowed an exceptional married fellow in 1860 – 1. Most of the rest waited till the early 1880s, following the Commissioners' decision in 1879 to insist on the general abolition of the celibacy rules (Winstanley 1947, p. 347; Crawley 1976, p. 161; VCH Cambs, III, 339, 372, 403 – 4, 412, 427, 444, 470, 483; CC, p. 240). Trinity's statutes of 1552 had allowed Regius Professors to marry, and there were married praelectors in Trinity before 1882 (VCH Cambs, III, 463; Rothblatt 1968/81, p. 231; Parry 1926, pp. 25, 28). In Oxford the relaxation of the rules scarcely began before the late 1860s, and made little headway before the late 70s and 80s (Engel 1983, pp. 106 – 14, esp. pp. 111 – 13 for the adventures of Mandell Creighton who was engaged when Merton changed its statute to allow a small number of tutors to marry). In Caius there was a married fellow commoner in 1799 – 1800 (Venn, II, 133), but the only apparently married fellow I have discovered is R. D. Willis, father of Robert Willis, who was a Perse fellow from 1790 till his death in 1821; see p. 203; Venn, II, 101, checked in the Archives. R. D. Willis was a prosperous court physician; whether this led Davy to treat him with complacency or enabled him simply to ignore communications from the College, we cannot tell; but he received his stipend. The entry in Venn, II, 50, making Nelson's father a fellow after his marriage is, I fear, almost certainly due to confusion with his cousin and namesake, ibid. II, 53; Nelson's father was probably never a fellow.

5 Cf. Engel 1983, pp. 106 – 14, esp. 108 – 9, 111 – 113.

6 Stephen 1885, pp. 108 – 10, cited Crawley 1976, p. 161. The device by which Commissioners and senior fellows were held to ransom by a minority of young fellows was worthy of Jeeves.

who detailed the changes of the 1860s and the 1880s with such precision, failed to describe how they were achieved. By a paradox the period between his own youth in the 1850s and the 1880s, one of the most intriguing in the College's history, is singularly ill-recorded. Venn's reticence was doubtless partly tact to the older fellows, and above all to the Master, Dr Ferrers, who did not die till 1903; partly too, the present always seems so familiar that it is difficult to realise how much it needs to be recorded. We may also suspect that Venn's modesty prevented him from describing stirring events in which he had himself played a leading part. One could speculate whether the lively debates in Trinity Hall had any influence, through Stephen, on his young cousin; but Venn was still a junior fellow and not likely to have played a large role in the debates of the late 1850s. The only secure evidence I have found is in Ferrers' brief memoir of Dr Drosier.[7] This reveals Drosier as a promising young MD of the 1840s who had played his part in the University and the College in teaching medicine, but was essentially a man of leisure. 'His tastes lay chiefly in the direction of field sports . . . Though somewhat inert in his general habits, it was commonly remarked that skating would get him out of bed at any hour in the morning, and duck-shooting keep him out to any hour in the night. He was well known to the boatmen in the vicinity of the Wash, where he spent many nights shooting wild ducks, and it was a common remark in Combination Room that when the newly-reclaimed land in that neighbourhood was incorporated into a Parliamentary district, Drosier would be its representative'.[8] In short, he was one of the idle fellows, though not in the class of Hamnett Holditch; yet he was also a good man of business, well liked among his colleagues, 'an excellent whist-player', and a matrimonial pioneer.[9] In 1862 'he was married to Miss Purchas, being thus one of the first to avail himself of a change in the Statutes which he had zealously advocated'. Drosier married in 1862, Ferrers himself in 1866 – following his brother-in-law the bursar, John Lamb, who had married in 1865; and Venn followed in 1867.[10] But they had been anticipated. On 28 September 1859 the Master himself, Dr Guest, had married a colonel's widow, Anne Banner, while the new statutes were drafting.[11] True, the Master by tradition was exempt from the statute; true also, he had narrowly escaped extinction from another clause in the same statute

7 *Caian*, I (1891 – 2), 87 – 90.
8 Ibid., p. 88.
9 Ibid., p. 89; and for what follows, p. 88.
10 Venn, II, 233, 278, 313. John Sturdy has collected evidence as to where the early married fellows lived. A few were settled on College land in Gonville Place and Scroope Terrace, and a little later in Gresham Road; J. S. Reid was in West Road from 1887 (*Gesta*, 6 May). Otherwise they were scattered over the residential areas round Parker's Piece and in the south and south-west, a few further afield. There were none in early days in Harvey Road – nor in Mortimer Road, where one or two lived in the 1920s and later, and a group of three for a time in the 50s. The settlement of fellows in Gonville Place is reflected in a College order of 28 March 1882: 'To call the new road between Dr Drosier's and Mr Bensly's the "Gresham Road" ' (cf. p. 252).
11 Venn, III, 144.

at his election, and had his face rubbed in the words of Dr Caius that the Master must be both celibate and of the see of Norwich.[12] We have no direct evidence of his involvement, but it is hard to credit that it was pure coincidence that the most liberal of matrimonial decisions was taken as the Master was taking a wife. What is certain is the note under Anthony W. W. Steel in the *Biographical History*: 'married, Jan. 1, 1861: the first to take advantage of the new statutes'.[13] Steel, who had been brought up in India under the tuition of an ex-fellow, was himself a fellow from 1859 till his sudden death in 1885, at the age of 48; he had been for a time curate and vicar of the Round Church in Cambridge, and a notable figure in the town, but also mathematical lecturer, and in his last years a popular and successful tutor. Memorial windows, side by side in the chapel, pleasantly record the memories of Guest and Steel;[14] but it is curious to observe that Guest's shows a celibate monk (Pope Gregory the Great) sending monks to convert the English, and Steel's honours St Paul, most bachelor of apostles.

Norman Ferrers as Master

Thus the statutes of 1860 swept into oblivion for a while the Norfolk and Norwich connection and the names and memory of Mrs Frankland, Mr Wortley and their like, and cleared away much else which was genuine lumber, enabling the estates and revenues to be more rationally administered and allowing the fellows to marry. But Charles Clayton was still tutor and little change took place for some years to come in the academic arrangements of the College. When Guest resigned in October 1880 — only a few weeks before his death — the leading tutor, Dr Ferrers, FRS, was elected to succeed him.[15] Ferrers had done notable work as a mathematician, including an edition of the writings of George Green.[16] Ferrers had a sharp clear mind, and in the 1850s he was reckoned a reformer — but not in the world of teaching or curriculum, nor in the relations of college and University. On Easter Day 1882 he mounted the pulpit of Great St Mary's and denounced the work of the second Royal Commission. 'This sermon', said Winstanley, 'is one of the curiosities of pulpit oratory. It was out of place in a church and singularly inappropriate to Easter Day . . . Yet as indicating the reaction of an enlightened and moderate man to the work of the Commissioners, it has

12 See p. 214.
13 Venn, II, 323; Reid 1912, p. 18.
14 Venn, III, 173—4. The two memorial windows on the north side are to Sir George Paget and to the distinguished zoologist, physiologist and philosopher G. J. Romanes, whose career lay mainly in Edinburgh and London, and who founded the Romanes lecture at Oxford; but he was a scholar of Caius 1870—3 and hon. fellow 1892—4 (*DNB*; Venn, II, 380).
15 On Ferrers, see Venn, II, 278; IV, 150—6 (E. S. Roberts); below, p. 234; on the estates, pp. 251—2.
16 See pp. 195—6.

an interest'.[17] He took as text 'I am not come to destroy but to fulfil' and bitterly regretted that the Commissioners had not acted in this spirit. It seemed to him that the power and demands of the University had come to override the traditional rights and loyalties of the colleges; above all, at a time when Caius, like every college, was suffering from the ravages of the agricultural depression, it had laid hands on the colleges and taxed them for the University's supposed needs. Ferrers and his like had been prepared for 'a reform and were confronted with a revolution'.[18]

Cambridge in the late 19th century

The nature and effect of external intervention in the affairs of Oxford and Cambridge in recent centuries is at first sight contradictory. In the 16th and 17th centuries the Chancellor and the royal court intervened directly in appointments and management; in the 18th century the duke of Newcastle spread a net of intrigue and corruption which also had a direct effect on the way the University was run — but a very modest one. In the 19th century far greater changes were effected, but by means more indirect. Royal Commissions and Statutory Commissions were appointed — three times each for Oxford and Cambridge between 1849 and 1926, and over the late 19th and early 20th centuries almost without intermission in the University of London. But the Commissioners included local notables such as Adam Sedgwick in the 1850s and J. B. Lightfoot in the 1870s — and were governed by men with a long knowledge and sympathy for the Oxford and Cambridge colleges; and looking back it is astonishing to see how much of the old differences between university and university and college and college survived their ministrations. Thus celibacy abandoned Caius in a rush — but lingered and hovered in most other colleges for decades; whereas democracy among the fellows limped slowly into Caius while it had long existed elsewhere. In 1882 the grip of the twelve seniors was slightly relaxed: the Governing Body came to have an element of four elected fellows. Early in this century there was the beginning of a swing to include more elected fellows and more by virtue of their offices; only in 1920 was it established that all the members of the Council should be elected, save only the Master, the senior tutor and senior bursar; but even then no substantial attempt was made to create a Governing Body more widely representative of the fellowship, as in other colleges: only when changing the statutes is a General Meeting of fellows 'the Governing Body',[19] though in practice the Council, now a small oligarchy in a fellowship well over twice as large as in

17 Winstanley 1947, pp. 358—9.
18 Ibid.
19 Statute 5(6). The changes in the composition of the Council were made in 1904 and 1920.

1920, nearly three times as large as in 1882, regularly consults the General Meeting on major issues. In this way the historical *persona* of the seniority still survives — it is a striking illustration of the power of tradition in Cambridge which, contrary to Dr Ferrers' anxious fears, was by no means overcome by the Commission. By an interesting compensation, the Caius fellowship is in other respects more democratic, more equal, than in many other colleges: every fellow, male or female, research, teaching, professorial or life, has an equal vote in the election of a Master and of the College Council, in the passage of a statute, or in a motion to the General Meeting. Since 1926 the intervention of government through commissions has ceased — Oxford established its own Franks, Cambridge its Bridges, London its Murray Committees. But since the First World War, and far more since the Second, the finance of the universities has come to depend increasingly on Government grants; and through its control over finance the Government can send a tremor through the universities more instant and deadly even than those inspired by King Henry or King Oliver.

Thus if we look at the reforms of the 19th century it is a nice question whether they came more from without or within; for Oxford and Cambridge were encompassed with a cloud of witnesses mostly enjoying Oxbridge degrees; and for some this meant a nostalgia for the courts and gardens; for others a revulsion from the idleness of the dons and their ignorance of the new trends in scholarship. The great change in Oxford in the mid and late 19th century has been traced by A. J. Engel in the transformation *From Clergyman to Don*; and the similar phase in the history of Cambridge by Sheldon Rothblatt as *The Revolution of the Dons*.[20] Neither of these titles quite answers to the history of Caius, for the Master and some of the leading seniors had often not been clergy, and one would hardly cast E. S. Roberts — or John Venn — in the role of a revolutionary. Yet these very differences are instructive. In Oxford the power of the clerical fellows came to be replaced in the third quarter of the century by a more complex pattern with three groups or nuclei in the intense debate on the future of the University: the clerical party which wished to see reform indeed, but with as little diminution of clerical power and privilege as possible; the group to whom the essential function of a university lay in learning and research, and was inclined to admire the German universities a great deal more than Oxford, and which wished to see professors as leaders and governors instead of mere shadows of a famous name; and the tutors.[21] As we contemplate Oxford today we can see that the tutors won — not without compromise and concession, for by some mysterious means university departments of immense prestige were formed, some of which owed very little allegiance to the colleges. But the Oxford tutors are the centre of a coherent

20 Engel 1983; Rothblatt 1968/81.
21 Engel 1983, esp. pp. 142−3, 150 (the savage parody of the research party's programme by Lewis Carroll, the wit of the church party), 156−7.

educational programme in which they manage the admission, welfare, and teaching of their pupils — and they reappear in a large majority of cases on Faculty Boards and elsewhere as managers of the affairs of the University too. This has led to what many regard as an excessive dominance of the colleges over the University even in times of rapid change, and few doubt that there are many stresses and strains in the system. But it is also clear that the tutors' authority has preserved a degree of common action and harmony between University and colleges which must be the envy of many in Cambridge. The greater freedom of manoeuvre that the University enjoys in Cambridge has always been hampered by the barrier which the changes of the late 19th and early 20th centuries have set between University and college; so that although it remains broadly true in Cambridge too that one sees the same faces at college meetings and in Faculties, university and colleges very rarely make joint appointments, and a like office in a college and the University are clean different things.

The use of the word 'tutor' in Cambridge is the key to much of the history that we are now trying to penetrate; for the Cambridge tutor has never recovered, except by accident, the ancient role of teacher which is the major feature of his Oxford counterpart — has indeed deliberately avoided being caught in the professional net of teacher. Here is the account of a devout Caian describing in the late 1970s his memories of his Cambridge tutor of the years 1919—22. 'In the Cambridge system the Tutor is a sort of "housemaster", keeping an eye, in an extremely unobtrusive way, upon the welfare and demeanour, and the assiduity, of about 80 men. The term "Tutor" is misleading, as it is not he, but one's Director of Studies who organizes and supervises one's programme of lectures and work; the latter is expert in the subject being read; (one "swots" in the prep school, "works" in the Sixth, and "reads" at the university). Formal contact with the Tutor is minimal: you call on him at the beginning of term — "Had a good vac?" and at the term's end to get an exeat — "Have a good vac"; perhaps a word about work, about rooms; these exchanges suffice until you know each other better. But should you be in trouble, about work, unwell, in financial or disciplinary difficulty, he will be on hand to help. This was preeminently true of Arnold McNair.'[22] — And he goes on to describe some of the multifarious ways in which McNair helped and befriended his pupils. Superficially there are strong resemblances between this account and Venn's or Francis's of Clayton; and they serve to show the element of historical continuity in the story of the Cambridge tutor and why it is that Cambridge has had to coin the word 'supervision' for college tuition, where every other university in this land (so far as I know) says 'tutorial'. But the differences were not the less profound — for when McNair was tutor there was a whole apparatus of teaching in college and University for a young history student, and a Seeley Library to read in; and though Clayton was a good man and a

22 Warr 1979, pp. 113—14.

notable preacher, McNair was an academic lawyer of immense distinction. This symbolises many changes since the 1850s, and we must try to get a clear view of them one by one.

Religion in Caius

After the abolition of celibacy came the end of the religious tests. It had been a scandal widely felt that Oxford and Cambridge were still the privileged homes of the established Church in the mid-19th century. So deep were the scars this left behind that the new University of Liverpool in its Charter of 1903 stated that it was a fundamental principle that there should be no religious discrimination — and no teaching of theology. The clause was modified in the new Charter of the 1960s, for no university can win recognition in this country in the mid or late 20th century which does not have religious and political freedom written into its constitution, and the persecution of theology ceased in principle, though with modest practical result. Acts of Parliament in 1856 and 1871 abolished religious tests first for students then for fellows and all members of the Universities of Oxford and Cambridge save those whose posts were tied to religious duties.[23] As a member of the established Church, I suppose that I should be one of the slender band left in the fellowship if the act of 1871 were suddenly repealed; but to all of us now — so great a change has come — freedom of belief and practice is a fundamental part of an academic society; for those of us of religious faith a part of our creed.

It is no chance that the act of 1871 followed hard on the first celibacy debates. When fellows could hope not to lose their fellowships by marriage, they began to lose their faith. In the mid-century the central figure for those who relished advanced religious and political discussion was F. D. Maurice, who was both inspiring and disquieting; and from the 1850s, and especially for the more sceptically inclined, the age of Darwin had arrived. In 1859 *The Origin of Species* was published and the story goes that Whewell banned it from the Trinity Library for a time.[24] In 1862 Robert Willis presided over a great meeting of the British Association in the Caius Hall which debated the issue of the origin of man, and decided, by a handsome majority, that the apes were the key to it all.[25] Looking back, much of the debate seems trivial or absurd; but it was not so in the 1860s. Agnosticism and atheism were nothing new; but Darwin gave them new direction; liberal Protestantism meanwhile gained new force and direction from the mingling of Biblical criticism and the search for a Christian faith in which dogma gave way to morality. This gospel was eloquently presented in a

23 Winstanley 1947, chap. 3. For the whole of this section see especially Green 1964.
24 Clark 1900, p. 75 n.
25 Francis 1923, p. 118.

book published anonymously in 1865 called *Ecce Homo*, which offered a naive view of the historical Jesus but a very moving exposition of the social gospel, of Jesus as a preacher of morality.[26] In a few months it became known to his friends that its author was J. R. Seeley, and H. B. Swete of Caius was among those first in the secret. In 1869 Seeley was to write to Henry Sidgwick, commiserating with him on the need to resign his fellowship owing to religious doubt — but also very much commending him for it and rejoicing in it, for Seeley had just returned to Cambridge as Regius Professor of Modern History and had no college ties — and reckoned 'that *the* abuse at Cambridge is the College' and looked to the formation of 'a class of residents without College ties' for the salvation of the University.[27] The issues were closely linked.

John Venn meanwhile was close to Seeley and friendly with Sidgwick, and had been much swayed by a Caius contemporary, C. H. Monro, who had a speculative and philosophical cast of mind.[28] As his own studies in logic developed, and as he observed his friends' minds swaying, he gradually moved further from the evangelical faith of his family and his youth in Caius. He had been ordained and served as a curate here and there; but in course of time he ceased to practise his orders and in the 1880s was able formally to renounce them.[29] Yet he did not become an agnostic: rather he moved with Seeley and Sidgwick into an undogmatic Christianity. He even felt in later life that if the movement of the Church at large in this direction had gone further sooner, he need never have given up his orders. He was fortunate in his College. After the departure of Clayton, dogmatic Evangelicalism ceased to prosper in the College, although the earnest missionary zeal did not depart. C. F. Mackenzie, inspired by Livingstone's famous speech in the Senate House in 1857, set off to become the first bishop of the Mission to Central Africa, and to die of fever by the Zambesi in 1862, still a junior fellow. Later in the century, in Bishops Wallis and Knight of Wellington and Rangoon, the fellowship continued to flourish in distant parts of the world, if not quite such classic centres of the Victorian mission as Central Africa.[30] Nor were Mackenzie and Harvey Goodwin, Bishop of Carlisle (1869–91), the chief Caian bishops of the 1860s, Evangelicals; Harvey Goodwin was a notable high churchman. In any case, the tendency in College seems for a while to have been towards a religion both undogmatic and unostentatious; and when the Reverend Norman

---

26 On Seeley see Wormell 1980, esp. pp. 22–32; Rothblatt 1968/81, chap. 5 (on *Ecce Homo*). For the discovery of his authorship see Venn 1895, pp. 167–8; Swete 1918, p. 17; Chadwick 1970, pp. 64–6, esp. 64 n. 2. Seeley appears in a group mainly of Caians in a photo of 1857 in Swete 1918, facing p. 17.
27 Wormell 1980, p. 73.
28 Francis 1923, p. 113.
29 Venn, II, 313; Francis 1923, p. 123.
30 Chadwick 1959, esp. pp. 16–20; Swete 1918, pp. 22–3; Venn, II, 271, 403, 523; IV, 130, 139; V, 17, 52; VI, 16; for Harvey Goodwin, above, p. 221. Venn (II, 370) and Crockford both note that E. S. Roberts was ordained in 1877–9 by the bishop or in the see of Carlisle — evidently by Harvey Goodwin.

Ferrers was Master, the Reverend J. B. Lock bursar and the Reverend E. S. Roberts tutor, few could determine what the religious complexion of the College officers might be. Roberts, at least, was a devout man; perhaps all of them were. But they provided an ambience in which men did not have to search their consciences so long as they were prepared to go sometimes to chapel; and by the mercy of providence John Venn was not under pressure to resign his fellowship nor — especially after the abolition of the tests — was there substantial resistance, so far as we can tell, to receiving men of doubtful religious opinions into the fellowship.[31] As for chapel, it remained compulsory in principle, though with declining effect, for undergraduates till 1914; the old rules for fellows were finally swept away in 1860.

The educational programme of the 1860s and 1870s

In the 1870s there was teaching in classics and mathematics and a lecturer in law; there was from 1872 a chemistry 'praelector', and since 1862 there had been a lecturer in moral science.[32] Classics and mathematics were long to remain the heart of the matter; what was changing was that the College lecturers were beginning to take over from the coaches — a process not finally concluded in many subjects till the 1940s or 50s. The chemistry lab had been a theme of debate since the 1840s. It finally arrived — still a discreet distance from the old courts — following a decision taken in December 1871, on an island of college property behind the Blue Boar.[33] Under the second chemical praelector, later fellow, Mr Pattison Muir, who was also a writer of influential textbooks, it flourished; but even in 1871−2 there were rumours that the University might one day make provision. Indeed the first University laboratories came in the 1860s. But it was not until the Chancellor, the duke of Devonshire, endowed the Cavendish Laboratory and the University established the Cavendish Chair in 1871 that serious advance in the physical sciences seemed possible; doubtless this was the immediate stimulus which led the College Council to provide for chemistry in December of the same year.[34] It was still a much debated question whether the colleges or the University should provide in such matters. It must already have been evident that no simple answers could be given: in Caius it must have been particularly evident in the 1870s and 80s that the medical school under Sir George Paget — with its physiological department expanding rapidly under the great organiser Sir Michael Foster, and already

31 E.g. Seeley; for Roberts's religious views, see Reid 1912, pp. 38−9. Compulsory chapel for undergraduates seems never to have been formally abolished: see below, p. 290 and n.
32 For chemistry and law, Venn, III, 200; Francis 1923, p. 117.
33 Venn, III, 199−200, citing *Gesta*, 12 Dec. 1871. The chemistry laboratory had a brief but distinguished career: the celebrated German chemist, Siegfried Ruhemann (Venn, II, 495) taught in it.
34 Winstanley 1947, p. 194−8.

by the 1880s drawing such brilliant young scientists as Charles Sherrington — must be primarily a university centre of healing and research.[35] But the relative calls of college and University, of teaching and research, were to be hotly debated for another century and more.

Over the centuries Caius had produced its share of eminent lawyers, and never more than in the early and mid-19th century. Yet it is hard to discern traces of serious teaching before the era of C. H. Monro. Monro was a classic who revived the tradition of Legge and studied and taught Roman law through the era when the Law Tripos was created; and he taught law from 1872 till the turn of the century — remaining a fellow till his death in 1908 — but passing on the mantle meanwhile to W. W. Buckland, one of the most eminent Roman lawyers Cambridge has produced in recent centuries.[36]

The reforms of 1848 had issued in the Moral Sciences and the Natural Sciences Triposes; but they were slow to impinge on the studies of Caians. John Venn began the process, so far as can now be discerned, by teaching for the Moral Sciences Tripos in the 1860s, and bringing Caius into the range of influence and discourse of the leading minds of the University of the day, including Sidgwick and Leslie Stephen.[37] Venn was at first a mathematician and it is Venn's diagram which has made him a household word among the schoolchildren of the present century. His chief interest in the 60s and 70s, and down to the late 80s, lay in philosophy; and he was one of the pioneers of logic, and especially of probability theory, in the University. He greatly influenced the study of logic and built up a splendid library, which he presented to the University in 1888.[38] This was perhaps a signal of changing direction; yet the logical studies continued for a while longer; but by the late 1880s his chief interest lay in the prosopographical history of the College — and later, of the University.[39] When the coats of arms of benefactors were put in the hall windows in the early 20th century, Venn's was placed among them, a benefactor on account of his immeasurable contribution to our past and our knowledge of it, which has been acknowledged at every point in this *History*. Venn's work as historian has perhaps obscured his notable contribution to the College in other ways, and we may see his hand behind the successful extension of College teaching from the 1870s on, and in the efforts of the College to contribute to the University in the 80s, including the election of Seeley to a professorial fellowship.[40]

---

35 Cf. Geison 1978; Roach 1959, p. 263; Cohen 1958, pp. 2—5.
36 On Monro, Venn, II, 310; IV, 126; *Caian* XVII (1907—8), 79, 161—71 (by Venn and Buckland); Francis 1923, pp. 112—13. On Buckland, below, pp. 243, 247.
37 Francis 1923, pp. 117—19; on Venn, I am also indebted to an unpublished paper by Dr A. Edwards.
38 Francis 1923, p. 122.
39 Venn; and Venn's *Alumni*, completed under the direction of his son, J. A. Venn, President of Queens', 1932—58.
40 On Venn's friendship with Seeley, see Venn 1895; Venn 1913, p. 281.

E. S. Roberts

But the major catalyst of change was undoubtedly E. S. Roberts, who arrived as an undergraduate in 1865.[41] He had been brought up in Swineshead in Lincolnshire and educated at Boston. Reading between the lines of the tactful obituary notices, it seems that the headmaster quarrelled with his father and he was withdrawn from the school – he later took pleasure in entertaining his old headmaster in Caius – and was rescued by the classics master, Mr Dunn, who taught him in his spare time. Roberts, meanwhile, had to walk nine miles from Swineshead to Boston for the purpose.[42] He remained a moderate but firm adherent of muscular Christianity all his days. As an undergraduate he tried the services of the leading classical coach, Mr Shilleto, but most of what he had to teach he had already learned from Dunn; and he always preferred to read for himself – and, like Venn, laid up in his mind a determination that his successors should not be dependent on the coaches. He was a hard reading man who had little time at first for relaxation; but once he had secured his fellowship in 1870, he took to the water – it was not uncommon then for fellows to row – and stroked the second boat in the Mays of 1872, by which time he was already Senior Treasurer.[43] From 1870 he was a College lecturer in classics, and the direction of his own studies was already philological. Reid recalls the excitement of philology with Professor Cowell, at whose feet they sat with W. W. Skeat, and which ran notionally from 2.30 to 3.30 but rarely ended before 5.[44] Cowell was an orientalist and professor of Sanskrit, and his pupils included the eminent Sanskrit scholar Cecil Bendall, who was a fellow of Caius from 1879 – 86. But Roberts and Reid stayed faithful to the classics. Roberts also later turned his attention to Greek epigraphy and in the rare leisure – if such it can be called – of a busy life, in the small hours of the morning, he embarked on a substantial *Introduction to Greek Epigraphy*, which he eventually completed with the help of E. A. Gardner.[45] In research and teaching and sport he fervently believed and played his role in each according to his strength and opportunity; in 1877 he was ordained, and although he rarely exercised his ministry outside the College, save in his enthusiastic support for the birth and progress of the College Mission, he embodied as completely as any Cambridge figure of his day the ideal of education, religion, learning and research. In 1876 he became tutor, and when Ferrers was elected Master, in effect, senior tutor – and more than that, for Ferrers in his later years was struck down by rheumatoid arthritis, and Roberts as Senior Tutor and, from 1894, President; was Master in everything but

41 For what follows, Reid 1912; Roberts 1934; Venn, II, 370; etc.; VI, 505 – 14.
42 Reid 1912, pp. 2 – 3; Venn, VI, 505; Roberts 1934, pp. 116 – 17.
43 Reid 1912, p. 6; Scott 1927, p. 84.
44 Reid 1912, pp. 9 – 10.
45 Roberts 1887 – 1905; cf. Reid 1912, pp. 33 – 5; Roberts 1934, p. 111. On Bendall, see Venn, II, 429; *DNB*.

name.[46] When Ferrers died in 1903 and the fellows were known to be in conclave, the Master of Jesus trotted to the Caius Porter's Lodge (so he assured Mrs Roberts) with a letter of congratulation already in his pocket.[47] Reid's memoir of Roberts is a fascinating document – the warmth of lifelong friendship burns clearly through it, and also a certain reserve on academic policy; Reid was more the type of the academic, fervent on matters of principle, hating compromise; Roberts the committee man, who in the first golden age of academic committees, by clarity of vision and readiness for give and take knew how to move business forward and get things done. Reid clearly implies that his friend could go too far in compromise, had too strong a sympathy with other men's views.[48] The issues are hidden from us now; we cannot judge between them; but we can admire the scale of Roberts' achievement.

The other notable source is his widow's autobiography, which is a fascinating revelation of the entry of women into University society. Roberts worked strenuously for Girton and the Perse Girls' School in his day, but we shall learn nothing of either from his widow. Though the daughter of an Oxford Head and immersed in universities all her life, and evidently a person of lively mind as well as exceptional charm, she was studiously unacademic – at least in her reminiscences – and it is for the quality of life in Cambridge, and for the entry of the fellows' wives into Caius that she is peculiarly valuable evidence; and she lived in the College as tutor's and Master's wife for twenty-six years or so, longer than any other woman so far. Her criticism of her husband, to whom she was devoted, was that his conscience was 'so terribly despotic' that even though they were under the same roof almost continuously, she still saw much less of him than she wished.[49] Roberts, in a favourite phrase, used to refer to the contribution of the Boat Club to the wholesomeness of College life. One cannot help feeling that she and her like have also contributed, and as much.

The title 'Senior Tutor' is sometimes used in references to Roberts and his predecessors. But in some formal sense it was only instituted in 1898 for him; and when he became Master he carried it into the Lodge. W. W. Buckland in fact succeeded as senior of the tutors, but he only achieved the formal status after Roberts' death in 1912 – or so the College's official record assures us; but it confuses us abominably by also telling us that from 1904 the Governing Body came to comprise three seniors, six elected fellows and the senior bursar, the senior tutor and the senior dean – if space could be found for them and they were not otherwise provided for – a provision by no means easy to put into practice, especially when the terms 'senior'

46 Venn, IV, 155; Roberts 1934, pp. 163 – 4 (dated 1905 for 1896; see Reid 1912, p. 49).
47 Roberts 1934, pp. 152 – 3.
48 Reid 1912, pp. 39 – 40.
49 Roberts 1934, pp. 111 – 12.

were not normally applied either to bursars or to deans.[50] But through this mist a great truth shines. In Caius, as in most colleges, great authority may reside in bursars and presidents; but the traditional seats of power are the offices of Master and senior tutor. While Roberts lived they were not divided.

This is far from suggesting that J. B. Lock, the bursar, or the much younger W. W. Buckland, were nonentities; both were remarkable men who made, in their very different ways, a deep impression on the College. But Roberts had the authority born of unique experience in every field of university activity, and the authority of a man who respected all men — and was respected by them in his turn. He would have relished the notion propounded, according to a favourite story of Joseph Needham, by Conrad Noel from his pulpit at Thaxted on Trinity Sunday — that the universe was governed by a committee.[51]

Education and learning, c. 1900

In 1853, Venn tell us, there were twenty-nine fellows, plus the Master, all of them elected for their prowess in the Mathematical or Classical Tripos; and he attempted a comparison of the state of the fellowship in 1900, when there were twenty-seven, which is candidly a little confusing.[52] For it is based on grounds of election, but these had shifted in the interval. In 1853 a fellowship was a piece of property — 'Does Lord John Russell know that I can mortgage my fellowship?' asked an Oxford don in 1854 protesting against the Prime Minister's threats to interfere with his rights — which could be held till death or marriage overtook the fellow.[53] In the Middle Ages a fellowship had been a stipend for a man engaged in study and teaching; in the late 19th and 20th centuries it has become so (for many) once again. But in the 18th and early 19th centuries it was simply a possession, a prize. In 1860 the new statutes had made most fellowships into prizes for success in tripos, but limited their tenure — not by marriage — but to ten years; this could be extended indefinitely if the fellowship was combined with a College office, including a lectureship, and thus the way was cleared for making college teaching posts a profession for life.[54] In 1882 the basic tenure was reduced to six years, but much more flexibility was allowed the College in other elections, and the notion of the professorial fellow was introduced.

50 Statutes (1904), c.3.2; Venn, VI, 511; cf. ibid. 506, which also talks of Buckland as senior tutor; but the *Caian* XXIII (1913−4), 82, is specific that the title was conferred on him after Roberts's death, and this is confirmed by the official College lists of this period in *CUCaI*.
51 Needham 1976, p. 37.
52 Venn, III, 153; Venn 1901, pp. 239−40, which specifies that his figures relate to 1900.
53 Engel 1983, p. 65.
54 For these details, Venn, III, 151−4.

Thus the fellowship of 1901 was like an archaeological trench with different strata. The resident research fellows were still to come; the senior fellow, Mr Wiglesworth, who had been elected in 1850 and held his fellowship till his death in 1918, lived in London where he was an equity draftsman, and had been for many years steward of the College manors; he had been elected for prowess in classics, but that was a remote event in 1900.[55] The three juniors were engaged in teaching and tutoring in London and elsewhere.[56] Venn himself had retired from teaching, though not from service to the College: his great work came to a climax in 1901 and from 1903 till his death in 1923 he was President. The effective teaching strength comprised, first of all, three classics and two mathematicians. Apart from the Master and Reid, who was later Professor of Ancient History, there was a young Irish scholar called Lendrum, who later changed his name to Vesey, and became a celebrated Cambridge eccentric. Once every week in the hunting season he was to be seen marching out of College in scarlet hunting costume; the evidence is conflicting as to whether it was a Wednesday or a Saturday.[57] Joseph Needham recalls falling sick in the dangerous 'flu epidemic of 1918, when Vesey was the only resident fellow — with characteristic kindness he brought him a bunch of grapes, and with equal caution handed it to him on the end of a walking stick. It is also alleged that being worsted in argument by Ridgeway in the Combination Room he had his revenge soon after by asking Ridgeway to put his head through the window of his room: — he pilloried him before his class and then dismissed him, 'That will do, Ridgeway'. But as so often in such sagas there are rival versions in which Buckland and Roberts were the victims.[58] Legend is moderately consistent, however, that Reid and Ridgeway and Vesey were fairly often at loggerheads. My father claimed that his election to a fellowship in history in 1908, with a reputation based on the study of ancient history, represented a rare accord between Ridgeway and Reid.

Sir William Ridgeway had been elected a fellow from 1880−7, and returned to the fellowship when he was elected Disney Professor of Archaeology in 1892. He was a vivid personality, a charismatic teacher, and a man of fierce academic energy. His first book, *The Origin of Metallic Currency* (1892), though it has its oddities, remains a classic — nor has the dust gathered on *The origin and influence of the Thoroughbred Horse* (1905); but he had trampled on many of the frontiers between archaeology and anthropology with a polemical fierceness which took the breath away; and though this sometimes limited the quality of his scholarship, he greatly

---

55 Venn, II, 268; V, 2.
56 F. A. E. Trayes, G. M. Buck, T. M. Taylor: Venn, II, 502, 505, 517; etc. Trayes was later editor of Venn, V.
57 Warr 1979, p. 113; Peters 1980, p. 34. It is said that he changed his name when he inherited a country estate. On Reid, *Caian* XXXIV (1925−7), 143−55; Venn, II, 432; V, 24.
58 Peters 1980, p. 34: the Buckland and Ridgeway versions are based on hearsay.

stimulated the study of anthropology and archaeology in their infancy.[59] As time passed his eyesight narrowed, until he could only see plainly out of the corner of his right eye; his sweeping gestures could be a hazard to an inexperienced waiter offering soup on his blind side — and to a friendly undergraduate trying to prevent him from walking through a window which he supposed to be a door, he rejoined — 'Thankee, my boy, I know very well where I am'.[60] There was a warmth there too, as is reflected in the *Festschrift* his pupils and admirers gave him; and his home in Fen Ditton was long remembered as a haven of good talk and hospitality.[61]

Many of the seniors had once been mathematical wranglers; but by 1900 two young lecturers sufficed to teach the subject. E. G. Gallop, who had been brought from Trinity in the late 1890s, and J. F. Cameron, who was a wrangler and a fellow in 1899 and a lecturer in mathematics in 1900, performed this role for many years.[62] Cameron, however, soon turned his hand to teaching applied mathematics to the students of mechanical sciences, whose work he directed. He studied in Göttingen, and spent two long vacations in large engineering works. He was for many years an efficient, lucid and zealous teacher; he lived in that side of the tradition of Roberts which set a special price on total immersion in the teaching and tutorial work of the College. He was a tutor from 1909, senior tutor from 1919. But already he had shown a shrewd interest in the financial management of the College, and from 1921, when J. B. Lock died after thirty years as bursar, he stepped into the bursary; and although he rose higher still, to be Master from 1928 till 1948, yet just as Roberts had carried the senior tutor's office into the Master's Lodge, so Cameron remained in substantial measure bursar till near the end of his life.

Venn distinguishes four biologists, two chemists and a medical fellow, but the borderlines, as we look back, seem oddly drawn. It seems to underplay the medical tradition of the College, which had clearly revived under Paget and Drosier. Sir Clifford Allbutt had succeeded Sir George Paget as Regius Professor of Physic in 1892; like Paget he was a man of wide culture and varied interests; he was an Antiquary as well as an FRS; and later in life he gave the College an enchanting boat — a 19th century imitation of a 15th century French nef, which he believed had been designed by Pugin.[63] He was also a prolific writer on medical science and a distinguished head of the Medical School. But needless to say the immediate care of the medical students lay with younger men. The College in the late 19th century

59 Venn, II, 432, etc.; *Caian* XXXIV (1925−7), 134−42.
60 Warr 1979, p. 112.
61 The *Festschrift* is *Essays and Studies presented to William Ridgeway*, ed. E. C. Quiggin (Cambridge, 1913).
62 On Gallop, Venn, II, 504; V, 45; *Caian* XLV (1936−7), 4−8; for Cameron, Venn, VI, 528−40, and below, chap. 13.
63 Pl. 12; Venn, VI, 524; on Allbutt, Venn, II, 325; V, 6−7; *Caian* XXXIII (1924−5), 57−67.

attracted a galaxy of young physiologists. The first and greatest of these, Charles Sherrington, had come and gone well before 1900, but his memory survived, and he was one of those which gave the College an ideal of excellence in the field which was to remain the natural mark of a medical college.

'I was an undergraduate at Cambridge in the opening 80s of the last century' wrote Sherrington when he was approaching ninety, 'and was at Gonville and Caius College. The Master was then the Rev. Dr Norman Ferrers, whom we saw but little;' — and he goes on to talk of his real theatre, the Medical School, astir under 'Michael Foster, George Humphry and George Paget . . . "the great triumvirate" ' — but more especially a younger group in 'that then small and ramshackle haunt of Physiology'.[64] Sherrington held a junior fellowship in Caius from 1887 to 1893, but he was already spending much of his time in London; and he is one of the great Caians, like Harvey himself, whose main work lay in distant and infidel places, in Liverpool — where the mystery and perception of this marvellous man were caught in one of the most brilliant portraits of Augustus John, a portrait Sherrington himself heartily disliked — and in Oxford.[65] Three brief glimpses of a long life may catch a little of the varied treasury of an experimental scientist who was also a poet and a philosopher.

About the time he ceased to be a fellow, while working in London in pathological research, word came to him and the colleague with whom he worked, of the development of diphtheria inoculation in Paris at the Institut Pasteur. 'I had a spare stall in the stable . . . and we got a horse and began inoculating it with gradually increasing doses of diphtheria cultures . . . Then oddly enough, one Saturday about seven in the evening, came a telegram from my brother-in-law in Sussex. "George has diphtheria". George, a boy of eight, was the only child . . .' When at last he found his colleague, who was dining out, he said ' "By all means, you can use the horse, but it is not yet ripe for trial!" Then by lantern light . . . I bled the horse into a great four-litre flask duly sterilised . . . By Sunday's early train I reached Lewes. Dr Fawssett of Lewes was waiting at the railway station in a dog-cart . . . "You can do what you like with the boy, but he will not be alive at tea-time". We drove out to the old house . . . The boy was breathing with difficulty. He did not know me. The doctor helped with injecting the serum' and then left. 'Early in the afternoon the boy was clearly better. At three o'clock I sent a messenger to the doctor. Thence forward progress was uninterrupted . . .' And there is a charming epilogue in which Sherrington went to tell Sir William Lister, who insisted on interrupting a dinner party to hear the story. 'Unlike as he and Pasteur were in some ways, they both as part of their inspiration had an unshakable confidence in the

---

64 Cohen 1958, p. 4; cf. Venn, II, 446; V, 27; VI, 5. What follows owes much to Lord Cohen's book.
65 Cohen 1958 — John's portrait is pl. 14.

immense future before Medicine'.[66]

In 1901 at Liverpool he was joined by a young man called Harvey Cushing, who later became an eminent brain surgeon and a reverent disciple. But his diary opens a window into the real world of scientific research, not cumbered with the stained glass of obituary notices. 'Sherrington is a great surprise. He is young, almost boyish if 36 (?) [actually 43], nearsighted, wearing when he has not lost them a pair of gold spectacles. He operates well for a "physiolog" but it seems to me much too much. I do not see how he can carry with any accuracy the great amount of experimental material he has under way.'[67] The young man was deceived; the marvellous capacity to keep together a thousand projects and see them as parts of a single scheme of research was one of the secrets of this remarkable magician. Just such a complex world he gathered together in his most famous book, *The Integrative Action of the Nervous System* (1906), which summarises a part of his most spectacular research.

If one peruses his entry in *Who's Who* in 1952[68] — the last of his life — and sees the long list of appointments, as professor in Liverpool and Oxford, as President of the Royal Society, as honorary member, fellow, associate and doctor, in innumerable institutions the world over, one sees the College taking a modest place in an amazing galaxy of honours. But one entry catches the eye: 'Address: Gonville and Caius College'. For when he was in his mid-80s, a widower and in wartime, Mrs Cameron opened the hospitable doors of the Master's Lodge and gave him asylum for some years, until he needed constant help and went to a nursing home, first in Cambridge then in Eastbourne, to die. Many undergraduates of the late 1940s can recall him as a shrivelled, charming little old gentleman — very short-sighted as he always had been — seeking his favourite chair in the Reading Room, observing it filled, continuing to observe till its occupant lept to his feet to offer it to him — a nightly comedy which usually ended in his being happily installed in the chair: a revered honorary fellow who had come home to the College which had seen him too little. As a scientist and physiologist Sherrington is one of the immortals. As with Harvey, the College can hardly claim a major share in his achievements; but he never forgot it, and in its turn his scientific genius has been an inspiration to many Caians and his breadth of culture — his vision of *Man on his Nature* (1946) — has given his name to a flourishing College society.

After Sherrington one may expect an anti-climax — but it is only of a modest dimension. Probably few physiologists now study the work of the American scientist A. S. Lea, who was brought from Trinity in 1881 to be director of medical students, and from 1885 a fellow; but he was an eminent physiologist and biochemist in his day, and the title of his book

66 Quoted Cohen 1958, pp. 8–9.
67 Quoted Cohen 1958, pp. 9–10.
68 Reprinted in Cohen 1958, pp. 107–8.

The Chemical Basis of the Animal Body (1892) foreshadows the amazing line of physiologists and biochemists which followed; and he gave it human expression by serving as deputy steward of the College for many years.[69]

Lea came in 1881 and not a moment too late, for not only was Sherrington already in residence, but the freshmen of 1884 were to include both Hugh Anderson and William Hardy.[70] Anderson was to make fundamental contributions to his science by the study of nerve physiology, and to the College and University as Master and Commissioner. Hardy was to make an even greater name as chemist and physicist and serve the College for twenty years as tutor. But the pattern of their careers was oddly different. Anderson's father was an eminent shipowner, a major figure in the history of what we would call P. and O.; both his grandfathers had been surgeons; and these two heritages deeply influenced his life. In the first half of his career, down to his election as Master in 1912, he was a devoted teacher and research scientist, advancing knowledge of the central nervous system and of the neural effects of nicotine, though flashes of financial acumen had already been perceived. From 1912 to his early death in 1928 he was a dedicated administrator in College and University, with a special flair for financial administration. It is not an absolute division. He was a man of charm and whimsical humour, and a culture widely spread, all his days; his appreciation of music was always with him. His warm humanity was expressed in his fluffy manner of lecturing as a young man. 'He argued with us as though he felt it was his own fault if he could not convert us . . . but perhaps after all we might know more about it than he did. He wrote countless little jottings and diagrams on the blackboard, lost the duster and rubbed them out with his gown, and ended smothered in chalk and apologetic at having given such a bad lecture . . . The main impression that remains is of one eager to help and convince but teaching us all as colleagues rather than pupils – and there can have been very few that did not appreciate the compliment'.[71] Anderson passed on in 1912 to another chapter of his life, and of this book.[72]

Hardy, meanwhile, was a very popular senior treasurer of the Boat Club from 1892 for many years, a tutor from 1900 to 1920, and senior tutor throughout the First World War (1914 – 19), though absent on government service part of the time.[73] But in the early 1920s he became immersed in his research and in public work of various kinds – director of the Low Temperature Research Station in 1922, and a knight in 1924 – and the care for medical students passed for a time into the exceedingly capable hands of R. A. Peters.[74]

69 Venn, II, 474; V, 36.
70 For Anderson, Venn, VI, 514 – 28; Barcroft in *Caian* XXXVII (1929), 113 – 22.
71 Lord Adrian, quoted Venn, VI, 515 – 16.
72 See pp. 264 – 7.
73 Venn II, 472; V, 35 – 6; *DNB*. On Hardy as scientist, see *DSB*, XV, 201 – 2 (J. S. Fruton); as treasurer of the Boat Club, Scott 1927, pp. 104 – 5, and below, p. 255.
74 Peters 1980.

These three names — Anderson, Hardy and Peters — were examples of a notable feature of the College at this time: the Master and tutors were men of scientific eminence, who combined a lofty reputation as scientists with dedicated work in the College. Many thought they showed an inspiring example; others reckoned their talents wasted in administration — that their place was in the lab, administration for administrators. There are no eternal verities in this region, but an argument without end — yet not a fruitless argument, for the College's life has been much enriched by examples to prove all the rules: by tutors who were eminent scholars and devoted to their pupils; by tutors and directors of studies too involved to be productive scholars, yet sometimes bringing qualities of mind and understanding to match or surpass many of the scholars; and by specialist or professional administrators. No doubt as with every such institution, it has had its examples too of laziness and inefficiency; though I can think of none of the 20th century to match the outstanding record of Hamnett Holditch. Meanwhile, from being a neuro-physiologist of high acclaim, Anderson became a brilliant university administrator; and Hardy, from being an excellent tutor, a national figure in his world of research.

Thus at the turn of the century the drift of Caius science was plainly on the borders of natural sciences and medicine. There was chemistry of diverse kinds and there were lectures in physics; but there seems to have been no warning of the later eminence of the College in physics much before the advent of Chadwick in 1919 and the conversion of Hardy at about the same epoch. There was a geologist among the lecturers, but he was not a fellow. From 1898 there was a zoologist among the fellows, Stanley Gardiner, who combined overseas adventure — to the Coral Seas, to the Maldive Islands, to the Seychelles — with the office of lay dean, representing stability and discipline at home. He was indeed a man of many sciences — botany and geography and oceanography among them; in 1908–9 he was the first and only College lecturer in oceanography; and the last of his honours, the year before his death in 1946, was the Darwin Medal of the Royal Society — a fitting bow from the Galapagos to Funafuti.[75] In 1901 he was joined by R. C. Punnett, also at first a zoologist, but eventually, after some mutations, Professor of Genetics from 1912 to 1940 — to be soon succeeded by R. A. Fisher — and a notable expert on *Mimicry in Butterflies* and *Heredity in Hens*.[76]

The humanities and music — Charles Wood

Apart from archaeology and the fine array of classics, the humanities were not extensively represented in the fellowship in 1900. There were naturally

75 Venn, II, 519; IV, 138; V, 50–1; VI, 16.
76 Venn, II, 539; V, 59; VI, 19; VII, 3.

divines: Frederic Wallis had departed in 1895 to be bishop of Wellington in New Zealand, but he remained a fellow till his death in 1928 — having returned to this country in time to preach at the funeral of Roberts in 1912, and to enjoy two archdeaconries in the diocese of Salisbury in his retirement; A. M. Knight was dean in 1900, and soon after went as bishop to Rangoon (1902 — 10).[77] The most distinguished theologian the College produced in the 19th century was Henry Barclay Swete, Regius Professor of Divinity. This kindly man of prodigious learning, whose 'placid lectures' soothed the Cambridge students still in Edwardian days, and who has blinked down upon many generations of Caians from his portrait in Hall, taught theology in the 1870s; but his chief place in College history is as an early example of the genus professorial fellow and as a major figure in the religious history of the College.[78] The law was represented by W. W. Buckland, an army in himself, and modern languages were on the march since 1900, when E. C. Quiggin, soon to be lecturer in Celtic, became a fellow.[79] But it was Edward Bullough who created modern languages in Caius. He only became a member of the College a month before Roberts's death, in May 1912, and a fellow in December. Of Lancashire descent but born at Thun in Switzerland, and educated in Germany at Dresden, he brought a European culture to Caius. First he taught German, then Italian; and was remembered by many who were not linguists for his teaching and writing on aesthetics; he died Professor of Italian in 1934. His wife was a daughter of the great actress Eleonora Duse, and they built for themselves a fine Italian villa in Cambridge, which Mrs Bullough gave to the Dominican Order after his death and is now the nucleus of Blackfriars; for he became in later life the first of many devout Roman Catholic fellows who have brought back the doctrines of Edmund Gonville into Caius.

The fellow of this epoch whose memory is most constantly refreshed in the College today is Charles Wood the musician. Wood was one of the notable group of Irishmen who have adorned the fellowship between the 1890s and the present day; he came to Selwyn in 1888, and on to Caius as 'organist scholar' in 1889.[80] In 1894 he was promoted fellow, and directed the College music in this role from then until his death in 1926 — though his election as professor in 1924 somewhat muted him as College musician. It is not too much to say that Wood created the tradition of music in Caius. He was one of the founders of the Scales Club in the 1890s — at first a small coterie of music makers, later opened more widely to the music lovers of the College. But he was not sole founder, and his success owed much to the whole-hearted support of Roberts, of Anderson as cellist and Master, of

77 See above, p. 231.
78 Green 1964, p. 344; Swete 1918; and see below, p. 291.
79 On Buckland, above, pp. 233 — 6; on Quiggin, Venn, II, 533; V, 56; on Bullough, Venn, V, 132 (and I am indebted to personal reminiscences of Michael Oakeshott and Father Kenelm Foster, OP).
80 Venn, II, 504; V, 45; Warr 1979, pp. 116 — 18; Caian XXXIV (1925 — 7), 156 — 65.

Peters as violinist and tutor — and many others. He had been a pupil of Stanford at the Royal College, and he himself taught there; 'many later composers were his pupils. He was a great teacher, and possibly for that reason never realised his potentiality as a composer' — wrote one who enjoyed his patronage in the early 1920s. 'After Scales Club or College concerts we would get him to reminisce about the great days of the College, when the number of . . .' cellos available for the College concerts in the 1890s or so 'would increase as the whisky went down' — the record was seventeen. 'And at that moment he would look one in the eye, challenging one's disbelief.'[81]

He is familiar today as the composer of much sacred music still sung by cathedral and college choirs, and of domestic music still well known to innumerable Caians: the chimes of the College clock, the grace used after major feasts, a sheaf of music still performed in chapel. In the year that he became a fellow the 'venerable Senior Fellow', Mr Drury, retired to Torquay; but this did not prevent a notable collaboration in the *Carmen Caianum*, which is a remarkable document of that period. Following an appeal from Roberts in the *Caian*, old Mr Drury, a Harrovian who had taught for a time at Harrow and was doubtless familiar with its tradition of notable songs, composed the words, and Wood the tune, of the *Carmen*. Benjamin Drury and his brother had been among the first holders of the scholarship for Harrovians to Caius established by John Sayer at his death in 1831. Since the money was in the hands of the Governors of Harrow this closed scholarship survived the reforms of the 1850s; and it has helped a number of fellows younger than Drury, from C. H. Monro in the 1850s to Hugh Anderson in the 1880s and Mark Buck in the 1970s, on their path to Caius. As for the *Carmen*, it 'has been sung for many years, in every part of the globe', as Reid said in his memoir of Roberts.[82] I doubt if the *Carmen* is sung in many parts of the globe today, and it is wholly unfamiliar to many younger Caians. But after an Annual Gathering this most stirring period piece of the 1890s gives an immense deal of warm and unsophisticated pleasure — and many who hear it have listened a few hours before to the subtler enchantment of Wood's setting of Jeremy Taylor's 'Heaven' in the service of the Commemoration of Benefactors. The mystical quality of 'Heaven', however, disturbed Wood's successor, Patrick Hadley. But Hadley could show his appreciation too to his distinguished predecessor, as by incapsulating Wood's chimes into his own suite in honour of the Coronation of 1953.

To the modern student of the arts in Caius the most surprising gaps in this list will perhaps be history and English. English philology indeed was

81 Warr 1979, p. 116.
82 Reid 1912, p. 28. On Drury, Venn, II, 235; IV, 124; *Caian* XII (1902−3), 18−23. On Sayer and his scholars, see M. C. Buck in *The Harrovian*, XCIV (1981), 131−2. The full text of the *Carmen* is in Venn, III, 393. It is sung at Annual Gatherings and the dean's Christmas parties. On Hadley see below, pp. 288−9.

represented in a distinguished way by the young Allen Mawer, the eminent philologist, fellow from 1905 to 1909; and later one of the founding fathers of the English Place-Name Society.[83] But his career lay elsewhere, in Sheffield and Newcastle and London; and the other notable English scholar of that era, John Dover Wilson, was never a fellow — though an honorary fellow in his later years.[84] It is a little characteristic of Cambridge, and highly characteristic of the Caius of the 1930s and 40s, that English was not professionally taught by a fellow until the 1950s. History is a very different tale. Sir John Seeley himself had been a fellow from 1882 to 1895, and it is somewhat surprising that there was no professional historian in the fellowship after his death until the election of Zachary Brooke in 1908. The history tripos had been founded in the 1870s — after an uneasy start among the moral sciences — and it was taught in Caius by a lecturer called G. E. Green, who was or had been a master at the Leys, from 1893;[85] and ancient history flourished in the person of J. S. Reid.

Professorial fellows

Thus there were gaps and inequalities in the provision of teaching and learning in the fellowship; but yet the range of studies in the College had been transformed; so too its relation to the University as a centre of teaching and learning. The Royal Commission of the 1870s, and its child and successor the Statutory Commission, when it settled down to revising college statutes in the early 1880s, insisted first and foremost that it was the duty of the colleges to foster the University itself, much more poorly endowed for its tasks than the richer colleges. In Oxford in this epoch the colleges retained the initiative, and tightly bound the professors new and old to the colleges which supported them. There were similar moves in Cambridge, but much less systematic; and in both places there were noisy grumbles that professors were drones, a useless, if not pernicious, infection from the German system of universities dominated by professors. These feelings, shared by old tutors and young Turks, were summed up in a brilliant pamphlet by the young fellow of All Souls, Hensley Henson — later to be a celebrated and controversial divine — who attacked the whole fabric of professorial stipends, and the sinister spread of science and research — 'nor is it surprising that . . . busy college tutors and lecturers should chafe against the existence of well-paid professors, whose lectures nobody attends, and whose researches nobody cares about.'[86]

This was not the view taken by E. S. Roberts. He realised — and J. B.

83 Venn, IV, 23.
84 Venn, IV, 17–18; V, 77; VI, 30; VII, 5.
85 Venn, II, 529; V, 54; he was afterwards a master at Charterhouse (1916–29).
86 Quoted in Engel 1983, p. 231. Owen Chadwick, *Hensley Henson* (Oxford, 1983), p. 31, lists some of the professors at whose feet he sat.

Lock, the bursar, was at his elbow to remind him — that the agricultural depression was eroding the College's income, and resources were limited. But within that limit he was keen to see the College play its part — and this meant, in the 1880s, to pay its share of the stipends of professors. In 1881 Sir George Paget, Regius of Physic, was restored to his fellowship. 1882 was the year of the new statutes; the year when Emmanuel College took the first steps toward the appointment of the first Dixie Professor of Ecclesiastical History, and Caius elected the Regius of Modern History, J. R. Seeley of Christ's. By 1890, when Swete returned to Cambridge and to Caius as Regius Professor of Divinity, Caius had three Regius Professors in its fellowship. Paget and Swete were ex-fellows. The story behind Seeley's election is not known. But it can hardly be coincidence that Reid had once been his pupil and Venn and he had long been intimate friends.[87] Seeley had made his fortune, and won his place in the history of religious sentiment, by *Ecce Homo*. Meanwhile — though his most scholarly work was on the text of Livy and *Ecce Homo* is very naive history — he came to be known as a leading modern historian — not for any original contribution to historical scholarship (as we understand it), but for his highly intelligent and lucid expositions of history as a practical subject: for the contributions that history might make to moral problems, to politics, and above all, to the problems and opportunities of Empire. His *Expansion of England* (1883) was a classic statement of a moderate Victorian imperialism, its historical roots and practical consequences; it was one of the great educating forces of its age, and it was still read in the 1930s. It gathers dust today. The view that history has lessons to teach is widely held; but few will agree what they are. The view of history as a practical science is not popular with working historians. Yet if it be true — as many historians would agree — that popular assumptions about politics and morality are partly based on the comparison of prejudices about the present and illusions about the past, the students of history ought to be better equipped than other folk to meditate on them. I doubt it they are. Seeley has failed, anyway for the time; but it was a noble failure.

Meanwhile, there entered with Zachary Nugent Brooke in 1908 a history no less integrated to strongly held convictions, but a scientific history with its root deep in the German scholarship of the 19th and early 20th centuries; for though my father never visited Germany and only studied abroad for any length of time in Rome — and although circumstances compelled him to spend four years of his early maturity at war with the Germans in the First World War — he was characteristic of the young British medievalists of his day in founding his studies on the best German medieval scholarship. And scientific history, from whatever source and fountainhead, inspired the junior historians of the early 20th century in Cambridge, and a type of

87 Reid in *Caian* V (1895–6), 33–41; Venn 1895. On Seeley, see esp. Wormell 1980; and above, pp. 222, 231. On Z. N. Brooke, below, see p. 282.

history, much closer to the texts and to the frontiers of knowledge than Seeley's, came in as a tide to sweep Seeley and his works away.

The election of Seeley bears witness to a remarkable appreciation of the possible role of the professorial fellow. Seeley himself had once been contemptuous of the college link; but after his election to Caius he wrote 'I am much pleased with what I see of my new College [he had formerly been a fellow of Christ's] and of the improvement which has taken place there in a quarter of a century.'[88] The colleges had to support the University in teaching and research — in Seeley's case, essentially in practical teaching — if it was to be revived as an academy which could vie with the best in Britain and Europe. But at the same time the colleges might be fructified by the presence of professors in their midst — for the professor was no longer the amateur teacher he had often been in the 18th and early 19th centuries — though some were still thought to hanker after sinecures. There is a warm optimism about the Caius revival of the late 19th century of which this may be taken as a happy example. For it is doubtful if the professorial fellows, then or later, have fulfilled this role. When Buckland became Regius Professor of Civil Law early in 1914, an appreciation of him appeared in the *Caian*, and it was hoped that the former senior tutor 'will not lapse into professorial exile, as some professors are apt to do, but that, even if only from force of habit, his familiar figure will still continue to flit about our Courts and Combination Rooms' — and so it did, to good purpose, for Buckland was an active President from 1923 till the 1940s.[89] But the image did not change, and Hedley Warr, speaking of the early 1920s, while noting the 'happy closeness of relationship between dons and students', said of the older fellows 'some held professorships and did little in the College except occasionally dine at High Table; with these august gentlemen I certainly had no contact.'[90] This impression is, I hope, a little unfair; and there is a contrary view which holds that professorial fellows are meant only to be a modest adornment; and that the illustrious among them may be much more — and no-one doubts the role of McNair or Grierson or Hawking. Some again have given the College a less enviable fame by their notoriety.

The entry of women to Cambridge

Among these must be counted Sir William Ridgeway, who was a leader of the opposition to the entry of women into the University.[91] The place of women in Cambridge was a serious issue in the 1880s and 1890s — and until the denouement in 1948. Ridgeway, however, could make any cause

88 Wormell 1980, p. 73 — also to Henry Sidgwick (see p. 231).
89 *Caian* XXIII (1913—14), 85.
90 Warr 1979, p. 112.
91 See above, pp. 237—8; for what follows, see Howarth 1978, pp. 35, 39; and for Ridgeway as teacher, p. 133.

ludicrous by his advocacy; and one cannot help feeling that in the long run his utterances must have hastened many sensible men into support of the female cause. If one strives objectively to consider the role of Caians in the advance of women's education in Cambridge, one cannot set aside the famous peroration to Ridgeway's speech in the Senate discussion in 1897: 'our pilots have given ear to the sirens of Girton and Newnham and unless we take heed will wreck this great University'.[92] Roberts and Reid, however, thought differently: both had lectured for Girton while it was still in Hitchin, and Roberts in later years served on the Girton Council — Anderson was to be chairman of its Executive Committee.[93] The Perse Girls' School was the happy outcome of the sad divorce of the College from that area of Perse's Trust. With the Boys' School some official connection was preserved; there has been none with the Girls', but characteristically, Roberts was the chairman of its governors.[94] The admission of women to Caius was hardly foreseen in this era: I do not believe it was seriously considered within the College before the 1960s; and meanwhile the bedmakers and the fellows' wives were the sole precursors of the civilising movements of the 1970s.

The bedmakers have a long and honourable history whose early passages are quite obscure. But as a part of a corps of College servants they date truly from the late 19th century. Until the 18th century the College butler, the waiters, the personal servants of the fellows, had been student sizars, and they only slowly disappeared. At the other end of the scale the major College officials, like the cook, were independent tradesmen — doubtless their independence was a manner of speaking, but they were not salaried officials; they were (as we should say) contractors to the College. All this was swept away in the 1880s;[95] and then began the formation of that massive cadre of College servants so movingly represented in the photograph of Joseph Needham's retirement party — a gathering of College servants and officials old and new nearly 100 strong. They form an element in the College community gravely under-represented in this book. Caius would not be a College, it could not exist without them. In the College staff there has always been a female element so strong that in the 1930s the Christmas Party was still 'the Bedmakers' Party' — and when I hear talk of the political 'complexion' of the College — as if a body many hundred strong in a democratic society could have such a thing — I call to mind the senior bedmaker of the early 1950s who appeared in the electiontide of 1951, one day all in scarlet, the next in black — 'in mourning', as she said with a twinkle, 'for my best friend — the government'.

The fellows' wives began to arrive in 1861.[96] Before that Mrs Brady and

92 Quoted in Howarth 1978, p. 35.
93 Venn, VI, 504; Reid 1912, p. 11; *VCH Cambs*, III, 492 (Jean Lindsay).
94 Venn, VI, 504; Reid 1912, pp. 11–12.
95 Venn, VI, 509. Venn, VII, pl. XI, shows a group of College staff of 1953.
96 See p. 226.

the successive wives of Dr Gooch had visited the Lodge; and it had been presided over by Dr Smith's sister-in-law; Davy was married only briefly, Chapman not at all; and even Guest had only married in 1859. So the wives of the community were few and lonely before the arrival of Mrs Roberts in 1886. As her husband transformed the College as a place of education and learning — and wholesome sport — so she brought a lively female presence to its courts and transformed its society; and her delightful *Recollections — Sherborne, Oxford and Cambridge*, published in extreme old age in 1934 — are our chief source for this undervalued element in the history of the College. She was the daughter of Dr Harper, former Headmaster of Sherborne, Principal of Jesus College, Oxford; she grew up in the Oxford of Lewis Carroll and Oscar Wilde and brought a breath of a wider world to the close knit courts of Caius. Roberts was already married to the College and his marriage to Mary Harper could not separate him from it; all the more because the Master, Dr Ferrers, was by then an invalid, and a beleaguered College could not find the space others found in the ampler grounds for building a detached tutor's house.[97] So a house was devised with what is now the Monro Reading Room as its centre, and there she lived and reared her family till she moved into the Lodge in 1903 — cheerful and friendly to all, thoroughly happy in her extremely inconvenient house, sending forth the small children into Gonville Court, to mingle with the peace of September and the noisy chatter of term; a gracious presence and a devoted wife — if always a little jealous of his other partner. She lived in College all her married life — yet 'I never in my life had him enough with me; his sense of duty was so strong, and his various avocations so numerous and exacting, that his family's share of him was cut down, in common, as I like to think, with other pleasures he would have himself enjoyed if his conscience hadn't been so terribly despotic'.[98] Meanwhile her lively, chatty presence must have formed a charming contrast to the great tutor of few words, whom the stranger thought dour, whose warmth and imagination hardly found expression in speech.

When the Roberts moved into the Lodge the tutor's house was preserved for a time, but soon its centre was converted into the Monro Library.[99] Yet indeed with Mrs Roberts in the Lodge — still more with Mrs Cameron — no tutor's wife could have held a candle to the hospitality of the Lodge. Mrs Roberts describes a little of this: the great College parties which she arranged with dancing in the Panelled Room and sitting out in the Lodge. She describes the origin of the bedmakers' party. 'Another kind of entertainment we always found great fun was a big College Servants' Party we generally gave at Christmas.' Every servant and pensioner was invited — the numbers were 'nearly 200' — and 'the tutors and their wives and any

97 Roberts 1934, pp. 123–4, 137–9; Venn, VI, 506.
98 Roberts 1934, pp. 111–12.
99 Venn, VI, 506.

fellows who were in College'. It lasted from 8 to 12, 'and the first part was a play, indifferently acted by our family and guests, but cordially appreciated. Then followed tea' and dancing, 'in which all were supposed to join, and many, even amongst the stoutest bedmakers, were persuaded to. We ourselves danced vigorously, and I remember seeing Mr Cameron, now Master of Caius and Vice-Chancellor dancing merrily, with Mr Stratton (now an Astronomy Professor) acting as his lady.'[100] Thus Mrs Roberts started what came to be known in the 1930s as the Bedmakers' Party. It still began with a play, acted by the fellows' children to the astonishment and (I hope) the pleasure of the guests; if a dance followed, I have forgotten it — and doubtless the younger children were discreetly removed at this stage. But the play was one product of a cooperative movement among the fellows' wives.

Mrs Roberts also started another tradition. We have seen from time to time that dynasties were formed within the families from which the College was recruited — Henry Wharton came from a line of Caians, and in his day another family, the Dades, proliferated beyond number in Caius; Robert Willis was a fellow's son — and the examples can be freely multiplied. But the changes of 1860 enabled a more intimate kind of succession to grow up. Roberts himself was the first of the family to be a Caian, but like St Bernard arriving at the gate of Cîteaux he brought several brothers with him, including H. A. Roberts (1864–1932), who late in life became one of the effective founders of the University Appointments Board and a fellow. Three children of E. S. Roberts flourished in Gonville Court, and Caroline and Margaret became known to Caians as Caia and Gonvillia. Caia married the dean, Arthur Duncan-Jones, whose grandson has brought back the fourth generation of this notable dynasty into the fellowship.

When Roberts died and his widow departed from the Lodge, tradition has it that Lady Anderson was a gracious and kindly hostess; but the mantle most evidently passed to Mrs Cameron, first as senior tutor's wife (1919–21) and then in the Lodge from 1928 to 1948. The changes of the 19th century can be seen as it were in a mirror in the marriage of the Presbyterian (Church of Scotland) Cameron to his Quaker wife, Elfrida Sturge. In her presence the College itself became a Society of Friends, though no-one could have been more correct in attending College chapel, less ostentatious of the communion in which she had been born. Her genius for friendship was perhaps most easily and naturally displayed with the very young and the mature. To the wives and families of the fellowship she was a friend dearly loved; and to the children a by no means supernumerary aunt. To a shy Cambridge child of the 1930s the great children's parties arranged by the hospitable Heads could be nightmare occasions — and there is a college hall in Cambridge which I rarely enter still without the shudder of such a memory. But not Caius. In recent decades the Master's

100 Roberts 1934, pp. 179–80. On H. A. Roberts (below), see Venn, II, 460; V, 31.

Lodge has shed some of its outer limbs and flourishes; but Mrs Cameron not only had a growing family but an army of maids in the Lodge, and it was a great rabbit-warren of a house. Here we gathered to eat sumptuous teas and to flow into every corner of the house, playing sardines. With undergraduates her touch was not quite so sure, for her mingling of charm and logic was a little bewildering to the freshman. She knew well that they did not know what to do with their hands and so provided them with pipe-cleaners to arrange in novel shapes. She knew they never could make up their minds to depart, so at the right time she invited all to view the portrait of Dr Caius, which then hung next to the door into Caius Court — and there she held out her hand to say farewell. It was a little contrived; and though her husband, who was almost as shy as the freshmen, enjoyed playing the servant on such occasions, her style had been devised for the world of the 20s and 30s, and could not have survived her departure. But much remains. Her warmth towards the society dictated that fellows and other senior members — and the senior college staff — ought to gather for a party as the academic year was starting; and the logical part of her mind characteristically observed that Dr Caius was born on 6 October 1510.[101] Thus grew up the immemorial tradition that the senior members of the College and their wives gather on the Saturday morning nearest before the start of the Michaelmas Term to eat his birthday cake and be entertained — since the time of Francis Bennett — by the President. But more than this: a College is a palimpsest in which buildings relatively timeless are marked by many generations of inhabitants, by the memory and presence of its striking personalities. For those of us who grew up in the 1930s and 40s she was a central figure of the community: to the tradition begun by Mrs Roberts she added the enchanting combination of candour and sensibility and warmth which is the mark of the Society of Friends.

The Barnwell estate and the age of timber

The buildings are not really timeless. The transformation we have surveyed would be sufficient to mark the age of Roberts as one of revolutionary change. Yet it is also true that few eras since the days of Caius have seen so many changes to our buildings as his.

Doubtless the bursar, Mr Lock, also the founder of a notable dynasty, played as large a part as Roberts in this — and certainly he and his predecessors — especially John Lamb, who had presided over the transformation following the statutes of 1860, and E. J. Gross, who lived to compile the 'Chronicle of the College Estates' (ER) — fostered the resources to realise it. In the reforms consummated in the statutes of 1860 the old endowments had all been swept into a common College fund — save only the Perse

101 Venn, III, 30.

Trust, too complex to be integrated, and the Davy Trust, still personal to the Master. Even the Perse fellows and scholars had lost their name and identity, along with those of Frankland and Wortley and all the other names of early benefactors. But new benefactions came to take their place, and so the accounts now include special heads for Drosier and Tapp and Comyns Berkeley and S. A. Cook and many others, too recent to be caught in the tidal wave of 1860. Now it is essential to the normal working of a college that most of its income be flexibly handled, and the reforms of 1860 in their general drift (though not in their obliteration of benefactors' names) were necessary. The fellowships ceased to be pieces of property, the income of the corn rents and their kin ceased to be divisible among the seniors; reserve funds for repairs and building and other necessary purposes were put on a much sounder footing. The rapid decline in the price of farm produce and the value of land in the late 1870s and 1880s brought the shock of the agricultural depression; but now the College was in better shape to face it than twenty years before. Yet it was bad enough, for the major part of the College's investment lay in agricultural land; and indeed until 1964 all its transactions had to be approved by the Ministry of Agriculture and Fisheries.

The College had a little property in the City of London, including a very profitable house in Philip Lane which paid an ample rent from the formation of the Frankland bequest in the late 16th century to the great fire of 1940 - followed by a sorry epilogue in 1956 when the City Corporation compulsorily bought it for a modest price.[102] But the first signs of a substantial shift into town property came after the enclosure of the east fields of Cambridge in 1807−11, which gave the College a consolidated plot — the Barnwell estate as it was called — in the area beyond Parker's Piece and Gonville Place. In 1827 the College began letting plots on building leases; and as the century went on the amount of development steadily increased. The railway station marks the point to which the expansion of Cambridge had reached in the 1840s, over the land of the colleges in the old east field; but there was still much green land about it then. In 1852 Caius parted with a great plot in the centre of its holding to form Fenners' Cricket Ground. St Paul's church is built on land sold in 1839, St Barnabas on a plot given in 1867. From 1877, as the agricultural depression was beginning to be felt, the College began to build roads within its estate — and the names of Lyndewode, Glisson, Harvey, Gresham, Mortimer and Wollaston adorn what were desirable residential regions of the 1880s. The development stretched further in due course, into the area of artisan dwellings (as they then were — though fashionable now among academics too) on and beyond Mill Road; and here may be found more recent names in College history, Willis and Guest and Mackenzie.

---

102 *ER*, p. 58; Archives, *Copy Conveyance Book 5*, no. 56 (1956); for what follows, *ER*, pp. 17−20.

Thus the bursars prepared for the expansion and the building works of the turn of the century; and we may reckon that Lock's share in all this work was large. But Roberts was deeply in it too: as tutor he was one of a group who constantly worried about the cramped nature of the site. 'And the surprising discovery was made that both sides of Rose Crescent were in one ownership. I shall never forget the excitement of a visit', writes Reid in his memoir of Roberts, 'which Mr Gross [the bursar before Lock] and I paid together to a London suburban villa, to interview the representative proprietor, when he declared himself ready to treat for a sale.' Roberts was as excited as he; but the cost 'was honestly believed by some seniors to spell certain ruin to the College . . . But for this, we might have secured, to the lasting benefit of the College, both sides of the Crescent'.[103] This took place in 1887−8, and the buildings which then gathered round St Michael's Church were immediately occupied and given the cheerful name of 'Newgate'. In 1901 Aston Webb and Ingress Bell began to rebuild Newgate, forming thus the present 'old' St Michael's Court, 'in the Tudor style', but with windows and adornments showing 'some typical liberties in the Arts and Crafts taste.' The arrangements of the interior were made with loving care — and, as has been profanely thought, with more ingenuity than domestic sense — by J. B. Lock himself.[104] The Waterhouse building had already gravely diminished the gardens in the old courts, and Reid describes how he and Roberts searched the Backs for a site for a fellows' garden.[105] A plot was found at the southern end of the meadowland beyond Queens' Road which Anne Scroop had bequeathed to the College. In the late 19th century this, like all her meadow, was intended for development: it had not then occurred to the fellowship that it could afford to use the land now occupied by Harvey Court and Finella and Springfield for itself. So the College sacrificed the value of development, and the fellows subscribed the cost of laying out the beds and lawns in what is still the Fellow's Garden.

Through the decade 1900−10 new schemes were coming forward. We have encountered the baths in St Michael's Court in 1904 and the spread of the infection to Tree and Gonville Courts. Serious plumbing did not reach Caius Court till the 1930s, when the old Physics Lab in the basement of I staircase was converted into baths;[106] it is a modest incursion, and no user could believe them so recent. In 1905 the panelled Combination Room was

103 Reid 1912, p. 26. In more recent years the College acquired much of the north side too; and under the inspiration of the present Senior Bursar has pioneered a restoration of both sides — the north as Regency shop-fronts, the south as revived Edwardian Tudor to the designs of David Roberts and Geoffrey Clarke (*Caian* 1980, pp. 51−4).
104 Pevsner 1970, p. 81; Venn, III, 148−9; IV, 160−1; VI, 509.
105 Reid 1912, pp. 26−7.
106 Venn, VI, 535.

formed by reconstructing the shape of the 15th century library and refitting it to the designs of Arnold Mitchell. Every timber in the roof was exposed, and the panelling of the state cabin of HMS Wellington acquired – a beautiful, relatively plain example of panelling made about 1815 in the style of the early 17th century – by the munificence of Lock himself and Hugh Anderson.[107] The result is a magnificent Edwardian smoking room, one of the finest in Cambridge. In 1908 – 10 new panelling was made for Salvin's Hall to the designs of Edward Warren which has made it a good deal more urbane, but altered its character and abbreviated its windows.[108] All this, and the panelling on the staircases to Hall and Combination Room, and reuse of the original Hall panelling for the JCR when it was created in its present site in 1909, witness to the love of good timber so characteristic of the taste of the day and in particular of that generation of fellows of Caius. The most dramatic witness – and alas, the most questionable – came in 1909 when Monro's bequest was used to revive the ancient hall and refurbish it as an extension to the library. So far so good; but the plaster ceiling by Soane, which survived till 1853, all that remained of the work of the man now reckoned the most distinguished architect to work for Caius down to the 20th century, had been destroyed in the 1850s. The decor and furnishing of the Monro Reading Room were essentially of 1909 – with its restored 15th century ceiling and its Edwardian bookcases – though a rebellion among the teaching fellows led to its being converted into an effective under-graduate reading room in 1928, and it has been refurbished in the 1980s [and Soane's ceiling restored in the 1990s].

Clubs, societies and the Mission

A characteristic section on the College Boat Club was written by Roberts himself for Venn's third volume. 'Of the various clubs and societies which largely contribute to the vigour and wholesomeness of College life on its lighter side the Boat Club is . . . the most important'.[109] He justified this claim for his own favourite sport by pointing out that down to the 1870s only the Boat Club and the Cricket Club existed and football was confined to 'the members of this or that public school' and those 'who did not row could only take walking or riding exercise'.[110] Only! – It was a singular act of forbearance by Venn to allow such words in his *magnum opus*; and by the time Roberts was writing the whole gamut of College societies and extramural activities had sprung into existence, and with them, the

107 Venn, IV, 162.
108 Venn, IV, 163 – 4 (and for what follows, ibid., pp. 162 – 7 *passim*); Pevsner 1970, p. 80. The changes included the addition of the gallery.
109 Venn, III, 306.
110 Venn, III, 309.

Amalgamated Clubs.[111] As treasurer of the Boat Club Roberts had a leading part in paying off the cost of the Boat House between 1878 and 1888, and he attempted to lead a reform in the College style of rowing. In these regions his efforts were not at first appreciated; but in the early 1880s he had a powerful ally in R. W. Michell, who was captain and later for many years coach until his death in action in 1916.[112] In 1892 Roberts handed over the treasurership to W. B. Hardy, but 'continued to show the keenest interest in its welfare: and it may be doubted whether any freshmen came away from his first interview with him without an intimation that it was his bounden duty to support the Boat Club.' What Roberts did by precept, Hardy attempted to encourage by example. 'His activities were manifold. Whenever a glee or a part song was afoot he was in request, and whenever the CURV (Rifle Volunteers) marched out, he, as Sergeant of Pioneers, wearing the imposing beard he grew for the purpose, led the way'. He was a famous sailor 'on broader and deeper waters than the Cam . . . He selected a set of rooms on the top floor in old St Michael's court [before the Webb building was built] where neither doors nor windows fitted, by a matter of inches, and where accommodation approximated as nearly as might be to the conditions of a yacht deck.'[113]

In 1891, on Roberts' initiative, came the first number of the *Caian* — 'There was a want and there was an egg; though day by day becoming older, it had all the while kept wholesome' as the first editor, his nominee, observed in his first editorial, with more attention to the tutor's language than to embryology.[114] And so it was hatched, and it already comprised, with College news and belles lettres, an article on College history by Venn and reports of the Boat Club, of Rugby and Association Football, Athletics, Cricket, Lawn Tennis, the Rifle Volunteers, the Science and Art, Fortnightly, Debating and Musical Societies; last but not least, the Chess Club; and following the College clubs, a report on the recently formed Caius House, 'the College Settlement in Battersea'. In most of these Roberts had taken a personal interest, especially in the Rifle Volunteers and the Mission. It seems a startling revelation of the Victorian Church Militant when we meet the Reverend E. S. Roberts, tutor of Caius, in the guise of Lieut.-Col. Roberts, officer commanding the University Corps — he had been involved since 1871, Captain of the College Company since 1875; he was in command of the Corps from 1889 to 1897 and recruited most of the younger fellows into it, led by Bandmaster Charles Wood.[115] In 1896 the Honorary Colonel, the Prince of Wales (Edward VII to be) inspected the Corps and the lunch for him in the Combination Room was a highlight of Mrs Roberts'

---

111 On whose origin, see Reid 1912, p. 7; Reid himself was first treasurer.
112 For all this, Scott 1927, pp. 95 ff.; for Michell see also Venn, II, 445; V, 27; Scott 1927, pp. 141—2.
113 Scott 1927, pp. 104—5.
114 *Caian* I (1891—2), 1.
115 Venn, VI, 509—10; Roberts 1934, pp. 161—6; Col. Edwards in Reid 1912, pp. 48—51.

reminiscences.[116] This is the background from which sprang the ready response of so many Caians to the First World War.

Yet Roberts' religion was neither militant nor muscular, in the full sense of the words. I have little doubt that he was aware when he used the word 'wholesome' of the Boat Club and its kin that Charles Kingsley would have said 'manly';[117] Roberts' 'wholesomeness' is almost a signature tune of his beliefs. It is easy to smile at his enthusiasm for his own particular sport, and shudder at the reverend rifleman. But he was not a medieval prince-bishop riding to war; he honestly believed that arming the fellows helped to keep the peace; and in its world and its context he was reflecting, in a characteristically moderate, unexaggerated form, one of the most powerful impulses of his day. The influence of Kingsley and Leslie Stephen and their like made Christianity a branch of public morals and manliness its most outspoken virtue — and of this we may reckon 'wholesomeness' a moderate version.

The boats and the rifles live in another context too, for they were part of a more total vision of the life of Caius and of the 'greater Caius', the *alumni*, beyond the bounds of Cambridge than any previous tutor or Master had desired. In the early 1880s Reid suggested to Roberts, and the tutor carried to the Governing Body with his enthusiastic support, the idea of an annual gathering of *alumni*; and with various changes and adaptations and inter-missions in periods of war, it has been held ever since.[118] In the 1890s there began to be regular meetings of a group of old Caians in London which turned into an annual dinner to which the Master was first invited in 1904 — and from this stemmed the College Club, formed in 1906, to whose dinners he invariably came. In all these activities, and in the Mission, he took the closest interest, yet that never diverted his attention from the young Caius at home; and when he carried the *persona* of senior tutor into the Mastership, he still reckoned to know every Caian by sight and name.[119] His achievements all reflect a quality noted by Reid — the serene optimism which looked confidently forward to 'the complete abolition of complaints about the dinner in the College Hall'.[120]

116 Ibid., pp. 163−5 (and see above, n. 46).
117 Newsome 1961, chap. iv, esp. pp. 207−11. For the combination 'manly and wholesome', see John Buchan, *Brasenose College* (London, 1898), p. 76, cited Rothblatt 1975, p. 260.
118 For this and what follows, Reid 1912, pp. 29−30.
119 Reid 1912, p. 28.
120 Reid 1912, p. 25. For what follows on the 19th−20th century benefactors, see details in Venn, III, 219−20, 235; IV, 168; VI, 523−4, 535−9; VII, 503−4. These describe many not included in the text, such as Lord Rhondda and Dr Martin Smith (VI, 523), T. H. Riches (IV, 168; VI, 539). The benefactions by and on behalf of fellows have continued in the legacies of E. K. Bennett and S. A. Cook (pp. 273−4, 281) and others; and among the most recent a gift in memory of F. J. Stopp by his widow Dr Elisabeth Stopp. For Smart see Venn, II, 364; IV, 168; for Teichman (originally Teichmann), II, 559; V, 71; VI, 538; for Berkeley, II, 463; V, 32; VI, 7, 539; for Tapp, II, 430; V, 23; VI, 539; for Salomons, II, 391; IV, 168; V, 15; VI, 523−4.

Benefactors

Much of the cost of the building work of this period was borne by a group of generous Caians; and the age of Roberts saw a blossoming of gifts and benefactions hard to parallel since the 16th century. We have noted the example set by fellows, Drosier and Monro in their legacies, Lock and Anderson in the panelled Combination Room. Frank Smart (who came in 1863) and Sir David Salomons (of 1870) were already mature Caians when Roberts became tutor; they contributed to the refurbishing of the hall and, very substantially, of the scholarship and studentship funds. W. M. Tapp came in 1877; Comyns Berkeley, later an eminent gynaecologist, in 1883; Oskar Teichman, doctor and soldier to be, in 1898. Smart, Berkeley and Teichman all came to Caius to study medicine, though their benefactions spread more widely — Smart's to botany and biology, Teichman's (in his sons' honour) to history and law. Tapp and Salomons were men of unusually wide interests. Tapp was a solicitor who took to business in middle life, investing in commerce and property. He was an accomplished geologist — the Woodbridge Water Company seems to have sprung from a combination of his commercial and geological zeal; he was also a man of strong antiquarian tastes, a fellow of the Antiquaries and a collector of Korean pottery. While he lived he contributed to many College causes, and presented the portraits of Ridgeway (his contemporary), Roberts and Cameron; when he died in 1936, he left the College some £200,000, half for the study of law, half for the general fund.

Salomons came of a rich Anglo-Jewish family, and was already a baronet before he was a BA. His uncle, the first baronet, Sir David Salomons, was an eminent banker who by his moral courage, charm and diplomatic skill and sheer persistence, rose to be the first Jewish Lord Mayor of London and an MP, and a leader in the movement to win full legal and political rights for the Jews in Britain. The nephew, Sir David Lionel Salomons, devoted similar diplomatic skills to a lesser cause — to overcoming the obstacles to the rise of the motor car; but though not a heroic figure like his uncle, he was a very remarkable and beneficent man. He heads the line of Jews who have lent much and various distinction to the College over the last hundred years, in commerce and athletics and above all in intellectual, academic and cultural endeavour. He was a brilliant electrical engineer, whose scholarships greatly encouraged the growth of engineering in Caius. If Ridgeway did honour to the thoroughbred horse, Salomons prepared for his supplanting, for he was one of those who brought the horseless carriage, the first electric cars, into this country, and founded the RAC. He was also something of a pioneer in the study of Japanese art in England, and the pieces of plate which — like so many of his generation — he gave to the College, are substantial examples of the taste of their period. All these men kept a close and lively interest in the College, giving generously over long periods of time.

On 6 June 1912 Roberts, now sixty-five and in indifferent health, went, as he always did, to 'start the first boat in the May races . . . and he had to hurry there on his bicycle, as he was late. He had a terrible heart attack, and was brought home by two of his faithful pupils and friends.'[121] He lingered for ten days, but died on 16 June — to the end, in the words of Vesey's epitaph, 'strenuus, vigilans, misericors, benevolus' — 'strenuous, watchful, merciful and kind';[122] few have served the College more devotedly, and fewer still have embodied the contemporary model and ideal of a College and a University more fully than he.

121 Roberts 1934; pp. 216–17; cf. Reid 1912, p. 40; Venn, VI, 510.
122 Venn, VI, 511.

13

1912 – 1984 – I – The Masters

Prologue – the historian's dilemma

A College historian is at his most vulnerable as he approaches his own day. A brief inspection of similar histories soon reveals his plight. He wades knee-deep in rich material; if he strives to be complete he falls into a catalogue of men and events 'which is as easy to read as a telephone directory'. He is talking about people many of whom are still alive, and a reasonable delicacy must hedge his choices – yet amid the numberless trees of contemporary history the principles of selection can be most subjective, the wood hopelessly elusive. No-one knows exactly how many Caians are alive at this moment, but the visible part of the 'Greater Caius' comprises 7000 Caians whose addresses are known. No sensible system of sampling can be devised with such numbers and one recoils from the kind of College history which echoes the Grand Inquisitor's song in the *Gondoliers*, making ambassadors 'crop up like hay', and multiplying 'bishops in their shovel hats'. One would dearly like to honour the explorers such as Edward Wilson (1872 – 1912), physician and artist, who died with Scott in the Antarctic with a Caius flag, embroidered by Mrs Roberts, now a poignant memorial in the Hall; or Charles Doughty, geologist, poet and author of *Arabia Deserta* (1843 – 1926), whose notes and manuscripts adorn the library; or listen to the younger poets, that other Arabian James Elroy Flecker, a member of the College from 1908 till his death in the orient in 1915, or the war poet H. E. Monro (1879 – 1932). We might witness the triumphs of the sportsmen and athletes, N. H. Tubbs and Geoffrey Conway on football fields, Harold Abrahams in the Olympics. We could ponder the careers of those who have struggled to preserve the world's environment, exploring the desert forests planted under the inspiration of Richard St Barbe Baker – whose *My Life – My Trees* of 1980 recorded eighty years of energetic life. In surveying the history of Christ Church, Oxford, Lord Dacre has spoken of the 'crowded statesmen and ceaseless bishops' the House has bred – we have encountered a modest but noble group of bishops, and our statesmen have mercifully been far from crowding, though perhaps Iain McLeod and Lord Carr, and above all our second Lord Chancellor, Lord Elwyn-Jones, have done something in the 20th century to redeem the sins of Lord Thurlow in the 18th. An academic community must take particular pride in its Nobel Laureates: two Masters, Sir James Chadwick and Sir Nevill Mott, and five honorary fellows (three of them one-time fellows), Sir

Charles Sherrington, Francis Crick, Anthony Hewish, Sir John Hicks and Sir Richard Stone — and Milton Friedman, once a visiting fellow, also a member of the College. To go on in this vein, however, though it may reflect a legitimate pride, also serves to obscure a proper and equal feeling for 'those who have left no memorial'. Yet to be silent about the recent past is equally wrong. What would we think of a history of the College which stopped short of the admission of women in 1979? I have therefore been ruthlessly selective: after a brief chronological canter through the last sixty years and six Masters, I shall seek (in chapter 14) to expound areas of the College's recent past, not as flowing narrative, but as variations on a theme — the elements in the idea of a university and a college canonised in the statutes of the late 19th century (1897) — and still enshrined in the Caius College statute (6,1) which enjoins the whole body of fellows to elect a Master 'best qualified to preside over the College as a place of education, religion, learning and research'. I am sure that the reader who observes so many of the highlights of contemporary Caius lost in the twilight of my narrative will honour my purpose and pity my predicament.

Sir Hugh Anderson

Anderson and Cameron had both served their apprenticeship as fellows under Roberts; both were men who devoted their utmost energies to the College's service; and both combined the Mastership — not, as Roberts had done, with the senior tutor's role, but with a strong control of College finance, almost as bursars. Anderson had also a brilliant record in research and carried to the end of his day a sympathy for it which grew out of personal memory — Cameron's respect for learning was more external, though no less genuine for that. Anderson's original work ceased when he became Master, and, especially after the First World War, he was deeply involved in every aspect of College administration and numberless good causes in the University and beyond.[1]

The war years brought a caesura, unsought, unlooked for, in the life of the College. Numbers were drastically diminished; many of the younger fellows were away on war service. F. J. M. Stratton, the astronomer, later professor, and in later years known to many generations of Caians the world over as Chubby, rose to be a Lieutenant-Colonel.

An immense number of Caians, well over 1000, served in the forces — all other forms of war work apart; and 240 of them and six College servants, were killed in action or died on service. In 1915 the College became for some

---

1 On Anderson, see Venn, VI, 514—28; *Caian* XXXVII (1929), 91—122 (including J. Barcroft, 'Scientific Work', pp. 113—22) *Proc. of the Royal Society*, Series B, CIV (1929), Obituaries, pp. xx—xxv (W. B. Hardy and C. S. Sherrington). For the First World War, Venn, VI, 541—9.

months the headquarters of the First Army; and various groups of officers were billeted in it from time to time — especially those on staff courses between 1917 and 1919, who presented a massive silver standing salt as a memorial to their stay. From late 1916 Vesey was the College Pooh-Bah, tutor, dean, praelector and steward, and sole resident fellow.[2] In 1917 the numbers in residence fell to thirty-two. Early in 1919 they were picking up fast, swollen by numerous naval officers and twenty-three American soldiers — from thirteen different states — waiting for transport home.[3] The years after the war saw an extraordinary expansion of numbers, and a gathering of all the talents. The entries of 1918 and 1919 have been made famous by T. E. B. Howarth: it 'included Joseph Needham, a product of Sanderson's Oundle, biochemist and sinologist, who would one day hold the Chinese Order of the Brilliant Star, and be Master of the College; A. B. Cobban, a great historian of France; R. Cove Smith, an outstanding rugby international, who became a celebrated paediatrician; Hamish Hamilton the publisher, who stroked a British Olympic crew; two notable Olympic athletes in Harold Abrahams and H. B. Stallard, who became Hunterian Professor of the Royal College of Surgeons; a future star of the musical comedy stage, Claude Hulbert, and a notable radio producer Eric Maschwitz; and G. F. Hopkinson, perhaps the most daring and original paratroop commander of the Second World War [and hero of the affair of the Jesus Gun], dropped into the sea off Sicily and picked up by a boat commanded by a fellow member' of a Caius VIII.[4] By the time it had grown to its full extent the post-war generation was a remarkable mixture of ex-schoolboys and retired soldiers, who met and mingled at work and play.

Sir Rudolph Peters, who left Caius in 1923 to be Professor of Biochemistry at Oxford, but returned to Cambridge in his retirement and to Caius as honorary fellow and president of the Music Club, recalled in the interview published in the *Caian* when he was ninety the immense burden of work which fell on him as a young teaching fellow and tutor in the opening 20s.[5] 'One night I found the class I was supervising in physiology and biochemistry rather inattentive. I dismissed them and went to bed. In the morning I woke up to find a large gun outside my window. When I asked my bedmaker about it, she answered: "It caim from Jaisus!"'[6] The incident of the Jesus Gun has entered deeply into folklore, and no history of Caius could be complete without it. It must serve as a symbol of the wholesome

2 Venn, VI, 547.
3 Venn, VI, 546, 548.
4 Howarth 1978, p. 68; *CC*, p. 289. On Hopkinson, see Venn, VI, 59. Also contemporary with these (1919–22) was Geoffrey Conway, a celebrated Rugby international, son of an ex-fellow and honorary fellow, father and grandfather of Caians (Venn, V, 174–5 and below, p. 308). Cf. the remarkable pp. 432–3 of Venn, VII, for 1953–4, which include Sir Edward Parkes, Professor Christopher Zeeman, and the present archbishop of Canterbury and bishop of Birmingham — but none of these entered as undergraduates.
5 Peters 1980, esp. pp. 39–40; cf. Venn, IV, 97; V, 106; VI, 41; VII, 14.
6 Peters 1980, pp. 39–40.

riots and escapades which punctuate a college's history — the siege of Caius in 1838, when a mob of undergraduates from other colleges were foiled in the attempt to seize an unpopular proctor, or the hoisting of a van by way of Tree Court onto the Senate House roof in 1958[7] — and excuse us from giving particulars of others and for passing over the unwholesome ones in silence.

The affair of the Jesus gun was organised by the Caius Co-optimists — a society inspired by the dean, Joseph Hunkin, in an attempt to divert the livelier elements in College from beer-drinking.[8] The War Office had been distributing guns as souvenirs, and Caius had been promised a modern gun while an ancient gun was bound for Jesus; a confusion arose which gave Jesus an object reckoned by the ex-military of Caius much beyond its worth, and the Co-optimists planned to 'retrieve the gun by night. The operation was master-minded by a young soldier who became a major general in the next war . . . called Hopkinson. He planned the operation on military lines . . .'.[9] We have indeed a letter written by one of the conspirators on the night of the exploit, F.S. (later Sir Frederick) Russell. [10]

'Sunday 6th November 1921

'Dear Mother and Father,

. . . We have had another meeting of the Co-optimists, it was a sort of 'war council' to decide about the Jesus gun. The Proctors have distributed propaganda asking that there should be no rags on Armistice night so we are going to get to work the night before. It has been very thoroughly planned out.

Hopkinson, the Secretary of the club, is G.O.C. and directs operations.

Geoff Conway is O.C. gunrunning party, H.K.P. Smith O.C. fighting patrols with three lieutenants under him. Philcox, the boat captain, is O.C. railing removal party. I am on the last named party and we have rather the most difficult job: we have to remain behind and put the railings in place if possible!

The show is to take place about 10.30 and there will be about 60 people in the gun moving party as it is going to be a very heavy job shifting it off the concrete blocks.

The fighting patrol is to attack police, proctors, and members of other colleges to prevent them joining the rag which is purely an inter-college show.

The gun is going to be taken through the streets and into one of the

7 *Caian* I (1891–2), 40–2; *Caian* LVI (1959–61), 4–12 (Nigel Balchin and Peter Davey).
8 Warr 1979, p. 122. There are many accounts of the Jesus gun, including a good one by Warr, loc. cit.; see *Caian* XXX (1921–2), 30–40; *Caian* 1981, pp. 75–76, and Sir Frederick Russell's letter, below.
9 Warr 1979, p. 122; for Hopkinson, see n. 4, and Venn, VII, 59.
10 *Caian* 1981, pp. 75–6.

court yards in Caius. To get into the court, big gates which are not used now have to be opened. Wax impressions have been taken of the keys and they have already been found to work!

It is quite an undertaking and like the blocking of Zeebrugge will depend chiefly on the element of surprise. It is going to be a bit of a job getting 60 people into another college grounds! It takes place after 10 so that men in Jesus will not be able to get out to protect their property.

The utmost secrecy is maintained and none of the members chosen to swell the numbers of the various parties are to be told till the day before.

Thursday 10th November 12.30 (midnight) I am awfully sorry I did not send this off before but meant to finish it on Monday and have not had a minute to spare. I was out last night and the night before from 9–12 sawing through iron railings. It was hard work as two of the bars we had to cut were buried under the ground and we had to dig holes. Also it was very slow work as people kept passing and we had to stop work.

However all has turned out well, things went without a hitch and now the gun is in Caius and has been taken down 4 steps into an inner court. Seeing that it weighs 5 tons, they will have a nice job getting it up the steps again if they want it back!

It was a wonderful show and not a soul seemed to hear us. The gun and 120 people got through the big gates and they were pushed to just as the prog. arrived.'

The Master had a guest that night, T. B. Strong, bishop of Ripon. They must have sat up late, for when they returned to the Lodge for a nightcap, 'the Master went to the window to draw the curtain, and suddenly called to the bishop: "Bishop, do you see anything?" "Yes, Master, I think I see a gun." "Thank goodness", said the Master, "so do I".'[11] Next morning the tutors felt bound 'to make some sort of gesture of disapproval' and 'therefore gated the whole College'; but the pretence was thin.[12] Hedley Warr's recollection over fifty years later was that: 'We . . . enlisted the support of a senior don, Stratton, who had been a brigadier in the war, and thought the whole affair splendid; and for weeks afterwards the Co-optimists mounted night guards armed with flour bombs and other missiles' but 'the enemy' were foiled and attempted no reprisals. Chubby Stratton in fact had become a Lieut.-Colonel and was a Lieut.-Colonel again in the Second World War; but in late 1921 he was senior tutor — and though he often proudly rejoiced in the tale of the gun in later years, one may doubt if his support was so openly confessed at the time.[13]

11 See the letter of G. McKerrow in *Caian* 1981, p. 75 (for Bishop Strong, *DNB*). For a variant version, see Wigglesworth 1979, p. 32 n.
12 Peters 1980, p. 40.
13 Cf. Venn, IV, 26; V, 81; VI, 31; VII, 6.

Over this lively community Anderson presided with dignity and quiet charm. He may not have known the undergraduates individually as Roberts had – who could? – but he was on friendly terms with many, and to the young fellows he showed the intense interest in their concerns and their work which so many of us have enjoyed from our seniors in the Caius SCR. 'My contacts with him were naturally infrequent' wrote one undergraduate of him, 'though always delightful . . . The University sermon, to which the Heads of Houses were expected to go,' was at 2.00 p.m. on Sundays. 'I once commiserated with him about this; "Yes indeed Warr; I always fall asleep, and the trouble is I always wake up with a snort".'[14]

A natural tendency to sleep in the afternoons marks the Cambridge committee man, and Anderson, humane, cultivated, brilliant scientist that he was, was also a great committee man. He was a leading University Commissioner, he was for some years chairman of the Press Syndicate – and he was deeply involved in the negotiations with the Rockefeller Foundation which were to lead to the princely benefaction which made possible the building of a new University Library after his death. One fears that few who have worked in the Anderson Room have recalled the years of patient, dedicated committee work and negotiation which it records – nor even known that it was named after him. So deep was the respect in which he was held that when he died the flag of Trinity flew at half-mast in his honour, a very rare tribute to the Head of another House.

His most characteristic work for the University was as a member of the Royal Commission and of many of the boards and syndicates which converted its Report into the immortal prose of university and college statute.[15] It was set up late in 1919 to enable Oxford and Cambridge to meet the challenge of the post-war world, and above all to justify, by detailed enquiry into their circumstances, the first major payments of state aid. It contained G. M. Trevelyan, Miss Clough, and M. R. James as well as Anderson and a group of noted politicians, and it spoke the language of courtesy and respect not so audible in more recent exchanges between governments and ancient universities. And the university itself, not without forebodings of the effects of state subsidy, but with few major dissentients, welcomed the majority of its findings.

Some have a distant ring, for one states that the statutes of the university should prohibit men and women from living in the same college; but for the most part it recommended the establishment of familiar landmarks in the Cambridge scene: the General Board, the Faculties, the corps of fully paid university lecturers and the like; it enlarged and clarified the contribution of the richer colleges to the poorer.[16] It was not until 1926 that the work of the

14 Warr 1979, p. 115.
15 On the Library and the Royal Commission, see esp. Venn, IV, 519 – 20; cf. Howarth 1978, pp. 84 – 6.
16 *Royal Commission 1922.*

Statutory Commissioners who followed in its wake was complete, and the new statutes under which the College is still governed — though a number have since been amended — brought into force. There was an attempt to follow Oxford in bringing colleges and University together in paying staff — but none to achieve the much fuller integration which had grown up in Oxford in the wake of the 19th century reforms; and the separation of the University and college in staffing and organisation proceeded steadily down to the early 1950s. This left the role of the college in some respects more clearly defined, in others less so — but it was of the essence of the new dispensation in university finance that college revenues should not be used in ways which overlapped with state aid where this could be avoided; and that it should not be possible for the colleges to waste their resources — or for public figures eager to save the nation's funds to discern pockets of college income which might be diverted to university uses. Anderson was a great master of public finance and administration, and he was evidently a central figure in the planning of college accounts, and his faithful ally Cameron, now bursar of Caius, devised the Caius pattern which was thought at the time a model of its kind.[17] To those of us who came first to study it in the 1950s or later it seems an almost impenetrable labyrinth, and it is for that reason all the more a fascinating historical document of the 1920s. Caius was already the fourth richest college (after Trinity, St John's and King's), and it was naturally felt by so conscientious a man as Anderson peculiarly important that it should foster and use its resources in the way most beneficial to its ends, as he saw them.

In recent years state aid for higher education has come by two routes — by direct subsidies through the University Grants Committee and by grants to students. The second category provides an education notionally free (subject to parental contribution according to means) to all British citizens who are admitted. In the 1920s such subsidies were modest but important. The first anticipation of student grants were for those who had served in the war, and these naturally tailed off very soon; between the wars government aid to students was by our standards still relatively slight. Far the greater part of the aid to students came from within the colleges or from trusts and private charities. Thus one of the major purposes of the new direction of college finance was to ensure a steady flow into scholarship and similar funds. Major heads in the accounts reveal the external revenue liable to university taxation; and the great internal accounts comprise the cost of living and eating, and of tutorial and educational expenses — the tuition account, which was directed to be kept in reasonable balance.[18] The colleges were not to subsidise junior members in the lab or lecture room by direct means; waste and misdirection (as they were then conceived) were to be avoided.

17 Venn, VI, 530.
18 Statutes of 1926, 45 (8).

The rest of the College accounts, in Caius as elsewhere, are largely concerned with the support of the fabric and estates, and the separate trusts which cannot be accounted in the common pool.[19] By developing the Barnwell estate in Cambridge,[20] by larger investment in government stocks, and by prudent economy, J. B. Lock brought the College through his long bursarship, which started in the agricultural depression of the 1880s and ended soon after the First World War, with his death in 1921 — and won him a legendary fame as a shrewd man of business.[21] Anderson himself came from a rich home, but he and Cameron had both studied college finance at the feet of Lock and in the wake of the depression, and the mark of their hand on the College finances is extreme prudence and a love of intricate administration. The development of the Barnwell estate was complete by 1910, when it was yielding a rental of approximately £3330.[22] From such sources — and from the 1920s on the development of the town of Rickmansworth — came a substantial element in College income;[23] and gilt edged securities came to play an increasing role in it in the 1920s and 30s; yet a major share of college investment, and the principal role of the bursar's administration, still lay in farm property until much later; and the College was not permitted to move freely in the stock markets and invest in equities until the early 1950s. This explains why, when Cameron became Master in 1928, an expert on estate management, and especially on the management of farm properties, was appointed as bursar in E. P. Weller.

Thus the College accounts to this day are a monument to a man and a generation who wished to see cautious, prudent government, and the direction of all that could be spared to scholarships and needy students — some too for learning and research, for the current system of research fellowships springs from the 1920s — though the money spent on research has been much enlarged in the last thirty years, especially since the advent of much more extensive student grants has greatly diminished the economic function of scholarships. But a whole generation had reason to bless the care of Anderson and his colleagues in this regard, for still in the late 1940s an undergraduate who was not an ex-serviceman, who came from a poor home,[24] could owe his university degree almost entirely to a scholarship and the funds at the tutors' discretion.

No-one who has studied the system of finance represented by the accounts of the colleges today can doubt that they were partly devised by canny bursars. A colleague of Anderson's among the Statutory

19 See above, pp. 251—2.
20 See above, p. 252.
21 Venn, II, 383; V, 14.
22 ER, p. 19.
23 See Index to Archives, *Copy Conveyance Books* 1—3 (1917—37), esp. for the years 1924—37.
24 Or, as was my own case in my second and third years, was supported by an impoverished widowed mother, helped by generous friends.

Commissioners spoke thus of Anderson's own contribution: 'The plan ultimately adopted was his, but he realised from the first that it must be worked out in co-operation with the bursars and others versed in University finance. Many were the meetings and discussions in his study, the Master ever acute, but ever ready to consider most carefully the arguments of others and to assign to them their full weight. And thus, when some agreement had been reached, it was he who explained it in all its bearings to his colleagues, who prepared and wrote out in his own hand the sheets of figures needed to make clear the plan which he put forward as fair and equitable to Colleges and University alike. . . . Always quiet and unobtrusive, never rattled or flurried, silent until he felt sure, unless at times he spoke to point out his doubts and hesitations . . ., he has died as he lived, a great son of the University, thinking only of its welfare, anxious to promote its interest as a place of learning and research'.[25]

J. F. Cameron

Anderson died after an operation on 2 November 1928. On the 23rd of the same month the fellowship hastened to translate the other shrewd and canny and amiable Scotsman among its seniors from the Bursary to the Lodge.[26] John Cameron had been a fellow since 1899 and a College officer since 1909, when he first became a tutor; and apart from a spell as a civil servant in the First World War he was a college man all his days. He had no pretence to scholarship nor an easy social manner, but in other ways he much resembled Anderson, with whom he had worked very intimately as commissioner for the College in statute making and as bursar; and he shared too his utter devotion to College and University, and his warmth and conscience and something of his dry wit — always a little unexpected coming from so inarticulate a man. He delighted in the paradox that a Presbyterian could enjoy the ultimate authority in matters spiritual: 'I am the bishop of this College' he used to say, in the quiet of drawing room or study. Like Anderson again he was a great committee man and a man of affairs: he presided over the Town Gas Company for twenty-one years, and followed Anderson at the University Press. Quiet, unspectacular administration was his forte, and in College a pastoral care in which his wife so conspicuously shared[27] over every element in its life, spreading to the oldest pensioners among the College servants and the widows and children of fellows long dead. A characteristic event of his reign is the happy alliance with Brasenose College, Oxford, the other home of Joyce Frankland's sons

25 Venn, VI, 520.
26 Venn, VI, 521, 530; on Cameron, VI, 528—40.
27 See above, pp. 250—1. The link with Brasenose, below, is documented in the *Gesta* for 27 May 1932 and *Reports to Governing Body*, s.a. 1932.

— cemented with breathtaking speed in 1932. The Principal of Brasenose wrote (perhaps after informal discussion) on 26 May; the College Council met on the 27th; and on the 28th the Master was able to reply to the Principal, cordially agreeing to the scheme. Cameron was not a man to look for spectacular adventures, but two very notable events occurred in his reign, one largely of his choosing, the other very much not.

The tumble of buildings between St Michael's Court and the Market Place was converted into the New Building, or, more statistically, into staircases G and H, St Michael's, to the designs of J. Murray Easton. Fairly or unfairly, this is the only College building since the days of Caius, which has won general acclaim from modern architectural critics. 'Its front faces the Market Place, and that has no doubt influenced its design and influenced it in the most gratifying way', wrote Pevsner. It sets a face of white Portland stone, raised over piers, above a shopping arcade — with a front slightly curved to emphasize (as I would think) the modesty and elegance of its proportions. But 'where Mr. Easton had to face St Michael's Court and the church his courage deserted him and he recanted' — that is, showed signs of sympathy with an earlier world, with Georgian windows and 'in one place even Tuscan columns'; the whole in 'honey-coloured Ketton stone'.[28] Here 'soap and education'[29] came into their own at last, with baths on every landing.

The building was begun in 1934, and in the same year Cameron had the satisfaction, while he was Vice-Chancellor, of welcoming King George V to the opening of the new University Library — thus celebrating the completion of a great enterprise in which his predecessor had been particularly involved.

His term as Vice-Chancellor, 1933–5, was perhaps the busiest of his life; but he was able to watch over the building project in St Michael's Court with a prudent and auspicious eye. It was completed in 1936. Three years later again came the outbreak of the Second World War which formed as it were a barrier in Cameron's later years: in 1943 he was reelected to serve to the age of seventy-five, which is now the ultimate limit of a Master's tenure, and he retired in 1948 as the era of renewal and reconstruction was getting under way. The Second, as in so many spheres, was less catastrophic than the First. It is true that many of the fellows departed to war service, civilian and military, at home and abroad, from Lieut.-Colonel Stratton in the Signals to Dr Needham on a scientific mission to China.[30] But the student population fell only to about 60% of its normal size; and the casualties, though horrifying, were far fewer — 102 compared with 240 killed in

---

28 Pevsner 1970, p. 81; Venn, VI, 535–6. The choice of colour was influenced by Dr F. C.
   Powell: see *Caian* 1984, p. 37.
29 See p. 217.
30 Venn, VI, 550–1. Needham was scientific counsellor at the British Embassy in Chungking.

action.[31] St Michael's Court was taken over by the Master in Lunacy and his staff,[32] an event which gave rise to a flow of College wit, concluding with a doubt, occasionally heard from the other side of Trinity Street in the later 1940s, as to when or whether the 'lunatics' had departed. On 8 May 1945 the war in Europe came at last to an end, and the widow of J. S. Reid was able to compare the bonfire on Midsummer Common with 'a similar event some ninety years earlier at the close of the Crimean War'.[33] Cameron's career as Master was brought to a triumphant conclusion by the celebration of the sexcentenary in 1948; at the Annual Gathering the theme of continuity was carefully displayed — first by Joseph Hunkin, then bishop of Truro, who preached on a text few but he would have had the courage to grasp for such a feast — 'No man also having drunk old wine straightway desireth new; for he saith the old is better'; and the senior fellow, R. C. Punnett, proposed the toast of the younger members of the College, to which he had himself replied fifty years before — and to it the response came from J. B. Lock's grandson, Michael Lock, 'grandson, son and brother of Fellows'.[34] It was a fitting close to the career of a Master who had striven to keep the College moving gently through troubled waters with the minimum of change. In his retirement he characteristically edited the *Biographical History* and the *Annual Record*, but he died soon after, in 1952.[35]

Sir James Chadwick

Between Cameron, the devoted College administrator, and Chadwick, the world-famous nuclear physicist, there is a striking contrast — which Chadwick himself failed to diminish by many efforts to carry on where Cameron had left off, and by a devout interest in Venn's *Biographical History* — an interest some of the younger fellows profanely thought a falling off in the intellectual activity of a great scientist. Chadwick is one of the outstanding intellectual figures in the history of Cambridge and Caius, but as Master he was in many ways a fish out of water, partly because he found it peculiarly difficult to communicate with ordinary folk in the rough and tumble of community life, partly because he harked back, ever and anon, to the Caius of his dreams in the days of Anderson and Cameron.[36] He came from a relatively poor home in Macclesfield and Manchester, and had won early

31 They are listed in the Roll of Honour in the library and in the memorial in the ante-chapel: and see p. 260.
32 Venn, VI, 553.
33 Venn, VI, 553–4.
34 Venn, VI, 533.
35 Ibid., p. 534.
36 There is a very balanced account by J. B. Skemp in Venn, VII, 485–502; see also H. Massey and N. Feather in *Biographical Memoirs of Fellows of the Royal Society*, XXII (1976), 11–70; Sir Nevill Mott in *Caian* 1975, pp. 48–54.

recognition from the famous New Zealander, Ernest Rutherford, who by singular good fortune was his professor in Manchester. After a spell in Germany — and internment there during the war of 1914–18 — he returned to Manchester in time to be transferred to Cambridge with Rutherford in 1919, when Anderson, by an inspired act of patronage, nominated him for a studentship in Caius. Chadwick, who developed in later years an almost mystical devotion to the memory of Dr Caius, described Anderson as 'the best Master Gonville and Caius has ever had since John Caius'.[37] For those who met Chadwick casually, or failed — as many of his colleagues in Caius were to do through no fault of theirs — to penetrate his shy exterior, the warmth of feeling for the College and the man who brought him there comes as a surprise. In 1921 Chadwick became a fellow — one of a remarkable line of distinguished physicists to mature in Caius;[38] in 1925, with Kapitza as his best man, he married Aileen Stewart-Brown, who came from a family of Liverpool patricians. Throughout the years till his departure to Liverpool in 1935 he was Rutherford's principal lieutenant, arranging everything for an increasingly charismatic and absent head, striving to overcome Rutherford's notorious reluctance to acquire and spend the large sums of money modern physics requires. In these years he was developing Rutherford's remarkable discoveries on his own lines too, and in 1931–2 came the central event of his scientific career, the discovery — or, as medieval calendars speak of the relics of the saints — the invention of the neutron. For this he had rapid recognition, and in 1935 both a Chair at Liverpool and a Nobel Prize. In Liverpool he won the respect and friendship both of the younger physicists and of the Liverpool patriciate, to whom his wife had naturally the entrée; and in 1937 he was joined by his senior in the Caius fellowship, Arnold McNair, who was appointed Vice-Chancellor.

In the early 1940s, under circumstances of great strain, mental and physical, he became the central figure in British research clearing the ground for the making of an atom bomb; and from 1943 until 1946 he was leader of the British mission to Washington, working in close collaboration with General Groves, leader of the American nuclear research team, towards the holocaust of 1945. After the end of the war he returned to England full of honours — he was knighted in the summer of 1945 a few weeks before the first bomb fell. He returned to Liverpool; but the urge of creative science was shrivelling — partly with the passage of years, partly with the impact on a lonely, sensitive mind, of what he had achieved. In 1948 he accepted with evident delight the invitation to return to Caius as Master — to escape from the nuclear world back to the one corner of his universe which he believed had never changed.

A man of science of his quality must have a special imaginative gift, and

---

37 Venn, VII, 487.
38 Sir William Hardy had by this time become a physicist, or else one might have said, the first.

Chadwick evidently had a vision of Caius as it had been in Dr Caius' own time and as it has been under Anderson. From the former he seems to have distilled the notion of authority and paternalism that had more to do, perhaps, with the office of Head of Department or Vice-Chancellor in Liverpool in the 1930s than with the role of Master in the late 1940s, and he never accommodated himself to change – nor perhaps had seen the College so intimately in the 30s as he was compelled to do in the late 40s and 50s. After the war many fellows returned and many new ones were elected: the fellowship of 1948 was very different from the body which had worked with Cameron in the 30s and early 40s. In particularly, there had been an inner core of officers, the bursar and three tutors, who had long formed a kind of informal cabinet;[39] and with their support Cameron had run the Council and the College benevolently, but on a tight rein. The Council is the Governing Body for all but changes of statute;[40] and however much it may consult the General Meeting of Fellows – or in more recent times, representative bodies of students – it has almost absolute power over elections, appointments and the normal management of affairs. We have seen that its number, twelve fellows and the Master, was an accident of Tudor history perpetuated in the heyday of committee government.[41] Between the thirteen who govern and the whole body of the fellowship some strain and stress can easily arise, especially if the thirteen become a sort of self-perpetuating oligarchy. Three are *ex officio*; and the remaining ten places on the Council were only fully opened to election by the statutes of 1920, and the tendency had always been to keep a substantial nucleus of seniors and officials on it.

In a similar way the office of President had been opened to election by the fellowship early in the century, but in practice it had been regarded as a life appointment for Venn and Gross and Buckland, till Buckland died in 1946.[42] Thereafter Stratton held it till he wished to retire in 1948, and E. K. Bennett – Francis Bennett as he was universally known – from 1948. A number of fellows felt strongly that the Council could only represent the whole society if its membership changed and rotated; and many too thought that in the long run the Presidency should rotate, at least sufficiently to open it to a wider circle of the most senior, most respected fellows. At first neither the Master nor the reigning officials showed any understanding or sympathy for this point of view; but indeed the mixture of academic idealism and personal feelings which such a situation unleashes would have been hard for the most adroit of Masters to have handled.

39 Venn, VII, 495, citing P. Grierson and G. T. Griffith in *Caian*, pp. 54 – 7 at p. 56.
40 See Statutes 4 – 5: 5(4) does envisage a situation in which the General Meeting of fellows can override the Council, but it has never, so far as I know, been invoked since the Statute came into force. In practice it is normal for the Council to accept decisions of the General Meeting. A characteristic statement of the relationship occurs in Statute 39(8), which declares that the Council *passes* the Accounts and then *submits* them to the General Meeting.
41 See p. 97.
42 See Appendix 2.

Chadwick had many qualities of greatness which most of his colleagues recognised at least from a distance; but when faced with a serious personal difficulty with a colleague, he was liable to retire to bed, feeling 'very ill'.

These tensions came to a head in the 'Peasants' Revolt', an episode now deeply entrenched in the mythology and folklore of the College. At a hastily summoned gathering two days before the General Meeting in October 1950, a group of fellows, mostly, but not all, natural scientists, and mostly, but far from all, under forty, made a plan to change the composition of the Council and support two of their number for election to it. The Peasants' Revolt came in on a tide of genuine academic idealism which was to generate an admirable enthusiasm for lofty aims; it also generated hard feelings, personal misunderstandings, misery and faction which were only finally laid to rest under the Mastership of Needham. When I left Caius in 1956 the fellowship was still a divided, factious body; no trace of this was to be seen when I returned in 1977. But it will not do to exaggerate the revolt: with very few exceptions the fellowship remained personally friendly, the high table a cheerful place, throughout the early 1950s; the majority of the fellowship were never, I fancy, members of a 'party'; and the junior members of the College had hardly an inkling of the intrigues of the seniors. And it had a Cinderella, or perhaps an Iolanthe touch, as well. Our opening campaign in October 1950 brought onto the Council two fellows who thus became the Wat Tyler and the John Ball of the movement, if I may so term them – and both are now members of the House of Peers.[43]

The discussions among the fellowship in the opening 1950s placed before the younger fellows an idea of a College with some very positive elements – as a place in which academic excellence, teaching, learning and research of the highest order lived cheek by jowl with the rest of the community, so that the highest excellence was at the service of the whole fellowship and the students were brought face to face with the leading exponents of their craft – and a sense of academic values stimulated by intercourse with experts in many different fields. This feeling went much wider than the movement of the Peasants. Many of us rejoiced in the width of academic achievement and interests of men like Sir Ronald Fisher and Joseph Needham, and felt that they should have more recognition in the College's life. So far so good; but a doctrine came also to be developed (or revived – for it was hardly original) that there was an inherent conflict between the academic and the administrative approach to College affairs. This opposition was lent a certain colour by the central figures of the 'Old Guard', Cameron's lieutenants. E. P. Weller was an extremely conscientious bursar with a wide knowledge of the complexities of his office; but he had been much under Cameron's wing and had little natural understanding of academic values; he was an estates bursar by training, furthermore, and was hesitant over the College's entry into equities, which was a central point with the College's economists

43 Lord Swann, later honorary fellow, and Lord Bauer, fellow (see p. 299).

and a plank in the Peasants' platform. His position on the Council was *ex officio*; not so that of H. E. Tunnicliffe and H. T. Deas, both experienced teachers and tutors, directors of studies in medicine and classics – Tunnicliffe, extrovert, oblivious of the winds that blew, Deas more sensitive, but closely bound by the methods and traditions of Cameron, his father-in-law.[44] In 1950 Tunnicliffe failed to secure reelection to the Council, in 1951 Deas followed him. Efforts were made to convince them that the revolt was not a matter of personal animosity, and with Tunnicliffe this had some success; his naturally cheerful, friendly temperament broke through and he returned to the Council at a later election. But Henry Deas, whose wit and learning should have led him to write this *History* thirty years ago, had already been afflicted by a 'deeper disenchantment',[45] and abandoned the society of his colleagues, though not the shrewd and lucid exposition, to undergraduates, of his subject, which continued even after retirement till his death. With such personal difficulties Chadwick was quite out of his depth; and the difficulties were much compounded by the issue whether tutors should be renewed in office till they dropped – or the tutorship itself be made to rotate. Chadwick accepted, with many misgivings, the strongly held opinion of many that a tutor should work for a limited term, but in practice became much entangled in the issue of choosing suitable tutors, and the role of the Master's nomination to the office.

The Peasants had tried to dissociate their aims from personal feelings by establishing certain principles of College government; but principle and personality became inextricably confused in their attitude to Francis Bennett, President and Senior Tutor, whom all loved and revered and whose administration few admired. Quill pen in hand, with the aging tutor's clerk, Mr Rutherford, at his side, he struggled with the rising tide of paper – and it was not difficult to see that his struggles were not always effective. Edwin Keppel Bennett – but always Francis to his pupils and colleagues and friends – had grown in the College, which had been his home from 1914 – 16 and continuously from 1919, into the very image of traditional, civilised standards – with a mind richly stored from a range of literature and reading deep and wide; a German scholar, but indeed, shrewd and learned though he was, he was essentially a man of letters more than a scholar.[46] He combined with this a warmth of feeling and kindness, which meant that, even though his rooms and his conversation were most fully at the disposal of a coterie – the Shadwell Society as it was in his day, which under his guidance listened to papers, composed sonnets and performed charades – he was universally known and respected and liked. He watched more efficient tutors take over from him without complaint, and he was

44 See the admirable memoir of Deas in *Caian* 1972, pp. 54 – 7.
45 Venn, VII, 496.
46 On him see esp. E. M. Forster in *Caian* LV (1956 – 8), 123 – 7; Venn, V, 159 – 60; VI, 50;
   VII, 21.

succeeded in 1952 as Senior Tutor by Stanley Dennison, later Professor of Economics at Belfast and Newcastle, and Vice-Chancellor of Hull. Francis's colleagues at first held back from deposing him as President when he came up for reelection. It was not until 1956 that Francis was succeeded by Ronald Fisher as President — to be followed in his turn by Joseph Needham in 1959, twin symbols on the peaks of science and scholarship of the values of the Peasants — but very obviously supported and respected by many who had no care for politics or the revolt. Meanwhile, a young fellow, naively seeking reassurance of Bennett's reactions from one of his closest friends outside the College, enquired of E. M. Forster whether Francis was upset by these démarches. Some show of reassurance he received; but also — 'You see, Francis has all these feelings, but is too *grand* to show them'; he was indeed a person of great inner dignity.

It would be wrong to conclude, however, that Chadwick went unappreciated. With a few of the older and many of the younger fellows he could unbend, and if they sought it they found a warmth and an interest — and a shrewd appreciation of a variety of disciplines. Under his cold exterior there lay a warmer region, sometimes deeply hidden. On a dramatic day in June 1956 the College Council held its first interview for Tapp fellows — for the first time candidates for research fellowships had been sought from outside Caius; this went much further soon after, to the great enrichment of the fellowship, but the first step was perhaps the most crucial.[47] This was common ground between Chadwick and many of the Peasants; and he took infinite trouble to see that the election was soundly and fairly made. By the natural irony of human affairs the Council, later the same day, turned to an extremely contentious domestic issue, of 'soap and education' — the provision of larger accommodation, and a bathroom, for a fellow's set. The Council normally rose, at the latest, about 7.00; at 11 o'clock that night the Master still held that it was an unreasonable proposal. 'It may be unreasonable, Master', said Francis Bennett, the President, 'but I do not think we shall get to bed tonight until we accept it' — and thus it was decided.

Admirable in his loyalty to his own austere principles, warm in his feeling for young fellows of every type and discipline, Chadwick found a rumbustious fellowship no place for his declining years. He resigned on a point of principle in 1958, but the evidence suggests he had long had it in mind to do so — and he left a deeply divided fellowship which took many months to select his successor. Meanwhile, in the summer of 1956, a young fellow leaving Cambridge for a provincial chair called in his study; found him, as often, deep in a volume of Venn, contemplating a note or memo which had fallen from its pages — doubtless he was struggling to recall if he had fulfilled the task to which it pointed. 'Master, I have come to say goodbye'. A pause, as he solved his problem: 'Well, that's a relief', said Chadwick —

47 *Gesta* 8 June 1956, nos. 1, 2.

then his face was suffused with the charming smile it wore when he really wished to show the face of friendship, and which was the nearest to an apology he could normally muster. For thus he was, a brilliant scientist, a devout lover of Liverpool and Caius, warm beneath a cool, remote exterior, surpassingly gauche.

Harvey Court

In the late 1940s the rapid expansion of numbers was felt to be a temporary bulge to handle an exceptional generation of ex-servicemen. By the 50s and 60s the expansion in numbers seemed rather a fact of life. It was no longer possible to contemplate providing two years' lodging out of three in College for undergraduates, and in the 60s and 70s the traditional landladies and a generation of students more inclined to assert their adult independence almost parted company altogether. In the long run this was solved by converting more college houses into college-run student bed-sitters and flats – and many houses in Mortimer Road and Harvey Road in particular have been taken hand in this way; and in the process a somewhat different relation between landlady or caretaker and student has been forged. But from the start the College lifted its eyes to Anne Scroop's pastures. It was an extraordinary stroke of fortune for a College so constrained on its central site – and yet, since the mid and late 19th century, so large – that it possessed this lung, this stretch of land beyond the Backs – not as near the College as would be ideal, but nearer than could readily have been acquired. The old pasture closes stretched from West Road to the Fellows' Garden; and after the enclosure of 1804 – 5 arable land up the south side of West Road was added to it; in 1872 the College converted a substantial part of the land further south towards Barton Road into the cricket ground, originally bought by the 'Wortley Purchase' of 1782.[48] In the 20th century Selwyn College has expanded to the far end of West Road, the University has taken much of the West Road property as part of its Sidgwick Avenue site; but the College has gained something in the process – and the result is a strip of land running with little break from West Road to Barton Road.

At the corner nearest to the College, where West Road and Queen's Road meet, it was decided to form a new College court – not a hostel, but an integral part of the College. The essential decisions were taken in Chadwick's later years as Master, though the building of Harvey Court was only accomplished under Sir Nevill Mott in 1960 – 2.[49] It was designed by Sir Leslie Martin and Colin St John Wilson, and Pevsner calls it 'the most sensational new building up to that date in Cambridge . . . a valid statement by a man (or two men) of radical convictions . . . the raison d'être for the court

48 *ER*, pp. 28 – 30.
49 Venn, VII, 529 – 33 (P. T. Inskip).

arrangement is that the architects wanted to have students' rooms in stepped tiers with terraces in front – a system which Sir Leslie Martin in his plans for Whitehall has carried to extremes. Here there are only three tiers, and by cantilevering the top tier back . . . reasonable room sizes and shapes could be secured. So the court appears more spacious than it is, and the front terraces have great advantages, even if not that of a view. On the other hand they tend to be used as public walks and make it impossible to sport one's oak successfully' – a modest statement of the problems of this interesting and imaginative building, so difficult to keep dry and warm and to adapt to all the needs of real life.[50]

Sir Nevill Mott

A fellowship sometimes proceeds by reaction; but the three elections which have followed the resignation of Chadwick – of Sir Nevill Mott in 1959, of Joseph Needham in 1966 and of Sir William Wade in 1976 – have all brought into the Lodge a scholar eminent in his field. All, to our pleasure and continuing profit, are still alive; to write of them, and of their terms of office, as we have written of their predecessors from John Colton to James Chadwick, would be premature. Suffice it to say that in Mott the College received a physicist of like eminence to Chadwick; but very different in the progress of his work. For Chadwick had resigned serious research to come back to Caius as Master; while Mott, who was Cavendish Professor throughout his Mastership, presently resigned the Mastership, then retired from his Chair, and rose to still greater heights of scientific discovery – from wave mechanics and atomic structure to solid state physics, to whose inner cave of mystery he has penetrated. For this he received the Nobel Prize in 1977, an event which brought hope and life to many a scholar past the first prime of life.[51]

Darwin College

The 1960s witnessed a ferment of discussion in Cambridge about the provision of College membership and fellowships for the numerous and increasing groups of university teachers and officers who had no fellowships – and with it also much discussion of the destiny of research students and post-doctoral fellows from overseas, not readily found homes within the Cambridge system. There was also much discussion, after the Robbins Report, of the size of the university itself and whether new colleges should

50 Pevsner 1970, p. 82.
51 Venn, V, 382; VI, 94 – 5; VII, 62 – 3; *Caian* 1978, p. 10. For a brief summary of Sir Nevill Mott's achievement, see Sir Sam Edwards in *Nature*, 269 (1977), 744 – 5.

be provided – and above all of the place of women in Cambridge. From this came new foundations, such as Clare Hall and Darwin College for postgraduates, and Robinson for undergraduates too – eleven colleges in all have been founded or re-founded since 1954. In Darwin and Robinson Caius has been closely involved.[52] Darwin was founded by a joint enterprise in 1965 by Caius, St John's and Trinity in the group of houses between Silver Street and the mill streams, including Newnham Grange, made famous by Gwen Raverat as the home of Sir George Darwin and his family and so of her childhood.

Joseph Needham as Master (1966 – 76)

Joseph Needham has become a symbol of the College and its meaning for a whole generation.[53] There are few academies which combine such cosmopolitan and such parochial flavour as the University of Cambridge. Few of our recent fellows have been so deeply read in the history of the College or so devoted to aspects of its traditions as Needham, the devout Caian and romantic Anglo-Catholic. There is no Englishman of our generation but he who is so completely a citizen of both Britain and China; and it is exceedingly rare for a man to be a master both in the sciences and the humanities over so wide a stretch of country as to be both FRS and FBA in his own right. When his 80th birthday was celebrated, two dinner parties were served in College within the octave – first for a gathering of professors from the Chinese Academy of Sciences; then a domestic evening for the fellowship alone, in which it was joined by the Ambassador of the Chinese People's Republic. In the 18th century it was often supposed that Cambridge might avoid parochialism by involvement in politics, and there are journalists still who seek to discover the political complexions of colleges – from which they have perhaps had some encouragement in Caius from the active presence of a brilliant Conservative philosopher in Dr John Casey. But let them contemplate the two senior fellows of 1985, Joseph Needham and Michael Oakeshott, and they will be shown that the fellowship is large enough to comprise a lifelong friend of Christian socialism and modern China and the doyen of conservative philosophical historians. As we shall see when we ponder the religious scene, a large and complex community cannot be painted in simple colours.

---

52 See Young 1967. For Robinson see Needham 1976, p. 36; and see below, p. 279. The new colleges are New Hall, Churchill, Clare Hall, Darwin, Wolfson, Lucy Cavendish and Robinson; Fitzwilliam has been converted from a House of non-collegiate students to a College; and St Edmund's House, Hughes Hall and Homerton have changed their status to Approved Foundations and Approved Societies.

53 See esp. Needham 1976; Venn, V, 188; VI, 55; VII, 26.

Sir William Wade

In 1976 Needham retired from the Mastership after seven years as President and ten as Master, when his capacious, friendly presence and a grandeur surpassing temporal strife, were steadily used to help the passions of the 50s to subside. However it was achieved, it was a peaceful community which elected H. W. R. Wade to succeed him.[54] The present Master is a Caian sure enough — one of the most distinguished of the pupils of his namesake (but not a relative) Emlyn Wade; but his life has been spent in a larger world, in Trinity and Oxford. As a gardener he has brought colour and life to the Master's garden, and greatly encouraged the College gardeners to beautify the courts. As a lawyer he first chronicled the arcane labyrinth of English land law in Megarry and Wade's *Law of Real Property* (now, in 1984, in its 5th Edition) — and then turned, not only to describe, but to clarify and civilise, *Administrative Law* — an achievement deeply impressive to those of us who have a regard for our legal system well this side of idolatry. Not only so, but he combines his stable base in Cambridge with occasional visits to exotic parts of the world which he advises on their constitutions, in a manner superficially reminiscent of Henry Bickersteth's friend Mr Bentham. He has not yet, however, provided Caius with a new constitution; and only one major change of statute has been passed in his time — or indeed, in the last thirty years.

The admission of women

The proposal to admit women to Caius was discussed in the 1960s and 70s amid a great cloud of witnesses. The Robbins report carried in its wake a ferment of new proposals for expansion and change; by the late 60s the chief topic in such discussions was the admission of women to the men's colleges. This was a movement far wider than a single college; and it started amid another ferment, the demand for a student presence in the committees and councils of the universities and colleges of the land. When I returned to Caius in 1977 from many years in other universities, it seemed astounding that Cambridge had changed so little; those within believed they had lived through stirring times. A structure of committees in which students could meet fellows and discuss their common problems, especially domestic problems, had indeed been formed; but there was no student on the Council. Since then a student presence has been established as normal during discussion of matters not reserved to senior members — those reserved include appointments or the more confidential areas of finance and student welfare. But more than this, there had been a steady flow of discussion between the SCR, the MCR and the JCR on the admission of women to Caius. After

54 See Wade 1977; Venn, VI, 167; VII, 80.

some preliminary skirmishes and a great deal of careful thought and discussion, the first major debate among the fellows — gathered as the Governing Body to consider a change of statute — took place in 1969. To succeed, a majority of two-thirds was required, and by a narrow margin this was not achieved. But throughout the eight years which followed a majority of the fellowship, and at times a fairly large majority, remained in favour of the change; a series of vociferous memos from the student body urged it; and the Master, Joseph Needham, made no secret of his support. Meanwhile, an attempt was made to find an outlet for the wishes of the majority by sharing in the foundation of a new college. It was thus that Caius was deeply involved in the early negotiations which led eventually to the endowment of Robinson College. Although its initiatives produced no tangible College contribution as had originally been proposed, Caius contributed in another way — for, after a brief initial period, the chairman of Trustees through many years leading to the grant of its charter in 1984 has been Professor Charles Brink of Caius; Needham himself has also been a Trustee; and two of the fellows migrated to Robinson.

In the autumn of 1977, after various attempts had failed, many thought the issue of 'co-residence' was for a while quiescent; but a tentative enquiry at a General Meeting by some of those who had often debated it before made clear that the fellows were prepared for yet another full-dress discussion. This was held in January 1978, and to a newcomer to this particular exercise, though not to College General Meetings, it was an extremely unusual and heartening occasion — if evidently rehearsed. A great issue was seriously debated, and many kinds of argument deployed, on this side and on that. It soon became apparent that some swing of opinion had taken place among those who had been neutral or hostile before, and the statute was voted by a majority well over the two-thirds needed. The College was led by the new Master, very discreetly, to follow the many who had already marched across the frontier; for Caius, which might have led the van in 1969, found itself leading the regiment from a less advanced position in 1978. What was especially impressive to a veteran from the early 1950s, was the lack of bloodshed in the process. Large issues were involved; feelings were deep; but the change was effected without open rancour and with the minimum of tears. Dorothy Needham was fittingly chosen to lead the first regiment of women, and was duly elected an honorary fellow at the earliest moment the change of statute allowed, in October 1979. Since then many have come as undergraduates and research students; and three as fellows. All three are natural scientists. Dr Mary Astle and Dr Nicola Nichols are chemists — and Mrs Nichols has added a further dimension to our story in 1984 by becoming the mother of Henry Charles Gonville Nichols. Laura Garwin is a geologist, and so studies the past: her special interest lies in the events of a hundred million years or so ago. Her time scale puts the history of the College in perspective: it is still young; it may have — we trust it will — a much longer future ahead.

14

1912 – 1984 — II — Education, Religion and Learning

Education

A while ago we inspected in some detail the teaching resources of the College in the early 1900s. We could carry this forward and list the expanding resources of the College, in teaching fellows and directors of studies, in numerous branches of natural science and medicine, in mathematics, applied and pure, and engineering; in law, where the tradition of John Colton, Thomas Legge, W. W. Buckland and Emlyn Wade has been kept alive by Michael Prichard and Leonard Sealy and their younger colleagues, in modern languages and history; and the rise of English and the decline, but not the extinction, of classics. We could study the active help the College receives, not only from the fully organised systems of University teaching, but from directors of studies who are not fellows, many of whom give it expert, dedicated service none the less — in such subjects as archaeology, history of art, Anglo-Saxon and geography. But such a catalogue would become a prospectus, and the dry bones of it merely. Pursuing the principle of ruthless selection I have put together some sketches from the other side — brief descriptions of the College as it seemed to students of varied interests and background, in the 1920s and the 1940s and 50s.

'One day, during the First World War,' a young schoolboy destined to study medicine at Cambridge, was 'lying in the long grass near Oundle doing OTC open-order drill . . . I happened to be next to Charles Brook, and he said "What College are you going to in Cambridge?" I said "I haven't the faintest idea", and he said, "Well, you'd better come to Caius, that's the one with the greatest medical reputation; that's where I'm going, so why not put your name down for Caius?" So I did, and that's how' Joseph Needham came to Caius.[1] 'My first Tutor was Bill Hardy (Sir William Hardy) the famous physiologist who became afterwards a physicist . . ., he it was who prevented me from doing entirely biological subjects. I wanted to do zoology, anatomy and physiology, and he wouldn't have it. He said, "No, my boy, that's not the way of the future at all. Atoms and molecules, atoms and molecules, my boy, that's what you should study. You'll never do anything in biology if you don't have that chemical and physical basis." So I was therefore pitchforked into chemistry, anatomy and physiology, and that of course affected the whole of my life. And similarly later Peters . . .

---

1 Needham 1976, p. 38; for what follows, pp. 38–9. Cf. Venn, V, 185; VI, 55; VII, 26.

was my director of studies and supervisor, and he had a great influence too'. And the College influenced the future Master in other ways — through Hunkin, the dean, and Anderson the Master who had 'the same charming interest in what one was doing, which is hard to describe but which was so very real'; and his undergraduate contemporaries. None the less, as one contemplates Needham reminiscing with the editor of the *Caian*, two impressions obtrude. First, that it was the lab and Sir Gowland Hopkins which formed him as a scientist and gave him intellectual excitement and companionship. 'The enormous problem of seeing the connections between . . . the atoms and molecules . . . and the organs and tissues of the body . . ., indeed the whole structure of the developed human organism, that was a really tremendous intellectual challenge.'[2] So a brilliant research biochemist was formed; but Needham's intellectual horizons were always wide, in religion, philosophy and politics. In his interest in Marxism, growing in the late 20s and 30s and his love of China in the 30s and 40s, he felt very isolated — to a degree difficult for us who know a little of the intellectual history of Cambridge in the 1930s to comprehend. 'I was very isolated in Cambridge, in fact I was altogether an Ishmael in College society . . . The older fellows regarded me as an absolute outsider, quite out of sympathy with their miscellaneous Edwardian and Victorian conventions. That is why I have a specially warm corner in my heart for Stanley Cook . . . Among those older fellows there were plenty of professionals, but very few people whom you might call dedicated intellectuals, and of these Stanley Cook was one. He was Regius Professor of Hebrew, but he was always pumping me about Freud or Marx, or Frazer or Hopkins . . .'.[3] There was still some echo of this isolation in the early 1950s, and one of the aims of the young insurgents of that era — with great impertinence — was to bring the revered Ishmael nearer to the centre of the stage; they hardly guessed, however, they were helping him on the path to the Master's Lodge. Meanwhile in 1936 a group of Chinese research biochemists came to work in Cambridge, and they included Dr Lu Gwei-Djen who has become the closest collaborator in his great work *Science and Civilisation in China*.

Needham's near contemporary, Hedley Warr, one of the most devoted Caians of his generation, could never distinctly recall 'how I got to Caius . . . I think it was' the body which later became the Advisory Council for the Ministry which 'secured me a place in Caius as an Ordinand'.[4] Warr was to be, like Needham, a lifelong devout Anglican and lay reader, but was never ordained; he was a schoolmaster, for many years headmaster of

2 Needham 1976, p. 40.
3 Needham 1976, p. 43. On S. A. Cook, see Venn, II, 519; V, 50; VI, 16; *Proc. of the British Academy*, XXXVI (1950), 261—76 (D. Winton Thomas). He left the residue of his estate to the College for the furtherance of the disciplines in which he was particularly interested — and to foster these the S. A. Cook Bye-Fellowships have been established, and have brought a series of distinguished scholars to the College.
4 Warr, 1979, p. 108.

King Edward VI School at Louth in Lincolnshire. 'My tutor was Arnold McNair, whose subject was law' — and was another striking example of the eminent scholar-tutors of the epoch. Warr recalled the quiet, kindly eye he kept on his pupils; and how after a sharp illness, early in the vacation, 'a letter followed me from McNair, saying that the College Council wanted me to have a good holiday, and enclosing a cheque for £30 — which in those days gave me a whole month cycling round the Loire châteaux. Years after, when he was President of the International Court at the Hague and a peer, McNair came for the Louth Grammar School Speech Day (as also did Sir Rudolph Peters) . . .' — and he goes on to instance other signs of recognition of his former pupil. 'He had a career of great distinction, . . . as Vice-Chancellor of Liverpool University, as Judge and later President of the Hague Court, as member of the House of Lords, and chairman of various government commissions [and be it said, as fellow of Caius from 1912 till his death in 1975]; yet quiet, kind and utterly unpompous, he was always at the service of his friends and pupils; a jewel of a man'.[5]

'My Director of Studies was Zachary Brooke', recently returned from the war; 'he was a medievalist whose particular field of research was the struggle of Empire and Papacy'; and he tells one of the many stories of Brooke on the road to Canossa.[6] The most celebrated of these, quoted in Philip Grierson's moving memoir in the *Caian*, was of the supervision on Bismarck which suddenly came to life when Zachary Brooke fell to explaining how Bismarck — in his famous saying 'to Canossa we *shall* not go' — had misunderstood the events of 1077.[7] Since 1908 Zachary Brooke (who came to Caius from St John's) had felt himself something of a lone wolf, representing Clio in a medical College, and to the end of his days he was liable to protest if too much was made of the College's medical fame. But already in the 1920s the first of his two pupils who still represent history among the senior fellows was reading the Tripos. Michael Oakeshott, director of studies in the late 40s and later Professor of Political Science at LSE, is a sublime philosopher-historian; Philip Grierson, fellow from 1935, director of studies in the 1950s, and now one of the world's greatest numismatists, was always a master of facts and their relation. They formed an extremely stimulating contrast to those who studied under both in the 40s, but were alike in this, that they accepted the tradition passed on by Z. N. Brooke that a teaching fellow should try to teach the whole of history. Thus the subject had a fine tradition; its apotheosis came later. My own departure from Cambridge in 1956 made way for the arrival of the present director of studies, Neil McKendrick, and with him came the transformation of history teaching in Caius and in many respects in Cambridge at large; it became

5 Warr 1979, pp. 113–14. On Lord McNair, see Venn, IV, 72; V, 96; VI, 37; VII, 11; *Proc. of the British Academy*, LXII (1976), 507–12 (Emlyn C. S. Wade); De Visscher 1977.
6 Warr 1979, p. 114.
7 *Caian* LI (1946), 95–105, at p. 101. For Grierson and Oakeshott, see pp. 297–9.

more of a professional skill drawing expertise from all over the University; and Caius achieved a position of preeminence in history in Cambridge. This lay far in the future in the 1920s, when the young Hedley Warr was making friends with his director of studies, who, though 'a shy, sensitive man, . . . was extremely kind to me, had me early to lunch with his charming young wife at his house in Milton Road, and admitted me to friendship . . .'[8] Warr was deeply involved in the religious life of the College, and a keen amateur musician. 'I became an unofficial chapel precentor, . . . sang in the college choral society and ran a "Caius quartet" specializing in pieces written for it by Charles Wood . . . But the standard of music was very modest and so was its scope — utterly unlike later times' under Hadley and Tranchell.[9] None the less, 'I worked hard, usually putting in four hours' work each morning and another three or four after Hall at night. My assiduity was rewarded with a "First" in the "Mays" . . . and . . . a college scholarship . . . In my second and third years I worked equally hard, but only secured a second in both parts of the Tripos . . .'[10]

The year 1919 saw the admission to the College of another newcomer, Thomas Okey, who has left us in his *Basketful of Memories* a fascinating vision of the transformation of English life in the late 19th and early 20th centuries. Sprung from a line of master basketmakers, craftsmen aristocrats of the east end of London, from a modest school which yet helped him to the passion for learning which moulded his life — he became a devoted member of Toynbee Hall, the friend of Bernard Shaw, a guide and leader in many Italian journeys, in the end a noted exponent of Italy and her literature; a poor man's son who made *The Little Flowers of St Francis* accessible to the English-speaking world. Only occasional flashes — as of the kind bookseller who let him have an old French dictionary for 4d — illuminate the way he came to his fluent knowledge of European languages on which his later life was built; it is the mixture of lucidity with mystery — the mystery of this search for French and German and Italian in Spitalfields and Whitechapel in the 1860s — which lends the book its special charm. For us its central interest is in the denouement. In 1919 at the age of sixty-six — by now author of a basketful of books — he was elected professor of Italian and received his first degree; he was admitted to Caius where his brother-in-law was a fellow, and in 1920 himself received a fellowship. He notes as his first, overwhelming impression of Cambridge one which has not been universal — its equality. 'Money . . . social position as such, count for nothing.' And he basked in 'the consciousness that one stands for what one is worth as a scholar and a man . . . All stand on an equality of worth, from the porter at the gate to the Master in the lodge . . .' But he also noted the

8 Warr 1979, p. 114 (where Mill Rd is a slip for Milton Rd).
9 Warr 1979, pp. 117–18.
10 Ibid., pp. 119–20. For what follows, see Okey 1930, esp. pp. 17, 139–41; Venn, V, 199 (T. Okey, 1852–1939).

slow invasion of modern conveniences, of baths and bells or telephones. 'A further relic of medievalism survives in the status of women' and it was difficult to explain to an academic friend from a Latin country why women were excluded from a dinner in Trinity at the installation of the Chancellor in 1930. He noted that in the conversation of the Combination Room with a visiting headmaster about possible recruits, 'The whole conversation related to their prowess at Rugby . . . Not a word was said as to their learning' — Though he hastened to add they all worked when they came up; all went in for honours; 'some gain double firsts . . .; but this is not talked about'. He flattered the students a little, if not the conversation of the fellows; and there is much about work, almost nothing about rugger, in the *Reminiscences* of the young Hedley Warr.

Thirty years after the entry of Okey and Warr another young ex-serviceman came to read history, as Warr had done in 1919; and Stanley Price, now a well-known playwright and television writer, has put on record his impression of the shifting scene.

'In October, 1951, I do not know if Caius was a welcoming place in reality. For that majority who had suffered the basic boredoms and grubbiness of National Service the mere sight of Tree Court, not to mention the tranquillity of Caius and Gonville beyond, was welcome enough. No red carpets or beaming dons were necessary. The initial euphoria of freedom lingered well beyond the first term. It may have made us a grateful, respectful, even pliable regiment of undergraduates.

'In the comparative tables of those times Caius seemed a middling sort of college; middle-sized, middling hearty, and predominantly middle-class. It was a more socially cohesive community than its near neighbours, King's, Trinity and Magdalene. If the social division between the Public and Grammar school undergraduate, the commissioned and the non-commissioned, tended to disappear over three years, the gap between science and arts faculties remained unbridgeable then as now . . .

'Such divisions as there were in Caius came as little surprise to an undergraduate in the 50s. They merely reflected the society outside with its educational distinctions based on income or the Eleven Plus exam, and the social definition of "officers and their ladies, other ranks and their women" of recent military service. Despite the conservative return of 1951, the Labour Club had a large following both in the University and the college and, for some, a more socialist egalitarianism may still have seemed around the corner. The Public Schools were bound eventually to be abolished, and a scheme was aired to turn the major Public Schools, with their fine locations and historic buildings, into universities as the only practical way to offset the traditional primacy of Cambridge and Oxford.

'Despite a Communist on "O" staircase, neighbour to two possessors of M.G.s and matching flat-caps, political passions did not run high among contemporary Caians. Suez and C.N.D. were still in the future. In a recent retrospective chronicle of Cambridge I have seen our characteristics stigmatized as "the meritocratic ambitiousness of the early 50s". I remember fashionable apathy rather than burning ambition; a fine, optimistic vagueness about the possibilities of the future. Medics and lawyers would be all right, some of us would teach, and, for the rest, there was ultimately a date with the Appointments Board, where a man in a suit would patiently explain what really went on in the offices of Lever Brothers, Cadbury's, and the seemingly glamorous world of advertising and public relations. The media explosion had not yet happened, the lucrative fruits of consultancy were unripened, and Harold Wilson was still a decade away with his "white heat" of technological revolution. There appeared to be no short-cuts to the top. Best advised then to line-up a well-fitting pair of dead man's shoes.

'College politics at an undergraduate level were not an issue. Student democracy was a concept limited to the Complaints Book in the J.C.R., much used for cellotaping in foreign bodies found in one's dinner. It was to come as a shock to discover later that during this whole period there were passionate political upheavals in the S.C.R. . . .

'In the lottery of obtaining a supervisor and Tutor some of us were lucky to establish a relationship outside the weekly reading of the essay. On the whole, however, the fellows were a distant breed; men to whom one applied for a limited number of termly exeats, or accounted for one's misdemeanours. It was not fashionable to expose one's problems or deeper feelings to anyone much older than oneself. The term "pastoral care" was still used only in an agricultural sense.

'I dare say "in extremis" one would have sought out Francis Bennett, coming to the end of his time as Senior Tutor. With his mane of silver hair, black jacket and striped trousers, he was everyone's ideal of a benign favourite uncle, . . .

'On the less avuncular side was a French lector called André Michel. . . . He gave the best parties in college. By "best" one invariably meant a reasonable proportion of female guests, and wine, provided exclusively by the host, that actually came in bottles from France itself. His influence was to be seen, long after his departure, in the clothing and the discarded Gaulloise packets of a generation of modern linguists, and the plaintive sound of Piaf in the courtyards. The Beatles had not yet ascended, and Paris still sounded more romantic than Liverpool.

'For most of us, having achieved the necessary separation from school and home during National Service, Caius confirmed an easy-going indepen- dence. Only on the question of what went on, or might have gone on at night did the college enforce an old morality. We were expected to be in college by midnight, though climbing in was accepted if accomplished with silence and geographic discretion. It was heinous to be found next morning trapped in the Master's walled garden. Ladies had to be out of the college by 10 p.m. Among my yellowing memorabilia I find a letter clipped from the columns of "Varsity" in March 1953. The delicate balance of its style between facetiousness and pomposity gives some insight into the undergraduate literary style of the time.

Sir,

The announcement that Pembroke had decided to extend its visiting hours for ladies till 11.30 p.m. on Saturday nights brings into focus again the whole iniquitous system of ladies' visiting-hours. The system is riddled with discrepancies. At some colleges the deadline for female visitors is 10 p.m., at others 11 p.m., and, at Trinity, 12 p.m. This would imply that the authorities believe a woman to be safe in Trinity two hours after she has ceased to be so in Caius or Clare. This seems to be either faulty logic, or else the most unreasonable optimism.. . .

As it is, we may roam the streets, or haunt the restaurants between 10 and 12 p.m., but are unable to offer the simple hospitality of a cup of coffee to a lady after 10 p.m. It is time the system was drastically revised. This is not a plea for "licensed" rooms, but purely to be allowed a fundamental liberty in them.

Yours, etc.,

Stanley Price

(Gonville and Caius College)

It was clearly manly pride that made me skirt round a greater contemporary problem — how to get ladies into one's room rather than when to get them out. The male-female ratio in Cambridge was over 10 to 1. The female bastions of Newnham and Girton were still a decade away from permissiveness, and female admission was not yet even a glint in the eye of the most progressive Fellow. The social life of Caius was only slightly less monastic than that of Gonville Hall. . . . On the credit side, and if one had a partner, a double ticket for a May Ball was five guineas. It is now £75. In retrospect I suppose we were a peculiar sandwich generation, too young for the War, too old for the permissive society.

'I graduated on the 29th June, 1954. Thirty years later, to the day, I stood in the Senate House watching my son graduate from the same college in the same subject, "déjà vu" a generation apart. From the gallery, I had an aerial view of a hundred or so young Caians, male and female, thanks be to Progress. What, I wondered, distinguished this '84 vintage? Certainly their hair. Viewed from above, it was the most neatly brushed and combed hair I had ever seen assembled under one roof. Where I could see their faces they looked serious but happy. I remembered feeling the same way.'

A revered senior colleague has read the last two chapters of this book, and surveying the last fifty or sixty years observed that I 'had not made it quite parochial enough . . .; the famous men . . . seemed to blot out all those . . . characters who made a College what it was.' Where are the head porters and the cooks? Where the men outside the gates on whom everyone depended? — the College doctor; the coach to whom the rank and file still hastened as a present help in trouble well into living memory? One could extend this list, for Cambridge has always teemed with tradesmen and men of the professions on whom the life of the College and University depends — tailors and solicitors, bankers and money-lenders, wine merchants and pastry-cooks . . . I have said that in a formal sense a college is run by the Master or the Senior Tutor, but in truth it is commonly a very diffuse establishment in which much responsibility and much initiative has been laid on the College staff, who are grievously under-represented in this book; and if we had to answer the question — who above all keeps the threads in his hand? Who is the anchor man on whom the organisation turns? — There is a school of thought which sees him among the tutors or the bursars; but there is a school, perhaps more numerous, which looks first to the head porter and the chef. I have tried to do justice to every point of view; and I have given the Boat Club its place and the other clubs their mention — but there are many who will think the most serious omissions are the grounds-men and the boatmen.

Among the most evocative of the photographs in volume VII of the *Biographical History* for Caians who remember the 1940s and 50s are those of Pepper the porter, Muggleton the gardener and Lionel Rumbelow, the butler (all in plate XII). Lionel was promoted butler from pantry boy at an early age; and this led many of us to view him as a friend and colleague — with less of that distant awe the college butler of legend once inspired, but with a deep respect. He was the type of the College servant on whom the community had been supported — who have given it its stability and its character over many generations, and can be amply illustrated from the staff today — whose life is dedicated to the work of the College. He was more devoted to the tradition in which he had grown up, more resistant to change, more determined to preserve the service which inspired him, than any man I have known.

A College historian must be constantly aware of what he has left out; but if he is to tell a coherent story, it must be the tradition of teaching and learn-ing in the College which defines his ultimate theme — though that does not mean that he forgets or undervalues the contribution of every element in the community which makes and serves the College, within and without its walls — or, in E. S. Roberts's favourite phrase, the 'Greater Caius' throughout the world.

What is its academic tradition? Since the days of Dr Caius, so we all assume, it has been primarily a medical College. With this I have no wish to quarrel, but only to encourage future historians to look, more closely than I have been able, to the significance and meaning of a well-recorded, yet obscure, tradition of this kind. The galaxy of Regius Professors and royal physicians in the 17th century kept alive a reputation which Caius had kindled and Harvey set aflame; and there were medical scholarships and fellowships to attract those to whom mere tradition (as they might think it) had little meaning. But in the 18th century this subsided, essentially (one may suppose) because there was no medical teaching worth the name to be had in Cambridge. Dr Wollaston was one of only two medical students in the early 1780s. He and Mr Bickersteth, the future Master of the Rolls, who came in 1802 expecting to study medicine, doubtless came primarily in search of scholarships. Yet somehow the torch was rekindled. From 1803 to 1839 a successful physician, Dr Davy, was Master. Another Caius physician, Sir George Paget, was a central figure in the revival of the University medical school in the mid and late 19th century. By the 1880s, as the figures in Appendix 3 testify, and — more eloquently still — the life story of many notable Caians from Sherrington to Needham and beyond — the notion was abroad that Caius was the place for a young doctor to begin his studies.

But medicine has not ruled alone. I have emphasised at various dates that this was not an excessively clerical college — Caius himself and his successor were laymen, for example. Yet the majority of its fellows down to 1900 have been clergy, and its theological tradition has been far from negligible: Cosin, Jeremy Taylor, Samuel Clarke, H. B. Swete, Charles Raven, J. M. Creed, Geoffrey Lampe would make a formidable team — and there are many other distinguished names to set beside them. One could pursue this hunt through other plantations, such as the law, from Lyndwood, Legge, Bickersteth, Alderson, to Buckland and McNair and the galaxy of their younger colleagues; and in more recent times through many disciplines and sciences. Most continuous of all, I have found, rather to my surprise, has been the tradition of antiquarian and historical scholarship in various forms — from Caius himself, through Brady and Wharton and Collier, Blomefield and Fenn, J. J. Smith and Guest and Venn and Seeley, down to the day when Z. N. Brooke brought from St John's a novel brand of professional scholarship. And one could continue these themes in other fields.

One abiding impression of Caius for many of us is as a home of good music; and this it has been since the 1890s — a home of all kinds of music, doubtless, but it is the music of the Scales Club, the College concerts, the Chapel and the organ that I speak. It had been so already in the late 16th century when the Puritan fellows grumbled at the Master's chamber organ and sent Thomas Mudde to Peterhouse. It is hard to be sure it was ever so again till the days of Charles Wood. Since his death, after a gap when the organ scholars held the fort, it has been fostered by a succession of professional musicians in the fellowship.

Patrick Hadley, who came in the late 1930s and fostered the musical life of Caius, especially in choir and chorus within and without the Chapel, till the early 1960s, was an Irishman like Wood, and a personality rich and warm; one of the most accessible and hospitable of men. Generations of undergraduates recall the friendly welcome in Paddy's rooms. He had his quirks and fancies, and suspected the Magnificat of a socialistic tendency; but the music of Chapel greatly flourished under his baton, and he built up a male-voice choir after the era of treble choirboys came to an end in 1939. For the chorus he adapted many classical works, including such as Verdi's *Te Deum*, and made a substantial corpus of folk-song arrangements. He was Professor of Music from 1946 to 1962, and during his tenure the Music Tripos was established, the Faculty grew fourfold and the first steps towards the new Music School were taken. The succession of professional musicians is now secure, and music in Caius has flourished in the 70s and 80s under Peter Tranchell, precentor and director of studies, and Robin Holloway, our composer in residence — but happily in permanent residence, and a teacher as well as an artist among us; and indeed all our four music fellows have been composers. This has helped the music of the College to become steadily more professional. In such an institution high professional standards can inhibit the free expression of the less gifted. However this may be, the proportion of students in Caius who join in the College music — or the musical life of Cambridge outside the walls - is impressive; and to many of us who enjoy music only as listeners not performers the range of opportunity College music offers for our indulgence is astonishing. It has come to be a meeting point of many different elements in Caius; and this was remarkably illustrated in the story of the new organ, installed in the Chapel in 1981.[11] It was the first organ in England made by the distinguished house of Johannes Klais of Bonn, and was inaugurated by a team of eminent organists on and about the feast of St Cecilia. This was the culmination of years of discussion and hard work, both in Cambridge and Bonn. Some may regret that we have not a far larger chapel for so great an instrument to deploy its range of talents; others have dropped a tear for yet another Victorian organ sent on its way; others blenched at the cost. But there was a strong body of opinion in the fellowship, widely spread, in favour of this imaginative investment; the hard work of the precentor, Peter Tranchell, and of Konrad Martin, who adapted the skills of an experienced admissions tutor to prepare the coming of a demanding newcomer, and many others in the College, and of Herr Klais and his colleagues in Bonn, brought a complex enterprise to a triumphant conclusion; and an ample reward both to those who can appreciate the subtleties of its making and performance, and the far larger band who can enjoy an instrument of exquisite quality.

11 On the new organ see *Caian* 1981, pp. 39 — 44, and the programme for 'The Inauguration of the New Organ, 20, 21, 22 November 1981', pp. 31 — 8.

Religion

There is no aspect of the life of a college in the present century more elusive than religion. To many it has meant almost everything, to many more almost nothing at all. In a sense this has always been so. The early fellows were members of a chantry; chapel was one of the centres of their work, essential to their raison d'être — and attendance at it was notionally compulsory for Master and fellows till 1860, and to undergraduates much longer — well into the 20th century.[12] That did not make them more religious. But indifference, which has been a common feature of all Christian communities in every century since the 4th at latest, is much easier and more acceptable today than before 1900. The indifferent and the agnostic (often very different people) are always with us and have their share in this chapter — though they will be forgiven if they skip it — for it is to the agnostic and the atheist that we primarily owe the happy fact that every university and college in this land — unlike many in other parts of the world — is sworn to avoid any kind of religious discrimination: those of all faiths and of none are equally welcomed, equally at home in Caius. But this ecumenism is not a purely negative thing: the width and variety which has been a notable feature of the College chapel itself in this century, and especially since the First World War, reflect a positive ecumenical concern at least among the deans and chaplains and senior fellows who have been interested. All this makes the theme bewilderingly complex; yet it cannot be evaded. Both Needham and Warr, two of our principal witnesses to Caius in the 20s, were deeply involved in the religious life in the College; and for some of us it played a like and crucial part, not only in our personal lives but in the intellectual and scholarly standards and interests we developed, when Eric Heaton was chaplain and dean in the late 1940s — and I am sure it has been so for many since.

We have seen that the fervent evangelicalism of Clayton of the 1850s and 60s had passed away in the late 19th century, and the religion of Roberts and a number of his colleagues seems to have been a characteristic Victorian liberal protestantism — more concerned with practice, both the practice of the services within the chapel and of the wholesome Christian virtues without, than with the sharper edges of theological debate.[13] The 1880s saw the formation of the College Mission — boys club and Mission house — in

12 The rules were revised in 1890 (*Gesta* 13 Mar. 1890, no. 9, following a letter from the dean now preserved in the library), including the rule that all undergraduates attend twice on Sunday; and again in 1909 (*Gesta* 19 Nov. 1909), making it compulsory for freshmen once on Sunday, twice in the week; for Junior Sophs, once on Sunday, once in the week. I have found no later Orders, and assume it fell into abeyance after the First War, as I believe in several colleges, without a formal Order. It is doubtful if the College chapel could have seated a full turnout of the years 1919—20, especially as down to the Second World War the choir was augmented on Sunday by boy choristers; and it seems certain that the rule of 1890 was unpracticable.
13 See pp. 230—2.

close association with the parish of Battersea, and this won devoted support from Roberts and was a characteristic endeavour of its day — and has happily been a concern of many of the College from every generation since.[14] My own solitary experiment in pantomime was made there in the 1940s. Meanwhile in 1890 the College received back its one major theologian of that era, H. B. Swete.[15] Theology had been intermittently an element in the College's scholarly tradition, and over the last hundred years it has fielded a remarkable succession of notable biblical scholars and theologians including two more Regius Professors, Charles Raven and Geoffrey Lampe. Lampe came to Caius as professorial fellow, but also was acting dean for a year, and became an energetic elder statesman in some college debates; he was an enthusiastic secretary of the Patronage Committee, and became more of a College man than most of his kind.[16] He gave lustre to the fellowship as editor and inspirer of the Patristic Lexicon and author of his characteristically liberal, far-seeking Bampton Lectures, *God as Spirit*.

Caius in the 1890s had by chance a remarkable group of young churchmen on their way, Charles Raven, later Master of Christ's and honorary fellow of Caius, a brilliant theologian and naturalist, S. C. Carpenter and A. S. Duncan-Jones, later deans of Exeter and Chichester.[17] In 1904 the young Duncan-Jones became first chaplain, then in 1906 junior dean of Caius. Lively and quick in mind, he made a very marked impact on the ordinands and theologians, and a rather wider circle, though not apparently well known to undergraduates at large. He became an energetic member of the liberal catholic group in Cambridge which had a powerful influence in many colleges, Caius included — and issued in *Essays Catholic and Critical*. S. C. Carpenter (soon to be warden of the College Mission) recalls a visit from Charles Raven, probably in the Lent of 1906, much disturbed by Duncan-Jones' excessive austerities[18] which he feared were making him ill. He may have misread the symptoms. In June Mrs Roberts wrote to her mother about a dance in honour of a Japanese prince — 'Mr Duncan-Jones — who does not dance since he has been ordained — hunted Caia up at the end of the evening and made her cut her partner and dance with him instead . . .' — and so his cure was effected;[19] they were married at Heacham in August 1907 — and towards the end of her life Mrs Roberts charmingly described the event, the costumes and the flowers, and how she had later helped to plan the marriage of Jane Cameron and Henry Deas in 1934. By

14 Reid 1912, p. 30. There is much information on the Mission in an unpublished paper by P. C. W. Anderson (1950).
15 Swete 1918; Srawley 1917 (J. H. Srawley was one of the notable list of theologians the College fostered in the late 19th and 20th centuries).
16 Sturdy 1981; Venn, VII, 227.
17 Venn, II, 547, 558; IV, 51, 144, 148; etc; Dillistone 1974; Carpenter 1956.
18 Carpenter 1956, pp. 23−4, dated by Carpenter's career, and by what follows. Carpenter was vice-principal of Westcott House 1906−8, then warden of the College Mission (Venn, IV, 144, where Westcott House is called by its older name, the Clergy Training School).
19 Roberts 1934, p. 189; cf. pp. 209−11.

Caia's marriage the dynasty of Roberts was continued; and Raven himself soon after married her cousin, who lived also in the Lodge.

When Duncan-Jones left Caius for Blofield in Norfolk in 1912 — the first step on a path which led eventually to the deanery of Chichester — he was, I believe, the last fellow of Caius to be presented to a College living.[20] It was the end of an epoch. The patronage committee has continued its work ever since — and received a kind of rebirth at the hands of Geoffrey Lampe who became the central figure in the resistance in the national synod in the 1970s to the total abolition of such patronage. But its role as an outlet for marriageable fellows has sharply declined since the abolition of celibacy; and the conversion of fellows of Caius from a predominantly clerical to a predominantly lay community was complete by 1912. Equally complete, we may suppose, was the passing of any regrets that the Test Act had been abolished.[21]

In 1919 Joseph Hunkin returned to Caius as dean — an enchanting, warm, puckish man, whose approach was liberal-evangelical, in marked contrast to Duncan-Jones' high church sympathies; a man always aware of his background in Methodist Cornwall, never more than when he came to succeed the Anglo-Catholic, ascetic scholar W. H. Frere as bishop of Truro. Joseph Needham has paid warm tribute of affection and admiration for 'a wonderful person . . . He seemed to have a really vivid interest in whatever you were doing and encouraged you in it'[22] — the more striking that Needham's spiritual home has long been in Anglo-Catholic Thaxted, the lovely Essex church beautified by Conrad Noel — the vicar who preached the beauty of holiness combined with communism, in a manner inspiring to some and bewildering to others, and who also enjoyed the friendship of G. K. Chesterton. Hunkin had no love for incense or socialism. Hedley Warr 'saw more of him than any of the dons' and tells a characteristic tale of his methods. 'When he had invited an interesting preacher he would send a note round to the more notable undergraduates (usually "Blues") in the College, and would give them a grin and friendly nod as he proceeded up the chapel in procession . . .'[23] He had returned from the war with an MC and bar, remarkable trappings for a chaplain; and he was indeed one of the bravest of men — he almost seemed to have lived without the experience of fear; and this led him into some scrapes. He was a zealous disciplinarian, a famous proctor in his time, and not all appreciated his warmth and kindness. Yet when I came to know him towards the end of his life one could still

20 Carpenter 1956, p. 27; cf. Venn, IV, 561 — for the later history of College livings, ibid., pp. 558–63; VII, 545–7.
21 There may have been lingering doubts among a few — but mercifully the gates of Caius have now been for over a century wide open to the Roman Catholics, free churchmen and Jews, and folk of many other persuasions, who have added notably to its breadth of vision and intellectual (and athletic) distinction.
22 Needham 1976, p. 39; for Hunkin, see Venn, IV, 71; V, 96; VI, 37.
23 Warr 1979, p. 117.

instantly feel the spell which had caught even members of the STC – the high church confraternity – like Needham and Warr – as well as the evangelicals and the free churchmen; one could hear also the echo of his direct and candid methods. In 1948 or so Hunkin visited the College, now as an honorary fellow. Many a man is judged by his capacity to restrain himself from criticising his successors; but Hunkin, always open and direct, could not dwell in this region of merit. Since his departure some modest high church practices had crept in, including a bell to summon the faithful to communion. 'That little bell – I would lose it, if I were you', he said to the dean amid other episcopal injunctions; but all with a charm and merry twinkle calculated to disarm and to captivate. The bell has been lost.

Let us set beside Hunkin, confident, assured for all his liberal ecumenism, a young contemporary, who represented the inarticulate faith that had survived from the age of Venn, yet emerging from a very articulate mind: here is Francis Bennett, preaching in chapel in 1947. 'I prefer to say "I believe in Love" rather than to say "I believe in God", for the word love has for me more precise significance than the word God . . . Love is the only power which makes human life in community possible . . . But love as a general feeling of benevolence is not enough . . . It has to be transformed into a principle of conduct and maintained as such'. He outlines its enemies, selfishness, impatience, envy, obstinacy, laziness . . . 'But love has its auxiliary forces too: sympathy and gratitude and endurance and the willingness to see the point of view of others and readiness to accept correction. And there is one other, courtesy, that gracious handmaiden of love. I have a great fondness for her.'[24]

Some of the religious fervour of Caians over the last fifty years has been poured into churches and societies outside the College; for a few in the STC down to the 40s; for far more in CICCU, the conservative evangelical society which has long prospered in Cambridge; fluctuating numbers in the more liberal SCM. For the Catholics Fisher House has been for many years now a natural centre, though in recent decades occasional masses have restored the chapel to something like its original function. It is commonly supposed that practising chapelgoers have formed increasingly a minority

24 *Caian* 1983, p. 57; cf. 1985, pp. 92–3. To help explain what follows, John Sturdy has kindly furnished the following specimen figures from the chapel records now in the Archives. They give numbers of communicants at five-yearly intervals on the second Sunday of the Michaelmas Term (1) and on Whit Sunday (2), the one major festival to fall in term. Details for the 40s and 50s are missing, and so 1955–6 has been given instead of 1954–5; 1983–4 is the last full year.

	1924-5	1929-30	1934-5	1939-40	1955-56	1959-60	1964-5	1969-70	1974-5	1979-80	1983–4
1	28	20	28	13	76	74	36	25	34	34	40
2	58	41	30	38	101	71	43	41	48	28	44

It should be borne in mind that 1 is a normal Sunday, and better reflects the general pattern, but that 2 also reflects the old customs of communicating only or particularly at Easter, Whitsun and Christmas.

even among the believers, as in most walks of life in Britain over the last fifty years. To the general rule, indeed, there have been many exceptions. The proportion of Caius undergraduates who go to chapel with some regularity has probably always been greatly in excess of what is common in most English parishes and in some other colleges; and in recent decades the ecumenical nature of the chapel has been a great encouragement. The years from the mid-40s to the early 60s saw a modest revival of churchgoing everywhere, and a major revival in Caius when Eric Heaton and Hugh Montefiore were deans. Although Caius shared in some measure in the numerical decline of the 60s, the historian of religion must always be wary of statistics; and the only ones we possess of any authority are of communicants, which seem to show figures substantially higher for the 1980s than for the 20s and 30s, though both areas were eclipsed in the 50s. These numbers are not easy to interpret, for fashions change and there has been a greater emphasis on the Eucharist, as the central, uniting act of Christian worship, since the 1940s. It may be that chapel was more crowded at other Sunday services in the 1920s and 1930s. But the figures help to counter the view that the religious life of Caius has suffered decline in the 20th century. They speak mainly of undergraduates.

The fellows who were sworn in former centuries to constant daily observance in chapel have made up for this excess throughout my lifetime; the large majority have only come to chapel for admissions of fellows and special occasions. Yet this gives a superficial view of the feeling of the fellowship for the chapel — dramatically revealed by very strong support for the new organ in the 1980s — and the religious life of College; and even more — if I may so put it — the pastoral and intellectual influence of successive deans and chaplains, which has often been profound.

Yet if religion is now for many more for the courts and chambers, the lab, the discussion group, the every day life of our community than for the chapel, it remains a symbol, and a centre for a substantial few, of the faith in which the College was founded. Twice a year that part of our community who find meaning in it recites the tale of our benefactors, gives thanks to God for each and every one and the blessings they have made possible in Caius — and asks in Caius' own prayer: 'O Lord the Holy Spirit, who art the author of all good and the giver of all wisdom, bestow on us thy servants the power of learning, the desire of wisdom, and grace to do good . . .'[25]

Learning and research

In an interview with the editor of the *Caian* in 1983, John Lehman, who rose from commanding the College boats in the 1960s to be Secretary of the

25 Benefactors Commemoration, translated from Venn, III, 369 (an addition to the service by the present dean in 1969).

United States Navy in the 1980s, explained his spectacular transformation thus: 'To combine the intellectual life with the life of decision-making and policy is for me the highest satisfaction, and this is what really I first learned here at Caius.' — and he went on to describe the balance preserved in Cambridge between intellectual growth — in his case, the Law Tripos followed by a PhD in Philadelphia — with other activities. 'At the end of every day I think back to what I would have done as we were rounding Grassy Corner and I put on that extra surge of effort to close the gap, as we always did in the Caius Boat Club. I am sure NATO will follow suit.'[26]

Every College club could produce its modest versions of this story, and we must keep Mr Lehman in mind when we consider the College's most specialised role in recent intellectual history; for he is one of a long line who have combined prowess on the field or the river with distinction elsewhere. Sportsmen and others have come to Cambridge to trifle; Mr Lehman was clearly not one of them. The Caius entrants of 1918 included Claude Hulbert who — in distinction from his elder brother Jack who had been at times almost a hard-reading man — greatly added to the lustre of the Footlights and the ADC, and to the laughter in Z. N. Brooke's room in Caius, while hardly burdening his mind with any serious history at all. And I can recall a few sportsmen still in the 1940s who came to play games and do little else. They were already marked out as an interesting and rare species; the vastly increased seriousness of student life and competition — so different from the popular image fostered by the riots of the 60s — had almost driven them out. But it is still for many the Boat Club, the Debating Society, the buttery and the chapel that form the centre of the impressions and memories of Caius; and it is still a wholesome thing, within limits, that it should be so. The limit is this. A College is a place of education in the broadest sense, sure enough. But what sets it apart from a school or a poly is its specific function as a centre of learning and research. This is not to make any exclusive claim — learning and research have flourished in innumerable other places, in schools and polytechnics and private homes, not to mention a London club called the Royal Society. Nor can a college be the centre of research in most fields today. Gone is the time when teaching even in the medical sciences consisted of Dr Drosier, in procession with his gyp, marching to the summit of the staircase above the Gate of Virtue to lecture to the more athletic and virtuous of the medical students; the College labs are 'a distant, if not fragrant, memory'.[27] Research in the humanities may indeed be conducted in a College, especially those which depend more on speculation than on data. But that is not the point. A College is a meeting place of men and women and ideas, within the wider context in which all scholars work. This book has been studded with case histories of intellectuals who have found in Caius, some of them much, some of them little,

26 *Caian* 1983, pp. 34−42, at pp. 34, 42. Cf. Venn, VII, 340.
27 See pp. 232, 253.

intellectual life and stimulus. Indeed it is of the very nature of scholarship that it cannot be confined in a small room — nor stir without human agency and human intercourse. Here we can only survey a few of the giants who have lived or worked here in the last two generations — and such is the longevity of Caians that all but one of them are still alive.

Sir Vincent Wigglesworth's qualifications for making his mark in the College in 1919 were a brief career in the artillery, which enabled him to help in the handling of the Jesus gun, and in the signals, which gave Chubby Stratton 'the impression that I was a person of much greater merit than he had supposed when I was one of his students' — for they discovered late in Stratton's life that Wigglesworth had served in Stratton's unit in the First World War.[28] But his real career began sooner: 'by the age of five I was keeping a large collection of caterpillars and other insects, and spending hours and hours watching them' — and from this has grown an intimacy which is still actively pursued in his 80s.[29] Acting on advice from Anderson and Peters Wigglesworth tried his hand at research in biochemistry under Sir Gowland Hopkins, before completing his medical training in London; and it was through medicine, specifically tropical medicine, that he came again to the study of insects. In 1946 he returned to Caius as professorial fellow, 'the back door into the College. My main occupation was necessarily with the Unit and with the Department. The relation of a professorial fellow with the College is a social one and there are times when he may feel that he is in the nature of a parasite'[30] — observed the world's leading expert on the tsetse fly and similar creatures; but he hastened on (for the comfort of his kind) to describe much too modestly his own services as a member of the College Council and in other ways. The most notable of these is reflected in many a page of his volume of essays on *Insects and the Life of Man* (1976).

'Man is an arrogant animal. In the euphoric state engendered by her Centenary in 1969, even *Nature* was betrayed into claiming that "the directions of scientific advance are no longer left to chance but, rather, are charted almost deliberately in advance". In his famous address to the combined Darwin Centenary and International Congress of Zoology in the Albert Hall in 1958, Julian Huxley assured us that man was no longer subject to natural selection. As one who does not believe any of these things I hold that there are still unexpected discoveries to be made, and that there is still room for the enquiring mind and the untrammelled research of the experimental biologist.'[31] His major contribution has lain for many of his colleagues in the presence and example and conversation of a great scientist still living in the midst of the community, still at work.

28 Wigglesworth 1979, pp. 31—44, at pp. 31—2.
29 Ibid., p. 31.
30 Ibid., pp. 40—1.
31 Wigglesworth 1976, p. 194.

In 1920 came Michael Oakeshott: he read history, became a fellow, and after Zachary Brooke's promotion to a Chair and his own return from war service, directed studies in history; and lectured meanwhile on the history of political ideas from Plato to Hegel or so — a course which gave a whole generation of students a sense of how history can be grasped and handled unique in British universities in its time; my own notes from it were carefully kept and have been more often consulted than any other notes I made in that era save those relating to my own research. But his published work has lain mostly in two adjacent fields. His first major book on *Experience and its modes* (1933) was a Hegelian study which instantly set him apart from all that was fashionable in British philosophy at that time; and although the reputation he had acquired in Cambridge won him the Chair of Political Science at LSE in 1951, where his influence as a teacher and thinker has steadily progressed, it is only in his later years that he has found himself in the unexpected role of a revered doyen of a philosophical tradition not generally ignored.[32] The world thought that his appointment to a Chair formerly held by an eminent socialist, Harold Laski, was an astonishing lurch to the right; he himself explained that the real difference was that he had no claim to infallibility — 'I am not the pope'. In the 1930s he also put experience to work in a more practical way, and published a book in collaboration with Guy Griffith, fellow and ancient historian, called *A Guide to the Classics* (1936); this book has earned them the reputation of being the new Machiavellis of the turf; for its sub-title is 'How to pick the Derby Winner' — and it is profanely believed that it has been the most studied of their books among the fellows of Caius.

R. A. Fisher's first entry to the College was as long ago as 1909; he was a fellow for some years in the 1920s; but his lasting career in Caius was as a professorial fellow from 1943 until his death in 1962.[33] He was the father of a very large family, and the title of an early paper on the 'Frequency Distribution of the values of the correlation coefficient in samples from an indefinitely large population' is calculated to trip the layman — the last word is a mathematical construct not a gathering of folk — which yet seems to unite statistics and population, the first and last loves of his academic life. For he was a mathematician of immense distinction who spent much of his life in the study of genetics, at Rothamsted, London and Cambridge. But indeed he used his statistical genius to change the direction of several scientific fields, and the traditional study, for example, of physical anthropology nearly perished in his hands. *The Design of Experiments*, marvellously simple in its language, and equally subtle in its thought, can give exquisite pleasure to a scholar who has never done an experiment in his life. I recall an evening in the Combination Room, as a very young fellow, with

32 Cf. Venn, V, 228—9; VI, 62; VII, 34.
33 Venn, IV, 105; V, 109; VI, 42—3; VII, 15. Joan Fisher Box, *R. A. Fisher: the Life of a Scientist* (New York, 1978).

Needham on one side, Fisher on the other, both characteristically, from the warmth of their interest in their colleagues, engaged in talk about the middle ages. In such discussions — whatever the topic — it always seemed that Joseph Needham knew more than one did oneself. Ronald Fisher knew little about the middle ages, but from a very slender base of fact could build a mightly edifice of inference, and defeat the expert who had only facts at his disposal. In *The Genetical Theory of Natural Selection* he propounded, among a series of dazzling sociological studies growing out of the purer genetical analysis, a theory about the fall of the Roman Empire, much more alluring than most of those fashionable at the time. It has now attracted the attention of historians — after a long interval — and been challenged; and it did not escape notice among his irreverent junior colleagues that it was part of an elaborate argument for the benefits of providing handsome allowances to members of the middle-class intellectual elite who, like himself, had large families of children. Fisher could be provoking and petty; but warm and friendly too; and young men of whatever discipline who came into contact with him were given a unique revelation of the nature of science and the range and power of the human mind.

My next two case histories are of men far younger than any of these three. Philip Grierson was born in Dublin in 1910, but he came to school in England and has been resident in Caius since 1929, a fellow since 1935, and is the unique symbol of stability in the present fellowship.[34] Yet from this base he has travelled more widely than most of his colleagues, and his only known unfulfilled ambition is to travel to the moon. In the mid 1940s he began to collect medieval coins, and as historian and numismatist he is a towering figure now among those who study the coinage and economic history of Europe, of the east and west, from the decline of Rome to the fall of Byzantium — and beyond. He has never been impoverished except temporarily after an international auction; but he has made a modest inheritance and the income of a university professor work quite outside the rules of economics to such purpose that, having parted with a half of his collection — the Byzantine coins — to the great American Institute, Dumbarton Oaks in Washington, he still possesses the finest representative collection of medieval coins from western Europe that has yet been known. In earlier days many of his coins were housed in College and his pupils could touch and handle and enjoy them; now they are safely locked in the Fitzwilliam Museum, where he and his colleague Mark Blackburn are engaged in composing the catalogue of his collection. This will be at once the unique conspectus and manual of medieval currency and one of the most formidable works of scholarship to have been inspired and planned and drafted within the walls of the College. This immense effort of scholarship has required, and excused, a vast amount of travel — and a certain concentration of time. He is a sociable, hospitable man whose colleagues delighted to make him

34 Venn, V, 361; etc.; Brooke and Stewart 1983.

President; and he in turn taught them to eat and drink at a pace compatible with an evening's research, or at the cinema. His portrait by George Bruce catches the dignity of a man who graces his doctoral scarlet, and the informal warmth which generations of pilgrims have encountered on G staircase, St Michael's.

Lord Bauer was born in Budapest in 1915, and came to Caius in 1934.[35] If a man would understand how the medieval economy worked, he must first grasp the history of its coinage from Grierson — preferably starting with 'The monetary reforms of 'Abd al-Malik', which turned the western economy of the 9th century upside down, or seems to have done if Grierson's reasoning is correct — and then turn to the opening chapters of Bauer's *West African Trade* (1954), whose teaching is deployed before a wider audience in Bauer and Yamey, *The Economics of Under-developed Countries* (1957), a brilliant distillation of that gloomy science, in which, as in a mirror, one sees many aspects of the medieval economy our economic historians had missed. *West African Trade* is a work of profound scholarship by a brilliant economist. Yet Peter Bauer is best known in the world as the critic of current modes of aid to the Third World; and in Caius he is known as the College's investment adviser — in virtue of which he resumed his fellowship in 1968. Most of his colleagues would probably confess to feeling uneasy in the presence of his economic doctrines, an unease ironically mingled with delight in the success of his practical advice. Those of us who shared his company in the 40s and 50s had a rare intellectual pleasure — and it is a remarkable experience still to see him at work with the present Senior Bursar, Air Vice-Marshal Reginald Bullen, two great professionals of very different background and training investing in harmony together.

In 1977 the fellowship included eight fellows of the Royal Society and ten of the British Academy; in 1983 these were reversed, at ten and eight — making a total of seventeen since Needham doubled in two roles. Only by ruthless and invidious selection have I reduced these pages to any reasonable proportion. We could have dwelt in the cold (in low temperature physics) with David Shoenberg or seen new meaning in Horace with Charles Brink — impressive instances of active scholarship beyond the psalmist's hurdle — and many other adventures would be open to us. I make no defence of my selection save that no person of good will can doubt the scholarly genius of these men, in a positive way; in that sense they can represent the fellowship of recent decades. But if we ask the question — with what names will the fellowship and the College of the late 20th century be most clearly remembered in the history of learning and research, many of us, I think, would hazard the guess — as the College of Hawking and Needham.

Stephen Hawking's spectacular investigations of black holes in the

---

35 Venn, VI, 119–20; VII, 72. For 'Abd al-Malik see Grierson, *Dark Age Numismatics* (Variorum reprint, 1979), no. xv.

universe are placed beyond the comprehension of ordinary men by the legendary distances involved, by the fact that his discoveries have been made by the mind alone — not by such telescopes as John Smith set upon the chapel roof in the 18th century, or Stratton handled in the 20th, but by mathematics — and by his physical disability. His work is mainly done in the Department of Applied Mathematics, where he sits in his invalid chair holding the baton of Newton, as Lucasian Professor of Applied Mathematics.[36] But he lives in college with his wife and family — albeit a part of the college disguised as a house in West Road — and ever and anon he comes with his wheel chair through the Gate of Honour to Hall with his wife or a colleague at hand to help — for he is a cult figure to his colleagues not only for his scientific genius, but for the Motor Neurone Disease which encompasses him — the human mind seems never more mysterious than in a frame desperately crippled; and Stephen Hawking is to his colleagues both a very friendly and a very awe-inspiring presence.

In October 1984 the Chinese Ambassador brings the history of scholarship in Caius — and for the time being the history of the College — to a fitting close by laying the foundation stone of the Needham Research Institute in the garden of Robinson College. In the pagoda, as his colleagues impertinently call it, a permanent home can be given to the collections on which his greatest book is based, and an institute formed where his studies may continue. A practical person contemplating the question — where can the whole range of the history of Chinese science and civilisation be studied? — would be bound to answer, in China, and in China alone; it is inconceivable (one would think) that the materials and the skills for the task could be gathered in Western Christendom. That is a part of the miracle which Joseph Needham has performed; and for a crucial period in the formation of the work the collection was housed in K1 and K2, Caius Court. I can recall few occasions which tested the inner convictions of the fellowship on the function and meaning of the college more sharply than the debate in 1956 whether Needham might have a second room in which to house his books.[37] It was widely accepted that this was one of the great works of scholarship on which the fame of Caius would depend; it was accepted that he was in great straits for space — and extremely economical in its use, for already his single room was filled with bookcases between which only the most diminutive of his assistants (so we thought) could move. But space in the old courts is very scarce; the fellowship was growing; if non-resident fellows who did little teaching were given such privileges, fewer and fewer undergraduates would ever have the chance to live in the ancient courts. These are not trivial arguments; it is a real debate — though it must be said that the College speaks more kindly of its non-resident fellows in such discussions than it used to — and Harvey Court was then only a gleam in

36 Venn, VII, 329.
37 *Gesta* 18 July 1956, no. 5; cf. 10 June 1956, no. 11.

the eye. But it was a symbolic decision none the less — not a decision that one fellow's research might outweigh all other criteria, nor indeed a special favour to a senior colleague; but a modest contribution to a great work of scholarship and a genuine appreciation of one of the values for which a college exists and of a man who expounded them. It specially concerns this book that so much of Needham's research has been done within the College. But that would be a fact of little moment if the project began and ended there. Just as the College lives and thrives in 'the greater Caius' scattered throughout the globe, so *Science and Civilisation in China* is now a vast international enterprise, the work of many collaborators in most countries of the world where science and scholarship are valued.

Epilogue

The two outstanding changes of recent years have been the transformation of the College from a male to a mixed community and the growth and enhancement of its buildings. Women were first admitted to Caius in 1979; by 1985 the University of Cambridge itself – which had been a male university with two distinguished women's colleges within it till the foundation of New Hall in 1954 – had become a mixed university. In 1996 there are still three colleges mainly or wholly for women, but none are wholly male. Great changes do not come overnight: the sexes are not yet evenly balanced in the College; there are only 14 women fellows. But if we recall that the idea of mixed colleges was only effectively born in the 1960s, we can realise how substantial is the transformation we have witnessed.

By 1950 the College had allowed itself to grow into a large modern academic community hemmed in on a tiny island site in the heart of Cambridge. In its future annals the late twentieth century will be remembered as the era when it found means to escape from the extreme constriction of its boundaries, and to expand both on the former meadow land beyond the river and the Backs – the lung which formed the most beneficial part of Dame Anne Scroope's bequest in 1500 – and around its homeland in the city centre.

In the 1960s the College built Harvey Court, a building which won awards for its aesthetic merits, but with its immense cellars made wasteful use of a prime site. In the following twenty years the College took in hand the row of houses stretching south along Dame Anne's meadows to Sidgwick Avenue: two houses on West Road; the noble villa built by William Wilkins senior in 1798 for his family, Newnham Cottage; Finella – celebrated for the decor of the 1920s added under the patronage of Mansfield Forbes – 'a milestone in the coming of what might be called Expressionism in decoration' in Pevsner's words; and Springfield, once the home of Gwen Raverat's formidable Aunt Cara, Lady Jebb. In Harvey Court and the neighbouring houses many students and fellows now live and work.

Between 1950 and 1995 the community has almost doubled: there has been a large increase in student numbers, especially among postgraduate students, now over 250 in number; the fellowship has nearly trebled; the College numbers well over 900 men and women, including the staff of 150 or so. This has meant an urgent need for more accommodation – both for rooms for students and fellows, and for public rooms. In *The Caian* for 1995, the Librarian J. H. Prynne recalls how his twenty-five years as Librarian

302

have been filled with schemes for a new College Library: while the fruitless search for a new site went on, the books filled the space of the existing Library and expanded elsewhere in the recesses of Gonville Court; and reading space for students grew ever more inadequate.

In 1987 it was recognised that the Squire Law Library – the most recent tenant of the princely wing of the old University Library added by C. R. Cockerell in the 1830s and 40s – must find another home. Plans were afoot for a new building for the whole Law Faculty. But if it was to move, how were funds to be raised for the building – and who was to occupy Cockerell's Library? Fine as it is, the Cockerell Building has overlooked and dominated Caius Court for 150 years, and poetic justice – as well as practical good sense – suggested that Caius be offered it for its College Library. For a great price the College has acquired a 350-year lease of the Cockerell Building, and Caius enjoys the most notable addition to its buildings for many generations. Its restoration has been supervised by the architects Donald Insall and Partners, leading experts in the sympathetic treatment of historic buildings: their partner Peter Locke had already given the College much help in the past; Mark Wilkinson has been principally in charge of the Cockerell restoration. The opportunity has been taken to revive the fine Waterhouse lecture room of 1883 – 5 as an auditorium, designed by Robert Dunton of the same Partnership.

After Cockerell, the other additions to our property in the heart of Cambridge – houses in Green Street, additional space in Rose Crescent – might seem of less importance. But every step we can take to expand the ancient centre is vital; and the purchase of the old corner houses – formerly Bowes and Bowes, now the Cambridge University Press bookshop – completes our holdings opposite Great St Mary's, adds valuable rooms in its upper storeys, and a notable building with a Georgian exterior and a sixteenth-century core to the College.

All these changes have taken place under the last years of Sir William Wade as Master, and in the tenure of his successor Peter Gray – a devoted Caian of the 1940s, who had been a Fellow in the early 1950s, and then for 30 years Lecturer and Professor of Chemistry in Leeds. The refurbishment will be completed in the Mastership of Neil McKendrick, for well over thirty years a celebrated Director of Studies in History, and recently Chairman of the Committee which has directed it. The acquisition of the Cockerell Building and the bookshop have been negotiated by Robin Porteous, Senior Bursar. They all represent the faith and determination of the whole community of Master and Fellows.

Meanwhile, the move of the Library to its new home releases vital space to expand and replenish public rooms for fellows and students alike. More than that, the College has had an exciting opportunity to refurbish its public rooms, and in particular to restore the exquisite plasterwork of Sir John Soane in the old hall, recently the Monro Reading Room. To restore

Soane's work and re-design the interior of the old inner library in a classical idiom sympathetic to Soane's work – and to provide a more ample and attractive setting for the public rooms of the whole community – the College has set the distinguished architect John Simpson to work; and – while this book itself is being refurbished – the transformation of the public rooms is under way.

Addenda

When this book was published in 1985, college history was still a relatively neglected subject: happily it is no more, and what follows indicates some of the studies of the intervening years – as well as some of my errors and omissions.

Friendly critics have observed that the later chapters of the book form more of a domestic chronicle – with less sense of the context in Cambridge and the wider world – than the earlier chapters. I have tried to provide such a context in my *History of the University of Cambridge*, IV, *1870 – 1990* (Cambridge, 1993) – cited below as Brooke 1993: in the same series Damian Leader's I, *The University to 1546* (1988) and Peter Searby's III, *1750 – 1870* (now in the press) have also enlarged the context – as have several volumes of *The History of the University of Oxford*. For a wider audience, Roger Highfield and I provided – with photographs (as here) by the late Wim Swaan, *Oxford and Cambridge* (Cambridge, 1988).

Chapter 1   I have written more extensively on Edmund Gonville in *Studies in Clergy and Ministry in Medieval England*, ed. D. M. Smith (York, 1991), pp. 1 – 11.

pp. 4, 7   An exciting new dimension to our knowledge of Gonville as patron has been provided by C. Norton, D. Park and P. Binski, *Dominican Painting in East Anglia: The Thornham Parva Retable and the Musée de Cluny Frontal* (Woodbridge, 1987): they argue that these splendid pieces of fourteenth-century art were made for Gonville's first foundation, the Dominican Priory at Thetford, under his patronage. They have also corrected in detail my account of Gonville's relation to his own patrons: it was John de Warenne, earl of Surrey, on whose behalf Gonville was acting in Thetford; the estate only effectively passed to the younger Henry of Lancaster – later the nominal founder of Corpus – in 1347 (ibid. pp. 87 – 8 n.; on Henry see above, p. 6).

pp. 5, 11   Gonville's death is dated November 1351, probably 17 November 1351, by C. Brooke in *The Caian* 1994, p. 67.

pp. 34 – 5 n. 64   It has been noticed that T. James wrote numbers in many of the volumes he listed, and this will greatly facilitate study of the history of the MS collection before 1600.

p. 36   Linda Voigts has shown that it is not certain that Marshall's books came as a single bequest: 'A doctor and his books: the manuscripts of Roger Marchall (d. 1477)' in *New Science out of Old Books: Studies in Manuscripts and Early Printed Books in Honour of A. I. Doyle*, ed. R. Beadle and A. J. Piper

(Aldershot, 1995), pp. 249 – 314, esp. 267, 300 n. 84. But the survival of perhaps eighteen in contrast to three in Peterhouse still illustrates the grip Gonville Hall kept on its MSS.

p. 37 Historically, the glossed Gratian of the 1190s from the Oxford schools, MS 283/676 (apparently a medieval accession) and the twelfth century Greek Gospels with the hand of Robert Grosseteste in it, MS 403/412, which came to Caius in the sixteenth century, are items of exceptional interest (see L. Boyle in *History of the University of Oxford*, I, 531 – 2; *Byzantium: Treasures of Byzantine Art and Culture from British Collections*, ed. D. Buckton (British Museum, London, 1994), pp. 183 – 4, no. 197).

pp. 43, 46 On John Fisher see now *Humanism, Reform and the Reformation: the Career of Bishop John Fisher*, ed. B. Bradshaw and E. Duffy (Cambridge, 1989); and on the Lady Margaret Beaufort, M. K. Jones and M. G. Underwood, *The King's Mother* (Cambridge, 1992).

p. 55 n.1 Vivian Nutton's reappraisal of Caius as humanist is *John Caius and the Manuscripts of Galen* (Cambridge Philological Soc., Supplementary vol. 13, 1987).

pp. 55, 65 Paul Binski has in preparation a new study of Caius' symbolism of the gates, revealing its origins in medieval friars' sermons as well as in 'humanist' themes.

p. 55 n. 5 See now Catherine Hall, 'Dr Caius' counting house', *The Caian* 1987, pp. 49 – 55.

p. 66 The *simplicity* of the main design of Caius Court was evidently designed to emphasise the traditional, medieval aspect of Caius' inspiration: there is a striking contrast between the interior of the court, with its two-storeyed elevation in the fourteenth century mould, and the exterior, now in Tree Court and the Master's Garden, which reveals that it is truly a three-storeyed design.

pp. 79, 85 Peter Stein has now set Legge in his context as a civil lawyer in 'Thomas Legge, a sixteenth-century English civilian and his books', in *Satura Roberto Feenstra*, ed. J. A. Ankum *et al.* (Fribourg, 1985), pp. 545 – 56. Legge's role as commissary in the university and diocese of Ely still awaits full investigation. The legal context of the church courts has been brilliantly brought to life by R. Helmholz, *Roman Canon Law in Reformation England* (Cambridge, 1990).

p. 80 n. 6 See now C. Brooke, 'Allocating rooms in the sixteenth century', *The Caian* 1987, pp. 56 – 67.

p. 89 John Fingley was beatified by the Pope in 1988, an event celebrated with a mass in Caius Chapel: see *The Caian* 1988, pp. 110 – 14.

p. 97 The figures for the seniorities of King's etc. are not quite consistently presented: as in most other cases, the Caius seniority (and the modern College Council) was a body of 13 persons, twelve fellows plus the Master.

p. 103 The act of 1576 obliged the colleges to collect one-third of their rents in kind – *or* in a cash equivalent based on current prices in

Cambridge, Oxford, Windsor or Winchester: see G. E. Aylmer in *History of the University of Oxford*, III (1986), 534 – 7; Sarah Bendall in Bendall et al., *A History of Emmanuel College*, forthcoming.

p. 128 and n. 4 the whole context of this chapter has now been illuminated by J. Twigg, *The University of Cambridge and the English Revolution, 1625 – 1688* (Woodbridge, 1990).

p. 130 n. 17 See J. Twigg, 'The limits of "Reform": some aspects of the debate on university education during the English Revolution', *History of Universities*, IV (1984), 99 – 114.

pp. 157 n. 57, 215 n. 103 See now J. C. T. Oates, *Cambridge University Library, A History*, I; D. McKitterick, *Cambridge University Library, A History*, II (Cambridge, 1986).

pp. 167 – 8 and n. 41 See C. N. L. Brooke, J. M. Horn and N. L. Ramsay, 'A canon's residence in the eighteenth century: the case of Thomas Gooch', *Journal of Ecclesiastical History*, 39 (1988), 545 – 56.

p. 189 n. 4 To these studies can now be added, e.g. Searby (see above); J. Twigg, *A History of Queens' College, Cambridge* (Woodbridge, 1987); R. Hyam in P. Cunich et al., *A History of Magdalene College, Cambridge* (Cambridge, 1994).

p. 195 and n. 29 The second centenary of George Green's birth in 1993 was celebrated by a service and plaque in Westminster Abbey (see *The Caian* 1993, p. 53) and D. Mary Cannell's *George Green* (London, 1993). On Bromhead, see M. Cannell in *The Caian* 1996, forthcoming.

p. 200 n. 50 Lord Langdale's work for the PRO has been fully described by J. Cantwell in *The Public Record Office 1838 – 1958* (London, 1991), chaps. 1 – 6.

pp. 215 – 16 On Waterhouse see now the massive study by Colin Cunningham and Prudence Waterhouse, *Alfred Waterhouse, 1830 – 1905* (Oxford, 1992), esp. pp. 66 – 8, 231 (no. 268), 257 (no. 502).

p. 224 and n. 4 On the decline and fall of celibacy, Peter Searby has kindly pointed out to me the full statement of intended statutes of the early 1860s in Parliamentary Papers 1861, H.C. xx [2852], *Report of the Cambridge University Commissioners*, pp. 17 – 24; and see Brooke in S. Bendall et al., *A History of Emmanuel College*, forthcoming.

pp. 232, 290 and n. 12 On the decline of compulsory chapel see now Brooke 1993, pp. 111 – 21, esp. pp. 114 – 16 (the attempt to breathe new life into it in 1890), 119 and n.54. Caius attendance records from 1918 on show a dramatic decline in attendance – it is clear that there was no systematic attempt to enforce it after the return of the veterans of the First World War.

p. 233 Venn and Venn's diagram are now honoured in a window in hall: see A. W. F. Edwards in *The Caian*, 1990, pp. 67 – 8.

pp. 259 – 60 The count of Caian Nobel Laureates left out Max Born, who was awarded the Nobel Prize in Physics in 1954.

pp. 260 – 7 Maisie Anderson's memoirs of her father, and of life in the Caius Lodge in the 1910s and 20s – 'Time to the Sound of Bells' – were serialised in *The Caian* from 1988 to 1993. On Sir Hugh Anderson, see also Brooke 1993, chap. 11.

p. 262 The Co-optimists' own record of the Jesus gun has been published, with photographs, in *The Caian* 1994, pp. 55 – 60; see also *The Caian* 1992, pp. 85 – 7, for Maisie Anderson's recollection of it.

p. 272 n. 43 On Lord Swann, see the memoir by Charles Goodhart in *The Caian* 1991, pp. 105 – 10.

pp. 276 – 7, 300 – 1 Sadly, it is no longer true that 'all [three recent masters] are still alive': Joseph Needham died on 24 March 1995; Sir Nevill Mott on 8 August 1996. See *The Caian* 1995, pp. 104 – 38; 1997, forthcoming.

p. 279 In 1985 the admission of women was still a recent event. Now (1996) some 35% of the students are women, and we have had 21 women fellows – of whom 14 are currently fellows – still only 14% of the total fellowship.

p. 283 l. 11 On music under Tranchell, see the notices of Peter Tranchell by Harry Porter and Raymond Leppard in *The Caian* 1994, pp. 95 – 9. A wider audience can now appreciate how greatly Caius music flourishes under Geoffrey Webber in the series of CDs he has recorded.

pp. 302 – 6 The lists of Masters and Presidents have been brought up to date in this reprint. On p. 304 it should have been noted that there is evidence that Lawrence Maptid (1546) and Hugh Glyn (1559) bore the title President before the statutes of Dr Caius (Venn, I, 29, 42).

Appendix 1

The Masters

For the dates from 1348 to 1559, see Hall and Brooke 1983; from 1559 to 1880, Venn, III, 30–145; from 1880–1976, above, chaps. 12–14.

Gonville Hall, 1349–1558

JOHN COLTON	1349 – c.1360/1
RICHARD PULHAM	Before 1366 – after 1394
WILLIAM SOMERSHAM	Before 1401 – 1416
JOHN RICKINGHALL	Before 1421 – 1426
THOMAS (ATTE) WOOD	1426 – 1456
THOMAS BOLEYN	c.1456 – 1471/2
EDMUND SHERIFFE	1472 – 1476/7
HENRY COSTESSY	c.1477 – 1483
JOHN BARLEY	1483 – 1504/5
EDMUND STUBB	1504/5 – 1513/14
WILLIAM BUCKENHAM	1513/14 – 1536
JOHN SKIPP	1536 – 1540
JOHN STYRMIN	1540 – 1552
THOMAS BACON	1552 – 1558 (and see below)

Gonville and Caius College, 1558–1976

THOMAS BACON	1558 – 1559
JOHN CAIUS	1559 – 1573
THOMAS LEGGE	1573 – 1607
WILLIAM BRANTHWAITE	1607 – 1619
JOHN GOSTLIN	1619 – 1626
THOMAS BATCHCROFT	1626 – 1649 (and see below)
WILLIAM DELL	1649 – 1660
THOMAS BATCHCROFT	(restored) 1660

ROBERT BRADY	1660 – 1700
JAMES HALMAN	1700 – 1702
SIR JOHN ELLYS	1702 – 1716
SIR THOMAS GOOCH, Bart.	1716 – 1754
SIR JAMES BURROUGH	1754 – 1764
JOHN SMITH	1764 – 1795
RICHARD BELWARD (formerly FISHER)	1795 – 1803
MARTIN DAVY	1803 – 1839
BENEDICT CHAPMAN	1839 – 1852
EDWIN GUEST	1852 – 1880
NORMAN FERRERS	1880 – 1903[1]
E. S. ROBERTS	1903[1] – 1912
SIR HUGH ANDERSON	1912 – 1928
J. F. CAMERON	1928 – 1948
SIR JAMES CHADWICK	1948 – 1958
SIR NEVILL MOTT	1959 – 1966
JOSEPH NEEDHAM	1966 – 1976
SIR WILLIAM WADE	1976 – 1988
PETER GRAY	1988 – 1996
NEIL MCKENDRICK	1996 –

1 Given as 1902 by a slip in Venn, VI, 507.

Appendix 2

The Presidents

Nicholas Shaxton is called President in Caius' *Annals*, p. 14, which may be a confusion with his office as President of Physwick Hostel (Venn, I, 19). Otherwise the President first appears in Caius' later years and in his statutes (Venn, III, 364, c. 31). He was appointed by the Master until 1904, and in early days, like other officers, normally, it seems, for a year at a time (see p. 137). But in the late 17th and 18th centuries it became in effect an office for life — or for as long as the President remained a fellow. In theory, the President's tenure under the statutes of 1860 lapsed at the Master's death or resignation, and when election by the General Meeting of fellows was introduced in 1904 (see Statutes) the sitting President, John Venn, was not subject to reelection until the Master's death in 1912. In practice he was reelected until his death. The term from 1904 to 1920 was 3½ years; since 1940, 4 years (see Statutes).

This list has been compiled by Dr Mark Buck (fellow, 1977—82). In several cases the office is not noted in Venn.

'Nom.' signifies that the Master's nomination was announced at a College Meeting on the day named.

JOHN TRACIE	was fellow 1569—73 and President for some time during that period (Venn, I, 65).
EDMUND HOWND	1573—1576 (Venn, I, 62).
RICHARD SWALE	occurs in 1582, and as 'nuper presidis' in 1589 (Venn, I, 85 and above, p. 88: *Annals*, p. 206): otherwise the Presidents of Legge's Mastership are difficult to trace and the office seems to have been vacant over the period 1609—36 (cf. the Bursars' Books).
THOMAS GOSTLIN	Nom. 28 May 1636 and again for a year on 25 January 1642 (*Gesta*; cf. Venn, I, 189—90).
JOSEPH LOVELAND	1643—1644 (Venn, I, 243). Vacant 1644—55 (see p. 137).
WILLIAM BAGGE	Nom. October 1655—1657 (*Gesta*; see pp. 137—40). Vacant 1657—1660.

JAMES WHEELER	Nom. 4 April 1660; ejected 1661 (*Gesta*; Venn, I, 376; see p. 135).
WILLIAM BLANCKS	Nom. 16 July 1661–1676 (*Gesta*; Venn, I, 204). Vacant 1676–9 (cf. Bursar's Books; Gostlin's Book as Bursar).
JOHN GOSTLIN	Nom. 22 July 1679–1705 (Venn, I, 369: his tomb in chapel gives his death as 1 Feb. 1704, i.e. 1705, after 25 years as President. He was alive on 12 Jan., *Gesta*).
JOHN LIGHTWINE	Nom. 21 February 1705–1729 (*Gesta*; cf. Venn, I, 441).
JAMES HUSBAND	Nom. 18 June 1729–1737 (*Gesta*; Venn, I, 524).
JOHN BERNEY	Nom. 15 August 1737–14 January 1738, when his fellowship finally expired (*Gesta*; Venn, II, 8). Vacant 1738–51 (Venn, III, 120–1; cf. Bursars' Books).
JAMES BURROUGH	Nom. 9 January 1751–1754: elected Master (*Gesta*; Venn, III, 126–9).
JOHN SMITH	Nom. 27 February 1754–1764: elected Master (*Gesta*; Venn, III, 129–32).
JOSHUA WHITE	Nom. 17 August 1764–1766 (*Gesta*; Venn, II, 48).
CHARLES CARVER	Nom. 21 October 1766–1767 (*Gesta*; Venn, II, 49 — where, however, his fellowship is said to cease at Michaelmas 1766).
JAMES HICKS	Nom. 11 April 1767–1769 (*Gesta*; Venn, II, 51).
BARTHOLOMEW EDWARDS	Nom. 15 October 1769–1782 (*Gesta*; cf. Venn, II, 64; he evidently retained the office till he resigned his fellowship. He occ. as 'Mr Edwards President' on 9 October 1782).
SAMUEL REEVE	Nom. 25 December 1782–1789 (*Gesta*; he committed suicide in 1789, Venn, II, 72).
RICHARD FISHER	(from 1791, BELWARD) Nom. 3 June 1790–1795: elected Master (*Gesta*; Venn, II, 82–3; III, 132).
THOMAS BURROUGHES	Nom. 28 October 1795–1797 (*Gesta*; Venn, II, 93).
MARTIN DAVY	Nom. 25 May 1798–1803: elected Master (*Gesta*; Venn, II, 114, where his nom. is given wrongly as 1795; III, 133–7).
JOHN BORTON	Nom. 31 May 1803–1805 (*Gesta*; Venn, II, 110).

RICHARD LUCAS	Nom. 29 October 1805 – 1812 (*Gesta; CUCal.*; cf. Venn, II, 113).
BENEDICT CHAPMAN	Nom. 1 June 1812 – 1819; Master 1839 – 52 (*Gesta; CUCal.*; Venn, II, 114 – 15; III, 137 – 40).
JEREMY DAY	Nom. 15 December 1819 – 1821 (*Gesta*; Venn, II, 119).
ROBERT WOODHOUSE	Nom. 30 October 1821 – 1823 (*Gesta*: Venn, II, 119 – 20). Vacant 1823 – 6 (*CUCal.*; Bursars' Books).
THOMAS TURNBULL	Nom. 30 June 1826 – 1835 (*Gesta*; cf. *CUCal.*; Venn, II, 158 gives 1848).
HAMNETT HOLDITCH	Nom. *c.* 18 March 1835 – 1867 (*Gesta*, an entry not precisely dated; Venn, II, 170; see above, p. 195).
B. H. DRURY	First occurs 21 February 1868 – 1875 (*Gesta*; Venn, II, 235).
A. G. DAY	First occurs 10 June 1875 – 1877 (*Gesta*; Venn, II, 262).
B. H. DRURY	Reappointed 19 October 1877 – 1894 (*Gesta*; Venn, II, 235).
E. S. ROBERTS	Nom. 17 January 1894 – 1903: elected Master (*Gesta*; Venn, II, 370; VI, 505 – 14; above, chap. 12).
J. VENN	Nom. 20 February 1903 – 1923 (*Gesta*; Venn, V, 5; for reelections, see General Meeting Minute Book 6 Oct. 1912, etc.).
E. J. GROSS	Elected 27 April 1923; died 1923 (General Meeting Min. Bk.; Venn, V, 11).
W. W. BUCKLAND	Elected 11 October 1923 – 1946 (General Meeting Min. Bk.; Venn, V, 29; VI, 5).
F. J. M. STRATTON	1946 – 1948 (cf. Venn, VI, 31).
E. K. BENNETT	1948 – 1956 (cf. Venn, VI, 50).
SIR RONALD FISHER	1956 – 1959 (cf, Venn, VII, 15).
JOSEPH NEEDHAM	1959 – 1966: elected Master (cf. Venn, VII, 26).
PHILIP GRIERSON	1966 – 1976 (cf. Venn, VII, 59).
M. J. PRICHARD	1976 – 1980 (cf. Venn, VII, 121).
W. J. MACPHERSON	1980 – 1992 (reelected 1984, 1988).
SIR SAM EDWARDS	1992 –

Appendix 3

Notes on the Changing Pattern of Schools, Courses and Careers in the late 19th and 20th Centuries

It would be interesting to plot the schools where Caians have been taught and the backgrounds from which they have sprung over recent generations, and to tabulate their courses and destiny; and I have been advised to try my hand at a table or tables to give some indications of the shifting pattern. Statistics are fashionable, and where they can be accurately presented and objectively interpreted they can be extremely interesting. Often, however, the evidence on which they are based, and their interpretation, are like quicksands. In the Middle Ages the Bible could be interpreted literally, allegorically, mystically and in other ways; and the mystical and allegorical interpretation of statistics is much affected by journalists and politicians, and a few historians. These tables are presented therefore with diffidence.

I have given my figures as averages over five-year periods, according to a reasonable custom; but this gives them a deceptive air of precision. I am well aware of the imprecisions on which they are based, and that I myself have made some small errors in counting, in spite of my best endeavours. The averages minimise my failings, but exaggerate the scientific nature of the enterprise.

I have chosen a scatter of dates as follows: 1886—90, when E. S. Roberts was securely established as tutor and the late 19th century distribution should be clear; 1907—11, to illustrate the situation before, not not too long before, the First World War; 1932—6, similarly placed to the Second, but also mostly after the worst of the depression of the early 30s; 1951—5, when the 1944 Education Act and post-war trends — including more state support — had had time to be felt; and 1967—71, well after the full establishment of universal student grants and the Robbins Report, but before the changes of the 70s.

APPENDIX 3

TABLE 1

Sons of Caians

The figures are based on the entries in Venn, II—VII, and relate to sons only — nephews and grandsons etc. are not included; and failure of information may somewhat depress the figures; but they are not likely to be seriously misleading.

Year	Average[1] total entry	Average yearly intake who were sons of Caians	Percentage
1886—90	63	3.2	5.1
1907—11	87.8	4.4	5.0
1932—6	100.2	10.2	10.2
1951—5	124.4	17	13.7
1967—71	126.8	9.2	7.3

It is interesting to observe that the first four years of women, 1979—82, included twelve daughters of Caians, among them Ann Conway (1982), a fourth generation Caian.

TABLE 2

Schools from which Caians have come

The pattern of English secondary schools has changed dramatically over the last hundred years; yet if the tables are to reveal anything there must be some measure of comparison. I have therefore chosen three categories, with shifting frontiers and meaning indeed, but with less shift than others one can choose — the Public Schools in the sense of boarding schools, from which a substantial fraction of Caians came in the late 19th and early 20th centuries, and about a quarter now; what used to be called the Public day schools, most of which were Direct Grant Schools between the 1940s and the 1970s, though many were already Independent; and the Grammar Schools and other Secondary Schools which do not readily fall under the second category, the majority of which (though with many exceptions) are now Comprehensive. The changes of recent years make real comparison very hazardous, but two points should be emphasised. The distinctions are not, and never have been, of educational or cultural merit; and recent changes have been so rapid and fundamental that no-one (save political prophets of right or left or centre) knows what the present pattern really is. I

1 Throughout these tables, 'average' means annual average.

315

have limited the first two categories to members of the Headmaster's Conference listed in G. Kalton, *The Public Schools* (London, 1966), pp. 143–5; and I have added appropriate Scottish schools to these categories. I have included 'mainly boarding' in 1; 'mainly day' in 2. I have left in my third category (mostly of grammar schools) the relatively small number of Comprehensive Schools — of which, for example, Quarry Bank at Liverpool has been a steady source of Caians — already established and sending students to Caius by 1971. Normally the last school only is counted; but I have not taken account of the eight (1.6 a year) in 1932–6 who came via the Royal Military Academy at Woolwich; or the one (0.2) from Sandhurst in 1955; or the one (0.2) who came via the Royal College of Music in 1970.

Annual Average of	Average total	Category 1 Annual average	%	2 Annual average	%	3 Annual average	%	Educated overseas	From another university	Educated privately	Not known
								(annual averages only)			
1886-90	63	27.2	43	13.2	20.1	14.6	23.2	4.2	2	0.4	0.4
1907-11	87.8	58.4	66.5	12	13.7	9	10.3	7	1	0	0
1932-6	100.2	56.8	56.7	10.2	10.2	22	22	8	2.8	0.4	0
1951-5	124.4	57.2	45.9	21	16.9	38	30.5	7.4	0.6	0.2	0
1967-71	126.8	26	20.5	33.6	26.5	65	51.3	2.0	$0.2(+0.8)^2$	0	0

2 This represents students educated at overseas universities, so already included in the previous column.

TABLE 3

Subjects studied

This table shows the courses taken by undergraduates who entered in these years. The first category mainly consists of those who took pass degrees, etc., but may include a few where the information is incomplete. The figures refer to courses taken, so that a man who took parts of two triposes will appear twice, and in earlier years the MB/BChir figures duplicate BA or Natural Sciences. (Medical students in earlier times either combined their medical studies with a pass BA or with a part of the Natural Sciences Tripos.) Thus the table inevitably gives an unbalanced view of the distribution of subjects: and it does not separate out the elements in pass degrees, nor the rich variety of disciplines and courses gathered under 'Natural Sciences'.

| | Annual averages of: — | | | | |
	1886–90	1907–11	1932–6	1951–5	1967–71
Ordinary or Pass BA	15	27.4	10.6	12.2	1
MB/BChir (now Medical Sciences)	11.6	9	16.4	18.6	18.2
Natural Sciences	17.2	17.2	26.8	40.2	27.4
Mathematics	5	5.2	5.2	5.4	15.6
Classics	7.4	5.4	6	4.2	3.2
Moral Sciences (now Philosophy)	0.4	0.6	0.2	0.8	1.8
Mechanical Sciences (now Engineering		3.6	7.8	10.4	12
Chemical Engineering					1.2
Electrical Sciences					1.4
Modern and Medieval Languages, etc.	1.4	3.4	11.2	13.4	12
History	0.6	4	10.4	9.4	8.8
Theology	0.4	0.8	0.2	1.4	0.2
Law	3.2	5.4	9.6	14.2	9.4
Economics		2.2	6.4	9	8.6
Semitic Languages (later Oriental Languages and Oriental Studies)	0.6	0.2	0.4	0	0.4
English			4.2	4	9.6
Archaeology and Anthropology			1.2	0.8	3.2
Music	0.2	0.2	0.2	1.8	3.8
Geography			1.8	2.8	0.8
Social and Political Sciences					4.8
Other[3]				0.4	3.4
No Degree	11.6	14	8.2	5.2	5.2

3 In 1951–5, veterinary sciences (total) 2, (average 0.4); in 1967–71 (*totals only*), agriculture 1; Anglo-Saxon, Norse and Celtic 2; architecture 4; computer science 4; history of art 3; land economy 3 (total 17, average 3.4)

TABLE 4

Father's Professions

The professions of parents are taken from the tutorial records as recorded in Venn, II—VII. They give much positive information about fathers, especially about the traditional professions which dominated the scene in the 1880s, but very little about the mothers. Many of the entries cannot be interpreted in a way which would satisfy a social scientist; and categorising by income group or class (whatever that now means) is impossible on this evidence. I have done some violence to a few entries to make them fit my categories, but in most cases where the profession does not fit readily into any of them I have put them under 'Other' and listed them below. The business entries are doubtless misleading, and the shifting numbers in various categories are probably as much due to changing fashion in labels as to changing patterns in business methods. The 14.8 per year of no known profession in 1886—90 no doubt included a number of men of means or gentlemen too grand to name their professions; later entries under this heading are more likely to be due to a failure in the forms. One category particularly attracts my notice: the decline of clerical fathers. This partly reflects economic decline, perhaps; but it is also partly balanced by the rise of the schoolmasters, for the clergy took a major share in teaching in the 19th century. Where a parent was both a teacher and reverend, however, I have by an arbitrary dispensation placed him among the teachers. For the rest, though the figures are interesting and suggestive, any substantial interpretation of them is mystical, unless they are set among larger and more precise statistics for the University and the country as a whole. But we seem to see in the 1880s an era in which it was the members of the traditional professions, medicine, the bar, the army and the Church, and business men, who had the means and will to send their sons to Caius; and in 1967—71 an age in which opportunity has come to be spread much more widely; and if we may interpret the period 1951—71 as reflecting a trend, we seem to move altogether into a new world of opportunity. But we can also understand a little, if we reflect on these figures, some of the reasons why competition for entry to Cambridge and Caius has become so intense in recent decades.

The figures are for undergraduate entry: for fellows and research students such figures would not be significant until very recent times — but the pattern through this century has been more varied than for undergraduates.

	Annual averages of:—				
	1886–90	1907–11	1932–6	1951–5	1967–71
Unspecified	14.8	4	3.6	2.4	7
Overseas (also included in categories below)	3	8	12	8	1.4
Accountants	0	0.8	1.8	3.4	4.4
Architects	0.8	0.8	0.2	0.8	1.2
Armed forces (Army, Navy, RAF)	1.8	2	6.8	5.6	2.8
Authors	0	0	0.2	0.2	0.6
Bankers, Bank managers	0	2	1.4	3.4	2.4
Bank cashiers, clerks	0	0.2	0	1	0.2
Builders, decorators, bricklayers	0	0	0.6	1.2	1
Business: manufacturers	3.4	9	7.6	4.8	0.8
merchants, shipowners	7.2	9	7.2	4.8	0.8
other business (directors, company secretaries etc.)	0.4	3.4	5.6	14	18
Science in business	0	0	0	0.4	2
Civil servants	0.8	1.4	2	5.6	7.6
colonial, Indian civil service etc.	1.6	2.2	2.4	2.4	0.6
Clergy (including all denominations, lay missionaries; church administrators)	11.2	9.4	5.8	2.8	0.8
Clerks	0	0.4	1.4	3.2	2.4
Diplomatic service	0	0.2	0.4	0.2	1.2
Engineers	1.4	5.2	7.2	9	13
Factory workers			1.2	0.6	2.4
Farmers	0	2.2	1.8	1.6	1.4
Foremen				1.2	1
Inspectors of taxes			0.2	0.8	0.8
Insurance	0	1.2	1.6	1.4	2.2
Joiners, carpenters	0	0	0.4	1.2	0.8
Journalists	0	0	0.2	0.4	1.2
Land, estate agents surveyors	0	1.8	0.8	2	0.8
Landowners, 'gentlemen'	0.2	5.8	2.2	0.4	0.2
Lawyers: barristers	1.4	1.6	2.6	2.2	0.4
solicitors	0.8	5	3.6	2.4	3.4
Local government	0	0.8	1	1	2.6
Merchant navy	0	0.4	0.6	0.4	0.2
Opticians	0	0	0.4	0.4	0
Physicians and surgeons (and dentists)	8	11.8	13.2	16.2	11.2

	Annual averages of:—				
	1886–90	1907–11	1932–6	1951–5	1967–71
Sales managers, supervisors, etc.	0	0	0.2	2.4	3.2
Schoolmasters	1.4	0.8	5.6	4.8	8.4
Shopkeepers	0	0.4	2	4.4	2.6
Stockbrokers	0	1.2	0.6	1.4	0
Tailors	0	0	0.6	0	0
University teachers, higher education and senior scientific research	0	1.2	3	5.2	6

Other — as follows:

(1 each except where a number is given — all numbers are totals):

1886–90: actor, artist, dock surveyor, MP, Rabbi, surveyor of customs

1907–11   none

1932–6   agent, artist, bus owner, buyers (2), cabinet maker, colliery salesman, commercial traveller, hairdresser, hotel waiter, newspaper proprietor, policeman, post office sorter, railway employee, railway manager, saddler, Trinity House pilot. A politician is also entered above under physicians.

1951–5:   actor, analytical chemist, bookbinder, buyer, clinic technician, commercial travellers (3), draughtsman, hairdressers (2), hotel proprietors (4), laundry proprietor, miners (2), motor mechanic, photo-engraver, post office officials (2), printers (3), publisher, railway employees (2), station masters (3), secretary of NFU, shipwright, veterinary surgeon

1967–71: amusement caterer, antique and art dealers (3), BBC, British Council, bus driver, car park attendant, communications officer, customs officer, deputy director of Water Research Association, draughtsmen (2), information officer, innkeeper, interior designer, landscape gardener, lens maker, librarian, marine pilot, ordnance surveyor, policeman, postman, sub-postmaster, prison officer, project manager, publisher, research administrator, saddler, school caretaker, secretary, secretary of football club, security officer, social worker, springsmith, stewards (2), storeman, taxi driver, technical representative, telecommunications supervisor, traffic warden, veterinary surgeon.

TABLE 5

The Professions of Caians

Since this table has to be based on material readily available in Venn, II—VII, it is less complete as the years go on; and too little had been gathered when VII was published to make a significant picture for 1967—71. Where more than one career has been followed, so far as possible what seems the main career has been counted. It is clear that the selection of years shortly before the two World Wars, and the lack of information for many of the 1930s and 1950s, has seriously distorted the picture. It may well be that there are more Caian diplomats, solicitors, and civil servants, for example, than the table would suggest. The slight dip in physicians etc. in 1907—11 may reflect a number of medical students who failed to complete their studies owing to the First World war. Those who joined the forces in the World Wars and later had a different career are noted twice.

| | Annual averages of:— | | | |
	1886—90	1907—11	1932—6	1951—5
Unknown	4.8	4.6	25.8	32.2
Overseas (some included in categories below)	7.4	5.6	7	8.6
None (mostly died young)	1.4	1	0	0
Accountants	0	0.6	0.2	1.6
Actors	0	0.2	0.2	0.4
Architects	0	0.2	0.4	0
Armed forces (including service in World Wars: see above. Figures in italics mean: died on active service)	1.4	64.2 (*12*)	27 (*8.4*)	2.2
Authors	0	0.4	0	0.2
British Council	0	0	0.4	0.4
Broadcasting	0	0	0.6	0
Business	3.6	8.6	7	20.6
Science in business	0.8	0.8	0.8	1.8
Civil servants	1	2.4	4	1
Colonian and Indian civil service	1	3.6	4.8	1.6
Clergy (including medical. missionaries)	7.6	4.2	1.8	3.6
Diplomatic service	0.2	0.4	1.4	0.4
Engineers	1	1.8	2.4	1.8
Estate agents, surveyors	0	0.8	0.4	0.8
Farmers	0	0.2	0.2	0.6

	Annual averages of:—			
	1886−90	1907−11	1932−6	1951−5
Insurance	0	0	0.4	1
Journalists	0	0	0.4	0.2
Lawyers: barristers	1.2	2.4	1.6	1.8
solicitors	4.2	1.8	3	2.2
Local government	0	0	0	0.6
Musicians	0.2	0.6	0.4	0.6
Physicians and surgeons	17.6	13.6	18.8	18.2
Schoolmasters	8.8	2.2	5.8	9.2
Stockbrokers	0	0.6	0	0
University teachers, higher education, senior research	2.8	4.4	5.8	15.4
Veterinary surgeons	0	0	0.2	0.4

Other — as follows: (1 each except where a number is given — all numbers are totals):

1886−90: botanist, librarian, organist and lay helper (in father's church), plantation overseer, secretary, traveller and sportsman

1907−11: hospital administrator, landowner, museum service, police, Red Cross, secretary of golf club, stage director

1932−6: inspector of taxes, MP (Iain Macleod); one was killed in the International Brigade in Spain

1951−5: art critic, charity organisers (2), in film industry, general manager, Malayan railways, inland revenue, MP, museum service (2), patent agent, publisher, town planners (2)

Bibliography and
List of Abbreviations

A few books and articles cited only once, e.g. short papers in the *Caian*, are not noted here. Books and documents from the College Archives − including *Absence* and *Redit Books, Bursars' accounts, Libri Rationales, Registrum Magnum* − are also not listed here.

Allen 1969 − 70   W. Allen, *Translating for King James*, Nashville, 1969; London, 1970.

Allen 1978   P. Allen, *The Cambridge Apostles: the early years*, Cambridge, 1978.

Annals, Venn,   *The Annals of Gonville and Caius College by John*
Annals   *Caius*, ed. J. Venn, Cambridge Antiquarian Society, 1904.

Annan 1951   N. Annan, *Leslie Stephen, his thought and character in relation to his time*, London, 1951.

Aston 1977   T. H. Aston, 'Oxford's Medieval Alumni', *Past and Present*, no. 74 (Feb. 1977), 3 − 40.

Aston, Duncan and   T. H. Aston, G. D. Duncan and T. A. R. Evans, 'The
Evans 1980   Medieval Alumni of the University of Cambridge', *Past and Present*, no. 86 (Feb. 1980), 9 − 86.

Aubrey   J. Aubrey, *Brief Lives*, ed. A. Clark, 2 vols., Oxford, 1898.

Baker 1970   R. St˙Barbe Baker, *My Life − My Trees*, London, 1970.

Ball 1889   W. W. Rouse Ball, *A History of the Study of Mathematics at Cambridge*, Cambridge, 1889.

Ball 1901   W. W. Rouse Ball, *A short account of the History of Mathematics*, London, 1901.

Battely 1745   J. Battely, *Antiquitates S. Edmundi Burgi ad annum MCCLXXII perductae*, Oxford, 1745.

Baxter 1696   *Reliquiae Baxterianae; or, Mr Richard Baxter's Narrative of.the most memorable passages of his Life and Times*, ed. M. Sylvester, London, 1696.

Bennet 1887   E. K. Bennet, *Historical Memorials of the College of S. John Evangelist Rushworth or Rushford, Co. Norfolk*, Norwich, 1887, reprinted from *Norfolk Archaeology*, X (1888 − sic), 50 − 64, 77 − 382.

BL	British Library, London.
Black 1984	M. H. Black, *Cambridge University Press, 1584–1984*, Cambridge, 1984.
Blomefield 1739	F. Blomefield, C. Parkin *et al.*, *An Essay towards a Topographical History of the county of Norfolk . . .*, 5 vols., Fersfield etc., 1739–75.
Blomefield 1750	F. Blomefield, *Collectanea Cantabrigiensia*, Norwich, 1750.
Bolton 1958	F. R. Bolton, *The Caroline Tradition in the Church of Ireland*, London, 1958.
Brady 1684	R. Brady, *An Introduction to the Old English History*, London, 1684.
Brady 1685	R. Brady, *A Complete History of England from . . . Julius Caesar unto the end of the reign of King Henry III . . .*, London, 1685.
Brady 1700	R. Brady, *A Continuation of the Complete History of England: containing the lives and reigns of Edward I, II and III and Richard the Second*, London, 1700.
Brooke 1957	C. N. L. Brooke, 'The earliest times to 1485', in *A History of St Paul's Cathedral*, ed. W. R. Matthews and W. M. Atkins, London, 1957, pp. 1–99, 361–5.
Brooke and Stewart 1983	[C. N. L. Brooke and B. H. I. H. Stewart], 'Philip Grierson's contribution to numismatics', in *Studies in Numismatic Method presented to Philip Grierson*, ed. C. N. L. Brooke, B. H. I. H. Stewart, J. G. Pollard and T. R. Volk, Cambridge, 1983, pp. ix–xiv.
Buck 1982	M. C. Buck, 'The Fellows' Betting Books', *Caian* 1982, pp. 42–51.
Buck 1983	M. C. Buck, *Politics, Finance and the Church in the reign of Edward II: Walter Stapeldon, Treasurer of England*, Cambridge, 1983.
Burgon 1839	J. W. Burgon, *The Life and Times of Sir Thomas Gresham*, 2 vols., London, 1839.
Buxton and Williams 1979	*New College Oxford, 1379–1979*, ed. J. Buxton and P. Williams, Oxford, 1979.
Caian	*The Caian* was first published in 1891 as a separate journal (see p. 255), and references up to July 1965 are by vol. and year; it was then amalgamated with the *Annual Record* and later references are by year of publication.

Caius, *Works*	*The Works of John Caius, M.D., . . .*, ed. E. S. Roberts, Cambridge, 1912 (works separately paginated; and see Venn 1912).
Carpenter 1936	E. Carpenter, *Thomas Sherlock, 1678—1761*, London, 1936.
Carpenter 1956	S. C. Carpenter, *Duncan-Jones of Chichester*, London, 1956.
Catto 1984	*The History of the University of Oxford*, ed. T. H. Aston, I, *The Early Oxford Schools*, ed. J. Catto, Oxford, 1984.
CC	*Cambridge Commemorated: an anthology of University Life*, ed. L. and H. Fowler, Cambridge, 1984.
CClR	*Calendar of Close Rolls* (Public Record Office, Texts and Calendars).
Chadwick 1959	O. Chadwick, *Mackenzie's Grave*, London, 1959.
Chadwick 1970	O. Chadwick, *The Victorian Church*, II, London, 1970.
Cheney 1973	C. R. Cheney, *Medieval Texts and Studies*, Oxford, 1973.
Chibnall 1963	A. C. Chibnall, *Richard de Badew and the University of Cambridge, 1315—1340*, Cambridge, 1963.
Clark 1900	J. W. Clark, *Old Friends at Cambridge and elsewhere*, London, 1900.
Clark 1901	J. W. Clark, *The Care of Books: an essay on the development of libraries from the earliest time*, Cambridge, 1901.
Clark 1964	G. N. Clark, *A History of the Royal College of Physicians of London*, I, Oxford, 1964.
Clark 1978	J. Clark, 'The Decline of Party 1740—1760', *English Historical Review*, XCIII (1978), 499—527.
Clark 1982	J. Clark, *The Dynamics of Change: the crisis of the 1750s and English party systems*, Cambridge, 1982.
Clark 1983	J. Clark, 'The Politics of the Excluded: Tories, Jacobites and Whig Patriots, 1715—1760', *Parliamentary History*, II (1980), 209—22.
Cobban 1969	A. B. Cobban, *The King's Hall within the University of Cambridge in the later Middle Ages*, Cambridge, 1969.
Cobban 1975	A. B. Cobban, *The Medieval Universities*, London, 1975.
Cobban 1976	A. B. Cobban, 'Decentralized teaching in the medieval English universities', *History of Education*, V (1976), 193—206.

Cobban 1980	A. B. Cobban, 'The medieval Cambridge colleges: a quantitative study of higher degrees to *c*. 1500', *History of Education*, IX (1980), 1–12.
Cobban 1982	A. B. Cobban, 'Theology and Law in the medieval colleges of Oxford and Cambridge', *Bulletin of the John Rylands Library*, LXV (1982), 57–77.
Cocke 1984	T. Cocke, *The Ingenious Mr Essex, Architect, 1722–1784* (Catalogue of an Exhibition at the Fitzwilliam Museum), Cambridge, 1984.
Cohen 1958	Lord Cohen of Birkenhead, *Sherrington, Physiologist, Philosopher and Poet*, Sherrington Lectures, IV, Liverpool, 1958.
Cole 1765–7	*The Bletchley Diaries of the Reverend William Cole, 1765–67*, ed. F. G. Stokes, London, 1931.
Colley 1977	L. Colley, 'The Loyal Brotherhood and the Cocoa Tree: the London organisation of the Tory Party 1727–60', *Historical Journal*, XX (1977), 77–95.
Colley 1982	L. Colley, *In Defiance of Oligarchy: The Tory Party 1714–60*, Cambridge, 1982.
Colvin 1978	H. M. Colvin, *A Biographical Dictionary of British Architects, 1600–1840*, London, 1978.
Constable 1964	G. Constable, *Monastic Tithes from their origins to the Twelfth Century*, Cambridge, 1964.
Cooper, *Annals*	C. H. Cooper, *Annals of Cambridge*, 5 vols. (V, ed. J. W. Cooper), Cambridge, 1842–1908.
Coote 1804	[C. Coote,] *Sketches of the Lives and Characters of eminent English Civilians . . .*, London, 1804.
Cosin 1869	*The Correspondence of John Cosin, D.D., Lord Bishop of Durham . . .* [ed. G. Ornsby], I, Surtees Society, 1869.
CP	*The Complete Peerage*, revised edn. ed. Vicary Gibbs *et al.*, 12 vols., London, 1910–59.
CPR	*Calendar of Patent Rolls* (Public Record Office, Texts and Calendars).
Crawley 1976	C. Crawley, *Trinity Hall: the history of a Cambridge College, 1350–1975*, Cambridge, 1976.
Cressy 1970	D. Cressy, 'The social composition of Caius College, Cambridge, 1580–1640', *Past and Present*, no. 47 (May 1970), 113–15.
Cressy 1972	D. A. Cressy, 'Education and Literacy in London and East Anglia 1580–1700', Cambridge PhD Thesis, 1972.

Cressy 1979   D. Cressy, 'School and College admission ages in seventeenth-century England', *History of education*, VIII (1979), 167–77.

Cruickshanks 1979   E. Cruickshanks, *Political Untouchables: the Tories and the '45*, London, 1979.

CSPD   *Calendar of State Papers, Domestic Series* (Public Record Office, Texts and Calendars).

CTPC   *Cambridge University Transactions during the Puritan Controversies of the 16th and 17th centuries*, ed. J. Heywood and T. Wright, 2 vols., London, 1854.

CUCal   *Cambridge University Calendar* (by year).

CUL   Cambridge University Library.

Cule 1969   J. Cule, 'A note on Hugo Glyn and the statute banning Welshmen from Gonville and Caius College', *National Library of Wales Journal*, XVI (1969–70), 185–91.

Cuming 1961   *The Durham Book*, ed. G. J. Cuming, Oxford, 1961.

Cuming 1982   G. J. Cuming, *A History of Anglican Liturgy*, 2nd edn., London etc., 1982.

Cuming 1983   G. J. Cuming, *The Godly Order: Texts and Studies relating to the Book of Common Prayer*, Alcuin Club Collections 65, London, 1983.

Curtis 1959   M. H. Curtis, *Oxford and Cambridge in transition 1558–1642*, Oxford, 1959.

Davis 1971   *Paston Letters and Papers of the Fifteenth century*, ed. N. Davis, I, Oxford, 1971.

De Visscher 1977   P. De Visscher, 'Lord McNair (1885–1975)', *Académie Royale de Belgique: Bulletin de la Classe des Lettres*, sér. 5, LXIII (1977), 414–22.

Dewar 1968   L. Dewar, *An Outline of Anglican Moral Theology*, London, 1968.

Dillistone 1974   F. W. Dillistone, *Charles Raven, Naturalist, Historian, Theologian*, London, 1974.

DNB   *Dictionary of National Biography* (reference by name).

Documents 1852   *Documents relating to the University and Colleges of Cambridge . . .*, published by direction of the [University] Commissioners, 3 vols., London, 1852.

Douglas 1951   D. C. Douglas, *English Scholars 1660–1730*, London, 1939, cited from the 2nd edn., 1951.

Dowling 1984   M. Dowling, 'Anne Boleyn and Reform', *Journal of Ecclesiastical History*, XXXV (1984), 30–46.

D'Oyly 1821	G. D'Oyly, *The Life of William Sancroft, Archbishop of Canterbury*, 2 vols., London, 1821.
DSB	*Dictionary of Scientific Biography*, ed. C. C. Gillespie, 16 vols., New York, 1970−80.
Emden	A. B. Emden, *A Biographical Register of the University of Cambridge to 1500*, Cambridge, 1963.
Emden, *Oxford*	*A Biographical Register of the University of Oxford to 1500*, 3 vols., Oxford, 1959.
Emmanuel statutes	*The Statutes of Sir Walter Mildmay Kt. . . . authorised by him for the government of Emmanual College founded by him*, ed. F. Stubbings, Cambridge, 1983.
Engel 1975	A. J. Engel, 'Emerging concepts of the academic profession at Oxford 1800−1954', in Stone 1975, I, 305−52.
Engel 1983	A. J. Engel, *From Clergyman to Don: The Rise of the Academic Profession in nineteenth-century Oxford*, Oxford, 1983.
ER	*Estates Record*, ed. E. J. Gross, in Venn, IV, part II (separately paged).
Fasti 1300−1541	J. Le Neve, *Fasti Ecclesiae Anglicanae 1300−1541*, revised edn., ed. J. M. Horn, B. Jones and H. P. R. King, London, 1962−7. See also Horn 1969, 1971, 1974.
Feingold 1984	M. Feingold, *The Mathematician's Apprenticeship*, Cambridge, 1984.
Ferguson 1976	J. P. Ferguson, *An Eighteenth Century Heretic: Dr Samuel Clarke*, Kineton, 1976.
Fletcher 1984	J. M. Fletcher, 'The Faculty of Arts', in Catto 1984, pp. 369−99.
Foxe	John Foxe, *Acts and Monuments*, cited from ed. S. R. Cattley, 8 vols., London, 1837−41.
Francis 1923	H. T. Francis, Memoir of John Venn, *Caian* XXXI (1922−3), 100−24, with additions by H. P. Stokes, J. N. Keynes and J. S. Reid, pp. 124−9.
Froissart	J. Froissart, *Chroniques*, ed. S. Luce *et al.*, 15 vols. so far, Société de l'Histoire de France, 1869−1975.
Fuller 1662	T. Fuller, *The History of the Worthies of England*, (I), London, 1662.
Gabriel 1955	A. L. Gabriel, *Student Life in Ave Maria College*, Notre Dame, 1955.
Gabriel 1962	A. L. Gabriel, *The College system in the 14th century universities*, Baltimore, 1962.
Garland 1980	M. M. Garland, *Cambridge before Darwin: the ideal of a liberal education, 1800−1860*, Cambridge, 1980.

Gaskell and Robson 1971	P. Gaskell and R. Robson, *The Library of Trinity College, Cambridge: a short history*, Cambridge, 1971.
Geison 1978	G. L. Geison, *Michael Foster and the Cambridge School of Physiology*, Princeton, 1978.
Gransden 1982	A. Gransden, *Historical Writing in England*, II, c. *1307 to the early sixteenth century*, London and Henley, 1982.
Gray 1921	J. M. Gray, *A History of the Perse School, Cambridge*, Cambridge, 1921.
Green 1957	V. H. H. Green, *Oxford Common Room, a study of Lincoln College and Mark Pattison*, London, 1957.
Green 1964	V. H. H. Green, *Religion at Oxford and Cambridge*, London, 1964.
Grierson 1959	P. Grierson, 'Gonville and Caius College' in *VCH Cambs*, III (1959), 356 – 62.
Grierson 1960	P. Grierson, 'The monetary reforms of 'Abd Al-Malik . . .', *Journal of Economic and Social History of the Orient*, III (1960), 241 – 64 = Grierson, *Dark Age Numismatics*, Variorum Reprint, 1979, no. XV.
Grierson 1978	P. Grierson, 'John Caius' Library', in Venn, VII, 509 – 25.
Grisbrooke 1958	W. J. Grisbrooke, *Anglican Liturgies of the 17th and 18th centuries*, London, 1958.
Guest 1838	Edwin Guest, *A History of English Rhythms*, 2 vols., London, 1838.
Guest 1883	Edwin Guest, *Origines Celticae*, 2 vols., London, 1883.
Gunning	H. Gunning, *Reminiscences of the University, Town and County of Cambridge, from the year 1780*, 2 vols., London and Cambridge, 1854.
Hackett 1970	M. B. Hackett, *The Original Statutes of Cambridge University*, Cambridge, 1970.
Hall and Brooke 1983	C. Hall and C. N. L. Brooke, 'The Masters of Gonville Hall', *Caian* 1983, pp. 43 – 50.
Hans 1951	N. Hans, *New trends in Education in the 18th century*, London, 1951.
Hardy 1852	T. Duffus Hardy, *Memoirs of the Right Honourable Henry Lord Langdale*, 2 vols., London, 1852.
Hargreaves-Mawdsley 1963	W. N. Hargreaves-Mawdsley, *A History of Academical Dress in Europe until the end of the eighteenth century*, Oxford, 1963.

Hector and Harvey 1982	*The Westminster Chronicle 1381–1394*, ed. L. C. Hector and B. F. Harvey, Oxford Medieval Texts, 1982.
Hennell 1979	M. Hennell, *Sons of the prophets*, London, 1979.
Highfield 1964	J. R. L. Highfield, *The early rolls of Merton College, Oxford*, Oxford Historical Society, New Series 18, 1964 for 1963.
Highfield 1984	J. R. L. Highfield, 'The early colleges' in Catto 1984, chap. 6, pp. 225–63.
Hill 1965	C. Hill, *The Intellectual Origins of the English Revolution*, Oxford, 1965.
Hinnebusch 1951	W. A. Hinnebusch, *The Early English Friars Preachers*, Rome, 1951.
Horn 1969, 1971, 1974	John Le Neve, *Fasti Ecclesiae Anglicanae 1541–1857*, revised edn., I–III, ed. J. M. Horn, London, 1969, 1971, 1974. See also *Fasti*.
Howarth 1978	T. E. B. Howarth, *Cambridge between Two Wars*, London, 1978.
Hughes 1960	H. Trevor Hughes, *The piety of Jeremy Taylor*, London, 1960.
Hunter 1981	M. Hunter, *Science and Society in Restoration England*, Cambridge, 1981.
Hutchins	J. Hutchins, *The History and Antiquities of Dorset*, 3rd edn., 4 vols., Westminster, 1861–74.
James 1899	M. R. James, *A Descriptive Catalogue of the Manuscripts in the Library of Peterhouse*, Cambridge, 1899.
James 1905	M. R. James, *A Descriptive Catalogue of the Western Manuscripts in the Library of Queens' College, Cambridge*, Cambridge, 1905.
James 1907–8	M. R. James, *A Descriptive Catalogue of the Manuscripts in the Library of Gonville and Caius College*, 2 vols., Cambridge, 1907–8, with *Supplement* (cited as III), 1914.
James 1909–12	M. R. James, *A Descriptive Catalogue of the Manuscripts in the Library of Corpus Christi College, Cambridge*, 2 vols., Cambridge, 19[09–]12.
Jean le Bel	*Chronique de Jean le Bel*, ed. J. Viard and E. Déprez, Société de l'Histoire de France, 2 vols., Paris, 1904–5.
Jordan 1959	W. K. Jordan, *Philanthropy in England, 1480–1660*, London, 1959.
Jordan 1960	W. M. Jordan, *The Charities of London, 1480–1660*, London, 1960.

Jordan 1961   W. K. Jordan, *The Charities of Rural England, 1480 – 1660*, London, 1961.

Kearney 1970   H. Kearney, *Scholars and Gentleman: Universities and Society in pre-industrial Britain, 1500 – 1700*, London, 1970.

Kenyon 1972   J. P. Kenyon, *The Popish Plot*, London, 1972.

Kersting and Watkin 1984   A. F. Kersting and D. Watkin, *Peterhouse, 1284 – 1984: An Architectural Record*, Cambridge, 1984.

Keynes 1949   G. Keynes, *The portraiture of William Harvey*, Cambridge, 1949.

Keynes 1966   G. Keynes, *The life of William Harvey*, Oxford, 1966.

Knowles and Grimes 1954   D. Knowles and W. F. Grimes, *Charterhouse*, London, 1954.

Lake 1982   P. Lake, *Moderate puritans and the Elizabethan church*, Cambridge, 1982.

Leader 1981   D. R. Leader, 'The Study of Arts in Oxford and Cambridge at the end of the Middle Ages', PhD Thesis, University of Toronto, 1981.

Leader 1983   D. R. Leader, 'Grammar in late-medieval Oxford and Cambridge', *History of Education*, XII (1983), 9 – 14.

Leedham-Green 1981   E. Leedham-Green, 'A catalogue of Caius College library, 1569', *Transactions of the Cambridge Bibliographical Society*, VIII, i (1981), 29 – 41.

Lewis 1855   J. Lewis, *The Life of Dr John Fisher*, 2 vols., London, 1855.

Liscombe 1980   R. W. Liscombe, *William Wilkins 1778 – 1839*, Cambridge, 1980.

Lovatt 1983 – 4   R. Lovatt, 'The first century of the College Library', *Peterhouse Record 1983 – 4*, pp. 60 – 73.

Lytle 1975   G. F. Lytle, 'Patronage patterns and Oxford Colleges c. 1300 – c. 1530', Stone 1975, I, 111 – 49.

McAdoo 1949   H. P. McAdoo, *The Structure of Caroline Moral Theology*, London, 1949.

McConica 1975   J. McConica, 'Scholars and Commoners in Renaissance Oxford', Stone 1975, I, 151 – 81.

McNair 1969   A. McNair, 'Why is the doctor in "The Merry Wives of Windsor" called Caius?', *Medical History*, XIII (1969), 311 – 39.

Macself   A. J. Macself, *Plant Portraits and Plant Names*, II, L – Z, London, n.d.

Maddison, Pelling and Webster 1977   *Essays on the Life and Work of Thomas Linacre c. 1460 – 1524*, ed. F. Maddison, M. Pelling and C. Webster, Oxford, 1977.

Maitland 1898   F. W. Maitland, *Township and Borough*, Cambridge, 1898.

Matthews 1934   A. G. Matthews, *Calamy Revised*, Oxford, 1934.

Matthews 1948   A. G. Matthews, *Walker Revised*, Oxford, 1948.

Mayor 1911   *Cambridge under Queen Anne*, ed. J. E. B. Mayor, Cambridge, 1911.

Mitchell 1976   S. J. D. Mitchell, *Perse: A History of the Perse School 1615—1976*, Cambridge, 1976.

Mommsen, *Digesta*   *Digesta Iustiniani Augusti*, ed. T. Mommsen, 2 vols., Berlin, 18[66—]70.

Monk 1830   J. H. Monk, *The Life of Richard Bentley, D.D.*, London and Cambridge, 1830 (cited from 1 vol. edn.).

Morey 1978   A. Morey, *The Catholic subjects of Elizabeth I*, London, 1978.

Morgan 1975   V. Morgan, 'Cambridge University and "The Country" 1560—1640', Stone 1975, I, 183—245.

Morgan 1984   V. Morgan, 'Country, Court, and Cambridge University, 1558—1640: A Study in the Evolution of a Political Culture', PhD Thesis, University of East Anglia, 1984.

Mullinger 1873   J. B. Mullinger, *The University of Cambridge from the earliest times to the Royal Injunctions of 1535*, Cambridge, 1873.

Mullinger 1884   J. B. Mullinger, *The University of Cambridge from the Royal Injunctions of 1535 to the accession of Charles the First*, Cambridge, 1884.

Mullinger 1911   J. B. Mullinger, *The University of Cambridge, volume III, from the election of Buckingham to the Chancellorship in 1626 to the decline of the Platonist movement*, Cambridge, 1911.

Mynors 1963   R. A. B. Mynors, *Catalogue of the Manuscripts of Balliol College, Oxford*, Oxford, 1963.

Needham 1954—   J. Needham *et al.*, *Science and Civilisation in China*, I— , Cambridge, 1954— .

Needham 1976   Interview with Joseph Needham, *Caian* 1976, pp. 34—49.

Newsome 1961   D. Newsome, *Godliness and Good Learning*, London, 1961.

Nias 1951   J. C. S. Nias, *Gorham and the Bishop of Exeter*, London, 1951.

Nutton 1979   V. Nutton, 'John Caius and the Linacre tradition', *Medical History*, XXIII (1979), 373—91.

Okey 1930   T. Okey, *A Basketful of Memories*, London, 1930.

O'Malley 1955	C. P. O'Malley, 'The relations of John Caius with Andreas Vesalius and some incidental remarks on the Giunta Galen and on Thomas Geminus', *Journal of the History of Medicine*, X (1955), 147 – 72.
Osmond 1913	P. H. Osmond, *A Life of John Cosin, bishop of Durham 1660 – 1672*, London etc., 1913.
Outhwaite 1982	R. B. Outhwaite, *Inflation in Tudor and early Stuart England*, 2nd edn., London, 1982.
Overton 1902	J. N. Overton, *The Non-Jurors*, London, 1902.
Pantin 1955	W. A. Pantin, *The English Church in the Fourteenth Century*, Cambridge, 1955.
Pantin 1959	W. A. Pantin, 'Chantry priests' houses and other medieval lodgings', *Medieval Archaeology*, III (1959), 216 – 58.
Pantin 1964	W. A. Pantin, 'The halls and schools of medieval Oxford: an attempt at reconstruction', in *Oxford Studies presented to Daniel Callus*, Oxford Historical Society, 1964 for 1959 – 60, pp. 31 – 100.
Parker 1853	*Correspondence of Matthew Parker*, ed. J. Bruce and T. T. Perowne, Parker Society, 1853.
Parry 1926	R. St John Parry, *Henry Jackson O.M.*, Cambridge, 1926.
Peters 1980	Interview with Sir Rudolf Peters, *Caian*, 1980, pp. 31 – 50.
Pevsner 1970	N. Pevsner, *The Buildings of England: Cambridgeshire*, 2nd edn., Harmondsworth, 1970.
Pevsner, *Willis*	N. Pevsner, *Robert Willis*, Smith College Studies in History 46, Northampton, Mass., 1970.
Pocock 1950 – 2	J. G. A. Pocock, 'Robert Brady, 1627 – 1700. A Cambridge historian of the Restoration', *Cambridge Historical Journal*, X (1950 – 2), 186 – 204.
Pocock 1957	J. G. A. Pocock, *The Ancient Constitution and the feudal law*, Cambridge, 1957.
Pollard 1911	*Records of the English Bible*, ed. A. W. Pollard, London, 1911.
Porter 1958	H. C. Porter, *Reformation and Reaction in Tudor Cambridge*, Cambridge, 1958 (corr. repr. 1972, with new preface and bibliography).
Porter 1979	H. B. Porter, *Jeremy Taylor Liturgist* (Alcuin Club 61), London, 1979.
Powicke 1931	F. M. Powicke, *The medieval books of Merton College*, Oxford, 1931.
PRO	London, Public Record Office.

Raven 1947   C. E. Raven, *English Naturalists from Neckham to Ray*, Cambridge, 1947.

RCHM Cambridge *Royal Commission on Historical Monuments, England, City of Cambridge*, 2 parts, London, 1959.

Reid 1912   J. S. Reid, Memoir of E. S. Roberts, with appendices by R. St J. Parry and Col. Edwards, *Caian, Special Number* (1912).

Richmond, Hall H. Richmond, C. Hall and A. Taylor, 'Recent Dis-
and Taylor 1981 coveries in Gonville and Caius College', *Proceedings of the Cambridge Antiquarian Society*, LXXI (1981), 95–110.

Roach 1959   J. P. C. Roach, 'The University of Cambridge', in *VCH Cambs*, III (1959), 150–312.

Roberts 1887–1905 E. S. Roberts, *An Introduction to Greek Epigraphy*, 2 vols. (II with E. A. Gardner), Cambridge, 1887–1905.

Roberts 1934   Mrs Ernest Stewart Roberts, *Sherborne, Oxford and Cambridge*, London, 1934.

Robson 1967   R. Robson, 'Trinity College in the Age of Peel', *Ideas and Institutions of Victorian England, Essays in Honour of George Kitson Clark*, ed. R. Robson, London, 1967, pp. 312–35.

Robson and   R. Robson and W. F. Cannon, 'William Whewell,
Cannon 1964   F.R.S.', *Notes and Records of the Royal Society of London*, XIX (1964), 168–91.

Romilly   *Romilly's Cambridge Diary, 1832–42*, ed. J. P. T. Bury, Cambridge, 1967.

Rothblatt 1968/81 S. Rothblatt, *The Revolution of the Dons: Cambridge and Society in Victorian England*, London, 1968, cited from the edn. of Cambridge, 1981.

Rothblatt 1975 S. Rothblatt, 'The student sub-culture and the examination system in early 19th century Oxbridge', Stone 1975, I, 247–303.

Royal Commission *Reports of the Royal Commission: Report of Her*
1852, 1874, 1922 *Majesty's Commissioners appointed to inquire into the . . . University and Colleges of Cambridge, 1852; Report of the Commissioners appointed to inquire into the property and income of the Universities of Oxford and Cambridge, 3 vols., 1874; Royal Commission on Oxford and Cambridge Universities. Report, 1922.*

Russell 1977   E. Russell, 'The influx of commoners into the University of Oxford before 1581: an optical illusion?', *English Historical Review*, XCII (1977), 721–45.

Salter 1925   F. R. Salter, *Sir Thomas Gresham*, London, 1925.

Schneider 1928   G. A. Schneider, *A Descriptive Catalogue of the Incunabula in the Library of Gonville and Caius College*, Cambridge, 1928.

Scott 1927   A. Claughton Scott, *The History of the Caius College Boat Club 1827–1927*, Cambridge, 1927 (= *Caian* XXXV).

Scott 1981   M. A. Scott, *The Perse School for Girls, Cambridge: the first hundred years, 1881–1981*, Cambridge, 1981.

Scrivener 1884   F. H. A. Scrivener, *The Authorized Edition of the English Bible (1611)*, Cambridge, 1884.

Searle 1864   W. G. Searle, 'Catalogue of the Library of Queens' College in 1472', *Cambridge Antiquarian Society Communications*, II (1864), 165–93.

Searle 1867–71   W. G. Searle, *The History of Queens' College of St Margaret and St Bernard in the University of Cambridge, 1446–1662*, Cambridge Antiquarian Society, 2 vols., Cambridge, 1867–71.

Serpell 1983   M. F. Serpell, 'Sir John Fenn, his friends and the Paston Letters', *Antiquaries Journal*, LXIII (1983), 95–121.

Sheriffe, Sheriffe's Evidences, Caius Library MS 706/692 (see pp. 39–40).

Sherrington 1957   C. E. R. Sherrington, *Charles Scott Sherrington 1857–1952: Memories*, privately printed, 1957.

Simon 1963   J. Simon, 'The social origins of Cambridge students, 1603–1640', *Past and Present*, no. 26 (Nov. 1963), 58–67.

Smith 1849   J. J. Smith, *A Catalogue of the Manuscripts in the Library of Gonville and Caius College, Cambridge*, Cambridge, 1849.

Squibb 1977   G. D. Squibb, *Doctors' Commons: A History of the College of Advocates and Doctors of Law*, Oxford, 1977.

Srawley 1917   J. H. Srawley, Memoir of H. B. Swete in *Caian* XXVI (1916–17), 101–12.

Stanwood and   P. G. Stanwood and A. I. Doyle, 'Cosin's Correspon-
Doyle 1969   dence', *Trans. of the Cambridge Bibliog. Society*, V, i (1969), 74–8.

Stanwood and   J. Cosin, *A Collection of Private Devotions*, ed.
O'Connor 1967   P. G. Stanwood and D. O'Connor, Oxford, 1967.

Statutes   *Statutes of Gonville and Caius College*: for the statutes of Gonville, Bateman and Caius, see Venn, III, 341–89; for the printed statutes between 1860–

1926, I have used the complete copy, with amend-
ments, in the Bursary (and see Index, s.v. Gonville
and Caius College, Statutes).

Stephen 1885   L. Stephen, *Life of Henry Fawcett*, 2nd edn., London, 1885.

Stephenson and   M. Stephenson and Z. N. Brooke, 'Notes on an early
Brooke 1933   deed with the seal of Edmund Gonville', *Caian* XLI
(1933), 59–65.

Stevenson 1902   W. H. Stevenson, 'Dr Guest and the English Conquest of South Britain', *English Historical Review*,
XVII (1902), 625–42.

Stokes 1924   H. P. Stokes, *The mediaeval hostels of the University
of Cambridge*, Cambridge Antiquarian Society,
1924.

Stone 1975   *The University in Society*, ed. L. Stone, 2 vols.,
Princeton, 1975.

Stranks 1952   C. J. Stranks, *The Life and Writings of Jeremy
Taylor*, London, 1952.

Streeter 1931   B. H. Streeter, *The Chained Library*, London, 1931.

Strype 1711   J. Strype, *The Life and Acts of Matthew Parker*, London, 1711.

Strype 1812   J. Strype, *Memorials of Thomas Cranmer*, edn. of
Oxford, 1812, with corrections by Henry Ellis.

Stubbings 1983   F. Stubbings, *Forty-Nine Lives: an anthology of portraits of Emmanuel men*, Cambridge, 1983. See also
Emmanuel Statutes.

Sturdy 1981   J. V. M. Sturdy, Memoir of G. W. H. Lampe, *Caian*
1981, pp. 63–9.

Swete 1918   *Henry Barclay Swete: A Remembrance*, London,
1918.

Tanner 1917   *The Historical Register of the University of Cambridge*, ed. J. R. Tanner, Cambridge, 1917.

Thompson 1935   A. Hamilton Thompson, 'William Bateman, bishop
of Norwich, 1344–1355', *Norfolk Archaeology*,
XXV (1935), 102–37.

Thomson and Porter   *Erasmus and Cambridge*, ed. D. F. S. Thomson and
1963   H. C. Porter, Toronto, 1963.

Toulmin Smith 1980   *The Itinerary of John Leland . . . parts IV and V*, ed.
L. Toulmin Smith, London, 1908.

Trevor-Roper 1973   H. Trevor-Roper, *Christ Church Oxford: the portrait
of a College*, Oxford, 1973.

Turner 1975   R. S. Turner, 'University Reforms and professional
scholarship in Germany 1760–1806', Stone 1975, II,
495–531.

Twigg 1983   J. D. Twigg, 'The University of Cambridge and the English Revolution, 1625 – 1688', University of Cambridge PhD Thesis, 1983.

Ullmann 1967   W. Ullmann, 'A decision of the Rota Romana on the benefit of clergy in England', *Studia Gratiana*, XIII (1967), 457 – 89 = Ullmann, *The Papacy and Political Ideas in the Middle Ages*, Variorum Reprints, London, 1976, no. IX.

VCH Cambs, III   *The Victoria History of the Counties of England: A History of the County of Cambridge and Isle of Ely*, III, ed. J. P. C. Roach, London, 1959. See also Roach. Other vols. of *VCH* are also referred to.

Venn   *Biographical History of Gonville and Caius College*, I – III, ed. J. Venn, Cambridge, 1897 – 1901; IV, Part I, ed. E. S. Roberts, Part II, *Chronicle of the College Estates (ER)*, ed. E. J. Gross, 1912; V, ed. F. E. A. Trayes, 1948; VI, ed. F. J. M. Stratton, 1958; VII, ed. M. J. Prichard and J. B. Skemp, 1978.

Venn 1887   J. and S. C. Venn, *Admissions to Gonville and Caius College . . . March 1558/9 to June 1678 – 9*, London and Cambridge, 1887.

Venn 1891   *The Register of Baptisms, Marriages and Burials in St Michael's Parish, Cambridge (1538 – 1837)*, ed. J. Venn, Cambridge, 1891.

Venn 1895   J. Venn, 'Some personal reminiscences of J. R. Seeley', *Caian* IV (1894 – 5), 164 – 70.

Venn 1901   J. Venn, *Caius College* (University of Cambridge, College Histories), London, 1901.

Venn 1904   J. Venn, *Annals of a clerical family*, London, 1904.

Venn 1912   J. Venn, 'John Caius', repr. with corrections and additions, from Venn, III, in Caius, *Works*, pp. 1 – 78.

Venn 1913   J. Venn, *Early Collegiate Life*, Cambridge, 1913.

Venn, *Alumni*   *Alumni Cantabrigienses*, ed. J. and J. A. Venn, 2 Parts (to 1751, 1752 – 1900), 4 + 6 vols., Cambridge, 1922 – 54.

Venn, *Annals, see Annals.*

Wade 1977   Interview with Professor H. W. R. Wade, *Caian* 1977, pp. 32 – 42.

Walker 1970   E. C. Walker, *William Dell: Master Puritan*, Cambridge, 1970.

Walsh 1981   K. Walsh, *Richard FitzRalph in Oxford, Avignon and Armagh*, Oxford, 1981.

Warr 1979   Hedley Warr, *Memoirs*, Cheltenham, 1979.

Warren's Book   *Warren's Book*, ed. A. W. W. Dale, Cambridge, 1911.

Watt 1981   J. A. Watt, 'John Colton, Justiciar of Ireland (1382) and Archbishop of Armagh (1383–1404)' in *England and Ireland in the late Middle Ages*, ed. J. Lydon, Dublin, 1981, pp. 196–213.

Westcott 1905   B. F. Westcott, *A general view of the history of the English Bible*, 3rd edn., rev. W. A. Wright, London, 1905.

Wharton 1691   *Anglia Sacra*, ed. H. Wharton, 2 vols., London, 1691.

Whiston 1730   W. Whiston, *Historical Memoirs of the Life of Dr Samuel Clarke*, London, 1730.

Whitteridge 1959   William Harvey, *De motu locali animalium*, ed. G. Whitteridge, Cambridge, 1959.

Whitteridge 1964   *The Anatomical Lectures of William Harvey*, ed. G. Whitteridge, Edinburgh, 1964.

Wigglesworth 1976   V. B. Wigglesworth, *Insects and the Life of Man*, London, 1976.

Wigglesworth 1979   Interview with Sir Vincent Wigglesworth, *Caian*, 1979, pp. 31–44.

Willis 1845, 1 and 2   R. Willis, *The Architectural History of Canterbury Cathedral*, London, 1845; 'The Architectural History of Winchester Cathedral', in *Proceedings at the Annual Meeting of the Archaeological Institute of Great Britain and Ireland at Winchester, September, 1845*, London, 1846, repr. by Friends of Winchester Cathedral, 1980.

Willis 1869   R. Willis, *The Architectural History of the conventual buildings of the monastery of Christ Church, in Canterbury*, London, 1869.

Willis and Clark   R. Willis and J. W. Clark, *The Architectural History of the University of Cambridge and of the Colleges of Cambridge and Eton*, 4 vols., Cambridge, 1886.

Winnett 1958   A. R. Winnett, *Divorce and remarriage in Anglicanism*, London, 1958.

Winstanley 1922   D. A. Winstanley, *The University of Cambridge in the Eighteenth Century*, Cambridge, 1922.

Winstanley 1935   D. A. Winstanley, *Unreformed Cambridge: a study of certain aspects of the University in the Eighteenth Century*, Cambridge, 1935.

Winstanley 1940   D. A. Winstanley, *Early Victorian Cambridge*, Cambridge, 1940.

Winstanley 1947   D. A. Winstanley, *Later Victorian Cambridge*, Cambridge, 1947.

Wordsworth 1877   C. Wordsworth, *Scholae Academicae*, Cambridge, 1877.

Wormald and Wright *The English Library: Studies in its History before*
1958   *1700*, ed. F. Wormald and C. E. Wright, London, 1958.

Wormell 1980   D. Wormell, *Sir John Seeley and the uses of History*, Cambridge, 1980.

Yates 1978   T. E. Yates, *Venn and Victorian Bishops abroad*, London, 1978.

Young 1967   F. G. Young, *Darwin College 1963—66, and the University of Cambridge*, Cambridge, 1967.

Index

The numbers in italics refer to *plates*. Most references to the College have been gathered under Cambridge, Gonville and Caius College. With place-names counties are given as they were before the changes of the 1970s. The following abbreviations are used:

b   bursar
f   fellow
h f   honorary fellow
M   Master
p   president
t   tutor

'Chancellor' means chancellor of the University of Cambridge.

'Abd al-Malik, 299
Abel, 52
Aberdeen, Lord, 192
Abergwili, canon of, 39
Abraham, 88
Abrahams, Harold, 259, 261
Adamson, William, f, 128, 132, 135
advowsons, 159 – 61
agricultural depression (1870s), 227, 252, 266
Aiguillon, 1
Alabaster, Thomas, 53 – 4
Albert, prince, chancellor, 191 – 2
Albon, Edmund, f, 32n.
Alcock, John, bishop of Ely, 45
Alderson, Sir Edward Hall, f, 200, 207, 213, 288
Alderson, Samuel, f, t, 207
Aldus, 105n.
Allbutt, Sir Clifford, Regius Professor of Physic, f, 219, 238
Allen, John, f, 108 – 9; Thomas, f, 138
Amherst, Lord, 186
Amiens, Treaty of, 198
Anderson, Sir (H. K.), f, 254, 257; M, 241, 243 – 4, 248, 260 – 7, 269 – 70, 281, 296, 310; and James Chadwick, 270 – 1

Anderson, Lady, 250; Maisie, 307 – 8
Andrewes, Lancelot, 111, 113
Anne (Boleyn), queen, xii, 27, 49 – 51, 56, 73
Anne, queen, 159
Antwerp, 60
Apollodorus, 211
Apostles, the, 190
Archer, T. W., 212
Argentein, John, Provost of King's, 48; *see also* Sheriffe
Arians, 154 – 5
Aristophanes, 211
Armagh, archbishops of, *see* Colton, FitzRalph
Arminians, 110
Arras, Congress of, 26
Ashdon (Essex), 161, 213
Askew, Anne, 53
Astle, Mary, f, 279
Aston, T. H., 41
Athanasian Creed, 154
Aubry, John, 94, 126
Augustine, St, 73, 117
Austen, Jane, 101, 184 – 5; *Emma*, 200; *Mansfield Park*, 102
Avignon, and papal court, 5, 18 – 19, 21

Babbage, Charles, 195
Bacon, Francis, 197
Bacon, Thomas, M, 51, 59, 63 – 4, 68, 309; his brother, 51
Badger, Dr Bayham, 197
Bagge, William, f, t, p, 128, 131 – 40, 311
Baldus, 109
Balfour, A. J., 220
Balsham, Hugh of, bishop of Ely, 9
Bancroft, Richard, archbishop of Canterbury, 107
Banffshire, Caian from, 207
Bangor, bishop of, see Sherlock
Bankes, Mr, 193
Banner, Anne, Mrs Guest, 225
Barbary pirates, 157
Barber, Robert, 146 – 7
Barber, Thomas, 146 – 7
Bardi, Adriano dei, 33
Barham (Suffolk), 186
Barker, Edmund, f, 132 – 3, 135n.
Barker, William, f, 50
Barley, Barly, John, f, M, and rector of St Michael Coslany, Norwich, xii, 40, 309
Barley, William, 32n.
Barnham, 90 – 1
Barnstaple (Devon), 108
Baronius, Cardinal, 106, 147
Barrett, William, f, 92 – 3
Bartolus, 109
Basel, Council of, 27
Batchcroft, Thomas, f, t, M, 110, 121 – 4, 126 – 7, 132, 141, 145, 309; ex-Master, 130
Bateman, William, bishop of Norwich, formerly archdeacon of Norwich and dean of Lincoln, founder, 3 – 6 passim, 13 – 18, 22, 45; as dean, 5, 18; as founder of Trinity Hall, 6, 11 – 13; his statutes, see Cambridge, Gonville and Caius College
Bath, earls of, 116
Battely, John, 177
Batty, Dr, 197
Bauer, Lord (Peter T.), f, 272n, 299
Baxter, Richard, 129, 130
Beaufort, Edmund, 27
Beaufort, Lady Margaret, 17, 40, 43, 45, 46
Becke, Katherine, half-sister of Stephen Perse, and her husband William Becke, 101

Bedford, duke of, 38
Belfast, Queen's University, 274
Bell, Ingress, 253
Belward, Richard, formerly Fisher, f, p. 188 – 9, 312; M, 188 – 9, 194, 210, 310
Bendall, Cecil, f, 234
Bennett, E. K. (Francis), f, Senior Tutor, p, 251, 256n., 271, 273 – 4, 285, 313; his sermon, 293
Bensly, R., 225n
Bentham, Jeremy, 197, 200
Bentley, Richard, Master of Trinity, archdeacon of Ely, Regius Professor of Divinity, 127, 153, 163 – 9 passim, 174, 176; his son, 166; his grandson, 166
Berkeley, Comyns, 257; fund, 252
Berkshire, earl of, 121
Bernard, St, 106, 250
Berney, John, f, p, 169, 305
Bertram, Sir Thomas and Lady, 102
Betts, William, 49n.
Beverley, John, f, 34
Beza, 90, 93
Bible, 104 – 6; Authorised version, 104 – 5; Apocrypha in, 104 – 5; Vulgate, 106; biblical critics, 230 – 1
Bickersteth, Henry, Lord Langdale, f, 186, 196 – 203, 208 – 9, 288; 9c; as Master of the Rolls, 196, 200
Bilney, Thomas, 48 – 9, 52
Bincombe (Dorset), 160, 183
Binski, P., 67n., 215n., 216n.
Birmingham, bishop of, see Montefiore
Bismarck, 282
Blackall, Samuel, 185n.
Blackburn, Mark, 298
Black Death, 1, 12, 45
Blaeu's Atlas, 153
Blanckes, William, f, p, 133, 204, 312
Blofield (Norfolk), 292
Blois, château, 216
Blomefield, Francis, 4, 6, 153, 177 – 9, 288; on Caius chapel, 172 – 3
Blomfield, C. J., bishop of London, 201
Boethius, MS of, 25
Bois, John, 104
Boleyn, Anne, see Anne
Boleyn, Thomas, M, 16, 27, 32n., 39, 49, 309; his brother the Lord Mayor, 27
Bologna, 27
Bonaventura, St, 106

Booth, Bothe, Hamond, 16, 39
Booth, Bothe, John, bishop of Exeter, 39
Booth, Bothe, Laurence, Master of Pembroke, bishop of Durham, archbishop of York, 39, 46, 64
Booth, Remigius, f, 90
Booth, Bothe, William, archbishop of York, 39
Borton, John, p, 312
Bost, Henry, 27
Boston (Lincs), 234
Bottisham, Nicholas, f(?), 23 – 4, 31
Boult, John, f, 138 – 9
Bourgchier, Thomas, cardinal, archbishop of Canterbury, 27
Bourne, James, 182n.
Boxall, John, 61
Boyle lectures, 154
Bracknell, Lady, 67
Bradford, Samuel, Master of Corpus and vice-chancellor, bishop of Carlisle, 165
Brady, Edmund, 145
Brady, Mrs Jane or Jean, 69, 146, 248
Brady, Robert, M, Regius Professor of Physic, 126, 128, 131, 141 – 2, chap. 8, 310; early life, 141, 145; as historian, xii, 143 – 5, 214, 288; as professor, 114, 141, 145, 147; as royal physician, 115, 141, 146; his death, 159; his legacy, 160, 172
Branthwaite, William, M, 104 – 10, 113 – 14, 116, 129, 153, 309; as vice-chancellor, 109 – 10; his library, 36, 58n., 105 – 6
Branthwaite, William (II), 139
Brassie, Robert, provost of King's, vice-chancellor, 63
Bratton Fleming (Devon), 151, 160 – 1
Bridges, John, 107
Bridges Commission (Cambridge), 228
Brink, Charles, f, 279, 299
Brinkley, John, f, Professor of Astronomy, Dublin, bishop of Cloyne, 185 – 7
Bristol, 130, 147; bishopric of, 166, and see Gooch
British Association, meeting in 1862, 230
Bromhead, Sir Edward, 196
Brook, Charles, 280
Brooke, Dorothea, 125

Brooke, M. Z. and N. S., 131n.
Brooke, Zachary (d. 1788), 162, 176
Brooke, Zachary N. (d. 1946), xv, 205n., 245 – 6, 282, 288, 295, 297; on William Bagge, 131 – 40
Browne, John, f, t, 110 – 11, 114
Bruce, the Hon. George, 299
Bucer, Martin, 51
Buck, G. M., f, 237n.
Buck, M. C., f, 244; Appendix by, 311 – 13
Buckden (Hunts), 110
Buckenham, Nicholas, 29
Buckenham, William, f, M, rector of St Michael Coslany, Norwich, xii, 29, 48 – 9, 309; as vice-chancellor, 48
Buckingham, duke of, chancellor, 121
Buckland, W. W., f, senior tutor, p, Regius Professor of Civil Law, 235 – 7, 247, 271, 280, 288, 313
Budapest, 299
Buddhist studies, 218n.
Bullen, Air Vice-Marshal Reginald, f, Senior Bursar, 253n., 299
Bullough, Edward, f, 243; his wife, 243
Bunyan, John, 101, 130
Burdett, Sir Francis, 200
Burgate (Suffolk), 122n.
Burghley, Lord (William Cecil), chancellor, Secretary of State, Lord Treasurer, 47, 82, 84, 87 – 8, 89n., 91 – 3, 104, 162; and Caius' foundation, 59 – 61; and Caius' troubles, 70 – 3
Burney, Charles, 157n.
Burnham Wyndhams (Norfolk), 62
Burrough, Sir James, f, t, p, M, xii; earlier career and as architect, 170 – 2, 177; as esquire bedell, 174; t, 175, 178, 182; p, 170, 312; M, 161, 170, 173 – 4, 175, 310; as vice-chancellor, 173 – 4
Burroughes, Thomas, p, 312
Burton, Edward, f, 92
Bury St Edmund's (Suffolk), 65, 99, 177
Butts, William, 49 – 50, 56 – 7, 70, 73; 13a
Byng, Dr, vice-chancellor, 76

Cabold, Thomas, f, 32n.
caduceus, 63 – 4; 3a
Caesar, 58
Cain, 52

CAIUS, John, f, M, founder, chap. 4; his life, 55 – 60, 78; as f, xii, 48 – 59; and Norwich, 84; and Physwick Hostel, 28; at Padua, 57, 123

and the College, as founder, xi, 12, 41 – 2, 45, 52, 61 – 4; as M, 64, 70 – 8, 309; and Sir J. Chadwick, 270 – 1; and Legge, 84; troubles, 70 – 7; his *Annals*, 56, 60, 63, 66; on T. Bacon, 51; his buildings, 14, 65 – 7; his caduceus, 63 – 4; *3a*; his fellowships and scholarships, 62, 210; grant of arms, 64; matriculation register and sources of Caians, 16, 80, 86; his portrait, 251; *2*; his salver, 188; his statutes *see* Cambridge, Gonville and Caius College; and the Trapps, 95; and women, 69

as physician, and medical tradition, 31, 46, 62, 82, 94 – 5, 115, 187, 288; and College of Physicians, 59 – 60, 62 – 5

his library, 37, 72; his works, as antiquary, 10, 23 – 4, 28 – 9, 74 – 5, 144, 288; on Cambridge, 75; on dogs, 75; *De Libris Propriis*, 58; on natural science, 58

his tomb, 55, 67, 73, 78, 122; *6*; his Birthday Party, 251

Caius, Thomas, 74

Calais, 1 – 2

Calvin, Calvinism, 90, 93, 105

Cam, river, 9, 255

Camborne, Stephen, 136, 160 – 1

CAMBRIDGE, City, *passim*; Blomefield on, 177; Cambridge men at Caius, 155; MPs for, 127; and Stephen Perse, 99 – 101, 103

churches and parishes in, Great St Mary's, 9, 42, 45, 123, 133, 226; Holy Trinity, 124, 221; St Barnabas', 252; St Benet's, 22, 100; St Edward's, 100, 221; St Giles, 194n.; St Michael's, 33, 100, 146, 253; *21*; St Paul's, 252; St Sepulchre, Round Church, 226; religious houses, chaplaincies, etc., Austin Friars, 100; Barnwell priory, 10; Blackfriars, 243; Dominicans (medieval), 7, 104; Fisher House, 293; St John's Hospital, 45; St Radegund's nunnery, 10

gilds, 13, 45

places, streets in, Barnwell, 32, 62, 100, 251 – 2; Barnwell Gate, 45;

Barton Rd, 151; Chesterton, 100; Christ's Pieces, 204; Fenners, 252; Foule Lane, 24; Free School Lane, 10, 12 – 13, 22, 100; Glisson Rd, 252; Gonville Place, 32, 225n.; Gresham Rd, 225n., 252; Guest Rd, 252; Harvey Rd, xii, xiii, 32, 225, 252, 275; Henney Lane, 14; 'High St', 14, 45; Hobson's Conduit, 100; King's Ditch, 45; Lyndewode Rd, 32, 252; Mackenzie Rd, 252; Maids Causeway, Newmarket Rd, 100 – 1; Market Place, 51, 268; Mill Rd, 252; Mortimer Rd, 32, 225n., 252, 275; Newnham, 32; Newnham Grange, 279; Parker's Piece, 221, 225n., 252; Queen's Rd, 253, 275; Rose Crescent, 253; School of Pythagoras, 9; Scroope Terrace, 32, 225n.; Senate House Passage, 65; Sidgwick Avenue, 275; Trinity Hall Lane, 14; Trinity Lane, 14, 24 – 5, 65, 166; Trinity St, 14; West Rd, 32, 275; Willis Rd, 252; Wollaston Rd, 252; Worts Causeway, 192

schools, Leys School, 245; Perse School (Boys), 100 – 1, 155, 185, 193, 202 – 3, 248; Perse Girls' School, 235, 248

CAMBRIDGE, Colleges, Christ's, 17, 45, 90, 181n., 184; Master, *see* Carey, Raven; Churchill, 277n.; Clare Hall, later College, 10, 45, 86, 107, 129, 178, 180, 286; Clare Hall, 277; Corpus Christi, 5, 6, 11n., 12 – 14, 22, 49, 86, 192 – 3, 208; Master, 175, *and see* Maptid, Parker; Darwin, 277; Downing, 189, 192 – 3, 208; Emmanuel, 60, 84, 92, 96, 104 – 5, 107, 129, 168, 181n., 246; Master, *see* Chaderton, Sancroft; Fitzwilliam, 277n.; Girton, 216, 235, 248, 286; God's House (later Christ's), 12, 44.

CAMBRIDGE, GONVILLE AND CAIUS COLLEGE, formerly GONVILLE HALL, *passim*; alumni, the 'greater Caius', x, 25, 259, 287, 301; annual gathering, 256; professions of, 156, 321 – 2, and of fathers, 318 – 20; schools of, 314 – 16, sons of, 308, sources of, *see* East Anglia, Norfolk, Suffolk, and other counties

archives, etc., *absence books*, 200; accounts, 102, 139; *Annals*, 95, 97,

109, 114 – 15 *and see* Caius, John; *Exiit and redit books*, 145 – 6; *Gesta*, 134 – 5; matriculation register, 80 – 4, 86, 140; *Registrum Magnum*, 128, 135; seal, 11, 18, 62

benefactors, *passim*, esp. 257 – 8, *and see* Bateman, Berkeley, Brady, Branthwaite, Caius, Camborne, Davy, Drosier, Frankland, Gonville, Legge, Perse, Salomons, Tapp, Teichman, Trapps, Wendy, Wortley; commemoration of benefactors, 125, 244, 294

buildings, 302 – 3; Barraclough's, 152, 208, 214, 217; Caius Court, 65 – 7, 83, 306; *5*; chambers, 21 – 2, 118, 138 – 9, 156; *15*; chapel, 14th – 15th cent., 14, 22 – 4, 72n.; 16th – 17th cent., 63, 66, 78 – 80, 112 – 113, 122 – 3; 18th cent., 172 – 3, 181; 19th – 20th cent., 221, 231 – 2, 288, 290 – 5; *6 – 8, 9a – b*; compulsory chapel, 290; organ, 216 – 17, 289, 294; *7*; combination room (formerly parlour), 25, 53, 184 – 5, 255; panelled, 24, 253, 257; *22 – 3*; fellows' garden, 32, 209, 253; Finella, 253; Gates of Honour, Humility and Virtue, 21, 55, 65 – 7, 79, 108, 212, 217, 295; *Frontispiece, 1, 5, 24*; Great Gate, 65, 151; *18*; Gonville Court, chap. 2 *passim*, esp. 29, 64 – 7, 80n., 172 – 3, 249; *4*; hall (15th cent.), 23, 25, 184, 220; (1853 – 4), 215, 220, 254; *17*; Harvey Court, xii, 32, 253, 275 – 6, 300; *19*; JCR, 254, 295; laboratories, 232, 253, 295; Legge and Perse buildings, 21, 80, 83, 101, 109, 138, 208, 220; library (old), 19, 21, 25 – 7, 33 – 7, 54, 62, 77, 132, 135, 153, 178; *22*; (1853 – 4 and Monro), 214 – 15, 249, 254; (1996), 302 – 3; Master's lodge, 24, 28, 38, 66, 69, 70, 166, 211; *16*; Newnham Cottage, 192, 194n.; Physwick Hostel, 24, 28 – 9, 33, 53, 61, 83, 311, *and see* Fiswick; St Margaret's Hostel, 24; St Michael's (and St Mary's) Court, 253, 268 – 9; *21*; Tree Court, 65, 80, 151, 193, *and see* Waterhouse

Clubs: Amalgamated, 255; Boat Club and boathouse, ix, 190, 205, 206, 241, 254 – 5, 287, 294 – 5; cricket, 254; other sports, 221 – 2; other clubs, 255; Co-optimists, 262 – 3; Music Club,

261; Scales Club, 243 – 4, 288; Shadwell Society, 273; Sherrington Society, xiii

College Council, Governing Body, senior fellows, 96 – 8, 117 – 18, 137, 227, 235, 256, 268, 271 – 3, 279; General Meeting of fellows, 228, 271 – 3, 279

Fellows and officers: bursars, 100, 102 – 4, 139, 152, 168, 195, 227, 235, 251 – 3, 260, 265 – 7, 272; chaplain, 92 – 3; dean, 152, 183, 185, 235, 243, 281, 290 – 4; lay dean, 242; directors of studies, 229; fellows, senior, *see above under* Coll. Council; junior, 96 – 8, 128; Frankland, 96 – 8, 100; Perse, 98, 100, 124, 202 – 3, 252; Master, 9, 17 – 19, 38 – 40, 47 – 51, *and passim*, esp. 100, 173, 227, 235 – 6, 287; list, pp. 309 – 10; president, 70, 170, 173, 271, 311; list, 311 – 13; professorial fellows, 236, 245 – 7; registrary, 81, 137, 139; steward of the manors, 237; tutors, 81, 83, 86, 99, 118, 134, 142, 229; senior tutor, 227, 235 – 6, 241, 274, 287

Finance and estates, 102 – 3, 126, 134, 138, 251 – 3, 265 – 7; *and see* benefactors *above*

Staff, 248, 287; bedmakers' party, 248 – 50; butler, 155, 248; cook, 147, 248

Statutes: Gonville's 11 – 12, 17, 30, 32; Bateman's, 16 – 17, 30, 32, 63, 68, 108, 169; Caius', xi, 67 – 70, 75 – 7, 97, 102, 108, 133, 137, 192, 205, 226, 311; of 1860, 223 – 5, 311; 1882, 227 – 8; 1897, 260; 1904, 227, 235; 1920, 227 – 8; 1926, 265; texts of, 335 – 6

Subjects studied and taught, in Gonville Hall, arts, 12, 19, 30 – 5 *passim*; law, canon and civil, 14, 19, 23, 25 – 7, 29 – 35 *passim*; medicine, 12, 14, 19, 23, 29 – 35 *passim*; theology, 14, 19, 25, 27, 29 – 35 *passim*; in Gonville and Caius College, Anglo-Saxon, 317n.; archaeology and anthropology, 317; architecture, 317n.; biology, 257; botany, 257; chemistry (incl. biochemistry), 186 – 7, 242, 261; classics, 234, 237, 280, 317; economics, 317; engineering, mechanical sciences, 196, 238, 257, 317;

English, 244 – 5, 280, 317; genetics, 242, 297 – 8; geography, 317; history, 237, 245 – 7, 257, 282 – 3, 288, 297, 317; history of art, 317n.; law, 257, 280, 288, 295, 317; mathematics, 92, 186, 189, 194 – 5, 226, 237 – 8, 297 – 8, 317; medicine (and physiology etc.), 186, 197, 225, 238 – 42, 257, 280, 287, 295 – 6, 317; modern languages, 243, 273, 317; music, 90, 243 – 4, 317; natural sciences, 280, 317; numismatics, 298; oceanography, 242; philosophy (moral sciences), 317; physics, 242, 269 – 70, 276; social and political sciences, 317; theology, 186, 243, 288; veterinary science, 317n.; zoology, 242.

Other themes: alliance with Brasenose, 267 – 8; the *Caian*, 255; Catholics, recusants, in Caius, 75, 87 – 92, 173, 292n.; celibacy, 68 – 9, 223 – 7; college livings, 159 – 61; dedication to Annunciation, 2, 13; foundation, chap. 1; and foundation of Darwin College, 277; gown, 205; Jews in, 257, 292n.; religion in, 8 – 9 and *passim*, esp. 230 – 2, 290 – 4; siege (1838), 262; student numbers and statistics, 207, 314 – 22; women in, 248 – 51, 286, admission of women, 260, 278 – 9, 302, 308

CAMBRIDGE, cont. (Colleges, cont.)
Jesus, 45, 47, 77, 86, 88, 216, 235, *and see* Sterne; Jesus gun, 261 – 3; King's College, 12, 22, 27, 44 – 5, 107, 118 – 19, 129, 178, 284; Chapel, 42, 45, 171 – 2; gate, 191; library, 36; Provost, *see* Argentein, Brassie; senior fellows, 97; and Wilkins, 192 – 3, 208; King's Hall (later Trinity), 10 – 11, 24, 37, 42, 44 – 5, 53; wardens, 27, 40, *and see* Redman; Lucy Cavendish, 277n.; Magdalene, 128, 180, 284; Michaelhouse (later Trinity), 24, 45, 53; New Hall, 277n.; Newnham, 248, 286; Pembroke, 10, 22, 25 – 7, 216; and Laurence Booth, 39, 64; Peterhouse, 9 – 10, 33, 36 – 7, 91, 113, 178; Master, *see* Cosin, Law, Wren; Queens', 33, 36n., 44, 46, 47, 66, 107, 224n.; presidents, *see* Fisher, May, Venn; librarian, 206n.; Robinson, 277, 279, 300; St Catharine's, 178; Masters, 138, 189, *and see* Sandys, Sherlock;

St Edmund's House, 277n.; St John's, 17, 44, 70n., 82 – 3, 104 – 5, 168, 189 – 90, 207, 221, 277, 282, 288; Long Gallery, 46; Master, *see* Whitaker; senior fellows, 97; Sidney Sussex, 224n.; Trinity, foundation and 16th cent.; 29, 44 – 5, 47, 53, 61, 86 – 7, 93; 17th cent., 104 – 5, 118 – 9; Newton at, 152 – 3, 157; 18th – 20th cents., 178, 180, 183, 189 – 90, 199, 200, 221, 238, 261, 277, 284; Great Court, 24, 83; Nevile's Court, 83, 85, 157; New Court, 192, 208; Gates, 24, 66, 157; library, 153, 215; Masters, *see* Bentley, Nevile, Redman, Whewell, Whitgift; Trinity Hall, 6, 11, 13, 15 – 16, 22, 36n., 220; 'amicable concord' with Gonville Hall, 13; and celibacy, 224 – 5; Wolfson, 277n.

Clubs: Boat Club and boat race, 190, 209, 221; other sports, 221

Departments and buildings: Arts School, 219; Cavendish Laboratory, 232; Downing Site, 219; Fitzwilliam Museum, 298; Geological Museum, 219; Old Schools, 42, 45n., 171 – 4; Regent House, 29, 171; Senate House, 171 – 2; University Library, 34, 42, 141, 213, 215, 264

Officials and bodies: Caput, 210 – 11; chancellors, 10 – 11, 17, 205, 227, *and see* Albert, Booth, Buckingham, Burghley, Cromwell, Devonshire, Fisher, Holland, Manchester, Newcastle, Rickinghall, Rotherham, Salisbury, Somerset, Suffolk; Council of the Senate, 211n.; esquire bedells, 100, *and see* Gunning; General Board, 264; Heads of Houses, 9, 68, 70, 134, 165, 264; High Steward, 175; librarian, *see* Moore; preachers, 43; proctors, 91, 131; professors, 191, 207, 228; Cavendish, 232; Dixie, 246; Italian, 243; Lady Margaret, 43, *and see* Brooke; Regius, 43; Regius of Divinity, 43, 154, *and see* Bentley, Lampe, Raven, Watson; of Hebrew, *see* Cook; of Physic, 198 *and see* Brady, Glisson, Gostlin, Green; Senate, 166; vice-chancellors, 64, 71, 91, 100 – 1; 165, 172, *and see* Brassie, Byng, Cameron, Gooch, Legge, Whitgift; Vice-Chancellor's Court, 85, 99

Subjects, Triposes and Faculties: astronomy, 181, *and see* Smith; Classics Tripos, 191, 219; study of Greek, 48; Hebrew, 48; humanist studies, 55 – 9, 82; law, 82, 84 – 6; mathematics, 128; Mathematics Tripos, 157, 181, 191, 219; medicine, 82, 197 – 8; Medical Faculty, 108; Moral Sciences (philosophy) Tripos, 91, 219, 233; Natural Sciences Tripos, 191, 219; ordinary, pass degree, 207, 219; *and see* Caius, J., *and* Gonville and Caius College

Other themes: antiquity of, 75; university in 14th – 15th cent., chaps 1, 2; 1450 – 1550, 41 – 7; in 16th, chaps 3 – 5; in 17th, chaps 6 – 8, esp. 132 – 4; in 18th, chap 9; in 19th – 20th, chaps 10 – 14; and celibacy, 68 – 9, 224 – 6; chambers for students, 21 – 2; hall and hostel, 41; and royal court and government, 227; regents, 42 – 3; tutors, 42 – 3, 228; *and see* coaches, Gonville and Caius College; women in, 277 – 9, 284, 286

Cambridgeshire, Caians from, 86, 140; Perse's debtors in, 98

Camden's *Britannia*, 120

Cameron, J. F., f, t, b, M, 250; as t, 267; as b, 265, 267; as M, 238, 250, 267 – 9, 272 – 3, 310; and Heacham, 212; as vice-chancellor, 250, 268

Cameron, Mrs (Elfrida Sturge), 224, 240, 249 – 51, 267

Cameron, Jane (Mrs Deas), 291

Canossa, 282

Cantaber, king, 75

Canterbury, archbishop of, 170, *and see* Bancroft, Bourgchier, Chichele, Cranmer, Grindal, Islip, Laud, Morton, Parker, Pole, Runcie, Sancroft, Sheldon, Ufford, Warham; vicar general of, 74; cathedral, 205; dean, *see* Nevile; deanery, 84n.; King's School, 93

Carey, Valentine, Master of Christ's, dean of St Paul's, 92, 101, 110

Carlisle, bishop of, *see* Bradford, Laws, Goodwin

Carmen Caianum, 244

Caroline, queen, formerly Princess of Wales, 155, 164n.

Carpenter, S. C., dean of Exeter, 291

Carr, Lord, 259

Carroll, Lewis, 228n.

Carstone, Richard, 196 – 7, 199

Carter, John, 32n.

Cartwright, Thomas, 87

Carver, Charles, f, p, 312

Casey, John, f, 277

Cassin, Henry, 182n.

Cassiodorus, 57

Castle Hedingham (Essex), 59

Catherine, St, 18

Catherine of Aragon, queen, 49

Catholics, Roman, 82, 88 – 92, 123, 156, 292n.; Cosin's controversies with, 111

Cave, William, 148

Cecil, *see* Burghley, Salisbury

celibacy, *see* Cambridge, Gonville and Caius College

Celsus, 58

Chaderton, Laurence, Master of Emmanuel, 89n., 90, 105, 107, 110, 113

Chadwick, Sir James, f, M, 242, 259; as professor at Liverpool, 270; as Nobel laureate, 270; as M, 269 – 76, 310; his wife (Aileen Stewart-Brown), 270

Chamberlayne, Edward, 178 – 9

Chambord, château, 216

Champeneys, Geoffrey, 27

Chancellors, Lord, 160, *and see* Elwyn-Jones, Thurlow

Chancery, and court of, 99, 160, 172, 176, 183, 189, 200; Master in, 86, 88

chantries, 7 – 8, 32, *and see* Rushford

Chapman, Benedict, f, t, p, M, as t, 199, 207; as p, 313; as M, xii, 192, 212 – 13, 249, 310

Charles I, king, 94, 121, 132; wife, *see* Henrietta Maria

Charles II, king, 143, 146

Charlestown, Carolina, 182

Charterhouse school, 245n.

Chartres, Bernard of, xiv

Chatteris (Cambs), 161

Chaucer's Boethius, 25

Chenonceau, château, 216

Chester, 70

Chesterton, G. K., 292

Chichele, Henry, archbishop of Canterbury, 26

Chicheley, Henry, 140; Thomas, 140

Chichester, and Gooch, 172; archdeacon of, *see* Doket; bishop of, *see* Rickinghall; cathedral chapter, 25;

canon of, 211, *and see* Gooch; dean, *see* Sherlock

China, 186, 218, 281; Chinese Academy of Sciences, 277; Chinese People's Republic, ambassador of, 277, 300

Chungking, British Embassy at, 268n.

Church, Robert, f, 90, 92

CICCU, 293

Cicero, 105, 117, 180

Cîteaux, 250

Civil War, 101, 156

Clark, J. W., 204–5

Clark, Jonathan, 126n., 150n., 154n., 162n., 164n., 174n.

Clarke, G., architect, 253n.

Clarke, John (I), f, 157

Clarke, John (II), 154–5

Clarke, Samuel, 153–5, 288; Whiston's *Life*, 152

Clarke, William, f, 71, 74

Clavius, on Euclid, 126

Clayton, Charles, f, t, 208, 218–21, 226, 229, 290

Clement VI, Pope, 5

Clements, John, 73

Clere, Elizabeth, 29, 31

Clough, Miss B. A., 264

Cloyne, bishop of, *see* Brinkley

Clynt, Henry, 25; John, f, 25

Clynt, Mary, 25

coaches, tutors, private, 208, 219–20

Cobban, A. B., 261

Colchester (Essex), 115

Cole, William, 6, 164, 167–8, 174, 183

Collier, Jeremiah or Jeremy, 147, 150, 288

Colton, John, of Terrington, M, xi–xii, 11, 18–19, 21, 23, 30, 38, 276, 309; career in Ireland and as archbishop of Armagh, 19n.

Colvin, H. M., 193

Compton, Henry, bishop of London, 164

Congreve, 150

Coniston (Lancs), 197

Constable, Luke, 146

Constantinople, 169

Conway, Ann, 315

Conway, Geoffrey, 259, 261n., 262

Cook, S. A., f, Regius Professor of Hebrew, and his trust, 252, 256n., 281

Cooke, Thomas, f, 108, 126

Copperfield, David, 85

Cornwall, archdeacon of, *see* Marke

Cosin, John, f, 101, 106, 110–16 *passim*, 118, 120–1, 184, 288; as canon of Durham, 111; as Master of Peterhouse, 111, 122, 124; in France, 111; as bishop of Durham, 112; and Sancroft, 148

Costessy, Henry, M, fellow of King's Hall, Master of Rushford, 28, 40, 309

Cotton, Sir John, 164

Cotton, Sir Robert, 144

Cowell, E. B., professor of Sanskrit, 234

Cranmer, Thomas, archbishop of Canterbury, 47

Creed, J. M., 288

Creighton, Mandell, 224n.

Cressy, David, 81

Crick, F., h f, 260

Crome, Edward, 49

Crome, Walter, f, 34

Cromwell, Henry, 65

Cromwell, Oliver, 127, 129–30, 134, 228

Cromwell, Thomas, chancellor, 47–9

Croppe, Thomas, 32n.

Crowcher, John, f, 25

Crowfoot, J. W., f, 213–14

Crowley, Robert, 53–4

Croxley (Herts), 62

Cruso, Aquila, f, 114

Cudworth, Ralph, 129, 134

Cumberland, earl of, 92

Cushing, Harvey, 240

Curtis, M. H., 84

Dacre, Lord, 259

Dade, family, 147, 250; John, f, 147

Dalai Lama, 186

Danbury, Elizabeth, 15

Darwin, Charles, 190, 230; centenary, 296; Medal (Royal Society), 242

Darwin, Sir George, 277

David, 88

Davis, Norman, 177n.

Davy, Charles (I), 185n.

Davy, Charles (II), 185

Davy, Martin, f, t, p, M, as t, 187, 198; as p, 187, 210, 312; as M, 187, 189–212 *passim*, esp. 208–12, 249, 310; as physician, 198, 211, 288; as vice-chancellor, 198, 210–11; his death, 212; his Trust, 212, 223, 251; 13d

Davy, Mrs (Anne Stevenson), 211
Davys, Simon, 86
Day, A. G., f, p, 313
Day, Jeremy, f, p, 313
Deane, Andrew, f, 49
Deas, Henry T., f, 273, 291
De la Pole, Geoffrey, 28, 33; Humphrey, 22, 28, 33
Dell, William, M, 69, 94, 127 – 31, 132, 137, 140, 152, 159, 309; his wife, 131
DeMorgan, Augustus, 195
Dennison, S. R., f, vice-chancellor of Hull, 274
Denver (Norfolk), 128, 146, 160, 172
Dereham, Richard, f, Warden of King's Hall, 30n., 40
Descartes, Cartesian philosophy, 154
Despenser, Henry, bishop of Norwich, 23
Dethick, Henry, f, 71, 74
Devon, 80; Caians from, 108 – 9, 155
Devonshire, 7th Duke of, as chancellor, 232
Dickens, *Bleak House*, 183, 196 – 7, 199; *David Copperfield*, 85
Dioscorides, 58
Dixie, Sir Wulstan, 60
Doket, John, archdeacon of Chichester, 27
Domesday Book, and Dr Brady, 144
Donne, J., 125
Dorset, Caians from, 114; countess of, 150
Douai, 89
Doughty, Charles, 259
Dover (Kent), 57
Dover, Thomas, 147
Down and Connor, bishop of, *see* Taylor
Dowsing, William, 127
Dresden, 243
Drosier, W. H., f, 225, 238, 295; as benefactor, 223, 252, 257; and marriage, 225; his wife (Elizabeth Purchas), 225
Drury, B. H., f, p, 244, 313
Dryden, J., 140 – 1
Dublin, 298; St Patrick's, 19; Trinity College, 124, 147
Ducket, Tinkler, f, 169
Duffy, E., 154n.
Dugdale, W., *Baronage* etc., 147, 153
Duncan-Jones, Arthur, dean of Caius and Chichester, f, 161, 250, 291 – 2

Duncan-Jones, Richard, 250
Dunn, T. W., 234
Durham, bishop of, 115n., *and see* Cosin, Neile; bishopric, 112; canon of, 111, 113, *and see* Cosin; county, 219
Duse, Eleonora, 243

East Anglia, and the College, 10, 15 – 16, 40, 51, 86, 126n., 141, 155, 207; *and see* Norfolk, Norwich, Suffolk
Easton, J. Murray, architect, 268
Edinburgh, 174, 196 – 7, 199, 210, 226n.
'Education, religion, learning and research', 234, 260, chap. 14
Education Act (1944), 314
Edward the Confessor, king, 144
Edward III, king, 1 – 2, 5
Edward IV, king, 28
Edward VI, king, 73, 104
Edward VII, as Prince of Wales, 255
Edwards, A., f, 233
Edwards, Bartholomew, f, 178; p, 312
Eliot, George, *Middlemarch*, 125
Elizabeth I, queen, 47, 50, 65, 73, 75, 81 – 4 *passim*, 105; and celibacy, 68
Ellys, Sir John, f, t, M; as f, 155; t, 140, 152, 154, 157 – 8, 164; M, xii, 140, 152, 159 – 60, 161, 183, 310; the 'Devil of Caius', x, 152
Ellys, John (II), his nephew, 160
Elsworth (Cambs), 39
Elveden, Walter of, 15
Elwyn-Jones, Lord, Lord Chancellor, h f, 259
Ely (Cambs), 204n.; bishop of, 53, *and see* Alcock, Andrewes, Balsham, Louth, Wren; Commissary of, 85; cathedral, 173
Elyott, Adam, 157
Emden, A. B., 29
Engel, A. J., 228
Erasmus, 48, 50
Essex, archdeacon of, *see* Gooch; Caians from, 86
Essex, James, 171, 173
Eton (Bucks), 27, 190, 221
Euclid, 126, 197
Euripides, *Medea*, 197
Evangelicals, influence of in Caius, 208, 218 – 19, 221, 231
Exeter (Devon), 108, 130; bishop of, 201, *and see* Booth, Stapeldon; canon of, 26; dean, *see* Carpenter

Eywood (Herefs), 198

Fagius, 51
'Family', the, dining club, 209 – 10
Fawsett, Dr, 239
fellow-commoners, 121, 139 – 40, 153,
  156, 185
Fen Ditton (Cambs), 238
Fenn, Sir John, f, 177 – 8, 288
Ferrara, 50
Ferrers, Norman, f, t, M; f, 207; t, 196,
  223; M, 205, 223, 225 – 8, 231 – 2, 234,
  239, 249, 310; death of, 235
Fersfield (Norfolk), 177
Fingley, John, 89, 306
Fisher, John, St, cardinal, bishop of
  Rochester, 17, 52; as President of
  Queens', Lady Margaret's confessor
  and preacher, 46; and founding of
  Christ's and St John's, 45 – 6; as
  Chancellor, 40, 43, 46, 48, 62; his
  death, 47
Fisher, Richard, see Belward
Fisher, Sir Ronald (R.A.), f, p, 242,
  272, 274, 297 – 8, 313
Fiswick, Fishewicke, William, founder
  of Physwick Hostel, 24
FitzRalph, Richard, archbishop of
  Armagh, 19
Flanders, and count of, 23
Flecker, James Elroy, 259
Florence, 198
Forster, E. M., 274
Fortune, 65; 3b
Foster, Sir Michael, 232, 239
Foulden (Norfolk), 15, 69, 139
Foxe's Book of Martyrs, 106
France, 145; king of, see François I,
  Philip VI
Francis, H. T., f, 218, 223, 229
Franciscan friar, 89
François I, king of France, 216
Frankland, Mrs Jocosa or Joyce,
  daughter of J. and R. Trapps, 95 – 6;
  her legacy and fellows, 96 – 8, 100,
  102, 108, 116, 204, 226, 252, 267; her
  son, see Saxey
Frankland, William, 96
Franks Commission (Oxford), 228
Frederick, Prince of Wales, 168
Freeman, E. A., 143
Frere, Eleanor, 178
Frere, John, f, 178 – 9

Frere, Sheppard, 178
Frere, W. H., bishop of Truro, 292
Friedman, Milton, 260
Froissart, John, 1 – 2
Fuller, Thomas, 13
Furness Abbey (Lancs), 197

Gairdner, James, 177 – 8n.
Galen, 57 – 9, 64
Gardiner, Stanley, f, 242
Gardner, E. A., f, 234
Garter, Order of, 1, 6
Garwin, Laura, f, 279
Gawdy, family, and their letters, 119 –
  21; Framlingham (I), 119 – 120;
  William, 120 – 1
Genetics, professors of, 242
George I, king, 174
Geore II, king, 174
Germany, 198; German professors and
  universities, 174, 191, 228, 245 – 6;
  German visitors in 18th cent., xi
Gerrard, Richard, f, 90
Gesner, Conrad, 58, 70, 73
Geynes, John, 64
Gibbs, James, 171
Giggleswick (Yorks), 86
Gladstone, W. E., 222n.
Glasgow, University of, 147
Glisson, family, 121; Francis, f, Regius
  Professor of Physic, 114 – 15, 145
Glyn, Hugh, f, 69 – 70
Goade, Roger, provost of King's, 76
Godmanchester (Hunts), 127
Göttingen, 174, 238
Gonville, family, 2, 32, 196; Edmund,
  career, 2 – 5, 177; as founder, xi, 1 – 6,
  14 – 15, 40, 243, 305; and Thetford
  and Rushford, 7 – 8; as king's clerk,
  rector of Thelnetham, Rushford and
  Terrington St Clement, 1 – 2; and J.
  Colton, 18; his death, 305
Gonville, Nicholas and William, 2
Gooch, John, 166, 169, 170n.
Gooch, Sir Thomas, bart. (I), f, M,
  archdeacon of Essex etc., bishop of
  Bristol, Norwich and Ely: 153; as M,
  161 – 71, 183, 310; as vice-chancellor,
  168, 170 – 1; as archdeacon, 168; as
  canon of Chichester, xi, 168; as
  bishop, of Bristol, 166 – 7, of
  Norwich, 6, 167 – 8, of Ely, 6, 163,
  168 – 9; his stable, 215; his death, 173;

his wives: Mary Sherlock, 169, 149; Hannah Miller, 169, 249; Mary Compton, 169, 249
Gooch, Thomas (II), 169n.
Gooch, Sir William, 163
Goodall, Henry, 170
Goodwin, Harvey, f, bishop of Carlisle, 221, 231
Gorham case, 201
Gostlin, John, (I), f, M, Regius Professor of Physic, early life 106 – 9; and Legge, 79 – 80, 84n.; M, 106, 108, 110, 114 – 17, 121, 126, 159; election as M, 109 – 10; as vice-chancellor, 116; as physician, 95
Gostlin, John (II), f, p, 159 – 60, 312
Gostlin, Thomas, f, p, 311
Grand Junction Canal, 188
Grantchester, Adam or Anthony of, 10 – 11
Gratian, *Decretum*, 106; MSS of, 28, 306
Gray, P., f, M, 303, 310
Great Massingham (Norfolk), 86, 100 – 1
Greece, Wilkins in, 192
Green, Christopher, f, Regius Professor of Physic, 115, 147, 155
Green, George, F, 195 – 6, 226, 307; Green's functions, 196
Green, G. E., 245
Green, John (I), 86; (II), 155
Gregory, I, the Great, Pope, 226
Grene, William, f, 27 – 8
Gresham, Sir Thomas, and Gresham College, 60
Grey, Lord, 197
Grierson, Philip, f, p, 33n., 58, 72, 94n., 188, 247, 282, 313; as scholar, 298 – 9; his portrait, 299
Griffith, Mr, 147
Griffith, Guy, T., f, 297
Grimm, brothers, 214n.
Grimshaw, Mr, 188
Grimstone, Thomas, f, 95
Grindal, Edmund, as bishop of London, 71; as archbishop of Canterbury, 74
Gross, E. J., f, b, p, 251, 253, 271, 313
Grove, General, 270
Guest, Benjamin, 190n.
Guest, Edwin, f, M, 16n., 190n., 206, 213 – 17, 223, 288, 310; and building, 204n., 214 – 17; his marriage, 225 – 6; his resignation, 226; memorial window, 206n., his wife, *see* Banner

Gunning, Henry, esquire bedell, 164, 187 – 8, 198, 209 – 11, 220
Gunpowder Plot, 107

Hadleigh (Suffolk), 53
Hadley, Parrick, f, Professor of Music, 244 – 5, 283, 288 – 9
Haileybury (Herts), 193
Hainault, 1
Hakluyt, 92
Hall, Catherine, xv, 13 – 15nn., 21n., 23n., 31n., 33n., 35n., 102n., 135n., 205n., 217n.
Halman, Holman, James, f, M, 159, 161, 310
Hamilton, Hamish, 261
Hampden, John, 144
Harcock, Harcocks, Henry, 136 – 7
Hardwicke, Lord, 175
Hardy, Sir Thomas Duffus, on Lord Langdale, 196 – 203 *passim*
Hardy, Sir William B., f, t, 241, 255, 280
Harley, Lady Jane (Lady Langdale), 198, 200
Harley, Robert (earl of Oxford), 166 – 7; *and see* Oxford
Harper, Dr, 249; Mary, *see* Roberts
Harpley (Norfolk), 100 – 1
Harrington, William, f, 133
Harrow, 221; and Sayer scholars, 244
Hartstongue, Francis, John and Standish, 147
Harvey, William, xii, xiii, 93 – 5, 114, 123, 127, 153, 158, 239; as Warden of Merton, 94; and medical tradition, xii, xiii, 82, 187, 288
Haveus, Theodore, 66 – 7, 78
Hawking, Stephen, f, Lucasian Professor, 247, 299 – 300
Heacham (Norfolk), and lodge, 211 – 12, 291
Heaton, Eric, dean of Caius and of Christ Church, 290, 294
Hegel, 297
Henderson, Alexander, 197, 199
Henrietta Maria, queen, 111
Henry VI, king, and King's College, 12, 22, 44 – 5, 170
Henry VII, king, 52
Henry VIII, king, 43, 73; and Christ Church, 44 – 5, 84; and King's, 45; and Physwick Hostel, 29; and Trinity, 44 – 5, 47, 53, 84

Henry, earl of Lancaster, 4, 6, 7; (II), earl and duke, 4–7, *passim*, 13
Henslow, J. S., Professor of Botany, 190
Henson, Hensley, 245
Henty, G. A., xii, 221–2
Herbert, George, 113, 125
Hereford, archdeacon of, *see* Styrmin; bishop of, *see* Skipp; canon of, 26, 39
Herefordshire, Caians from, 86
Hervey, Henry, 94n.
Heslop, A., 18
Hethersett (Norfolk), 160
Hewish, Anthony, h f, 260
Heydon (Norfolk), 141
Hickhorngill, Edmund, f, 133
Hicks, James, f, p, 312
Hicks, Sir John, f, 260
Hillington (Norfolk), 140
Hinchinbrooke (Hunts), 65
Hinson, Thomas, 116; William, 116n.
'Hippelaphus', the, 58
Hippocrates, 57–8
Hitchin (Herts), 248
Hobbes, Thomas, 94
Hoddesdon (Herts), 96
Holditch, Hamnett, f, p, 194–5, 203, 225, 242, 313
Holland, earl of, chancellor, 132
Holloway, Robin, f, 289
Holman, *see* Halman
Holtby, Richard, 89
Homer, 180
Hopkins, Sir Gowland, 281, 296
Hopkins, John, 192n.
Hopkins, William, coach and esquire bedell, 219–20
Hopkinson, G. F., 261–2
Horace, 180, 299
House of Commons, 164; House of Lords, 163
Housman, A. E., 163
Hovell, Sir Richard, 140; William, 139–40
Howarth, T.E.B., 261
Howden (Yorks), 86
Howe, earl, 187
Howlett, David, 70n.
Hownd, Edmund, f, p, 311
Hoyle, David, 121n., 122
Huddleston, John, 90–1
Hulbert, Claude, 261, 295; Jack, 295
Hull University, vice-chancellor of, *see* Dennison

humanism, humanist studies, 27, 48, 50, 56–60, 82
Humfrey, Charles, architect, 204; *and see* Willis
Humphrey, George, 239
Hundred Years' War, 5, 6, 26
Hunkin, Joseph, dean of Caius, bishop of Truro, 262, 269, 281, 292–3
Huntingdon, 102
Husband, Christopher, 116
Husband, James, f, p, 312
Huxley, Julian, 296
Huys, Dr, 62

Ickleton (Cambs), 198
India, 226
inflation, 120–3
Iolanthe, 67, 272
Ipswich (Suffolk), Dominican house, 7
Ireland, Caians in, 147; Irish scholars in Caius, 237–8, 243, 298–9; Chancellor, Justiciar, Treasurer of (John Colton), 19
Ishmael, 281
Isis, river, 9
Islip, Simon, archbishop of Canterbury, 1–2
Italy, Italian studies, 62, 198, 283; Italian MSS, 57

Jacobites, 151, 162
Jamaica, 182
James I, king, 75, 108
James II, king, 115, 126, 143, 148–9
James the Old Pretender, 126
James, John, architect, 172
James, M. R., 33, 264
James, Thomas, 34–5, 305
Japanese art, 257
Jason, 109
Jean le Bel, 1–2
Jellyby, Mrs, 219
Jesus gun, the, 261–3
Jews, Jewish benefactors, and Caius, 257, 292n.; medieval Jews, 9
John of Cambridge, 14, 21
John, Augustus, 239; 14
Johnson, Samuel, 163
Josephus, 120
Josselin, J., 74
Judicial Committee of the Privy Council, 201

Kapitza, Peter, 270
Kearney, Hugh, 83
Kenilworth (Warwicks), 60n.
Kent, 51
Kerrich, Thomas, 179 – 82
Kidman, Mr, 188 – 9
Kimbolton (Hunts), 127
King's Bench, Court of, 166
Kings' Cliffe (Northants), 65n.
Kingsley, Charles, 256
Kirby, William, f, 186
Kirkby Lonsdale (Westmorland), 196 – 7
Klais, Johannes, of Bonn, 289
Knight, A. M., f, dean, bishop of
Rangoon, 231, 243
Knight, John, 147n.
Knightley, Mr, 200
Korean pottery, 257

Lake District, 196
Lamb, John (I), Master of Corpus, 205
Lamb, John (II), f, b, 205, 225, 251
Lampe, Geoffrey W. H., f, Regius
Professor of Divinity, 161, 288, 291 – 2
Lancaster, duchy of, 4n.; duke, see
Henry
Lane, Sir Robert, 121
Langdale, Langdale Pikes, 196; Lord
Langdale, see Bickersteth
Larling (Norfolk), 2
Laski, Harold, 297
Latimer, Hugh, bishop of Worcester,
48 – 9, 51
Latin, spoken, 133, 136
Laud, William, archbishop of
Canterbury, 107, 113 – 14, 133, 206;
and Cosin, 111; and Jeremy Taylor,
124; reports to (1636), 113 – 14,
118 – 19, 122 – 3; Laudians, 110
Lavenham (Suffolk), 161
Law, Edmund, Master of Peterhouse,
bishop of Carlisle, Knightbridge
Professor of Divinity, 175 – 6
Lawshall (Suffolk), 106
Lea, A. S., f, 240 – 1
Legge, Thomas, 111, 288; as tutor, 83;
M, chap. 5 passim, esp. 77, 79,
84 – 93, 302; as vice-chancellor, 92;
and Doctors' Commons, 82; and
drama and his plays, 79, 90; and law,
223, 280, 306; as Commissary of Ely
and Vice-Chancellor's court, 85; and
recusants, 88 – 92, 120; and Gostlin,

114 – 15; his death, 106; his tomb,
79 – 80, 99; 9b
Lehman, John, 294 – 5
Leibniz, G. W., 143, 155
Leicester, earl of, 94; (Newark)
Hospital at, 6; Wigston Hospital, 155
Lendrum, see Vesey
Le Neve, Peter, 177 – 9
Lewes (Sussex), 239
Lhasa, 186
Lichfield, bishop of, see Overall
Lightfoot, J. B., 227
Lightfoot, Mrs Joan, 138
Lightwine, John, f, p, 172, 312
Linacre, Thomas, 59, 60, 78
Lincoln, 5; bishop, see Montaigne;
cathedral, canon, 34, 40; chancellor,
see Smith; dean, see Bateman; cath-
edral close, xi
Ling, William, f, 122
Linwood (Lincs), 26
Lister, Sir William, 239
Liverpool, Quarry Bank School, 316;
University, 230, 239 – 40, 269 – 70,
275; and see McNair
livings, see advowsons
Livingstone, David, 231
Livy, 246
Llandaff, bishop of, see Watson
Lock, J. B., f, b, 232, 236, 238, 245 – 6,
266, 269; and buildings, 251 – 4
Lock, Michael, 269
Loggan, David, 14, 23, 28, 65; front
endpaper
Loire, château, 266, 282
LONDON, 115n., 120, 130, 133, 146,
226n., 237, 239, 296 – 7; the City, 252;
goldsmith of, 95; Lord Mayor, 164; Dr
Caius in, 46, 58, 60, 64, 84
bishops of, see Blomfield, Compton,
Grindal, Northburgh, Sandys,
Sheldon, Sherlock
churches, religious houses in:
Charterhouse, 2; St Andrew's
Holborn, 27 – 8; St Bartholomew's
Hospital, 59, 77; St George's Hanover
Sq., 172; St James's Piccadilly,
154 – 5; St Mary Aldermary, 49; St
Paul's Cathedral, dean of, see Carey,
Nowell; Westminster Abbey, 157n.,
Westminster, St Stephen's, canon of,
39
places and institutions in: Albert

Hall, 296; Barber Surgeons' Hall, 59; Battersea, College Mission, 234, 256, 290 – 1; Doctors' Commons, 85, 88; Ely House, Holborn, 169; Exchequer of Receipt, Tally Court, 144; Fleet Prison, 87, 91; Inns of Court, 83, 85; Inner Temple, 120; Lincoln's Inn, 196, Middle Temple Hall, 215; Kensington Palace, 155; King's College, *see* Swete; Lambeth Palace, 47, 59, 73, 75, 77, 149; Library, 213; LSE, *see* Oakeshott; National Gallery, 193; Natural History Museum, 216; Public Record Office, 200; Royal Archaeological Institute, 204; Royal College of Music, 244, 309; Royal College of Physicians, 55, 59 – 60, 62 – 5, 94, 115, 138, *and see* Caius; Royal Society, 115, 157, 186 – 7, 211, 214, 295; Presidents, Sherrington, 240; Wollaston, 187; St James's Palace, 174; Society of Antiquaries, 177 – 9, 211, 214; Spitalfields, 283; Toynbee Hall, 283; University College, 193; Westminster, 71, 75, 122, 162, 170; Whitechapel, 283; Whitehall, 276; Woolwich, Royal Military Academy, 316
London, Richard, f, 122 – 3
Longfellow, Henry, 214
Lotto, Lorenzo, 62n.
Louth (Lincs), King Edward's School, 282
Louth, William of, bishop of Ely, 37
Loveland, Joseph, f, p, 311
Lovering, Thomas, 101
Lu, Gwei-Djen, 281
Lucas, Richard, f, p, 313
Lynch, Thomas, 182
Lyndwood, Lyndewode, William, of Gonville Hall, canon lawyer, pluralist, bishop of St David's, 21 – 2, 26 – 7, 29, 31, 37, 288; Keeper of the Privy Seal, 26; his *Provinciale*, 26
Lynn, King's (Norfolk), 38, 99, 203; Dominican house, 9

Mabillon, Jean, 149
Macclesfield (Cheshire), 269
McKendrick, Neil, f, M, 282, 303, 310
Mackenzie, C. G., f, bishop of Central Africa, 231
McLeod, Iain, 259, 322
McNair, Lord (Arnold D.), f, t, 79n.,

229 – 30, 247, 282, 288; vice-chancellor of Liverpool, 270, 282
Macpherson, W. J., f, t, p, 313
Maitland, F. W., 75, 220
Malines, 73
Manchester, 216, 269, 270; earl of, Henry Montague, 1st earl, 127; Edward Montague, 2nd earl, 127 – 9; as chancellor, 132
Manilius, 163
Manning, Thomas, 186
Manny, Mauny, Walter, 1 – 2, 4 – 6
Manwood, Sir Roger, 95
Maptid, Laurence, f, Master of Corpus, 49, 51
Maratta, Carlo, 172
Marke, Thomas, archdeacon of Norfolk and Cornwall, 27
Market Rasen (Lincs), 26
Marshall, Roger, 36, 305 – 6
Martin, Konrad, f, t, 289
Martin, Sir Leslie, architect, 275 – 6
Martin, Thomas, 178
Mary I, queen, 47, 51, 53, 61 – 2, 73, 104
Mary II, queen, *see* William
Mattishall (Norfolk), 15, 19, 31, 38, 170
Maurice, F. D., 190, 203
Mawer, Sir Allen, f, 245
May, William, president of Queens', 47
Medfield, student in Physwick Hostel, 33n.
Mediterranean, Wilkins' travels in, 193
Melbourne, Lord, 197
Merionethshire, Caian from, 86
Merton, Walter of, 9
Michel, André, 285
Michell, Edmund, f, 116
Michell, R. W., 255
Middleton, Conyers, 165
Mildmay, Sir Walter, 60, 104 – 5
Mill, James, 197
Milton, John, 125, 130, 133
Mitchell, Arnold, architect, 254
Monro, C. H., f, 222, 231, 233, 244, 251, 257
Monro, H. E., 259
Montague, Richard, 121; *and see* Manchester
Montaigne, George, bishop of Lincoln, 107, 109 – 10
Montanus, J. B., 57
Montefiore, Hugh, f, dean, bishop of Birmingham, 261n., 294

Moore, William, f, university librarian, 114, 132, 135, 141
Mortimers, manor of, 32
Morton, John, cardinal, archbishop of Canterbury, 27
Mott, Sir Nevill, f, M, 275 – 6, 308, 310; as Cavendish Professor and Nobel laureate, 259, 276
Mudde, Thomas, 91, 288
Muggleton, F., 287
Muir, Pattison, f, 232
Murphy, Robert, f, 194
Murray Committee (University of London), 228
Mutford (Suffolk), 15, 19, 38

Namier, Sir Lewis, 162
Napoleon, 198
Nash, John, architect, 193
Nature, 296
Naylor, Oliver, f, 115 – 16, 184
Naylor, William, f, 140
Needham, Dorothy, h f, 279
Needham, Joseph, f, p, M: 186n., 236 – 7, 272, 298, 308; as student, 261, 280 – 1, 288; as scholar and scientist, 299 – 301; as p, 274, 313; as M, x, xii, 272, 276 – 9 *passim*, 311; on Dell, 130; on Hunkin, 292; and religion, 290, 293; and socialism, 277, 281; and China, and Science and Civilisation in China, 277, 281, 301; Needham Research Institute, 300
negative vote, 91, 159, 169
Neile, Richard, bishop of Durham, 111
Nelson, Edmund, I and II, 193, 224n.
Nelson, Horatio (Lord), 193, 224n.
Nevile, Thomas, Master of Trinity, dean of Canterbury, 46, 83
Nevis, West Indies, 182n.
Newcastle-upon-Tyne, University of, 274
Newcastle, 1st duke of, as high steward and chancellor, 162, 167 – 9, 173 – 4, 210, 227
Newmarket (Suffolk), 109, 146, 182
Newport (Essex), grammar school, 96
Newton, Sir Isaac, Lucasian Professor, 127, 143, 148, 152 – 4, 155, 157, 176, 300
Nichols, Henry, 279; Nicola, f, 279
Nicholson, Sygar, 50n.
Nobel laureates, 259 – 60, 270, 276

Noel, Conrad, 236, 292
non-jurors, 149 – 51
Norfolk, antiquaries, 177 – 9, archdeacon of, *see* Marke, Sponne; and Gonville Hall, 16, 29, 38, 40, 47 – 8; and Caius College, 86, 89, 104, 108, 121, 140, 159, 178, 226; and college livings, 161; and the election of Guest, 206, 213 – 14
Norman Conquest, and Dr Brady, 144
Normandy, duke of, 1
Normanton, Normington, John, f, 122n., 123
Norris, John, 178 – 9
Northburgh, Michael, bishop of London, 2
Northey, Sir E., 163
Northumberland, archdeacon of, *see* Rickinghall
Norway, 58
Norwich, church: archdeacon of, 27, *and see* Bateman; bishop of, *see* Bateman, Despenser, Nykke, Repps; cathedral of Holy Trinity, 13; canon of, 49; Dominican house, 9; St Michael Coslany, 40, 48 – 9, 160, *and see* Barley, Buckenham, Stubb; diocese, and the college, 15, 23, 25, 213; and mastership, 226
  city: 6, 27, 40, 99, 130; and John Caius, 56; and Legge, 84; and the college, 47 – 8, 86, 110, 194, 203, 226; charities, 6, 168, 170; schoolmaster of, 210
Nottingham, 195
Nowell, Alexander, dean of St Paul's, 96
Nykke, Richard, Bishop of Norwich, 51 – 2

Oakeshott, Michael, f, professor at LSE, 277, 282, 297
Oates, Titus, 157 – 8
Okey, Thomas, f, 283 – 4
Olympic sportsmen, 261
Orleans, 1
Orrell, Thomas, 114
Osborne, John, f, 30n.
Osburne, Edward, 89
Oundle, School (Northants), 280
Overall, John, bishop of Lichfield, 111
Overy, Roger, f, 49
Owen, Heather, 147n.

OXFORD University: antiquity of, 74 – 5; in 13th – 14th cent., 8 – 9, 42; in 15th – 16th, 41 – 2; in 16th, 52, 82, 98; in 17th, 94, 133; in 19th, 44, 98, 207, 228, 236, 245; in 20th, 229, 239 – 40, 261, 264, 278; and celibacy, 68 – 9, 224n.; chambers for students, 21 – 2; hall and hostel, 41; and government, 227; university regents, 29; Romanes lecture, 226n.

Colleges: college libraries, 36; tutors, 42, 228 – 9; All Souls, 73, 124, 245; Balliol, 44; library, 33, 36n., 37; Brasenose, 96; alliance with Caius, 267 – 8; Christ Church, 44, 259; Exeter (Stapeldon Hall), 10, 15; Lincoln, 96; Magdalen, 44, 143; Merton, 9, 23, 224n.; library, 33 – 4, 37; New College, 22, 42, 44

Oxford, countess of, 59 – 60; 1st earl (of Oxford and Mortimer, Robert Harley), 166 – 7; 5th earl (Edward Harley), 198

Padua, 27, 48, 50, 52, 57, 63, 94, 123

Paget, A. C., 206n.

Paget, Sir George, f, Regius Professor of Physic, 206 – 7, 212 – 14, 220, 226n., 232, 238 – 9, 246, 288

Paige, Donald, 131 – 40 *passim*

Palgrave, Sir Francis, 200

Paman, John, f, 87, 90

Pantin, W. A., 22

Paris, 1, 8, 111, 194, 198, 239

Parker, Matthew, Master of Corpus, archbishop of Canterbury, 47 – 50 *passim*, 52, 55 – 6, 60, 87, 213; and troubles in Caius, 70 – 7; letters of, 70 – 2, 74; his library, 34; his scholarship, 94; his wife, 68

Parkes, Sir Edward, f, 261n.

Parkin, Charles, 177

Parliament, and bishopric of Durham, 112; and Cambridge, 132; history of, 144; *Modus tenendi parliamentum*, 144

Parr, Queen Katherine, 84

Parr, Samuel, 210

Pasteur, Louis, 239

Paston letters, 177n., 178

Paul, St, 53, 226

Peacock, George, 195

'Peasants' Revolt', 272 – 4, 281

Peking, 186

Pennington, Sir Isaac, Regius Professor of Physic, 198

Pepper, F. W., 287

Perse, John (Stephen's father), 86, 98 – 9; his wife (Stephen's stepmother), 98 – 9

Perse, Martin (cousin and brother-in-law), 98 – 9, 101, 124; his wife (Stephen's sister), see Beche

Perse, Stephen, f, b, xii, 22n., 79 – 80, 90 – 1, 98 – 103, 106; his entry to Caius, 86; his chamber, 99, 118; his wealth, 95 – 6, 99 – 103; as physician, 79, 95, 99; and Barrett, 93; his death, 108; statue of, 152; tomb of, 79 – 80, 99; *9a*

his will, 100 – 1, 152, 201 – 3; his Trust, 101 – 2, 201 – 3, 223, 248, 251 – 2; his almsfolk, 100; Perse feast, 99 – 100; Perse fellows and scholars, 99 – 100, 116, 124; his schools, 100 – 1, 155, 185, 193, 202 – 3, 235, 248; the Perse scandal, 101 – 2, 201 – 3

Peter the Lombard, 106

Peter Martyr (Pietro Martire Vermigli), 93

Peters, Sir Rudolph (R.A.), f, t, h f, 241, 244, 261 – 2, 280, 282, 296

Peters, William, f, 155

Pevsner, Sir N., 216, 268, 275 – 6

Philadelphia, 150, 295

Philcox, W. A., 262

Philip II, king of Spain, etc., husband of Mary I, 51, 61 – 2, 73

Philip VI, king of France, 1

Philippa of Hainault, queen, 1 – 2

Phillips, Thomas, 183

Philostratus, 211

Physwick, see Cambridge, Gonville and Caius College, buildings; *and see* Fiswick

Pickeril(l), Robert, f, 122 – 3

Pisa, 57

Pitt, William, Prime Minister, 187, 210 – 11

Pius V, Pope, 75

Plato, 27, 62, 297

Platonists, Cambridge, 129

Pole, Reginald, cardinal, archbishop of Canterbury, 50

Popish Plot, the, 158

Porphyrius, 211

Porson, Richard, 211

Porter, H. C., 93
Powell, F. C., f, 66, 268n.
Powell, W. S., Master of St John's, 183
Prayer Book, Cranmer's, 112; of 1662, 112, 117
Presbyterians, 112, 124, 129, 250, 267
Preston, John, see Warrock
Price, John, 86; Stanley, 284 – 6
Prichard, M. J., f, p, Senior Tutor, 280, 313
Protestants and reformation, 48 – 54, chaps. 4 – 7 passim, and see Evangelicals, Puritans; literature and theology, 104 – 7, 112; liberal protestantism, 230 – 1, 290, 293
Prynne, J., f, 33n., 302
Prynne, William, 143, 145
Pugin, A. W. N., 238; 12
Pulham, Richard, f, M, xii, 23 – 4, 30, 38, 309
Punnett, R. C., f, 242, 269
Purchas, Elizabeth F., see Drosier
Puritans, 72, 88 – 90, 92 – 3, 104 – 5, 107, 110, 122 – 3, chap. 7; Puritan Directory, 127
Pym, John, 144

Quakers, 250
Quebec, 173
Quiggin, E. C., f, 243

Ramsey abbey (Hunts), 65
Ramus, Pierre de la Ramée, 105
Rande, Roger, f, 30n.
Rant, Humphrey, 139
Rant, John, f, 135 – 6, 138 – 9
Raven, Charles, Master of Christ's, Regius Professor of Divinity, h f, 288, 291
Raverat, Gwen, 277
recusants, see Catholics
Redman, John, Warden of King's Hall, Master of Trinity, 47, 52 – 3
Reeve, Samuel, f, p, 312
Reform Act (1832), 202 – 3
Reid, J. S., f, t, 225n., 235, 237, 245, 248, 256; Mrs Reid, 269
Rembrandt, 94
Renaissance influence on John Caius, 55 – 6
Repps, William, of Gonville Hall, bishop of Norwich, 49, 56
Restoration, the (1660), 119, 145

Reynolds, Sir J., 177, 183 – 4, 13c
Rheims, 89
Rhondda, Lord, h f, 256n.
Riches, T. H., 256
Rickinghall, John, M, chancellor, chancellor of York, archdeacon of Northumberland, bishop of Chichester, 25, 31, 38 – 9, 309
Rickmansworth (Herts), 62, 266
Ridgeway, Sir William, f, Disney Professor of Archaeology, 237 – 8, 247 – 8, 257
Ringrose, J., 21n.
Ripon, bishop of, see Strong
Ritz, painter, 172
Robbins Report, 276, 278, 307
Roberts, D., architect, 253n.
Roberts, Ernest Stewart, f, t, p, M: 207, chap. 12 passim, esp. 234 – 6; t, 217, 223, 234 – 5, 255, 314; p, 223, 234 – 5, 313; M, 217, chap. 12, 310; ordination and religion, 231n., 232, 290; portrait, 257; death, 258
    and Boat Club, 190, 254 – 5; and 'Greater Caius', 256, 287; and Girton, 235; and Perse Girls' School, 203, 235; and rifle volunteers, 255
Roberts, Mrs E. S. (Mary Harper), 249 – 51, 259, 291; her autobiography, 235, 249, 255 – 6; their daughters, Caroline (Caia, Mrs Duncan-Jones), 291 – 2; Margaret (Gonvillia), 291
Roberts, H. A., 250
Rochester, bishop of, see Fisher
Rockefeller foundation, 264
Rockingham, marquis of, 179
Romanes, G. J., h f, 226n.
Rome, 57, 123, 126, 246; Roman Catholics, see Catholics
Romilly, Joseph, 209 – 10
Roos, Lord, 112n.
Rothamsted, 297
Rothblatt, Sheldon, 228
Rotherham, Thomas, archbishop of York, Chancellor, 46
Rougham, William, f, 21, 23 – 4, 30n., 31, 38
Rous, John, 41
Royal Commissions and Statutory Commissions: 1840s – 50s, 68, 192, 213, 227; 1870s – 80s, 226 – 7, 245; 1920s, 264 – 7
Rubin, Miri, 2n.

Rugby, school, 221
Ruhemann, Siegfried, 232
Rumbelow, Lionel, 287
Runcie, Robert, archbishop of Canterbury, 261n.
Runcton Holme (Norfolk), 62
Rushford (or Rushworth, Norfolk), College, and parish, 7 – 8, 28, 32, 40; rector, see Gonville
Ruskin, John, 204n.
Russell, Sir Frederick, h f, 262 – 3
Russell, Lord John, 236
Rutherford, Lord, 270

St Bees (Cumberland), 86
St David's, bishop of, see Lyndwood
Salisbury, archdeacon of, 243; bishop of, see Shaxton, Sherlock; canon of, 26; dean of, 107
Salisbury, earl of (Robert Cecil), Chancellor, 106 – 7
Salisbury, John of, 166
Salomons, Sir David, 257; Sir David Lionel, 257
Salvin, A., architect, 214 – 16, 254
Sancroft, William, Master of Emmanuel, archbishop of Canterbury, 106, 112n., 148 – 50
Sandhurst (Berks), 316
Sandwich (Kent), school, 95; earl of, 175
Sandys, Edwin, Master of St Catharine's, bishop of London, archbishop of York, 75 – 6, 88
Sarum Manual, 28, 73n.
Saxey, William, 95 – 6
Sayer, John, 244
Scarburgh, Sir Charles, f, xiii, 94, 126 – 7, 133n.
Schuldham, Francis, f, and Schuldham Plate, 182, 204
Scilly Isles, 145
Scotsmen in Caius, 267; Scottish episcopalian liturgy, 150
Scott, H. Claughton, 190
Scott, Capt. Robert, 259
Scroop(e), Anne, 32, 253, 275
Sealy, Leonard, f, 280
Sedbergh (Yorks), 197
Sedgwick, Adam, 199, 227
Seeley, Sir John (J.R.), f, Regius Professor of Modern History, 222, 231, 233, 245 – 7, 288

senior wranglers, 178, 189, 200, 202
Serlio, Sebastiano, 66
Serpell, Michael, 178
Shadwell, Thomas, 140 – 1
Shakespeare and Dr Caius, 55
Shaw, Bernard, 283
Shaxton, Nicholas, f, bishop of Salisbury, suffragan bishop of Ely, 22n., 48 – 9, 51 – 4, 56, 311; his wife, 53 – 4; Bishop Shaxton's Solace, 54
Sheldon, Gilbert, bishop of London, archbishop of Canterbury, 112n.
Sheriffe, al. Argentein, Edmund, M, and archdeacon of Stow, 17, 39 – 40, 309; his Evidences, 34n., 39 – 40
Sheringham, Robert, f, 133 – 4
Sherlock, Thomas, Master of St Catharine's, dean of Chichester, bishop of Bangor, Salisbury and London, 164 – 5, 167
Sherrington, Sir Charles, f, h f, 124, 233, 239 – 41, 260; and medical tradition, 288
Shilleto, R., coach, 234
Shoenberg, David, f, 299
Shoubridge, William, 212
Shrewsbury (Shropshire), 59, 60n.
Sicily, 192, 261
Sidgwick, Henry, 222, 231, 233, 247n.
Siena, 57
silver robberies, 188 – 9
Simeon, Charles, 218
Simon, Mrs J., 81
sizars, 117, 121, 128, 140, 248
Skeat, W. W., 234
Skinner, Quentin, f, 65n.
Skipp, John, M, archdeacon and bishop of Hereford, chaplain to Queen Anne, 49 – 51, 56, 309
Smart, Frank, 257
Smith, H. K. P., 262
Smith, J. J. (great-nephew of John), f, t, 205, 213 – 14, 288
Smith, Jane, 195
Smith, John, f, t, p, M, professor of astronomy; xii, 174 – 6, 182 – 7, 194, 205, 210, 300, 309, 312; as Vice-Chancellor, 175; and Reynolds, 177; 13c; as chancellor of Lincoln, xi, 183
Smith, Mrs, his sister-in-law, 183, 249
Smith, Joseph, his nephew, f, 183n., 210
Smith, Martin, 256

Smith, R. Cove, 261
Smith, Stephen, 31
Soane, Sir John, architect, 177, 194, 254, 303 – 4
Somerset, duke of, Chancellor, 162, 168
Somersham, William, of Lynn, M, 30n., 38, 309
South Cave (Yorks), 86
Spain, king of, *see* Philip
Spelman, Charles, 141 – 2; Sir Henry, 141 – 2, 144; Sir John, 141; Roger, 141
Spenser, Robert, f, 70
Spicer, Robert, 101
Sponne, William, archdeacon of Norfolk, 25, 31
Stallard, H. B., 261
Stanford, Sir C. V., composer, 244
Stapeldon, Walter of, bishop of Exeter, 10
Steel, A. W. W., f, t, vicar of St Sepulchre, 226
Steerforth, 85
Stein, Peter, 79n., 85n.
Stephen, Leslie, 220, 222, 224 – 5, 233, 250
Sterne, Edward, Master of Jesus, 113n.
Stevenson, Anne, *see* Davy
Stockport (Cheshire), St Mary's church, 161
stocks, 55, 74
Stockton, Owen, f, 133
Stoke by Clare (Suffolk), 86
Stoke by Nayland (Suffolk), 31
Stokes, Matthew, f, 95, 148
Stokes, Professor (Sir G. G.), 219
Stokes, W. H., f, dean, 212
Stone, Sir Richard, h f, 260
Stopp, Elisabeth, and F. J., 256
Stow (diocese of Lincoln), archdeacon of, 26; *and see* Sheriffe
Stratton, F. J. M. (Chubby), f, senior tutor, p, 260, 263, 271, 296, 300, 313
Stratton, Robert, Master of Trinity Hall, 18
Strong, T. B., bishop of Ripon, 263
Stubb, Edmund, M, rector of St Michael Coslany, Norwich, 48, 309
Students' Christian Movement, 293
Sturdy, John, f, dean, 74n., 110n., 124n., 212n., 225n., 293n.
Styrmin, John, M, archdeacon of Hereford, 49, 51, 302
Sudbury (Suffolk), Dominican house, 7

Suffolk, and the college, 16, 38, 86, 121, 178; college livings, 161
Suffolk, duke of (John de la Pole), 28; earl of (Robert of Ufford), 22 – 3; earl of (Thomas Howard), chancellor, 109
Surrey, 222
Swaffham (Norfolk), 146
Swale, Richard, f, p, 88 – 92, 311
Swann, Lord (M.M.), f, h f, 272n.
Swete, H. B., f, t, professor at King's London, Regius Professor of Divinity, 161, 231, 243, 246, 288, 291
Swift, Jonathan, 167
Swineshead (Lincs), 234
Synod, National, of the Church of England, 161

Tancred, Christopher, 186
Tanner, Thomas, 177
Tapp, W. M., 223, 257; Tapp Trust, 252, 274
Tavistock (Devon), 115n., 116
Taylor, Jeremy, f, bishop of Down and Connow, 101, 110n., 114, 124 – 5, 206, 288; his 'Heaven', 125, 242
Taylor, T. M., f, 237n.
Terrington St Clement (Norfolk), *see* Gonville
Terrington, John of, f, 14n.; *and see* Colton
Thackeray, Frederick, 198 – 9
Thames, river, 72, 74
Thaxted (Essex), 236, 292
Thelnetham (Suffolk), *see* Gonville
Thetford (Norfolk), Dominican house, 4, 7, 305
Thomas Aquinas, St, 106, 123
Thomas, earl of Lancester, 7
Thompson, Henry, f, 31
Thucydides, 62
Thun, 243
Thurloe, John, secretary of state, 134
Thurlow, Lord (Edward), Lord Chancellor, 182-3, 259
Thurston, Malachi, f, 151
Tilney, Alan, f, 30n.
Tilney, Henry, f, 185
Tinckler, Isaac, 123
tithes, 3 – 4, 10, 19, 28, 31
Todhunter, Isaac, coach, 220
tolerance, 87 – 8, 92, 129
Tories, 150 – 1, 162 – 8 *passim*, 170, 173 – 4, 210 – 11

INDEX

Tracie, John, f, p, 311
Tranchell, Peter, f, 283, 288 – 9
Trapps, Joan and Robert, 95; *and see* Frankland
Trayes, F. A. E., f, 237n.
Trevelyan, G. M., 264
Trinity, doctrine of, 154 – 5
Trollope, A., 184
Trott, Matthew, f, t, 99
Trumpington (Cambs), 100
Truro, bishop of, *see* Frere, Hunkin
Tubbs, N. H., 259
Tunnicliffe, H. E., f, t, 273
Tunstall, Robert, f, 30n.
Turnbull, Thomas, f, p, 313
tutors, 229, *and see* coaches; *see also* Cambridge, Gonville and Caius College; Oxford
Twain, Mark, 217

Ufford, John of (I), archbishop of Canterbury, 1 – 2; (II), 22 – 3
Unitarian thought, 154
University Grants Committee, 265
Urswick, Christopher, 27

Valladolid, Jesuit College, 158
Vanbrugh, Sir John, 150
Vavisore, George, 86; Ralph, 86; Thomas, 88 – 9
Venice, 198
Venn, Henry (father of John), 208
Venn, J. A. (son of John), President of Queens', xiii, 233n.
Venn, John, f, p, 228, 231 – 2, 293; and Leslie Stephen, 224; as mathematician and philosopher, 233, 237; his diagrams, xiii, 233; as p, 237, 271, 311, 313; as college historian, xiii – xiv, 80 – 1, 233, 288; his *Biographical History*, 29, 153, 254, 269, 274; his statistics, 68, 156; on 14th – 15th cent., 10, 31; on John Caius, 52, 56; on Legge and recusants, 89 – 90; on Harvey, 94; on Brady, 145; on Ellys, 159; on Gooch, 170; on Holditch, 194; on Guest, 214; on marriage of fellows, 224 – 5; on college in the 1850s, xii, 184, 206, 217, 218 – 22, 223, 229, 236; on college in 1900, 236
Verdi, G., 289
Vesalius, 57

Vesey, W. T., formerly Lendrum, f, t, 237, 258, 261
Virginia, Lieut.-Governor of, 163
Virtù, Virtue, and Dr Caius, 65 – 6, 73, 78

Wade, Emlyn C. S., f, 278, 280
Wade, Sir William (H. W. R.), M, 276, 278 – 9, 310; Foreword by, ix – x
Wake, Thomas, f, 116 – 17
Wales, 124; Welshmen and Dr Caius' statutes, 69 – 70; Welsh mountains, 212
Walker, Henry, 50
Walker, J. W. and Sons, 216
Wallis, Frederic, f, bishop of Wellington, 231, 243
Walpole, Christopher, 89; St Henry, 89
Walpole, Sir Robert, 155, 163, 210
Walsingham (Norfolk), 182
Walsingham, Thomas, f, 31n.
Wangford (Suffolk), 135
Wapping (Middlesex), 158
Warenne, earl of, 4, 7
Warham, William, archbishop of Canterbury, 51
Waring, Edward, Lucasian Professor, 181
Warner, Stephen, f, 70
Warner, Thomas, f, 25
Warr, Hedley, 229, 247, 281 – 4, 290, 293
Warren, Edward, 254
Warrock, John, *al.* Preston, *al.* William Warrock, 25
Wars of the Roses, 39, 170
Warwick, 60n.
Wash, the, 225
Washington, DC, 270; Dumbarton Oaks, 298
Waterhouse, A., architect, xiii, 21, 151, 193, 214 – 17
Watson, Richard, f, 101
Watson, Richard, Regius Professor of Divinity, bishop of Llandaff, 176
Waynflete, William, bishop of Winchester, 44
Webb, Aston, 253
Weller, E. P., f, b, 266, 272
Weller, the elder Mr (in *Pickwick Papers*), 218
Welles, Robert, f, 95
Wells, canon of, 26; precentor, 27

Welton, Richard, 150
Wendy, Thomas, f, 50, 56, 59, 62, 64,
  70; his fellow, 97
Westley, John, builder, 122
Wharton, Henry, 143, 147 – 50, 153,
  214, 250, 288; his family, 147; his
  Anglia Sacra, 149
Wheeler, James, f, p, 135, 137, 312
Whewell, William, Master of Trinity,
  189, 191, 204, 220 – 1, 230
Whichcote, Benjamin, 129
Whigs, 162 – 8 *passim*, 174, 187, 208,
  210 – 11
Whiston, William, 152, 154
Whitaker, William, Master of St John's,
  90, 92
White, Joshua, f, p, 312
Whitgift, John, Master of Trinity and
  vice-chancellor, archbishop of
  Canterbury, 76, 87, 93, 96
Wigglesworth, Sir Vincent, f, 296
Wiglesworth, T. W., f, 237
Wilkins, Harriet (Mrs Woodhouse), 194
Wilkins, William (I), architect, 188, 194
Wilkins, William (II), f, architect, 186,
  192 – 4, 200, 203, 208; and Perse
  School, 202
William III, king, and Queen Mary, 149
Williams, Joseph and Lewis, 182
Willis, Framlingham, f, and his letters,
  179 – 82, 184
Willis, Robert (I) (R. D.), f, 203, 224n.
Willis, Robert (II), son of R. D., f,
  Jacksonian Professor, 21, 191, 203 – 5,
  214 – 15, 219, 224n., 230, 250; his wife
  (Mary Ann Humfrey), 204
Willowes, Thomas, 31
Wilson, Colin St John, architect, 275
Wilson, Edward, 259
Wilson, Harold, 285
Wilson, John Dover, h f, 245
Wilson, Sir Thomas, 109
Wilton (Norfolk), 15
Wiltshire, Caian from, 207
Wimpole (Cambs), 140
Winchester (Hants), 146; archdeacon
  and canon, 49; bishop of, *see* Wayn-
  flete, Wykeham; cathedral, and
  Willis, 205; college, 11
Windsor (Berks), 146

Windsor, Dixie, 167
Winstanley, D. W., 173 – 4, 183, 189
Witan, Anglo-Saxon, 143 – 4
Wollaston, William, f, 156, 186 – 7, 288
Wolsey, Thomas, 44
women in Cambridge, 69, 235; *and see*
  Cambridge, Gonville and Caius
  College
Wood, Charles, f, 125, 216, 242 – 4,
  283, 288
Wood, atte Wode, Thomas, f, M, xii,
  39, 309; as builder, 24 – 6
Woodbridge Water Co., 257
Woodhouse, John, f, 212 – 13
Woodhouse, Robert, f, 186, 194 – 5,
  200, 203, 209, 213; his wife (Harriet
  Wilkins), 194
Woodroofe, the joiner, 122
Worcester, bishop of, *see* Latimer
World Wars, I, 37, 228, 246, 256, 260,
  266 – 8, 296, 321; II, 212, 228, 261,
  263, 268 – 9, 314, 321
Wortley, Bartholomew, f, 150 – 2,
  160 – 1, 226; bequest and purchase
  from, and Wortley fellows, 151, 184,
  208 – 9, 252, 275; statue of, 217
Worts, William, 192
Wren, Matthew, Master of Peterhouse,
  bishop of Ely, 112n.
Wright, Edward, f, 92
Wright, Jermyn, and his son, 138
Wright, Stephen, architect, 173
Wyclif, John, 9
Wykeham, William of, bishop of Win-
  chester, 3 – 4, 13, 16, 19, 22, 42, 44

Yarmouth (Norfolk), 193; Dominican
  house, 7
Yelden (Beds), 129 – 30
York, 89, 130; archbishop, 47, *and see*
  Rotherham, Sandys; chancellor, *see*
  Rickinghall
Yorkshire, Caians from, 86, 88 – 9;
  dales, 222

Zambesi, river, 231
Zanchius, 93
Zeebrugge, 263
Zürich, 58, 61

GONVILLE & CAIUS COLLEGE

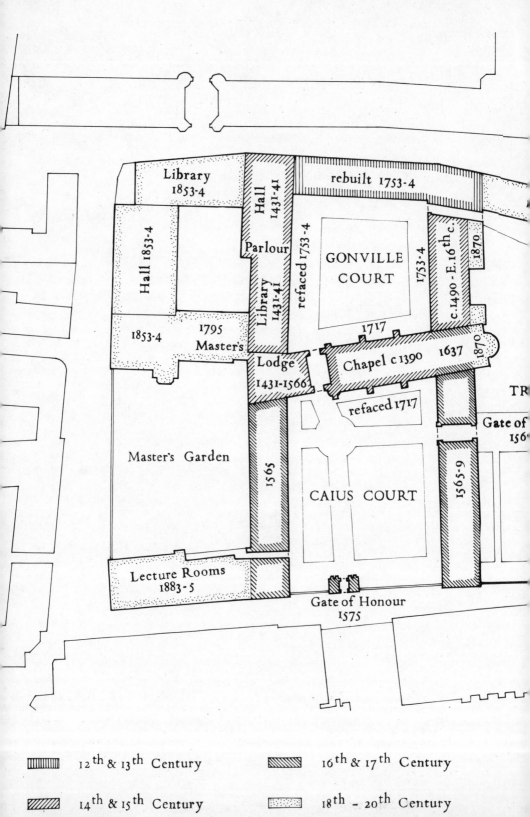

Library 1853-4

Hall 1853-4

1853-4

1795 Master's

Hall 1431-41

Parlour

Library 1431-41

Lodge 1431-1566

refaced 1753-4

rebuilt 1753-4

GONVILLE COURT

1753-4

c. 1490 - E. 16th c.

1870

1717

Chapel c 1390

1637

1870

refaced 1717

Master's Garden

1565

CAIUS COURT

1565-9

Gate of 156...

TR

Lecture Rooms 1883-5

Gate of Honour 1575

|||||||| 12th & 13th Century   ⧄⧄ 16th & 17th Century

⧄⧄ 14th & 15th Century   ⋰⋰ 18th - 20th Century